Lecture Notes in Computer Science 12880

More information about this subseries at http://www.springer.com/series/7409

K. Selçuk Candan · Bogdan Ionescu ·
Lorraine Goeuriot · Birger Larsen ·
Henning Müller · Alexis Joly ·
Maria Maistro · Florina Piroi ·
Guglielmo Faggioli · Nicola Ferro (Eds.)

Experimental IR Meets Multilinguality, Multimodality, and Interaction

12th International Conference of the CLEF Association, CLEF 2021
Virtual Event, September 21–24, 2021
Proceedings

Editors
K. Selçuk Candan
Arizona State University
Tempe, AZ, USA

Lorraine Goeuriot
Université Grenoble Alpes
Saint-Martin-d'Hères, France

Henning Müller
HES-SO Valais-Wallis
Sierre, Switzerland

Maria Maistro
University of Copenhagen
Copenhagen, Denmark

Guglielmo Faggioli
University of Padua
Padova, Italy

Bogdan Ionescu
Politehnica University of Bucharest
Bucharest, Romania

Birger Larsen
Aalborg University Copenhagen
Copenhagen, Denmark

Alexis Joly
University of Montpellier
Montpellier, France

Florina Piroi
TU Wien
Vienna, Austria

Nicola Ferro
University of Padua
Padova, Italy

ISSN 0302-9743 ISSN 1611-3349 (electronic)
Lecture Notes in Computer Science
ISBN 978-3-030-85250-4 ISBN 978-3-030-85251-1 (eBook)
https://doi.org/10.1007/978-3-030-85251-1

LNCS Sublibrary: SL3 – Information Systems and Applications, incl. Internet/Web, and HCI

This Springer imprint is published by the registered company Springer Nature Switzerland AG
The registered company address is: Gewerbestrasse 11, 6330 Cham, Switzerland

Preface

Since 2000, the Conference and Labs of the Evaluation Forum (CLEF) has played a leading role in stimulating research and innovation in the domain of multimodal and multilingual information access. Initially founded as the Cross-Language Evaluation Forum and running in conjunction with the European Conference on Digital Libraries (ECDL/TPDL), CLEF became a standalone event in 2010 combining a peer-reviewed conference with a multi-track evaluation forum. The combination of the scientific program and the track-based evaluations at the CLEF conference creates a unique platform to explore information access from different perspectives, in any modality and language.

The CLEF conference has a clear focus on experimental information retrieval (IR) as seen in evaluation forums (like CLEF Labs, TREC, NTCIR, FIRE, MediaEval, RomIP, TAC) with special attention to the challenges of multimodality, multilinguality, and interactive search ranging from unstructured to semi-structured and structured data. The CLEF conference invites submissions on new insights demonstrated by the use of innovative IR evaluation tasks or in the analysis of IR test collections and evaluation measures, as well as on concrete proposals to push the boundaries of the Cranfield/TREC/CLEF paradigm.

CLEF 2021 [1] was organized by the University "Politehnica" of Bucharest, Romania, during September 21–24, 2021. The continued outbreak of the COVID-19 pandemic affected the organization of CLEF 2021. The CLEF steering committee along with the organizers of CLEF 2021, after detailed discussions, decided to run the conference fully virtually. The conference format remained the same as in past years and consisted of keynotes, contributed papers, lab sessions, and poster sessions, including reports from other benchmarking initiatives from around the world. All sessions were organized and run online.

CLEF 2021 continued the initiative introduced in the 2019 edition during which the European Conference for Information Retrieval (ECIR) and CLEF joined forces: ECIR 2021 hosted a special session dedicated to CLEF Labs where lab organizers present the major outcomes of their labs and their plans for ongoing activities, followed by a poster session to favour discussion during the conference. This was reflected in the ECIR 2021 proceedings, where CLEF Lab activities and results were reported as short papers. The goal was not only to engage the ECIR community in CLEF activities but also to disseminate the research results achieved during CLEF evaluation cycles as submission of papers to ECIR.

[1] http://clef2021.clef-initiative.eu/.

Naila Murray (Facebook AI Research) was invited to deliver a keynote talk about video understanding and multi-modal search. Further keynote talks were in the process of being confirmed and were not final at the writing of this editorial.

CLEF 2021 received a total of 21 scientific submissions, of which a total of 11 papers (10 long, one short) were accepted. Each submission was reviewed by three Program Committee members, and the program chairs oversaw the reviewing and follow-up discussions. Twelve countries are represented in the accepted papers, as several of them were a product of international collaboration. This year, researchers addressed the following important challenges in the community: application of neural methods for entity recognition as well as misinformation detection in the health area, skills extraction in job-match databases, stock market prediction using financial news, and extraction of audio features for podcast retrieval. Evaluation remains a strong interest with papers on the evaluation of 1) pseudo-relevance feedback based on web-based data enrichment, 2) evolving datasets using pivot systems, and 3) multitask learning models for relevance assessment. Creating shareable open datasets is also a strong focus this year with datasets or frameworks created for 1) linguistic uncertainty in NLP, 2) an Italian corpus for subjectivity detection in newspapers, and 3) personalized type-based facet ranking tasks.

Like in previous editions since 2015, CLEF 2021 invited CLEF lab organizers to nominate a "best of the labs" paper that was reviewed as a full paper submission to the CLEF 2021 conference according to the same review criteria and PC. Five full papers were accepted for this "best of the labs" section.

The conference integrated a series of workshops presenting the results of lab-based comparative evaluations. CLEF 2021 was the 12th year of the CLEF conference and the 22nd year of the CLEF initiative as a forum for IR evaluation. A total of 15 lab proposals were received and evaluated in peer review based on their innovation potential and the quality of the resources created. The 12 selected labs represented scientific challenges based on new datasets and real world problems in multimodal and multilingual information access. These datasets provide unique opportunities for scientists to explore collections, to develop solutions for these problems, to receive feedback on the performance of their solutions, and to discuss the challenges with peers at the workshops. In addition to these workshops, the labs reported results of their year long activities in overview talks and lab sessions. Overview papers describing each of the labs are provided in this volume. The full details for each lab are contained in a separate publication, the Working Notes[2].

The 12 labs running as part of CLEF 2021 comprised mainly labs that continued from previous editions at CLEF (ARQMath, BioASQ, CheckThat!, CheMU, CLEF eHealth, eRisk, ImageCLEF, LifeCLEF, Lilas, PAN, and Touché) along with a new pilot/workshop activity (SimpleText). In the following we give a few details for each of the labs organized at CLEF 2021 (ordered alphabetically):

---

[2] Faggioli, G., Ferro, N., Joly, A., Maistro, M., and Piroi, F. editors (2021). *CLEF 2021 Working Notes*. CEUR Workshop Proceedings (CEUR-WS.org), ISSN 1613-0073.

ARQMath: Answer Retrieval for Mathematical Questions[3] considers the problem of finding answers to new mathematical questions among posted answers on the community question answering site Math Stack Exchange. The goals of the lab were to develop methods for mathematical information retrieval based on both text and formula analysis. Objectives to reach these goals include creating test collections for training and evaluating Math IR systems, establishing a state-of-the-art set of retrieval solutions on these test collections to be used as future baselines, and promoting Math IR to the research community. Compared to the 2020 ARQMath edition, this year the test collection size has doubled, the same being observed in the number of participants.

BioASQ[4] challenges researchers with large-scale biomedical semantic indexing and question answering (QA). The challenges include tasks relevant to hierarchical text classification, machine learning, information retrieval, QA from texts and structured data, multi-document summarization, and many other areas. The aim of the BioASQ workshop is to push the research frontier towards systems that use the diverse and voluminous information available online to respond directly to the information needs of biomedical scientists. Four tasks were organized in 2021, two on biomedical semantic indexing, one on QA, and a new task on COVID-19 QA. For the Spanish semantic indexing task, a continuation of a task introduced in previous years, new data was added that contained Spanish clinical trials and Spanish patents. Participant systems generally outperformed strong baselines, with participant solution clearly shifting towards the use of deep neural approaches. As such approaches, however, necessitate large amounts of training data, which were not available for BioASQ tasks, participants were investigating knowledge and model transfer from other resources.

CheckThat!: Detecting Check-Worthy Claims, Previously Fact-Checked Claims, and Fake News[5] aims to foster the development of technologies capable of both spotting and verifying check-worthy claims in short messages and political debates in various languages. This year there were three main shared tasks where participants were to estimate the check-worthiness of a claim in a short message (tweet) and in political texts (debates/speeches), to check if a detected claim was previously verified, retrieve evidence to fact-check a claim, and verify the factuality of a claim. The data in 2021 included more languages than in the previous year, with some teams addressing the challenges for all languages, while others tackling one language only.

ChEMU: Cheminformatics Elsevier Melbourne University[6] proposes two key information extraction tasks over chemical reactions from patent texts. The ChEMU corpus builds on the one used in the previous lab edition, being extended to provide data for two distinct 2021 tasks: reference resolution for chemical reactions and anaphora resolution to identify relationships (i.e. coreference and bridging relationships) between expressions in descriptions of chemical reactions. Out of 19 originally registered teams, only two manged to submit experiments. The tasks proved to be complex, the submitted experiments barely over-performing the baseline results.

---

[3] https://www.cs.rit.edu/dprl/ARQMath.

[4] http://www.bioasq.org/workshop2021.

[5] https://sites.google.com/view/clef2021-checkthat.

[6] http://chemu2021.eng.unimelb.edu.au/.

CLEF eHealth[7] aims to support the development of techniques to aid laypeople, clinicians, and policy-makers in easily retrieving and making sense of medical content to support their decision making. The goals of the lab are to develop processing methods and resources in a multilingual setting to enrich difficult-to-understand eHealth texts and provide valuable documentation. Organized since 2012, the CLEF eHealth labs have provided a recurring contribution to the creation and dissemination of text analytics resources, methods, test collection, and evaluation benchmarks that support both medical professionals and laypersons when dealing with health-related information. The 2021 CLEF eHealth edition organized two tasks. The first one was a multilingual Information Extraction task, focusing on Spanish language ultrasound reports. The second task, Consumer Health Search, was a continuation of previous CLEF eHealth IR tasks with a new representative web corpus and layperson medical queries. From the 67 teams that originally registered, 11 of them submitted runs to the two tasks.

eRisk: Early Risk Prediction on the Internet[8] explores challenges of evaluation methodology, effectiveness metrics, and other processes related to early mental health risk detection. Early detection technologies can be employed in different areas, particularly those related to health and safety. Over the years these evaluations have taken place, it has become evident that the interplay between psychological disorders and the users' expression through language is a very challenging task, with currently available solutions not reaching satisfactory performance levels. The 2021 edition of the lab contained three tasks, two being continuations of tasks organized in the previous years (self-harm and depression severity detection), and a new one on the topic of pathological gambling. The data provided to campaign participants consisted of texts written in social media. From the 76 teams that originally registered to this lab, 18 had submitted experiments, with a total of 117 runs (26 for Task 1, 55 for Task 2, and 36 for Task 3).

ImageCLEF: Multimedia Retrieval[9] provides an evaluation forum for visual media analysis, indexing, classification/learning, and retrieval in medical, nature, security, and lifelogging applications with a focus on multimodal data, that is data from a variety of sources and media. The 2021 ImageCLEF edition consisted of four main tasks dedicated to multimedia retrieval in four areas: medical, nature, identification of hand-drawn components, and social media, with the latter being newly introduced this year. The first task consisted of three subtasks related to radiology images (visual question answering, CT-based tuberculosis evaluation, and captioning concepts across radiology images). The nature-related task contained training and test data to form 3D reconstructions of coral environments. The task on hand-drawn images focused on user interface drawings as well as screenshot images (new this year) which, by segmentation and labeling steps, are to provide additional support for code developers. The social media-related task aimed to assess the vulnerability potential and real-life effects of users sharing personal visual data. 42 participating groups submitted over 250

[7] https://clefehealth.imag.fr/.

[8] https://erisk.irlab.org/.

[9] https://www.imageclef.org/2021.

experiments to these tasks, with results varying in performance improvements over previous task editions.

LifeCLEF: Multimedia Life Species Identification[10] aims at boosting research on the identification and prediction of living organisms in order to solve the taxonomic gap and improve our knowledge of biodiversity. Through its biodiversity informatics related challenges, LifeCLEF is intended to push the boundaries of the state of the art in several research directions at the frontier of multimedia information retrieval, machine learning, and knowledge engineering. LifeCLEF in 2021 organized four challenges (PlantCLEF, BirdCLEF, GeoLifeCLEF, and SnakeCLEF) involving image data, audio data, and geolocations. In terms of participating teams that submitted runs, the Bird-CLEF task (a bird sound recognition task) stands out with over 800 teams submitting experimental results. The main LifeCLEF outcome is that, taken together, the solutions used by the participants to solve the lab tasks provide a new snapshot of state-of-the-art systems' performances in computer vision, audio analysis techniques, and machine learning algorithms that can be part of a real-world biodiversity monitoring system.

LiLAS: Living Labs for Academic Search[11] aims to bring together researchers interested in the online evaluation of academic search systems. The long term goal is to foster knowledge on improving the search for academic resources like literature, research data, and the connections between these resources in fields from the life sciences and the social sciences. The immediate goal of this lab is to develop ideas, best practices, and guidelines for a full online evaluation campaign at CLEF 2021. The first LiLAS iteration as a workshop-lab provided participants exclusive access to real-world academic data search systems, LIVIVO for scientific literature search and GESIS Search for data sets and open access publication search, for each of which a use case was defined. STELLA was introduced as the living lab framework to assess participant submissions which were provided either as static search results sets or as Docker images to be integrated in the live search systems. Nine experimental systems were evaluated with metrics designed for assessing interleaved results, combining results from the participants with baseline results provided by the search systems.

PAN: Digital Text Forensics and Stylometry[12] is a networking initiative for digital text forensics, where researchers and practitioners study technologies that analyze texts with regard to originality, authorship, and trustworthiness. PAN provides evaluation resources consisting of large-scale corpora, performance measures, and web services that allow for meaningful evaluations. The main goal is to provide for sustainable and reproducible evaluations, to get a clear view of the capabilities of state-of-the-art algorithms. This year, PAN organized three shared tasks: detecting authors of hate speech spreaders, authorship verification, and multi-author writing style analysis. Each of the tasks made use of its own specifically designed collection of documents. For the first task, focusing on profiling hate speech spreaders, a data set of social media postings (i.e. Twitter) was created, with manually annotated tweets as hater/not-hater labels. For the second task, authorship verification, the lab organizers

[10] https://www.imageclef.org/LifeCLEF2021.

[11] https://clef-lilas.github.io/.

[12] http://pan.webis.de/.

aimed for a scaled up benchmark setting using fan-fiction literature. Finally, the multi-author style analysis task, a task that evolved over the years PAN was organized as a lab, used a collection of Q&A postings from StackExchange where paragraphs from different answers were joined into one text, thus creating a document with mutiple authors.

SimpleText: (Re)Telling Scientific Stories to Non-specialists via Text Simplification[13] aims to create a community interested in generating a simplified summary of scientific documents and to contribute in making the science really open and accessible for everyone. The goal is to generate a simplified abstract of multiple scientific documents based on a given query. SimpleText was organized as a workshop which discussed three pilot tasks on text simplification for scientific information access, all contributing steps towards arriving at a simplified text summary of an input scientific text. The first pilot task addressed the passage selection challenge, i.e. which parts of a document are appropriate for inclusion into a simplified summary. The second pilot task aimed to decide which terms in a selected passage require a simplifying explanation and contextualisation. Finally, the last pilot task discussed aimed to obtain simplified text passages derived from input scientific text passages. The document collection used for these tasks was compiled from preprint and open access repositories, Wikipedia, and science journalism article resources.

Touché: Argument Retrieval[14] is the first shared task on the topic of argument retrieval. Decision making processes, be it at the societal or at the personal level, eventually come to a point where one side will challenge the other with a "why" question, which is a prompt to justify one's stance. Thus, technologies for argument mining and argumentation processing are maturing at a rapid pace, giving rise for the first time to argument retrieval. In its second year, Touché has organized two shared tasks: an argument retrieval for controversial questions task and an argument retrieval for comparative questions task. The two tasks used different document collections: for the first task the args.me corpus was provided, while for the second one argument retrieval was performed on the ClueWeb12 collection. Out of 36 registered teams, 27 sent in their retrieval experiments, where relevance judgements from the 2020 lab edition could be used for training.

As a group, the 152 lab organizers were based in 22 countries, with Germany, and France leading the distribution. Despite CLEF's traditionally Europe-based audience, 44 (28.9%) organizers were affiliated with international institutions outside of Europe. The gender distribution was biased towards 75% male organizers.

The success of CLEF 2021 would not have been possible without the huge effort of several people and organizations, including the CLEF Association[15], the Program

[13] https://www.irit.fr/simpleText/.

[14] https://touche.webis.de/.

[15] http://www.clef-initiative.eu/association.

Committee, the Lab Organizing Committee, the reviewers, and the many students and volunteers who contributed.

Finally, we thank the generous support of the H2020 AI4Media project, Facebook AI Research, Keysight Technologies Romania, and Siemens Romania R&D, who provided general funding support.

July 2021

K. Selçuk Candan
Bogdan Ionescu
Lorraine Goeuriot
Birger Larsen
Henning Müller
Alexis Joly
Maria Maistro
Florina Piroi
Guglielmo Faggioli
Nicola Ferro

Organization

CLEF 2021, Conference and Labs of the Evaluation Forum – Experimental IR meets Multilinguality, Multimodality, and Interaction, was hosted (online) by the University "Politehnica" of Bucharest, Romania.

General Chairs

K. Selçuk Candan — Arizona State University, USA
Bogdan Ionescu — University "Politehnica" of Bucharest, Romania

Program Chairs

Lorraine Goeuriot — Université Grenoble Alpes, France
Birger Larsen — Aalborg University, Denmark
Henning Müller — University of Applied Sciences Western Switzerland (HES-SO), Switzerland

Lab Chairs

Alexis Joly — Inria Sophia-Antipolis, France
Maria Maistro — University of Copenhagen, Denmark
Florina Piroi — Vienna University of Technology, Austria

Lab Mentorship Chair

Lorraine Goeuriot — Université Grenoble Alpes, France

Publicity Chairs

Liviu-Daniel Ştefan — University "Politehnica" of Bucharest, Romania
Mihai Dogariu — University "Politehnica" of Bucharest, Romania

Outreach Program Chairs

Yu-Gang Jiang — Fudan University, China - Asian Liaison
Hugo Jair Escalante — Instituto Nacional de Astrofisica, Optica y Electronica, Mexico - Central American Liaison
Fabio A. Gonzalez — National University of Colombia, Colombia - South American Liaison

Ben Herbst	Praelexis, South Africa - African Liaison
Abdulmotaleb El Saddik	University of Ottawa, Canada - North American Liaison

Industry and Sponsorship Chairs

Şeila Abdulamit	Vodafone, Romania
Mihai-Gabriel Constantin	University "Politehnica" of Bucharest, Romania
Bogdan Boteanu	University "Politehnica" of Bucharest, Romania

Website and Social Media Chair

Denisa Ionaşcu	University "Politehnica" of Bucharest, Romania

Finance Chair

Ion Marghescu	University "Politehnica" of Bucharest, Romania

Proceedings Chairs

Guglielmo Faggioli	University of Padua, Italy
Nicola Ferro	University of Padua, Italy

Program Committee

Martin Braschler	ZHAW, Switzerland
Fabio Crestani	University of Lugano, Switzerland
Elöd Egyed-Zsigmond	LIRIS, France
Sebastien Fournier	LSIS, France
Norbert Fuhr	University of Duisburg-Essen, Germany
Teresa Goncalves	University of Evora, Portugal
Gareth Jones	Dublin City University, Ireland
Jaap Kamps	University of Amsterdam, The Netherlands
Jussi Karlgren	Spotify, UK
Liadh Kelly	Maynooth University, Ireland
Christina Lioma	University of Copenhagen, Denmark
David Losada	University of Santiago de Compostela, Spain
Josiane Mothe	IRIT, France
Irina Ovchinnikov	Haifa University, Israel
Martin Potthast	Leipzig University, Germany
Paolo Rosso	Universitat Politècnica de València, Spain
Eric Sanjuan	Université d'Avignon, France
Benno Stein	Bauhaus-Universität Weimar, Germany
Theodora Tsikrika	Information Technologies Institute, CERTH, Greece
Christa Womser-Hacker	University of Hildesheim, Germany
Md Zia Ullah	CNRS, France

CLEF Steering Committee

Steering Committee Chair

Nicola Ferro	University of Padua, Italy

Deputy Steering Committee Chair for the Conference

Paolo Rosso	Universitat Politècnica de València, Spain

Deputy Steering Committee Chair for the Evaluation Labs

Martin Braschler	Zurich University of Applied Sciences, Switzerland

Members

Khalid Choukri	Evaluations and Language resources Distribution Agency (ELDA), France
Paul Clough	University of Sheffield, UK
Fabio Crestani	Università della Svizzera italiana, Switzerland
Carsten Eickhoff	Brown University, USA
Norbert Fuhr	University of Duisburg-Essen, Germany
Lorraine Goeuriot	Université Grenoble Alpes, France
Julio Gonzalo	National Distance Education University (UNED), Spain
Donna Harman	National Institute for Standards and Technology (NIST), USA
Evangelos Kanoulas	University of Amsterdam, The Netherlands
Birger Larsen	University of Aalborg, Denmark
David E. Losada	Universidade de Santiago de Compostela, Spain
Mihai Lupu	Vienna University of Technology, Austria
Josiane Mothe	IRIT, Université de Toulouse, France
Henning Müller	University of Applied Sciences Western Switzerland (HES-SO), Switzerland
Jian-Yun Nie	Université de Montréal, Canada
Eric SanJuan	University of Avignon, France
Giuseppe Santucci	Sapienza University of Rome, Italy
Jacques Savoy	University of Neuchâtel, Switzerland
Laure Soulier	Pierre and Marie Curie University (Paris 6), France
Theodora Tsikrika	Information Technologies Institute (ITI), Centre for Research and Technology Hellas (CERTH), Greece
Christa Womser-Hacker	University of Hildesheim, Germany

Past Members

Djoerd Hiemstra	Radboud University, The Netherlands
Jaana Kekäläinen	University of Tampere, Finland

Séamus Lawless	Trinity College Dublin, Ireland
Carol Peters	ISTI, National Council of Research (CNR), Italy (Steering Committee Chair 2000–2009)
Emanuele Pianta	Centre for the Evaluation of Language and Communication Technologies (CELCT), Italy
Maarten de Rijke	University of Amsterdam, The Netherlands
Alan Smeaton	Dublin City University, Ireland

Supporters and Sponsors

Supporter

Funded under the European Union's Horizon 2020 research and innovation programme, ICT-48-2020, grant #951911, the AI4Media project—A European Excellence Centre for Media, Society and Democracy—aspires to become a Centre of Excellence engaging a wide network of researchers across Europe and beyond, focusing on delivering the next generation of core AI advances and training to serve the media sector, while ensuring that the European values of ethical and trustworthy AI are embedded in future AI deployments (https://www.ai4media.eu/).

Gold Sponsor

FACEBOOK AI

Facebook AI Research seeks to further our fundamental understanding in both new and existing domains, covering the full spectrum of topics related to AI, with the mission of advancing the state of the art of AI through open research for the benefit of all. Along with the key principles of Facebook AI - openness, collaboration, excellence, and scale - we believe FAIR researchers also need to have the freedom and autonomy to design and follow their own research agendas so they can take on the most impactful work and develop the most disruptive projects, all while sharing their results with the community (http://ai.facebook.com).

Silver Sponsor

Keysight Technologies Romania is a leading test and measurement equipment provider for electronic design, e-mobility, network monitoring, 5G, LTE, IoT, connected cars, and more. The company's nearly 12,600 employees serve customers in more than 100 countries (https://www.keysight.com/).

Silver Sponsor

SIEMENS

Located in Braşov, Cluj-Napoca, and Bucureşti, the Siemens R&D activity is represented in Romania by the Siemens Advanta Development and Siemens Technology teams. The programmers, engineers, and researchers in our teams work with Siemens divisions and business units to identify and implement tomorrow's technologies. The world is constantly changing and we're always thinking about what's next. Siemens Advanta Development is involved in the development of hardware, software, and automation products and solutions in the fields of energy, industry, healthcare, mobility, building technologies, and e-business. The IT Services and Solutions teams provide internal support services for various Siemens platforms. It is also involved in the automated development and testing of applications on Web, mobile, or SAP platforms. The teams from the Technology group carry out their research activity on new design methodologies and advanced verification of the implementations made in ASIC and FPGA, analytics and Big Data, IT Security Software and Systems Innovation, applied research based on computational models, and Artificial Intelligence (https://new.siemens.com/ro/ro.html).

Contents

Full Papers

Audio Features, Precomputed for Podcast Retrieval and Information Access Experiments

Abigail Alexander[1], Matthijs Mars[1], Josh C. Tingey[1], Haoyue Yu[1], Chris Backhouse[1], Sravana Reddy[2,3], and Jussi Karlgren[2,3](✉)

[1] University College London, London, UK
[2] Spotify, Boston, USA
jkarlgren@spotify.com
[3] Spotify, Stockholm, Sweden

Abstract. This paper describes how an existing collection of podcast material has been enriched with precomputed audio features. The feature set which is described in the paper is made available to facilitate more convenient information access experimentation to collections that include both audio and text data. A simple example analysis is given to demonstrate how the audio features can be used to score podcast segments for being entertaining, discussion oriented, or subjective, to fit the current TREC Podcast Track task.

Keywords: Information access · Audio analysis · Podcasts

1 Podcasts are a New Medium

Access to podcasts involves new research and development challenges. Most of the starting points of current retrieval technology for both speech and text take departure in (1) topical search being the primary access path to a collection and (2) in transcribed text being the most convenient way to represent the content of spoken material. This is arguably true for most task-oriented information access use cases, but for entertainment and enjoyment, use cases which are at the forefront of attention for podcast listeners, the ranking criteria for candidate items are likely to be broader than topical relevance [9].

Speech, which in general is less conventionalised and less rule-bounded than writing, is a richer communicative channel than text. Podcast material is different from previous spoken language material in several ways—the production circumstances, the intended use cases, and the distribution technology conspire to render the language in podcasts different from known related genres such as radio broadcasts, recorded lectures, conversations, or written interactive usage such as chats or forum discussions.

Some podcasts track closely to genre conventions known from text or previous practice, where others are more conversational with rapid exchanges of

K. S. Candan et al. (Eds.): CLEF 2021, LNCS 12880, pp. 3–14, 2021.
https://doi.org/10.1007/978-3-030-85251-1_1

ideas, quick conversational moves, argumentation, and overlapping speech. Podcasts can be monologues, lectures, conversations, interviews, debates, and chatty multi-party conversations. They may contain historical clips, and the range of emotions expressed by participants can range across most human sentiments: in fact, one of the apparent attractions of podcasts as a medium is that the constraints of other media can be and often are breached with impunity by the participants in a podcast conversation.

Transcriptions normalise much of this type of variation since text is designed to express emotions in explicit terms rather than intonation and to render topical content in an orderly way. Most transcription technologies will handle linguistic variation—dialectal and sociolectal variation, e.g.—badly and will fail entirely in the face of e.g. rapid multi-party discourse, overlapping speech, disfluency and repair, or ambient noise. These various variational dimensions are not irrelevant to listeners, however: listeners do pay attention to various auditive characteristics of a podcast when they assess the qualities of an episode or a show [10].

This means that information access technology for podcast material cannot entirely be based on current text-based retrieval technology. Retrieval systems and exploration tools for podcasts must in some way take into account such information that would be lost when transcribing the audio content to text. This paper presents a set of precomputed audio features to lower the threshold to systematic experimentation on information access—retrieval, clustering, classification, summarisation, and related applications—for podcast material.

2 The Spotify English-Language Podcast Dataset

In 2020, Spotify released a large dataset of podcasts[1] with the view of enabling researchers from various fields to test their theories and hypotheses on realistic scale collections of spoken audio, particularly podcast material. The dataset consists of 105,360 English language podcast episodes collected from Spotify's catalogue between late 2019 and early 2020. Each episode includes the audio (sampled at 44.1 kHz), an automatically generated transcript, and some associated metadata, including the episode and show names and descriptions. In total, the dataset contains approximately 60,000 h of audio and 600 million transcript words, corresponding to a total of 2 TB worth of data [2].

3 The TREC Podcasts Track

For this purpose, TREC, the annual Text Retrieval Conference, in 2020 organised a Podcasts Track with two information access tasks to experiment on podcast material [8]. There have been previous speech retrieval tracks both in TREC and in CLEF, but this is the first initiative to address the specifics of podcast material, recognising the challenges outlined above.

[1] https://podcastsdataset.byspotify.com/.

The Podcasts Track attracted great interest but not all registered participants submitted results and no participant made direct use of the audio data, except to provide alternative transcriptions. A post-participation questionnaire indicated that the size of the collection and technical challenges with audio analysis were considerable thresholds for participants. The objective for the second year is to lower participation thresholds in general and to specifically provide the participants with precomputed audio features to encourage experimentation on the audio data rather than the transcripts.

3.1 Task 1: Fixed-Length Segment Retrieval

The segment retrieval task asks participants to, given a query, retrieve appropriate two-minute segments from the data set. In 2020, the queries were of three types: *topical*, *known-item*, and *refinding* queries, all based on topical relevance as the primary target criterion. These were all addressable using text retrieval techniques on the transcripts, and the participants' approaches were well aligned, using text retrieval, reranked using deep learning models.

In 2021, to encourage participants to use the audio material, the task types have been modified. The refinding queries and the known-item queries, which overlapped to some extent, have been combined into one type. The topical queries will be assessed differently: the participants will be asked to submit results for the topical queries separately ranked by several different target notions: as before, by *relevance*, but also, separately ranked by if the segment is *entertaining*, such that the segment presents the topic in a way which the speakers intend to be amusing and entertaining to the listener, if the segment is *subjective*, such that the speakers explicitly and clearly make their approval or disapproval of the topic evident, and if the segment contains *discussion* with more than one speaker contributing to the topic. In addition, a *speaker* query type is added, for which the participants will be asked to find episodes where some given speakers participate. For speaker queries, a clip of the intended speaker taken from another recording will be given for reference.

We expect that these reranking criteria will be better served by making use of the audio data in addition to the topical retrieval (which presumably will continue best being executed by using the transcript).

3.2 Task 2: Summarisation

The summarisation task asks of participants to, given a podcast episode, its audio, and transcription, return a short text snippet capturing the most important information in the content. Returned summaries should be grammatical, standalone utterances of significantly shorter length than the input episode description. The user task is to provide a short description of the podcast episode to help the user decide whether to listen to a podcast. In 2021, the participants will be asked to provide, in addition to the textual summary, up to three audio clips from the podcast to give the user a sense of what the podcast sounds like. The audio clips will be assessed by human assessors to answer the question "Do the clips give a sense of what the podcast sounds like, (as far as you can tell from listening to it)?"

We expect that this task will benefit greatly from using audio features.

We look forward to seeing how these tasks will be addressed by participants using audio features alongside textual features, and expect to see various levels of utility for the precomputed features. We expect that in coming years, the feature sets and tools to extract them from the speech signal will evolve in capacity and effectiveness for downstream tasks. This effort is a step in that direction: by sharing precomputed audio features for the English-language Podcast Data Set suitable for the TREC tasks, we hope to see more experimentation on audio as well as new features and audio analyses be made available.

4 Feature Extraction

As all the podcasts in the English-language Podcast Data Set are sampled at 44.1 kHz, a 30-min long podcast contains approximately 80 million data points. This is illustrated in Fig. 1 which shows an example of the audio waveform from a podcast with both speech and music segments. While there is some difference seen between the different segments, this is mainly due to the loudness of the section with music. In order to extract useful information from the podcast audio, the data needs to be processed into more informative high-level features that act to summarise the raw audio signal.

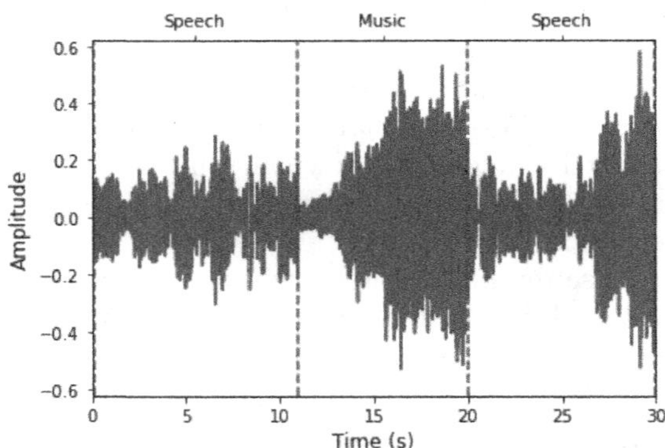

Fig. 1. The audio waveform of a 30-second clip from a podcast containing sections of both speech and music.

To provide a large set of useful high-level features which are both understandable and cover a broad range of use cases, we have extracted two complementary feature sets. The first, employing the Geneva Minimalistic Acoustic Parameter Set (GeMAPS) [4], uses established features in phonetics and speech sciences.

The second uses the learned features of the Yet Another MobileNet (YAMNet)[2] model to label the data with labels from the AudioSet ontology [6].

4.1 The Geneva Minimalistic Acoustic Parameter Set

The Geneva Minimalistic Acoustic Parameter Set or GeMAPS is an attempt by Eyben et al. [4] to design a minimalistic and standardised parameter set of acoustic features that are useful for machine learning problems. These features include parameters in the time domain (e.g. speech rate), the frequency domain (e.g. pitch), the amplitude domain (e.g. loudness) and the spectral energy domain (e.g. relative energy in different frequency bands). Importantly, all are calculated in a clearly defined, standardised manner, such that the values are reproducible and results can be easily compared.

The feature set is designed to be minimalistic in that it calculates the least amount of features required to generate relatively strong results. This way, classifiers trained on the features are less likely to over-adapt to the training data and instead generalise well. The interpretation of the parameters and results from a minimalistic set is also more straightforward since the features and derived models are relatively simple.

The minimal set contains 18 Low Level Descriptors (LLDs) describing vocal features such as intonation, stress, rhythm, excitation, as well as various spectral descriptors that analyse the base frequency and harmonics of speech. The selected LLDs are chosen based on their relative importance from previous research results. This minimal set is referred to as GeMAPS. In addition, an extension set with seven further LLDs, all cepstral descriptors which analyse the periodic structures in frequency data [3], is also defined. These features have been shown to consistently improve results on automatic affect recognition tasks with respect to the features in the minimal set of GeMAPS. The extension of this set in combination with the minimal set is called the extended Geneva Minimalistic Acoustic Parameter Set (eGeMAPS).

In designing this recommended parameter set, the GeMAPS authors compared both the minimal and the extended set with large-scale brute-force baseline acoustic feature sets on binary arousal and binary valence classification. The results show that eGeMAPS always matches or outperforms GeMAPS, which indicates that the added features can help in some predictive tasks. Classification with eGeMAPS achieves similar (if somewhat reduced) performance to the large scale parameter sets, yet the size of the parameter set is only 2% of the most extensive set included in the comparison [4].

The eGeMAPS features can be computed from the raw audio waveform using the openSMILE feature extraction toolkit [5]. The openSMILE toolkit is a tool for Speech and Music Interpretation by Large-space Extraction (SMILE) and contains feature extraction algorithms for speech processing and music information retrieval[3]. Figure 2 shows a subset of the eGeMAPS features for the same podcast segment as shown before in Fig. 1.

[2] https://github.com/tensorflow/models/tree/master/research/audioset/yamnet.

[3] https://github.com/audeering/opensmile-python.

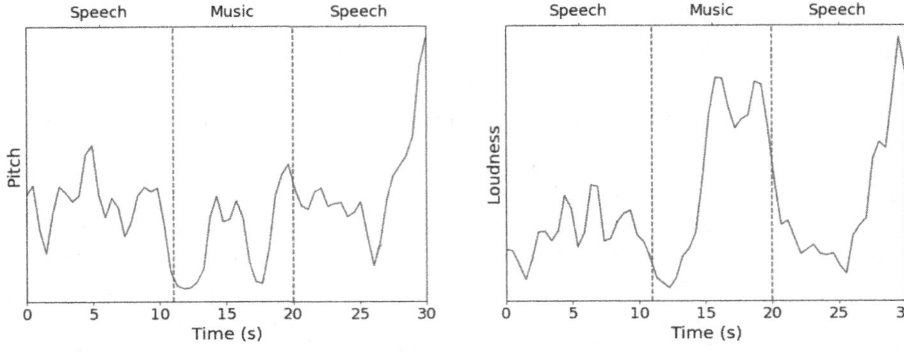

Fig. 2. The pitch and loudness averaged over 0.96 s of audio for a clip of 30 s from the Podcast Dataset. The data is sampled every 0.48 s.

4.2 YAMNet

The second feature set uses learned features that are inferred from a labelled dataset. Yet Another MobileNet or YAMNet is a neural network based audio feature extractor based on the Mobilenet_v1 convolutional architecture [7], which is trained on the AudioSet corpus. AudioSet [6] contains audio from approximately 2 million 10-second YouTube clips, labelled by humans into 521 audio event classes. The complete AudioSet ontology covers sound classes such as humans, animals, and music, amongst many other common everyday environmental sounds.

The network pre-processes audio input into mel spectrograms—spectrograms where the frequency spectrum is transformed to fit human perception—and uses a convolutional neural network (CNN) to analyse these spectrograms in a similar manner to image recognition tasks.

The output of the MobileNet architecture is pooled into a 1024-dimension embedding vector, before a single logistic layer is used to predict the 521 AudioSet event labels.

Besides using the AudioSet labels from YAMNet as an audio event classifier, the 1024-dimensional embedding vector can be used as a general-purpose audio feature representation. The pre-trained YAMNet model can then be used as a feature extractor for a smaller network trained on top of the embedding vector on a small set of labelled data for a particular task without retraining the complete network from scratch. Figure 3 shows the vectors for a podcast segment from the Podcast Dataset.

The output scores of YAMNet are not calibrated between the different classes, so they cannot be used directly as probabilities. Instead, for a specific task, one needs to perform calibration across the classes to determine the appropriate scaling and thresholding of the classes. Since the data is trained on YouTube video clips using 10-second AudioSet clips, there is a risk of mismatch if the task data are different or if the events of interest occur on a smaller timescale.

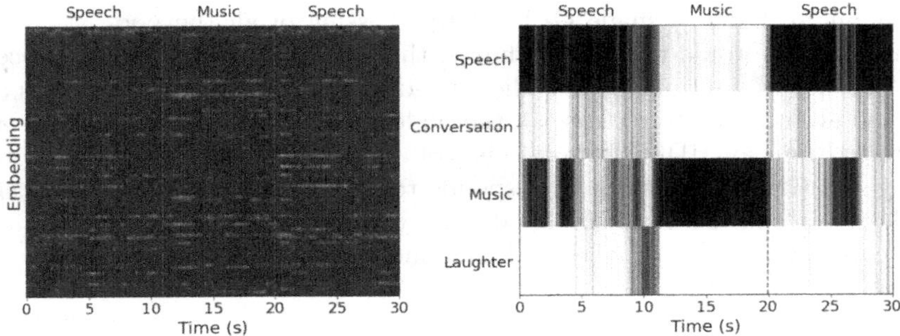

Fig. 3. *(Left)* The first 100 components of the 1024 dimensional vector for a 30 s clip of a podcast containing both speech and music. *(Right)* The logarithm of the class scores for the event labels speech, conversation, music, and laughter for the same podcast segment.

The YAMNet features are particularly useful because they are very interpretable. The audio event labels translate directly to sounds we can hear and recognise as humans. Therefore, using these labels, a segment with a particular audio event can be easily found without considering its underlying acoustic characteristics [10, cf].

4.3 Extracted Features

We have extracted both above sets of features for every episode in the Podcast Dataset.

Using the openSMILE toolkit, we have calculated each podcast's eGeMAPS functionals. In our implementation, the functionals are aggregations (mean, standard deviation, etc.) of the eGeMAPS LLDs over a time window of 1.01 s[4] starting every 0.48 s, such that all the windows overlap both their neighbours by approximately half their length. In total, there are 88 functionals in the eGeMAPS feature set. The computation of the eGeMAPS features for the complete Podcast Dataset would take ~5500 hours on a single CPU core. Therefore, the processing was sped up by running the extraction process in parallel on multiple CPU cores. The resulting eGeMAPS feature set is saved as 16-bit floats and compressed into an HDF5 format to reduce the storage size. The resulting total file storage size of the eGeMAPS features for all the podcasts is approximately 75 Gigabytes, which is ~4% the size of the raw audio data.

Using the pre-trained YAMNet model, we extracted the 1024-dimensional embedding vectors and the audio event class scores from the podcast audio. These are calculated for every 0.96 s long window of the podcast starting every 0.48 s, such that all the windows overlap both their neighbours by approximately half their length. GPU acceleration was used to speed up the processing of the

[4] This window length was chosen to provide a time window which is as close as possible to the 0.96 s windows of the YAMNet features.

podcast audio. Using a single GPU, the processing of all the podcasts in the Podcast Dataset would take ~2500 hours; therefore, it was sped up by processing in parallel on multiple GPUs. The 1024-dimensional embedding vectors and the audio event class scores from all the podcasts are saved as 16-bit floats and compressed into an HDF5 format. The total size of all the vectors is approximately 400 Gigabytes, which corresponds to ~20% of the original audio size. The class scores have a total size of 60 Gigabytes for the entire Podcast Dataset, which corresponds to ~3% of the original audio size.

5 Example Analysis: TREC 2021 Reranking Tasks

5.1 Creating Labelled Data

In order to devise some example mood-based metrics to fit the target notions for the TREC tasks, labelled audio data are required. To create the labelled data, mood labels were manually assigned to a sample of 200 2-minute-long podcast segments. To enrich the sample used, we selected the segments based on a search of an Elasticsearch[5] index containing all the possible Podcast Dataset segment transcripts. For example, to find funny segments, the phrase "that's so funny" was used as the query; for subjective segments, the phrases "I agree" and "I disagree". The authors performed the labelling by listening to a subset of segments each and noting down any of the relevant labels detailed in Table 1. A label was assigned if an expression of a mood occurred at any given time during the two-minute segment; multiple labels for a segment were allowed.

5.2 Creating Mood Metrics

The mood metrics were subsequently manually formulated using the labelled data and their corresponding audio feature scores. Due to the small size of the data set, we did not employ traditional machine learning techniques. Instead, a more exploratory approach was employed on a case-by-case basis to establish preliminary, "proof of concept" mood target notion metrics. These results and metrics are not definitive and serve only to demonstrate that it is possible to use the audio data to gain mood-based insights to improve the search task. For each target notion category (Entertaining, Discussion and Subjective), one specific label was chosen and explored: *funny*, *debate*, and *disapproval*, respectively.

Entertaining: Funny Metric. To find funny podcast segments, we used the "Laughter" feature from YAMNet. By tabulating how often the "Laughter" score is the highest (or second-highest to only "Speech") for each time step in the data, we can find the amount of laughter in a podcast. Figure 4 shows the distribution of this feature for both the funny and non-funny segments in our labelled set. The figure indicates that if a segment has parts where "Laughter" gets the highest

[5] https://www.elastic.co/elasticsearch.

Table 1. Table detailing the range of mood labels, their definitions, and the number of podcast segments out of the 200 segment sample that had these labels assigned. The labels are not mutually exclusive.

Mood category	Label	Definition	No. segments
Entertaining	Funny	Funny, or supposed to be funny	103
	Storytelling	Someone is telling a story	111
	Excitement	Someone is excited about something	35
	Angry	Someone is angry at something	9
	Sad	Someone is sad about something	3
Discussion	Narration/monologue	Segment with no discussion	81
	Conversation	Segment with conversation (chit chat, two people or more actively in conversation)	140
	Interview	Segment with interview style conversation (more one-sided, someone asks a question and someone answers in monologue)	30
	Debate	Segment where people debate about something (opinions being voiced)	35
Subjective	Approval	Clearly voiced approval (e.g. I like X, I love Y)	76
	Disapproval	Clearly voiced disapproval (e.g. I don't like X, I hate Y)	30

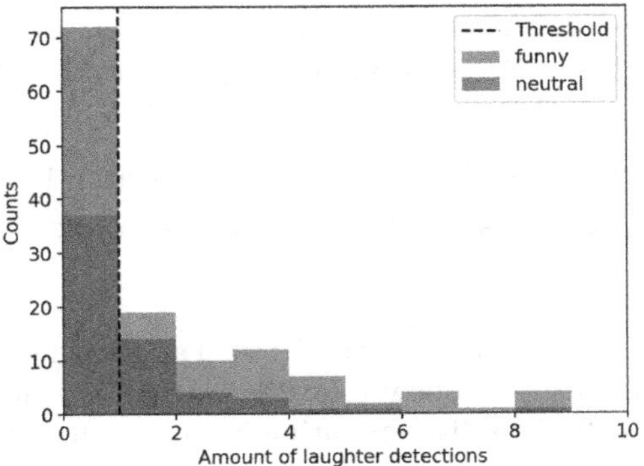

Fig. 4. Histogram for the laughter metric with its chosen threshold cutoff value.

score, it is more likely to be funny than not. Using a greater than or equal to one threshold for the score to classify our labels results in predicting 69% of the *funny* labels in the Podcast Dataset correctly.

Discussion: Debate Metric. The Opensmile eGeMAPS features were used to investigate the discussion and subjective notions, where it is predicted their presence will be more uniform across the podcast segment. The mean, standard deviation, maximum and minimum were computed for each eGeMAPS feature

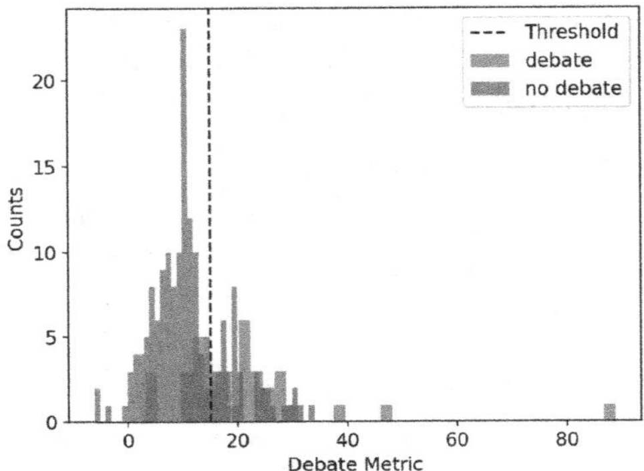

Fig. 5. Histogram for the debate metric with its chosen threshold cutoff value.

across the sample of two-minute segments. Then, the Pearson correlation coefficients were computed for each of these features with their corresponding "debate scores" (score = 1 if labelled as debate and 0 otherwise) so that discriminating features could be roughly identified. Using a trial and error approach, a metric for debate was subsequently hand-crafted by linearly combining the features with the most significant correlations. This resultant metric is given by Eq. 1 with a distribution as shown in Fig. 5. A selection on debate segments can be performed by rejecting all segments below a threshold of debate_metric = 15. Using this threshold, we succeed in predicting 74% of the *debate* labels in the Podcast Dataset correctly.

$$\begin{aligned} \text{debate metric} = &\ \mathit{std\_dev}(\text{MFCC4\_SMA3\_STDDEVNORM})/143 \\ &+ 12 \times \mathit{max}(\text{SLOPEUV500\_1500\_SMA3NZ\_AMEAN})/0.0156 \end{aligned} \tag{1}$$

Subjective: Disapproval Metric. An identical approach to the determination of the above debate metric was followed for the disapproval metric. The resultant metric is given by Eq. 2. The discriminating power of this metric is illustrated by Fig. 6, and a selection on disapproval segments can be performed by rejecting all segments below a threshold of disapproval_metric = 4.2. This cutoff value corresponds to an accuracy of 0.700 on the training data.

$$\begin{aligned} \text{disapproval metric} = &\ 2 \times \mathit{mean}(\text{SPECTRALFLUX\_SMA3\_STDDEVNORM})/0.824 \\ &+ \mathit{mean}(\text{F1FREQUENCY\_SMA3NZ\_AMEAN})/556 \\ &+ \mathit{mean}(\text{F2FREQUENCY\_SMA3NZ\_AMEAN})/1590 \end{aligned} \tag{2}$$

5.3 Performance and Limitations

The above classification performance scores were computed for each metric and are detailed in Table 2. In general, all metrics yield reasonable accuracy, even

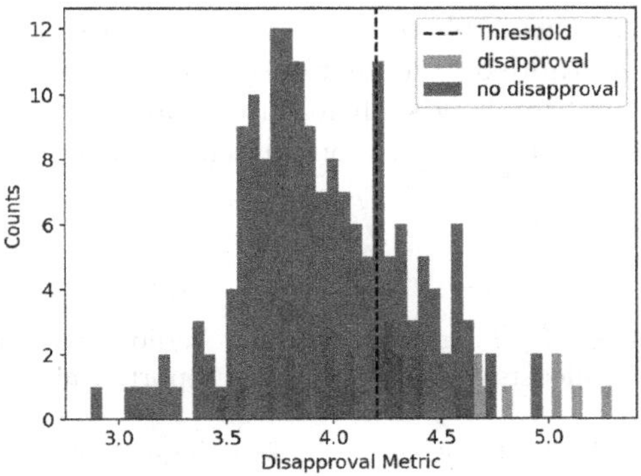

Fig. 6. Histogram for the disapproval metric with its chosen threshold cutoff value.

for this small and subjectively labelled training set of only 200 segments. The *funny* metric also maintains good recall and precision. However, the *debate* and *disapproval* metrics show low precision scores due to the amount of false positives associated with the simple linear cuts. This indicates that more sophisticated classification methods, larger training sets, and possibly more consistent labelling of the training set are necessary. In addition, it is worth to note the likely systematic effect of segment and sentiment granularity mismatch. Here, we assigned labels to the entirety of the 2-minute segment, but the moods in question may only feature in a fraction of that time, and this will be reflected in the segment features accordingly. Averaging over the 2-minute range risks missing distinguishing features.

Table 2. Mood metric classification performance for manually labelled training data.

Mood metric	Accuracy	Recall	Precision
Funny	0.690	0.641	0.725
Debate	0.745	0.686	0.375
Disapproval	0.700	0.567	0.266

6 Concluding Remarks

We wish to encourage more researchers to use audio data for podcast analysis, e.g. in the TREC Podcasts Track. All the extracted features presented here are available in a simple format with the entire Podcast Dataset[6] and the code used

[6] https://podcastsdataset.byspotify.com/.

to extract the features is available on GitHub[7] [1]. We expect to see other audio analyses and feature sets added to further enrich the Podcast Dataset and intend our effort to be a model for how such features and analyses can be shared to facilitate audio-based experimentation on speech at realistic scale.

References

1. Alexander, A., Mars, M., Tingey, J., Yu, H.: Audio-enhanced segment retrieval within the Spotify podcasts dataset. Technical report, University College London (2021)
2. Clifton, A., et al.: 100,000 podcasts: a Spoken English document corpus. In: Proceedings of the 28th International Conference on Computational Linguistics (COLING) (2020)
3. Devlin, J., Chang, M.W., Lee, K., Toutanova, K.: BERT: pre-training of deep bidirectional transformers for language understanding. In: Proceedings of the 2019 Conference of the North American Chapter of the Association for Computational Linguistics: Human Language Technologies. Association for Computational Linguistics (2019)
4. Eyben, F., et al.: The Geneva Minimalistic Acoustic Parameter Set (GeMAPS) for voice research and affective computing. IEEE Trans. Affect. Comput. **7**(2), 190–202 (2016)
5. Eyben, F., Wöllmer, M., Schuller, B.: Opensmile: the Munich versatile and fast open-source audio feature extractor. In: Proceedings of the International Conference on Multimedia - MM 2010. ACM Press (2010)
6. Gemmeke, J.F., et al.: Audio set: an ontology and human-labeled dataset for audio events. In: 2017 IEEE International Conference on Acoustics, Speech and Signal Processing (ICASSP). IEEE, New Orleans (2017)
7. Howard, A.G., et al.: MobileNets: efficient convolutional neural networks for mobile vision applications. arXiv:1704.04861 [cs], April 2017
8. Jones, R., et al.: TREC 2020 podcasts track overview. In: Voorhees, E.M., Ellis, A. (eds.) Proceedings of the Twenty-Ninth Text REtrieval Conference (TREC). NIST (2021)
9. Jones, R., et al.: Current challenges and future directions in podcast information access. In: Proceedings of the 44th International ACM SIGIR Conference on Research and Development in Information Retrieval (2021)
10. Martikainen, K.: Audio-based stylistic characteristics of Podcasts for search and recommendation: a user and computational analysis. Master's thesis, University of Twente (2020)

[7] https://github.com/trecpodcasts/podcast-audio-feature-extraction.

A Hybrid Approach for Stock Market Prediction Using Financial News and Stocktwits

Alaa Alhamzeh[1,2](✉), Saptarshi Mukhopadhaya[2], Salim Hafid[1,2], Alexandre Bremard[1], Előd Egyed-Zsigmond[1], Harald Kosch[2], and Lionel Brunie[1]

[1] INSA de Lyon/LIRIS, 20 Avenue Albert Einstein, 69100 Villeurbanne, France
{alaa.alhamzeh,salim.hafid,alexandre.bremard,elod.egyed-zsigmond, lionel.brunie}@insa-lyon.fr

[2] Universität Passau, Innstraße 41, 94032 Passau, Germany
{saptarshi.mukhopadhaya,Harald.Kosch}@uni-passau.de

Abstract. Stock market prediction is a difficult problem that has always attracted researchers from different domains. Recently, different studies using text mining and machine learning methods were proposed. However, the efficiency of these methods is still highly dependant on the retrieval of relevant information. In this paper, we investigate novel data sources (Stocktwits in combination with financial news) and we tackle the problem as a binary classification task (i.e., stock prices moving up or down). Furthermore, we use for that end a hybrid approach which consists of sentiment and event-based features. We find that the use of Stocktwits data systematically outperforms the sole use of price data to predict the close prices of 8 companies from the NASDAQ100. We conclude on what the limits of these novel data sources are and how they could be further investigated.

Keywords: Stock market · Sentiment analysis · Online news · Stocktwits · Classification

1 Introduction

Stock market prediction has been always a challenging task as it depends on various factors and is positioned at the intersection of linguistics, machine learning and behavioral economics [1]. The prediction task can be addressed as a binary classification problem, i.e. whether a particular stock price will rise up or fall down, or as a regression problem where the goal is to predict the future stock price. Generally, two main approaches are considered [2]:

- Technical Stock Analysis: based on the historical numerical values of the stock such as the opening price, the closing price, the traded volume, etc.

K. S. Candan et al. (Eds.): CLEF 2021, LNCS 12880, pp. 15–26, 2021.
https://doi.org/10.1007/978-3-030-85251-1_2

- Qualitative Stock Analysis: based on external financial factors like the textual information contained in social media, financial news articles and company profiles.

In our work, we ran experiments using both types of analyses. The stocks on which these experiments were run correspond to 8 different companies from the NASDAQ100 stock exchange.

Our contribution essentially consists in a novel combination of several data sources for stock market prediction, namely Stocktwits in combination with online News, and in running different experiments to compare the quality of these data sources and the predictiveness of the textual features.

Furthermore, our work is mainly a sentiment-analysis-based approach performed on the textual data, though we do also run hybrid-based experiments that involve an event-based approach. The main challenges of sentiment-based approaches to stock market prediction are the finance-specific language and the lack of labeled data. General purpose sentiment-models are not effective enough.

In this paper, we aim to run experiments that seek the answer of the following questions:

- Can the use of textual data systematically improve the performance of models based on numerical data?
- Is there an optimal observation period that a model should consider before giving a price movement prediction?
- How can one combine the information retrieved from different data sources?

The paper is organized as follows: in Sect. 2, we take a close look at the conceptual background of our work as well as the state-of-the-art studies considering stock market prediction. In Sect. 3, we come to our contribution details. We validate the results in Sect. 4. Finally, we discuss the overall research questions and future work in Sect. 5.

2 Related Work

Stock market prediction is not a new problem, therefore many approaches have been tested involving various techniques. In [3], Fung et al. have proposed a method based on the *efficient market hypothesis* [4] which states that the current market is the assimilation of all the information available. They first found the trend using a piece-wise linear segmentation algorithm based on a t-test. Using agglomerative hierarchical clustering they grouped the useful trends. They then used guided k-means clustering to align the useful news with the trends. A special weighting scheme was then proposed to give importance to the news which support only one type of trend. Finally, the news and trends were aligned and given to an SVM (Support Vector Machine) [5] predicition model.

In 2010 Kaya and Karsligil [6] proposed an approach where each news is labeled based on the change in the stock price for the considered company. They considered Noun-Verb combinations, instead of single words, as features. News articles were divided into samples, with each sample corresponding to a single day. Feature selection was then performed using the Chi-square method. An SVM model was finally used for classification.

Dang and Doung [7] proposed an approach where they labeled the news using a price label (positive, negative and neutral). Furthermore, they created their own financial dictionary for Vietnamese language and tagged the words with parts of speech tags. Only adjectives and verbs were used, and the words in the dictionary were labeled with positive and negative scores based on their frequency in the positive and negative news. They used delta TF-IDF (Term Frequency Inverse Document Frequency) to give an importance degree to the words that are unevenly distributed between positive and negative classes. Term reduction was performed using the OCFS algorithm. This algorithm finds the centroid of the training corpus and scores each word accordingly. After all the processing, they used a SVM to classify the stock price movement.

Deep learning is another way of making stock market predictions. In [8], the authors predicted the stock price using news sentiment score and historical stock prices. Each news article was given a sentiment using python NLTK library. Neutral news were discarded, and for each of the other news the maximum polarity score between positive and negative was taken, then the average score of all the news for each particular day was calculated. The final model used the past prices and the sentiment scores as inputs for the prediction.

Although plenty of research work has been done on the problem of Stock Market Prediction, there is yet to be a single benchmark against which all experiments can be compared. That means that most published works have used different datasets and different evaluation approaches. For example some research works [8] considered stock prediction as a regression problem, while other papers [7] considered it as a classification problem. Some research [9] also focused more on evaluating the correlation between price change and sentiment change and did not even try to predict the price change. Due to these reasons it's very difficult to compare our work to the state of the art research.

3 Contribution

We present in this section the details of our model. First, we introduce the different data sources we consider in our experiments in Sect. 3.1. We go through their filtering and cleaning process in Sects. 3.3 and 3.2. Later on, we describe our system architecture and the configuration of its different parameters in Sect. 3.4. Finally, we present individually the sentiment-based score and the event-based score for our proposed hybrid approach in Sect. 3.5.

3.1 Datasets Description

The data used in this paper can be divided into 3 separate categories: price data, stocktwits and news articles. This data has been collected through API channels and Python scraping scripts for a period of 19 months (from 01/02/2019 to 30/09/2020).

3.1.1 Price Data

The price data used in this study is collected by the Alphavantage API[1], which has partnered with major institutions, exchange platforms and brokers around the world. As mentioned in the official API documentation, the historical data is derived from the Securities Information Processor (SIP) market-aggregated data, which contains the standard Open-High-Low-Close-Volume time series. The split and dividend events are taken into account using a split/dividend-adjustment in order to prevent misleading price change signals, thus to ensure that the data represents the true movements of the market which can then be used as an input for our technical analysis. The collected price data were the daily prices (Open, High, Low, Close and Volume) for a total of 8 companies from the US NASDAQ100:

AAL (American Airlines Group Inc), AAPL (Apple Inc), AMGN (Amgen Inc), AMZN (Amazon.com Inc), FB (Facebook Inc Common Stock), GOOG (Alphabet Inc Class C), GOOGL (Alphabet Inc Class A), MSFT (Microsoft Corporation), NFLX (Netflix Inc).

3.1.2 Stocktwits

The stocktwits data has been collected directly from the official Stocktwits API[2] symbol stream endpoint. The original data contains the message body itself as well as some meta-data such as the timestamp, the likes, the author's information (username, name, followers, following, likes, etc.) in addition to a sentiment hashtag the author has given to his/her tweet. This sentiment can only be "Bullish" (the user is confident that the price will rise in the near future) or "Bearish" (the user is confident that the price will fall in the near future). This sentiment label is optional, so the user may or may not add it before sending his tweet.

The stocktwits have been collected for the same 8 companies as for the price data as detailed in Table 1.

Table 1. Stocktwits distribution by company

Company	Count
AAPL	508,940
AMZN	335,327
FB	183,048
MSFT	172,258
NFLX	165,000
AAL	114,182
GOOGL	41,522
AMGN	7,565

[1] https://www.alphavantage.co/documentation/.
[2] https://api.stocktwits.com/developers/docs/api.

3.1.3 News

The news were collected from various resources and stored into an ElasticSearch index. Some examples of the news' sources are The Wall Street Journal, The Washington Post, USATODAY, and CNN. There are around 800K news articles. Each article has a publication date, a title, a message and a full-text, collected using RSS feeds and a full text scrapper. The message part represents a short description snippet that is contained in the RSS feed for the articles. Therefore, we have chosen them as the textual data input for our prediction model since the titles may not provide enough information and the full-texts are very long to process. Moreover, full-texts are not proven to systematically perform better than the messages.

However, this news data is not labeled. In other words, we do not know which events or which sentiment an article contains. Furthermore, companies records very different frequencies in terms of news articles. The distribution of the news data per company is detailed in Fig. 1.

3.2 Data Pre-processing

The collected news data and the stocktwits have to be cleaned as they contain noise such as HTML tags and extra spaces (Fig. 2. **step 1**). We use Vader [10] as the Sentiment Analyzer for the sentiment-based approach. Therefore, we do not need to remove punctuation as Vader is capable of handling sentences as they are. Vader is also capable of handling emojis contained in Stocktwits, so those were also not removed. The details about Vader will be discussed in Sect. 3.5.1. However, we did have to run a preprocessing pipeline for the event-based feature. The pipeline involved tokenizing, lemmatizing, removing stopwords, removing non-alphabetical characters, and removing time-related words (daytime, months, days of the week). For the news articles, we replaced all the company names with company symbols, for example - "American Airlines" and "American Airlines INC" would both be replaced with "AAL". And for the news articles, we removed company names once the data was filtered. The reason for that was to avoid introducing a frequency bias, since the articles are filtered in such a way that they systematically contain the company name (see Sect. 3.3), and having the same words systematically present would bias the word embedding (details on the usage of the word embedding will be explained in Sect. 3.5.2).

3.3 Data Filtering

As our news are taken from various resources, they hold no guarantee of being firm-specific. Therefore, to make sure the news articles are relevant to the 8 companies whose stocks we're predicting, we filtered the news using the company name(Fig. 2. **step 2**).

For Stocktwits in order to reduce the noise we filtered the twits and only kept ones which have at least 10 followers and 100 likes and that contain at least 20 words.

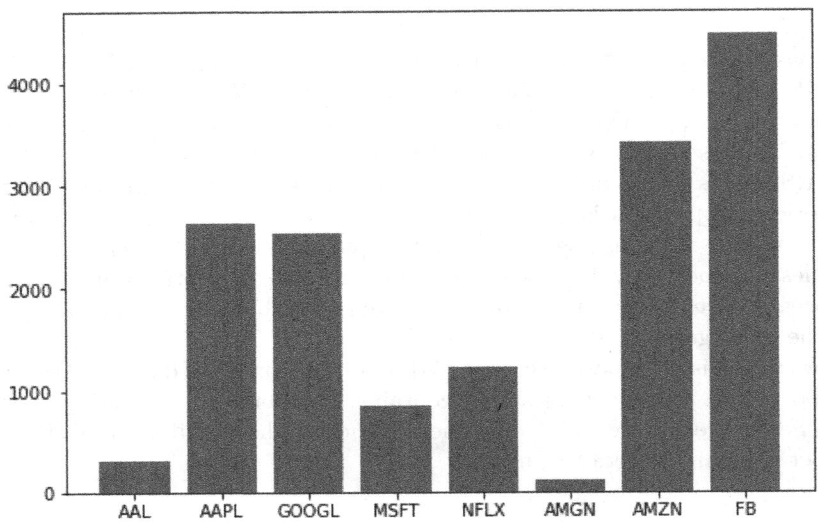

Fig. 1. News distribution based on company name

3.4 System Architecture and Parameters

There are two important parameters to our experiments. The first one is the Press Observation Period (pop), which defines the number of previous days of news articles/stocktwits fed into the model in order to make a prediction. The second one is the Price Change Period (pcp), which determines the day of the close price prediction with regards to the day the prediction is done. For example, if we have (**pop = 3**, **pcp = 1**) and the current date is the day d then we are feeding the model the news/stocktwits of days **d-2,d-1,d** till the closing time of the stock market on day d in order to predict the price movement of **d + 1**.

3.5 Text Based Features and Models

3.5.1 Sentiment-Based Score

Sentiment analysis plays a significant role in extracting the essence of textual data. When it comes to stock movement prediction, it is interesting to study how the stock price movement changes based on the sentiment tone of the news articles and the stocktwits. However, there are many approaches to find the sentiment of a text:

1. Rule based approach: the sentiment is predicted using lexicons and grammatical rules.
2. Machine learning based approach: the sentiment is predicted using a model which has learned through examples.

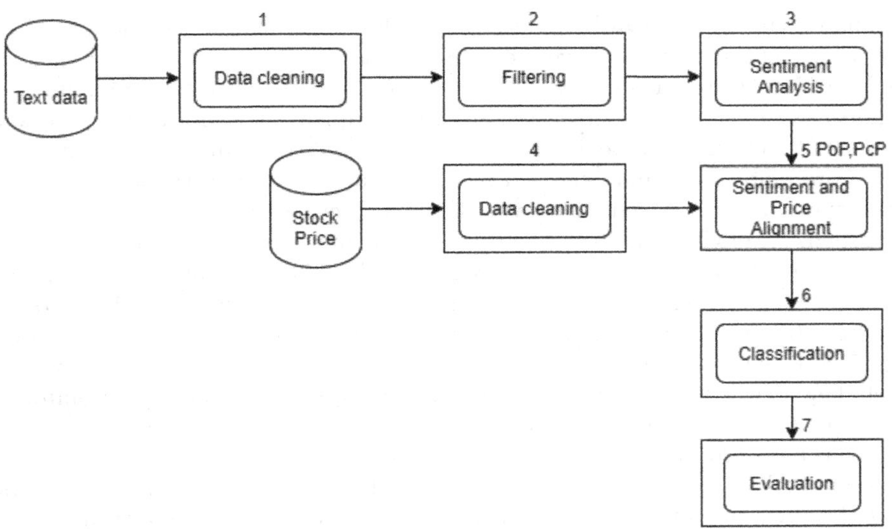

Fig. 2. Overall system architecture

Machine-learning-based approaches require data labeled by domain experts. On the other hand, rule-based sentiment analyzers[3] use patterns and lexicons and therefore do not need any labeled data. Since our news dataset is unlabeled, we will be using a rule-based sentiment analyzer to get the sentiment score. Vader is a very well known sentiment analyzer. It has the capacity to handle grammatical rules such as negation, conjunction and punctuation along with a gold standard sentiment lexicon.

The lexicons used by Vader have a score for each word in the vocabulary between −4 to +4. In [10] it has been shown that Vader has outperformed other rule-based sentiment analyzers and machine-learning-based sentiment classification models. Although it was initially created for classifying twitter sentiment, in [11] the author has used Vader for financial sentiment analysis and has shown that Vader outperforms the machine-learning-based approaches. In [9] the author has shown good correlation between the sentiment change and the stock price change using Vader. As we are dealing with the financial domain, we updated Vader's lexicon with a financial lexicon called SentiBignomics [12–14].

Inspired by [9], we used Vader in our experiment to calculate sentiment scores (Fig. 2. **step 3**). In our experiments we added temporal weights to the sentiment scores, that are linearly decreasing with time. Indeed, the further an article is published from the day we want to predict the price change, the less it counts.

3.5.2 Event-Based Score

With the advances in the field of event-extraction, many published studies have used event-based features to solve the problem of stock market prediction.

[3] Vader (https://pypi.org/project/vaderSentiment/), Textblob (https://textblob.readthedocs.io/en/dev/).

Feldman et al. [15] proposed a hybrid approach to stock market prediction using both sentiment analysis and event extraction, the events were extracted using a predicate-level semantic business event extractor designed by a team of linguistic engineers and financial experts. Han et al. [16] implemented an event-extraction approach for online Chinese news based on an event-trigger dictionary combined with word embedding and deep learning. The current state-of-the-art on event-extraction works at the sentence-level, that is, detecting not only the event (what happened) through a rule-based pattern or a trained model, but also the relevant entities (to whom the event happened). While this kind of approach is the one that currently yields the state-of-the-art results, it usually requires lots of resources (access to rich extensive labeled data sources). In this paper, we will approach event-extraction in a more simple way as we will work at the word-level. The idea is to see how much improvement we can get out of combining a relatively simplistic event-based feature with sentiment-based features.

It has been proven that the events with most affect on stock market prices are the events related to firm-fundamentals. Shao et al. [17] demonstrated that news related to firm-fundamentals explained, on average, 39% of annual returns in the early 2010s, and Kogan et al. [18] found that fundamental firm-level information present in public news accounts for 20–40% of stock price volatility. Therefore, we started by defining a list of seven events closely related to firm fundamentals:

- Product launch.
- Product recall.
- Merge or acquisition.
- Price change.
- Legal related event.
- Bankruptcy related event.
- Financial related event.

We assign a score to each event according to its impact on the stock market. The scores were initially assigned using online finance literature on the impact of corporate events on the stock market. We then performed a series of tests on the training datasets to fine-tune the scores for each event.

Furthermore, inspired by Peng et al. [19], we define an initial list of 10 seed words for each event-category. For example, the seed words for the event-category product-launch were: *product, launch, publish, release, unveil, announce, reveal, introduce, unseal, relaunch.* Once we had a list of seed words for each event-category, we extended those lists using both a financial ontology[4] and a Word2Vec word embedding trained with our finance-specific dataset. The closest words to the initial seed words were generated based on both the financial ontology and the word embedding using cosine similarity. We then kept the top 50 most relevant words for each event-category. Finally, we calculated a vector V = (logN1, ..., logNm) where Nm is the number of words in the news article/stocktwit that belong to the event-category m. If the word count is equal to zero we replace it with a large negative number (e.g. -100).

[4] FIBO: The Financial Industry Business Ontology.

In order to determine to which event-category, if any, a news article/stocktwit belongs to, we compute the V vector and then pick the event that corresponds to its maximum value. However, if two events have the same word count, we pick the event whose weight is the highest. We also defined a minimum threshold (initially set at a high value, e.g. 10, then fine-tuned) for the word count.

3.5.3 Combined Score

While we know which events can impact the stock market, for some events it is not obvious to know if the impact will be positive or negative (e.g. price-change event). To avoid introducing a bias by giving the event-weight a positive/negative value, we give all the events positive values and we let the sentiment analyzer decide on the score's polarity. To calculate the final score feature, we multiply the sentiment analyzer score by the detected-event's weight.

$$combinedScore = detectedEventScore * sentimentScore \tag{1}$$

If no event is detected, the *detectedEventScore* is equal to 1 and the *combinedScore* is equal to the *sentimentScore*.

4 Evaluation

In this section we report the results of seven experiments which evaluate the ability of the system to predict the price change direction (i.e. price moving up or down) of the next day (pcp = 1) for 8 different companies from the US NASDAQ100 based on various price observation periods (pop). The goal of the experiments is to define the most efficient prediction pipeline (i.e. to find, given our datasets and our proposed features, the most efficient combination of data input, model features, price observation period and prediction model to optimize the close prices prediction).

Different models were tested (Linear Regression, SVM, Ensemble models, LSTM) before settling on a Random Forest (RF) model optimized using a Grid search algorithm. The hyperparameters that were optimized using the Grid search algorithm are the number of trees in the RF, the number of features considered before splitting at each leaf node, the maximum depth of the RF and whether or not bootstrapping is used for sampling data points. The RF prediction model is common to all experiments. The experiments differ however in the input datasets and in the features used to train the prediction model.

The first experiment uses only the price data (i.e. historical daily close prices for the 8 companies) as a feature for the prediction, and serves as a benchmark to see how the model's performance improves when stacking up more complex features. The second experiment uses only sentiment scoring based on the news data. The third experiment uses only sentiment scoring based on the stocktwits data. The fourth experiment uses a combination of price data and sentiment scoring using only the news data for sentiment analysis. The fifth experiment uses the same combination of price data and sentiment scoring but uses only the stocktwits data for sentiment analysis. The sixth experiment uses a combination of price data, sentiment scoring and event weights based only on the news data. The seventh and last experiment uses a combination of price data, sentiment scoring and event weights based only on the stocktwits data.

Table 2. F1-scores for American Airlines (AAL) for different pop

pop	3	8	13	18	23	28	33	38	43	48
Stocktwits count	6	14	22	30	38	46	54	61	68	75
News count	2	5	7	10	12	15	17	19	22	24
Price-based only	0.33	0.33	0.32	0.34	0.34	0.39	0.32	0.32	0.27	0.26
Sentiment-only (news)	0.44	0.54	0.46	0.43	0.45	0.48	0.51	0.45	0.46	0.52
Sentiment-only (stocktwits)	0.52	0.54	0.47	0.52	0.52	0.50	**0.56**	0.49	0.48	0.46
Price+Sentiment (news)	0.51	0.47	0.54	0.47	0.55	0.54	0.51	0.51	0.5	0.44
Price+Sentiment(stocktwits)	0.48	0.47	0.51	0.50	0.54	0.54	0.55	0.56	0.53	0.52
Price+Sentiment+Events(news)	0.51	0.47	0.51	0.44	0.52	0.53	0.47	0.53	0.50	0.42
Price+Sentiment+Events(stocktwits)	0.53	0.51	0.53	0.52	0.51	0.51	**0.57**	0.52	**0.57**	0.49

The evaluation metric used to evaluate the results of the experiments is the F1-score, which is the harmonic mean of precision and recall. The benefits of using the F1-score instead of a mere accuracy score is that the F1-score is less sensitive to class imbalance and is more sensitive to False Negatives and False Positives, both of which are important in a real trading scenario. The results of the experiments are presented in Table 2. As the results show consistent F1-scores (in terms of min, max, average and standard deviation) across all 8 companies we only show the results for American Airlines (AAL).

To train the model, we assign to each sample (corresponding to the day d) a price-change label of $\{-1, 0, 1\}$ to indicate whether the price will have moved down, not moved, or moved up on the day d+pcp (e.g. d + 1 with pcp = 1 in our case).

The prediction and evaluation pipeline goes as the following: for example, for American Airlines, when predicting the price change movement for a pcp = 1, we obtain the highest F1-Score of 0.57 with a pop equal to 32 using the price-based, sentiment-based and event-based features (see results in Table 2). For example, to obtain the price change movement prediction for October the 1st 2020, we used a pop of 32 days, i.e. from August 29th 2020 to September 30th 2020. In this time period, we first retrieved all of AAL's daily closing prices to make our price-based feature. Then, we retrieved our textual data (news articles or stocktwits, in this example only stocktwits were considered) and made it go through our preprocessing and filtering pipelines (see Sects. 3.2 and 3.3). Once the textual data was preprocessed and filtered, we grouped them based on the publication day and the company name they refer to form the samples. Each sample contains all of the textual data published on a given day and that refers to a single company. To extract the sentiment-based feature, we ran the Vader sentiment analyzer on each sample and got a score that is the average sentiment score across all textual data contained in a single sample. To extract the event-based feature, we construct the event vector V (see Sect. 3.5.2) based on all the textual data contained in a sample. If the maximum value of the vector is superior to the minimum detection threshold, we assign to the sample the event-weight that corresponds to the event who had that maximum value. If no event was detected (i.e. no value of the event vector was superior to the minimum detection threshold) then no event-weight is assigned to the sample. Finally, for each sample, we calculated the compound score (see Sect. 3.5.3). This compound score will be the sentiment-based + event-based feature. For the AAL example, the F1-Score of 0.57 was then obtained by calculating the harmonic mean of the precision and recall when predicting whether the stock price of AAL will go up, down, or won't change from day d to day (d + 1) for all the days within the testing period (which accounts for 30% of the whole dataset timespan of 19 months, see Sect. 3.1), using the price-based, sentiment-based and event-based features.

5 Discussion and Conclusion

Different conclusions can be drawn from the results of our experiments. First, using sentiment score as a feature of the prediction model systematically increases the performance of the model (both when using filtered news or stocktwits) in comparison with its performance using solely price-based features, which means that we can affirm that the use of textual data can systematically improve the performance of a price-based model. Second, there is no clear conclusion as to which dataset (news articles or stocktwits) generates the most predictive sentiment scores. Third, using event-based features does not systematically improve the model's performance. However, that could be because the extracted event-features are not sophisticated enough. Further experiments ought to be done using state-of-the-art event-extraction methods to conclude whether or not event-based features systematically improve the model's performance. Fourth, our experiments didn't prove the existence of any optimal price observation period (which is defined as the number of previous days of news articles/stocktwits fed into the model as input in order to make a prediction output). It is possible, though not proven, that such an optimal value does not exist, given that the amount of impact that the news articles/stocktwits have on the stock market and the delay for that impact to take place both depend highly on the individual context of the situation and the content of the news articles/stocktwits around.

References

1. Nassirtoussi, A.K., Aghabozorgi, S., Wah, T.Y., Ngo, D.C.L.: Text mining for market prediction: a systematic review. Expert Syst. Appl. **41**(16), 7653–7670 (2014)
2. Hur, J., Raj, M., Riyanto, Y.E.: Finance and trade: a cross-country empirical analysis on the impact of financial development and asset tangibility on international trade. World Dev. **34**(10), 1728–1741 (2006)

3. Fung, G.P.C., Yu, J.X., Lam, W.: News sensitive stock trend prediction. In: Chen, M.-S., Yu, P.S., Liu, B. (eds.) PAKDD 2002. LNCS (LNAI), vol. 2336, pp. 481–493. Springer, Heidelberg (2002). https://doi.org/10.1007/3-540-47887-6_48
4. Fama, E.F.: Efficient market hypothesis. Dissertation Ph.D. thesis, Ph.D. dissertation (1960)
5. Cortes, C., Vapnik, V.: Support-vector networks. Mach. Learn. **20**(3), 273–297 (1995)
6. Yasef Kaya, M.I., Elif Karsligil, M.: Stock price prediction using financial news articles. In: 2010 2nd IEEE International Conference on Information and Financial Engineering, pp. 478–482. IEEE (2010)
7. Dang, M., Duong, D.: Improvement methods for stock market prediction using financial news articles. In: 2016 3rd National Foundation for Science and Technology Development Conference on Information and Computer Science (NICS), pp. 125–129. IEEE (2016)
8. Mohan, S., Mullapudi, S., Sammeta, S., Vijayvergia, P., Anastasiu, D.C.: Stock price prediction using news sentiment analysis. In: 2019 IEEE Fifth International Conference on Big Data Computing Service and Applications (BigDataService), pp. 205–208. IEEE (2019)
9. Agarwal, A.: Sentiment analysis of financial news. In: 2020 12th International Conference on Computational Intelligence and Communication Networks (CICN), pp. 312–315. IEEE (2020)
10. Hutto, C., Gilbert, E.: Vader: a parsimonious rule-based model for sentiment analysis of social media text. In: Proceedings of the International AAAI Conference on Web and Social Media, vol. 8 (2014)
11. Sohangir, S., Petty, N., Wang, D.: Financial sentiment lexicon analysis. In: 2018 IEEE 12th International Conference on Semantic Computing (ICSC), pp. 286–289. IEEE (2018)
12. Consoli, S., Barbaglia, L., Manzan, S.: Fine-grained, aspect-based sentiment analysis on economic and financial lexicon. Aspect-Based Sentiment Analysis on Economic and Financial Lexicon (January 14, 2021) (2021)
13. Barbagliaa, L., Consolia, S., Manzanb, S.: Forecasting with economic news. Available at SSRN (2020)
14. Barbaglia, L., Consoli, S., Manzan, S.: Monitoring the business cycle with fine-grained, aspect-based sentiment extraction from news. In: Bitetta, V., Bordino, I., Ferretti, A., Gullo, F., Pascolutti, S., Ponti, G. (eds.) MIDAS 2019. LNCS (LNAI), vol. 11985, pp. 101–106. Springer, Cham (2020). https://doi.org/10.1007/978-3-030-37720-5_8
15. Feldman, R., Rosenfeld, B., Bar-Haim, R., Fresko, M.: The stock sonar—sentiment analysis of stocks based on a hybrid approach. In: Twenty-Third IAAI Conference (2011)
16. Han, S., Hao, X., Huang, H.: An event-extraction approach for business analysis from online Chinese news. Electron. Commer. Res. Appl. **28**, 244–260 (2018)
17. Shao, S., Stoumbos, R., Frank Zhang, X.: The power of firm fundamental information in explaining stock returns. Rev. Account. Stud. 1–41 (2021)
18. Boudoukh, J., Feldman, R., Kogan, S., Richardson, M.: Information, trading, and volatility: evidence from firm-specific news. Rev. Finan. Stud. **32**(3), 992–1033 (2019)
19. Peng, Y., Jiang, H.: Leverage financial news to predict stock price movements using word embeddings and deep neural networks. arXiv preprint arXiv:1506.07220 (2015)

Dataset Creation Framework for Personalized Type-Based Facet Ranking Tasks Evaluation

Esraa Ali[1(✉)], Annalina Caputo[2(✉)], Séamus Lawless[1], and Owen Conlan[1]

[1] ADAPT Centre, School of Computer Science and Statistics, Trinity College Dublin, Dublin, Ireland
{esraa.ali,seamus.lawless,owen.conlan}@adaptcentre.ie
[2] ADAPT Centre, School of Computing, Dublin City University, Dublin, Ireland
annalina.caputo@adaptcentre.ie

Abstract. Faceted Search Systems (FSS) have gained prominence in many existing vertical search systems. They provide facets to assist users in allocating their desired search target quickly. In this paper, we present a framework to generate datasets appropriate for simulation-based evaluation of these systems. We focus on the task of personalized type-based facet ranking. Type-based facets (t-facets) represent the categories of the resources being searched in the FSS. They are usually organized in a large multilevel taxonomy. Personalized t-facet ranking methods aim at identifying and ranking the parts of the taxonomy which reflects query relevance as well as user interests. While evaluation protocols have been developed for facet ranking, the problem of personalising the facet rank based on user profiles has lagged behind due to the lack of appropriate datasets. To fill this gap, this paper introduces a framework to reuse and customise existing real-life data collections. The framework outlines the eligibility criteria and the data structure requirements needed for this task. It also details the process to transform the data into a ground-truth dataset. We apply this framework to two existing data collections in the domain of Point-of-Interest (POI) suggestion. The generated datasets are analysed with respect to the taxonomy richness (variety of types) and user profile diversity and length. In order to experiment with the generated datasets, we combine this framework with a widely adopted simulated user-facet interaction model to evaluate a number of existing personalized t-facet ranking baselines.

Keywords: Type-based facets · Faceted search · Personalization · Dataset collection · Evaluation framework · Simulated users

1 Introduction

In Faceted Search Systems (FSS), facets associated with the information objects being searched are used to decompose the information space into compounds

K. S. Candan et al. (Eds.): CLEF 2021, LNCS 12880, pp. 27–39, 2021.
https://doi.org/10.1007/978-3-030-85251-1_3

of subjects [9]. They allow users to filter and narrow down the search space quickly. However, as the size of the collection increases, so does the number of facets, making it impractical to display them all at once. To tackle this problem, FSS usually employ ranking methods to find and promote relevant facets. Personalized facet ranking approaches exploit current user interactions as well as historical feedback to identify and rank facets of interest to the user. This paper looks at this problem by focusing on the specific approaches to type-base facet (t-facet) ranking, in which facets are further organised in a hierarchy for better readability. T-facets are derived from structured data organised in hierarchies, such as ontologies or taxonomies, and are usually extracted from `isA` or `type` attributes associated with the information objects.

Although the current literature presents a wealth of research in FSS, this area lacks standard datasets with relevance judgments for the specific problem of *personalised* facet ranking. This problem is even more relevant for personalized t-facet ranking tasks. Personalized FSS vary on the experimental setup they use to evaluate their ranking methods. Furthermore, none of the existing setups involves a rich hierarchical type-based taxonomy nor deals with the hierarchical nature of t-facets. A unified systematic methodology to build and evaluate collections suitable for this task is needed.

This research solves this problem by introducing a framework that customizes existing data collections to make them suitable for the assessment of such methods. It is dedicated to evaluate personalized t-facet ranking approaches where the past user's selections are used in the ranking process. The ranking methods focuses on type-based facets to leverage both their categorical and hierarchical nature. We study how datasets for personalised t-facet ranking should be selected and customized to fit the purpose of this task, and which simulation methods and IR metrics should be adopted to evaluate such FSS.

The proposed framework is concerned with search tasks that aim at minimizing user effort in precision-oriented FSS. The assumption is that the search task is fulfilled as soon as the user finds their intended search target. T-facet ranking approaches are evaluated by using a simulation-based methodology proposed by Koren et al. [8], which is well established and widely used in faceted search literature. The evaluation assumes that the searcher can identify the intended target and their associated facets as soon as they see it.

We contribute to this research area by proposing a dataset creation framework to evaluate personalized t-facet ranking methods using simulated interaction models. The framework outlines the eligibility criteria for existing collections, as well as the required data structure of the underlying documents (or information objects) and associated taxonomy of types. The framework also details the pre-processing and transformation steps required to implement this customization. Using this framework, we introduce two datasets created for this evaluation task. Finally, we show the feasibility of the proposed framework by analysing the generated datasets and using them to evaluate several personalized t-facet ranking baselines.

2 Related Research

Personalized t-facet ranking is an unexplored area in literature, hence we give a brief overview of existing personalized facet ranking evaluations. Chantamunee et al. [4] suggested a personalized facet ranking based on Collaborative Filtering (CF). They used user ratings and Matrix Factorization via SVM to learn facet ranks. The MoviesLens dataset was used in their evaluation. The average rating given by the user to the facet is used as ground truth, they reported RMSE values to measure the effectiveness of the ranking method. This experimental setup might be useful in prediction tasks, but it does not assess how the final facet list will assist the user in reaching their target.

Koren et al. [8] argues that task-based studies, while undoubtedly useful, are very limited, because they are expensive to conduct, hard to repeat, and the number of users is usually limited, which makes their results inconclusive and not reproducible, especially in personalized search systems. They instead suggest an approach that simulates the clicking behavior of users in the FSS. They attempt to measure the amount of effort required by users to satisfy their search needs. A User information need is considered fulfilled when the target resource is located by using the ranked facets. Based on this idea, the proposed evaluation counts users actions taken towards finding this intended target. The goal of the evaluation is to minimize the effort needed by the users to fulfill their search needs.

This is the most adopted simulation model for precision-oriented FSS present in literature [1, 10–12] and others have followed. Adaptive Twitter search system [1] adopted this approach for finding tweets. User profiles were built from users' previous tweets, and the evaluation assessed whether or not the personalized ranking approach could predict the latest retweets. Also non-personalized FSS adopted the same simulated user evaluation method. Vandic et al. [10] suggested an approach to rank facets based on query relevance and information structure features in the e-commerce domain. Different models for clicking behavior were used and metrics measuring user effort to scan facets and their values were computed.

In general, existing literature seems to follow two different paths to obtain evaluation collections in faceted search. The first is to utilize existing ad-hoc IR datasets with relevant judgments provided on the resource level. In this case, it is assumed that relevance travels from the resource (document) to the facets to which they belong. This is the path followed by the INEX 2011 Data Centric Track [12]. The task consisted of two sub-tasks: an ad-hoc search task and a faceted search one. In the faceted search track, the evaluation metrics measured the effort needed to reach the first relevant result. The evaluation was based on the user simulation interaction model proposed by Koren et al. [8]. We follow this path in transforming the TREC-CS 2016 dataset in Sect. 4.1. Our framework customizes the dataset to fit to the type-based facet ranking task, existing personalized relevance judgments were useful to evaluate the facet ranking approach based on the same INEX 2011 Data Centric track assumptions.

The second path is to transform existing real-life datasets to fit facet ranking evaluation. This path was followed by Koren et al. [8] on the MovieLens evaluation. In order to generate query requests, they used the most recent user's ratings as search targets. The simulation approach was used to measure the user effort to reach those targets. The MovieLens dataset is not suitable for our task as movies genre (types) are limited and do not have a multilevel hierarchical taxonomy.

Following the steps in this last approach, our framework customizes real-life collections into a TREC-like format and then applies the INEX evaluation method. The customization framework formalizes the dataset generation process and extends it to suit the case of type-based facets. As an example of the second path, we adopt The Yelp dataset described in Sect. 4.2. In both paths, the same aspects need to exist in the dataset in order to be a good fit for this research task, these are discussed in section (Sect. 3.2).

For both use cases, we adopt the metrics proposed in the INEX 2011 task: 1) The number of actions (#Actions), which counts how many clicks the user has to perform on the ranked facets in order to reach the first relevant document in the top results; 2) The faceted scan (F-Scan), which measures the user's effort to scan facets and documents until the user reach the same first relevant document in the top results.

3 Dataset Customization Framework

Before formalising the desiderata of the data and the processing procedure to generate a ground-truth dataset, we define the personalised t-facet ranking problem in the context of a FSS. We assume that when the user submits a search query, the underlying search engine starts by retrieving and ranking the top relevant documents.[1,2] Then, the FSS collects the t-facets associated with all retrieved documents. These collected t-facets are reckoned to be relevant and represent the input for the t-facet ranking approach. This research assumes that the ranking of t-facets occurs during the initial population of the result page, and that the t-facets are not reshuffled during the navigation process unless the user submits a new query, which will re-initiate the facet ranking step.

3.1 Eligibility Criteria

The applicability of the proposed framework is subjected to a number of criteria that pertain the domain, search task and type of data, listed as follows:

1. The underlying data collection is structured. It contains objects and each object has properties and types, which can be used as type-based facets.

[1] In the scope of this work, the term 'documents' is used to refer to the information objects being searched. According to the FSS domain, documents can be places, web pages, products, books or images, etc.

[2] How the document ranking is performed is outside scope of this research.

2. The searchable objects belong to a rich taxonomy of categories, from which stems the need for ranking. This is a crucial requirement, as the categories act as type-based facets.
3. Data contain plenty of user feedback, ratings and reviews, which are also useful for personalization.
4. The data is accessible and available online, as some datasets needs further data collection or have no pre-defined taxonomy of types, which makes them unsuitable for this task.
5. The dataset's domain should be suitable for faceted search, e.g. product shopping, digital libraries, venue suggestion, social event search, etc.
6. There is room for personlization in both facet ranking and search result ranking.

3.2 Designated Data Structure

The intended dataset contains a collection of documents, or resources, to be searched. Each document has:

1. Textual description, for example a web page content or a description written by the document's owner.
2. A set of reviews and ratings given to this document by the users. The reviews reflect users' experiences or opinions about this document.
3. A set of categories assigned to the document by the document owners or system admins. The categories belong to a large hierarchical taxonomy of categories and they are treated as type-based facets.

Every document in the collection must be associated to at least one category. Documents may belong to more than one category. Each category must match with only one node in the hierarchical taxonomy. The FSS operates on a single unified taxonomy of categories for all the documents in the collection. When the facet types belong to a large, multilevel taxonomy, the FSS need to select the appropriate levels in the t-facet taxonomy to present to the user. In that case, we refer to them as level-n t-facets, where n is the level of the t-facet in the original taxonomy.

This hierarchical taxonomy can be seen as an directed acyclic graph, or tree, of categories, meaning that each node must have exactly one parent and can have zero or multiple children. Figure 1 demonstrates the tree structure with an emphasis on the levels. The taxonomy tree has a single root at level zero, this is the top of the tree. Level-n is the lowest level and contains the end leaf nodes. Categories (types) at the same level have the same distance from the root node.

This categorical taxonomy serves as the type hierarchy from which all the type-based facets are derived. Defining this taxonomy, its levels and the relationship between its nodes is crucial as this governs the t-facet ranking process.

Since this research is concerned with evaluating t-facet ranking rather than facet generation, the t-facets are directly collected and aggregated from the data. How the t-facets taxonomy is created or assigned to documents is outside of the

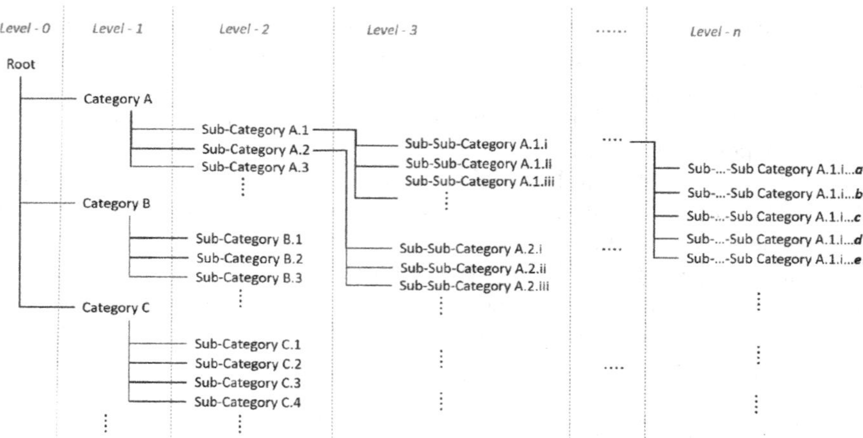

Fig. 1. Example of a multilevel hierarchical taxonomy of categories.

scope of this research. However, the ordering of t-facets is decided by the ranking algorithm.

The desired dataset should also includes user profiles. Each profile might contain basic information about the user, like name, age and gender, if available. It also has historical ratings the user gave to a number of documents within the collection. User ratings reflect whether they favored this document or not. Rating values belong to a numerical scale where the minimum value means dissatisfaction, and the maximum value reflects complete satisfaction. This scale values can also be mapped or classified to `positive`, `negative`, or `neutral` labels. We assume the middle point of the scale to be neutral, while values above it are positive, and values below it are considered as negative.

3.3 Required Preprocessing

The pre-processing, performed on the document categories, ensures that all the categories and their ancestors are linked to the document. Missing ancestors are added to the list of linked document categories. Ancestors common to multiple categories associated with the document are added only once. Pseudo-code explaining this preprocessing is shown in Algorithm 1.

This preprocessing step is mandatory to ensure that the ranking method uses consistent category levels during the ranking process, as the ranking approaches consider a pre-configured number of levels. Let us consider the case of a document originally assigned to a fifth level category with a system operating at only the first two levels of the taxonomy. The pre-processing will ensure that the second level parent of the level-5 category is also included in the list. Without this step, the ranking approach might disregard this document and its t-facets from the ranking process.

Algorithm 1: Pre-processing Document Categories

```
Input: document, taxonomy_tree
Result: Expanded categories list
categories_list = retrieve_categories(document);
;                              // Returns list of categories for document
complete_category_list= {};
for category ∈ categories_list do
    complete_category_list.append(category);
    ancestors_list = find_ancestors(category);
    ;            // Returns all ancestors of category but the root node
    for ancestor ∈ ancestors_list do
        if ancestor ∉ categories_list then
            complete_category_list.append(ancestor);
        end
    end
end
Output: complete_category_list
```

3.4 Generating Evaluation Requests

Typically, existing IR datasets already contain requests and their relevance judgments at document level. In addition, datasets like the TREC-CS, provide the current search context and the user's historical ratings. However, datasets adapted from real-life require an additional step to create requests that imitate this type of information.

To achieve this, user information including user historical picks[3] can be utilized. Lets assume the users has m historical picks recorded in the original collection. We consider the most recent n picks as the intended search target. The n picks are then grouped according to their context (for example venues in the same city, or season of visit). Each context group that has a minimum threshold of t candidates will form a separate request. In order to produce a relevance judgment for each candidate in a request, the candidate's user rating is mapped into a relevance score; i.e. if the user rated this pick positively then it is considered relevant, otherwise it is considered irrelevant.

The personalized t-facet ranking task consists then in predicting the type-based facet sub-tree to which these relevant picks belong. The remaining of the ratings are part of the user's history and added to the user profile in the request. To avoid creating poor user profiles, only users with a minimum of r ratings in their profile are considered for this setup.

When the dataset under consideration does not provide explicit information needs, the framework generates artificial queries for each user. The queries are collected from the text associated with documents that the user has positively favored in the past (excluding the documents considered as candidates for eval-

[3] User picks are the user's interaction with the system that expresses a preference, like a rating, review, or feedback.

uation). For this purpose, NLP methods for extracting keywords or tags can be employed to generate the top phrases which reflects the user's interests.

The contexts and the textual query will be used as input to the search engine. Both the quality of the generated queries and the retrieval model affect the evaluation of the facet ranking method. The search engine must be able to retrieve the intended search target in the relevant document set, otherwise, the appropriate facet needed to reach that document could be omitted in the ranked sub-tree. On the other side, assuming that such a document is in the initial pool retrieved by the search engine, it is the objective of the t-facet ranking approach to promote it at the top of the result list.

4 Experiments

In this section we demonstrate how the proposed framework can be applied in two different scenarios to obtain appropriate datasets for personalised t-facet ranking evaluation. The tourism domain, specifically the point of interest (POI) suggestion task, is chosen for the search task. In addition to the availability of several online datasets, POI suggestion is a well-known personalization task where categories have already proven to play an important role [2,3]. Moreover, we were able to identify two datasets in this domain that satisfy all the criteria listed in Sect. 3.2: TREC-CS [7] and the Yelp datasets[4]. The following two subsections describe the two datasets, how they meet the criteria, and how they were customized to fit the t-facet ranked process.

4.1 Use Case 1: TREC-CS Dataset

The first dataset to which apply the proposed framework is the TREC Contextual Suggestion (TREC-CS) track dataset [7]. TREC-CS is a personalized Point-Of-Interest (POI) recommendation task in which participants develop systems to provide a ranked list of suggestions related to a given user profile and a context. We tackle the POI suggestion problem by ranking the types of venues as t-facets. The t-facet taxonomy is derived from the Foursquare venue category hierarchy[5]. To link as much Foursquare venues to TREC-CS POIs as possible, we complement the original data with three Foursquare supplementary datasets from [2,3] and our own crawled POIs.

The contexts and requests are given by the dataset. In order to implement the document ranking, the input queries are formed by combining the user's tags weighed by their most common ratings provided by the same user. For the document ranking step, POIs web pages and reviews are indexed with Solr using BM25 with a NDCG value of 0.4023. The existence of relevance judgments makes it possible to evaluate our approach against a well established ground-truth. We follow the evaluation strategy used in the Faceted Search task of INEX 2011 Data-Centric Track [12].

[4] https://www.yelp.com/dataset, accessed June 2021.

[5] https://developer.foursquare.com/docs/resources/categories, version:20180323.

4.2 Use Case 2: Yelp Dataset

In this use case, we apply the framework to the Yelp Open Dataset. In order to be comparable to TREC-CS dataset, we use it as a POI suggestion dataset. The user reviews, ratings, and POIs information are provided with the original dataset. POIs are assigned to categories derived from Yelp categories tree[6], which we use as t-facet taxonomy.

To ensure rich user profiles, only users with more than 170 reviews are included ($r = 170$). This threshold is suitable to have lengthy user profiles and a reasonable number of users in the dataset. We cap the user review at 1000 most recent reviews. For each user, we take the most recent 50 reviews ($n = 50$). To create visit context, we group the reviews by their city and state. Any context with more than 20 candidates is considered as a separate request ($c = 20$), this ensures a high number of relevant search targets for each request.

Unfortunately the Yelp dataset does not provide textual description for the POIs. Instead, we index all reviews, tips and attributes collected for each POI with Solr. The location is used as the initial filter to the search engine. In order to build a query, for each user we generate the top keywords from the latest 20 reviews in the user history (excluding all candidate target POIs). The query keywords are created using the Rapid Automatic Keyword Extraction algorithm (Rake)[7].

We created the relevance judgment for each request by mapping the user rating in the candidate target POIs into relevance score ($score = rating - 2$), thus POIs rated 2 and 1 will be considered irrelevant. This is useful to evaluate the document ranking separately. Also in this case the search engine is implemented in Solr using BM25, resulting in a NDCG value of 0.1608.

4.3 Personalized T-Facet Ranking Baselines

This section introduces the personalization baselines used to experiment with the two generated datasets. For methods that do not handle the hierarchical nature of the t-facets, we followed the two-step approach suggested by Ali et al. [6]. The first step scores each individual type-based facet. The second step uses the generated score to build the final t-facet tree to be displayed to the user.

T-Facet Scoring Methods

Probabilistic Scoring (Prob. Scoring) [6]. This is a probabilistic model to personalize t-facet ranking. Topic-based user profiles are collected from users' historical interactions with the system. The method assigns a score to the t-facet according to its relevancy to the user and query. We experiment using the no-background model with cosine similarity.

---

[6] https://www.yelp.com/developers/documentation/v3/all_category_list/categories.json.

[7] https://github.com/csurfer/rake-nltk.

Rocchio-BERT [5]. A lightweight method which utilizes Rocchio formula to build a vector representing the user interests. In this model, the user's profile is expressed in a category space through vectors that capture the users' past preferences. The BERT embeddings are used as t-facet representation in vector space. The t-facet score is the cosine similarity between its BERT vector and the user profile vector.

Most Prob. (Person) [8]. Most probable scoring method utilizes the user historical ratings. It is defined as the probability that the user will rate this facet positively. It is the number of time a t-facet was associated with a positive review by the user divided by the total number of POIs rated by the user.

Most Prob. (Collab). Also suggested by Koren et al. [8]. It is similar to the previous method, but computes the probabilities considering all the ratings from all the users in the system. It counts how many times this t-facet was rated positively by all the users divided by the number of POIs rated in the system.

MF-SVM. Matrix Factorization (MF) using SVM [4]. The matrix is built by adding the users and their t-facet ratings. T-facet ratings are collected from the POIs' ratings to which they are associated. Usually, the same facet may be associated with several POIs, thus has multiple ratings from the same user. In this case, this method takes the mean of the t-facet rating values.

T-Facet Tree Building Method
The tree construction algorithm re-orders the original taxonomy tree by using the generated scores from the previous step [6]. It follows a bottom-up approach where the t-facets at the lower level in the taxonomy are sorted first, followed by all the ancestors of those t-facets, and so on up to the root of the hierarchy.

To build a final t-facet tree with v levels, we adopted a *fixed level* strategy [6]. The strategy respects the original taxonomy hierarchy and uses a predefined fixed page size for each t-facet level. It starts by grouping t-facets at level-v by their parent. Then, it sorts the parent nodes at level-$(v-1)$ by aggregating the scores of their top k children, the children are ordered by their relevance score generated in the previous step, and so on, up to level-1. We use *Max.* aggregation function to keep the top ranked t-facet at the top of the final tree.

5 Results and Discussion

Table 1 shows the statistics for the two generated datasets, Yelp and TREC-CS 2016. Both datasets operate on large multilevel taxonomies. Yelp taxonomy provides more categories, which make the ranking task more challenging. The statistics also show that the user profiles generated from Yelp dataset contain larger number of rated POIs per user; as a result we have more diverse t-facets rated by users. This provides richer data for the ranking algorithms to use in building the personalization model.

Table 1. Comparison of Yelp and TREC-CS 2016 statistics after customization with the proposed framework.

Item	TREC-CS 2016	Yelp
Total number of POIs	778K	160K
Total number of Taxonomy Types	942	1,566
Total number of Taxonomy Types in first two levels	459	994
Number Taxonomy Levels	5	4
Total number of Users	27 (209)	1,456
Average number of POIs rated per user	35.5 (54.1)	247.69
Total number of unique POIs rated by users	60 (4072)	81,163
Average number of Rated T-Facets in user history	38.18	135.8
Total Number of Requests	61	1495
Average number of t-Facets to be ranked per request	208	168.14

Yelp dataset also overcomes the limited availability of user profiles in TREC-CS 2016, in which users always rated the same 60 POIs. This affected the category distribution of the rated t-facets. In order to minimize the limited profile issues, we included users and ratings from TREC-CS 2015 dataset (statistics of this dataset are shown in the table between brackets). The results reported below use this improved user profiles.

Table 2 reports the evaluation results obtained for both datasets using the baselines mentioned in Sect. 4.3. All results are reported by adopting the Fixed Level-Max tree building strategy, with level-1 and level-2 page size set to three. Several methods behave consistently across both collection. Rocchio-BERT outperformed the other personalization baselines on both datasets. Second in performance is the Prob. Scoring method; it is the second best method with Most Prob. (Collab). On the Yelp dataset, it provides the second best #Actions while its F-Scan results are worse than the Most Probable (Person.).

Table 2. Results for baselines using Fixed-level (Max) strategy.

Scoring method	TREC-CS		Yelp	
	F-Scan	#Actions	F-Scan	#Actions
Rochio-BERT	**3.28**	**1.28**	**9.33**	**2.66**
Prob. Scoring	3.45	1.33	10.32	2.98
MF-SVM	3.91	1.49	19.29	4.07
Most Prob. (Person)	3.73	1.61	9.65	3.03
Most Prob. (Collab)	3.35	1.33	10.49	3.00

The affect of the quality of personal profiles is more evident in the Most Probable (Person.) performance, since this ranking method mainly depends on the individual user historical ratings. The approach improved with respect to both metrics in the Yelp dataset. On the other hand, MF-SVM performances dropped in the Yelp dataset; this indicates that the adoption of the average of documents rating as a t-facet rating is a poor heuristic to rate t-facets when many diverging ratings need to be aggregated.

6 Conclusions

This work presented a framework to generate benchmarks that can be used in evaluating personalized type-based facet ranking methods. The framework employs a fixed predefined t-facet taxonomy, which avoids propagating errors from the t-facet generation step to the facet ranking step. This enables the assessment and evaluation of the t-facet ranking process in isolation from other FSS components. We demonstrated the feasibility of this customization method by applying it in two different datasets. The first is TREC-CS dataset with existing relevance judgment at the document level, and the other is a larger dataset released by Yelp. In this last dataset, users' historical interactions are employed to compensate the lack of relevance judgments. As future plan, we intend to experiment with additional datasets in other domains, like product shopping or digital libraries.

Acknowledgements. This work was supported by the ADAPT Centre, funded by Science Foundation Ireland Research Centres Programme (Grant 13/RC/2106; 13/RC/2106_P2) and co-funded by the European Regional Development Fund.

References

1. Abel, F., Celik, I., Houben, G.J., Siehndel, P.: Leveraging the semantics of tweets for adaptive faceted search on twitter. The Semantic Web (2011)
2. Aliannejadi, M., Mele, I., Crestani, F.: A cross-platform collection for contextual suggestion. In: SIGIR. ACM (2017)
3. Bayomi, M., Lawless, S.: ADAPT_TCD: an ontology-based context aware approach for contextual suggestion. In: TREC (2016)
4. Chantamunee, S., Wong, K.W., Fung, C.C.: Collaborative filtering for personalised facet selection. In: IAIT. ACM (2018)
5. Ali, E., Annalina Caputo, S.L., Conlan, O.: Personalizing type-based facet ranking using BERT embeddings. In: SEMANTiCS (2021)
6. Ali, E., Caputo, A., Lawless, S., Conlan, O.: A probabilistic approach to personalize type-based facet ranking for POI suggestion. In: Brambilla, M., Chbeir, R., Frasincar, F., Manolescu, I. (eds.) ICWE 2021. LNCS, vol. 12706, pp. 175–182. Springer, Cham (2021). https://doi.org/10.1007/978-3-030-74296-6_14
7. Hashemi, S.H., Clarke, C.L., Kamps, J., Kiseleva, J., Voorhees, E.M.: Overview of the TREC 2016 contextual suggestion track. In: TREC (2016)
8. Koren, J., Zhang, Y., Liu, X.: Personalized interactive faceted search. In: WWW. ACM (2008)
9. Tunkelang, D.: Faceted search. Synth. Lect. Inf. Concepts Retrieval Serv. **1**, 1–80 (2009)

10. Vandic, D., Aanen, S., Frasincar, F., Kaymak, U.: Dynamic facet ordering for faceted product search engines. IEEE Trans. Knowl. Data Eng. **PP(99)**, 1 (2017). https://doi.org/10.1109/TKDE.2017.2652461
11. Vandic, D., Frasincar, F., Kaymak, U.: Facet selection algorithms for web product search. In: Proceedings of the 22nd ACM International Conference on Conference on Information & Knowledge Management, pp. 2327–2332. ACM (2013)
12. Wang, Q., Ramírez, G., Marx, M., Theobald, M., Kamps, J.: Overview of the INEX 2011 data-centric track. In: Geva, S., Kamps, J., Schenkel, R. (eds.) INEX 2011. LNCS, vol. 7424, pp. 118–137. Springer, Heidelberg (2012). https://doi.org/10.1007/978-3-642-35734-3_10

SubjectivITA: An Italian Corpus for Subjectivity Detection in Newspapers

Francesco Antici, Luca Bolognini, Matteo Antonio Inajetovic, Bogdan Ivasiuk, Andrea Galassi(✉), and Federico Ruggeri(✉)

DISI, University of Bologna, Bologna, Italy
{francesco.antici,luca.bolognini3,matteo.inajetovic, bogdan.ivasiuk}@studio.unibo.it, {a.galassi,federico.ruggeri6}@unibo.it

Abstract. We present SubjectivITA: the first Italian corpus for subjectivity detection on news articles, with annotations at sentence and document level. Our corpus consists of 103 articles extracted from online newspapers, amounting to 1,841 sentences. We also define baselines for sentence- and document-level subjectivity detection using transformer-based and statistical classifiers. Our results suggest that sentence-level subjectivity annotations may often be sufficient to classify the whole document.

Keywords: Subjectivity detection · Italian language · News articles · Natural language processing · Deep learning

1 Introduction

Subjectivity detection (SD) consists of understanding whether a given piece of text is biased by its creator or not. As highlighted by Chaturvedi et al. [6], SD is a very complex task because the perception of subjectivity is subjective in itself and may derive from different levels of expertise, different interpretations of the language, and also conscious and unconscious biases linked to the personal background. Moreover, domains characterized by the lack of context, such as Tweets, or by references and quotes, such as news articles, pose an additional challenge.

The ability to detect subjectivity in textual documents can greatly help other tasks [31] such as fake news detection, information extraction, question answering, sentiment analysis, and argument mining. The recent success of machine learning techniques based on deep neural networks in many NLP tasks has partially relieved the need for structured knowledge, but it has increased the need for labeled corpora for training. While many resources exist for the English language, the same can not be said for other ones. Projection techniques [12,17] can be used to create new corpora in an unsupervised fashion, but they usually need parallel corpora or they rely on automatic translation processes that

F. Antici, L. Bolognini, M. A. Inajetovic, B. Ivasiuk—Equal contribution.

K. S. Candan et al. (Eds.): CLEF 2021, LNCS 12880, pp. 40–52, 2021.
https://doi.org/10.1007/978-3-030-85251-1_4

Table 1. Nonexhaustive list of SD and SSA corpora. The Size column refers to the type of elements in the Granularity column.

Dataset	Task	Domain	Language	Granularity	Size
Wiebe et al. [30]	SD	News	English	Sentence	~500
Chesley et al. [8]	SSA	News	English	Document	~1,000
Movie Review [21]	SSA	Reviews	English	Document	~2,000
MOAT [7,26]	SSA	News	English	Sentence	~3,500
MPQA [7,32]	SSA	News	English	Sentence	~16,000
NoReC$_{fine}$ [20]	SA	News	Norwegian	Sentence	~8,000
MSA [1]	SSA	News	Arabic	Sentence	~3,000
Odia [18]	SSA	News	Odia	Sentence	~2,000
Volkova et al. [29]	SSA	Twitter	Eng, Spa, Rus	Tweet	~4,500,000
Senti-TUT [4]	SSA	Twitter	Italian	Tweet	~3,000
Felicitta [3]	SSA	Twitter	Italian	Tweet	~1,000
SubjectivITA	SD	News	Italian	**Sent.+Doc.**	1,841 S; 103 D

may compromise the subjective form that some words have in the original language. Additionally, the lack of non-English corpora hinders the evaluation of any cross-lingual technique.

For these reasons, we have created SubjectivITA, the first corpus for SD made of newspaper articles in the Italian language. The corpus has been manually annotated at two different levels of granularity, therefore it is suitable to perform the task both at sentence and document level. To guarantee the quality of the corpus, we followed an iterative process of discussion and modification of the guidelines, so as to align the opinions of the annotators and increase their agreement. We report the problems that emerged during this process and discuss how to address specific ambiguous cases. Finally, we used our corpus as a benchmark to evaluate a set of machine learning techniques that range from basic methods such as Logistic Regression, to state of the art NLP models like BERT [11].

In Sect. 2 we survey related works and present a comparison between existing corpora. In Sects. 3 we describe our labeling process and our guidelines. In Sect. 4 we present our experimental evaluation, while in Sect. 5 we draw conclusions and discuss possible future developments.

2 Related Work

SD is a well-known task, and over the years many resources and methods to address it have been developed. We focus our attention on existing corpora, in particular on those that address this task specifically and those that are not in the

English language, framing them in Table 1 according to multiple aspects. A more comprehensive overview of the topic, including the evolution of SD over the years and the relation with other tasks, is covered by the excellent survey of Chaturvedi et al. [6]. To the best of our knowledge, Wiebe et al. [30] are the first to create a corpus for SD. They annotate a set of news articles and also describe an iterative process to improve inter-annotator agreement and annotation guidelines, from which we draw inspiration for our own process.

Since subjective sentences and documents usually express a stance towards a topic, SD and sentiment analysis (SA) can be performed together. Chesley et al. [8] present one of the first Subjectivity and Sentiment Analysis (SSA) corpora, a multi-class classification task where labels specify whether a subjective sentence conveys a positive or negative sentiment. In recent SSA corpora based on news sources in non-English languages [1,18,20], documents are tagged at the sentence level to obtain more fine-grained labeling than the one achievable by using only document-level tagging. In our corpus, documents are labeled both at the sentence and document level, but we use only two labels (*Subjective* and *Objective*). Concerning the Italian language, existing SSA corpora are mainly based on Twitter [3,4], while our proposed corpus has been obtained from Italian newspapers. Our annotation process is very similar to the one described by Bosco et al. [3], except for some differences in the partition of tasks assigned to the annotators.

3 Creation of the Corpus

Our SubjectivITA corpus was created by manually gathering articles from Italian online newspapers, chosen so as to cover a wide spectrum of styles and topics. The choice fell on outlets of national importance and usually considered as politically impartial, but also on local outlets, columns, and blogs, hoping thus to include more subjective content. The articles were collected between the 20th of January 2021 and the 1st of February 2021 and were chosen randomly among those that contained less than 40 sentences. Both the corpus and the guidelines (in the Italian language) are publicly available.[1]

3.1 Annotation Process

The articles were annotated using two labels, *Objective* (**OBJ**) and *Subjective* (**SUBJ**),[2] defined in Sect. 3.2. Following an initial guidelines draft, four Italian native speakers (A1, A2, A3, A4) independently annotated the same set of 6 articles, totalling 80 sentences, obtaining a preliminary small corpus named $\mathbf{P}_1^{\mathbf{I}}$. The annotation phase consisted of the following step:

1. *Segmentation*: the articles are manually split into separate sentences.[3]

[1] https://github.com/francescoantici/SubjectivITA.

[2] The original Italian terms and labels are "OGGettivo" and "SOGgettivo".

[3] Since different authors have different styles of writing and follow different conventions regarding punctuation symbols, we preferred to not rely on automatic segmentation tools since they may introduce errors.

Table 2. Cohen's kappa results on **sentences** tags.

(a) Corpus $\mathbf{P_1^I}$.

	A1	A2	A3	A4
A1	–	0.38	0.21	0.44
A2	0.38	–	0.41	0.36
A3	0.21	0.41	–	0.51
A4	0.44	0.36	0.51	–

(b) Corpus $\mathbf{P_1^F}$

	A1	A2	A3	A4
A1	–	0.52	0.59	0.52
A2	0.52	–	0.66	0.82
A3	0.59	0.66	–	0.73
A4	0.52	0.82	0.73	–

(c) Corpus $\mathbf{P_2}$

	A1	A2	A3	A4
A1	–	0.52	0.50	0.51
A2	0.52	–	0.65	0.66
A3	0.50	0.65	–	0.76
A4	0.51	0.66	0.76	–

Table 3. Cohen's kappa results on **articles** tags.

(a) Corpus $\mathbf{P_1^I}$

	A1	A2	A3	A4
A1	–	0.67	0.33	0.67
A2	0.67	–	0.67	0.25
A3	0.33	0.67	–	0.00
A4	0.67	0.25	0.00	–

(b) Corpus $\mathbf{P_1^F}$

	A1	A2	A3	A4
A1	–	0.25	0.57	0.25
A2	0.25	–	0.57	1.00
A3	0.57	0.57	–	0.57
A4	0.25	1.00	0.57	–

(c) Corpus $\mathbf{P_2}$

	A1	A2	A3	A4
A1	–	0.53	0.37	0.53
A2	0.53	–	0.78	0.55
A3	0.37	0.78	–	0.78
A4	0.53	0.55	0.78	–

2. *Sentence Labeling*: each sentence obtained from step 1 is labeled independently of the context (i.e. the other sentences).
3. *Document Labeling*: after all the sentences have been labeled, the article is evaluated in its entirety and the appropriate label is assigned.

Then, a guideline improvement phase followed, achieved through group discussion and the annotators' feedback. In this phase, guidelines were refined and expanded to cover unforeseen situations and clarify the ambiguities on which the annotators were either doubtful or disagreeing on. Such a process on annotation and guidelines improvement was iterated multiple times, monitoring the annotators' agreement, until the quality of the annotations was considered satisfactory.

The agreement between the annotators was measured using *Cohen's Kappa* and *Fleiss' Kappa*, and it is shown in Tables 2, 3 and 4. The agreement between each pair of annotators was assessed through Cohen's Kappa, to study the correlation between the annotators, monitor interpretation biases, and make the evaluation transparent. For example, Table 3a clearly shows that after the first iteration, annotators A3 and A4 had no agreement on document annotation. Fleiss' kappa was instead used to monitor the agreement of the whole group, and was used as the stopping criterion: the iterative process finished once substantial agreement ($\kappa \geq 0.6$) [16] on the sentence-level annotation was reached.

This process significantly improved the agreement between the annotators, as clearly shown in Table 4, and led to the final version of this preliminary corpus, named $\mathbf{P_1^F}$. Once the guidelines were finished, they were validated by creating a new preliminary corpus **P2** and evaluating the agreement between the annotators. Such a corpus was composed of 9 articles, amounting to 145 sentences, on which the agreement between the annotators both at sentence- and article-level was close to substantial. The guidelines were therefore considered a reliable tool and were used to annotate the remaining articles. Each annotator

Table 4. Fleiss' kappa values on tags.

Level	$\mathbf{P_1^I}$	$\mathbf{P_1^F}$	$\mathbf{P_2}$
Sentence	0.24	0.65	0.61
Article	0.30	0.53	0.58

Table 5. Summary of the guidelines for sentence tagging.

Objective rules	Subjective rules
O1) Report, historic events, or statistics	S1) Explicit personal opinion
O2) Report of a third subject's emotions	S2) Ironic or sarcastic expression
O3) No conclusions without supporting data	S3) Personal wishes and hopes
O4) Conclusions supported by data	S4) Discriminating expressions
O5) Public and commonly used nicknames	S5) Exaggerated expressions
O6) Common sayings	S6) Conclusions not supported by data
O7) Absence of explicit personal opinions	S7) Expression of subjective emotion
O8) No other rule applies	

received 22 different articles, which they tagged individually, resulting in a final corpus of 103 articles with a total of 1,841 sentences.

3.2 Definition of Objective and Subjective

We define a sentence as subjective whenever it shows its author's point of view or opinion on the matter, even if it's only using irony or sarcasm. Otherwise, the sentence is considered objective. The same definition applies when labeling documents: they are considered subjective when they express, to some degree, the author's personal opinions on the topic at hand, and objective otherwise. The labelling of the documents must not rely on a quantitative evaluation of the number of objective and subjective sentences, but instead on the characteristics of the document as a whole. These general definitions have been further developed in the guidelines as a set of specific rules that have been used by the annotators to discriminate ambiguous cases. We list these rules in Table 5, while in Table 6 we report examples of sentences from the corpus and the guidelines, specifying which rule was applied to label them.

It is important to underline some aspects related to these rules and our decisions regarding ambiguous cases. First of all, since the context of the sentences is not considered for their annotation, sentences that are objective by themselves are labeled as such, even if they would be considered subjective in the specific context of the article where they belong. This may be the case, for example, of sentences that contain subtle irony. Moreover, any fact or data reported in the articles is assumed to be true, unless they concern something that is widely known as incorrect (e.g., *The Sun revolves around the Earth*).

Table 6. Examples of sentences (translated from Italian) with their respective tag and the annotation rule that was applied.

Sentence	Tag	Rule
Without school, Andrew's day is never ending	OBJ	O2
I hope Renzi sues him	SUBJ	S3
They celebrated as if there was no coronavirus	SUBJ	S1
28 December 1977: the New Partisans kill Angelo Pistolesi	OBJ	O1
The consumer expressed his disappointment in a web post	OBJ	O2
You are the worst administration	SUBJ	S4
Supplies seems to be available at international level, but it isn't clear yet	OBJ	O3

One of the most controversial cases of discussion is how quotes influence the subjectivity of an article. Quotes in news articles usually report the words of a person that expresses their personal and subjective perspective on a topic. Since sentences are annotated independently of the context, those that contain quotes are likely to be classified as subjective. In cases where a journalist addresses a topic without expressing their own perspective and only reporting other people's opinions, we can say that the article, in its entirety, is objective. That will therefore result in a document that contains mostly subjective sentences, but it is objective in itself. It can be argued that the best practice to address a controversial topic is to report quotes from parties with different opinions. However, when only one of those parties' opinion is considered by the author, neglecting the others, then the article may aim to influence the reader and skews the perspective towards being subjective. We have chosen to not address this specific case due to its complexity, and to leave it as subject for future work.

Another ambiguous case is whether hypotheses brought up by the author without supporting data should be considered subjective. We decided to distinguish two cases. If the author proposes a hypothetical development of the considered matter and presents it as the only possible scenario, the sentence is considered subjective (rule S6). Conversely, if the development is proposed just as a possible interpretation yet no accent is placed on the veracity of this hypothesis, then the sentence is labeled as objective (rule O3). Obviously, in cases where hypotheses are directly supported by reported facts and data, the sentence is considered objective (rule O4).

Table 7. Classification performance for sentence-level subjectivity detection. We report precision, recall and F1-score for the subjective class **SUBJ**. Additionally, we also consider summary metrics like accuracy and F1-macro scores.

Model	P-SUBJ	R-SUBJ	F1-SUBJ	Accuracy	F1-macro
GRU	0.46	**0.73**	0.56	0.63	0.62
MulilingualBERT	**0.62**	0.67	**0.64**	**0.76**	**0.73**
AlBERTo	**0.62**	0.65	0.63	0.75	0.72
MAJ-B	0.0	0.0	0.0	0.67	0.40
WR-B	0.33	0.30	0.32	0.57	0.50

Table 8. SubjectivITA corpus statistics for subjectivity detection.

(a) Dataset statistics for sentence-level SD.

Split	SUBJ	OBJ	Total
Train	401	998	1,399
Validation	81	134	215
Test	75	152	227

(b) Dataset statistics for document-level SD.

Split	SUBJ	OBJ	Total
Train	28	46	74
Test	10	19	29

4 Subjectivity Detection

Subjectivity detection can be tackled at different levels of granularity depending on the considered textual units that have to be classified. In our experimental setup, we explore the tasks of sentence- and document-level subjectivity detection. We formulate both tasks as a binary classification problem where an input example x can either be subjective or objective.

In particular, document-level classification is a task that comes with multiple valid formulations, where the simplest of them consists in aggregating sentence-level predictions into a single result. Certainly, subjective sentences may have an impact on the overall document label, but when we increase the scope to whole documents, we have also to consider other relevant factors, such as each sentence context, relations, and overall contribution to the gist of the document itself. For instance, a document may contain some subjective sentences that have a marginal contribution to its narrative point of view, thus, not sufficiently impacting the discourse to alter the perceived perspective. Conversely, a document that contains mostly objective sentences may end with a very subjective conclusion, shifting towards subjectivity. Nonetheless, solely focusing on sentence-level subjectivity annotations still represents a valuable baseline worth considering.

4.1 Sentence-Level Detection

Problem Description. In the context of sentence-level subjectivity detection, an input x is represented by a sentence contained in our corpus. Our approach follows an end-to-end perspective by considering deep learning models that directly encode x via an embedding layer and assign it a label $\tilde{y} \in \{\mathbf{SUBJ}, \mathbf{OBJ}\}$.

Models. We consider two major classes of deep learning models in our experimental setup: a) recurrent neural networks and b) transformer-based architectures. Due to the unbalance of our corpus, we also consider a majority baseline, namely **MAJ-B**, and a weighted random baseline based on class distribution, **WR-B**. The models we evaluate are the following:

- **Bi-GRU**: a single-level bi-directional GRU [9] followed by a single dense layer for classification. The employed configuration is as follows: 16 units for the GRU layer with 0.1 dropout rate and 1 unit with sigmoid activation for the dense layer. We consider pre-trained GloVe [22] with embedding dimension set to 200.
- **MulilingualBERT**: the pre-trained `bert-base-multilingual-uncased` version of BERT.[4] As in most of NLP task, fine-tuned BERT [11] models have been successfully used to address SD [14] and related NLP tasks [10,15,19].
- **AlBERTo** [23]: a pre-trained version of BERT for the Italian language, initially fine-tuned on Italian tweets for the task of sentiment analysis (see footnote 4). We consider this model due to the success of BERT-based models on Italian language tasks [27].

Methodology. We divided the corpus sentences into three splits, by randomly assigning the documents to train (75%), validation (12.5%), and test set (12.5%). Table 8a reports a summary of the dataset composition. As a preliminary step, we carried out a hyper-parameter calibration routine by picking the best configuration based on the performance achieved on the validation set. Given the small amount of available data and the non-deterministic aspect of neural networks [24], we repeatedly trained each neural model on the train set with different random seed initialization. We set the number of repetitions to 3. We regularized by early stopping the training phase based on the validation accuracy score. Concerning model optimization, each model was trained to minimize a binary cross-entropy loss. The **Bi-GRU** baseline had the learning rate set to 0.01 and uses Adam optimizer. Both **BERT** and **AlBERTo** had their learning rate set to 1e-5 after the calibration phase. All models were trained for a maximum of 30 epochs and had the early stopping patience is set to 3.

Results. Table 7 summarizes the results of the sentence-level subjectivity detection task. Each metrics is to be considered as the average over three individual

[4] For all the transformer architectures we considered the implementations available at http://huggingface.co/.

Table 9. Classification performance for document-level subjectivity detection. We mainly report precision, recall, and F1-score for the subjective class **SUBJ**. Additionally, we also consider summary metrics like accuracy and F1-macro scores.

Model	P-SUBJ	R-SUBJ	F1-SUBJ	Acc	F1-macro
RF	0.56	0.50	0.53	0.69	0.65
DT	0.60	0.30	0.40	0.69	0.60
SVM	**0.83**	0.50	0.62	**0.79**	**0.74**
LR	0.80	0.40	0.53	0.76	0.69
MAJ-B	0.0	0.0	0.0	0.66	0.40
WR-B	0.39	0.43	0.41	0.57	0.54
r-SUBJ	0.77	**0.89**	**0.83**	0.76	0.71

model runs. All employed deep learning models are well above the majority baseline **MAJ-B**. In particular, the **GRU** baseline reaches satisfactory performance with a 0.62 F1-macro score and 0.56 F1-SUBJ score, but it is significantly outperformed by the BERT-based models. **MulilingualBERT** and **AlBERTo** achieve comparable performance, with the former achieving few percentage points more. Due to the challenging nature of the task and the imperfect agreement between annotators, it is difficult to evaluate what is the upper bound on this task and how much space for improvement there is.

4.2 Document-Level Detection

Problem Description. In the sentence-level setting, the inputs x are represented by the documents of our corpus. In this scenario, we opt for a more traditional machine learning approach, mainly due to the small corpus size. As already stated, document-level detection cannot be solely reduced to a function of sentence-level predictions because it involves multiple factors like contextual information and relevance to the document narrative. For this reason we hypothesize that deep learning approaches applied to the whole document would probably lead to better results. Nonetheless, in this stage of work we are mainly interested in presenting valuable baselines for the task. In particular, we evaluate to what extent features that mainly concern sentence-level subjectivity labels can be considered reliable. On this basis, we manually select a set of handcrafted features that sums up the content of each article concerning subjectivity information. More precisely, we consider for each article the following indicators: number of sentences, number of objective sentences, number of subjective sentences, and article source.

Models. We consider the following set of linear classifiers: Random Forest (**RF**), Decision Tree (**DT**), Support Vector Machine (**SVM**), and Logistic Regression

(**LR**).[5] We consider the same baselines described for sentence-level detection. In addition, we consider a threshold-based baseline, namely **r-SUBJ**, which discriminates between subjective and objective articles based on the average ratio of subjective sentences per article computed on the train set.

Methodology. We initially randomly split collected news articles into train (70%) and test (30%) sets, respectively, obtaining the dataset illustrated by Table 8b. Models are initially trained on the train set and later evaluated on the test set. No preliminary hyper-parameter calibration phase was considered in this scenario.

Results. Table 9 summarizes obtained results for each model. In particular, **SVM** significantly outperforms other machine learning models, achieving an F1-SUBJ and F1-macro scores of respectively 0.62 and 0.74. Surprisingly, the ratio-based baseline **r-SUBJ** achieves the highest F1-SUBJ score (0.83) and is second only to **SVM**. Such results favor the simplifying hypothesis that even summary sentence-level subjectivity information is a useful indicator for this task. Overall, all reported models would certainly benefit from a preliminary hyper-parameters calibration phase.

5 Conclusions

We presented a new Italian corpus for subjectivity detection in news articles. To the best of our knowledge, this is the first Italian corpus language to address this domain and also to have annotations both at document and sentence level. During the annotation we have encountered and discussed problems related to the inherent ambiguity of the task at hand, such as sentences involving quotes and irony, resulting in the creation of detailed guidelines that may help the creation new future resources. Finally, we produced a few baselines. Our results suggest that sentence-level information may be enough to properly classify documents, even if it may lead to misclassification of some ambiguous cases, such as documents with many quotes. We plan to test this hypothesis in future works.

Due to the scarcity of similar resources, the corpus is meant to contribute to research in SD, but it could also be used in multi-objective or transfer learning settings. This could be done across different dimensions, such as domains (news and tweets), languages, and related tasks (e.g., sentiment analysis [5], argument mining [2], and fake news detection [28]). Future research directions include extending the corpus, allowing a better and more robust evaluation of deep learning solutions and enriching the corpus with additional annotation layers concerning strongly correlated tasks like sentiment analysis. A further possibility would be to operate with a non-binary subjectivity scale in the hope that a richer annotation scheme might improve the effectiveness of SD as an auxiliary

[5] All mentioned models are employed with their default configuration as defined within the `sciki-learn` python library: http://scikit-learn.org/stable/.

task. However, the definition of such a scale would pose additional challenges. For what concerns the experimental part, we aim to apply more advanced techniques to the document-level detection, exploiting sentence embeddings [25] and hierarchical architectures based on neural attention [13,33]. Finally, we plan to perform experiments regarding transfer learning across corpora in different languages exploiting automatic translation of documents.

Acknowledgement. We would like to thank Paolo Torroni for his help and supervision.

References

1. Abdul-Mageed, M., Diab, M.T.: Subjectivity and sentiment annotation of modern standard arabic newswire. In: Linguistic Annotation Workshop LAW, pp. 110–118. The Association for Computer Linguistics (2011)
2. Basile, P., Basile, V., Cabrio, E., Villata, S.: Argument mining on Italian news blogs. In: CLiC-it/EVALITA, vol. 1749. CEUR-WS.org (2016)
3. Bosco, C., et al.: Detecting happiness in Italian tweets: towards an evaluation dataset for sentiment analysis in Felicitta. In: ES^{3}LOD@LREC, pp. 56–63. ELRA (2014)
4. Bosco, C., Patti, V., Bolioli, A.: Developing corpora for sentiment analysis: the case of irony and senti-tut. IEEE Intell. Syst. **28**(2), 55–63 (2013). https://doi.org/10.1109/MIS.2013.28
5. Caselli, T., Novielli, N., Patti, V., Rosso, P.: Evalita 2018: overview on the 6th evaluation campaign of natural language processing and speech tools for Italian. In: EVALITA@CLiC-it, vol. 2263. CEUR-WS.org (2018)
6. Chaturvedi, I., Cambria, E., Welsch, R.E., Herrera, F.: Distinguishing between facts and opinions for sentiment analysis: survey and challenges. Inf. Fus. **44**, 65–77 (2018). https://doi.org/10.1016/j.inffus.2017.12.006
7. Chenlo, J.M., Losada, D.E.: An empirical study of sentence features for subjectivity and polarity classification. Inf. Sci. **280**, 275–288 (2014). https://doi.org/10.1016/j.ins.2014.05.009
8. Chesley, P., Vincent, B., Xu, L., Srihari, R.K.: Using verbs and adjectives to automatically classify blog sentiment. In: AAAI Spring Symposium: Computational Approaches to Analyzing Weblogs, pp. 27–29. AAAI (2006)
9. Cho, K., et al.: Learning phrase representations using RNN encoder-decoder for statistical machine translation. In: EMNLP, pp. 1724–1734. ACL (2014). https://doi.org/10.3115/v1/d14-1179
10. Demszky, D., Movshovitz-Attias, D., Ko, J., Cowen, A.S., Nemade, G., Ravi, S.: Goemotions: a dataset of fine-grained emotions. In: ACL, pp. 4040–4054. Association for Computational Linguistics (2020). https://doi.org/10.18653/v1/2020.acl-main.372
11. Devlin, J., Chang, M., Lee, K., Toutanova, K.: BERT: pre-training of deep bidirectional transformers for language understanding. In: NAACL-HLT (1), pp. 4171–4186. ACL (2019). https://doi.org/10.18653/v1/n19-1423
12. Galassi, A., Drazewski, K., Lippi, M., Torroni, P.: Cross-lingual annotation projection in legal texts. In: COLING, pp. 915–926. International Committee on Computational Linguistics (2020). https://doi.org/10.18653/v1/2020.coling-main.79

13. Galassi, A., Lippi, M., Torroni, P.: Attention in natural language processing. IEEE Trans. Neural Netw. Learn. Syst. 1–18 (2020). https://doi.org/10.1109/TNNLS.2020.3019893
14. Huo, H., Iwaihara, M.: Utilizing BERT pretrained models with various fine-tune methods for subjectivity detection. In: Wang, X., Zhang, R., Lee, Y.-K., Sun, L., Moon, Y.-S. (eds.) APWeb-WAIM 2020. LNCS, vol. 12318, pp. 270–284. Springer, Cham (2020). https://doi.org/10.1007/978-3-030-60290-1_21
15. Kaliyar, R.K., Goswami, A., Narang, P.: FakeBERT: fake news detection in social media with a BERT-based deep learning approach. Multimed. Tools Appl. 1–24 (2021). https://doi.org/10.1007/s11042-020-10183-2
16. Landis, J.R., Koch, G.G.: The measurement of observer agreement for categorical data. Biometrics, 159–174 (1977). https://doi.org/10.2307/2529310
17. Mihalcea, R., Banea, C., Wiebe, J.: Learning multilingual subjective language via cross-lingual projections. In: ACL (2007)
18. Mohanty, G., Mishra, P., Mamidi, R.: Annotated corpus for sentiment analysis in Odia language. In: LREC, pp. 2788–2795. ELRA (2020)
19. Mozafari, M., Farahbakhsh, R., Crespi, N.: A BERT-based transfer learning approach for hate speech detection in online social media. In: Cherifi, H., Gaito, S., Mendes, J.F., Moro, E., Rocha, L.M. (eds.) COMPLEX NETWORKS 2019. SCI, vol. 881, pp. 928–940. Springer, Cham (2020). https://doi.org/10.1007/978-3-030-36687-2_77
20. Øvrelid, L., Mæhlum, P., Barnes, J., Velldal, E.: A fine-grained sentiment dataset for Norwegian. In: LREC, pp. 5025–5033. European Language Resources Association (2020)
21. Pang, B., Lee, L.: A sentimental education: sentiment analysis using subjectivity summarization based on minimum cuts. In: ACL, pp. 271–278. ACL (2004). https://doi.org/10.3115/1218955.1218990
22. Pennington, J., Socher, R., Manning, C.D.: Glove: global vectors for word representation. In: EMNLP, pp. 1532–1543. ACL (2014). https://doi.org/10.3115/v1/d14-1162
23. Polignano, M., Basile, P., de Gemmis, M., Semeraro, G., Basile, V.: Alberto: Italian BERT language understanding model for NLP challenging tasks based on tweets. In: CLiC-it, vol. 2481. CEUR-WS.org (2019)
24. Reimers, N., Gurevych, I.: Reporting score distributions makes a difference: Performance study of LSTM-networks for sequence tagging. In: EMNLP, pp. 338–348. Association for Computational Linguistics, Copenhagen (2017). https://doi.org/10.18653/v1/d17-1035
25. Reimers, N., Gurevych, I.: Making monolingual sentence embeddings multilingual using knowledge distillation. In: EMNLP (1), pp. 4512–4525. Association for Computational Linguistics (2020). https://doi.org/10.18653/v1/2020.emnlp-main.365
26. Seki, Y., Evans, D.K., Ku, L., Sun, L., Chen, H., Kando, N.: Overview of multilingual opinion analysis task at NTCIR-7. In: NTCIR. National Institute of Informatics (NII) (2008)
27. Tamburini, F.: How "BERTology" changed the state-of-the-art also for Italian NLP. In: CLiC-it, vol. 2769. CEUR-WS.org (2020)
28. Vedova, M.L.D., Tacchini, E., Moret, S., Ballarin, G., Pierro, M.D., de Alfaro, L.: Automatic online fake news detection combining content and social signals. In: FRUCT, pp. 272–279. IEEE (2018). https://doi.org/10.23919/FRUCT.2018.8468301

29. Volkova, S., Wilson, T., Yarowsky, D.: Exploring demographic language variations to improve multilingual sentiment analysis in social media. In: EMNLP, pp. 1815–1827. ACL (2013)
30. Wiebe, J., Bruce, R.F., O'Hara, T.P.: Development and use of a gold-standard data set for subjectivity classifications. In: ACL, pp. 246–253. ACL (1999)
31. Wiebe, J., Wilson, T., Bruce, R.F., Bell, M., Martin, M.: Learning subjective language. Comput. Linguist. **30**(3), 277–308 (2004)
32. Wiebe, J., Wilson, T., Cardie, C.: Annotating expressions of opinions and emotions in language. Lang. Resour. Eval. **39**(2–3), 165–210 (2005). https://doi.org/10.1007/s10579-005-7880-9
33. Zhang, X., Wei, F., Zhou, M.: HIBERT: document level pre-training of hierarchical bidirectional transformers for document summarization. In: ACL (1), pp. 5059–5069. Association for Computational Linguistics (2019). https://doi.org/10.18653/v1/P19-1499

Evaluating Elements of Web-Based Data Enrichment for Pseudo-relevance Feedback Retrieval

Timo Breuer(✉), Melanie Pest, and Philipp Schaer

TH Köln (University of Applied Sciences), Cologne, Germany
{timo.breuer,melanie.pest,philipp.schaer}@th-koeln.de

Abstract. In this work, we analyze a pseudo-relevance retrieval method based on the results of web search engines. By enriching topics with text data from web search engine result pages and linked contents, we train topic-specific and cost-efficient classifiers that can be used to search test collections for relevant documents. Building upon attempts initially made at TREC Common Core 2018 by Grossman and Cormack, we address questions of system performance over time considering different search engines, queries, and test collections. Our experimental results show how and to which extent the considered components affect the retrieval performance. Overall, the analyzed method is robust in terms of average retrieval performance and a promising way to use web content for the data enrichment of relevance feedback methods.

Keywords: Data enrichment · Web search · Relevance feedback

1 Introduction

Modern web search engines provide access to rich text data sources in search engine result pages (SERPs) and linked web page contents. In the effort of being comprehensive, search results should be diverse but also up-to-date. Although the search results themselves are intended for presentation to search engine users, they could be used to supplement automatic searching in a text collection, e.g., in the form of data enriched relevance feedback methods.

This work builds upon attempts that were first made by Grossman and Cormack (GC) at TREC Common Core18. The authors exploit the results of web search engines to enrich a pseudo-relevance retrieval method that ranks documents of the TREC Washington Post Corpus. More specifically, multiple pseudo-relevance classifiers are individually trained for each topic of the test collection. Each of these classifiers is based on training data retrieved from texts of scraped SERPs, which, in turn, depend on the query of the related topic. Depending on the topic, results of specific requests to web search engines may be subject to strong time dependencies, e.g., when related to breaking news. Likewise, the

K. S. Candan et al. (Eds.): CLEF 2021, LNCS 12880, pp. 53–64, 2021.
https://doi.org/10.1007/978-3-030-85251-1_5

geolocation or algorithmic changes in retrieval techniques and snippet generation can influence search results or the way they are presented. Thus, it is of special interest to investigate the reliability of this retrieval method that relies on ephemeral and constantly changing web content. On the other hand, the analyzed approach is a promising way to build cost-efficient classifiers that find relevant documents.

Our contributions are twofold. First, we address the following research questions: **RQ1** *How do the components of the workflow, i.e., the query formulation and the web search engine, affect the system performance over time?* and **RQ2** *To which extent are the original effects present in different contexts, i.e., with other newswire test collections?* Second, we provide an open-source implementation of the analyzed approach and make the scraped web contents and system runs available for follow-up studies. The remainder is structured as follows. Section 2 contains the related work. Section 3 explains how data enriched topics are used to train pseudo-relevance classifiers and provides details about the analyzed workflow components and the corresponding modifications to the experiments. Section 4 presents the experimental results that are based on reproducibility measures of system-oriented IR experiments. Section 5 concludes.

2 Related Work

Pointwise learning to rank (LTR) algorithms directly apply supervised machine learning approaches for predicting the relevance of single documents [12]. Usually, these approaches require training data with explicit class labels that are costly due to editorial efforts. Relevance feedback algorithms form another body of research in information retrieval (IR) literature correlated to pointwise LTR approaches [17]. Here, relevance feedback based on previously retrieved documents is exploited to improve the final ranking results. Pseudo-relevance feedback (PRF) algorithms - a specific type of relevance feedback - omit editorial labeling by assuming the top-k previously retrieved documents to be relevant [5]. Deriving training data with PRF mechanisms and applying it to LTR algorithms requires explicit positive and negative training samples. Raman et al. successfully showed that the assignment of explicit pseudo-irrelevant documents could improve the retrieval effectiveness [14]. Following a string of different text classification approaches based on machine learning, including spam-filtering [4] and cross-collection relevance classification [7], GC propose to train a logistic regression classifier with pseudo-ir/relevant tfidf-features from SERPs and linked web pages [8]. Similarly, Nallapati investigates different combinations of tf, idf, and combined statistics with discriminative classifiers [13]. Xu and Akella investigate the relevance classification based on the combination of relevance feedback with a logistic regression classifier [23].

Relying on the web as a large external corpus for query expansions has been extensively exploited by the top-performing groups at TREC Robust in 2004 and 2005 [18,19] or as part of TREC Microblog [1]. Kwok et al. showed that web-assisted query expansions could improve the retrieval effectiveness, especially for short queries or queries having only a semantic relation [10]. Similarly, Diaz and Metzler showed that query expansions from external corpora improve the mean average precision, especially when the external corpus is larger than the target collection [6]. As part of their experimental setups, they include web documents from Yahoo! web corpus. Like web documents, Wikipedia offers a resource for PRF via query expansions, as investigated by Xu et al. [22] and Li et al. [11]. Yu et al. showed that PRF techniques are more successful when considering the semantic structure of web pages [25]. When relying on hypertext documents, it is important to consider the markup removal before indexing, as shown by Roy et al. [16]. Otherwise, markup text affects the final results and the reproducibility.

The previously mentioned approach by GC is based on a PRF mechanism, and the principle of routing runs [8]. As defined by Robertson and Callan [15], a routing profile is constructed from existing judgments and used for assessing the relevance of documents. GC propose to derive this profile automatically by generating training data from SERPs scraped for specific topics. Subsequently, the profile ranks documents of the test collection. More specifically, the training data is retrieved from Google SERPs, and the resulting profile ranks the TREC Washington Post Corpus (Core18). GC submitted two alternative runs. In both cases, queries are concatenations of topic titles and descriptions. In order to derive the first run variant `uwmrg`, the entire content of web pages corresponding to the URLs of the SERP is scraped. In their second submission `uwmrgx`, GC propose using only the snippets from SERPs instead of scraping complete web pages. After having retrieved results for all topics of a test collection, text data is prepared as training samples and used for modeling a routing profile that ranks documents from Core18 scored by their probability of being relevant.

3 Approach

The workflow is concise and straightforward. Compressed files are extracted with GNU tools `tar` and `gzip`. Likewise, the required web content is scraped and freed from markup artifacts with the help of the `BeautifulSoup` Python package. The preprocessing removes punctuation and stop words, includes stemming (PorterStemmer), and is implemented with the help of the `nltk` Python package. The preprocessed text data of the scraped web content is used to derive a term-document matrix with tfidf-weights for which we use a sublinear scaling of term frequencies. For this purpose, we make use of the `TfidfVectorizer` of the `scikit-learn` Python package. This term-document matrix is also used for generating tfidf-feature vectors of documents from the test collection.

Training data is stored in `SVMlight` format. Class assignments of training features (to positive and negative samples) are based on a one-vs-rest principle. Depending on the topic, positive samples will be retrieved with the corresponding title (and description), while scraped results of other topics serve as negative samples. After training data and test collection features have been prepared, a model is trained for each topic. In this context, a logistic regression classifier is used. Again, we rely on `scikit-learn` when implementing the

`LogisticRegression` classifier. Adhering to the details given by GC we set the tolerance parameter to 0.0001 (default in `scikit-learn`) and the number of maximal iterations to 200, 000. Subsequently, documents are ranked by their likelihood of being relevant. The 10,000 first documents for each topic contribute to the final system run. For more specific and technical details, we refer the reader to our GitHub repository[1].

3.1 Modifications in the Experiments

As pointed out earlier, we are interested in the robustness of the introduced approach. **RQ1** includes multiple aspects that are addressed as follows. In our case, the *test of time* addresses possibly different web contents in comparison to the original experiments. SERPs are subject to a strong time dependency and the returned URLs, including how they are presented, change over time. In order to investigate the influence of time, we compare results with various time differences. First, we compare our results scraped in 2020 to the original experiment from 2018. On a more granular level, we compare results based on Core18 that were scraped every second day for 12 days in June 2020.

The original results were based on training data scraped from Google SERPs only. We investigate the influence of the *web search engine* by contrasting it with an alternative. In our study, we scrape training data from Google and DuckDuckGo, since the latter states not to include any personalized information except for optional localization contexts[2].

In the original experiment, the *queries* were made of concatenated topic titles and descriptions. However, we argue it might be interesting to contrast this approach with queries made of the topic title only. Users tend to formulate short queries for many web search tasks instead of thoroughly and explicitly formulating their search intents. Thus, we include both short (`title`) and longer (`title+desc`) queries in our experimental setup.

Addressing **RQ2**, we extend the investigations by considering four different *test collections* in total. Originally, runs were derived from the TREC Washington Post Corpus. We investigate and compare results retrieved from TREC Washington Post Corpus (Core18), New York Times Annotated Corpus (Core17), the AQUAINT collection (Robust05), and TREC disks 4 and 5 (minus the *Congressional Record*) (Robust04). All test collections contain newswire documents.

Finally, it has to be noted that SERPs are affected by personalization, as shown by Hannak et al. [9]. One major influence of personalization is the *geolocation* [24]. Throughout our experiments, we do not vary the geolocation parameter when querying the web search engines. We assume the original results to be retrieved with a Canadian geolocation parameter[3], and we also use an English

[1] https://github.com/irgroup/clef2021-web-prf/.

[2] https://spreadprivacy.com/why-use-duckduckgo-instead-of-google/, accessed: May 3rd, 2021.

[3] GC are affiliated with the University of Waterloo in Canada.

language code when querying the web search engine. Likewise, we keep the classifier's parameterization and how training data is preprocessed fixed to minimize their influence. As part of this study, we limit the training data to texts extracted from either web pages (`uwmrg`) or snippets (`uwmrgx`) corresponding to the ten first search results for each topic. While modern SERPs offer more comprehensive results than "ten blue links", we do not include other SERP sections like related queries/searches, entity cards, or advertisements. In the future, it might be interesting to include the influence of these elements.

4 Experimental Results

Our experimental evaluations are made with the toolkit `repro_eval` [3] that implements reproducibility measures of system-oriented IR experiments [2]. More specifically, we analyze the regression tests made with our reimplementation compared to the original results by GC. Even though this is not a reproducibility study in the true sense of the word, we see these measures as the right tool to answer how much the results vary over time considering the analyzed modifications. For some measures, a baseline and an advanced run are required. In the following, we consider `uwmrgx` as the baseline run based on SERP snippets and `uwmrg` as the websites' full text based advanced version of it (since the results were more effective in the original experiment)[4].

RQ1: Influence of the Web Search Engine and the Query Formulation. Table 1 shows the reimplemented results derived from the original test collection (`c18`) under variations of the web search engine (`g`: Google; `d`: DuckDuckGo) and the query formulation (`t`: Topic title only; `td`: Topic title and description). To the best of our knowledge, the run-type `c18_g_td` exactly corresponds to the original configurations. With regard to the nDCG scores, the reproduced results are fairly good. When using DuckDuckGo for retrieving web results (`c18_d_td` and `c18_d_t`), the reimplemented baseline scores are slightly higher than the original results. Even though the reimplemented advanced nDCG scores do not exceed the original scores in each of the four cases, we consider our reimplementations a good starting point for further investigations.

At the most specific level, we compare the reimplementations with the help of Kendall's τ Union (KTU) and the Rank-Biased Overlap (RBO) [21]. Table 1 and Fig. 1 compare the KTU scores of the reproduced results. In contrast to Kendall's τ, KTU lowers the restriction of comparing the actual documents by considering lists of ranks instead [2]. However, it is still a very strict measure, and as the results show, there is no correlation between the original and reimplemented rankings, neither for the baseline nor for the advanced runs. In addition, Fig. 1 shows the KTU scores across the different cut-off ranks. Likewise, the ordering of documents is low correlated across the different ranks.

[4] Most Tables and Figures contain results instantiated with nDCG. For results instantiated with other measures, please have a look at the online appendix at https://github.com/irgroup/clef2021-web-prf/blob/master/doc/appendix.pdf.

Table 1. Results of reproduced baseline and advanced runs derived from Core18.

Run	uwmrgx (baseline run)				uwmrg (advanced run)			
	nDCG	KTU	RBO	RMSE	nDCG	KTU	RBO	RMSE
GC [8]	0.5306	1	1	0	0.5822	1	1	0
c18_g_td	0.5325	0.0052	0.2252	0.1420	0.5713	0.0071	0.3590	0.0885
c18_g_t	0.5024	0.0024	0.2223	0.1697	0.5666	−0.0030	0.3316	0.0893
c18_d_td	0.5735	-0.0024	0.2205	0.1678	0.5633	−0.0001	0.3558	0.1014
c18_d_t	0.5458	-0.0020	0.1897	0.1387	0.5668	−0.0020	0.3357	0.1083

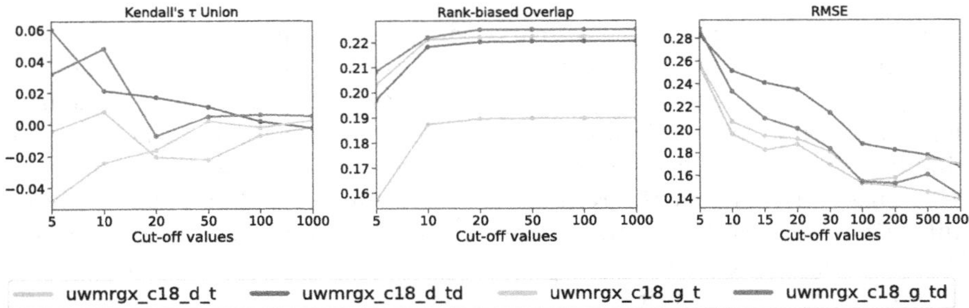

Fig. 1. Kendall's τ Union, Rank-biased Overlap, and the Root-Mean-Square-Error of the reproduced baseline uwmrgx averaged across the topics of Core18.

The RBO measure can be used to compare lists with indefinite lengths and possibly different documents. Table 1 and Fig. 1 show comparisons of the reimplemented RBO scores. The rankings based on training data from DuckDuckGo combined with short queries (uwmrgx_c18_d_t) result in lower RBO scores in comparison to the other baseline runs. The other three reimplementations of the baseline do not differ much across the cut-off ranks in terms of RBO. Similarly, there are differences between the reimplemented advanced runs. Runs based on queries with title and description achieve slightly higher RBO scores in comparison to the reimplementations with title-only queries. When comparing the advanced reimplementations to the baselines, there are higher RBO scores for the advanced runs (e.g. $\text{RBO}_{\text{uwmrgx\_c18\_g\_td}}$ 0.2252 vs. $\text{RBO}_{\text{uwmrg\_c18\_g\_td}}$ 0.3590). Combining Google and title-only queries results in the lowest RBO scores for the advanced runs, whereas in the case of baseline runs, it does not differ much from those runs based on queries with title and description.

At the level of effectiveness, the Root-Mean-Square-Error (RMSE), which is reported in Table 1 and Fig. 1, measures the closeness between the topic score distributions [2]. As a rule of thumb, the closer the RMSE to a value of 0, the smaller is the deviation. Interestingly, the baseline run uwmrgx_c18_d_t achieves the lowest RMSE (0.1387), despite its low correlation of document orderings in terms of RBO. With regard to the advanced reimplementations, uwmrg_c18_g_td (most

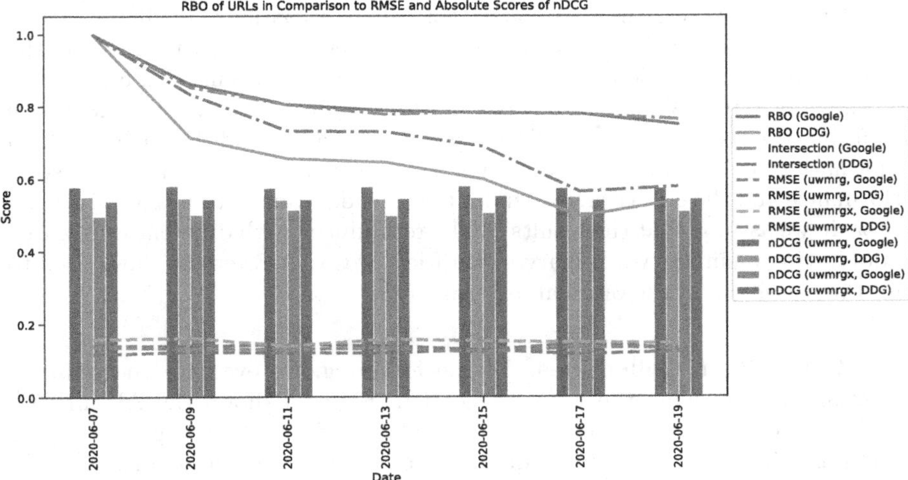

Fig. 2. RBO scores and relative amount of intersecting URLs in comparison to the nDCG and RMSE scores.

similar to the original experiment) achieves the lowest RMSE@1000 (0.0885). Figure 1 illustrates the decreasing RMSE scores with increasing cut-off values. For both baseline and advanced runs, there are almost consistently lower RMSE across the cut-off ranks. Similar to higher RBO scores of the advanced runs, there is a lower RMSE compared to those of the baselines.

Additionally, we conducted t-tests between the runs of our reimplementations to test for significant differences between the search engines or the query formulations (cf. Table 2). For each test collection, we either compared runs from different search engines with the same query (significant differences denoted with †) or compared runs with different queries but the same search engine (significant differences denoted with ∗). There are slightly lower absolute values but mostly insignificant differences with regard to the different query types. However, when using title-only queries, there are often significant differences between the search engines for those runs based on the snippets' texts only (`uwmrgx`).

RQ1: Influence of Time. In Table 1, we compare our reimplementations to the original results of approximately two years ago. However, as pointed out earlier, web content and especially SERPs are subject to several influences, and like the web content itself, they change frequently. Thus, it is worth investigating the robustness of our reimplementations on a more granular level. For this purpose, we retrieved training data from both web search engines for 12 days, starting on June 7th, 2020. Figure 2 shows the RBO, and the intersections between the URLs scraped at every second day compared to those scraped at the beginning on June 7th, 2020. Additionally, Fig. 2 includes the absolute nDCG scores and the RMSE scores of the reproduced baseline runs. While the RBO scores decrease over time, the nDCG and RMSE scores are robust with slight variations. We find a strong correlation between the RBO scores and the number of intersecting URLs in the search result lists[5] - the lower the RBO, the fewer URLs are in both SERP lists from different days. While it is out of this study's scope to reach any definitive conclusions, we see that the SERP's actual search results (and their URL orders) do not have to be the same as in the original experiment to reproduce the system performance and the effectiveness. Under the consideration of this "bag of words" approach, we assume that the results can be reproduced with different web search results having a similar vocabulary or tfidf-features that resemble those used to train the classifiers in the original experiments.

RQ2: Other Test Collections. In the following, we evaluate the reimplementations by replacing the target collection. Figure 3 shows the AP, nDCG, and P@10 scores of the baseline runs derived from four different newswire test collections with variations of the query type and web search engine. Our un-/paired t-tests (between the original runs and the reimplementations) show significant differences in very few cases (cf. online appendix), which is an indicator of robustness from a statistical perspective. When replacing the target collection, it is impossible to compare KTU, RBO, and RMSE since the runs contain different documents for possibly different topics. In this case, the experiment can be evaluated at the level of overall effects. Here, the Effect Ratio (ER) and the Delta Relative Improvement (DRI) measure the effects between the baseline and advanced runs [2]. Perfectly replicated effects are equal to ER 1, whereas lower and higher scores than 1 indicate weaker or stronger effects, respectively, than in the original experiment. The DRI complements the ER by considering the absolute scores of the effects. In this case, perfect replication is equal to DRI 0. Likewise, lower and higher scores indicate weaker or stronger effects, respectively. Table 2 shows the overall effects instantiated with nDCG.

Comparing both search engines, the reproduced and replicated overall effects tend to be higher in ER for training data retrieved with Google. Especially, training data from Google with title-only queries (`g_t`) results in ER > 1 across all test collections. This can be explained by lower replicability scores for baseline runs, while the advanced runs resemble the original scores fairly well. For instance, the `uwmrg_r5_g_t` run achieves nDCG 0.5865 while the corresponding baseline run `uwmrgx_r5_g_t` results in nDCG 0.5003. Consequently, this results in ER 1.6712 indicating larger effects between the baseline and advanced version than in the original experiment. For results based on training data from DuckDuckGo there are weaker overall effects with ER < 1 for each combination of test collection and query type. In most cases, the baseline scores are higher than the corresponding counterparts based on Google results, whereas the advanced scores are lower than those from Google or the original experiments. For instance, `c18_d_td` results in ER_{nDCG} -0.1985. Here, the baseline scores are higher than those of the advanced versions.

[5] Pearson's $r = 0.9747$ and $p = 0.0002$.

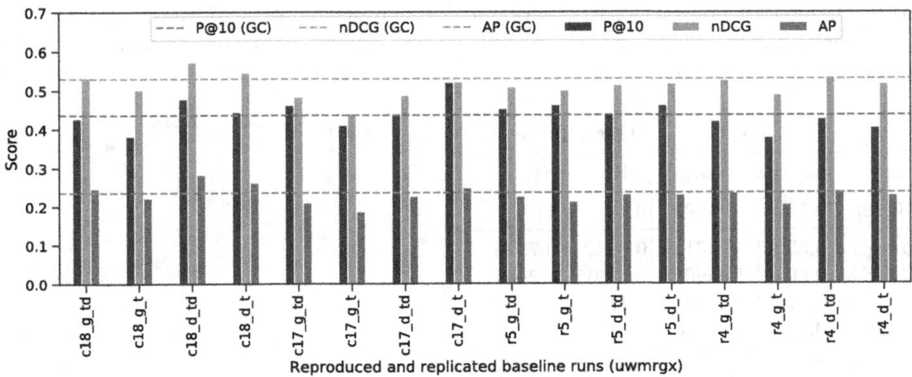

Fig. 3. Absolute scores of reproduced and replicated baseline runs derived from Core18 (`c18`), Core17 (`c17`), Robust04 (`r4`) and Robust05 (`r5`). (Color figure online)

Another way to illustrate the overall effects is to plot the DRI_{nDCG} against ER_{nDCG} for runs based on training data from Google or DuckDuckGo. In general, it can be said that the closer a point to (ER 1, DRI 0), the better the replication. The colors distinct runs with title-only queries (blue) from title and description queries (green). As can be seen, for Google, the data points are distributed over the second and fourth quadrants, whereas for DuckDuckGo all data points are in the second quadrant. With regard to Google, all title-only data points are in the fourth quadrant. This confirms the previous interpretations: training data from Google with title-only queries results in stronger overall effects than in the original experiment.

Further Discussions. Referring back to our research questions **RQ1** and **RQ2**, we reflect on the influence of the targeted aspects with regard to the reproducibility measures provided by `repro_eval` (KTU, RBO, RMSE, ER, and DRI). **RQ1** addresses the change of retrieval performance over time under the consideration of possibly different search engines and query formulations. Even though the experiments showed clear differences between the orderings of documents and the topic score distributions after two years, no substantial differences in average retrieval performance (ARP) are present. Even the more granular investigations of the temporal influence at intervals of two days (cf. Fig. 2) showed that the performance is robust and is independent of individual SERP ranking lists.

With regard to the *web search engine*, our reimplementations delivered higher baseline scores when training data is retrieved from snippets of DuckDuckGo-SERPs for each test collection. Especially for title-only queries, there are significant differences in comparison to the runs derived with Google results. Due to increased baseline scores, the overall effects were lower for DuckDuckGo than those runs based on Google results. At the level of overall effects, we can clearly distinct the results from two different web search engines, especially if the training data is retrieved from Google with title-only queries, where the over-

Table 2. Overall effects (with nDCG) of the search engines (SE) and queries (Q) consisting of `title` (blue) and `title+desc` (green) of different run versions. † and $*$ denote significant differences ($p < 0.05$) between SE and Q, respectively.

	nDCG		Overall Effects	
Run	uwmrgx	uwmrg	DRI	ER
GC [8]	0.5306	0.5822	0	1
c18_g_td	0.5325†	0.5713	0.0242	0.7538
c18_g_t	0.5024†	0.5666	-0.0305	1.2445
c18_d_td	0.5735†	0.5633	0.1150	-0.1985
c18_d_t	0.5458†	0.5668	0.0587	0.4067
c17_g_td	0.4836	0.5047	0.0534	0.4107
c17_g_t	0.4404†	0.5313	-0.1093	1.7637
c17_d_td	0.4870	0.5201	0.0291	0.6425
c17_d_t	0.5223†	0.5279	0.0864	0.1090
r5_g_td	0.5088	0.5613	-0.0061	1.0192
r5_g_t	0.5003	0.5865†	-0.0750	1.6712
r5_d_td	0.5134	0.5295	0.0659	0.3110
r5_d_t	0.5175	0.5509†	0.0325	0.6486
r4_g_td	0.5266*	0.5357*	0.0798	0.1772
r4_g_t	0.4886†*	0.5509*	-0.0304	1.2091
r4_d_td	0.5317*	0.5376	0.0861	0.1134
r4_d_t	0.5171†*	0.5411	0.0508	0.4651

all effects are much higher (cf. Table 2). When we conducted our experiments, DuckDuckGo had longer snippet texts that may lead to more expressive training data. We leave it as future work to investigate the interactions and effects between the query and the snippet length (volume of the training data).

How do the two different *query formulations* affect the final run results? In most cases, querying web search engines with titles only results in lower scores for the baseline runs than queries made from topic titles and descriptions. While it is a common finding, that retrieval performance can benefit from concatenation of titles and descriptions, e.g., as already shown by Walker et al. [20], it is interesting to see that these effects "carry over" in this specific setup, where the queries rather affect the quality of training data and are not directly used to derive the runs from the test collection.

RQ2 addresses the extent to which the original effects can be reproduced in different contexts with other newswire test collections. Comparing the ARP with different test collections does not show significant differences, which indicates that the procedure is robust in terms of ARP. It is impossible to compare some aspects with a different test collection, i.e., the ordering of documents and the topic score distributions cannot be directly compared. The ER and DRI measures are proxies that compare the effects between the baseline and advanced run. Using Google, shorter queries lead to stronger effects than in the original experiment. On the contrary, the resulting effects based on longer queries with Google and DuckDuckGo (with both query types) stay below those of the original experiments. This is consistent for all test collections.

5 Conclusion

We analyzed the topic-specific data enrichment of a pseudo-relevance method that is based on web search results. Motivated by Grossman and Cormack's submissions to TREC Common Core 2018, we reimplemented the original workflow and analyzed different influencing factors related to the web search that affect the constitution of the data enrichment, i.e., the training data. Our experiments demonstrate the influence of the web search engine and the query formulation. Even though the composition of SERPs (which are the foundation of the training data) changes over time, the average retrieval performance is not affected, and the results are robust. This shows that SERP snippets and linked web page content can be reliably used as an external corpus for the investigated ranking method. Furthermore, we analyzed the experiments in different contexts with other newswire test collections. In our experiments, we did not consider other elements of SERPs that might contribute to more effective retrieval results. It is of future interest to consider more targeted ways to extract texts from web pages or SERPs that improve the quality of the training data and investigate the influence of the classifier by replacing it with more sophisticated deep learning approaches. Besides our open-source reimplementation, we also provide the scraped artifacts and system runs in a public Zenodo archive[6].

Acknowledgments. This paper is supported by the DFG (project no. 407518790).

References

1. Bandyopadhyay, A., Ghosh, K., Majumder, P., Mitra, M.: Query expansion for microblog retrieval. Int. J. Web Sci. **1**(4), 368–380 (2012)
2. Breuer, T., et al.: How to measure the reproducibility of system-oriented IR experiments. In: Proceedings of SIGIR, pp. 349–358 (2020)
3. Breuer, T., Ferro, N., Maistro, M., Schaer, P.: repro_eval: a python interface to reproducibility measures of system-oriented IR experiments. In: Proceedings of ECIR, pp. 481–486 (2021)
4. Cormack, G.V., Smucker, M.D., Clarke, C.L.A.: Efficient and effective spam filtering and re-ranking for large web datasets. Inf. Retr. **14**(5), 441–465 (2011). https://doi.org/10.1007/s10791-011-9162-z
5. Croft, W.B., Harper, D.J.: Using probabilistic models of document retrieval without relevance information. J. Doc. **35**(4), 285–295 (1979)
6. Diaz, F., Metzler, D.: Improving the estimation of relevance models using large external corpora. In: Proceedings of SIGIR, pp. 154–161. ACM (2006)

[6] https://doi.org/10.5281/zenodo.4105885.

7. Grossman, M.R., Cormack, G.V.: In: MRG_UWaterloo and WaterlooCormack Participation in the TREC 2017 Common Core Track, vol. 500–324. National Institute of Standards and Technology (NIST) (2017)
8. Grossman, M.R., Cormack, G.V.: MRG_UWaterloo participation in the TREC 2018 common core track. In: Proceedings of TREC (2018)
9. Hannak, A., Sapiezynski, P., Kakhki, A.M., Krishnamurthy, B., Lazer, D., Mislove, A., Wilson, C.: Measuring personalization of web search. In: Proceedings of World Wide Web Conference, WWW, pp. 527–538 (2013)
10. Kwok, K., Grunfeld, L., Deng, P.: Improving weak ad-hoc retrieval by web assistance and data fusion. In: Proceedings of Asia Information Retrieval Symposium, AIRS 2005, pp. 17–30 (2005)
11. Li, Y., Luk, R.W.P., Ho, E.K.S., Chung, K.F.: Improving weak ad-hoc queries using wikipedia as external corpus. In: Proceedings of SIGIR, pp. 797–798. ACM (2007)
12. Liu, T.: Learning to rank for information retrieval. Found. Trends Inf. Retr. **3**(3), 225–331 (2009)
13. Nallapati, R.: Discriminative models for information retrieval. In: Proceedings of SIGIR, pp. 64–71. ACM (2004)
14. Raman, K., Udupa, R., Bhattacharya, P., Bhole, A.: On improving pseudo-relevance feedback using pseudo-irrelevant documents. In: Gurrin, C., et al. (eds.) ECIR 2010. LNCS, vol. 5993, pp. 573–576. Springer, Heidelberg (2010). https://doi.org/10.1007/978-3-642-12275-0_50
15. Robertson, S., Callan, J.: TREC - experiment and evaluation in information retrieval, pp. 99–122 (2005)
16. Roy, D., Mitra, M., Ganguly, D.: To clean or not to clean: document preprocessing and reproducibility. J. Data Inf. Qual. **10**(4), 18:1–18:25 (2018)
17. Ruthven, I., Lalmas, M.: A survey on the use of relevance feedback for information access systems. Knowl. Eng. Rev. **18**(2), 95–145 (2003)
18. Voorhees, E.M.: Overview of the TREC 2004 robust track. In: Proceedings of TREC, vol. 500–261 (2004)
19. Voorhees, E.M.: Overview of the TREC 2005 robust retrieval track. In: Proceedings of TREC, vol. 500–266 (2005)
20. Walker, S., Robertson, S.E., Boughanem, M., Jones, G.J.F., Jones, K.S.: Okapi at TREC-6 Automatic ad hoc, VLC, routing, filtering and QSDR. In: Proceedings of TREC, pp. 125–136 (1997)
21. Webber, W., Moffat, A., Zobel, J.: A similarity measure for indefinite rankings. ACM Trans. Inf. Syst. **28**(4), 20:1-20:38 (2010)
22. Xu, Y., Jones, G.J.F., Wang, B.: Query dependent pseudo-relevance feedback based on wikipedia. In: Proceedings of SIGIR, pp. 59–66. ACM (2009)
23. Xu, Z., Akella, R.: A Bayesian logistic regression model for active relevance feedback. In: Proceedings of SIGIR, pp. 227–234. ACM (2008)
24. Yi, X., Raghavan, H., Leggetter, C.: Discovering users' specific geo intention in web search. In: Proceedings of World Wide Web Conference, WWW, pp. 481–490 (2009)
25. Yu, S., Cai, D., Wen, J., Ma, W.: Improving pseudo-relevance feedback in web information retrieval using web page segmentation. In: Proceedings of World Wide Web Conference, WWW, pp. 11–18. ACM (2003)

End-to-End Fine-Grained Neural Entity Recognition of Patients, Interventions, Outcomes

Anjani Dhrangadhariya[1,2(✉)], Gustavo Aguilar[3], Thamar Solorio[3], Roger Hilfiker[4], and Henning Müller[1,2]

[1] University of Geneva (UNIGE), Geneva, Switzerland
anjani.dhrangadhariya@hevs.ch
[2] University of Applied Sciences Western Switzerland (HES-SO), Sierre, Switzerland
[3] University of Houston, Houston, TX, USA
[4] School of Health Sciences, HES-SO Valais-Wallis, Leukerbad, Switzerland

Abstract. PICO recognition is an information extraction task for detecting parts of text describing Participant (P), Intervention (I), Comparator (C), and Outcome (O) (PICO elements) in clinical trial literature. Each PICO description is further decomposed into finer semantic units. For example, in the sentence 'The study involved 242 adult men with back pain.', the phrase '242 adult men with back pain' describes the participant, but this coarse-grained description is further divided into finer semantic units. The term '242' shows "sample size" of the participants, 'adult' shows "age", 'men' shows "sex", and 'back pain' show the participant "condition". Recognizing these fine-grained PICO entities in health literature is a challenging named-entity recognition (NER) task but it can help to fully automate systematic reviews (SR). Previous approaches concentrated on coarse-grained PICO recognition but focus on the fine-grained recognition still lacks. We revisit the previously unfruitful neural approaches to improve recognition performance for the fine-grained entities. In this paper, we test the feasibility and quality of multitask learning (MTL) to improve fine-grained PICO recognition using a related auxiliary task and compare it with single-task learning (STL). As a consequence, our end-to-end neural approach improves the state-of-the-art (SOTA) F1 score from 0.45 to 0.54 for the "participant" entity and from 0.48 to 0.57 for the "outcome" entity without any hand-crafted features. We inspect the models to identify where they fail and how some of these failures are linked to the current benchmark data.

Keywords: Named entity recognition · Health · Evidence-based health

1 Introduction

Systematic reviews (SR) are cornerstones of evidence-based medicine (EBM) and aim to answer clinically relevant questions with utmost objectivity,

Supported by HES-SO Valais-Wallis.

K. S. Candan et al. (Eds.): CLEF 2021, LNCS 12880, pp. 65–77, 2021.
https://doi.org/10.1007/978-3-030-85251-1_6

transparency, and reproducibility. Primary relevance screening is a very resource-consuming process involving reviewers manually screening thousands of clinical trial abstracts for inclusion into an SR [20]. The criteria for including a study into an SR is decomposed into whether all or most predetermined PICO elements are present in the study [23]. Machine learning (ML) algorithms can help automate the recognition of PICO elements from clinical trial studies by directly pointing the human reviewers to the correct PICO descriptions in a document. However, the detected coarse-grained PICO descriptions (see Sect. 3.2) are further delineated into fine-grained semantic units (see Fig. 1). This means that even after a machine points a human reviewer to the correct coarse-grained PICO description, the reviewer requires to manually read and understand its finer aspects to screen the study for relevance. This leads to the semi-automation of the process. Fully automating the relevance screening process requires identifying, delineating, and normalizing the fine-grained PICO mentions allowing for machine reasoning over the extracted semantic units. Unlike in many biomedical journals, fine-grained PICO mentions in the broader health literature are neither clearly identified nor standardized as semantic units (e.g. naming conventions for interventions and outcome measurement) making it an even more tedious process for the reviewers [13]. This hampers machine reasoning over the semantic units leading to barriers for full automation.

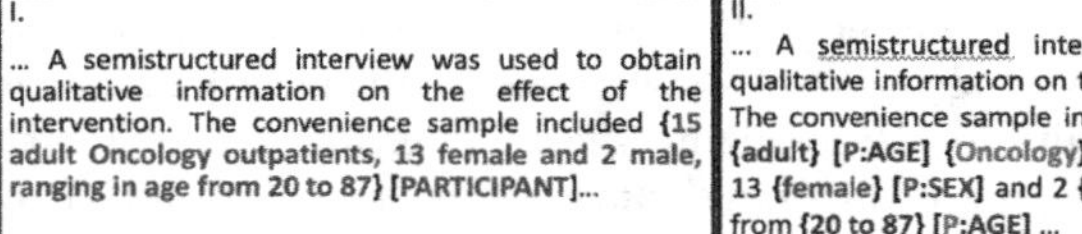

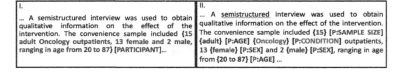

Fig. 1. Example of I. coarse-grained annotated participant span and II. further delineated fine-grained participant entities (P = Participant).

In this work, we test and propose end-to-end neural attention models that require no hand-engineered features unlike the previous approaches and are trained to improve recognition of fine-grained PICO entities. Our approach achieves state-of-the-art (SOTA) performance for fine-grained "Participant" and "Outcome" entity recognition. In our approach, fine-grained PICO recognition was considered as a sequence labeling task for which two different setups were tested: single-task learning (STL) and multi-task learning (MTL). We investigate if these model setups trained on the PICO benchmark corpus extend to reaching similar performance for an *in-house* PICO-annotated corpus from the physical therapy domain (hereafter: physiotherapy corpus). The key takeaway from the error analysis and corpus exploration is that the PICO benchmark corpus over-represents pharmaceutical entity labels leading to poor performance on any low-frequency entities especially the non-pharma entities coming from domains of physiotherapy, complementary therapies and in the more general health domain. Automating PICO recognition is far more challenging compared to open-domain

NER because there are disagreements even between human experts on the exact words that make up PICO elements. Additionally, PICO recognition cannot be purely labeled as an NER task because "Participant" entities span entire sentences.

2 Related Work

Research towards automatic PICO recognition peaked with exploration of several methods including rule-based lexical approaches [8], language models (LM) [3], support vector machines (SVMs) [4], graphical models like CRF [6], shallow neural (Multilayer Perceptrons) approaches [2], a combination of ML and rules [6] and deep neural approach like LSTMs [18]. These studies, however, used small annotated corpora, heavy text pre-processing, and hand-engineered features.

The availability of a comparatively large, and probably the only PICO benchmark corpus (EBM-PICO corpus hereafter) from [21] with multi-grained (fine and coarse-grained) PICO annotations opened up possibilities to explore the neural models. Nye *et al.* [21] used this corpus to train baseline models using hand-engineered features for separately detecting fine- and coarse-grained entities. Their baselines achieved a good performance on the coarse-grained PICO but a poor performance on the more difficult, semantic fine-grained entities.[1] SciBERT, through domain-adaptation, improved[2] the overall coarse-grained PICO recognition for the EBM-PICO corpus [1]. A few studies dived into the recognition of finer aspects of PICO but did not focus on all of them together. For instance, the DNER (Disease NER) [26] neural model focused on disease-mention recognition, [25] concentrated on recognition of patient demographics (sex, sample size, disease) and [7] explored recognition of different intervention arms from RCTs (randomized controlled trials). Except [21], prior work either focused on coarse-grained or sentence-level PICO recognition. Fine-grained PICO recognition has not yet garnered as much attention as it should given its potential for fully automating the SR screening phase.

The focus of our work is to improve recognition of fine-grained PICO entities, test feasibility and competency of MTL models utilizing joint information from the fine- and coarse-entity annotation, and improve generalization by introducing inductive bias [5]. The work stands out because both PICO corpus and the current SOTA automation methods focus on the overall entity recognition but do not explore domain differences. Both the MTL and STL models trained on the EBM-PICO benchmark corpus were used to evaluate fine-grained performance on the physiotherapy corpus.

[1] https://ebm-nlp.herokuapp.com/.
[2] https://paperswithcode.com/sota/participant-intervention-comparison-outcome.

3 Methodology

3.1 Multitask Learning

As fine-grained entities are nested under coarse-grained spans (see Fig. 1), we assume both entity extractions as closely related tasks that can serve as mutual sources of inductive bias for each other. This opens up the possibility to jointly training both tasks using the MTL approach [5,22]. MTL has previously shown to leverage performance on nested biomedical named-entities (NEs) for example for the GENIA corpus [11]. In contrast to an STL setup that requires a separate setup to recognize fine-grained and coarse-grained entities, an end-to-end MTL system jointly learns to recognize both by exploiting the similarities and differences between the task characteristics. MTL opens up the possibility to improve recognition of poorly performing[3] fine-grained recognition by sharing the hidden representation with the far better performing coarse-grained task. For comprehensive details on the MTL algorithms in NLP read [22].

In our MTL setup, fine-grained PICO recognition was considered as the main task and involved assigning each token in the input text with the fine-grained PICO class labels (see Table 1). Coarse-grained recognition was considered as an auxiliary task and involved assigning each token in the input text with either 1 ("Participant" or "Intervention" or "Outcome") or 0 ("No Label"). For both tasks, 0 ("No Label") was considered as the out-of-the-span or non-span label. We began training simple models and sequentially added more layers to understand the improvement effect. To probe the cumulative effect of the self-attention component on the tasks in the MTL setup two ablation experiments were performed [24].

Table 1. Coarse-grained P (Participant), I (Intervention) and O (Outcome) labels are delineated into respective fine-grained labels. Annotation counts are shown in the table.

	Participant	Count	Intervention/Comparator	Count	Outcome	Count
0	No label	124372	No label	120453	No label	115578
1	Age	708	Surgical	659	Physical	7215
2	Sex	157	Physical	1988	Pain	180
3	Sample size	661	Drug	4424	Mortality	261
4	Condition	3893	Educational	1328	Side effect	540
5			Psychological	62	Mental	1657
6			Other	323	Other	2064
7			Control	542		

[3] https://ebm-nlp.herokuapp.com/#Leaderboard.

3.2 Datasets

EBM-PICO Test Set: We used the EBM-PICO corpus comprising ~5000 coarse- and fine-grained PICO-annotated documents[4] to train and test the end-to-end system (see Fig. 1 and Table 1). A part of the dataset was annotated by crowd-sourcing and a small part by medical experts. It comes pre-divided into a training set comprising 4,993 documents and a test set comprising 191 that was used for evaluation. More details about the dataset can be found in [21].

Physiotherapy and Rehabilitation Test Set: An additional test set comprising 153 documents in an *in-house* SR titled "Exercise and other non-pharmaceutical interventions for cancer-related fatigue in patients during or after cancer treatment: a SR incorporating an indirect-comparisons meta-analysis" was manually annotated by the first author using the annotation instructions[5] available from [14,21]. The primary purpose of this additional test dataset was not to establish any inter-annotator agreement (IAA) but 1) to understand the complexity and noise encompassed in the multi-grained PICO annotation process, and 2) to test the feasibility of the proposed setups trained on the general medical (EBM-PICO) dataset to predict PICO classes for a corpus from physiotherapy and rehabilitation domains. The vitality of this annotation exercise will be apparent in the discussion section (see Sect. 5). IO (Inside, Outside) or raw labeling was used for both sequence labeling tasks.

3.3 System Components

1. Embeddings: Contextual representations like BERT, ULMFit, GPT encode rich syntactic and semantic information from the text into vectors eliminating the need for heavy feature engineering. They also tackle the challenge of out-of-vocabulary (OOV) words using the WordPiece tokenizer and byte pair encoding (BPE) [9,19]. The proposed model setups used BERT to extract dense, contextual vectors e_t from the encoded input text tokens x_t at each time-step t.

2. Feature Transformer: To encode long-term dependencies and learn a task-specific text structure from the input documents, the model stacked a single bidirectional LSTM (BiLSTM) layer on top of the embedding layer [15]. A forward LSTM ran from left-to-right (LTR) encoding the text into a ($\overrightarrow{h}$) vector using the current token embedding input e_t and the previous hidden state h_{t-1}. A backward LSTM does the same from right to left (RTL). Both outputs were shallowly concatenated ($[\overrightarrow{h}; \overleftarrow{h}]$) into h_t and used as the input for the next layer.

[4] A single document consists of a title and an abstract.

[5] https://www.ncbi.nlm.nih.gov/pmc/articles/PMC6174533/bin/NIHMS988059-supplement-Appendix.pdf.

3. Self-attention: Next, the model stacked a softmax-based multi-head self-attention layer that calculated for each token in the sequence a weighted average of the feature representation of all other tokens in the sequence [24]. Self-attention improves the signal-to-noise ratio by out-weighting important tokens. Self-attention weights for each token were calculated by multiplying hidden representation h_t with randomly initialized Query q and Key k weights, which were further multiplied with each other to obtain attention weighted vectors. Finally, the obtained attention weights were multiplied with the Value (V) matrix which was obtained by multiplication between a randomly initialized weight matrix v and h_t finally obtaining scaled attention-weighted vectors a_t.

4. Decoder: The attention-weighted representation a_t is either fed to a linear layer to predict the tag emission sequence followed by calculation of weighted cross-entropy loss or to a CRF layer along with the true tag sequence y_t. CRF is a graph-based model suitable for learning tag sequence dependencies from the training set and it has shown to outperform softmax classifiers [16] (Fig. 2).

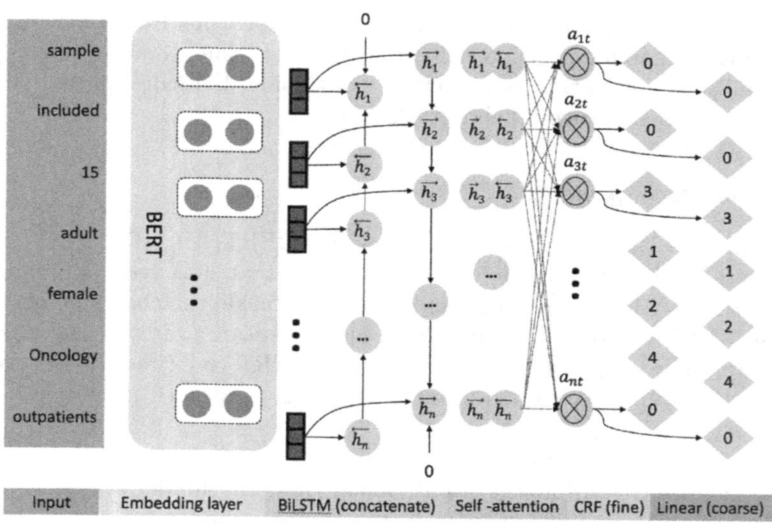

Fig. 2. The proposed end-to-end MTL approach with fine-grained recognition as the main-task and coarse-grained as the auxiliary task. Removing either of the CRF decoder heads gives the respective STL setup.

4 Experiments

To compare our proposed methodology on fine-grained PICO recognition, two strong baselines from Nye *et al.* were used. The baselines use a combination of n-grams, part-of-speech tags, and character embeddings as features and used them to separately train a logistic regression model and a neural LSTM-CRF. To demonstrate the feasibility of the MTL approach for improving fine-grained recognition using the auxiliary coarse-grained task and to compare the performance of each MTL setup, exactly identical STL setups were used. The setups are:

I. BERT Linear. setup includes a linear transformation layer stacked on top of the $\text{BERT}_{\text{BASE}}$ model followed by weight-balanced cross-entropy loss calculation.

II. BERT LSTM CRF. setup uses $\text{BERT}_{\text{BASE}}$ for feature extraction followed by an LSTM and a linear layer to generate emission probabilities that feed into the CRF decoder head that learns tag sequence dependencies and calculates loss.

III. BERT BiLSTM CRF. setup is identical to setup II, but BiLSTM replaces the LSTM layer.

IV. BERT LSTM Atten CRF. setup incorporates a single self-attention head. Attention weights calculated by the attention head are applied to the output of the LSTM layer followed by a linear transformation to generate emission probabilities. These probabilities feed into the CRF decoder.

V. BERT BiLSTM Atten CRF. setup is identical to the setup IV, but BiLSTM replaces the LSTM layer.

VI. BERT BiLSTM Multihead Atten CRF. setup differs from setup V in how attention-weights are applied. For MTL, this setup uses a single-head attention-weighted BiLSTM representation to decode coarse-grained entities while a two-head attention-weighted BiLSTM representation is used to decode the fine-grained entities. This was to over-weigh the fine-grained signals.

VII. BERT BiLSTM Multihead Atten: setup has specific settings for the MTL and STL. In the MTL setup, CRF is used as a decoder for the fine-grained task. The coarse-grained task includes a linear layer followed by a weighted cross-entropy loss calculation. As STL cannot have a coarse-grained task, the encoder setup was used with a linear layer as the decoder for the fine-grained task. Similar to the previous setup, to decode the coarse-grained sequence, a single-head attention-weighted BiLSTM representation was used, while it was a two-head attention-weighted BiLSTM representation to decode the fine-grained entities.

In the MTL setup, all except the final decoding layer shared the parameters for the main and auxiliary tasks. For decoding, the final shared hidden representations were fed to two separate decoding heads that calculated the losses separately for both tasks. The back-propagated loss was a linear combination of both task losses ($\mathcal{L}oss = \mathcal{L}oss_{coarse} + \mathcal{L}oss_{fine}$). For the STL setups without any shared representation between the tasks, the models were optimized using these individual task losses.

Ablation Experiments: To probe the effect of attention weights individually on the fine- and coarse-grained tasks in the MTL setup, two ablation experiments each were performed. For the experiments, the linear transformation was directly applied to the BiLSTM layer without attention-weighting and this unweighted BiLSTM output was first used for the main task and in the second experiment for the auxiliary task.

5 Results

Similar to the other PICO recognition studies, the F1 score was evaluated and reported per token for comparison. Each F1 score is an average of individual fine-grained categories for PICO. The F1 score serves to compare: 1) the performance of our methodology with the baseline, 2) the performance of STL *vs.* MTL for the fine-grained PICO recognition, and 3) the performance improvement brought by the additional functional layers for the MTL and STL setups. A t-test was applied as a significance test with a Bonferroni corrected p-value ($\alpha_{altered}$) threshold set to 0.007 to the normally distributed F1 scores for each MTL model and its corresponding STL counterpart for the fine-grained task [10,12]. F1 scores for the EBM-PICO and physiotherapy corpus are reported in Table 2. In most setups, STL significantly outperforms MTL. For the EBM-PICO corpus, in terms of the cumulative PICO F1, the MTL setup VII outperforms the STL counterpart, but only by gaining a 4% boost in F1 for the "Intervention" recognition while deprecating the performance on the "Participant" entity. Compared to the MTL setup V, setup VI gains 3% F1 on the "Participant" and "Outcome" recognition by exploiting the two-head attention-weighted BiLSTM outputs exclusively for decoding the fine-grained output *vs.* only a single head for decoding the coarse-grained output. Setup VII further improves the performance for the "Intervention" by switching to a linear decoding layer that uses the weighted cross-entropy loss. In comparison to the baseline, both setups outperform for "Participant" and "Outcome".

For evaluation on the physiotherapy corpus, MTL again seems to exploit the two-head self-attention exclusively on the fine-grained task (*vs.* only a single head on the coarse-grained task) and linear decoding followed by weighted cross-entropy loss calculation for the coarse-grained task to achieve a similar performance as STL. The MTL setup VII obtains 2% better F1 scores for the "Participant" and "Intervention" classes. MTL outperforms STL only by carefully exploiting task weights, weighted loss, task-specific decoder heads. Ablation experiments (see Table 3) show that the performance boost for the MTL setup is brought by cumulative attention weighting for both decoding tasks. Removing attention weights from either of the decoding heads reduces the F1 score. This effect of weights on the tasks was also observed in the experiments of [5] where the MTL benefited from the weighted hidden layers on the input, the rationale being that weighted input when backpropagated carried more information.

In general, it was observed that 1) using BERT alone gave very poor performance (See Table 2 Experiment I), 2) the addition of a single head self-attention

Table 2. F1-score comparison for the fine-grained (main task) PICO labels for multitask learning vs. single task learning for the EBM-PICO evaluation corpus and the physiotherapy corpus. The EBM-PICO baseline F1 scores for the fine-grained PICO recognition are annotated as b1 and b2. The best F1 score for an entity in its series of experiments is shown in bold. Underlined scores show that the setup performed significantly better than its counterpart.

	Setup	MTL F1			STL F1		
	Fine-grained	P	I/C	O	P	I/C	O
EBM-PICO evaluation corpus							
B1	Logistic regression	-	-	-	0.45	0.25	0.38
B2	LSTM-CRF	-	-	-	0.4	**0.5**	0.48
I	BERT Linear	0.21	0.07	0.09	0.20	0.08	0.12
II	BERT LSTM CRF	0.33	0.24	0.37	0.45	0.27	0.45
III	BERT BiLSTM CRF	0.39	0.28	0.40	0.52	0.27	0.53
IV	BERT LSTM attn CRF	0.34	0.28	0.47	0.53	0.25	0.49
V	BERT BiLSTM attn CRF	0.51	0.30	0.53	**0.54**	**0.30**	**0.57**
VI	BERT BiLSTM multihead attn CRF	**0.54**	0.30	**0.56**	**0.54**	0.29	0.55
VII	BERT BiLSTM multihead attn linear	0.52	**0.34**	**0.56**	**0.54**	**0.30**	**0.56**
Physiotherapy corpus							
I	BERT Linear	0.23	0.07	0.05	0.22	0.07	0.06
II	BERT LSTM CRF	0.36	0.15	0.20	0.52	0.15	0.27
III	BERT BiLSTM CRF	0.40	0.17	0.24	0.57	0.19	0.27
IV	BERT LSTM attn CRF	0.37	0.14	0.28	0.56	0.17	0.27
V	BERT BiLSTM attn CRF	0.57	0.17	**0.30**	**0.60**	0.19	**0.30**
VI	BERT BiLSTM multihead attn CRF	**0.62**	0.18	**0.30**	0.56	0.18	0.29
VII	BERT BiLSTM multihead attn linear	**0.62**	**0.23**	**0.30**	**0.60**	**0.21**	**0.30**

Table 3. F1 score for the ablation experiments in the MTL setup (BERT BiLSTM attention CRF) for both test corpora

Setup	F1 (Physiotherapy)			F1 (EBM-PICO)		
Fine-grained	P	I/C	O	P	I/C	O
BERT BiLSTM attn CRF	**0.57**	**0.17**	**0.30**	**0.51**	**0.30**	**0.53**
BERT BiLSTM attn (on coarse) CRF	0.44	0.11	0.19	0.39	0.21	0.37
BERT BiLSTM attn (on fine) CRF	0.43	0.15	0.23	0.31	0.29	0.42

layer brought a significant performance boost for both setups (See Table 2 Experiment V), 3) the approaches have poor generalization on the physiotherapy corpus for the "Intervention" entity, and 4) though most MTL setups did not outperform the STL setups, it cannot be concluded that MTL is ineffective.

These results warrant further investigation into task-weighting, appropriate task decoders, loss weighting strategies, especially for the label-imbalanced tasks.

6 Discussion and Error Analysis

As apparent from Table 2, the "Intervention" entity showed the most dissatisfying overall F1-score and was the only entity unable to pass the baseline. For the EBM-PICO corpus, performance on the "Intervention" entity had saturated at 0.30 F1 and was even worse for the physiotherapy corpus. Upon the confusion matrix inspection for "Intervention" for both setups and evaluation corpora it was identified that all the sequence taggers failed to correctly identify any of the "Other" and "Psychological" fine-grained classes (see red box in Fig. 3). The most obvious reason for this is the comparatively lower number of label annotations for these classes. It was apparent during the manual annotation of the physiotherapy corpus that the "Other" entity encompassed any intervention mention that did not fall into the rest of "Intervention" classes making this class highly heterogeneous with a mixture of diverse entities that followed several patterns (see Table 1). Heterogeneous entities are a challenge for IR [17].

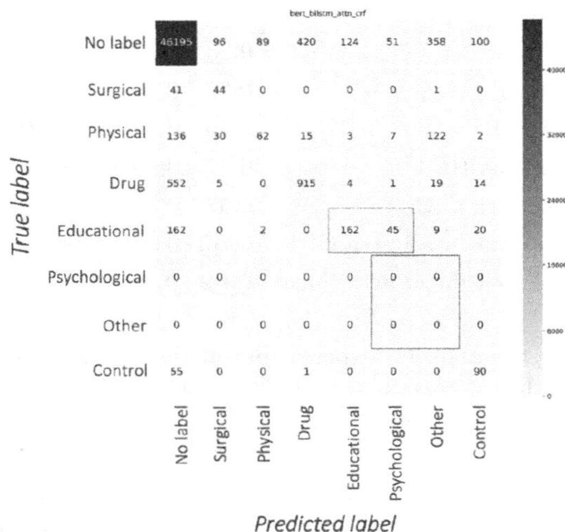

Fig. 3. "Intervention" entity example error matrix for the MTL experimental setup V (BERT BiLSTM attention CRF)

All the taggers were consistently confused between the physiological and educational intervention classes (see the blue box in Fig. 3), which are important for our field of interest. This challenge is related to the "Intervention" class definition. During manual annotation, it was rather difficult, even as a human annotator, whether to classify certain interventions as educational or psychological (for example, the psycho-educational intervention if administered by a psychologist is considered as psychological intervention and if administered by a nurse it is classified as an educational intervention). The performance of automatic labeling was just a direct reflection of the difficulty emanating from class definitions. General analysis of all the PICO confusion matrices shows several out-of-the-span entities were mislabelled as PICO and vice versa. If it was merely PICO being miss-tagged as out-of-the-span, it could have pointed to the class-imbalance problem given that out-of-the-span forms the majority class. However, consistently even the out-of-the-span entities were mislabelled as PICO which points to the class-overlap problem. Error inspection showed that the overall limited performance of these classifiers might result from the class-overlap between the PICO and out-of-the-span classes and ambiguities in how each coarse-grained PICO was divided further into fine-grained PICO classes, especially for the health entities.

7 Conclusion

We propose two end-to-end neural model setups for fine-grained PICO recognition that outperform the previous SOTA for the fine-grained "Participant" and "Outcome" entities without any need for hand-engineered features. We show that MTL is not only feasible but also a good alternative to the STL setup. However, combining even the seemingly related tasks in MTL might not directly boost the performance. To perform similar to or outperform its STL counterpart, MTL could require rather careful individual weighting of the involved tasks and task losses. We contribute a manually annotated dataset with multi-level PICO annotations adding to the currently available resources. Our error analysis warrants rethinking of semantically solid class definitions for fine-grained PICO entities along with ontology development for the health domain. The code and the annotated in-house dataset are available on Github[6].

References

1. Beltagy, I., Lo, K., Cohan, A.: Scibert: a pretrained language model for scientific text. arXiv preprint arXiv:1903.10676 (2019)
2. Boudin, F., Nie, J.Y., Bartlett, J.C., Grad, R., Pluye, P., Dawes, M.: Combining classifiers for robust PICO element detection. BMC Med. Inform. Decis. Mak. **10**(1), 1–6 (2010)
3. Boudin, F., Nie, J.Y., Dawes, M.: Clinical information retrieval using document and PICO structure. In: Human Language Technologies: The 2010 Annual Conference of the North American Chapter of the Association for Computational Linguistics, pp. 822–830 (2010)
4. Boudin, F., Shi, L., Nie, J.-Y.: Improving medical information retrieval with PICO element detection. In: Gurrin, C., et al. (eds.) ECIR 2010. LNCS, vol. 5993, pp. 50–61. Springer, Heidelberg (2010). https://doi.org/10.1007/978-3-642-12275-0_8
5. Caruana, R.: Multitask learning. Mach. Learn. **28**(1), 41–75 (1997)

[6] https://github.com/anjani-dhrangadhariya/multitask-pico-detection.

6. Chabou, S., Iglewski, M.: Combination of conditional random field with a rule based method in the extraction of PICO elements. BMC Med. Inform. Decis. Mak. **18**(1), 128 (2018)
7. Chung, G.Y.C.: Towards identifying intervention arms in randomized controlled trials: extracting coordinating constructions. J. Biomed. Inform. **42**(5), 790–800 (2009)
8. Dawes, M., Pluye, P., Shea, L., Grad, R., Greenberg, A., Nie, J.Y.: The identification of clinically important elements within medical journal abstracts: patient_population_problem, exposure_intervention, comparison, outcome, duration and results (PECODR). J. Innovation Health Inf. **15**(1), 9–16 (2007)
9. Devlin, J., Chang, M.W., Lee, K., Toutanova, K.: Bert: pre-training of deep bidirectional transformers for language understanding. arXiv preprint arXiv:1810.04805 (2018)
10. Dror, R., Baumer, G., Shlomov, S., Reichart, R.: The hitchhiker's guide to testing statistical significance in natural language processing. In: Proceedings of the 56th Annual Meeting of the Association for Computational Linguistics (Volume 1: Long Papers), pp. 1383–1392 (2018)
11. Fei, H., Ren, Y., Ji, D.: Dispatched attention with multi-task learning for nested mention recognition. Inf. Sci. **513**, 241–251 (2020)
12. Fuhr, N.: Some common mistakes in IR evaluation, and how they can be avoided. In: ACM SIGIR Forum, vol. 51, pp. 32–41. ACM New York, NY, USA (2018)
13. He, Z., Tao, C., Bian, J., Dumontier, M., Hogan, W.R.: Semantics-powered healthcare engineering and data analytics (2017)
14. Hilfiker, R., et al.: Exercise and other non-pharmaceutical interventions for cancer-related fatigue in patients during or after cancer treatment: a systematic review incorporating an indirect-comparisons meta-analysis. Br. J. Sports Med. **52**(10), 651–658 (2018)
15. Hochreiter, S., Schmidhuber, J.: Long short-term memory. Neural Comput. **9**(8), 1735–1780 (1997)
16. Huang, Z., Xu, W., Yu, K.: Bidirectional LSTM-CRF models for sequence tagging. arXiv preprint arXiv:1508.01991 (2015)
17. Jaseena, K., David, J.M.: Issues, challenges, and solutions: big data mining. CS IT-CSCP **4**(13), 131–140 (2014)
18. Jin, D., Szolovits, P.: PICO element detection in medical text via long short-term memory neural networks. In: Proceedings of the BioNLP 2018 workshop, pp. 67–75 (2018)
19. Joshi, A., Karimi, S., Sparks, R., Paris, C., MacIntyre, C.R.: A comparison of word-based and context-based representations for classification problems in health informatics. arXiv preprint arXiv:1906.05468 (2019)
20. Khangura, S., Konnyu, K., Cushman, R., Grimshaw, J., Moher, D.: Evidence summaries: the evolution of a rapid review approach. Syst. Rev. **1**(1), 1–9 (2012)
21. Nye, B., et al.: A corpus with multi-level annotations of patients, interventions and outcomes to support language processing for medical literature. In: Proceedings of the conference. Association for Computational Linguistics. Meeting. vol. 2018, p. 197. NIH Public Access (2018)
22. Ruder, S.: An overview of multi-task learning in deep neural networks. arXiv preprint arXiv:1706.05098 (2017)
23. Russell, R., et al.: Systematic review methods. In: Issues and Challenges in Conducting Systematic Reviews to Support Development of Nutrient Reference Values: Workshop Summary Nutrition Research Series, vol. 2 (2009)

24. Vaswani, A., et al.: Attention is all you need. In: Advances in Neural Information Processing Systems, pp. 5998–6008 (2017)
25. Xu, R., Garten, Y., Supekar, K.S., Das, A.K., Altman, R.B., Garber, A.M., et al.: Extracting subject demographic information from abstracts of randomized clinical trial reports. In: Medinfo 2007: Proceedings of the 12th World Congress on Health (Medical) Informatics; Building Sustainable Health Systems, p. 550. IOS Press (2007)
26. Zhang, T., Yu, Y., Mei, J., Tang, Z., Zhang, X., Li, S.: Unlocking the power of deep PICO extraction: Step-wise medical NER identification. arXiv preprint arXiv:2005.06601 (2020)

Comparing Traditional and Neural Approaches for Detecting Health-Related Misinformation

Marcos Fernández-Pichel[1(✉)], David E. Losada[1], Juan C. Pichel[1], and David Elsweiler[2]

[1] Centro Singular de Investigación en Tecnoloxías Intelixentes (CiTIUS), Universidade de Santiago de Compostela, 15782 Santiago de Compostela, Spain
{marcosfernandez.pichel,david.losada,juancarlos.pichel}@usc.es
[2] University of Regensburg, Regensburg, Germany
david@elsweiler.co.uk

Abstract. Detecting health-related misinformation is a research challenge that has recently received increasing attention. Helping people to find credible and accurate health information on the Web remains an open research issue as has been highlighted during the COVID-19 pandemic. However, in such scenarios, it is often critical to detect misinformation quickly [34], which implies working with little data, at least at the beginning of the spread of such information. In this work, we present a comparison between different automatic approaches of identifying misinformation, and we compare how they behave for different tasks and with limited training data. We experiment with traditional algorithms, such as SVMs or KNNs, as well as newer BERT-based models [5]. Our experiments utilise the CLEF 2018 Consumer Health Search task dataset [16] to perform experiments on detecting untrustworthy contents and information that is difficult to read. Our results suggest that traditional models are still a strong baseline for these challenging tasks. In the absence of substantive training data, classical approaches tend to outperform BERT-based models.

Keywords: Health-related content · Misinformation · Language · Neural approaches

1 Introduction

The everyday use of the Web and social media has resulted in increased information accessibility [28]. The quality of information acquired via these channels is not assured, however, and infodemics with unreliable [1], inaccurate [6], or poor quality [29] information have become more common. Previous research has evidenced that providing poor quality search results in this context, leads people to make incorrect decisions [27]. People are influenced by search engine results and interacting with incorrect information results in poor choices being made.

K. S. Candan et al. (Eds.): CLEF 2021, LNCS 12880, pp. 78–90, 2021.
https://doi.org/10.1007/978-3-030-85251-1_7

Since search engines are widely used as a mean to find health advice online [8], misinformation provided via these services can be especially damaging, and there is a need to develop retrieval methods that can find trustworthy, and understandable search results. The quest for such high quality retrieval results was the primary goal of evaluation campaigns such as the CLEF Consumer Health Search task [16]. The urgent need for effective quality filtering devices has only been underlined during the 2020 pandemic, when large quantities of information about COVID-19 and its treatments was of questionable or poor quality [15,26]. Moreover, the early detection of health-related misinformation is critical to avoid potential personal injury [34]. This leads us to a scenario in which prediction must be based on low training data.

The evidence suggests that language is a good indicator to discern trustworthy from untrustworthy information [22]. Information of varying quality tends to differ in writing style and in the use of certain words [25]. For example, the use of technical terms or certain formalisms is associated with documents of higher quality and, in many cases, more trustful. Moreover, several machine learning technologies have been used to exploit linguistic properties of text [2,33].

In this work, we evaluate the performance of traditional classification approaches, such as SVMs or KNNs, and newer BERT-based models for detecting health-related misinformation. To that end, we employed the CLEF 2018 Consumer Health Search task dataset. This task focuses on providing high-quality health-related search results to non-expert users. Different experiments were performed using target variables such as trustworthiness, readability, and the combination of both. Following Hahnel et al. [12], we consider that for a document to be useful it should not only be trustful but also understandable by non-expert users.

The main objective of our research is to provide a thorough comparison between recent deep Natural Language Processing (NLP) models and traditional algorithms for the identification of poor quality online contents (untrustworthy and difficult to read web pages). We pay special attention to the behaviour of the models under realistic conditions (low training data). To that end, our study includes a report on the influence of the amount of training data in the effectiveness and the training time of the different models.

2 Related Work

Several studies have analyzed how the credibility of online content is assessed [7, 24,36]. Some interesting conclusions are that subjective ratings depend on the user's background, like years of education or reading skills [12]. Ginsca and colleagues [10] presented a thorough survey on existing credibility models from different information seeking perspectives.

Other researches focused on determining how the search engine result page (SERP) listings are used to determine credibility through user studies [18] or on the association between different features and reliability. For example, Griffiths et al. [11] showed that algorithms like PageRank were unable to determine reliability on their own.

More specifically, some teams focused on assessing the credibility of health-related content on the web. For example, Matthews et al. [23] analysed a corpus about alternative cancer treatments and found that almost 90% contained false claims. Liao and Fu [19] studied the influence of age differences in credibility judgments and argued that older adults care less about the content of the site. Other teams focused on how to present medical information on a search engine result page to improve credibility judgments [31].

Sondhi and his colleagues presented an automatic approach, based on traditional learning algorithms, for medical reliability prediction at a document-level [33]. Other studies [37] proposed features, such as those based on sentiment or polarity signals, to better detect misinformation.

Recent advances have shown that new neural approaches can be effective tools for detecting health-related misinformation [4,9,14,32]. Most of these methods employ not only content-based features but other signals (e.g. network-based features).

In this work, we present an innovative comparison between traditional learning methods, such as SVMs or KNNs, and neural approaches for identifying health misinformation. We also test how the models behave with low training data, and our study is constrained to work with models that are fed with content-based features.

3 Dataset

To perform this comparison, we selected the CLEF 2018 Consumer Health Search task dataset [16], which focuses on the effectiveness of health-related information provided by search engines. The search task aims at helping non-expert users who are looking for health-advice. The dataset contains webpages obtained from CommonCrawl[1]. The creators of the dataset defined an initial list of potentially interesting sites and then, they submitted queries against a search engine to retrieve the final URLs. The initial list was manually extended by adding sites known to be either trustful or untrustful.

The assessments were provided by human assessors from Amazon Mechanical Turk. The turkers labelled the documents with respect to three different query-dependent dimensions: relevance, trustworthiness, and readability. In our experiments we consider only the latter two.

Both dimensions of interest were judged on an eleven point scale, from 0 to 10. In our case, we wanted to approach the problem as a two-class classification challenge and, thus, we converted the original scores into binary variables. To that end, we removed the middle values (from 4 to 6) and mapped the extreme values to trustful/untrustful and readable/non-readable respectively. Table 1 reports the main statistics of the resulting datasets. We also tested classifiers for the task of distinguishing between *useful* documents for non-expert end users (i.e., trustworthy and readable) and *non-useful* documents (the remaining

[1] http://commoncrawl.org/.

documents). With this goal in mind, we labelled useful documents as those that are both trustworthy and readable (third column in the table).

Table 1. Label distribution in the CLEF eHealth dataset.

	Trustworthiness	Readability	Useful (T& R)
# Positive	10,405	3,102	1,567
% Positive	73%	20%	12%
# Negative	3,820	12,455	11,488
% Negative	27%	80%	88%

4 Experimental Design

The experiments were conceived such that the aim was to uncover misinformative documents, as measured by the dimensions considered: trustworthiness, readability, and the combination of both. To that end, we compared the performance of traditional models against BERT models.

We employed a 5-fold stratified cross-validation strategy in all the experiments. To address the imbalance in data labels, we also applied a cost-factor strategy [13,21] in those learning methods whose implementation supports it[2]. We decided to set this cost-factor to the proportion between the classes for each experiment.

All experiments were conducted using the same docker container environment, an image with Ubuntu 18.04 and Python 3.7.3 version. The host machine also had 32GB of RAM, 240GB of storage, an Intel(R) Core(TM) i7-9750H CPU @ 1.60GHz, and a Nvidia Tesla V100S 32GB GPU, which was beneficial for the BERT experiments.

4.1 Traditional Models

We employed two variants for these experiments. The first consisted of a model where each word in a document was considered as a different feature, weighted by its normalized frequency. The second was equivalent, but stopwords were removed. The vocabulary was pruned to only consider terms present in at least 10% of the training corpus in both variants. We also applied a standardisation of the features (to get 0 mean and 1 standard deviation).

- **SVM.** Following [33], a classic reference for health information reliability detection, we used a support vector machine implemented as part of the SVMlight toolkit [17][3].

[2] We employed https://scikit-learn.org/stable/ (version 0.24.1).

[3] Using default parameter setting (kernel linear and $C = [avg.\ x * x]^{-1}$). We employed the SVMlight Python wrapper with this configuration.

- **Random Forest (RF).** We used Random Forest scikit-learn default implementation (100 trees were used and the Gini index was the criterion to measure the quality of a split).
- **Naive Bayes (NB).** We used Naive Bayes scikit-learn default implementation, utilising the Multinomial Bayes variant, which is particularly recommended for imbalanced data problems.
- **KNN.** We used scikit-learn default implementation of the KNN classifier ($k = 5$ neighbours).

For the models whose implementation supports cost weighting (SVM and RF) we also ran experiments with cost-weighting variants[4].

4.2 BERT-Based Models

For neural approaches, we considered BERT-based models [5]. These are pre-trained neural networks based on transformers architecture, and lead to state-of-the-art solutions for many NLP tasks.

More specifically, we used **DistilBERT base** model (uncased version) [30] and **DistilRoBERTa base** model from HuggingFace Transformers library [35]. The first has 6 layers, 768 hidden, 12 heads, and 66M parameters, while the second has the same number of layers, hidden and heads, but 82M parameters. These are light models obtained from larger ones, such as BERT base [5] or RoBERTa base [20]. The distilled models reduce the number of layers by a factor of 2, and the number of parameters by 40% while retaining 97% of the original performance [30].

These models were fine-tuned for our task in each fold. For the training process, 4 epochs and a 10% validation split were used, with a learning rate of 2^{-5}, a training batch size of 32, and a validation batch size of 64 instances.

We note that BERT models have an input limit of 512 tokens. This was a challenge since the majority of the documents were larger. We trained the models with the first 512 tokens of each training document. At testing time, two different approaches were evaluated: i) making the prediction using only the first 512 tokens of the test document, or ii) segmenting each test document into 512-token chunks, passing the classifier on each chunk, and returning a final score that is the prediction score averaged over all chunks (aggregation strategy). Both strategies are reported and compared in Sect. 5.

5 Experimental Results

A set of experiments was performed for each target classification problem. We report the results for each of the different dimensions and models, providing the F1-score (harmonic mean between precision and recall) for each class and the macro average F1 (unweighted mean of F1-score per class).

[4] Scikit-learn does not support cost-weighting for NB and KNN.

Table 2. Trustworthiness results obtained when setting or not the cost-factor to the proportion between classes.

	Cost factor	F1 macro	F1 trustful	F1 untrustful
SVM (stopword removal)	1	0.57	0.84	0.3
SVM	1	0.57	0.83	0.31
SVM n-grams (stopword removal)	1	0.57	0.84	0.29
SVM n-grams	1	0.57	0.84	0.3
RF (stopword removal)	1	0.57	0.84	0.3
RF	1	0.57	0.84	0.29
Naive Bayes (stopword removal)	1	0.59	0.76	0.41
Naive Bayes	1	0.59	0.78	0.39
KNN (stopword removal)	1	0.6	0.8	0.39
KNN	1	0.59	0.82	0.36
DistilBERT	1	0.61	0.82	0.39
DistilRoBERTa	1	0.59	0.82	0.36
DistilBERT (aggregation)	1	0.58	0.83	0.33
DistilRoBERTa (aggregation)	1	0.61	0.84	0.38
SVM (stopword removal)	2.72	0.56	0.7	0.42
SVM	2.72	0.57	0.71	0.42
SVM n-grams (stopword removal)	2.72	0.57	0.71	0.43
SVM n-grams	2.72	0.57	0.71	0.43
RF (stopword removal)	2.72	0.57	0.84	0.29
RF	2.72	0.56	0.84	0.27
DistilBERT	2.72	0.6	0.74	0.45
DistilRoBERTa	2.72	0.59	0.72	0.46
DistilBERT (aggregation)	2.72	0.57	0.69	0.45
DistilRoBERTa (aggregation)	2.72	0.58	0.7	0.46

5.1 Trustworthiness

The first dimension considered was trustworthiness. For this task, there is no substantial difference between the models (see Table 2). KNN and NB seem to be slightly superior to the other classic models and comparable to the best BERT-based variants.

With cost-weighting settings, the models tend to improve the detection of the minority class (untrustful), but the relative merits of the models remain essentially the same. Only RF shows here a distinctive behaviour, as its cost-weight variant decreases performance in terms of F1 untrustful.

Stopword removal had no substantial effect and the use of n-grams (bigrams and trigrams) did not bring any improvement (that is why it is only reported for SVMs). On the other hand, the aggregation strategy for BERT models did not yield any substantial advantage over a prediction that is solely based on the leading chunk. Making predictions with a single chunk of the test document is

Table 3. Readability results obtained when setting or not the cost-factor to the proportion between classes.

	Cost factor	F1 macro	F1 readable	F1 non-readable
SVM (stopword removal)	1	0.5	0.13	0.86
SVM	1	0.49	0.12	0.86
SVM n-grams (stopword removal)	1	0.49	0.11	0.86
SVM n-grams	1	0.49	0.12	0.86
RF (stopword removal)	1	0.51	0.16	0.86
RF	1	0.51	0.16	0.86
Naive Bayes (stopword removal)	1	0.59	0.33	0.84
Naive Bayes	1	0.59	0.33	0.84
KNN (stopword removal)	1	0.52	0.21	0.82
KNN	1	0.52	0.2	0.83
DistilBERT	1	0.5	0.19	0.81
DistilRoBERTa	1	0.49	0.16	0.81
DistilBERT (aggregation)	1	0.51	0.2	0.82
DistilRoBERTa (aggregation)	1	0.49	0.15	0.82
SVM (stopword removal)	4.02	0.51	0.3	0.72
SVM	4.02	0.5	0.31	0.68
SVM n-grams (stopword removal)	4.02	0.52	0.32	0.72
SVM n-grams	4.02	0.52	0.33	0.71
RF (stopword removal)	4.02	0.52	0.17	0.86
RF	4.02	0.53	0.18	0.87
DistilBERT	4.02	0.47	0.27	0.67
DistilRoBERTa	4.02	0.5	0.3	0.69
DistilBERT (aggregation)	4.02	0.49	0.28	0.7
DistilRoBERTa (aggregation)	4.02	0.48	0.27	0.69

computationally convenient, and our experiments suggest that this approach is comparable to a more thorough prediction based on the entire test document.

Overall, these results suggest that BERT models are unable to improve over simpler (and computationally less expensive) approaches. This could be related to the lack of large amounts of training data. In Sect. 5.4, we further analyze the models under varying training sizes.

5.2 Readability

In the readability experiments the objective was to detect the documents labelled as non-readable from the collection. The results in the readability experiments (see Table 3) show that the traditional algorithms perform better than BERT models. In particular, Naive Bayes achieves the best performance overall. When we set the *cost-factor* = 4.02 (notice that in this case the majority class was the non-readable), conclusions remain the same. Again, removing stopwords had no substatial effect on performance and the BERT-based models do not benefit from the aggregation approach.

Table 4. Usefulness results obtained when setting or not the cost-factor to the proportion between classes.

	Cost factor	F1 macro	F1 useful docs	F1 non-useful docs
SVM (stopword removal)	1	0.51	0.1	0.92
SVM	1	0.5	0.07	0.93
SVM n-grams (stopword removal)	1	0.51	0.09	0.93
SVM n-grams	1	0.5	0.07	0.93
RF (stopword removal)	1	0.5	0.07	0.92
RF	1	0.5	0.06	0.93
Naive Bayes (stopword removal)	1	0.59	0.3	0.88
Naive Bayes	1	0.6	0.32	0.88
KNN (stopword removal)	1	0.54	0.16	0.92
KNN	1	0.53	0.15	0.91
DistilBERT	1	0.56	0.2	0.91
DistilRoBERTa	1	0.53	0.12	0.93
DistilBERT (aggregation)	1	0.56	0.2	0.91
DistilRoBERTa (aggregation)	1	0.54	0.16	0.91
SVM (stopword removal)	7.33	0.57	0.3	0.84
SVM	7.33	0.54	0.29	0.79
SVM n-grams (stopword removal)	7.33	0.58	0.31	0.84
SVM n-grams	7.33	0.55	0.3	0.8
RF (stopword removal)	7.33	0.51	0.1	0.92
RF	7.33	0.51	0.09	0.92
DistilBERT	7.33	0.57	0.29	0.84
DistilRoBERTa	7.33	0.5	0.27	0.73
DistilBERT (aggregation)	7.33	0.55	0.29	0.81
DistilRoBERTa (aggregation)	7.33	0.49	0.26	0.72

These results suggest that determining readability can be effectively addressed with standard word-based technology. Even a simple bag-of-words model using a traditional learning method (like Naive Bayes or KNN) forms a solid classifier, comparable to the best neural models. One could argue that readability classification is essentially about distinguishing between the usage of simpler vs complex language. Our experiments show that such a goal can be competently tackled by classic NB technology.

5.3 Usefulness (Trustworthiness and Readability)

We also performed experiments combining readability and trustworthiness. To that end, we considered as *useful* documents the ones labelled as both trustful and readable. This seems reasonable since non-expert users look for trustworthy and understandable health-advice on the Web [12]. The remaining documents are regarded as *non-useful* documents (highly technical or untrustful).

The results (see Table 4) suggest that, as was the case in the trustworthiness experiments, there is no substantial difference between traditional and BERT models. Only a slight improvement of Naive Bayes over the rest was found.

Again, applying a cost-sensitive learning strategy, improves the minority class detection, but RF does not benefit from this technique.

5.4 Influence of the Training Set Size

In order to evaluate the influence of the training set size on effectiveness and efficiency, we report here two experiments: one for trustworthiness and another one for readability.

We selected **Naive Bayes**, **KNN**, and **DistilBERT base** (keeping stopwords and without any cost-factor), which were the best performing models in the experiments reported above. A 5-fold cross-validation strategy was applied again, but in this case models were only trained using a percentage of the training fold (always ensuring a stratified sample). We considered 1%, 5%, 10%, 30%, 50%, 70%, and 100% of the available data.

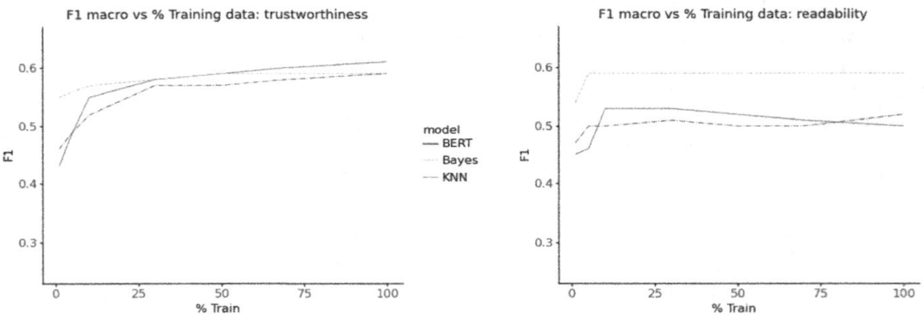

Fig. 1. Variation of the F1 macro precision with percent training data used in trustworthiness and readability tasks.

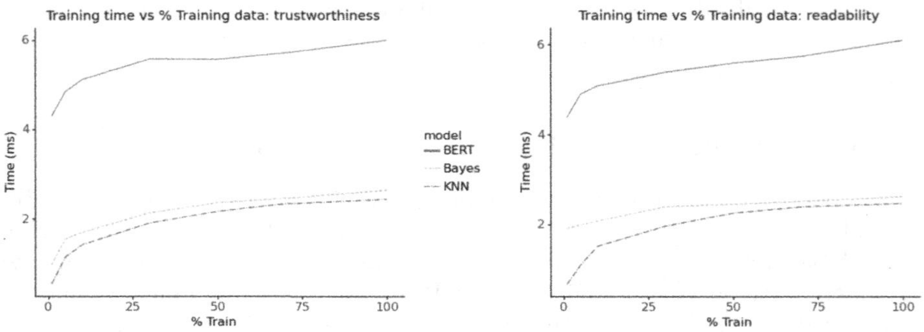

Fig. 2. Variation of the training time (ms) with percent training data used in trustworthiness and readability tasks. Y axis in log scale.

In Fig. 1, we depict how the F1 macro-precision of each model evolves with varying training data sizes. For trustworthiness (graph on the left), Naive Bayes clearly outperforms DistilBERT and KNN when training data is scarce. However, as we inject more training data, the performance of NB flattens, while the other models tend to benefit from the availability of more training examples. With the full training set, the three models perform roughly the same but the graph suggests that KNN and DistilBERT would keep improving and eventually beat the NB classifier.

For readability (graph on the right), Naive Bayes is the best performer over all training sizes. However, all models perform well even with few training examples. This supports the claim that few examples suffice to build a readability classifier. Observe that the performance of the three models tends to flatten (or even gets worse) with more than 20% of the training examples.

In Fig. 2, we report the training times required by each model against the percentage of the training data. In both tasks, the training time taken by DistilBERT is much longer than that taken by the other models (we had to use a logarithmic scale for the representation). KNN is faster than Naive Bayes since it is a *lazy* approach (in training time it only stores the examples and learns no model).

Finally, we also computed the prediction time (time needed to classify a test instance). On average, Naive Bayes took 4.9 µs to predict, KNN 300 µs, and DistilBERT 0.002 µs. These results make sense since KNN has higher computational load in prediction time (needs to search for the neighbours). The DistilBERT model shows a surprisingly low average time, which could be due to the fact that the underlying library is very optimized and takes advantage of the host GPU, while traditional models are only set to be executed in CPU.

6 Conclusions and Future Work

In this work, we presented a comparison between traditional learning methods, such as SVMs or KNNs, and neural approaches such as BERT models, for automatically identifying health-related misinformation online. We also tested how they behave with varying sizes of training data. The main lesson extracted from the study is that, for these tasks and dataset, the added complexity of a neural model does not seem to be worthwhile. Sophisticated neural models were outperformed here by traditional models and the advantage of these classic methods is even more apparent with small training sets.

The results are modest overall and there is still room for improvement, as the tasks are difficult and more research effort is required. The main conclusion is that a traditional model such as NB is consistent (with very different sizes of training data), is computationally efficient and should not be discarded considering that in many environments we have little training data.

This study opens up new lines of research related to how to detect health-related misinformation on the Web. A natural next step could be testing other strategies to deal with BERT input limit, such as generating summaries of the test documents and, subsequently predicting based on the summaries or, alternatively, using neural models that have no input limit, such as LongFormer [3].

Finally, we could also consider extending these experiments with BERT models already fine tuned for a document classification task.

Acknowledgments. This work was funded by FEDER/Ministerio de Ciencia, Innovación y Universidades – Agencia Estatal de Investigación/ Project (RTI2018-093336-B-C21). This work has received financial support from the Consellería de Educación, Universidade e Formación Profesional (accreditation 2019-2022 ED431G-2019/04, ED431C 2018/29, ED431C 2018/19) and the European Regional Development Fund (ERDF), which acknowledges the CiTIUS-Research Center in Intelligent Technologies of the University of Santiago de Compostela as a Research Center of the Galician University System.

References

1. Abualsaud, M., Smucker, M.D.: Exposure and order effects of misinformation on health search decisions. In: Proceedings of the 42nd International ACM SIGIR Conference on Research and Development in Information Retrieval. Rome (2019)
2. Adhikari, A., Ram, A., Tang, R., Lin, J.: Docbert: BERT for document classification. arXiv preprint arXiv:1904.08398 (2019)
3. Beltagy, I., Peters, M.E., Cohan, A.: Longformer: the long-document transformer. arXiv preprint arXiv:2004.05150 (2020)
4. Cui, L., Lee, D.: Coaid: Covid-19 healthcare misinformation dataset. arXiv preprint arXiv:2006.00885 (2020)
5. Devlin, J., Chang, M.W., Lee, K., Toutanova, K.: Bert: pre-training of deep bidirectional transformers for language understanding. arXiv preprint arXiv:1810.04805 (2018)
6. Eysenbach, G.: Infodemiology: the epidemiology of (mis) information. Am. J. Med. **113**(9), 763–765 (2002)
7. Fogg, B.J.: Prominence-interpretation theory: explaining how people assess credibility online. In: CHI 2003 Extended Abstracts on Human Factors in Computing Systems, pp. 722–723 (2003)
8. Fox, S.: Health topics: 80% of internet users look for health information online. Pew Internet & American Life Project (2011)
9. Giachanou, A., Rosso, P., Crestani, F.: Leveraging emotional signals for credibility detection. In: Proceedings of the 42nd International ACM SIGIR Conference on Research and Development in Information Retrieval, pp. 877880 (2019)
10. Ginsca, A.L., Popescu, A., Lupu, M.: Credibility in information retrieval. Found. Trends Inf. Retr. **9**(5), 355–475 (2015). https://doi.org/10.1561/1500000046
11. Griffiths, K.M., Tang, T.T., Hawking, D., Christensen, H.: Automated assessment of the quality of depression websites. J. Med. Internet Res. **7**(5), e59 (2005)
12. Hahnel, C., Goldhammer, F., Kröhne, U., Naumann, J.: The role of reading skills in the evaluation of online information gathered from search engine environments. Comput. Hum. Behav. **78**, 223–234 (2018)
13. Haixiang, G., Yijing, L., Shang, J., Mingyun, G., Yuanyue, H., Bing, G.: Learning from class-imbalanced data: review of methods and applications. Expert Syst. Appl. **73**, 220–239 (2017)

14. Hossain, T., Logan IV, R.L., Ugarte, A., Matsubara, Y., Singh, S., Young, S.: Detecting Covid-19 misinformation on social media. In: Workshop on Natural Language Processing for COVID-19 (NLP-COVID) (2020)
15. Islam, M.S., Sarkar, T., et al.: Covid-19-related infodemic and its impact on public health: a global social media analysis. Am. J. Trop. Med. Hyg. **103**(4), 1621–1629 (2020)
16. Jimmy, J., Zuccon, G., Palotti, J., Goeuriot, L., Kelly, L.: Overview of the CLEF 2018 consumer health search task. In: International Conference of the Cross-Language Evaluation Forum for European Languages (2018)
17. Joachims, T.: Making large-scale support vector machine learning practical. In: Advances in Kernel Methods: Support Vector Learning, pp. 169–184 (1999)
18. Kattenbeck, M., Elsweiler, D.: Understanding credibility judgements for web search snippets. Aslib. J. Inf. Manage. (2019)
19. Liao, Q.V., Fu, W.T.: Age differences in credibility judgments of online health information. ACM Trans. Comput.-Hum. Interact. (TOCHI) **21**(1), 1–23 (2014)
20. Liu, Y., et al.: A robustly optimized BERT pretraining approach. CoRR **abs/1907.11692** (2019). arxiv.org/abs/1907.11692
21. Madabushi, H.T., Kochkina, E., Castelle, M.: Cost-sensitive BERT for generalisable sentence classification with imbalanced data. arXiv preprint arXiv:2003.11563 (2020)
22. Matsumoto, D., Hwang, H.C., Sandoval, V.A.: Cross-language applicability of linguistic features associated with veracity and deception. J. Police Crim. Psychol. **30**(4), 229–241 (2015)
23. Matthews, S.C., Camacho, A., Mills, P.J., Dimsdale, J.E.: The internet for medical information about cancer: help or hindrance? Psychosomatics **44**(2), 100–103 (2003)
24. McKnight, D.H., Kacmar, C.J.: Factors and effects of information credibility. In: Proceedings of the Ninth International Conference on Electronic Commerce, pp. 423–432 (2007)
25. Mukherjee, S., Weikum, G.: Leveraging joint interactions for credibility analysis in news communities. In: Proceedings of the 24th ACM International on Conference on Information and Knowledge Management, pp. 353–362 (2015)
26. Pennycook, G., McPhetres, J., Zhang, Y., Lu, J.G., Rand, D.G.: Fighting Covid-19 misinformation on social media: experimental evidence for a scalable accuracy-nudge intervention. Psychol. Sci. **31**(7), 770–780 (2020)
27. Pogacar, F.A., Ghenai, A., Smucker, M.D., Clarke, C.L.: The positive and negative influence of search results on people's decisions about the efficacy of medical treatments. In: Proceedings of the ACM SIGIR International Conference on Theory of Information Retrieval, pp. 209–216 (2017)
28. Reuters Insitute, University of Oxford: Reuters Digital News Report (2020). https://www.digitalnewsreport.org/survey/2020. Accessed 16 November 2020
29. Rieh, S.Y.: Judgment of information quality and cognitive authority in the web. J. Am. Soc. Inform. Sci. Technol. **53**(2), 145–161 (2002)
30. Sanh, V., Debut, L., Chaumond, J., Wolf, T.: DistilBERT, a distilled version of BERT: smaller, faster, cheaper and lighter. ArXiv **abs/1910.01108** (2019)
31. Schwarz, J., Morris, M.: Augmenting web pages and search results to support credibility assessment. In: Proceedings of the SIGCHI conference on human factors in Computing Systems, pp. 1245–1254 (2011)
32. Sicilia, R., Giudice, S.L., Pei, Y., Pechenizkiy, M., Soda, P.: Twitter rumour detection in the health domain. Expert Syst. Appl. **110**, 33–40 (2018)

33. Sondhi, P., Vydiswaran, V.G.V., Zhai, C.X.: Reliability prediction of webpages in the medical domain. In: Baeza-Yates, R., de Vries, A.P., Zaragoza, H., Cambazoglu, B.B., Murdock, V., Lempel, R., Silvestri, F. (eds.) ECIR 2012. LNCS, vol. 7224, pp. 219–231. Springer, Heidelberg (2012). https://doi.org/10.1007/978-3-642-28997-2_19
34. Vigdor, N.: Man fatally poisons himself while self-medicating for coronavirus, doctor says (2020). https://www.nytimes.com/2020/03/24/us/chloroquine-poisoning-coronavirus.html. Posted 24 March 2020
35. Wolf, T., et al.: Transformers: state-of-the-art natural language processing. In: Proceedings of the 2020 Conference on Empirical Methods in Natural Language Processing: System Demonstrations, pp. 38–45. Association for Computational Linguistics, Online (2020). https://www.aclweb.org/anthology/2020.emnlp-demos.6
36. Yamamoto, Y., Tanaka, K.: Enhancing credibility judgment of web search results. In: Proceedings of the SIGCHI Conference on Human Factors in Computing Systems, pp. 1235–1244 (2011)
37. Zhao, Y., Da, J., Yan, J.: Detecting health misinformation in online health communities: incorporating behavioral features into machine learning based approaches. Inf. Process. Manage. **58**(1), 102390 (2021)

Towards the Evaluation of Information Retrieval Systems on Evolving Datasets with Pivot Systems

Gabriela Nicole González-Sáez(✉), Philippe Mulhem, and Lorraine Goeuriot

Univ. Grenoble Alpes, CNRS, Grenoble INP (Institute of Engineering Univ. Grenoble Alpes), LIG, 38000 Grenoble, France
{gabriela-nicole.gonzalez-saez,philippe.mulhem, lorraine.goeuriot}@univ-grenoble-alpes.fr

Abstract. Evaluation of information retrieval systems follows the Cranfield paradigm, where the evaluation of several IR systems relies on a common *evaluation environment* (test collection and evaluation settings). The Cranfield paradigm requires the evaluation environment (EE) to be strictly identical to compare system's performances. For those cases where such paradigm cannot be used, e.g. when we do not have access to the code of the systems, we consider an evaluation framework that allows for slight changes in the EEs, as the evolution of the document corpus or topics. To do so, we propose to compare systems evaluated on different environments using a reference system, called *pivot*. In this paper, we present and validate a method to select a pivot, which is used to construct a correct ranking of systems evaluated in different environments. We test our framework on the TREC-COVID test collection, which is composed of five rounds of growing topics, documents and relevance judgments. The results of our experiments show that the pivot strategy can propose a correct ranking of systems evaluated in an evolving test collection.

Keywords: Information retrieval evaluation · Test collection · Result delta

1 Introduction

Classical evaluation of Information Retrieval (IR) Systems is made using a common test collection: a set of documents, a set of queries, and a set of relevance judgments. Evaluation campaigns aim at building such test collections and help to improve search systems. At the end of an evaluation campaign, a Ranking of Systems (RoS) based on their performances is built. A search task defined in an evaluation campaign dictates the topics creation, the corpus of documents, the relevance judgments (such as pooling parameters, guidelines to measure the relevance), and the metrics used to rank systems. All these elements define an *Evaluation Environment (EE)*. Changes in the EEs may lead to changes in the

K. S. Candan et al. (Eds.): CLEF 2021, LNCS 12880, pp. 91–102, 2021.
https://doi.org/10.1007/978-3-030-85251-1_8

results of the systems. Sanderson et al. [7] has shown that evaluating IR systems on different subsets of the document collection affects the performance of the system. Hence, results obtained on varying document collections are not comparable.

In the Web search, the topics searched and the set of documents continuously evolve. In such settings, getting a regular update on a system's performances is very challenging. Constant evolution of the test collection makes it nearly impossible to apply a classical offline evaluation following the Cranfield paradigm. We address the case where the different versions of the system are no longer available, therefore we have different systems evaluated in different test collections without the possibility to re-evaluate older versions of itself.

How can we compare a set of systems evaluated on evolving versions of the evaluation environment? We hypothesize it is possible to create a ranking of systems evaluated in different EEs by measuring the difference between the evaluated systems and a pivot system that is evaluated on all the EEs.

This paper presents a method to select a pivot system from several candidates to create a correct ranking of systems evaluated on different test collections. Our experiments use the TREC-COVID test collection, that ran in five rounds. We test the pivot strategy over one round of the TREC-COVID and select one pivot to compare all the systems taking part in the five rounds.

2 State of the Art

We present now works on three topics related to our study: Sect. 2.1 focuses on comparing systems on dynamic test collections; Sect. 2.2 details the impact of different evaluation settings on the performance of the systems; and Sect. 2.3 presents works that evaluate systems in changing test collections.

2.1 Dynamic Test Collections

One of the most important constraints of the Cranfield evaluation is the use of a common test collection for all the systems in comparison. Assessing the quality of Web search needs a repeated or continuous evaluation given incremental document collections [4]. We present two papers that describe evaluation methods tackling the problem of continuous evaluation over evolving test collections.

Soboroff [8] addresses the need to create a dynamic test collection to evaluate the web search in realistic settings. Their experiments use a changing and growing document collection, with a fixed set of topics and relevant judgments. [8] shows that it is possible to compare the performance of systems from different versions of the test collection despite the decay in relevance data due to the changing document collection. According to the Bpref evaluation measure, the rankings of the systems in different versions of the test collection are similar to the RoS of the initial version of the test collection, leading to assess that systems are comparable across these versions. The difference with our proposal is that we compare different system evaluated in different versions of a test collection.

Tonon et al. [10] proposed a method to evaluate IR systems iteratively on the same test collection, increasing the judged documents according to systems that did not take part in the pool of documents. They focus on the bias on systems introduced by being included or not in the pooling systems. Such a bias makes it impossible to compare system accurately, because the test collection construction penalizes systems that did not take part in the pooling that might be more effective than systems that took part in the pool but retrieve different results [17]. Therefore, the pooling strategy must be considered in the EE, as being included in the pool of documents or not affects the evaluation of the system.

These papers rely on the need to create alternative methods to incorporate incremental test collections on the evaluation of IR systems, as the proper environment of the web search. Our proposal does not need to incorporate new resources into the test collection to compare systems across evolving EEs. Also, we integrate changes on any of EE elements, while guaranteeing those changes keeps the same RoS, then the EEs are comparable.

2.2 Performance on Different Evaluation Environments

In this work we define the EE as an extended test collection, that incorporates the elements involved in the IR evaluation and may affect the performance of the IR system: the document set, the topic set, the relevance judgment, the pooling strategy and the list of metrics evaluated. The papers described in this section analyse the impact of these elements on the performance measurements.

As shown in [7], evaluations conducted on different sub-collections (splits of the document corpus with the respective relevance assessments) lead to substantial and statistically significant differences in the relative performance of retrieval systems, independently from the number of relevant documents that are available in the sub-collections. Using the ANalysis Of Variance (ANOVA) model, [2] showed that changing the test collection (splits of the documents corpus) leads to varying system performances (inconsistently across metrics). In the same line, [3,13] model the system effect and the test collection effect on the performance metrics as separated factors, they define ANOVA models and GLMMs to analyse systems performances over several test collections with the goal of improving the measurement accuracy of retrieval system performance by better modeling the noise present in test collection scores.

Such studies are not aiming at system comparison, but rather at measuring the effect of the test collection on the system performance. They provide a better understanding of the measurement of performance, but do not allow to compare two systems that are evaluated using different EEs.

2.3 Meta-analysis of IR Evaluations Within Evolving Environments

Score standardization is an evaluation method that reduces the impact of the topic's difficulty on the IR system's performance [6,11,16]. It consists of normalizing the performance score for a topic by its observed mean and standard deviation over a set of runs/systems [15]. Urbano et al. [11] showed that even when the RoS between raw and standardized scores is the same, the RoS using mean scores may differ considerably.

Meta-analysis is another approach to compare the performance of systems over multiple test collections [9]. Meta-analysis consists in measuring a delta difference between one baseline and a target system, over multiple collections. This meta analysis allows the measurement of the mean difference between the systems with a confidence interval. This technique is strongly related to the measurement of the improvement across multiple test collections of a system with a specific modification that differences it from the baseline system. Our proposal addresses the problem of evaluation of different systems over evolving EEs. Therefore, the differences are not computed over one, but several retrieval systems that need to be compared. Both techniques make use of relative measurements to compare systems evaluated in different EEs. We extend this idea in our framework of evaluation with the use of a common pivot system that defines a reference to compute the relative distance between the systems' performance to rank the systems.

3 Pivot Evaluation of Continuous Test Collections

Our proposal focuses on the comparison of systems across different EEs. We assume that running a set of IR systems on two comparable EEs should give the same RoS, as showed by Soboroff [8] when RoS is built with bpref metric.

Our main goal here is to create a single RoS with systems evaluated on different (yet comparable) EEs. To get an accurate comparison of systems evaluated on varying EEs, we detail below a framework based on the difference between systems performances across comparable EEs.

3.1 Result Delta Definition

In this section, we present a method to measure the impact of EE variation on systems evaluation. Since we want to compare systems that are evaluated on different EEs, we cannot rely on absolute evaluation. Therefore, we propose to build our framework on differences between evaluation measures of performance, with **Result Deltas**. A result delta, $\mathcal{R}\Delta$, estimates the difference between the performance of two systems measured with a similar metric. Three kinds of $\mathcal{R}\Delta$ can be measured, according to the element that change in the evaluation task:

- $\mathcal{R}_s\Delta$: When we have two different IR systems evaluated in the same EE, as a classical IR evaluation.
- $\mathcal{R}_e\Delta$: If the same IR system is evaluated in two EEs, extracting mainly the environment effect on the system.
- $\mathcal{R}_{se}\Delta$: If both EEs and systems are different.

$\mathcal{R}_{se}\Delta$ can hardly be measured, as the two systems are not directly comparable: both the EEs and the systems are different. To get an estimation of this measure, we propose to use a reference system, called **Pivot system**, which would be evaluated within the two EEs considered. $\mathcal{R}_s\Delta$ would be computed between each system and the pivot within each EE considered. Finally, both $\mathcal{R}_s\Delta$ can be used to compute $\mathcal{R}_{se}\Delta$ and compare the two systems over the two EEs. The result delta value is measured using the relative distance between the pivot system and the evaluated system S_1:

$$\mathcal{R}_s\Delta(Pivot, S_1, EE_1) = \frac{M(S_1, EE_1) - M(Pivot, EE_1)}{M(Pivot, EE_1)} \tag{1}$$

Given a metric $M(S, EE)$ that evaluates the performance of a system S in a evaluation environment EE, we want to compare S_1 evaluated in EE_1 and S_2 evaluated in EE_2 (being comparable EEs). System performances are measured with $M(S_1, EE_1)$ and $M(S_2, EE_2)$. In order to compare S_1 and S_2, using a pivot system will help relating the systems across the EEs by comparing $M(S_1, EE_1)$ with $M(Pivot, EE_1)$ as $\mathcal{R}_s\Delta(Pivot, S_1, EE_1)$ and $M(S_2, EE_2)$ with $M(Pivot, EE_2)$ as $\mathcal{R}_s\Delta(Pivot, S_2, EE_2)$. According to the EE comparability assumption, the ranking of systems should be the same in both EEs. As an illustration, if $\mathcal{R}_s\Delta(Pivot, S_1, EE_1) > \mathcal{R}_s\Delta(Pivot, S_2, EE_2)$ then, $M(S_1, EE_1) > M(S_2, EE_1) \wedge M(S_1, EE_2) > M(S_2, EE_2)$.

3.2 Pivot Selection Strategy

The key point in our proposal lies in the choice of the pivot. To assess the quality of a pivot, we study whether the use of a given pivot to compute the result delta measures of systems evaluated on different EEs allows to obtain a *correct* RoS. The pivot-based RoS is validated using a ground truth reference RoS.

A system P is considered to be a good pivot according to a reference EE EE_{ref} if, using the result deltas measured with P to compare different systems evaluated across various EEs (EE_{splits}, a split of the EE_{ref}) we can get the same RoS as the reference one (got on EE_{ref}). To evaluate the correctness of a pivot, we compare:

- RoS_{ref} a reference RoS according to a ground truth, namely the official RoS in an evaluation campaign based on the whole corpus and topic set, and
- RoS_{pivot}, it is artificially built from two EEs created by splitting the whole corpus and/or whole topics set, and splitting the compared systems on these two EEs. RoS_{pivot} uses the result deltas of the pivot under consideration.

If the two rankings are the same, this means that the pivot is able to correctly support the indirect comparison of systems. To evaluate the correctness of a pivot, we measure the Kendall's Tau similarity between RoS_{pivot} and RoS_{ref}.

The correctness of a pivot must be compared to a baseline. To do that, we define a $RoS_{baseline}$ that is constructed under the same EEs created for the RoS_{pivot}. The $RoS_{baseline}$ orders the absolute performance values of the two system sets evaluated on each EE split. Then, we measure the similarity between the $RoS_{baseline}$ and RoS_{ref}. We expect higher similarity values using the pivot strategy than with the absolute performance values.

To assess the quality of a pivot, we must repeat the experiment: for instance, we may split the set of document Doc times, and the set of topics Top times, creating $Doc \times Top$ splits of the EE_{ref}. With these multiple experiments we build distributions of the correctness achieved by a pivot, and assess statistical significance of differences with the baseline. To evaluate the pivot strategy on systems already implemented, we filter the runs keeping only the documents and topics of the corresponding EE split. This process is described and validated in the work of Sanderson [7].

4 Methodology

Here, we describe how the strategy presented in Sect. 3.2 is implemented: firstly we describe the test collection we are using in Sect. 4.1, then we present how we validate the pivot strategy in Sect. 4.2.

4.1 TREC-COVID Evolutionary Collection

The data used to validate our proposal is the TREC-COVID collection [12], created in the COVID-19 pandemic by NIST and over 60 teams and 500 runs. The created test collection is available in TREC-COVID webpage[1]. TREC-COVID is a continuous test collection, organised on five rounds, where each round is composed of a specific release of CORD-19[2] documents collection [14], a set of incremental topics and a set of relevant judgments. CORD-19 is composed of an incremental list of scientific papers related to COVID-19. Topics correspond to information needs of clinicians and biomedical researchers during the COVID-19 pandemic. Round 1 has topics is 30, and five topics are added at each round, leading to 50 topics at round 5. The relevance judgments are repeated at each round for all the topics and the non-judged documents.

While the challenge did not compare the results from different rounds, we see the opportunity to apply our framework to this incremental dataset, creating round-based splits to validate the pivot method, then we create a result delta rank that includes the systems that took part on the five rounds.

4.2 Evaluation Method

The pivot selection strategy is validated on one round of the campaign, with 50%–50% splits of the topics and documents sets, over the set of participating systems. Figure 1a) shows an example with five systems (S1, ..., S5), the splits are EE1 (in orange) and EE2 (in blue). Then a ranking of the 5 systems is built using the result deltas (RD in Fig. 1) (S2, S4 and S5 in EE1, S1 and S3 in EE2),

[1] https://ir.nist.gov/covidSubmit/archive.html.
[2] https://www.semanticscholar.org/cord19.

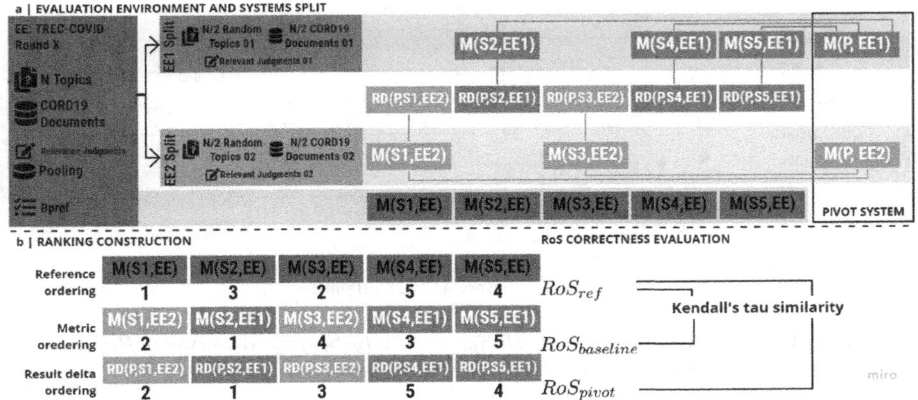

Fig. 1. a) EE split and result delta with pivot P. b) Similarity of RoS created (Color figure online)

namely RoS_{pivot}. This ranking is then compared, using Kendall's tau with the reference ranking RoS_{ref} (i.e., the ranking of all the systems participating on the corresponding round sorted by his performance metric.) and to the baseline ranking $RoS_{baseline}$. A good pivot should generate a ranking closer to the reference ranking than the baseline.

We use six pivot implementations, that are commonly used as baseline systems, using Terrier [5] system, BM25, DirichletLM, TF_IDF with default parameters, without and with pseudo relevance feedback (RF) using default parameters (DFR Bo1 model [1] on three documents, selecting 10 terms). We evaluate the correctness of these six candidate pivots. We run the experiment in 10 splits of documents and 10 splits of topics (leading to an overall of $10 \times 10 = 100$ pairs of EEs). Finally, per each EE pair we have six pivot-based RoS and one baseline RoS that are compared to the reference RoS with Kendall's tau similarity (Fig. 1b). The metric of performance used is BPref, one of the official metrics used on the campaign. Bpref is robust to incomplete relevance judgments, then it is appropriate to our experiment due to the split of documents.

Once validated, we can rank the result deltas of all the participant systems measured by the selected pivot, to create a final RoS that includes the 500 runs submitted on the five TREC-COVID rounds.

5 Experiments and Results

In this section, we present the results of two experiments. In the first one, we aim at *validating the pivot strategy*, by measuring the correctness of the ranking obtained with the different pivots presented in Sect. 4.2. In the second one, we apply the validated pivot strategy on a dynamic test collection (presented in Sect. 4.1) to observe the RoS obtained across several rounds.

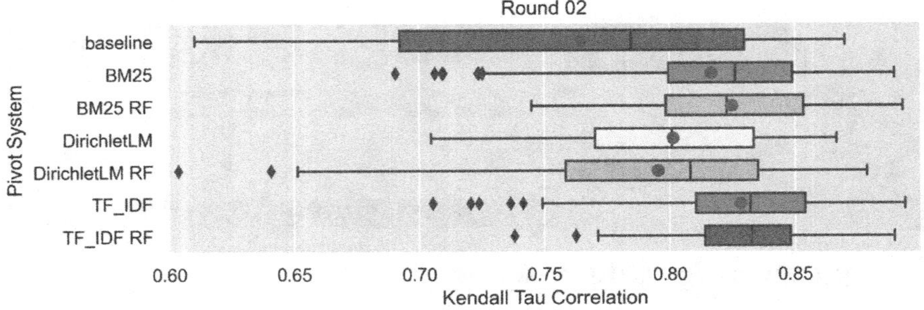

Fig. 2. Boxplot of similarity between RoS_{pivot} and RoS_{ref}, and between $RoS_{baseline}$ and RoS_{ref} on the first line. Gray circle represents mean value.

5.1 Pivot Selection

We describe our pivot selection on the round 2: EE_{split} is a half of round 2 test collection. We compare the correctness of the created pivot-based RoS with the reference RoS that considers the round's full set of documents and topics.

Figure 2 shows the correctness distribution for each created RoS over 100 EE splits. Each boxplot summarizes the Kendall's tau similarity distribution measured between the pivot-based RoS (obtained with the pivot's result delta of two sets of systems, where each set is evaluated on a EE split) and the reference RoS. We compare the boxplots of the pivots versus a baseline RoS (first boxplot). We see that the correctness mean (resp. standard deviation) of the baseline RoS is lower (resp. larger) than any pivot-based RoS. This reflects a higher uncertainty of the ranking created with bpref absolute values in comparison to the rankings created using result deltas. The result deltas of TF_IDF RF formed the RoS with the highest correctness (bottom boxplot).

Table 1 summarizes the results in the five rounds of TREC-COVID, a high correctness of pivot-based RoS is repeated in the five rounds (columns). Table 1

Table 1. Mean ± std. dev. of the similarity values between RoS and RoS_{ref}. In **bold** the higher similarity value. '*' if distribution difference is statistical significant from $RoS_{baseline}$ (Kolmogorov-Smirnoff test, p-value < 0.05).

RoS	Round1	Round2	Round3	Round4	Round5
Baseline	*0.819 ± 0.06*	*0.765 ± 0.08*	*0.857 ± 0.05*	*0.837 ± 0.08*	***0.892 ± 0.04***
BM25	0.837 ± 0.04	0.817 ± 0.04*	0.87 ± 0.03*	0.886 ± 0.03*	0.883 ± 0.05
BM25 RF	0.844 ± 0.03*	0.825 ± 0.04*	0.880 ± 0.03	0.884 ± 0.03*	0.882 ± 0.04
DirichletLM	0.841 ± 0.03*	0.801 ± 0.04*	0.865 ± 0.04	0.870 ± 0.05	0.880 ± 0.05*
DirichletLM RF	0.827 ± 0.05	0.795 ± 0.06*	0.840 ± 0.06	0.873 ± 0.05	0.841 ± 0.06*
TF_IDF	**0.852 ± 0.02***	0.828 ± 0.04*	0.887 ± 0.03*	**0.895 ± 0.03***	0.891 ± 0.04*
TF_IDF RF	0.846 ± 0.03*	**0.830 ± 0.03***	**0.890 ± 0.03***	0.888 ± 0.03*	0.883 ± 0.05*

Table 2. Bpref mean performance with complete test collection for each round

Run	Round1	Round2	Round3	Round4	Round5
Participants mean	0.31 ± 0.12	0.36 ± 0.10	0.43 ± 0.15	0.48 ± 0.13	0.44 ± 0.15
BM25	0.3965	0.3691	0.4234	0.4367	0.3399
BM25 RF	0.4173	0.3757	**0.4375**	0.4365	0.3440
DirichletLM	0.3530	0.3341	0.3193	0.3316	0.2558
DirichletLM RF	0.3555	0.3116	0.3105	0.2941	0.2245
TF_IDF	0.4115	0.3733	0.4221	0.4319	0.3483
TF_IDF RF	**0.4407**	**0.3919**	0.4348	**0.4395**	**0.3548**

presents the mean and standard deviation values of Kendall's Tau similarity between the seven created RoS (lines) and the reference RoS. The first row describes the correctness of the baseline RoS. Even when the ranking is based on absolute values, the similarity between the baseline RoS and the reference RoS is close 0.8, this high value could be related to our assumption of comparable EE (no modifications of the ranking across EEs). The standard deviation of the baseline RoS is the highest one on the first four rounds. Considering the five rounds, the pivot with the best correctness results are TF_IDF RF and TF_IDF. The similarity of these RoS and the reference RoS has the lowest standard deviation values and their distributions are significantly different from the baseline RoS similarity distribution in all rounds. In the five rounds the distribution of the Kendall's tau similarity got by sorting the systems with the result delta value measured by TF_IDF is significantly different to the similarity distribution of the rankings created with the Bpref values (denotes as * on Table 1). The distributions are significant different with 95% of confidence according to Kolmogorov-Smirnoff test, a non-parametric test useful to our experiment because the similarity data have non-normal distributions in most of the cases.

Table 2 shows the mean Bpref performance of participant runs (Participants mean row) and pivots considering the EE of reference (full set of documents and topics). TF_IDF RF is the pivot system with the highest performance in four rounds. DirichletLM RF is the pivot system with the lowest performance in all the rounds, and as is showed in Table 1 the RoS created with the result deltas of this pivot achieve the worst similarity values and the biggest standard deviation on all the rounds. The pivots presented the worst bpref performance on the final round, with lower values than the participants mean performance. Only in this round the baseline RoS is more similar to the RoS of reference than any pivot-based RoS. Finally, the selected pivot is TF_IDF RF, due to its result deltas values constructed a similar to the RoS of reference. Therefore, the correctness property is achieved in more than 83% of the RoS considering the five rounds by TF_IDF RF pivot.

Table 3. Best runs of the five rounds of TREC-COVID ranked with pivot strategy

Round	Best run per round	Official Bpref	Pivot result delta	Pivot rank
1	BBGhelani1	0.5294	0.2012	159
2	mpiid5_run3	0.5679	0.4491	47
3	mpiid5_run1	0.6084	0.3993	66
4	UPrrf38rrf3-r4	0.6801	0.5474	29
5	UPrrf102-wt-r5	0.6378	0.7976	1

5.2 Exploratory Experiment: Testing the Pivot in Real Settings

The pivot strategy has proved its ability to compare systems in comparable EEs, that were created splitting in half each test collection round. Now, we are interested in apply our method in a realistic setting, with a non-artificially evolving test collection. Our purpose is to observe within a realistic setting what ranking would our method give. Therefore, We apply our method in TREC-COVID to understand if the system's performance are improving across the rounds, even when the EEs are not completely comparable (Kendall's tau similarity of the pivot's rankings across the rounds ranges between 0.6 and 0.86).

As TF_IDF RF was the pivot with the best results in the rounds, we rank the result delta of all the system that participated on the five rounds of TREC-COVID challenge with TF_IDF RF using Bpref metric.

Table 3 presents the best runs of each round of TREC-COVID campaign and their rank using the pivot-based RoS. The best run of the fifth round was twice better than the pivot system, this is the largest difference between the best run and the pivot, and it explains why the fifth round's best run is at the first place of the pivot-based RoS. The best system of round4 is UPrrf38rrf3-r4, this system is submitted by the team that also presented the best bpref system in round5 UPrrf102-wt-r5. These runs are produced by Reciprocal Rank Fusion of three systems for UPrrf38rrf3-r4[3] and four systems for UPrrf102-wt-r5[4]. As the pivot-based RoS takes in consideration the pivot performance to compare the systems across the rounds, the relative improvement of the best system in round five is biggest than the improvement of the round four's best run, then we conclude that it should expected that UPrrf102-wt-r5 have better bpef performance than UPrrf38rrf3-r4 if they were evaluated in the same round.

6 Discussion

The ranking created with Bpref absolute values shows high similarity with the reference RoS, this could be due to the high similarity in the CORD-19 documents, all the documents are scientific papers from PubMed Central (PMC),

[3] https://ir.nist.gov/covidSubmit/archive/round4/UPrrf38rrf3-r4.pdf.

[4] https://ir.nist.gov/covidSubmit/archive/round5/UPrrf102-wt-r5.pdf.

bioRxiv, and medRxiv [14]. This similarity on the document collection, lead to similar ranking even when we consider only the half of the documents of the test collection to be retrieved by the IR systems.

Ranking the systems using result delta measured with a common pivot across the EEs is better than rank the bpref absolute values. The pivot-based RoS are more certain, because the standard deviation is lower than using bpref values to rank. Nevertheless, not all pivots work the same. We found one pivot system which ranking have lower similarity values than the baseline RoS. DirichletLM RF is the system with the lowest Bpref performance. Likewise, the RoS with the higher similarity values is constructed using the result deltas of the pivot with higher Bpref performance on the rounds. This lead to interpret that the performance of the pivot is related to the correctness achieved by the ranking created using the pivot's result deltas. To confirm this relation we will continue our work using more systems as pivot to create the ranking, attempting to explore pivots with higher and lower performances.

In the fifth round the baseline RoS is more similar to the reference RoS than any RoS created with the pivot strategy. In this final round the performance of the pivot systems decreased and it is far from the Bpref values achieved by the participant runs. We will continue exploring the impact of the distance between the pivot performance and the mean performance of the rounds to improve the correctness of the pivot-based RoS.

After the validation of the pivot strategy on each round of the TREC-COVID test collection we can propose a pivot to measure the result deltas with all the participating systems and create a final ranking of systems. Using this RoS we can evaluate the evolution of the results in the growing test collection. The best Bpref performance systems were evaluated on the final round followed by the fourth round. Table 2 shows that the highest Bpref mean performance is achieved in the fourth and fifth rounds. Because the pivot's Bpref performance (TF_IDF RF) is lower in round5 than in round4, the system with the overall highest Bpref value (achieved in round4) is ranked in position 29 with our framework. The difference on the pivot's bpref value across the rounds might be a measure of the EE difficulty.

7 Conclusion

We have presented a framework proposal to rank systems evaluated in different evaluation environments using result deltas and pivot systems. The proposed framework is evaluated on the TREC COVID test collection by assessing the correctness of the pivot-based RoS. The results show that, using the pivot strategy we can improve the correctness of ranking of systems that were evaluated in different EEs, compared to the RoS created with bpref absolute values.

In this paper we proposed only baseline systems as pivot, because of their easy implementation that guarantee the reproducibility of our framework. We shall explore other strategies, as pivots based on the participant systems, to achieve closer performances between the pivot and the evaluated systems. With these new pivots, we will explore the effect of the pivot performance on the proposed RoS. Also, we will analyse merging the result deltas of several pivots to create a meta-pivot. Additionally, we will study further EE comparability and investigate the impact of EE changes on the evaluation framework; Finally, we will define the guidelines to create a test collection for continuous evaluation based on the characteristics of comparable EEs.

Acknowledgements. This work was supported by the ANR Kodicare bi-lateral project, grant ANR-19-CE23-0029 of the French Agence Nationale de la Recherche, and by the Austrian Science Fund (FWF).

References

1. Amati, G.: Probabilistic models for information retrieval based on divergence from randomness. Ph.D. thesis, Glasgow University, Glasgow, June 2003
2. Ferro, N., Sanderson, M.: Sub-corpora impact on system effectiveness. In: Proceedings of SIGIR 2017, pp. 901–904 (2017)
3. Ferro, N., Sanderson, M.: Improving the accuracy of system performance estimation by using shards. In: Proceedings of SIGIR 2019, pp. 805–814 (2019)
4. Jensen, E.C., Beitzel, S.M., Chowdhury, A., Frieder, O.: Repeatable evaluation of search services in dynamic environments. ACM Trans. Inf. Syst. (TOIS) **26**(1), 1-es (2007)
5. Ounis, I., Lioma, C., Macdonald, C., Plachouras, V.: Research directions in terrier: a search engine for advanced retrieval on the web. CEPIS Upgrade J. **8**(1) (2007)
6. Sakai, T.: A simple and effective approach to score standardisation. In: Proceedings of ICTIR 2016, pp. 95–104 (2016)
7. Sanderson, M., Turpin, A., Zhang, Y., Scholer, F.: Differences in effectiveness across sub-collections. In: Proceedings of CIKM 2012, pp. 1965–1969 (2012)
8. Soboroff, I.: Dynamic test collections: measuring search effectiveness on the live web. In: Proceedings of SIGIR 2006, pp. 276–283 (2006)
9. Soboroff, I.: Meta-analysis for retrieval experiments involving multiple test collections. In: Proceedings of CIKM 2018, pp. 713–722 (2018)
10. Tonon, A., Demartini, G., Cudré-Mauroux, P.: Pooling-based continuous evaluation of information retrieval systems. Inf. Retr. J. **18**(5), 445–472 (2015)
11. Urbano, J., Lima, H., Hanjalic, A.: A new perspective on score standardization. In: Proceedings of SIGIR 2019, pp. 1061–1064 (2019)
12. Voorhees, E., et al.: TREC-COVID: constructing a pandemic information retrieval test collection. In: ACM SIGIR Forum, New York, NY, USA, vol. 54, pp. 1–12. ACM (2021)
13. Voorhees, E.M., Samarov, D., Soboroff, I.: Using replicates in information retrieval evaluation. ACM Trans. Inf. Syst. (TOIS) **36**(2), 1–21 (2017)
14. Wang, L.L., et al.: CORD-19: the COVID-19 open research dataset. arXiv (2020)
15. Webber, W., Moffat, A., Zobel, J.: Score standardization for robust comparison of retrieval systems. In: Proceedings of the 12th Australasian Document Computing Symposium, pp. 1–8 (2007)
16. Webber, W., Moffat, A., Zobel, J.: Score standardization for inter-collection comparison of retrieval systems. In: Proceedings of SIGIR 2008, pp. 51–58 (2008)
17. Webber, W., Park, L.A.: Score adjustment for correction of pooling bias. In: Proceedings of SIGIR 2009, pp. 444–451 (2009)

A Multi-Task Learning Model for Multidimensional Relevance Assessment

Divi Galih Prasetyo Putri, Marco Viviani(✉), and Gabriella Pasi

Department of Informatics, Systems, and Communication, Information and Knowledge Representation, Retrieval, and Reasoning (IKR3) Lab, Edificio U14, University of Milano-Bicocca, Viale Sarca, 336 – 20126 Milan, Italy
d.putri@campus.unimib.it, {marco.viviani,gabriella.pasi}@unimib.it
https://ikr3.disco.unimib.it/

Abstract. In recent years, deep learning models have been successfully applied to Information Retrieval (IR), mainly for assessing the topical relevance of documents with respect to queries. However, relevance is a multidimensional concept, which can be assessed based on several criteria, depending on the document type, the domain considered, the search task performed, etc. Given that recent advancements in deep neural networks enable several learning tasks to be solved simultaneously, in this paper we examine the possibility of modeling multidimensional relevance by jointly solving a retrieval task, to learn topical relevance, and a classification task, to learn additional relevance dimensions. To instantiate and evaluate the proposed model, we consider three query-independent relevance dimensions beyond topicality, i.e., readability, trustworthiness, and credibility. The reported findings show that the proposed joint modeling can improve the performance of the retrieval task.

Keywords: Multidimensional relevance · Neural information retrieval · Multi-Task Learning

1 Introduction

In recent years, deep neural networks have been employed in Information Retrieval (IR) for generating ranking models [14]. A neural model in an ad-hoc retrieval task is usually implemented to solve a matching problem between two texts [24], i.e., a *query* and each *document* in a document collection, in order to retrieve documents that are relevant to a user's information needs.

The concept of *relevance* constitutes the core notion in Information Retrieval; initially, this notion was made to correspond to that of *topicality*, which can be considered as the basic relevance criterion. However, topicality constitutes just one facet of relevance, which is, indeed, a multidimensional concept [4]. Several aspects related to the multidimensional nature of relevance have been discussed

K. S. Candan et al. (Eds.): CLEF 2021, LNCS 12880, pp. 103–115, 2021.
https://doi.org/10.1007/978-3-030-85251-1_9

for a long time by the research community. In [27], for example, the authors provide a global overview of several criteria based on document properties that can be exploited to assess document relevance. In [10], the authors denote document properties to be used in the IR task as "information nutrition labels". In [34], the authors make explicit reference to relevance criteria that can be considered in relevance assessment beyond topicality. In such a multidimensional context, an "overall" numerical relevance assessment can be obtained by the *aggregation* of the distinct numerical assessments associated with the considered criteria in a decision-theoretic setting [6]. *Learning-to-Rank* (L2R) has also been used to solve the problem of accounting for several relevance criteria together [30].

In this paper, we focus on assessing multidimensional relevance by means of a deep neural ranking model. To this purpose we assume a specific scenario, in which an additional relevance criterion besides topicality is considered; moreover, we assume that the additional relevance criterion is query-independent (i.e., document-centered). Specifically, given a query, we propose to employ a *Multi-Task Learning* (MTL) approach to assess the overall relevance of a document. In MTL, several tasks can be performed concurrently to enable sharing information between tasks, based on a deep neural architecture [5]. In our context, the assumption is to combine the classical retrieval task to learn topical relevance with a classification task to learn the assessment of the additional relevance criterion, by sharing the document representation, as it will be explained in Sect. 3. In other words, the global relevance of a document with respect to a user query can be learned by the MTL model that combines topicality with the additional, query-independent, relevance criterion. Such a model can, in addition, benefit from having more training data from multiple tasks, thus reducing potential overfitting in one task.

To illustrate and evaluate the proposed model, we consider the three following query-independent relevance criteria: *readability*, *trustworthiness*, and *credibility*, as defined in [13], which are assessed based on the properties of the documents.

2 Related Work

Over the years, several criteria have been considered besides the topical matching between queries and documents (i.e., topicality) to perform the retrieval task [4], e.g., *popularity* [21], *novelty*, *readability*, and *reliability* [15], etc. Among them, some are *query-dependent*, such as *topical authority* [16], while others can be considered *query-independent*, such as readability, *technicality* and *virality* [10], and popularity, as computed by the PageRank algorithm.

As briefly illustrated in the Introduction, to account for such criteria together, two families of approaches have been considered in the literature. The first family focuses on *aggregation*, in particular by performing a linear combination of – or by applying other aggregation strategies to – the distinct relevance assessments connected to the distinct relevance criteria; this constitutes a straightforward yet effective method [3,6,11]. In [3], in particular, the authors linearly combined the topicality assessment with another relevance assessment based on *document quality*, which is obtained by considering suitable quality features related to content readability. In [11], the authors addressed the issue of the incompatibility of relevance scores associated with topicality and *opinion* scores in linear combination functions, and compared several score transformation approaches. In [6], the authors proposed a prioritized aggregation scheme to combine four relevance dimensions, such as *aboutness*, *coverage*, *appropriateness*, and *reliability*, in the personalized IR task. An overview of the works using the aggregation approach in the context of IR can be found in [19]. The second family is based on the use of *Learning-to-Rank* (L2R). In L2R, several features are considered to account for distinct aspects (e.g., related to the document representation, its popularity, distinct IR models, etc.) that concur to the relevance learning process. Among L2R approaches, we can cite [23,30]. When using aggregation-based approaches, prior domain knowledge about the impact that different relevance criteria may have on the retrieval task is often required; when referring to approaches that rely on supervised learning, we deal with training datasets labeled with *relevance judgments*, which are difficult to be interpreted and used to capture the multidimensional aspect of relevance.

A possible solution to the above-mentioned issues is constituted by *Multi-Task Learning* (MTL), which *"improves generalization by leveraging the domain-specific information contained in the training signals of related tasks"* [5]. MTL has shown to be effective in many NLP tasks [37], and, in Information Retrieval, several works have tried to improve the effectiveness of the retrieval task using such approach [1,2,18,35,36]. Some works proposed to exploit the information related to the query to increase retrieval effectiveness by performing the *query classification task* [18] and the *query suggestion task* in search sessions [1,2], together with the retrieval task, to learn the relevance assessment. In [35] and [36], the authors showed the benefit of jointly learning relevance by performing together the *retrieval task* and the *recommendation task*. However, no MTL-based solution has focused on modeling multidimensional relevance to date.

3 Multi-Task Learning for Multidimensional Relevance Assessment

In this section we illustrate the proposed Multi-Task Learning model for learning multidimensional relevance in the presence of both relevance judgments (which refer to the topical relevance of documents with respect to queries) and other labeled data with respect to additional relevance criteria such as readability, trustworthiness, and credibility. Each of these additional relevance criteria is considered separately along with topicality in the proposed model.

Relevance judgments are employed as training data of the *retrieval task* that is performed by means of an existing neural model based on a *representation-focused architecture* [14], as detailed in Sect. 3.1.[1] The other labeled data, referred

[1] The use of more advanced neural ranking and classification models will be investigated in the future.

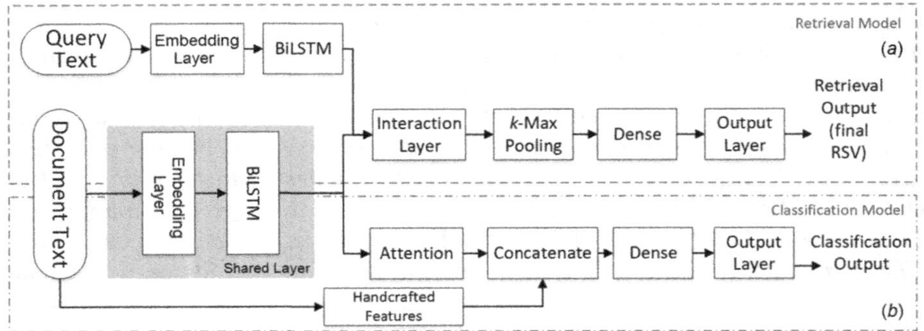

Fig. 1. The proposed Multi-Task Learning model for ranking, jointly performing the *retrieval task* and the *classification task.*

to each of the three considered additional relevance criteria, are employed as training data of another simple neural model that performs the *classification task*, as detailed in Sect. 3.2.

As illustrated in Fig. 1, which represents the high-level architecture of the proposed Multi-Task Learning model, the *ranking model* and the *classification model* operate simultaneously and share parameters in order to generate an assessment of relevance that is multidimensional, by taking into account both topical relevance and another relevance criterion at a time. To make this possible, in this work we adopted one of the most common approaches in Multi-Task Learning, called *hard-parameter sharing* [5]. Generally, in such an approach, several hidden layers are shared between tasks, while the output layers are task-specific. The tasks are usually related and might share a common underlying representation, as in the case of the proposed model.

The inputs of the model are the *query*, for the retrieval task, and the *document*, for both the retrieval and the classification tasks. The shared layer consist of an embedding and a Bi-LSTM layers, of which the document's semantic representation is learned across tasks.[2] The weights associated with the embedding representations in such layers are initialized using pre-trained word vectors,[3] and the weights are updated during the training process. In this way, learning parameters related to the retrieval and the classification task together allows to consider additional relevance dimension simultaneously, because it enables the obtained semantic representations capturing information from both tasks.

The non-shared layers are task-specific, and perform the tasks separately without sharing any parameters. Each of the task-specific layers returns separate outputs. However, the output of the retrieval task produces the final *Retrieval Status Value* (RSV) of the document, which takes into account also the additional relevance dimension beyond topicality due to the embedding and Bi-LSTM

[2] The technical choices behind embedding representations and, in general, the ranking and classification models will be detailed in Sects. 3.1 and 3.2.

[3] They are pre-trained on large text corpora, as it will be detailed in Sect. 4.

layers shared with the classification task. In fact, the Multi-Task Learning model is trained by minimizing a *global loss function* L, which is expressed as the weighted sum of the losses of both tasks. Formally:

$$L = \lambda_r L_r + \lambda_c L_c$$

where λ_r and λ_c are the weight parameters respectively for the loss L_r of the retrieval task and the loss L_c of the classification task. For both tasks, the *cross-entropy loss function* is applied.

3.1 The Retrieval Model

In this work, we followed the approach proposed in [33] to perform the retrieval task. As previously introduced, it is performed by employing a neural ranking model based on a so-called *representation-focused architecture*, which, given a *query* and a *document* as input, builds their word embedding representations and generate relevance assessments via a simple matching function such as the *cosine similarity*. The architecture of the retrieval model is illustrated in Fig. 1 (*a*). To transform the word sequences into fixed-length vector representations, a *Recurrent Neural Network* (RNN) with *Bidirectional Long-Short Term Memory* (Bi-LSTM) to encode the input texts are adopted. The Bi-LSTM layer in particular, provides as output a positional text representation of both the query and document. Then, the interactions between the two positional text representations are assessed by means of the cosine similarity function.[4] The top-k strong matching interactions are extracted by using k-max pooling, and aggregated by a multi-layer perception to output the final Retrieval Status Value. The sigmoid function is employed as activation function in the output layer.

3.2 The Classification Model

The classification model is used to learn the labels that can be associated with documents with respect to the additional relevance criteria considered in this article. As explained earlier, these relevance criteria are query-independent, and relate to a document's readability, trustworthiness, and credibility. By performing classification based on such criteria, it is possible, in fact, assign a document to suitable readability, trustworthiness and credibility classes (e.g., *credible*, *non-credible*, *unable to judge*), in a single-label multi-class way. A single classification task is performed with respect to each relevance criterion.

As illustrated in Fig. 1 (*b*), the classification model is constituted by a simple neural model widely used in Natural Language Processing tasks such as credibility assessment [12], but it can be generalized to other tasks. In the classification task, the only input is constituted by the *document*. The input pass through an embedding and a Bidirectional LSTM layer, and is treated by an attention layer

[4] In the positional representation of a textual document, the position of each word in the document is kept; the interaction between two positional representations is the matching between words at the same position in the documents.

that is introduced to increment the importance (the weight) of words identified as crucial, and decrease the importance (the weight) of less-crucial words. This is followed by a dense layer with a ReLU activation function.[5] The last layer employs a sigmoid function as the output activation function. To improve the effectiveness of the model, is also possible to incorporate additional hand-crafted features after the attention layer. Such solution has been employed both in [25], where the output of the Bi-LSTM layer is concatenated with linguistic feature vectors, and in [12], where emotional features are concatenated in the neural model. In our approach, we consider distinct groups of additional features that are suitable with respect to the relevance criteria taken into account, as it will be detailed in Sect. 4.2.

4 Experimental Evaluations

This section is devoted to presenting the experimental evaluation setting to assess the effectiveness of the proposed approach. In particular, we describe the employed datasets, the technical implementation details, the baselines and evaluation measures taken into consideration.

4.1 Datasets

At present, there are not many publicly available data collections to tackle the Information Retrieval task that also contain additional assessments on other relevance criteria beyond topicality. To both implement and evaluate the proposed approach, we used the 2018 and 2020 data collections from the CLEF eHealth - Consumer Health Search (CHS) task.[6] In particular, we focused on the *ad-hoc retrieval* subtask. The data consist of Web pages crawled by means of CommonCrawl,[7] related to the health-related domain. The data collections consider 50 topics/queries and associated documents. Besides relevance judgments, based on topical relevance, assessments on other relevance dimensions are also available in the collections. In the CLEF eHealth 2018 collection, the additional assessments are related to the document's readability and trustworthiness. In the CLEF eHealth 2020 collection, the additional relevance assessments consider the readability and credibility of the Web page. In this work, we used the readability assessments from both the 2018 and 2020 collections, the trustworthiness assessments from the 2018 collection, and the credibility assessments from the 2020 collection. In the original collections, while credibility assessments are expressed as discrete values (this is the most recent dataset), readability and trustworthiness assessments are expressed as values in the [0,1] interval. For this reason, we have mapped such values to discrete values, as similarly illustrated in [8], by associating the middle values, i.e., those in the interval [0.4,0.7], to 2: *unable to*

[5] We used ReLu as the most preferable activation function in the literature [12,32].
[6] https://clefehealth.imag.fr/.
[7] http://commoncrawl.org/.

judge, and the extreme values, i.e., those in the intervals [0,0.4) and (0.7,1], to 0: *non-readable/non-trustworthy* and 1: *readable/trustworthy*, respectively.

Furthermore, since the relevance judgments in the collections are not available for all the query-document pairs, we only considered in this work the documents for which such judgments and the considered additional relevance criterion assessments were available. This way, around thirty-five thousand documents labeled with both relevance judgments (i.e., topicality) and readability have been considered, whereas around twenty-six thousand and twelve thousand documents respectively have been considered for trustworthiness and credibility.

4.2 Additional Features in the Classification Model

As explained in Sect. 3.2, the classification task is modeled to perform classification with respect to a single relevance criterion at a time, by possibly considering additional feature sets (in addition to textual representation features) related to such criterion. In the following, for each criterion, we detail the additional features considered in this work.

Readability. Eight readability features from previous works [7,23] have been taken into account. Such features are computed by means of well-known readability indexes:[8] the Flesch-Kincaid Index, Automated Readability Index, Coleman-Liau Index (CLI), Dale-Chall Index (DCI), Flesch Reading Ease (FRE), Gunning Fog Index (GFI), Lasbarhetsindex (LIX), and Simple Measure of Gobbledygook (SMOG). References to each of these indexes are provided in [23].

Trustworthiness and Credibility. Some features proposed in [29] to assess the reliability of medical Web pages have been considered:[9]

1. *Link-based features*: the presence of links is considered an indicator of reliability. Reliable Websites are more likely to contain internal links, while less reliable Websites have more external links. Besides, the existence of privacy policy information and contact link are also taken into account.
2. *Commercial-based features*: the presence of commercial interests in a Website is a sign of low reliability. Therefore, the frequency of commercial words and of commercial links are used as features.

4.3 Experimental Setup

Experimental evaluations have been performed by taking as a baseline the single retrieval task performed by the neural model shown in Fig. 1 (*a*), and comparing

[8] By means of https://pypi.org/project/ReadabilityCalculator, the *ReadibilityCalculator* tool.

[9] Although the concepts of trustworthiness and credibility are only partially overlapping, they are closely interdependent [28,31]. However, it will be necessary in the future to provide more specific features relating to the two different criteria for relevance.

its results with those obtained by the Multi-Task Learning model when considering the three distinct additional relevance criteria separately in the classification model.

Implementation Details. From a technical point of view, we implemented all the models including the baseline using Keras.[10] For word embedding, we employed GloVe (trained on the Wiki+Gigaword dataset) with a vector size of 200.[11] For evaluation purposes, we performed 5-fold cross-validation and we tested the Adam optimizer with different learning rates and selected the optimal one.[12] Furthermore, we used the *TrecTools*[13] to compute evaluation metrics.

Evaluation Metrics. We evaluated the obtained rankings by considering: *Mean Average Precision* (MAP), *Precision@k* (with $k = 10$ and $k = 20$), and nDCG@10. Furthermore, to better assess the contribution of the additional relevance criteria to the final rankings, we considered other metrics, such as *understandability-biased* RBP (uRBP) [38], $\mathcal{MM}$ [22], and the *Convex Aggregating Measure* (CAM) [17]. uRBP is a measure based on *Rank-Biased Precision* (RBP) [20], and considers both topicality and readability in the evaluation process. The measure is formally defined as [38]:

$$\text{uRBP}(\rho) = (1 - \rho) * \sum^{k} \rho^{k-1} * r(d@k) * u(d@k) \tag{1}$$

where $r(d@k)$ and $u(d@k)$ are the gains for retrieving a document at rank k, respectively considering topicality and readability. ρ is the so-called *persistence parameter* of RBP, and indicates the user's persistence in search, or the probability of moving from a document in the rank k to the next document at rank $k + 1$. The use of this metrics is also suggested in the CLEF eHealth Evaluation Lab, with a ρ value equal to 0.8, the same employed in this work.

To assess the influence of trustworthiness and credibility, we considered two further metrics. The first metric is denoted as $\mathcal{MM}$ [22], and is computed as the *weighted harmonic mean* of the values produced by two metrics $\mathcal{M}_{rel}$ and $\mathcal{M}_{\kappa}$. Formally:

$$\mathcal{MM} = 2 * \frac{\mathcal{M}_{rel} * \mathcal{M}_{\kappa}}{\mathcal{M}_{rel} + \mathcal{M}_{\kappa}} \tag{2}$$

where $\mathcal{M}_{rel}$ and $\mathcal{M}_{\kappa}$ are any valid evaluation measures respectively for assessing (topical) relevance, and another additional criteria κ among trustworthiness and credibility. As illustrated in [26,38], in this work we consider nDCG.

---

[10] https://keras.io/.

[11] https://nlp.stanford.edu/projects/glove/.

[12] At the end, the selected learning rate was from {1E - 5, 1E - 4, 1E - 3}.

[13] https://github.com/joaopalotti/trectools/.

The second considered metric is the *Convex Aggregating Measure* (CAM), specifically proposed in [17] to consider the concept of credibility in evaluations of IR systems. CAM is expressed as the *convex sum* of the scores calculated for each relevance dimension, and is formally defined as:

$$\text{CAM} = \lambda \mathcal{M}_{rel} + \lambda \mathcal{M}_{\kappa} \tag{3}$$

As proposed in [26], also in this case we used nDCG for both $\mathcal{M}_{rel}$ and $\mathcal{M}_{\kappa}$, and set the λ value to 0.5.[14]

5 Results and Discussion

In this section, we report the results of the experimental evaluation against the evaluation measures outlined in the previous section. In Table 1 and 2, in particular, are reported the results obtained by the baseline (**STL**), which only considers the retrieval task (and, hence, only topicality), and those obtained by the Multi-Task Learning model considering readability, denoted as **MTL(R)**, the one considering trustworthiness, denoted as **MTL(T)**, and the one considering credibility, denoted as **MTL(C)**. In the tables, results that outperform the baseline, for each MTL model, are shown in bold. The symbol * denotes a p-value < 0.0125, by using the *two-tailed t-test* with Bonferroni correction as detailed in [9,39], i.e., for a p-value of 0.05, considering 4 models, $p = 0.05/4 = 0.0125$.

Table 1. Experiment results with respect to MAP, Precision, and nDCG.

System	Experiment Results			
	MAP	P@10	P@20	nDCG@10
STL	0.484	0.448	0.443	0.325
MTL(R)	**0.498**	**0.526***	**0.531***	**0.405***
MTL(T)	**0.491**	**0.488**	**0.51**	**0.364**
MTL(C)	**0.485**	**0.454**	**0.459**	**0.345**

In particular, in Table 1 we report the values of the standard retrieval evaluation measures including MAP, P@10, P@20, and nDCG@10. Overall, the performance of the Multi-Task Learning model improves with respect to the single-task model (baseline) for all of the experiments; hence, joint learning of retrieval and classification tasks proved beneficial.

[14] In both $\mathcal{MM}$ and CAM cases, is possible to use nDCG also for trustworthiness and credibility since we deal with graded scores and we can consider the ranking of trustworthy/credible information based on such scores.

Table 2. Experiment results for the readability-biased, trustworthiness-biased and credibility-biased evaluations.

Model	Readability-biased evaluation			Trust.-/Cred.-biased evaluation			
	URBP	URBP@10	URBP@20	$\mathcal{MM}_t$	CAM$_t$	$\mathcal{MM}_c$	CAM$_c$
STL	0.221	0.196	0.218	0.824	0.826	0.727	0.733
MTL(R)	**0.271**	**0.241**	**0.268**	**0.825**	**0.827**	**0.732****	**0.737***
MTL(T)	0.212	0.183	0.209	**0.829***	**0.830***	**0.734***	**0.739***
MTL(C)	0.205	0.181	0.202	**0.828**	**0.830**	**0.728**	**0.734**

Table 2 reports the results of the so-called *readability-biased*, *trustworthiness-biased*, and *credibility-biased* evaluations. For each considered metric, i.e., uRBP, $\mathcal{MM}$, and CAM, we evaluate the results by considering exactly one additional relevance dimension beyond topicality. Specifically, $\mathcal{MM}_t$ and $\mathcal{MM}_c$ denote the $\mathcal{MM}$ metric when applied to trustworthiness and credibility. The same holds for CAM$_t$ and CAM$_c$. By observing the results in Table 2, we may conclude that the proposed MTL model also performs better than the single-task model in all experiments, also when we have the possibility to investigate the effectiveness of additional relevance criteria by means of criteria-biased evaluation metrics.

The results considering the classification task applied to readability, i.e., the **MTL(R)** model, outperform those for the single-task baseline for almost all metrics. The effectiveness of the two latter models can best be appreciated by considering measures that are specifically designed to take trustworthiness and credibility into account. Both the **MTL(T)** and **MTL(C)** models increase the performance with respect to the single-task model when considering $\mathcal{MM}$ and CAM scores, in all configurations. With respect to these latter results, however, notwithstanding the positive contribution of such criteria, it is necessary to say that in the datasets used for experimentation the two concepts were rather overlapping, and that the number of credibility labels was much lower than the number of readability and trustworthiness labels, so the results obtained do not allow a clear disambiguation of their individual contribution.

6 Conclusions and Future Work

In this work, we proposed a deep neural model that incorporates more than one relevance criterion besides topicality in the context of Information Retrieval, by using supervised Multi-Task Learning (MTL); MTL jointly models the retrieval task, to learn topical relevance, and a classification task, to learn the assessments of an additional query-independent relevance criterion at a time. The proposed approach is based on the intuition that the joint optimization of some parameters during retrieval and classification tasks has an impact on the overall relevance value, which, in this way, is affected not only by topical relevance.

To verify this intuition, we have performed a set of experiments by considering readability, trustworthiness, and credibility as additional relevance criteria beyond topicality. We observed a substantial improvement compared to the single-task baseline, based on a simple neural model devoted to the retrieval task. We believe that these results may be useful for the subsequent investigation of other aspects related to the multidimensional nature of relevance in retrieval systems that rely on neural approaches. Future work should involve exploring more advanced neural models and considering the interplay between multiple criteria of relevance together. We also intend to perform extensive analysis on the results and compare them with other methods that consider multiple relevance criteria, such as Learning-to-Rank. Finally, it will be necessary to investigate more the relationship that may exist between the (topical) relevance judgments and the evaluations that are made with respect to the other relevance criteria considered.

References

1. Ahmad, W.U., et al.: Multi-task learning for document ranking and query suggestion. In: 6th International Conference on Learning Representations, ICLR 2018, Vancouver, BC, Canada, April 30 - May 3, 2018, p. 2018. Conference Track Proceedings OpenReview.net (2018)
2. Ahmad, W.U., et al.: Context attentive document ranking and query suggestion. In: Proceedings of the 42nd International ACM SIGIR Conference on Research and Development in Information Retrieval, pp. 385–394 (2019)
3. Bendersky, M., et al.: Quality-biased ranking of web documents. In: Proceedings of the Fourth ACM International Conference on Web Search and Data Mining, pp. 95–104 (2011)
4. Borlund, P.: The concept of relevance in IR. J. Am. Soc. Inf. Sci. Technol. **54**(10), 913–925 (2003)
5. Caruana, R.: Multitask learning. Mach. Learn. **28**(1), 41–75 (1997)
6. da Costa Pereira, C., et al.: Multidimensional relevance: prioritized aggregation in a personalized information retrieval setting. Inf. Process. Manage. **48**(2), 340–357 (2012)
7. Deutsch, T., et al.: Linguistic features for readability assessment. In: Proceedings of the Fifteenth Workshop on Innovative Use of NLP for Building Educational Applications, pp. 1–17 (2020)
8. Fernández-Pichel, M., et al.: Reliability prediction for health-related content: a replicability study. In: Proceedings of the 43rd ECIR Conference (2), pp. 47–61 (2021)
9. Fuhr, N.: Some common mistakes in IR evaluation, and how they can be avoided. ACM SIGIR Forum **51**(3), 32–41 (2018)
10. Fuhr, N., et al.: An information nutritional label for online documents. ACM SIGIR Forum **51**(3), 46–66 (2018)
11. Gerani, S., Zhai, C.X., Crestani, F.: Score transformation in linear combination for multi-criteria relevance ranking. In: Baeza-Yates, R., de Vries, A.P., Zaragoza, H., Cambazoglu, B.B., Murdock, V., Lempel, R., Silvestri, F. (eds.) ECIR 2012. LNCS, vol. 7224, pp. 256–267. Springer, Heidelberg (2012). https://doi.org/10.1007/978-3-642-28997-2_22
12. Giachanou, A., et al.: Leveraging emotional signals for credibility detection. In: Proceedings of the 42nd International ACM SIGIR Conference on Research and Development in Information Retrieval, pp. 877–880 (2019)

13. Goeuriot, L., et al.: Overview of the CLEF eHealth evaluation lab 2020. In: Arampatzis, A., et al. (eds.) CLEF 2020. LNCS, vol. 12260, pp. 255–271. Springer, Cham (2020). https://doi.org/10.1007/978-3-030-58219-7_19
14. Guo, J., et al.: A deep look into neural ranking models for information retrieval. Inf. Process. Manage. **57**(6), 102067 (2020)
15. Jiang, J., et al.: Understanding ephemeral state of relevance. In: Proceedings of the 2017 Conference on Conference Human Information Interaction and Retrieval, pp. 137–146 (2017)
16. Kleinberg, J.M., et al.: Authoritative Sources in a Hyperlinked Environment. Princeton University Press (2011)
17. Lioma, C., et al.: Evaluation measures for relevance and credibility in ranked lists. In: Proceedings of the ACM SIGIR International Conference on Theory of Information Retrieval, pp. 91–98 (2017)
18. Liu, X., et al.: Representation learning using multi-task deep neural networks for semantic classification and information retrieval. In: Proceedings of the 2015 NAACL Conference, pp. 912–921 (2015)
19. Marrara, S., et al.: Aggregation operators in information retrieval. Fuzzy Sets Syst. **324**, 3–19 (2017)
20. Moffat, A., Zobel, J.: Rank-biased precision for measurement of retrieval effectiveness. ACM Trans. Inf. Syst. (TOIS) **27**(1), 1–27 (2008)
21. Page, L., et al.: The Pagerank Citation Ranking: Bringing Order to the Web. Technical report, Stanford InfoLab (1999)
22. Palotti, J., et al.: MM: a new framework for multidimensional evaluation of search engines. In: Proceedings of the 27th ACM International Conference on Information and Knowledge Management, pp. 1699–1702 (2018)
23. Palotti, J., et al.: Consumer health search on the web: study of web page understandability and its integration in ranking algorithms. J. of medical Internet research **21**(1), e10986 (2019)
24. Rao, J., et al.: Bridging the gap between relevance matching and semantic matching for short text similarity modeling. In: Proceedings of the 2019 EMNLP-IJCNLP Conference, pp. 5373–5384 (2019)
25. Rashkin, H., et al.: Truth of varying shades: analyzing language in fake news and political fact-checking. In: Proceedings of the 2017 Conference on Empirical Methods in Natural Language Processing, pp. 2931–2937 (2017)
26. Roberts, K., et al.: Overview of the TREC 2019 precision medicine track. In: Proceedings of the Twenty-Eighth Text REtrieval Conference, TREC 2019, Gaithersburg, Maryland, USA, 13–15 November 2019, vol. 1250 (2019)
27. Schamber, L., Bateman, J.: User criteria in relevance evaluation: toward development of a measurement scale. In: Proceedings of the ASIS Annual Meeting, vol. 33, pp. 218–25. ERIC (1996)
28. Self, C.C.: Credibility. In: An Integrated Approach to Communication Theory and Research, 2nd Edition, pp. 22. Taylor & Francis (2008)
29. Sondhi, P., Vydiswaran, V.G.V., Zhai, C.X.: Reliability prediction of webpages in the medical domain. In: Baeza-Yates, R., de Vries, A.P., Zaragoza, H., Cambazoglu, B.B., Murdock, V., Lempel, R., Silvestri, F. (eds.) ECIR 2012. LNCS, vol. 7224, pp. 219–231. Springer, Heidelberg (2012). https://doi.org/10.1007/978-3-642-28997-2_19
30. Uprety, S., et al.: Modeling multidimensional user relevance in IR using vector spaces. In: The 41st International ACM SIGIR Conference on on Research and Development in Information Retrieval, pp. 993–996 (2018)

31. Viviani, M., Pasi, G.: Credibility in social media: opinions, news, and health information-survey. Wiley Interdisc. Rev. Data Min. Knowl. Discovery **7**(5), e1209 (2017)
32. Wadawadagi, R., Pagi, V.: Sentiment analysis with deep neural networks: comparative study and performance assessment. Artif. Intell. Rev. **53**, 6155–6195 (2020)
33. Wan, S., et al.: A deep architecture for semantic matching with multiple positional sentence representations. In: Proceedings of the AAAI Conference on Artificial Intelligence, vol. 30 (2016)
34. Xu, Y., Chen, Z.: Relevance judgment: what do information users consider beyond topicality? J. Am. Soc. Inf. Sci. Technol. **57**(7), 961–973 (2006)
35. Zamani, H., Croft, W.B.: Joint modeling and optimization of search and recommendation. In: Proceedings of the First Biennial Conference on Design of Experimental Search and Information Retrieval Systems, Bertinoro, Italy, 28–31 August 2018, vol. 2167 of CEUR Workshop Proceedings, pp. 36–41. CEUR-WS.org (2018)
36. Zamani, H., Croft, W.B.: Learning a joint search and recommendation model from user-item interactions. In: Proceedings of the 13th International Conference on Web Search and Data Mining, pp. 717–725 (2020)
37. Zhang, Y., Yang, Q.: A survey on multi-task learning. arXiv preprint arXiv:1707.08114 (2017)
38. Zuccon, G.: Understandability biased evaluation for information retrieval. In: Ferro, N., Crestani, F., Moens, M.-F., Mothe, J., Silvestri, F., Di Nunzio, G.M., Hauff, C., Silvello, G. (eds.) ECIR 2016. LNCS, vol. 9626, pp. 280–292. Springer, Cham (2016). https://doi.org/10.1007/978-3-319-30671-1_21
39. Miller, R.G.: Simultaneous Statistical Inference. New York, Springer-Verlag (1981). https://doi.org/10.1007/978-1-4613-8122-8

Skill Extraction for Domain-Specific Text Retrieval in a Job-Matching Platform

Ellery Smith(✉), Andreas Weiler, and Martin Braschler

Zürich University of Applied Sciences, Winterthur, Switzerland
{smil,wele,bram}@zhaw.ch

Abstract. We discuss a domain-specific retrieval application for matching job seekers with open positions that uses a novel syntactic method of extracting skill-terms from the text of natural language job advertisements. Our new method is contrasted with two word embeddings methods, using word2vec. We define the notion of a skill headword, and present an algorithm that learns syntactic dependency patterns to recognize skill-terms. In all metrics, our syntactic method outperforms both word embeddings methods. Moreover, the word embeddings approaches were unable to model a meaningful distinction between skill-terms and non-skill-terms, while our syntactic approach was able to perform this successfully. We also show how these extracted skills can be used to automatically construct a semantic job-skills ontology, and facilitate a job-to-candidate matching system.

Keywords: Domain-specific retrieval · Term extraction

1 Introduction

When building retrieval applications for domain-specific document collections that contain specialized terminology, handling such terminology correctly is essential on multiple fronts: the specialized concepts, which are often expressed as multi-word terms, are very good discriminators between relevant and irrelevant content, but are especially susceptible to the vocabulary mismatch problem between query and documents. Often, multi-word terms can be alternatively expressed in phrasal form as well. If we resort to matching individual parts of the multi-word term to address this issue, the retrieval process is prone to introduce many spurious matches. In the CLEF evaluation campaign these challenges of domain-specific retrieval were prominently addressed by concentrating on the use of controlled vocabularies to aid retrieval [12].

In this work, we describe our efforts to build a retrieval application for a job matching platform[1]. Working with content integrated from various Web sources, no controlled vocabulary is available for this purpose. As a substitute, we leverage the specialized terminology present in the documents of that platform, which

[1] This work was funded by CTI/innosuisse under contract no. 27177.2 PFES-ES.

K. S. Candan et al. (Eds.): CLEF 2021, LNCS 12880, pp. 116–128, 2021.
https://doi.org/10.1007/978-3-030-85251-1_10

often pertains to the "skills" that applicants offer or employers seek. Our goal is to extract these skills and treat them as integral retrieval units in the application. Whereas classic ad-hoc information retrieval is mature and has shown to be effective on many different forms of text, irrespective of the domains that the texts cover, fundamental challenges remain due to the state-of-the-art weighting schemes such as BM.25 [14] and Divergence from Randomness [1] essentially treating each word as a single token and not working on a semantic concept level.

In the following, we demonstrate the effectiveness of a syntactic headword-based method of skill extraction from natural language job advertisements, and compare it to two word embeddings-based methods. Our syntactic algorithm uses a small amount of manually-labeled data to construct grammatical dependency patterns, then applies these patterns to a larger unlabeled dataset to classify terms into skills and non-skills. The word embeddings methods use word2vec [11] to measure the similarity between known skill-terms and unseen terms.

Our algorithm relies on the linguistic homogeneity of job advertisement texts: while they are open-vocabulary, they have a low grammatical variance, which is exploitable with syntactic analysis, using the Stanford Dependencies model [10]. With this, we attempt to solve the vocabulary problem, and reduce the human effort required to construct a dataset of skills. In addition, while it is syntax-based, our algorithm does not require a syntactic parse of a job advertisement in order to extract skills. Only the training portion of the algorithm requires parsing, and the skill-extraction process is highly efficient and works on raw, unprocessed text.

We evaluate all three methods using both a single-term and a phrasal n-gram retrieval test. In both tests, the syntactic method significantly outperforms both word embeddings methods at all levels of recall, and, furthermore, we demonstrate that word embeddings were not able to model a meaningful distinction between skill-terms and non-skill-terms, while the syntactic method was able to model this successfully.

> You will be required to contribute to **research** on **financial modelling**. Your duties will include: assisting with **investment portfolio management**; ensuring correct and robust implementation of **bank securitization** in compliance with the internal methodologies. We require from you a strong academic record, with preference for a **PhD degree** in **Economics**. Strong **programming** skills in **Python** are desirable. Fluency in **English** and **German** is a necessity.

Fig. 1. Extract from a job advertisement, with skills in bold.

We also provide an analysis in Sect. 6, demonstrating the effectiveness of using syntactic headwords over word embeddings for this task. Finally, we demonstrate an application of these extracted skills in an end-to-end retrieval context, by constructing a job-skills ontology, and show how it can be used to match job advertisements to candidate CVs.

Our dataset consists of 10,000 unlabeled job advertisements, comprising 185,908 sentences and 3,441,093 terms, and 100 manually labeled job advertisements, comprising 2,191 sentences and 25,442 terms, obtained from crawling job search websites. For training, a portion of the labeled data in combination with the unlabeled data is used, with the remainder of the labeled data used for testing.

We define a "skill" as a tag (single- or multi-word expression) that is either directly (*e.g.*, "project management") or indirectly (*e.g.*, a degree) linked to skills that are offered by a candidate or requested in a job advertisement. A "skill-term" is a single token that comprises part or all of a skill. An example of a job advertisement, with skills highlighted, is shown in Fig. 1.

2 Related Work

Recent work has tackled the problem of skill-extraction from job advertisement in several ways, primarily based on the use of pre-made ontologies or databases.

Malherbe and Aufaure [9] attempt to automatically synthesize a skill database from candidates' social media profiles, augmented with information from DBpedia [2]. As a starting point, they use the skills submitted manually by employees, and map this onto DBpedia in order to create a semantically-sound ontology, enhanced with related concepts and synonyms.

Other approaches use web crawling to build up a skills database [4]; or create a subset of an existing ontology such as the Semantic Web [7] or Wikipedia [8]. In the case of Malherbe and Aufaure [9], Bastian et al. [4] and Kivimäki et al. [8], career websites were crawled for user-submitted skill-phrases. We argue that this can also be reliably achieved by extracting the skills directly from the natural language text of job advertisements themselves.

For labeling skills, Braun et al. [6] use a collaborative approach to build a larger crowd-sourced ontology, where users manually add self-annotated web pages to the corpus. However, we attempt to reduce the human effort involved in this process, and show that only a small amount of labeling can be used to build a corpus of skills.

3 Syntactic Headwords

Our syntactic method of finding skills is based around the notion of a skill-phrase's headword. We define a headword as a term that indicates the presence of a nearby skill-phrase, due to a syntactic connection to the skill-phrase. Some examples of this are shown in Fig. 2, where *degree*, *industry* and *experience* are the headwords.

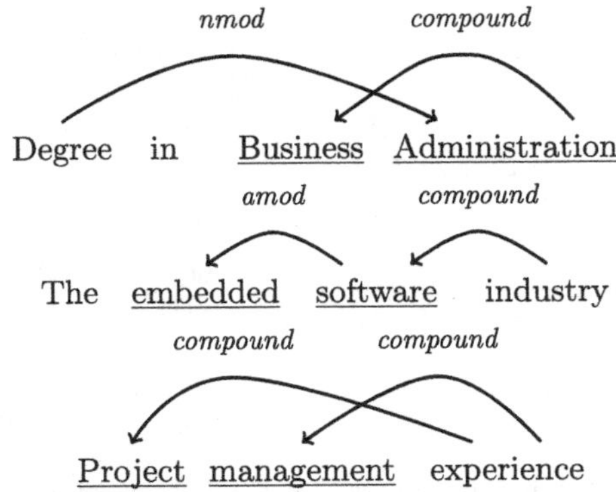

Fig. 2. Skill-phrases and their associated headwords.

Formally, to locate a headword, we first take a syntactic dependency parse of each sentence in the labeled data, using the Stanford Parser [10]. Next, we visit each node in the dependency graph that is marked as a skill-term, and walk backwards through the graph from that node until a non-skill-term is found. For example, in Fig. 2 we go from *business* to *administration* to *degree*, and from *embedded* to *software* to *industry*. Here, *degree* and *industry* are the headwords of each phrase. We collect all the possible headwords from the labeled data, and rank them by the normalized frequency of which they appear as headwords, as shown in Table 1.

Table 1. Top entries in the weighted headword table.

Experience	1.0000	Skill	0.4342	Manage	0.3421
Degree	0.8816	Industry	0.3816	Fluent	0.3289
Knowledge	0.6579	Years	0.3684	...	...

For each headword, we then construct a syntactic pattern tree, as shown in Fig. 3. This tree contains a branch for each dependency connected to that headword, and the probability of that dependency leading to a skill-term. To construct this, we walk forward in the dependency graph from each instance of a headword, along all paths, and add each path to the pattern tree. For instance, in Fig. 2, we would have (ADMINISTRATION, *nmod*) $\rightarrow$ (BUSINESS, *compound*), and thus we add the path *nmod* $\rightarrow$ *compound* to the pattern tree for *degree*.

We note how many times each path leads to a skill-term, and use this frequency as the weight for that branch in the tree. Each pattern tree is then linked to that headword's entry in the headword table.

In addition to constructing pattern trees from the labeled data, we also build a term-dependency index from the unlabeled job advertisements, as shown in

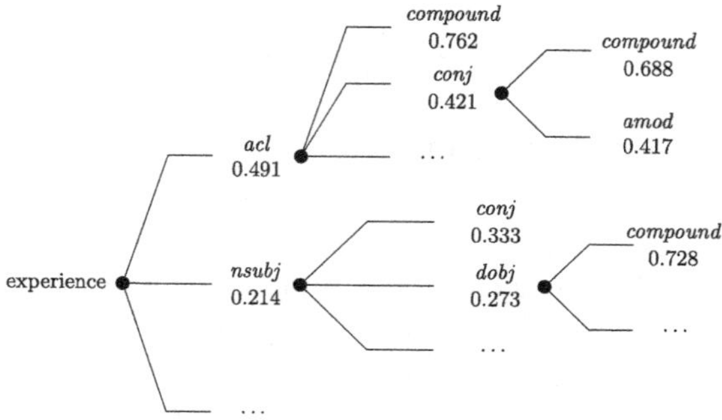

Fig. 3. Syntactic pattern tree for the headword *experience*.

Fig. 4. This is similar in structure to a standard inverted index [3]: each sentence is assigned a sequential ID number, and each term in the index contains a list of the sentence IDs in which it occurs. However, alongside each sentence ID, we also include a list of term-dependency pairs, representing its neighbors in the dependency graph for that sentence. Using this index, we can rapidly look up the dependencies associated with a given term.

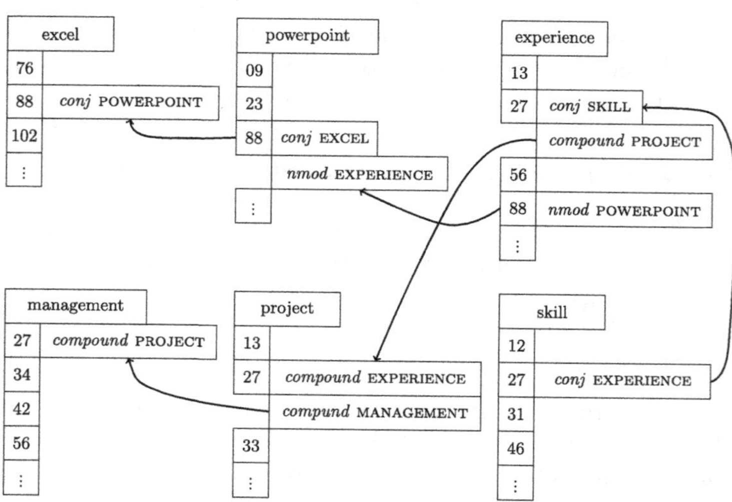

Fig. 4. Selected entries from the term-dependency index graph.

With these two data structures, we can now find new skill-terms in the unlabeled data. This procedure is detailed in Algorithm 1. For each headword, we look it up in the index, and for each occurrence, we walk the dependency paths for that sentence in parallel with the pattern tree. For every term encountered, we add the weight of the current branch in the pattern tree to that term's score.

When all headwords have been visited, we take the mean score for each term as the probability it is a skill-term.

In brief, this procedure learns which terms are skill-terms by how often they appear in a known grammatical context to a headword. Essentially, we find skills by how they are written in the text, without the need for semantic information.

Algorithm 1. Headword-based Skill Finder

Input: H, a table of headwords and their syntactic pattern graphs; I, a term-dependency index
Output: T, a confidence score for all terms

```
T ← {t : 0 | t ∈ I}
for all h ∈ H do
    for all i ∈ I[h] do
        TREESEARCH(i, H[h], h)
for all t ∈ T do
    T[t] ← T[t] / |I[t]|

function TREESEARCH(i, D, t)
    for all (t', d) ∈ I[t][i] do
        (D', w) ← D[d]
        T[t'] ← T[t'] + w
        TREESEARCH(i, D', t')
```

---

4 Word Embeddings

For the word embeddings methods, we train word2vec using Gensim [13] on the same unlabeled data as the syntactic method. For the first algorithm, we take the known skill-terms from the labeled data, and, for each unknown term, we calculate its mean similarity to the known skill-terms, S:

$$T(t) = \sum_{s \in S} \frac{sim(s,t)}{|S|}$$

If word2vec was able to correctly model the semantic similarity between skill-terms, then the probability of that term being a skill-term should be represented by this similarity metric.

For the second method, instead of measuring the similarity between unknown terms and skill-terms, we measure their similarity to the headwords obtained from our syntactic method, to see if word embeddings are more effective at modeling the relationship between headwords and skills than Algorithm 1.

We tune the dimensionality, d, on a development portion of 10% of the training data, optimising for average precision. We select $d = 300$, trialling

$100 \leq d \leq 1000$ with a step size of 100, and set the window size to 5, the maximal skill-phrase size used in our evaluation.

5 Evaluation

In a commercial job-matching platform, jobs are often tagged with skill-phrases, which drive the recommendation of jobs to potential candidates, or categorize them for searching. To this end, we evaluate our system's ability to automatically retrieve a set of relevant tags from the text of a job advertisement. The output of such a system is a set of phrases designed to describe the skills required to perform that job.

As such, we evaluate our system alongside the word embeddings methods using two retrieval tests. Given a job advertisement text as input, all systems produce a ranked list of terms, ordered by the confidence of it being a skill-term. We use two tests: individual skill-terms, and n-gram skill-phrases. In the skill-phrase test, any contiguous sequence of skill-terms in the text is grouped together as a skill-phrase.

Table 2. Results of the single-term test.

Recall	Precision		
	Syntax	Skill-word embeddings	Headword embeddings
0.1	.7115*	.4600	.3224
0.2	.7001*	.4568	.2896
0.3	.6703*	.3997	.2682
0.4	.5880*	.4020	.2608
0.5	.5266*	.3698	.2486
0.6	.5146*	.3448	.2415
0.7	.4300	.3139	.2313
0.8	.3807	.2732	.2158
0.9	.3249	.2175	.2023
1.0	.2322	.2018	.2018

To assess this, we use the relevance judgements of our labeled job advertisements. The relevant tags are manually labeled and represent the canonical set of skill-phrases for that job advertisement. One portion of the advertisements is used to bootstrap the skill extractor, and the other is used for evaluation. In both tests, we measure the precision at 10% recall intervals, and the results are obtained using 5-fold cross-validation on the labeled data. In all cases, the same set of 10,000 unlabeled job advertisements is used during training.

The results of the single-term test on all three algorithms is shown in Table 2, with * denoting statistically significant improvements ($p < 0.05$ using McNemar's test). The precision-recall curves are plotted in Fig. 5.

Our syntactic method significantly outperforms the skill-based word embeddings method at most levels of recall; however, the headword-based word embeddings method performs very poorly at all recall levels, suggesting that there is no meaningful correlation between headwords and skills in a semantic similarity context.

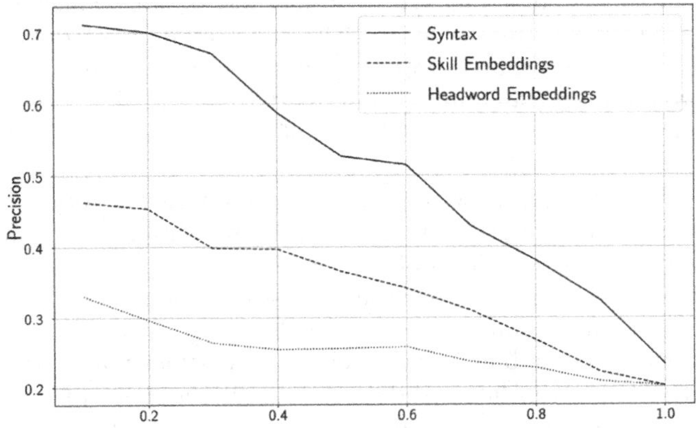

Fig. 5. Precision-recall curves for the single-term test.

The results of the skill-phrase test are shown in Table 3. The performance of the headword-based word embeddings method was similarly poor as in the single-term test, so we omit it from these results. Again, we can see that the syntactic method performs better at all recall levels.

Table 3. Results of the skill-phrase test.

Recall	Precision	
	Syntax	Skill embeddings
0.1	.6818*	.4693
0.2	.6241*	.3684
0.3	.5313*	.3038
0.4	.4623*	.2892
0.5	.4010*	.2584
0.6	.3743*	.2335
0.7	.3249*	.2136
0.8	.2900*	.1847
0.9	.2369	.1572
1.0	.1707	.1513

6 Analysis

Reflection of the results has to be in the context of the volume of data we are processing. Since we are working on a real-world data set in conjunction with our industry partner, the data volume is given. We think that in practice, many interesting problems are on this scale, thus effectively "small-data problems" [5]. We find that in this context our syntactic method performs better than word embeddings, when both are trained on the same amount of data. This does not contradict the notion that word embeddings methods often perform well in similar tasks when a large amount of training data is available (how they would compare to our approach on such volumes of data remains subject for future work).

The conclusions we can draw from our analysis is that a robust skill-phrase retrieval system can be trained with minimal human input, and that an open-vocabulary, but domain-specific, problem can be tackled with syntactic pattern recognition. This analysis shows that the process of bootstrapping a skill extractor with a very small amount of human-labeled data is sufficient for learning syntactic patterns of skills, but learning semantic relations via word embeddings is not. While the amount of labelled data does limit the scope of the evaluation, we show that our method can be used to solve a real-world data problem, where minimal human input is available.

In the task of retrieving relevant tags, it is clear from our evaluation that the syntactic headwords method outputs significantly more relevant tags than word embeddings. When determining whether a term is relevant or not, i.e. part of a skill-phrase, or not, we use the confidence score assigned to it by each algorithm. Thus, in order to determine why our algorithm outperforms the word embeddings methods, we look at the confidence scores assigned to each term or skill-phrase.

Table 4. Average confidence score for both term types.

	Average score		
	Skill terms	Non-skill terms	Ratio
Syntax	0.191	0.042	4.525
Skill-word embedding	0.196	0.190	1.032
Headword embedding	0.177	0.187	0.945

In Table 4, we take each term in the labeled data, and, for each algorithm, we calculate the average confidence score assigned to all skill-terms and non-skill-terms. We can see that the syntactic method gives a much greater statistical distinction between skill-terms and non-skill-terms than the word embeddings methods, and the skill-term word embeddings method does not succeed in finding a meaningful distinction between the two classes of terms. Thus, our method succeeds in disproving the null hypothesis.

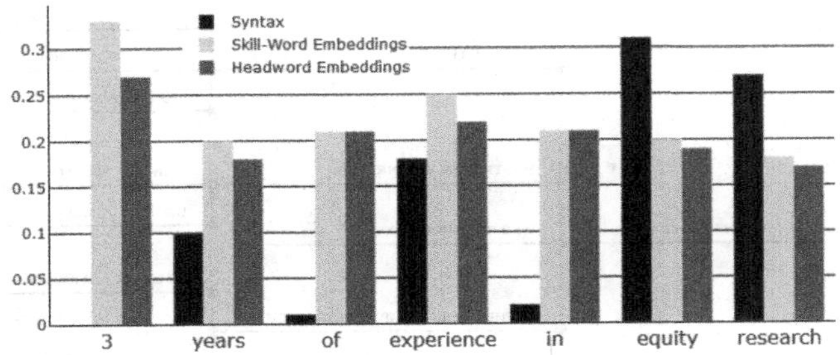

Fig. 6. Confidence scores assigned to each term, with the skill *equity research.*

By looking at the following example, we can see the advantages of the syntactic approach more clearly. For instance, Fig. 6 shows the scores of each of the algorithms for each term in the sentence "3 years experience in equity research", where the skill-phrase is *equity research.*

The confidence scores for both word embeddings methods is similar across all tokens, with minimal patterns being observed. We can see that the word embeddings methods were not able to find a significant distinction between the skill-terms and non-skill-terms, but the presence of the headwords *experience* and *years* allows the syntactic method to give a much higher score to the relevant terms, and ignore the irrelevant ones.

7 Applications

To apply this skill-extractor in an end-to-end retrieval setting, we have additionally designed a system which automatically constructs a semantic skills ontology for job-to-candidate matching. Since we can apply our skill extractor to both job advertisements and CVs, we can use these skills for a more robust matching algorithm than a purely term-based method. We show a sample of our automatically constructed skills-ontology in Fig. 7.

To build this, we firstly use the skill extractor to assign relevant skill-tags to a set of job descriptions. We then collect the total set of skill-phrases to form a skill-vector space. Thus, each job can be mapped to a skill-vector. Using these skill-vectors, we can then cluster jobs with similar skills to form an ontology of skills, where sub-skills are grouped together semantically under their parent skill. By mapping CVs and jobs to this ontology, via their extracted skills, we aim to create a deeper semantic job-matching engine, built on the foundation of the accurate relevant skills extracted in this work.

One example of a job-to-CV match is shown in Fig. 8, where the difference between a candidate's skills, extracted from the text of their CV by our extractor, is matched against the skills from a job advertisement. Using the distance between skills in our ontology, we can give a potential measure of how a qualified a candidate may be for a given job.

ROOT
SYSTEM AND SOFWARE DEVELOPMENT
SYSTEM TESTING
AGILE SOFTWARE DEVELOPMENT
TEST AUTOMATION ENGINEER
TEST DRIVEN DEVELOPMENT
MASTERS IN ENGINEERING
MANUFACTURING SYSTEMS DEVELOPMENT
DEGREE IN MECHANICAL ENGINEERING
WEB TECHNOLOGIES ...
BACHELOR IN COMPUTER SCIENCE
MACHINE LEARNING
MASTERS IN COMPUTER SCIENCE
CONTINUOUS SOFTWARE DEPLOYMENT
SOFTWARE PRODUCTS AND SERVICES
WINDOWS AND UNIX
DOCKER
REST API
MICROSERVICE ARCHITECTURE
PROJECT MANAGEMENT ...
MBA DEGREE ...
CORPORATE I.T. ...
FINANCIAL SERVICES
FINANCIAL ANALYSIS
FINANCIAL FORECASTING
MASTERS IN ECONOMICS AND FINANCE
FINANCIAL BUSINESS PLANNING
WEALTH MANAGEMENT ...
SALES AND PRODUCT MARKETING
BRAND MANAGEMENT
GERMAN MARKETS
MARKET RESEARCH
MEDIA MANAGEMENT
SALES OF TECHNICAL PRODUCTS
CHEMICAL PHARMACEUTICALS
MATERIALS SCIENCES
SALES AND MANUFACTURING

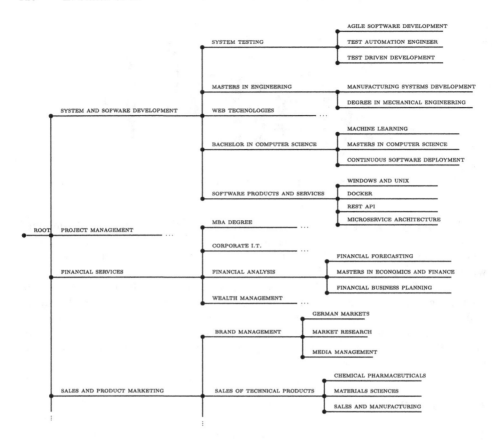

Fig. 7. Selected entries from a job-skills ontology.

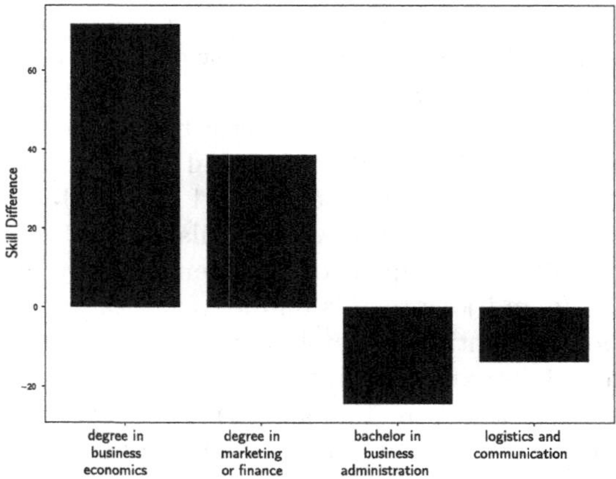

Fig. 8. Sample output from a job-to-CV matching procedure. This compares the skills needed with the candidate's skills for a "Product Marketing Manager" job.

8 Conclusions

In this work, we have demonstrated an effective method of extracting skills from job advertisement natural language text using syntactic headwords. We compared this to approaches based on word embeddings, and showed that syntactic methods are more effective at modelling the concept of a skill in a small-data setting. We additionally demonstrated an application of these extracted skills in an end-to-end job matching platform.

We have also shown that only a small amount of manual labelling is required to produce an open-vocabulary dataset of skills, which can potentially significantly reduce the human effort required for this task.

Additionally, our syntactic methods could be used to extract meaningful entities from other text domains, where the text is similarly linguistically homogeneous, or with low syntactic variance, such as newspapers or legal documents.

Acknowledgements. We thank our partners at Skillue AG, Basel, Switzerland, for their contributions to this work.

References

1. Amati, G., van Rijsbergen, C.J.: Probabilistic models of information retrieval based on measuring the divergence from randomness. ACM Trans. Inf. Syst. **20**(4), 357–389 (2002). https://doi.org/10.1145/582415.582416. http://doi.acm.org/10.1145/582415.582416
2. Auer, S., Bizer, C., Kobilarov, G., Lehmann, J., Cyganiak, R., Ives, Z.: DBpedia: a nucleus for a web of open data. In: Aberer, K., et al. (eds.) ASWC/ISWC 2007. LNCS, vol. 4825, pp. 722–735. Springer, Heidelberg (2007). https://doi.org/10.1007/978-3-540-76298-0_52
3. Baeza-Yates, R., Ribeiro-Neto, B., et al.: Modern Information Retrieval, vol. 463. ACM Press, New York (1999)
4. Bastian, M., et al.: Linkedin skills: large-scale topic extraction and inference, October 2014. https://doi.org/10.1145/2645710.2645729
5. Braschler, M.: The beauty of small data: an information retrieval perspective. In: Braschler, M., Stadelmann, T., Stockinger, K. (eds.) Applied Data Science, pp. 233–250. Springer, Cham (2019). https://doi.org/10.1007/978-3-030-11821-1_13
6. Braun, S., Kunzmann, C., Schmidt, A.: People tagging and ontology maturing: toward collaborative competence management. In: Randall, D., Salembier, P. (eds.) From CSCW to Web 2.0: European Developments in Collaborative Design, pp. 133–154. Springer, Heidelberg (2010). https://doi.org/10.1007/978-1-84882-965-7_7
7. Celik, D.: Towards a semantic-based information extraction system for matching résumés to job openings. Turkish J. Electr. Eng. Comput. Sci. **24**(1), 141–159 (2016)
8. Kivimäki, I., et al.: A graph-based approach to skill extraction from text. In: Proceedings of TextGraphs-8 Graph-Based Methods for Natural Language Processing, pp. 79–87 (2013)

9. Malherbe, E., Aufaure, M.A.: Bridge the terminology gap between recruiters and candidates: a multilingual skills base built from social media and linked data. In: 2016 IEEE/ACM International Conference on Advances in Social Networks Analysis and Mining (ASONAM), pp. 583–590. IEEE (2016)
10. de Marneffe, M.C., Manning, C.D.: The Stanford typed dependencies representation. In: Coling 2008: Proceedings of the Workshop on Cross-Framework and Cross-Domain Parser Evaluation, pp. 1–8. CrossParser '08, Association for Computational Linguistics, Stroudsburg, PA, USA (2008). http://dl.acm.org/citation.cfm?id=1608858.1608859
11. Mikolov, T., Chen, K., Corrado, G., Dean, J.: Efficient estimation of word representations in vector space. arXiv preprint arXiv:1301.3781 (2013)
12. Petras, V., Baerisch, S.: The domain-specific track at CLEF 2008. In: Peters, C., et al. (eds.) CLEF 2008. LNCS, vol. 5706, pp. 186–198. Springer, Heidelberg (2009). https://doi.org/10.1007/978-3-642-04447-2_23
13. Řehůřek, R., Sojka, P.: Software framework for topic modelling with large corpora. In: Proceedings of the LREC 2010 Workshop on New Challenges for NLP Frameworks, pp. 45–50. ELRA, Valletta, Malta, May 2010
14. Walker, S., Robertson, S.E., Boughanem, M., Jones, G.J.F., Jones, K.S.: Okapi at TREC-6 automatic ad hoc, VLC, routing, filtering and QSDR. In: Voorhees, E.M., Harman, D.K. (eds.) Proceedings of The Sixth Text REtrieval Conference, TREC 1997, Gaithersburg, Maryland, USA, 19–21 November 1997. NIST Special Publication, vol. 500–240, pp. 125–136. National Institute of Standards and Technology (NIST) (1997). http://trec.nist.gov/pubs/trec6/papers/city_proc_auto.ps

Linguistic Uncertainty in Clinical NLP: A Taxonomy, Dataset and Approach

Mark Turner[1(✉)], Julia Ive[1], and Sumithra Velupillai[2]

[1] Imperial College London, London, UK
mark.turner19@imperial.ac.uk
[2] King's College London, London, UK

Abstract. Linguistic uncertainty is prevalent in electronic health records (EHRs). The ability to handle and preserve uncertainty in natural language is an essential skill for clinicians, facilitating decidability and effective clinical reasoning processes despite incomplete knowledge in some situations. This has been addressed by previous research in clinical NLP by the development of algorithms that detect uncertainty expressions. However, existing rule-based algorithms have limited uncertainty detection capabilities. Therefore, we seek to reformulate uncertainty detection as a supervised machine learning problem by (i) reevaluating the concept of uncertainty, (ii) embedding this understanding in an improved linguistic uncertainty taxonomy and (iii) introducing a new dataset of EHRs annotated for nine types of uncertainty – the first publicly available dataset of its kind. Many of our classes are novel and emphasise implicit uncertainties – a form of uncertainty that is ignored by existing algorithms, yet has crucial functions in clinical settings. Through an evaluation of our dataset, we demonstrate the scalability of our approach and its utility in relation to research on clinical information extraction.

Keywords: Information extraction · Linguistic uncertainty · NLP

1 Introduction

Our premise is the observation that clinicians can do their jobs because they are able to process and operate alongside uncertainty. When treating a patient, uncertainty is omnipresent. Medical specialists are trained to reason *using* uncertainty and communicate in such a way so as to preserve the sense of uncertainty that might accompany their judgements and observations.

This behaviour pervades the written records that medical professionals produce while treating a patient. Consequently, the legacy of intellectual uncertainty defines the written sources that are constitutive of the input for a wide range of clinical natural language processing (NLP) tasks. Consequently, uncertainty detection is critical for reliable information extraction tools. That is, our machine learning models need to be able to identify uncertainty and crucially preserve

K. S. Candan et al. (Eds.): CLEF 2021, LNCS 12880, pp. 129–141, 2021.
https://doi.org/10.1007/978-3-030-85251-1_11

the sentiments that underpin it in whatever their subsequent operations happen to be. Currently the field lacks the datasets necessary to tackle such challenges.

Our main contributions are threefold: (1) we revise and expand existing uncertainty taxonomies to encompass new forms of linguistic uncertainty; (2) we present a new dataset of EHRs that are span-annotated according to these taxonomic foundations; (3) we evaluate our annotation scheme both intrinsically and extrinsically, demonstrating its scalability.

2 Related Work

2.1 Existing Rule-Based Uncertainty Detection

A very limited number of algorithms exist in the field of clinical NLP for linguistic uncertainty detection. They are predominantly rule-based and exist primarily to facilitate the labelling of corpora for medical computer vision tasks.

NegBio, introduced by Peng et al. [10], is a state-of-the-art example of a rule-based uncertainty classifier for clinical NLP. The pattern language, Semgrex, is used to create the dependency rules that facilitate superior uncertainty detection capabilities in comparison to previous approaches – for example, Chapman et al. [1] – that were limited to regular expressions and missed out on a syntactic level of analysis.

NegBio has been built upon by Irvin et al. [3] who introduced the CheXpert labeler. The CheXpert labeler specialises NegBio in the direction of uncertainty and negation detection for radiographic studies. Their mention extraction stage focuses on 14 common observations of interest – pneumonia, edema, lung opacity and more – that recur in radiographic studies. The result is that they achieve greater accuracy and faster run times across a more narrow medical domain.

To assess the skill of the NegBio/CheXpert algorithms we need to analyse the types of uncertainty that they are able to detect and the completeness of this schema. Here, two limitations of the NegBio/CheXpert algorithms are apparent:

1. These algorithms can only identify certain types of clinical uncertainties – specifically, those that are voiced explicitly in relation to a disease mention. This ignores uncertainty in causality, medical opinions and more.
2. These algorithms cannot distinguish between different types of uncertainty – a crucial aspect of clinical reasoning processes.

We see then that existing tools can *selectively identify, but not interpret* uncertainty. Our taxonomy and dataset seek to address these issues by reformulating uncertainty detection as a multiclass supervised machine learning problem.

Existing large-scale clinical linguistic uncertainty datasets – for example, the BioScope corpus [12] – maintain the limitations of a binary distinction between certainty and uncertainty, highlighting the relevance of new pilot taxonomisations of uncertainty to the task of clinical information extraction.

2.2 Existing Uncertainty Taxonomies: Content and Emphases

Mowery et al. [8] present an uncertainty and negation taxonomy that is based on a qualitative reading of both English and Swedish medical records. Their taxonomy differentiates between uncertainties on the basis of the position of lexical cue, opinion source and evidence evaluation mechanisms [8]. Their taxonomy extends beyond the scope of the above discussed NegBio [10] and CheXpert labeler [3] algorithms, because it moves beyond syntactic analysis: broader inference strategies – the ability to construe the relationship between people, infer confidence from written text and more – are drawn upon.

The purpose of the Mowery et al. [8] taxonomy is to differentiate between different *types* of uncertainty. By contrast, Velupillai [11] has formalised the taxonomic foundations for different *levels* of uncertainty, proposing six classes that should be visualised as a continuum: 'certainly positive', 'probably positive', 'possibly positive', 'possibly negative', 'probably negative' and 'certainly negative'. Velupillai's taxonomy is, therefore, agnostic to the type of uncertainty being voiced, focusing instead on the intensity of uncertainty that is being channeled in clinical text. These approaches are not contradictory and both have merit. Given our interest in the interpretability of uncertainty, the taxonomy presented in the next section develops the work of Mowery et al. [8].

3 Contribution: An Annotation Scheme

Here we present the system of distinctions that underlies our dataset. Our taxonomy (Fig. 1) separates uncertainty expressions into nine discrete subcategories. Each subcategory fits into one of four overarching categories. These parent categories indicate very different ways of expressing uncertainty that diverge significantly with regards to their clinical meaning contents.

Our taxonomy was constructed on the basis of an extensive study of unstructured clinical notes from the MIMIC datasets [2,6] – some of the largest publicly available EHR datasets. We have not been able to find an uncertainty expression in the MIMIC datasets that resists categorisation under our taxonomy and therefore suggest that the taxonomy is complete. An explanation of each type of uncertainty in our taxonomy now follows.

3.1 Implicit Uncertainty

We have seen that existing uncertainty detection algorithms are only able to detect uncertainties that are expressed via an *overt* lexical marker such as 'maybe' and 'possibly'. This is a consequence of the fact these algorithms are rule-based: the methodology is limited to a process of locating lexical markers that are constitutive of uncertainty and identifying their linguistic scope. Here we outline four categories of implicit uncertainty.

The category **Refusal to specify; certainty to a point** relates to the way caregivers approach key judgements, for example, a diagnosis, in steps through

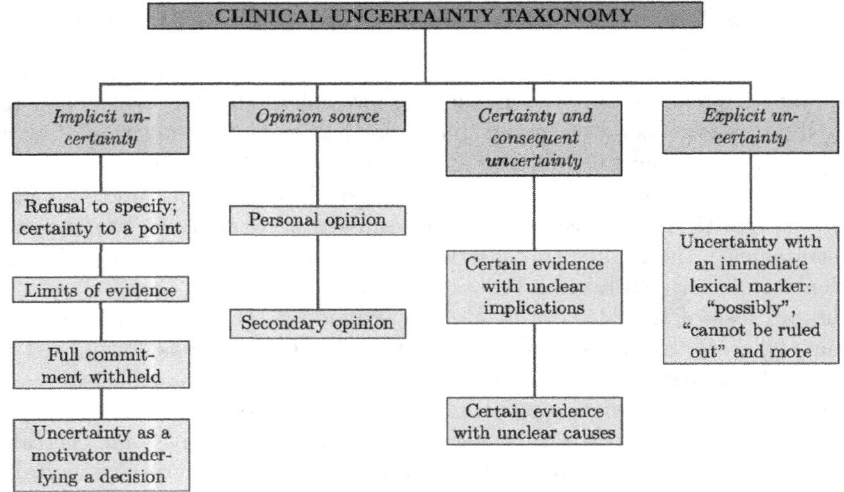

Fig. 1. A taxonomy for linguistic uncertainty in clinical language, presenting the types of uncertainty as found in MIMIC-III [4,6] and MIMIC-CXR [5,6].

an iterative process of observing and rethinking. A diagnosis is not always immediately forthcoming. In these stages uncertainty is omnipresent – the caregiver does not know why their patient is ill – but this uncertainty can manifest itself in language in concealed ways. The following phrases illuminate this phenomenon:[1]

1. *"Symptoms indicate a form of neurodegeneration"*
2. *"left lung, lower lobe is problematic"*

Caregivers are using a high level of generality to preserve uncertainty. Here we approach Mowery et al. [8] who emphasise the uncertainty inherent in expressions of "limitless possibilities".

We are looking for moments when caregivers use broad or vague terms so as to avoid implying they are certain about the specifics of something when, really, they are not. As such, we are tapping into a key dimension of clinical reasoning: the ability to slowly and methodically advance an argument, pushing back against uncertainty without jumping to conclusions.

Our second category, **Limits of evidence** is drawn from the Mowery et al. [8] taxonomy, where 'limits of evidence' is a parent category for a number of subclasses that make further distinctions within this category. To mitigate against data sparsity, we do not subdivide this class in our taxonomy. Further, while the Mowery et al. [8] taxonomy uses this category to record expressions where an explicit marker of uncertainty is used in conjunction with the evaluation of clinical evidence, we seek instead to group expressions where the uncertainty is implicit under this category.

[1] All examples hereinafter are from MIMIC and are paraphrased.

1. *"radiograph cannot confirm pneumonia"*

Clearly, there is a difference between ruling something out and saying that the data does not support a hypothesis conclusively. Caregivers are, nevertheless, able to use the latter case to slowly define the contours of a patient's condition and do so using the medium of implicit uncertainty.

Thirdly, the category **Full commitment withheld**, refers to occasions where caregivers resist offering full support for a particular hypothesis.

1. *"Denies use of hard drug"*

These forms of uncertainty expressions, often implicit, function to allow caregivers to convey their best guess without binding any future caregivers to the same conclusions; the possibility for new evidence and revised opinions is left open and a key dimension of the scientific method is preserved.

Finally, **Uncertainty as a motivator** covers expressions where uncertainty can be inferred as a context behind a clinical event's happening.

1. *"Needs a CT scan to confirm"*
2. *"Neuro was consulted"*

We gather uncertainties that implicitly underlie clinical decisions. Our taxonomy, therefore, encompasses occasions where clinicians allude to a context of uncertainty that may be motivating clinical events or sentiments.

3.2 Opinion Source

A binary distinction between a personal opinion and a secondary opinion suffices to preserve the significance of a statement's uncertainty value. Note: patient opinions are categorised above as 'full commitment withheld', because this better captures the way they are recorded and interpreted by clinicians.

Our category, **Personal opinion**, describes occasions when a clinician may qualify their judgements as a personal opinion. Typically this indicates that the background knowledge surrounding a patient's condition is making a decisive judgement difficult. This is a common and important linguistic device:

1. *"Impression:"*
2. *"It was felt that HCAP should be prioritised"*

In sum, where personal opinions are used, important uncertainty can be inferred. We see then this broader category of 'Opinion source' echoes some characteristics of the previously discussed category of 'Implicit uncertainty'. We create the distinct category, 'Opinion source', for practical reasons.

By contrast, **Secondary opinion** refers to occasions where a judgement sits within the scope of another clinician who has been called upon for their expertise.

1. *"Patient was assessed by the GI due to results from stool samples. The GI emphasised iron deficiencies over other factors."*

Expression **(1)** is interesting. On one hand, the reference to a specialist, adds certainty to the expressed opinion; on the other hand, the judgement remains an opinion amongst others which preserves a sense of uncertainty. The use of a secondary opinion means advice can be sought and revised when appropriate. In preserving something as an opinion, one allows for the situation in which one does not have to be ontologically committed to something until certainty is beyond reasonable doubt. Further, the fact the opinion of the GI was sought in the first place implies an uncertain context to this clinical episode; it betrays the challenges that accompanied a patient's care.

In sum, we provide a condensed version of the Mowery et al. [8] taxonomisation of clinical opinion sources with fewer opinion classes. The aim is to preserve linguistic uncertainty, while mitigating against the risks of data sparsity that might otherwise impede a machine learning task.

3.3 Certainty and Consequent Uncertainty

The category **Certain evidence with unclear implications** highlights formulations where an observation is declared with certainty, but its implications are not yet fully understood. This matters, because it indicates situations where a great deal of uncertainty still surrounds a given fact. It reflects times when our certainty is partial and improvable.

1. *"Clearly visible hila, might suggest prominence of c. pulmonary vessels"*
2. *"This observation could represent focal fat; secondary to that, a cystic tumor"*

Expression **(1)** is a good example of the generative relationship between certainty and uncertainty. The hilum are well understood, but the implications – i.e. the clinical meaning – of that observation are obscured. This form of uncertainty allows the caregiver to grasp towards a more reasoned assessment of the patient's condition and augment the knowledge that surrounds a given certainty. Expression **(2)** is analogous.

By considering certain evidence and unclear implications together we find a category that allows us to classify the common problem whereby a certain observation is actually not that certain after all. This is not a paradox: uncertainty persists in a certain observation when the implications of that observation remain *intractable despite the certainty* with which the subject is observed. Expression **(1)** demonstrated this.

The category, **Certain evidence with unclear *causes***, groups expressions where something is observed with certainty, but its cause cannot be determined.

1. *"Intrinsic right ventricular systolic function is depleted, probably more so because of the arterial BP"*

Expression **(1)** makes clear that the right ventricular function is undoubtedly weakened. But when interpreting the whole sentence, we learn that this observation is less certain than it might otherwise seem: clearly little is known about *why* the patient is suffering. The expression suggests there is more still to learn despite some basic certainties.

This category covers the cases where certainty brings *un*certainty into relief. This is common in everyday life: the moment we find conclusive evidence, we immediately encounter new questions that were inconceivable prior to our finding. Indeed, this dynamic is central to the research process.

3.4 Explicit Uncertainty

The final category of uncertainty from our taxonomy in Fig. 1 that remains to be discussed is **Uncertainty with immediate lexical marker**. Here we consider the most common and glaring form of uncertainty: uncertainty that is voiced using an overt lexical marker such as "possibly", "cannot be ruled out" and more. Unsurprisingly, this appears in the following forms:

1. *"Likely edema and mild vascular congestion"*
2. *"Suspected sepsis at admission. ITP or TTP cannot be ruled out"*

Mowery et al. [8] present a taxonomy with 'Position of lexical cue' as a meta-category that encompasses three subcategories referring to the position of lexical cues: 'pre-disorder', 'intra-disorder' and 'post-disorder'. Although this is of linguistic interest, our taxonomy blurs these distinctions classifying any uncertainties that are identifiable through lexical markers as 'explicit uncertainty'. This is because our taxonomy underpins and promotes a machine learning approach to clinical uncertainty detection. The exact position of the lexical cue is arguably redundant in relation to the *meaning* of an explicitly declared uncertainty expression, hence we chose to streamline our taxonomy in this area.

4 Dataset Overview

4.1 Sources and Data Selection

One native English speaker used the above described taxonomy to annotate unstructured EHR data from MIMIC-III v1.4 [4,6] and MIMIC-CXR [5,6]. Over 50 radiographic studies and discharge summaries ('Brief Hospital Course' section) were selected from these sources where it was empirically determinable that their linguistic uncertainty content was of interest. The documents in our dataset have an average word count of around 130 words.

4.2 Dataset Statistics

Across the nine uncertainty classes outlined in Sect. 3, our dataset contains 337 annotations each denoting a specific type of uncertainty expression. Table 1 presents the number of annotations and the average span of an annotation for each uncertainty class. Discontinuous annotations are rare, but necessary in a

Table 1. Here we present two types of data: first, dataset statistics and results, providing an overview of our dataset's annotations (average spans are given in number of words); second, random classifier results alongside F1 scores derived from an average over 5 fold cross validation are given for the experiments described in Sect. 5.2.

Uncertainty class	Count	Av. span	Ran. classif.	F1 score
Refusal to specify	25	5.7	0.11	0.35
Limits of evidence	18	7.6	0.11	0.32
Full commitment withheld	87	7.5	0.27	0.70
Uncertainty as a motivator	24	9.8	0.09	0.46
Personal opinion	33	6.7	0.14	0.65
Secondary opinion	26	13.0	0.10	0.73
Unclear implications	23	13.2	0.18	0.33
Unclear causes	29	12.9	0.12	0.18
Immediate lexical marker	72	7.2	0.20	0.53

minority of cases – for example, where an expression of 'unclear causes' makes use of or encompasses an 'explicit uncertainty'.

The annotation spans are of note. While our annotations very rarely extend beyond the sentence level, these are nevertheless long annotations. Consequently, the NLP tasks that we are seeking to facilitate are not limited to a search for individual trigger words that might represent uncertainty. Rather our dataset captures more complex dependencies between sets of words and pilots a method of data creation that would require NLP algorithms to learn the scope of an uncertainty annotation.

The classes 'secondary opinion', 'certain evidence with unclear implications' and 'certain evidence with unclear causes' have the longest spans ranging from an average of 12.9 to 13.2 words. This is a logical product of the fact that it takes more words to convey a relationship between people or a causal judgement in complex settings. The class 'personal opinion' where clinicians tend to document quick remarks or observations is accordingly defined by a shorter average span.

5 Results and Evaluation

It remains to evaluate our dataset and our annotation scheme. First, we must be able to demonstrate that the supervised machine learning tasks that our dataset invites are not trivial. Second, we must be able to prove that machine learning models can successfully learn from our dataset – i.e. that our annotations are consistent, coherent and distinguishable.

To construct this proof we begin with an *intrinsic* evaluation of our dataset that draws conclusions from the lexical diversity of our dataset's classes. Following this we conduct two supervised learning experiments on our dataset: first, we provide baseline results that show that an NLP algorithm can differentiate between individual classes; second, we provide further baseline results that show that uncertainty is distinguishable from certainty following training on our dataset. Together with the intrinsic evaluation, this *extrinsic* analysis completes the proof that: our approach to manufacturing data results in distinguishable, well defined classes with dependencies that can be learnt by supervised ML.

5.1 Intrinsic Evaluation: Lexical Diversity

When we look at the word and lemma counts for each of our uncertainty classes two points become clear:

1. The means of expressing a single type of uncertainty can vary broadly.
2. Unique word counts are very similar to unique lemma counts. This demonstrates that our dataset cannot be drastically simplified through lemmatisation in the pre-processing stage.

Further, n-grams show that our uncertainty classes are not defined by recurring word patterns. This is a key observation, because it shows that a supervised machine learning task that is trained to distinguish between our dataset's uncertainty classes cannot achieve strong results simply by memorising word patterns. This is a prerequisite of nontrivial supervised NLP tasks.

5.2 Extrinsic Evaluation: Differentiability of Classes

All 337 uncertainty annotations were extracted from our dataset and grouped by uncertainty class. We trained nine binary classifiers: each binary classifier was trained to differentiate one of the uncertainty classes from all other classes.

Following the work of Kim [7], a state-of-the-art single channel Convolutional Neural Network (CNN) for sentence classification was developed for use as a binary classifier. Appendix A presents more granular implementation details.

Experimental Setup. To assess the distinguishability of our dataset's classes, we extracted all of the dataset's annotations and train nine binary classifiers such that each of our nine uncertainty classes has its own binary classifier that differentiates between the uncertainty class in question (handled as the positive examples) and all other types of uncertainty expressions as defined by our taxonomy. All nine experiments are performed using 5-fold cross validation.

The natural imbalances between positive and negative examples is often in excess of 1 : 5 in the tasks we propose. The result is that during training the ratio of positive to negative examples is 1 : 2. This ratio was chosen empirically. Further hyperparameters are documented in Appendix A.

Results. For the purpose of analysis and comparison we present results from a random classifier in Table 1. The random classifier's results are notable for their very low F1 scores which are derived from poor precision and recall. Together with what we have said about the lexical diversity of our uncertainty classes in Sect. 5.1, they indicate that our dataset is not trivial.

The random classifier results are presented alongside our CNN's F1 scores in Table 1. The F1 score achieved by our nine models consistently and significantly outperforms the F1 scores attained by the random classifier. This is an important result, because it proves that an NLP model is able to learn the distinguishing features that are unique to each uncertainty class and, crucially, differentiate between them. This highlights the way our taxonomy and annotations are coherent and *useful* to machine learning practitioners seeking to build state-of-the-art information extraction tools for clinical NLP. This is a key finding that gives credibility to our dataset and annotation scheme and proves that a bigger version of the approach we pilot could be used productively within a supervised clinical NLP setting.

5.3 Extrinsic Evaluation: Discernibility of Uncertainty

Finally, it remains to be seen whether our dataset facilitates the training of NLP models that can differentiate between certainty and uncertainty. We define as certain all expressions that are not encapsulated by a shade of uncertainty. Again, this problem was approached as a binary classification task: examples were either certain or uncertain and the model was trained by supervised learning to draw this distinction. We use the CNN detailed in Appendix A.

Although our dataset contains nine uncertainty classes, for the purpose of this task all 337 examples of uncertainty were grouped together and labeled as the positive – i.e. uncertain – examples. As for the negative – i.e. certain – examples, we extracted 492 examples of certain expressions from our dataset and labeled these as the negative examples for our binary classification task. Any span in our dataset without an uncertainty annotation is regarded to be certain and was a candidate for extraction. It was ensured that the spans of our negative examples resembled the spans of our positive examples to prevent a misleading dependency being learnt by our model. Likewise, since our examples of uncertainty do not extend beyond the sentence level, the logic for extracting negative examples ensured that this property was common to both classes.

Crucially, given this method, it is clear that we are not proposing a task whereby a machine learning model is being trained to learn the scope of uncertainty expressions and label their precise location within a broader input string. Our positive examples already delimit the uncertainty expressions from their surrounding text and the task instead is to label whether or not uncertainty is a property of the given expression. While we acknowledge that this is less challenging, it is a critical to evaluating our dataset. Specifically, we can use this task to test whether our approach to manufacturing data for the supervised learning facilitates the distinguishability of uncertainty from certainty expressions – a necessary step when considering the prospects of scaling our approach.

Experimental Setup. We use 10-fold cross validation and downsample such that each positive example is accompanied by 1.2 other negative examples, a ratio that was determined empirically. Again, we downsample the training data after each split and leave the test data unmodified. Hyperparameters are documented in Appendix A. Test loss, accuracy, recall, precision and F1 score were used.

Results. The results for this task are presented in Table 2. Our F1 score of 0.75 improves decisively upon the score of 0.348 achieved by the random classifier on the same task. These results show that it is possible to create a well defined, distinguishable uncertainty class that incorporates a broad range of implicit uncertainties and simultaneously retains dependencies that can be learnt by supervised ML.

Table 2. Distinguishing uncertain and certain spans using a single channel CNN in the form of a binary classifier. Average scores from 10-fold cross validation are presented for each evaluation metric.

Metric	Score
Test loss	0.440
Accuracy (%)	79.97
Recall	0.78
Precision	0.81
F1 score	0.75

6 Conclusion

This paper lays the foundations for a supervised machine learning approach to linguistic uncertainty detection in EHR text. First, we present an improved uncertainty taxonomy that introduces new uncertainty classes and brings implicit, clinically important uncertainties to attention. Using these taxonomic foundations we present the first publicly available dataset that models linguistic uncertainty. The annotated data and annotation guidelines will be made available as a project in Physionet[2] pending their approval. Finally we show through extrinsic experimentation that our dataset and annotation scheme generates distinguishable, well defined classes that researchers could use productively. In providing evidence to support this case, we hope that the approach to data annotation that this paper introduces will be scaled in the future and that the data produced thus far will benefit efforts to improve patient care.

Ethics. This study has been carried out in accordance with all relevant guidelines and regulations for the use of MIMIC-III data. Assisting human medical experts to make

[2] https://physionet.org/.

better decisions in complex environments is the sole aim of this paper and the way we handle data in our dataset. Further, all annotators involved in the construction of our dataset were volunteers. Before deployment in an actual clinical setting, we plan to systematically evaluate our methodology under the supervision of expert clinicians.

A Model Implementation

Following the work of Kim [7], a state-of-the-art single channel Convolutional Neural Network (CNN) for sentence classification was used as a binary classifier.

For our experiments (see Sect. 5.2 and 5.3), the majority of hyperparameters were kept constant: the learning rate was set at 0.3; the dropout probability in the dropout layer was 0.1; BioWordVec embeddings were scaled by a factor of 0.65. The window sizes for our two convolutional layers were either 1 and 3 or 3 and 5. The number of training epochs ranged from 30 to 70. These hyperparameters were determined by monitoring the training loss. Random classifiers used as a baseline were drawn from the Scikitlearn library [9].

References

1. Chapman, W.W., Bridewell, W., Hanbury, P., Cooper, G.F., Buchanan, B.G.: A simple algorithm for identifying negated findings and diseases in discharge summaries. J. Biomed. Inform. **34**, 301–310 (2001). https://doi.org/10.1006/jbin.2001.1029
2. Goldberger, A.L., et al.: PhysioBank, PhysioToolkit, and PhysioNet: components of a new research resource for complex physiologic signals. Circulation **101**, e215–e220 (2000). https://doi.org/10.1161/01.cir.101.23.e215
3. Irvin, J., et al.: CheXpert: a large chest radiograph dataset with uncertainty labels and expert comparison. In: Proceedings of the AAAI Conference on Artificial Intelligence (2019). https://doi.org/10.1609/aaai.v33i01.3301590
4. Johnson, A.E., Pollard, T.J., Mark, R.G.: MIMIC-III clinical database (version 1.4). PhysioNet (2016)
5. Johnson, A.E., Pollard, T.J., Mark, R.G., Seth, B., Horng, S.: MIMIC-CXR Database (version 2.0.0). PhysioNet (2019)
6. Johnson, A.E., et al.: MIMIC-III, a freely accessible critical care database. Sci. Data **3**, 1–9 (2016). https://doi.org/10.1038/sdata.2016.35
7. Kim, Y.: Convolutional neural networks for sentence classification. In: EMNLP 2014 - 2014 Conference on Empirical Methods in Natural Language Processing, Proceedings of the Conference (2014). https://doi.org/10.3115/v1/d14-1181
8. Mowery, D.L., Ave, M., Chapman, W.W.: Medical diagnosis lost in translation – analysis of uncertainty and negation expressions in English and Swedish clinical texts. In: Proceedings of the 2012 Workshop on Biomedical Natural Language Processing (BioNLP 2012) (2012)
9. Pedregosa, F., et al.: Scikit-learn: machine learning in Python. J. Mach. Learn. Res. **12**, 2825–2830 (2011)
10. Peng, Y., Wang, X., Lu, L., Bagheri, M., Summers, R., Lu, Z.: NegBio: a high-performance tool for negation and uncertainty detection in radiology reports. In: AMIA Joint Summits on Translational Science Proceedings. AMIA Joint Summits on Translational Science (2018)

11. Velupillai, S.: Shades of certainty: annotation and classification of Swedish medical records (2012). http://su.diva-portal.org/smash/record.jsf?searchId=1&pid=diva2:512263
12. Vincze, V., Szarvas, G., Farkas, R., Móra, G., Csirik, J.: The BioScope corpus: biomedical texts annotated for uncertainty, negation and their scopes. BMC Bioinformatics **9**, 1–9 (2008). https://doi.org/10.1186/1471-2105-9-S11-S9

Best of 2020 Labs

Self-calibrating Neural-Probabilistic Model for Authorship Verification Under Covariate Shift

Benedikt Boenninghoff[1(✉)], Dorothea Kolossa[1], and Robert M. Nickel[2]

[1] Ruhr University Bochum, Bochum, Germany
{benedikt.boenninghoff,dorothea.kolossa}@rub.de
[2] Bucknell University, Lewisburg, USA
rmn009@bucknell.edu

Abstract. We are addressing two fundamental problems in authorship verification (AV): Topic variability and miscalibration. Variations in the topic of two disputed texts are a major cause of error for most AV systems. In addition, it is observed that the underlying probability estimates produced by deep learning AV mechanisms oftentimes do not match the actual case counts in the respective training data. As such, probability estimates are poorly calibrated. We are expanding our framework from PAN 2020 to include Bayes factor scoring (BFS) and an uncertainty adaptation layer (UAL) to address both problems. Experiments with the 2020/21 PAN AV shared task data show that the proposed method significantly reduces sensitivities to topical variations and significantly improves the system's calibration.

Keywords: Authorship verification · Deep metric learning · Bayes factor scoring · Uncertainty adaptation · Calibration

1 Introduction

Computational authorship verification (AV) is often described as the task to automatically accept or reject the identity claim of an *unknown* author by comparing a disputed document with a reference document written by a *known* author. AV can be described mathematically as follows. Suppose we have a pair of documents $\mathcal{D}_1$ and $\mathcal{D}_2$ with an associated ground-truth hypothesis $\mathcal{H}_a$ for $a \in \{0, 1\}$. The value of a indicates if the two documents were written by the same author ($a = 1$) or by different authors ($a = 0$). Automated systems usually calculate scores or likelihood ratios to distinguish between the same-author and the different-authors cases. The score-based task can formally be expressed as a mapping $f \colon \{\mathcal{D}_1, \mathcal{D}_2\} \longrightarrow s \in [0, 1]$. Usually, the estimated label $\widehat{a}$ is obtained from a threshold test applied to the score/prediction value s. For instance, we may choose $\widehat{a} = 1$ if $s > 0.5$ and $\widehat{a} = 0$ if $s < 0.5$. The PAN 2020/21 shared tasks also permit the return of a *non-response* (in addition to $\widehat{a} = 1$ and $\widehat{a} = 0$) in cases of high uncertainty [8], e.g. when s is close to 0.5.

K. S. Candan et al. (Eds.): CLEF 2021, LNCS 12880, pp. 145–158, 2021.
https://doi.org/10.1007/978-3-030-85251-1_12

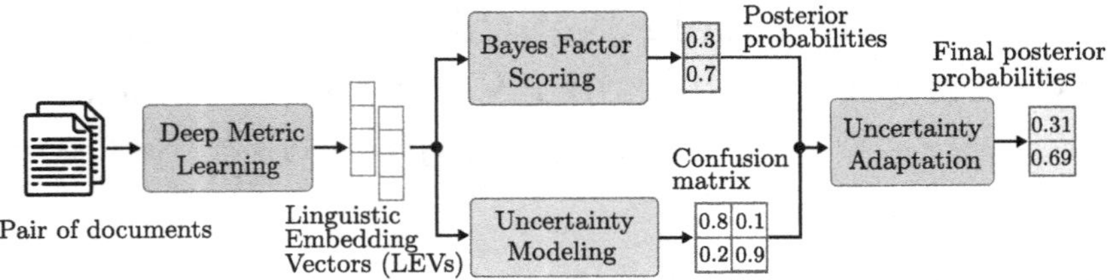

Fig. 1. Our proposed end-to-end neural-probabilistic model.

The current PAN AV challenge moved from a closed-set task in the previous year to an open-set task in 2021, i.e. a scenario in which the testing data contains *only* authors and topics that were *not* included in the training data. We thus expect a *covariate shift* between training and testing data, i.e. the distribution of the features extracted from the training data is expected to be different from the distribution of the testing data features. It was implicitly shown in [8] that such a covariate shift, due to topic variability, is a major cause of errors in authorship analysis applications.

Our proposed framework[1] is presented in Fig. 1. In [3], we introduced the concept of *linguistic embedding vectors* (LEVs), where we perform *deep metric learning* (DML) to encode the stylistic characteristics of a pair of documents into a pair of fixed-length representations, $\boldsymbol{y}_i$ with $i \in \{1, 2\}$. Given the LEVs, a *Bayes factor scoring* (BFS) layer computes the posterior probability for a trial. Finally, we propose an *uncertainty adaptation layer* (UAL) including uncertainty modeling and adaptation to correct possible misclassifications and to return corrected and calibrated posteriors, $p(\mathcal{H}_{\widehat{a}}|\boldsymbol{y}_1, \boldsymbol{y}_2)$ with $\widehat{a} \in \{0, 1\}$.

For the decision, whether to accept $\mathcal{H}_0/\mathcal{H}_1$ or to return a non-response, it is desirable that the concrete value or outcome of the posterior $p(\mathcal{H}_{\widehat{a}}|\boldsymbol{y}_1, \boldsymbol{y}_2) = s$ has a reliable *confidence* score. Ideally, this confidence score should match the true probability of a correct outcome. Following [11], our neural-probabilistic model is said to be well-calibrated if its posterior probabilities match the corresponding empirical frequencies. Inspired by [6], we take up the topic of calibration of confidence scores in the field of deep learning to the case of binary AV. A perfectly calibrated authorship verification system can be defined as

$$\mathbb{P}\left(\mathcal{H}_{\widehat{a}} = \mathcal{H}_a \middle| p(\mathcal{H}_{\widehat{a}}|\boldsymbol{y}_1, \boldsymbol{y}_2) = s\right) = s \quad \forall s \in [0, 1], \quad a \in \{0, 1\}, \quad \widehat{a} \in \{0, 1\}. \quad (1)$$

As mentioned in [6] we are not able to directly measure the probability in Eq. (1) and the authors proposed two empirical approximations, i.e. the *expected calibration error* (`ECE`) and the *maximum calibration error* (`MCE`) to capture the miscalibration of neural networks.

Another way to visualize how well our model is calibrated, is to draw the reliability diagram. The confidence interval is discretized into a fixed number

[1] The source code is accessible online: https://github.com/boenninghoff/pan_2020_2021_authorship_verification.

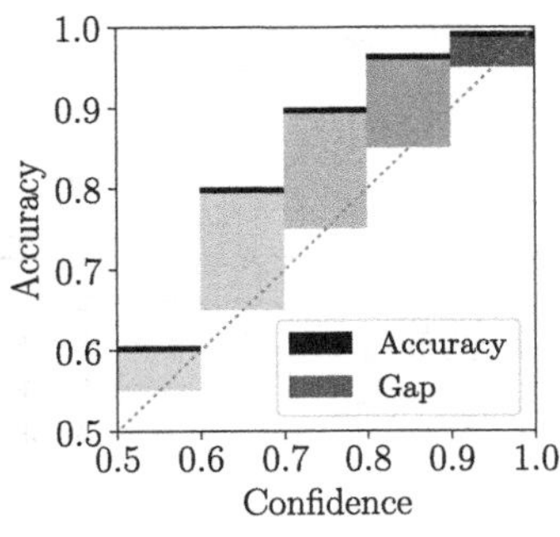

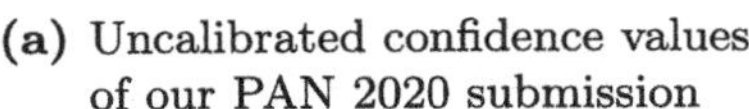
(a) Uncalibrated confidence values of our PAN 2020 submission

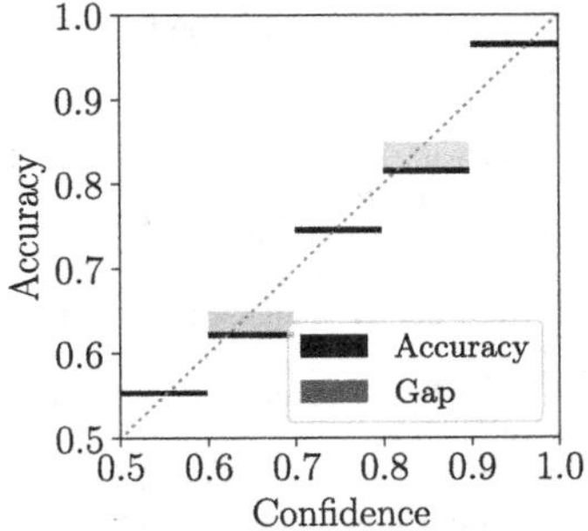

(b) Calibrated confidence values of our PAN 2021 submission

Fig. 2. Reliability diagrams for our PAN 2020 submission and the proposed 2021 submission. The red bars are darker for bins with a higher number of trials. (Color figure online)

of bins. Afterwards, we compute the average confidence and the corresponding accuracy for each bin. Figure 2 illustrates the differences between our PAN 2020 submission and our extended version for PAN 2021. The red gaps between accuracy and confidence in Fig. 2(a) indicate a miscalibration, meaning that the system delivers *under-confident* predictions since the accuracy is always larger than the confidence - resulting in a higher occurrence of false negatives. In contrast, the diagram in Fig. 2(b) shows that, for our proposed new method, accuracy and confidence are closer, if not equal.

In this work, we expand our method from PAN 2020 by adding new system components, evaluate performance w.r.t. *authorship* and *topical label*, and illustrate the effect of the fine-tuning of some core hyper-parameters. Our experiments show that, even though we are not able to fully suppress the misleading influence of topical variations, we are at least able to reduce their biasing effect.

2 Text Preprocessing Strategies

2.1 PAN2020 Dataset Split

The *fanfictional* dataset for the PAN 2020/21 AV [8] and contains 494,227 unique documents written by 278,162 unique authors, grouped into 1,600 unique fandoms. We split the dataset into two disjoint (w.r.t. authorship and fandom) datasets and removed all overlapping documents. The training set contains 303,142 documents of 1,200 fandoms written by 200,732 authors. The test set has 96,027 documents of 400 fandoms written by 77,430 authors.

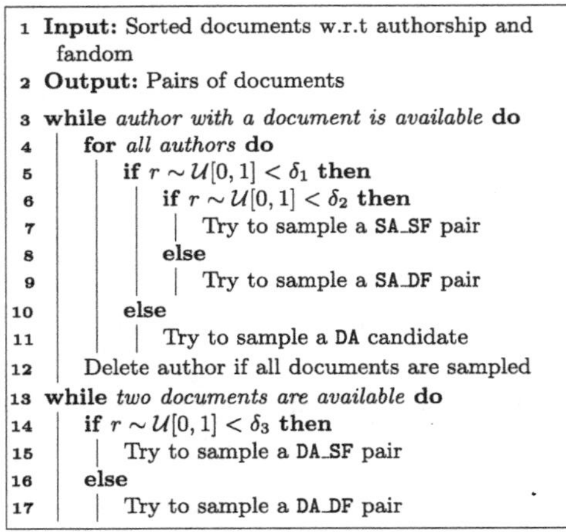

```
1  Input: Sorted documents w.r.t authorship and
   fandom
2  Output: Pairs of documents
3  while author with a document is available do
4    for all authors do
5      if r ~ U[0, 1] < δ1 then
6        if r ~ U[0, 1] < δ2 then
7          Try to sample a SA_SF pair
8        else
9          Try to sample a SA_DF pair
10     else
11       Try to sample a DA candidate
12   Delete author if all documents are sampled
13 while two documents are available do
14   if r ~ U[0, 1] < δ3 then
15     Try to sample a DA_SF pair
16   else
17     Try to sample a DA_DF pair
```

Fig. 3. Pair re-sampling procedure.

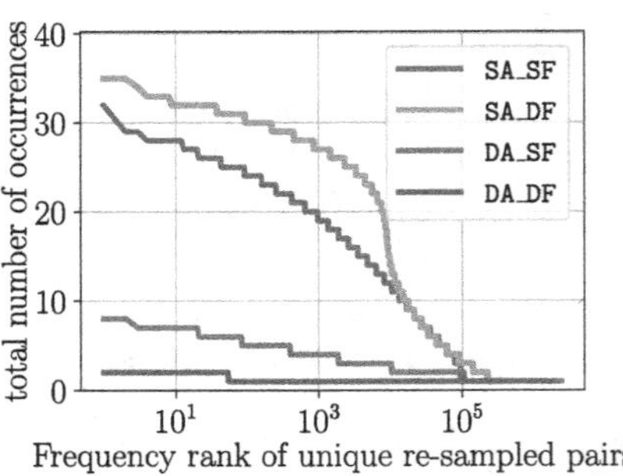

Fig. 4. Zipf plot of the pair counts.

2.2 Re-sampling Document Pairs

The size of the training set can be augmented by re-sampling new document pairs in each epoch, as illustrated in the pseudo-algorithm in Fig. 3. Each document pair is characterized by a tuple (a, f), where $a \in \{0, 1\}$ denotes the authorship label and $f \in \{0, 1\}$ describes the equivalent for the fandom. Each document pair is assigned to one of the subsets[2] SA_SF, SA_DF, DA_SF, and DA_DF in correspondence with its label tuple (a, f).

The algorithm in Fig. 3 follows three constraints: Firstly, all documents contribute equally to the neural network training in each epoch. Secondly, repetitively re-sampling of the same document pairs should be reduced. Thirdly, each document should appear in equal numbers in all subsets. Our re-sampling strategy roughly consists of two while loops, where $\mathcal{U}[0, 1]$ represents a uniform sampler over the half-open interval $[0, 1)$. In the first while loop (lines 3–12) we iterate over all authors until all documents have been sampled either to one of the same-author sets (SA_SF and SA_DF) or have been chosen to be a DA candidate. In the second while loop (lines 13–17), we take all collected DA candidates to sample DA_SF and DA_DF pairs. The parameters δ_1, δ_2, and δ_3 control the distributions of the subsets. We chose $\delta_1 = 0.7$, $\delta_2 = 0.6$ and $\delta_3 = 0.6$. As a result, the epoch-wise training sets are not balanced, rather, we obtain approximately 70% different-authors pairs and 30% same-author pairs.

Figure 4 shows a Zipf plot of the pair counts. It can be seen that there is still a high repetition regarding the same-author pairs since each author generally contributes only with a small number of documents.

During the evaluation stage, the verification task is performed on the test set only. The pairs of the test set are sampled once and then kept fixed. In Sect. 4,

[2] SA = same author, DA = different authors, SF = same fandom, DF = different fandoms.

we briefly report on the system performance for all subsets and then proceed with the analysis of a more challenging case: We removed all `SA_SF` and `DA_DF` pairs. Finally, we have 5,216 `SA_DF` pairs and 7,041 `DA_SF` pairs, resulting in a nearly balanced dataset of 12,257 test pairs.

2.3 Sliding Windowing

As suggested in [3], we perform tokenization and generate *sentence-like units* via a sliding window technique. An example is given in Fig. 5. With the sliding window technique we obtain a compact representation for each document, where zero-padding tokens only need to be added to the last sentence. Given the total number of tokens per sentence T_w, the hop length h and the total number of tokens N, the total number of sentence units per document is $T_s = \lceil \frac{N-T_w+h}{h} \rceil$. We choose $T_w = 30$ and $h = 26$. The maximum number of sentence units per document is upper bounded by the GPU memory and set to $T_s = 210$.

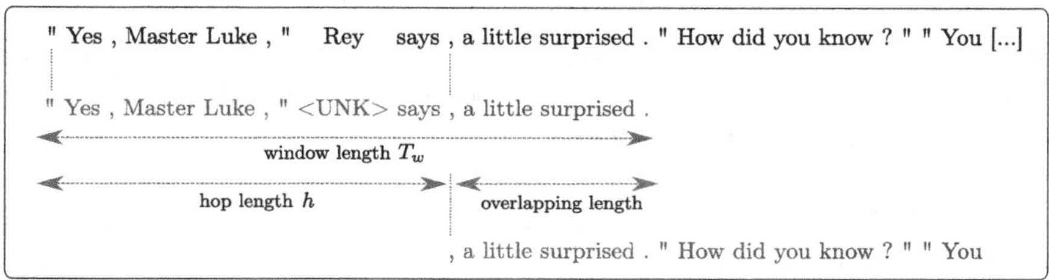

Fig. 5. Example of our sliding window approach.

2.4 Word Embeddings and Topic Masking

A disadvantage of the sliding window approach is that our sentence-like units differ from common sentence structures required by modern contextualized word embedding frameworks. Hence, we decided to represent a token by two different context-independent representations which are learned during training. Firstly, we initialize semantic word representations from the pretrained FastText model [4]. Secondly, we encode new word representations based on characters [2]. We further reduce the vocabulary size for tokens and characters by mapping all rare token/character types to a special *unknown* (`<UNK>`) token which can be interpreted as a topic masking strategy [14]. Finally we chose vocabulary sizes of 5,000 tokens and 300 characters. The embedding dimensions are given by $D_w = 300$ for words and $D_c = 10$ for characters.

3 Neural-Probabilistic Model

3.1 Neural Feature Extraction and Deep Metric Learning

Neural feature extraction and the deep metric learning are realized in the form of a *Siamese* network, mapping both documents into neural features through exactly the same function.

Neural Feature Extraction: After text preprocessing, a single document consists of a list of T_s ordered sentences. Each sentence consists of an ordered list of T_w tokens. Again, each token consists of an ordered list of T_c characters. As mentioned in Sect. 2.4, we implemented a characters-to-word encoding layer to obtain word representations. The dimension is set to $D_r = 30$. The system passes a fusion of token and character embeddings into a two-tiered bidirectional LSTM network with attentions,

$$\boldsymbol{x}_i = \text{NeuralFeatureExtraction}_{\boldsymbol{\theta}}\big(\boldsymbol{E}_i^w, \boldsymbol{E}_i^c\big), \tag{2}$$

where $\boldsymbol{\theta}$ contains all trainable parameters, $\boldsymbol{E}_i^w \in \mathbb{R}^{T_s \times T_w \times D_w}$ represents word embeddings and $\boldsymbol{E}_i^c \in \mathbb{R}^{T_s \times T_w \times T_c \times D_c}$ represents character embeddings. A comprehensive description can be found in [2].

Deep Metric Learning: We feed the document embeddings $\boldsymbol{x}_i$ in Eq. (2) into a metric learning layer,

$$\boldsymbol{y}_i = \tanh\big(\boldsymbol{W}^{\text{DML}}\boldsymbol{x}_i + \boldsymbol{b}^{\text{DML}}\big), \tag{3}$$

which yields the two LEVs $\boldsymbol{y}_1$ and $\boldsymbol{y}_2$ via the trainable parameters $\boldsymbol{\psi} = \{\boldsymbol{W}^{\text{DML}}, \boldsymbol{b}^{\text{DML}}\}$. We then compute the Euclidean distance between both LEVs,

$$d(\boldsymbol{y}_1, \boldsymbol{y}_2) = \|\boldsymbol{y}_1 - \boldsymbol{y}_2\|_2^2. \tag{4}$$

Probabilistic Contrastive Loss: In [2], we chose the modified contrastive loss,

$$\mathcal{L}_{\boldsymbol{\theta},\boldsymbol{\psi}}^{\text{DML}} = a \cdot \max\{d(\boldsymbol{y}_1, \boldsymbol{y}_2) - \tau_s, 0\}^2 + (1-a) \cdot \max\{\tau_d - d(\boldsymbol{y}_1, \boldsymbol{y}_2), 0\}^2, \tag{5}$$

with $\tau_s = 1$ and $\tau_d = 3$. With the contrastive loss all distances between same-author pairs are forced to stay below τ_s and conversely, distances between different-authors pairs are forced to remain above τ_d. A drawback of this contrastive loss is that its output cannot be interpreted as a probability. We therefore introduce a new *probabilistic* version of the contrastive loss: Given the Euclidean distance of the LEVs in Eq. (4), we apply a kernel function

$$p_{\text{DML}}(\mathcal{H}_1|\boldsymbol{y}_1, \boldsymbol{y}_2) = \exp\big(-\gamma\, d(\boldsymbol{y}_1, \boldsymbol{y}_2)^{\alpha}\big), \tag{6}$$

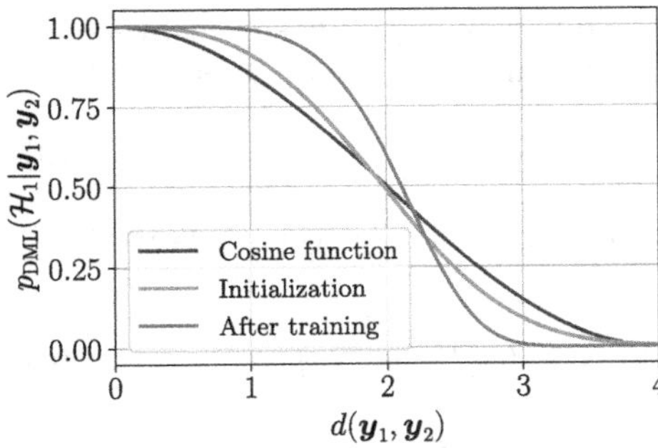

Fig. 6. Learned mapping function of the probabilistic contrastive loss. (Color figure online)

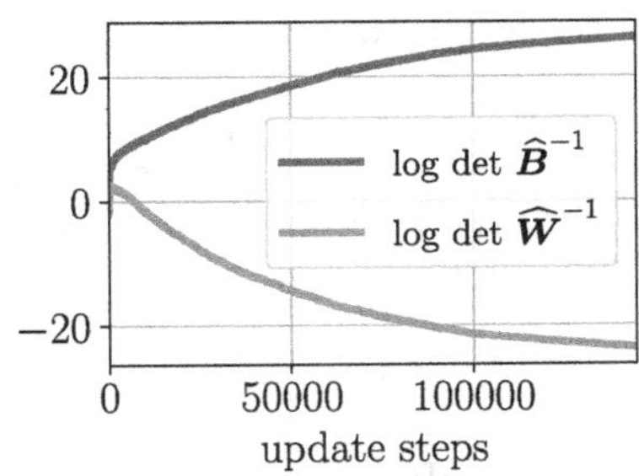

Fig. 7. Entropy curves during training. (Color figure online)

where γ and α can be seen as both, hyper-parameters or trainable variables. The new loss then represents a slightly modified version of Eq. (5),

$$\begin{aligned}\mathcal{L}_{\boldsymbol{\theta},\psi}^{\text{DML}} &= a \cdot \max\left\{\tau_s - p_{\text{DML}}(\mathcal{H}_1|\boldsymbol{y}_1, \boldsymbol{y}_2), 0\right\}^2 \\ &\quad + (1-a) \cdot \max\left\{p_{\text{DML}}(\mathcal{H}_1|\boldsymbol{y}_1, \boldsymbol{y}_2) - \tau_d, 0\right\}^2,\end{aligned} \tag{7}$$

where we set $\tau_s = 0.91$ and $\tau_d = 0.09$. Figure 6 illustrates the decision mapping of the new loss, transforming the distance scores into probabilities. The cosine similarity is a widely used similarity measure in AV [1]. Hence, we initialized α and γ to approximate the cosine function in the interval $[0, 4]$ (blue curve), which was the operating interval in [2]. During training, we optimized α and γ, resulting in the green curve. We will discuss the effect in Sect. 4.

3.2 Deep Bayes Factor Scoring

The idea of pairwise Bayes factor scoring was originally proposed in [5]. In [3], we adapted the idea to the context of AV. We assume that the LEVs in Eq. (4) stem from a Gaussian generative model that can be decomposed as $\boldsymbol{y} = \boldsymbol{s} + \boldsymbol{n}$, where $\boldsymbol{n}$ characterizes a noise term, caused by e.g. topical variations. We assume that the writing characteristics of the author, measured in the observed LEV $\boldsymbol{y}$, lie in a latent stylistic variable $\boldsymbol{s}$. The probability density functions for $\boldsymbol{s}$ and $\boldsymbol{n}$ are given by Gaussian distributions, $p(\boldsymbol{s}) = \mathcal{N}(\boldsymbol{s}|\boldsymbol{\mu}, \boldsymbol{B}^{-1})$ and $p(\boldsymbol{n}) = \mathcal{N}(\boldsymbol{n}|\boldsymbol{0}, \boldsymbol{W}^{-1})$, where $\boldsymbol{B}^{-1}$ defines the *between-author* covariance matrix and $\boldsymbol{W}^{-1}$ denotes the *within-author* covariance matrix. We outlined in [3] how to compute the likelihoods for both hypotheses. The verification score for a trial is then given by the log-likelihood ratio: $\text{score}(\boldsymbol{y}_1, \boldsymbol{y}_2) = \log p(\boldsymbol{y}_1, \boldsymbol{y}_2|\mathcal{H}_1) - \log p(\boldsymbol{y}_1, \boldsymbol{y}_2|\mathcal{H}_0)$. Assuming $p(\mathcal{H}_1) = p(\mathcal{H}_0) = \frac{1}{2}$, the probability for a same-author trial is calculated as [3]:

$$p_{\text{BFS}}(\mathcal{H}_1|\boldsymbol{y}_1, \boldsymbol{y}_2) = \frac{p(\boldsymbol{y}_1, \boldsymbol{y}_2|\mathcal{H}_1)}{p(\boldsymbol{y}_1, \boldsymbol{y}_2|\mathcal{H}_1) + p(\boldsymbol{y}_1, \boldsymbol{y}_2|\mathcal{H}_0)} = \text{Sigmoid}\big(\text{score}(\boldsymbol{y}_1, \boldsymbol{y}_2)\big) \tag{8}$$

Loss Function: The calculation of Eq. (8) requires numerically stable inversions of matrices [3]. Hence, we firstly reduce the dimension of the LEVs via

$$\boldsymbol{y}_i^{\mathrm{BFS}} = f^{\mathrm{BFS}}\big(\boldsymbol{W}^{\mathrm{BFS}}\boldsymbol{y}_i + \boldsymbol{b}^{\mathrm{BFS}}\big), \tag{9}$$

where $f^{\mathrm{BFS}}(\cdot)$ represents the chosen activation function (see Sect. 4). We rewrite Eq. (8) as follows

$$p_{\mathrm{BFS}}(\mathcal{H}_1|\boldsymbol{y}_1,\boldsymbol{y}_2) = \mathrm{Sigmoid}\big(\mathrm{score}(\boldsymbol{y}_1^{\mathrm{BFS}},\boldsymbol{y}_2^{\mathrm{BFS}})\big) \tag{10}$$

and incorporate Eq. (10) into the binary cross entropy,

$$\mathcal{L}_{\phi}^{\mathrm{BFS}} = a\cdot\log\left\{p_{\mathrm{BFS}}(\mathcal{H}_1|\boldsymbol{y}_1,\boldsymbol{y}_2)\right\} + (1-a)\cdot\log\left\{1-p_{\mathrm{BFS}}(\mathcal{H}_1|\boldsymbol{y}_1,\boldsymbol{y}_2)\right\}, \tag{11}$$

where all trainable parameters are denoted with $\boldsymbol{\phi} = \big\{\boldsymbol{W}^{\mathrm{BFS}},\boldsymbol{b}^{\mathrm{BFS}},\boldsymbol{W},\boldsymbol{B},\boldsymbol{\mu}\big\}$. We also consider the within-author and between-authors variabilities by determining the Gaussian entropy during training. As shown in Fig. 7, the within-author variability decreases while the between-author variability increases.

3.3 Uncertainty Modeling and Adaptation

We expect that the BFS component returns a mixture of correct and mislabelled trials. We therefore treat the posteriors as noisy outcomes and rewrite Eq. (10) as $p_{\mathrm{BFS}}(\widehat{\mathcal{H}}_1|\boldsymbol{y}_1,\boldsymbol{y}_2)$ to emphasize that this represents an estimated posterior. Inspired by [10], the idea is to find wrongly classified trials and to model the noise behavior of the BFS. We firstly have to find a single representation for both LEVs, which is done by

$$\boldsymbol{y}^{\mathrm{UAL}} = \tanh\big(\boldsymbol{W}^{\mathrm{UAL}}(\boldsymbol{y}_1-\boldsymbol{y}_2)^{\circ 2} + \boldsymbol{b}^{\mathrm{UAL}}\big), \tag{12}$$

where $(\cdot)^{\circ 2}$ denotes the element-wise square. Next, we compute a 2×2 confusion matrix as follows

$$p(\mathcal{H}_j|\widehat{\mathcal{H}}_i,\boldsymbol{y}_1,\boldsymbol{y}_2) = \frac{\exp\big(\boldsymbol{w}_{ji}^T\,\boldsymbol{y}^{\mathrm{BFS}} + b_{ji}\big)}{\sum\limits_{i'\in\{0,1\}}\exp\big(\boldsymbol{w}_{ji'}^T\,\boldsymbol{y}^{\mathrm{BFS}} + b_{ji'}\big)} \quad \text{for } i,j\in\{0,1\}. \tag{13}$$

The term $p(\mathcal{H}_j|\widehat{\mathcal{H}}_i,\boldsymbol{y}_1,\boldsymbol{y}_2)$ defines the conditional probability of the true hypothesis $\mathcal{H}_j$ given the assigned hypothesis $\widehat{\mathcal{H}}_i$ by the BFS. Here, vector $\boldsymbol{w}_{ji}$ and bias term b_{ji} characterize the confusion between j and i. We can then adapt the uncertainty to define the final output predictions:

$$p_{\mathrm{UAL}}(\mathcal{H}_j|\boldsymbol{y}_1,\boldsymbol{y}_2) = \sum_{i\in\{0,1\}} p(\mathcal{H}_j|\widehat{\mathcal{H}}_i,\boldsymbol{y}_1,\boldsymbol{y}_2)\cdot p_{\mathrm{BFS}}(\widehat{\mathcal{H}}_i|\boldsymbol{y}_1,\boldsymbol{y}_2). \tag{14}$$

Loss Function: The loss consists of two terms, the negative log-likelihood of the groundtruth hypothesis and a regularization term,

$$\begin{aligned}\mathcal{L}_{\boldsymbol{\lambda}}^{\mathrm{UAL}} &= -\log p_{\mathrm{UAL}}(\mathcal{H}_j|\boldsymbol{y}_1,\boldsymbol{y}_2) \\ &\quad + \beta \sum_{i\in\{0,1\}}\sum_{j\in\{0,1\}} p(\mathcal{H}_j|\widehat{\mathcal{H}}_i,\boldsymbol{y}_1,\boldsymbol{y}_2)\cdot\log p(\mathcal{H}_j|\widehat{\mathcal{H}}_i,\boldsymbol{y}_1,\boldsymbol{y}_2),\end{aligned} \tag{15}$$

with trainable parameters denoted by $\boldsymbol{\lambda} = \{\boldsymbol{W}^{\mathrm{UAL}}, \boldsymbol{b}^{\mathrm{UAL}}, \boldsymbol{w}_{ji}, \boldsymbol{b}_{ji}|j,i\in\{0,1\}\}$. The regularization term, controlled by β, follows the maximum entropy principle to penalize the confusion matrix for returning over-confident posteriors [12]. We observed that the probabilities are usually placed closer to zero or one, which is equivalent to a distribution with low entropy. Without regularization, either $p(\mathcal{H}_0|\widehat{\mathcal{H}}_0,\boldsymbol{y}_1,\boldsymbol{y}_2) \approx p(\mathcal{H}_0|\widehat{\mathcal{H}}_1,\boldsymbol{y}_1,\boldsymbol{y}_2) \approx 1$ or $p(\mathcal{H}_1|\widehat{\mathcal{H}}_1,\boldsymbol{y}_1,\boldsymbol{y}_2) \approx p(\mathcal{H}_1|\widehat{\mathcal{H}}_0,\boldsymbol{y}_1,\boldsymbol{y}_2) \approx 1$. The objective of the maximum entropy regularizer is to reduce this effect.

3.4 Overall Loss Function

The overall loss combines the model accuracy, as assessed in Bayes factor scoring, with the uncertainty adaptation loss:

$$\mathcal{L}_{\boldsymbol{\theta},\boldsymbol{\psi},\boldsymbol{\phi},\boldsymbol{\lambda}} = \mathcal{L}_{\boldsymbol{\theta},\boldsymbol{\psi}}^{\mathrm{DML}} + \mathcal{L}_{\boldsymbol{\phi}}^{\mathrm{BFS}} + \mathcal{L}_{\boldsymbol{\lambda}}^{\mathrm{UAL}}. \tag{16}$$

All components are optimized independently w.r.t. the corresponding loss.

4 Experiments

The overall score of the PAN 2021 shared task is given by averaging five metrics [8]: `AUC` measures true/false positive rates for various thresholds. `F1` is defined as the harmonic mean of precision and recall. In this work, the `c@1` score represents the accuracy, since we do not return non-responses. The `f_05_u` favors systems deciding same-author trials correctly. Finally, the `Brier` score rewards systems that return correct and self-confident predictions. To capture the calibration capacity, we provide the `ECE` and `MCE` metrics. The first one computes the weighted macro-averaged absolute error between confidence and accuracy of all bins. The latter returns the maximum absolute error [6].

4.1 Analysis of the Sensitivity to Topical Interference

In a first step, we evaluated the discriminative power of the DML component alone, for fixed parameters α and γ as described in Eq. (6). In Fig. 8, we show histograms of the posteriors including the accuracy and averaged confidence for a single run. All confidence values (also in Fig. 2) lie within the interval $[0.5, 1]$, since we solve a binary classification task. Hence, to obtain confidence scores, the posterior values are transformed w.r.t. to the estimated authorship label, showing $p(\mathcal{H}_1|\boldsymbol{y}_1,\boldsymbol{y}_2)$ if $\widehat{a}=1$ and $1-p(\mathcal{H}_1|\boldsymbol{y}_1,\boldsymbol{y}_2)$ if $\widehat{a}=0$.

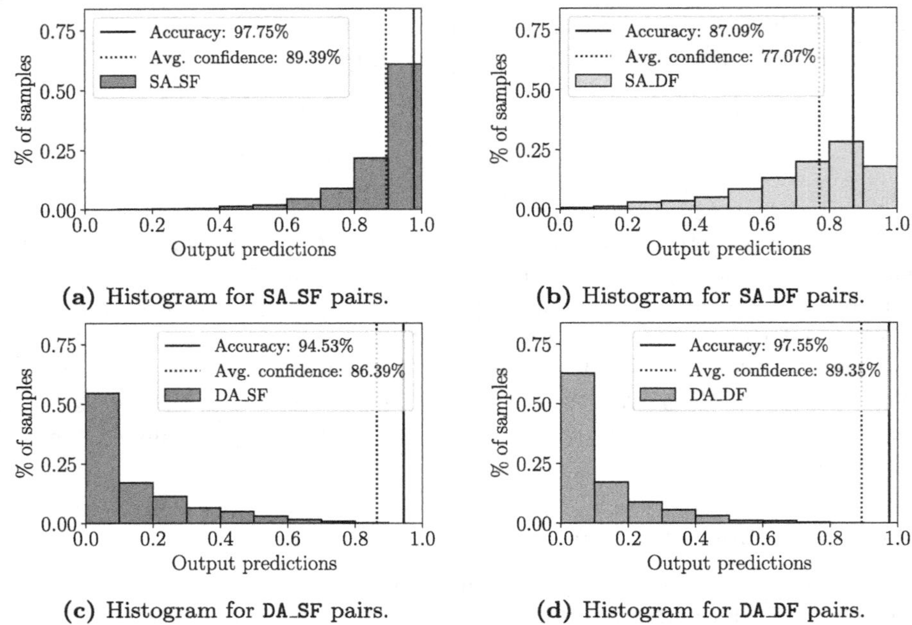

(a) Histogram for **SA_SF** pairs.

(b) Histogram for **SA_DF** pairs.

(c) Histogram for **DA_SF** pairs.

(d) Histogram for **DA_DF** pairs.

Fig. 8. Posterior histograms for DML with fixed kernel parameters.

It can be clearly seen that all subsets exhibit a high degree of miscalibration, where the accuracy is significantly larger than the corresponding confidence. For all subsets, the DML model tends to be under-confident in its predictions.

It is also worth noting that topical interference leads to lower performance. Comparing the histograms in Fig. 8(c) and (d), the accuracy of DA_SF pairs is 3% lower than the accuracy of DA_DF pairs. For SA_SF and SA_DF pairs in Fig. 8(a) and (b), the topical interference is even more obvious and the histogram of SA_DF pairs almost resembles a uniform distribution. Figure 9 displays the confidence histograms after the proposed uncertainty adaptation layer. We can observe a *self-calibrating* effect, where confidence is much better aligned with accuracy on average. However, plot (a) in Fig. 9 also reveals that the model returns a small number of self-confident but wrongly classified same-author trials.

Our most important discovery at this point is that our model analyzes different-authors pairs more readily. As illustrated in Fig. 4, this can be explained by the difficulty of re-sampling heterogeneous subsets of same-authors trials. Experiments conducted on a large dataset of Amazon reviews in [2], where we had to limit the total contribution of each author, have shown lower error rates for same-authors pairs.

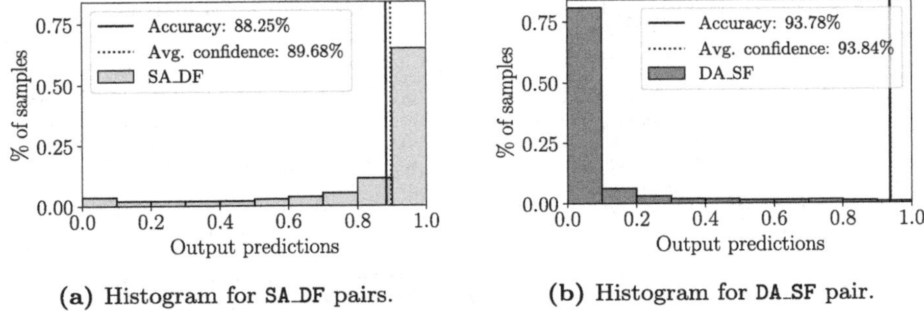

(a) Histogram for SA_DF pairs.

(b) Histogram for DA_SF pair.

Fig. 9. Posterior histograms after uncertainty adaptation ($\beta = 0.1$).

4.2 Ablation Study

Next, we focus on the more problematic SA_DF and DA_SF cases. All model components are analyzed separately to illustrate notable effects of some hyper-parameters. We observed that all runs generally achieved best results between epochs 29 and 33. To avoid cherry-picking, we averaged the metrics over these epochs and at least over four runs totally. All PAN metrics and the corresponding calibration scores are summarized in Table 1. Here, we also provide the averaged confidence, allowing us to characterize a system as over- (c@1 $<$ conf) or under-confident (c@1$>$conf).

In the first two rows, we see the performance of the DML component, showing the effect of learning the kernel parameters α and γ. The overall score slightly increases, which mainly follows from a better Brier score. As can be seen in Fig. 6, the learned mapping holds the distance $d(\boldsymbol{y}_1, \boldsymbol{y}_2)$ of a pair close to one or zero over a wider range, resulting in significantly reduced calibration errors.

The next two rows provide the results of the BFS component for two different activation functions f^{BFS} in Eq. (9). We tried some variations of the ReLU function but did not notice any performance differences and finally proceeded with the Swish function [13]. The ECE and MCE show further significant improvements for both activation functions and the overall score slightly increases using the Swish activation. Comparing the c@1, f_05_u and F1 scores, it is noticeable that the choice of activation function can clearly influence the performance metrics.

The last six rows provide a comparison of the UAL component[3]. The fourth row shows that the output of BFS returns slightly over-confident predictions (c@1 $<$ conf). The UAL without regularization ($\beta = 0$) only reinforces this trend. We varied the parameter β over the range $[0.05, 0.1, 0.125, 0.2]$. We observed that increasing β generally reduces the over-confidence of the model and with $\beta = 0.2$ in the 8th row, the influence of the regularizer becomes so strong that output predictions are now under-confident. In addition, the higher the β parameter is chosen, the lower the MCE values become for tanh activation while it remains on the same level for the Swish activation. This offers a mechanism to optimize the calibration, decreasing the ECE to approximately 0.7–0.8%.

[3] α, γ are learned, first four rows for tanh activation, last two rows for Swish activation.

Table 1. Results for PAN 2021 evaluation and calibration metrics.

Model		PAN 2021 evaluation metrics						Calibration metrics		
		AUC	c@1	f_05_u	F1	Brier	overall	conf	ECE	MCE
DML	Fixed	97.3 ± 0.1	91.2 ± 0.2	$\mathbf{91.7 \pm 0.2}$	89.2 ± 0.2	92.4 ± 0.1	92.4 ± 0.1	82.9 ± 0.1	7.9 ± 1.0	16.6 ± 0.5
	Learned	97.3 ± 0.1	91.5 ± 0.2	90.6 ± 0.7	89.9 ± 0.3	93.5 ± 0.3	92.6 ± 0.2	89.4 ± 0.2	2.2 ± 0.2	7.9 ± 1.0
BFS	Swish	$\mathbf{97.4 \pm 0.1}$	$\mathbf{91.6 \pm 0.2}$	90.9 ± 0.4	89.9 ± 0.3	93.7 ± 0.1	92.7 ± 0.1	91.4 ± 0.2	0.8 ± 0.1	4.4 ± 1.3
	tanh	97.3 ± 0.1	91.2 ± 0.2	91.5 ± 0.3	89.2 ± 0.4	93.4 ± 0.2	92.5 ± 0.1	91.8 ± 0.1	1.1 ± 0.2	4.7 ± 1.5
UAL (tanh)	$\beta = 0$	97.3 ± 0.1	91.5 ± 0.3	91.4 ± 0.4	89.8 ± 0.5	93.6 ± 0.3	92.7 ± 0.3	93.7 ± 0.2	2.3 ± 0.4	8.1 ± 1.5
	$\beta = 0.05$	97.3 ± 0.1	91.4 ± 0.2	91.0 ± 0.4	89.7 ± 0.3	93.7 ± 0.1	92.6 ± 0.1	92.7 ± 0.2	1.4 ± 0.2	6.7 ± 1.7
	$\beta = 0.1$	97.3 ± 0.1	91.5 ± 0.2	91.2 ± 0.4	89.8 ± 0.2	93.7 ± 0.1	92.7 ± 0.2	92.1 ± 0.2	0.8 ± 0.1	5.4 ± 1.5
	$\beta = 0.2$	$\mathbf{97.4 \pm 0.1}$	91.5 ± 0.2	91.1 ± 0.4	89.8 ± 0.3	93.7 ± 0.1	92.7 ± 0.1	90.2 ± 0.2	1.6 ± 0.2	$\mathbf{4.1 \pm 1.1}$
UAL	$\beta = 0.1$	97.3 ± 0.0	91.5 ± 0.1	90.9 ± 0.4	89.9 ± 0.2	$\mathbf{93.8 \pm 0.1}$	92.7 ± 0.1	91.9 ± 0.2	$\mathbf{0.7 \pm 0.1}$	4.8 ± 1.3
	$\beta = 0.125$	$\mathbf{97.4 \pm 0.1}$	$\mathbf{91.6 \pm 0.1}$	91.0 ± 0.3	$\mathbf{90.0 \pm 0.1}$	$\mathbf{93.8 \pm 0.1}$	$\mathbf{92.8 \pm 0.1}$	91.6 ± 0.1	0.8 ± 0.1	5.0 ± 1.6

4.3 Discussion

Our experiments yield two findings: First, as intended, the Bayes factor scoring together with uncertainty adaptation and maximum entropy regularization achieve a high agreement between model confidence and accuracy. Secondly, we are able to slightly increase the overall performance score. Our results from the PAN 2020 shared task, furthermore, show that our framework can better capture the writing style of a person compared to traditional hand-crafted features or compression-based approaches.

Nevertheless, our model is constrained by limits in the discriminative power of the employed LEVs, which serve as the input to all of the subsequent components. One critical point is that LEVs may only capture the surface structure of the writing style. The visualization of the attentions in [2] shows that the system primarily focuses on easily identifiable features, like orthography or punctuation. Another issue is the use of the chosen word representations, which are limited to represent the semantic meaning of a word only in a small context.

We can further improve our framework by addressing the two major types of uncertainty [7]: On the one hand, *aleatoric* or data uncertainty is associated with properties of the document pairs and captures noise inherent in each document. Examples are topical variations, the intra- and inter-author variabilities or the varying lengths of documents. Aleatoric uncertainty generally can not be reduced, even if more training pairs become available, but it can be learned along with the model. Aleatoric uncertainty can be captured by returning a non-response, when it is hard to decide for one hypothesis $\mathcal{H}_0$ or $\mathcal{H}_1$.

On the other hand, *epistemic* or model uncertainty characterizes uncertainty in the model parameters. Examples are the lack of knowledge, e.g. out-of-distribution document pairs or the described issue of re-sampling heterogeneous same-author pairs. This uncertainty obviously can be explained away given enough training pairs. One way to capture epistemic uncertainty is to extend our model to an ensemble. We expect all models to behave similarly for known authors or topics. But the predictions may be widely dispersed for pairs under covariate shift [9]. We will discuss our approaches for capturing these uncertainties and defining non-responses in the PAN 2021 submission paper.

5 Conclusion

In this work, we present a hybrid neural-probabilistic framework to address the task of authorship verification. We generally achieve high overall scores under covariate shift and we further show that our framework mitigates two fundamental problems: topic variability and miscalibration.

In forensic applications, the requirement exists to return suitable and well-calibrated likelihood-ratios rather than decisions. However, in the context of the PAN shared tasks, the evaluation protocol assesses decisions. Nevertheless, the experiments show that we are closing in on a well-calibrated system, which would allow us to interpret the obtained confidence score or posterior as the probability of a correct decision and to bridge the gap between computational authorship verification and traditional forensic text comparison.

Acknowledgment. This work was in significant parts performed on a HPC cluster at Bucknell University through the support of the National Science Foundation, Grant Number 1659397. Project funding was provided by the state of North Rhine-Westphalia within the Research Training Group "SecHuman - Security for Humans in Cyberspace" and by the Deutsche Forschungsgemeinschaft (DFG) under Germany's Excellence Strategy - EXC2092CaSa- 390781972.

References

1. Bevendorff, J., Hagen, M., Stein, B., Potthast, M.: Bias analysis and mitigation in the evaluation of authorship verification. In: 57th Annual Meeting of the ACL, pp. 6301–6306 (2019)
2. Boenninghoff, B., Hessler, S., Kolossa, D., Nickel, R.M.: Explainable authorship verification in social media via attention-based similarity learning. In: IEEE International Conference on Big Data, pp. 36–45 (2019)
3. Boenninghoff, B., Rupp, J., Nickel, R., Kolossa, D.: Deep bayes factor scoring for authorship verification. In: PAN@CLEF 2020, Notebook Papers (2020)
4. Bojanowski, P., Grave, E., Joulin, A., Mikolov, T.: Enriching word vectors with subword information. Trans. ACL **5**, 135–146 (2017)
5. Cumani, S., Brümmer, N., Burget, L., Laface, P., Plchot, O., Vasilakakis, V.: Pairwise discriminative speaker verification in the I-vector space. IEEE Trans. Audio, Speech Lang. Process. **21**, 1217–1227 (2013)
6. Guo, C., Pleiss, G., Sun, Y., Weinberger, K.Q.: On calibration of modern neural networks. In: 34th ICML, vol. 70, pp. 1321–1330. PMLR (2017)
7. Kendall, A., Gal, Y.: What uncertainties do we need in bayesian deep learning for computer vision? In: NeurIPS, vol. 30. Curran Associates, Inc. (2017)
8. Kestemont, M., et al.: Overview of the cross-domain authorship verification task at PAN 2020. In: CLEF 2020, Notebook Papers (2020)
9. Lakshminarayanan, B., Pritzel, A., Blundell, C.: Simple and scalable predictive uncertainty estimation using deep ensembles. In: NeurIPS, pp. 6405–6416 (2017)
10. Luo, B., et al.: Learning with noise: enhance distantly supervised relation extraction with dynamic transition matrix. In: 55th Annual Meeting of the ACL, pp. 430–439 (2017)
11. Pampari, A., Ermon, S.: Unsupervised calibration under covariate shift (2020)

12. Pereyra, G., Tucker, G., Chorowski, J., Kaiser, Ł., Hinton, G.: Regularizing neural networks by penalizing confident output distributions (2017)
13. Ramachandran, P., Zoph, B., Le, Q.V.: Searching for activation functions (2017)
14. Stamatatos, E.: Authorship attribution using text distortion. In: Proceedings of EACL (2017)

Priberam at MESINESP Multi-label Classification of Medical Texts Task

Rúben Cardoso(✉), Zita Marinho, Afonso Mendes, and Sebastião Miranda

Priberam Labs, Lisbon, Portugal
{rac,zam,amm,ssm}@priberam.com
http://labs.priberam.com

Abstract. Medical articles provide current state of the art treatments and diagnostics to many medical practitioners and professionals. Existing public databases such as MEDLINE contain over 27 million articles, making it difficult to extract relevant content without the use of efficient search engines. Information retrieval tools are crucial in order to navigate and provide meaningful recommendations for articles and treatments. Classifying these articles into broader medical topics can improve the retrieval of related articles [1]. The set of medical labels considered for the MESINESP task is on the order of several thousands of labels (DeCS codes), which falls under the extreme multi-label classification problem [2]. The heterogeneous and highly hierarchical structure of medical topics makes the task of manually classifying articles extremely laborious and costly. It is, therefore, crucial to automate the process of classification. Typical machine learning algorithms become computationally demanding with such a large number of labels and achieving better recall on such datasets becomes an unsolved problem.

This work presents Priberam's participation at the BioASQ task MESINESP. We address the large multi-label classification problem through the use of four different models: a Support Vector Machine (SVM) [3], a customised search engine (Priberam Search) [4], a BERT based classifier [5], and a SVM-rank ensemble [6] of all the previous models. Results demonstrate that all three individual models perform well and the best performance is achieved by their ensemble, granting Priberam the 6-*th* place in the present challenge and making it the 2-*nd* best team.

1 Introduction

A growing number of medical articles is published every year, with a current estimated rate of at least one new article every 26 s [7]. The large magnitude of both the documents and the assigned topics renders automatic classification algorithms a necessity in organising and providing relevant information. Search

K. S. Candan et al. (Eds.): CLEF 2021, LNCS 12880, pp. 159–172, 2021.
https://doi.org/10.1007/978-3-030-85251-1_13

engines have a vital role in easing the burden of accessing this information efficiently, however, these usually rely on the manual indexing or tagging of articles, which is a slow and burdensome process [8].

The MESINESP task consists in automatically indexing abstracts in Spanish from two well-known medical databases, IBECS and LILACS, with tags from a pool of 34118 hierarchically structured medical terms, the DeCS codes. This trilingual vocabulary (English, Portuguese and Spanish) serves as a unique vocabulary in indexing medical articles. It follows a tree structure that divides the codes into broader classes and more refined sub-classes respecting their conceptual and semantic relationships [9].

In this task, we tackle the *extreme multi-label (XML)* classification problem. Our goal is to predict for a given article the most relevant subset of labels from an extremely large label set (order of tens of thousands) using supervised training.[1] Typical multi-label classification techniques are not suitable for the XML setting, due to its large computational requirements: the large number of labels implies that both label and feature vectors are sparse and exist in high-dimensional spaces; and to address the sparsity of label occurrence, a large number of training instances is required. These factors make the application of such techniques highly demanding in terms of time and memory, increasing the requirements of computational resources. An additional difficulty is related with a large tail of very infrequent labels, making its prediction very hard, due to misclassification of these examples.

The MESINESP task is even more challenging due to two reasons: first, the articles' labels must be predicted only from the abstracts and titles; and second, all the articles to be classified are in Spanish, which prevents the use of additional resources available only for English, such as BioBERT [11] and ClinicalBERT [12].

This paper describes our participation at the BioASQ task MESINESP. We explore the performance of a one-vs.-rest model based on Support Vector Machines (SVM) [3] as well as that of a proprietary search engine, Priberam Search [4], which relies on inverted indexes combined with a k-nearest neighbours classifier. Furthermore, we took advantage of BERT's contextualised embeddings [5] and tested three possible classifiers: a linear classifier; a label attention mechanism that leverages label semantics; and a recurrent model that predicts a sequence of labels according to their frequency. We propose the following contributions:

- Application of BERT's contextualised embeddings to the task of XML classification, including the exploration of linear, attention based and recurrent classifiers. To the best of our knowledge, this work is the first to apply a pretrained BERT model combined with a recurrent network to the XML classification task.

[1] The task of multi-label classification differs from multi-class classification in that labels are not exclusive, which enables the assignment of several labels to the same article, making the problem even harder [10].

- Empirical comparison of a simple one-vs.-rest SVM approach with a more complex model combining a recurrent classifier and BERT embeddings.
- An ensemble of the previous individual methods using SVM-rank, which was capable of outperforming them.

2 Related Work

Currently, there are two main approaches to XML: embedding based methods and tree based methods.

Embedding based methods deal with the problem of high dimensional feature and label vectors by projecting them onto a lower dimensional space [8,13]. During prediction, the compressed representation is projected back onto the space of high dimensional labels. This information bottleneck can often reduce noise and allow for a way of regularising the problem. Although very efficient and fast, this approach assumes that the low-dimensional space is capable of encoding most of the original information. For real world problems, this assumption is often too restrictive and may result in decreased performance.

Tree based approaches intend to learn a hierarchy of features or labels from the training set [14,15]. Typically, a root node is initialised with the complete set of labels and its children nodes are recursively partitioned until all the leaf nodes contain a small number of labels. During prediction, each article is passed along the tree and the path towards its final leaf node defines the predicted set of labels. These methods tend to be slower than embedding based methods but achieve better performance. However, if a partitioning error is made near the top of the tree, its consequences are propagated to the lower levels.

Furthermore, other methods should be referred due to their simple approach capable of achieving competitive results. Among these, DiSMEC [10] should be highlighted because it follows a one-vs.-rest approach which simply learns a weight vector for each label. The multiplication of such weight vector with the data point feature vector yields a score that allows the classification of the label. Another simple approach consists of performing a set of random projections from the feature space towards a lower dimension space where, for each test data point, a k-nearest neighbours algorithm performs a weighted propagation of the neighbour's labels, based on their similarity [16].

We propose two new approaches which are substantially distinct from the ones discussed above. The first one uses a search engine based on inverted indexing and the second leverages BERT's contextualised embeddings combined with either a linear or recurrent layer.

3 XML Classification Models

We explore the performance of a one-vs.-rest SVM model in Sect. 3.1, and a customised search engine (Priberam Search) in Sect. 3.2. We further experiment with several classifiers leveraging BERT's contextualised embeddings in Sect. 3.3. In the end we aggregate the predictions of all of these individual models using a SVM-Rank algorithm in Sect. 3.4.

3.1 Support Vector Machine

Our first baseline consists of a simple Support Vector Machine (SVM) using a one-vs.-rest strategy. We train an independent SVM classifier for each possible label. To reduce the burden of computation we only consider labels with frequency above a given threshold f_{min}. Each classifier weight $\boldsymbol{w} \in \mathbb{R}^d$ measures the importance assigned to each feature representation of a given article and it is trained to optimise the max-margin loss of the support vectors and the hyper plane [3]:

$$\min_{\boldsymbol{w}} \frac{1}{2}\boldsymbol{w}\boldsymbol{w}^T + C\sum_{i=1}^{l} \xi(\boldsymbol{w}; \boldsymbol{x}_i, y_i) \qquad (1)$$
$$\text{s.t. } y_i(\boldsymbol{w}^\top \boldsymbol{x}_i + \boldsymbol{b} \geq 1 - \xi_i)$$

where $(\boldsymbol{x}_i, y_i)$ are the article-label pairs, C is the regularisation parameter, $\boldsymbol{b}$ is a bias term and ξ corresponds to a slack function used to penalise incorrectly classified points and $\boldsymbol{w}$ is the vector normal to the decision hyper-plane. We used the abstract's term frequency–inverse document frequency (tf-idf) as features to represent $\boldsymbol{x}_i$.

3.2 Priberam Search

The second model consists of a customised search engine, Priberam Search, based on inverted indexing and retrieval using the Okapi-BM25 algorithm [4].

As depicted in Fig. 1, it uses an additional k-nearest neighbours algorithm (k-NN) to obtain the set of k indexed articles closest to a query article in feature space over a database of all articles $\mathcal{A}$. This similarity is based on the frequency of words, lemmas and root-words, as well as label semantics and synonyms. A score is then given to each one of these articles and to each one of their labels and label synonyms, and a weighted sum of these scores yields the final score assigned to each label, as explicit in expression 2.

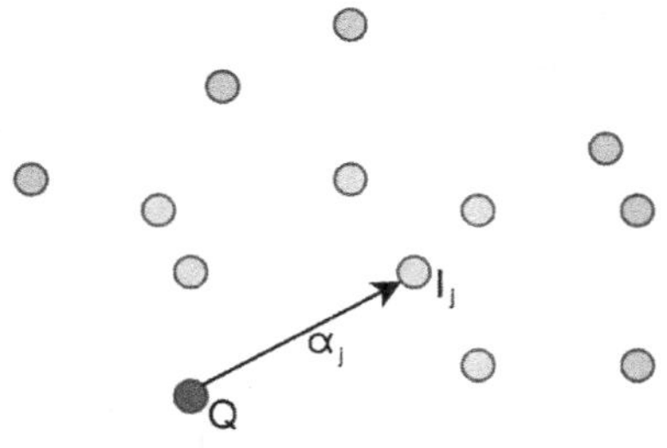

Fig. 1. K-NN to obtain K articles $I_j \forall j \in [K]$ closest to query article Q in feature space.

$$Score_{label\ i} = \sum_{j \in \mathcal{A}}^{K} \alpha_j \cdot \beta_{ji} \qquad (2)$$

α_j: score of neighbour article j
β_{ji}: score of label i for article j.

3.3 XML BERT Classifier

Language model pretraining has recently advanced the state of the art in several Natural Language Processing tasks, with the use of contextualised embeddings such as BERT, Bidirectional Encoder Representations from Transformers [5]. This model consists of 12 stacked transformer blocks and its pretraining is performed on a very large corpus following two tasks: next sentence prediction and masked language modelling. The nature of the pretraining tasks makes this model ideal for representing sentence information (given by the representation of the $[CLS]$ token added to the beginning of each sentence). After encoding a sentence with BERT, we apply different classifiers, and fine-tune the model to minimise a multi-label classification loss:

$$\text{BCELoss}(\boldsymbol{x}_i; \boldsymbol{y}_i) = y_{i,j} \log \sigma(x_{i,j}) + (1 - y_{i,j}) \log(1 - \sigma(x_{i,j})), \tag{3}$$

where $y_{i,j}$ denotes the binary value of label j of article i, which is 1 if it is present and 0 otherwise, $x_{i,j}$ represents the label predictions (logits) of article i and label j, and σ is the sigmoid function.

3.3.1 In-Domain Transfer Knowledge

Additionally, we performed an extra step of pretraining. Starting from the original weights obtained from BERT pretrained in Spanish, we further pretrained the model with a task of masked language modelling on the corpus composed by all the articles in the training set. This extra step results in more meaningful contextualised representations for this medical corpus, whose domain specific language might differ from the original pretraining corpora.

After this, we tested three different classifiers: a linear classifier in Sect. 3.3.2, a linear classifier with label attention in Sect. 3.3.3 and a recurrent classifier in Sect. 3.3.4.

3.3.2 XML BERT Linear Classifier

The first and simplest classifier consists of a linear layer which maps the sequence output (the 768 dimensional embedding corresponding to the $[CLS]$ token) to the label space, composed by 33702 dimensions corresponding to all the labels found in the training set. Such architecture is represented in Fig. 2. We minimise

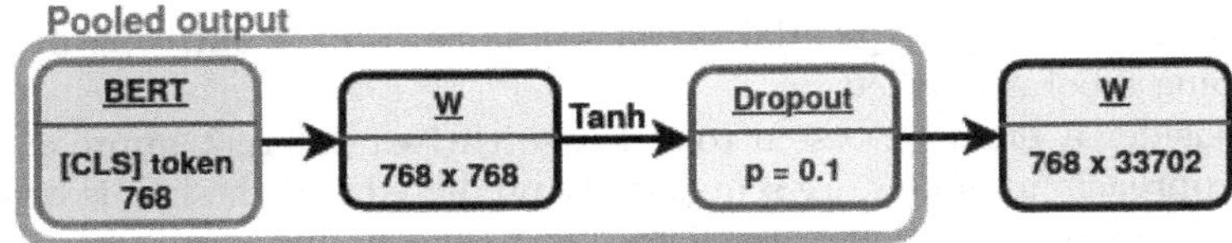

Fig. 2. XML BERT linear classifier: flowchart representing BERT's pooled output (in blue) and the simple linear layer (W in green) used as XML classifier. (Color figure online)

binary cross-entropy using sigmoid activation to allow for multiple active labels per instance, see Eq. 3. This classifier is hereafter designated LINEAR.

3.3.3 XML BERT with Label Attention

For the second classifier, we assume a continuous representation with 768 dimensions for each label. We initialise the label embeddings as the pooled output embeddings (corresponding to the $[CLS]$ token) of a BERT model whose inputs were the string descriptors and synonyms for each label. We consider a key-query-value attention mechanism [17], where the query corresponds to the pooled output of the abstract's contextualised representation and the keys and values correspond to the label embeddings. We further consider residual connections, and a final linear layer maps these results to the decision space of 33702 labels using a linear classifier, as shown in Fig. 3. Once again, we choose a binary cross-entropy loss (Eq. 3). This classifier is hereafter designated LABEL ATTENTION.

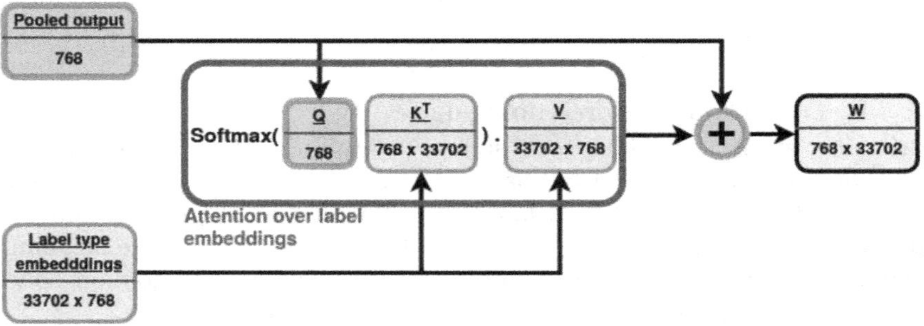

Fig. 3. XML BERT with label attention classifier: article's pooled output (blue) is followed by an extra step of attention over the label embeddings (red) which are finally mapped to a XML linear classifier over labels (green). (Color figure online)

3.3.4 XML BERT with Gated Recurrent Unit

In the last classifier, we predict the article's labels sequentially. Before the last linear classifier used to project the final representation onto the label space, we add a Gated Recurrent Unit (GRU) network [18] with 768 units that sequentially predicts each label according to label frequency. A flowchart of the architecture is shown in Fig. 4. This sequential prediction is performed until the prediction of a stopping label is reached.

We consider a binary cross-entropy loss with two different approaches. On the first approach, all labels are sequentially predicted and the loss is computed only after the stopping label is predicted, i.e., the loss value is independent of the order in which the labels are predicted. It only takes into account the final set. This loss is denominated Bag of Labels loss (BOLL) and it is given by:

$$\mathcal{L}_{BOLL} = \text{BCELoss}(\boldsymbol{x}_i; \boldsymbol{y}_i) \tag{4}$$

where $\boldsymbol{x}_i$ and $\boldsymbol{y}_i$ are the total set of predicted logits and gold labels for the current article i, correspondingly. The models trained with this loss are hereafter designated GRU BOLL.

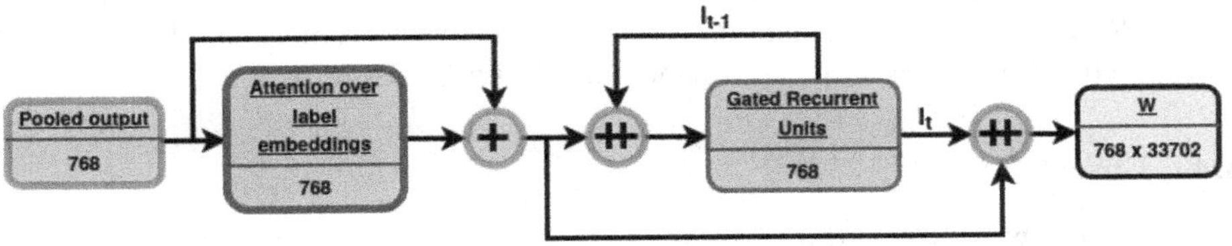

Fig. 4. XML BERT GRU classifier: the GRU network precedes the linear layer and sequentially predicts the labels. The symbol ++ stands for vector concatenation and l_t the label representation predicted by the GRU at time-step t.

The second approach uses an iterative loss which is computed at each step of the sequential prediction of labels. We compare each predicted label with the gold label, the loss is computed and added to a running loss value. In this case, the loss is denominated Iterative Label loss (ILL):

$$\mathcal{L}_{ILL} = \sum_{t \in T} \text{BCELoss}(\boldsymbol{x}_i^{(t)}; \boldsymbol{y}_i^{(t)}) \tag{5}$$

where T is the length of the label sequence, t denotes the time-steps taken by the GRU until the "stop label" is predicted, and $\boldsymbol{x}_i^{(t)}$ and $\boldsymbol{y}_i^{(t)}$ are the predicted logits and gold labels for time-step t and article i, respectively. Models trained with this loss are hereafter designated GRU ILL.

Although only one of the losses accounts directly for prediction order, this factor is always relevant because it affects the final set of predicted labels. This way, the model must be trained and tested assuming a specific label ordering. For this work, we used two orders: ascending and descending label frequency on the training set, designated GRU ASCEND and GRU DESCEND, respectively.

Table 1. Example of predictions for a particular abstract using the masking system which enforces a descending label frequency.

Prediction order	Label	Frequency
0	adulto	54785
1	niño	26585
...	...	...
13	prevención de accidentes	349
14	STOP-label	–

Additionally, we developed a masking system to force the sequential prediction of labels according to the chosen frequency order. This means that at each step the output label set is reduced to all labels whose frequency falls bellow or above the previous label, depending on the monotonically ascending or descending order, respectively. Models in which such masking is used are designated GRU W/MASK. Table 1 shows an example of the consecutive predictions obtained for a given abstract throughout the various predictive time-steps.

3.4 Ensemble

Furthermore, we developed an ensemble model combining the results of the previously described SVM, Priberam Search and BERT with GRU models. This ensemble's main goal is to leverage the label scores yielded by these three individual models in order to make a more informed decision regarding the relevance of each label to the abstracts.

We chose an ensembling method based on a SVM-rank algorithm [6] whose features are the normalised scores yielded by the three individual models, as well as their pairwise product and full product. These scores are the distance to the hyper-plane in the SVM model, the k-nearest neighbours score for Priberam Search and the label probability for the BERT model. This approach is depicted on Fig. 5.

An SVM-rank is a variant of the support vector machine algorithm used to solve ranking problems [19]. It essentially leverages pair-wise ranking methods to sort and score results based on their relevance for a specific query. This algorithm optimises an analogous loss to the one shown in Eq. 1. Such ensemble is hereafter designated SVM-RANK ENSEMBLE.

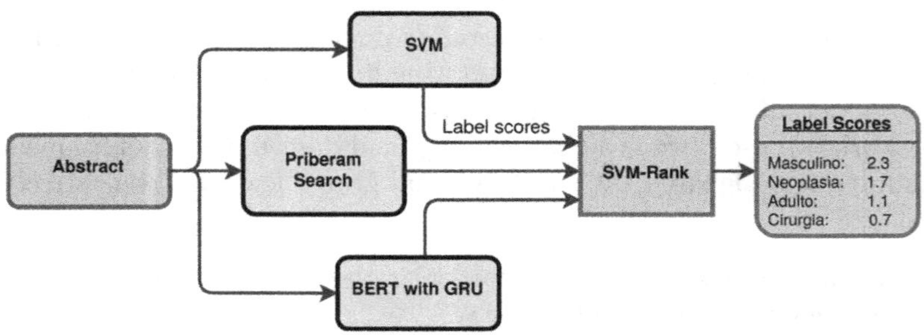

Fig. 5. SVM-Rank combines the three previous individual models.

4 Experimental Setup

We consider the training set provided for the MESINESP competition containing 318658 articles with at least one DeCS code and an average of 8.12 codes per article. We trained the individual models with 95% of this data. The remaining 5% were used to train the SVM-rank algorithm. The provided smaller official development set, with 750 samples, was used to fine-tune the individual model's and ensemble's hyper-parameters, while the test set, with 500 samples, was used for reporting final results. These two sets were manually annotated by experts specifically for the MESINESP task.

4.1 Support Vector Machine

For the SVM model we chose to ignore all labels that appeared in less than 20 abstracts. With this cutoff, we decrease the output label set size to ≈9200. Additionally, we use a linear kernel to reduce computation time and avoid over-fitting, which is critical to train such a large number of classifiers. Regarding regularisation, we obtained the best performance using a regularisation parameter set to $C = 1.0$, and a squared hinge slack function whose penalty over the misclassified data points is computed with an ℓ_2 distance.

Furthermore, to enable more control over the classification boundary, after solving the optimisation problem we moved the decision hyper-plane along the direction of $\boldsymbol{w}$. We empirically determined that a distance of -0.3 from its original position resulted in the best $\mu F1$ score. This model was implemented using scikit-learn[2] and the code was made publicly available[3].

4.2 Priberam Search

To use the Priberam Search Engine, we first indexed the training set taking into account the abstract text, title, complete set of gold DeCS codes, and also their corresponding string descriptors along with some synonyms provided[4]. We tuned the number of neighbours $k = [10, 20, 30, 40, 50, 60, 70, 100, 200]$ in the development set for the k-NN algorithm and obtained the best results for $k = 40$. To decide whether or not a label should be assigned to an article, we fine-tuned a score threshold over the interval $[0.1, 0.5]$ using the official development set, obtaining a best performing value of 0.24. All labels with score above the threshold were picked as correct labels.

4.3 BERT

For all types of BERT classifiers, we used the Transformers and PyTorch Python packages [20,21].

We initialised BERT's weights from its cased version pretrained on Spanish corpora, bert-base-spanish-wwm-cased[5].

---

[2] scikit-learn.org.
[3] github.com/Priberam/mesinesp-svm.
[4] https://temu.bsc.es/mesinesp/wp-content/uploads/2019/12/DeCS.2019.v5.tsv.zip.
[5] https://github.com/dccuchile/beto.

We further performed a pretraining step on the MESINESP dataset to obtain better in-domain embeddings. For the pretraining and classification task, Table 2 shows the training hyper-parameters.

For all the experiments with BERT, the complete set of DeCS codes was considered as the label set.

Table 2. Training hyper-parameters used for BERT's pretraining and classification tasks.

Hyper-parameter	Pretraining	Classification
Batch size	4	8
Learning rate	$5 \cdot 10^{-5}$	$2 \cdot 10^{-5}$
Warmup steps	0	4000
Max seq lenght	512	512
Learning rate decay	–	Linear
Dropout probability	0.1	0.1

4.4 Ensemble

Our ensemble model aggregates the prediction of all the individual models and produces a final predicted label set for each abstract. To improve recall we lowered the score thresholds used for each individual model until the value for which the average number of predicted labels per abstract was approximately double the average number of gold labels. This ensured that the SVM-rank algorithm was trained with a balanced set, and it also resulted in a system in which the individual models have very high recall and the ensemble model is responsible for precision.

We trained the SVM-rank model with the 5% hold-out data of the training set. This algorithm returns a score for each label in each abstract, making it necessary to define a threshold for classification. This threshold was fine-tuned over the interval $[-0.5, 0.5]$ using the official MESINESP development set, yielding a best performing cut-off score of -0.0233.

We also fine-tuned the regularisation parameter, C. We experimented the values $C = [0.01, 0.1, 0.5, 1, 5, 10]$ obtaining the best performance for $C = 0.1$. The current model was implemented using a Python wrapper for the dlib C++ toolkit [22].

5 Results

Table 3 shows the μ-precision, μ-recall and μ-F1 metrics for the best performing models described above, evaluated on both the official development and test sets.

The comparison between the scores obtained for the one-vs.-rest SVM and Priberam Search models shows that the SVM outperforms the k-NN based Priberam Search in terms of μF1, which is mostly due to its higher recall. Note that, although not ideal for multi-label problems, the one-vs.-rest strategy for the SVM model was able to achieve a relatively good performance, even with a significantly reduced label set.

Table 3. Micro precision (μP), micro recall (μR) and micro F1 (μF1) obtained with the 4 submitted models for both the development and test sets. For each metric, the best performing model is identified in bold.

Model	Development set			Test set		
	μP	μR	μF1	μP	μR	μF1
SVM	0.4216	0.3740	0.3964	0.4183	**0.3789**	0.3976
PRIBERAM SEARCH	0.4471	0.3017	0.3603	0.4571	0.2700	0.3395
BERT-GRU BOLL ASCEND	0.4130	**0.3823**	0.3971	0.4293	0.3314	0.3740
SVM-RANK ENSEMBLE	**0.5056**	0.3456	**0.4105**	**0.5336**	0.3320	**0.4093**

Table 4 shows the performance of several classifiers used with BERT. Note that, for these models, in order to save time and computational resources some tests were stopped before achieving their maximum performance, allowing nonetheless comparison with other models.

We trained linear classifiers using the BERT model with pretraining on the MESINESP corpus for 660k steps ($\approx$19 epochs) and without such pretraining (marked with *). Results show that, even with an under-trained classifier, such pretraining is already advantageous. This pretraining was employed for all models combining BERT embeddings with a GRU classifier. The label-attentive Bert model (GRU BOLL ascend) shows negligible impact on performance when compared with the simple linear classifier (LINEAR).

We consider three varying architectures of the BERT-GRU model: Bag of Labels loss (BOLL) or Iterative Label loss (ILL), ascending or descending label frequency, and usage or not of masking. Taking into account the best score achieved, the BOLL loss performs better than the ILL loss, even with a smaller number of training steps. For this BOLL loss, it is also evident that the ordering of labels with ascending frequency outperforms the opposite order, and that masking results in decreased performance.

On the other hand, for the ILL loss, masking improves the achieved score and the ordering of labels with descending frequency shows better results. The best classifier for a BERT-based model is the GRU network trained with a Bag of Labels loss and with labels provided in ascending frequency order (GRU BOLL ASCEND). This model was further trained for a total of 28 epochs resulting in a μF1 = 0.4918 on the 5% hold-out of the training set. It is important to notice the performance drop from the 5% hold-out data to the official development set.

This drop is likely a result of the mismatch between the annotation methods used in the two sets, given that the development set was specifically manually annotated for this task.

Table 4. μF1 metric evaluated for the 5% hold-out of the training set. All models have been pretrained on the MESINESP corpus, except for those duly marked. BOLL: Bag of Labels loss. ILL: Iterative Label loss. *****: not pretrained on MESINESP corpus. **†**: training stopped before maximum μF1 was reached.

BERT classifier	Training steps	μF1
LINEAR*	220k	0.4476
LINEAR	250k†	0.4504
LABEL ATTENTION*	700k	0.4460
GRU BOLL ASCEND	80k	**0.4759**
GRU BOLL DESCEND	40k	0.4655
GRU BOLL ASCEND W/MASK	100k†	0.4352
GRU ILL DESCEND	240k†	0.4258
GRU ILL DESCEND W/MASK	240k†	0.4526
GRU ILL ASCEND W/MASK	240k†	0.4459

Surprisingly, the BERT based model shows worse performance than the SVM on the test set. Despite their very similar μF1 scores for the development set, the BERT-GRU model suffered a considerable performance drop from the development to the test set due to a decrease in recall. This might indicate some over-fitting of hyper-parameters and a possible mismatch between these two expert annotated sets.

Additionally, as made explicit in Table 3, the ensemble combining the results of the SVM, Priberam Search and the best performing BERT based classifier achieved the best performance on the development set, outperforming all the individual models.

Finally, Table 5 shows additional classification metrics for each one of the submitted systems, as well as their rank within the MESINESP task. The analysis of such results makes clear that for the three considered averages (Micro, Macro and per sample), the SVM model shows the best recall score. For most of the remaining metrics, the SVM-rank ensemble is able to leverage the capabilities of the individual models and achieve considerable performance gains, particularly noticeable for the precision scores.

Table 5. Micro (μ), macro (Ma) and per sample (Eb) averages of the precision, recall and F1 scores, followed by score position within the MESINESP task. For each metric, the best performing model is identified in bold.

Metric	SVM	PRIBERAM SEARCH	BERT-GRUBOLL ASCEND	SVM-RANK ENSEMBLE
μF1	0.3976 (7°)	0.3395 (13°)	0.3740 (9°)	**0.4093 (6°)**
μP	0.4183 (17°)	0.4571 (10°)	0.4293 (15°)	**0.5336 (6°)**
μR	**0.3789 (6°)**	0.2700 (13°)	0.3314 (8°)	0.3320 (7°)
MaF1	**0.4183 (8°)**	0.1776 (13°)	0.2009 (11°)	0.2115 (10°)
MaP	0.4602 (9°)	0.4971 (8°)	0.4277 (11°)	**0.5944 (3°)**
MaR	**0.2609 (8°)**	0.1742 (16°)	0.2002 (11°)	0.2024 (10°)
EbF1	0.3976 (7°)	0.3393 (13°)	0.3678 (9°)	**0.4031 (6°)**
EbP	0.4451 (15°)	0.4582 (12°)	0.4477 (14°)	**0.5465 (3°)**
EbR	**0.3904 (6°)**	0.2824 (13°)	0.3463 (8°)	0.3452 (8°)

6 Conclusions

This paper introduces three type of extreme multi label classifiers: an SVM, a k-NN based search engine and a series of BERT-based classifiers. Our one-vs.-rest SVM model shows the best performance on all recall metrics. We further provide an empirical comparison of different variants of multi-label BERT-based classifiers, where the Gated Recurrent Unit network with the Bag of Labels loss shows the best results. This model yields slightly better results than the SVM model on the development set, however, due to a drop in recall, under-performs it on the test set. Finally, the SVM-rank ensemble is able to leverage the label scores yielded by the three individual models and combine them into a final ranking model with a precision gain on all metrics, capable of achieving the highest μF1 score (being the 6-th best model in the task).

Acknowledgements. This work is supported by the Lisbon Regional Operational Programme (Lisboa 2020), under the Portugal 2020 Partnership Agreement, through the European Regional Development Fund (ERDF), within project TRAINER (N° 045347).

References

1. Yi, X., Allan, J.: A comparative study of utilizing topic models for information retrieval. In: Boughanem, M., Berrut, C., Mothe, J., Soule-Dupuy, C. (eds.) ECIR 2009. LNCS, vol. 5478, pp. 29–41. Springer, Heidelberg (2009). https://doi.org/10.1007/978-3-642-00958-7_6
2. Shen, Y., Yu, H.F., Sanghavi, S., Dhillon, I.: Extreme multi-label classification from aggregated labels. arXiv preprint arXiv:2004.00198 (2020)
3. Fan, R.E., Chang, K.W., Hsieh, C.J., Wang, X.R., Lin, C.J.: LIBLINEAR: a library for large linear classification. J. Mach. Learn. Res. **9**, 1871–1874 (2008)
4. Miranda, S., et al.: Automated fact checking in the news room. In: The World Wide Web Conference (2019)

5. Devlin, J., Chang, M., Lee, K., Toutanova, K.: BERT: pretraining of deep bidirectional transformers for language understanding. In: Proceedings of the 2019 Conference of the North American Chapter of the Association for Computational Linguistics (2019)
6. Joachims, T.: Optimizing search engines using clickthrough data. In: Proceedings of the Eighth ACM SIGKDD International Conference on Knowledge Discovery and Data Mining (2002)
7. Garba, S., Ahmed, A., Mai, A., Makama, G., Odigie, V.: Proliferations of scientific medical journals: a burden or a blessing. Oman Med. J. **25**(4), 311 (2010)
8. Zhang, W., Yan, J., Wang, X., Zha, H.: Deep extreme multi-label learning. In: Proceedings of the 2018 ACM on International Conference on Multimedia Retrieval (2018)
9. VHL Network Portal. Red.bvsalud.org (2020). Decs. http://red.bvsalud.org/decs/en/about-decs/ Accessed 2 May 2020
10. Babbar, R., Schölkopf, B.: DiSMEC: distributed sparse machines for extreme multi-label classification. In: Proceedings of the Tenth ACM International Conference on Web Search and Data Mining (2017)
11. Lee, J., et al.: BioBERT: a pre-trained biomedical language representation model for biomedical text mining. Bioinformatics **36**, 1234–1240 (2020)
12. Alsentzer, E., et al.: Publicly available clinical BERT embeddings. arXiv preprint arXiv:1904.03323 (2019)
13. Tai, F., Lin, H.T.: Multilabel classification with principal label space transformation. Neural Comput. **24**, 2508–2542 (2012)
14. Prabhu, Y., Varma, M.: FastXML: a fast, accurate and stable tree-classifier for extreme multi-label learning. In: Proceedings of the 20th ACM SIGKDD International Conference on Knowledge Discovery and Data Mining (2014)
15. Agrawal, R., Gupta, A., Prabhu, Y., Varma, M.: Multi-label learning with millions of labels: recommending advertiser bid phrases for web pages. In: Proceedings of the 22nd International Conference on World Wide Web (2013)
16. Verma, Y.: An embarrassingly simple baseline for eXtreme multi-label prediction. arXiv preprint arXiv:1912.08140 (2019)
17. Vaswani, A., et al.: Attention is all you need. In: Advances in Neural Information Processing Systems, pp. 5998–6008 (2017)
18. Cho, K., et al.: Learning phrase representations using RNN encoder–decoder for statistical machine translation. In: Proceedings of the 2014 Conference on Empirical Methods in Natural Language Processing (2014)
19. Liu, T.Y.: Learning to Rank for Information Retrieval. Springer, Heidelberg (2011). https://doi.org/10.1007/978-3-642-14267-3
20. Wolf, T., et al.: HuggingFace's transformers: state-of-the-art natural language processing. ArXiv (2019)
21. Paszke, A., et al.: PyTorch: an imperative style, high-performance deep learning library. Adv. Neural Inf. Process. Syst. **32**, 8024–8035 (2019)
22. King, D.E.: Dlib-ml: a machine learning toolkit. J. Mach. Learn. Res. **10**, 1755–1758 (2009)

Herbarium-Field Triplet Network for Cross-Domain Plant Identification

Sophia Chulif and Yang Loong Chang(✉)

Department of Artificial Intelligence, NEUON AI,
94300 Kota Samarahan, Sarawak, Malaysia
{sophiadouglas,yangloong}@neuon.ai
https://neuon.ai/

Abstract. This paper presents the implementation and performance of a Herbarium-Field Triplet Loss Network to evaluate the herbarium-field similarity of plants which corresponds to the cross-domain plant identification challenge in PlantCLEF 2020. The challenge was designed to assess the use of digitized herbarium specimens on the automated plant identification of data deficient flora. The training data consisted of mainly herbarium images, while the test images were solely photos taken in the field. We trained a two-streamed triplet loss network to maximize the embedding distance of different plant species and at the same time minimize the embedding distance of the same plant species given herbarium-field pairs. The objective is to bring the embedding distance of the same herbarium-field pair closer together while moving the embedding distance of different herbarium-field pairs apart. We achieved a similar result in the test sets regardless of whether the species has many or very few field training data. We obtained a Mean Reciprocal Rank (MRR) of 0.121 on the whole test set and an MRR of 0.108 on the subset of species with fewer field training images, or in other words, rare species. Our main contribution is designing a triplet network for plant recognition based on herbarium-field pairs, which were empirically proven to be more effective in classifying species with fewer or no herbarium-field pairs.

Keywords: Cross-domain plant identification · Computer vision · Triplet loss · Convolutional neural networks

1 Introduction

Herbaria specimens have been used by novices and experts alike to study and confirm plant species, in addition to many other beneficial applications as described in [6]. Many works are being carried out to improve the access and preservation of these specimens, as they are considerably less expensive to

K. S. Candan et al. (Eds.): CLEF 2021, LNCS 12880, pp. 173–188, 2021.
https://doi.org/10.1007/978-3-030-85251-1_14

obtain than acquiring new field images. Despite the vast collection of herbaria, the detection and extraction of herbarium specimen characteristics require more research [23].

The PlantCLEF 2020 challenge was designed to assess to what extend automated identification of data-deficient Flora can be improved by using herbarium specimens [9]. In this paper, we present our approach using a two-streamed network, namely the Herbarium-Field Triplet Loss Network. It evaluates the similarity between digitized herbarium specimens and field pictures (herbarium-field pairs).

We adopt the triplet loss function to optimize the plant embeddings, which regulate the measure of plant similarity. The implemented network is trained to maximize the embedding distance of different herbarium-field species pairs and minimize the embedding distance of the same species pairs. It learns the similarity between herbarium sheets and field pictures instead of directly classifying plant species as conventional convolutional neural networks (CNN) [17].

Our main contribution is designing a triplet network for plant recognition based on herbarium-field pairs, which were empirically proven to be more effective in classifying species with fewer or no herbarium-field pairs.

2 Related Works

Past Challenges. The plant identification challenge was first introduced in 2011 with 71 tree species from the French Mediterranean area [10]. The amount of data gradually increased in the following years, along with the plant type included. The plant type extended to not only tree species but also herbs [11] and fern species [12]. From 2014 onwards, the test evaluation is observation-based with different views of the same plant, instead of a single-image identification. Consequently, participants can employ algorithms that model plants of various plant organ parts to give a unified prediction to increase the confidence in recognition. Finally, in 2015, the number of species introduced was increased to 1,000 classes [13]. This milestone increased the challenge's viability to employ large-scale machine learning solutions using deep learning [17], which brought about a paradigm shift in computer vision in early 2012. In the year 2016, all of the participants adopted a deep learning-based solution [7] and gave promising results. Coming to the year 2019, the focus of the challenge shifted to 10,000 species of Flora from the Guiana shield and the Amazon rainforest [8]. In this challenge, the participants' solutions were compared with human experts on Top-1 accuracy. The challenge results showed that some of the methods even surpassed the experts' results [5,19].

In 2020, the challenge introduced a new problem statement where the participants were required to identify plant species with limited field images or even no field images in the training dataset. In the absence of field images, these species were provided with a herbarium collection. The participants were expected to make use of the herbarium sheets to infer the correct species. Our proposed solution [4] managed to achieve a Mean Reciprocal Rank (MRR) of 0.121 for the whole test set (1st runner up) and 0.108 for difficult species (1st place) [9].

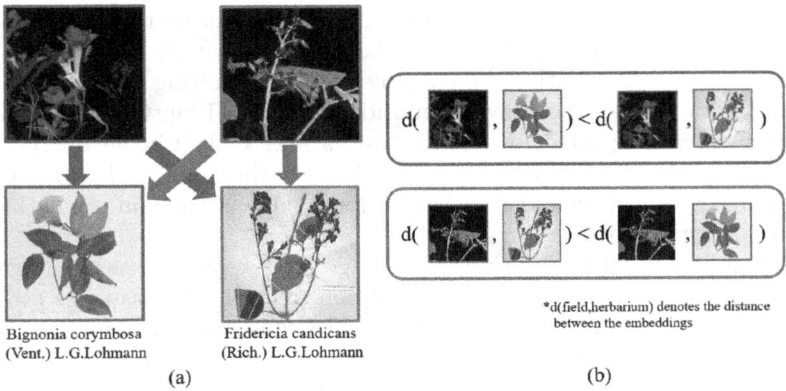

Fig. 1. The triplet loss concept mainly revolves around minimizing the distances between the same class and maximizing the distances between different classes. (a) shows two classes with its herbarium counterpart, the image embedding is compared with its own herbarium and the herbarium from another class (as indicated by the arrows). (b) The distances between herbarium-field pairs of the same species have to be less than the herbarium-field pairs of different species (red and blue box denotes the class label). (Color figure online)

FaceNet: A Unified Embedding for Face Recognition and Clustering. The authors in [21] introduce the triplet loss function that uses a CNN to optimize face embeddings, which correspond to a measure of face similarity. Instead of training an intermediate layer, the embeddings are directly optimized in the Euclidean space for face verification. Likewise, this triplet loss function is adopted in our networks to learn the optimized plant embeddings.

Plant Disease Recognition with Siamese Network. The authors in [2] introduce Few-Shot Learning algorithms that classify leaf images with deep learning. They employ Siamese Network with triplet loss that shows the possibility of achieving high accuracy with small datasets. In addition, the authors in [3] address the classification problem using real-world images. They also show that the image embeddings extracted from the employed Siamese Network are better than using transfer learning. In the same way, we employed a two-streamed triplet loss network which works similarly to classify plants utilizing the herbarium and field embeddings.

3 Methodology

3.1 Motivation

Conventional plant species identification [8] presents a straightforward, data-driven object classification problem, whereby input data are mapped with their labels by a learned feature that is most representative of their respective class. However, these mappings are based on the assumption that the training data have similar input distributions (input tensors) to the testing data, as in actual real-world data. Unlike the conventional identification, PlantCLEF 2020 introduced a classification problem where the test data were plant image queries (field pictures) while the training data are primarily herbarium images. In other words, the challenge revolved around transferring knowledge learned on the herbarium sheets to identify plant field images.

Although some of the herbarium-field image pairs were given as training data, not all of the classes had valid pairs in addition to the limited samples available in the dataset. With this in mind, class-to-class mapping becomes less reliable for plant species that do not have valid field images present in the dataset. Hence, our proposed network approaches the problem by designing a network that could focus on modeling features that are common between herbarium-field image pairs regardless of their labels.

Our proposed solution is inspired by the triplet network architecture [21] in the face recognition domain. With a limited training dataset, the triplet network aims to tackle face recognition of a presumably endless number of face identities. This problem shares a similar issue in the lack of specific class-to-class mapping. It is close to an open-set problem where more labels and classes are expected to be present even after the recognition model is produced.

The core concept of the triplet network is to present the machine with a triplets sample, whereby two samples share the same label and one sample having a different label. The machine is then required to minimize the feature distance between the identical label samples and maximize the feature distances otherwise.

3.2 Network Architecture

This section describes our approach in PlantCLEF 2020, the implemented network architecture, and the training stages involved. The training process is split into three stages: pre-trained herbarium network, pre-trained field network, and two-stream triplet loss network. The Herbarium and Field networks are trained individually to construct networks that could model generalized herbarium and field features. A triplet network is then employed to model the triplet distance between herbarium and field features. The objective is to train the network to behave: (i) herbarium features (or embeddings) of a species should be closer to the field features of the same class, (ii) herbarium features of a species should be further from field features of a different class. Figure 1 illustrates the concept of triplets learning for herbarium-field pairs.

The network architecture implemented in our approach is illustrated in Fig. 2. This Herbarium-Field triplet loss network is constructed with two Inception-v4 CNNs [22], namely Herbarium CNN and Field CNN which were initialized with weights pre-trained on PlantCLEF 2020 [9] and PlantCLEF 2017 [15] respectively. Both networks are formed to cater to the generalization of herbarium and

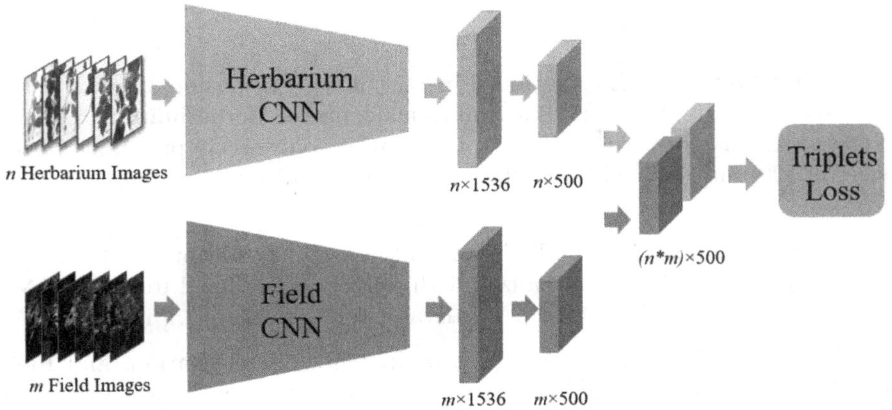

Fig. 2. Network architecture of the Herbarium-Field triplet loss network.

field features. At the final embedding layer of each network, a batch normalization layer is added and the output is fed into a fully-connected layer. The output size of the fully-connected layer is then reduced from 1536 to 500. Subsequently, these outputs are L2-normalized in the L2 layer and concatenated to give an output size of $(n * m) \times 500$ whereby n and m is the batch size of the Herbarium and Field networks respectively. This concatenated embedding is later passed into the triplet loss layer[1] through which the network learns to compute the herbarium and field embeddings with respective to their optimum embedding space. The network is trained to maximize the embedding distance of different species in herbarium-field pairs and minimize the embedding distance otherwise. The classification of species is dependent on the computed embedding space by which a large embedding distance denotes different species and a small embedding distance indicates the same species. There are two types of training methods investigated, i.e., frozen front layers and non-frozen front layers.

Frozen Front Layers. In this method, the front layers of the pre-trained Herbarium and Field network, or simply the extractor layer of the network, are frozen. So this allows only the weights in the newly added layer (triplet loss layer) to be updated.

Non-Frozen Layers. This method, on the other hand, trains all layers in the network. It allows the network to relearn and recompute the embeddings of herbarium and field images to their optimized embedding space from the triplet loss. The new layers are set to have a higher learning rate than the migrated layers.

[1] The triplet loss is computed using triplet_semihard_loss function provided in Tensorflow 1.13 [1].

3.3 Training Stages

Herbarium Network. As mentioned in Sect. 3.2, a Herbarium network based on the Inception-v4 model [22] is set up to make up the Herbarium-Field triplet loss network. The Herbarium network is initialized on weights pre-trained from ImageNet [20] and trained with PlantCLEF 2020 dataset (herbarium images) [9].

Field Network. Likewise, the Field network adopts the Inception-v4 [22] network architecture. It is also initialized with weights pre-trained from ImageNet [20] but trained with PlantCLEF 2017 dataset (field images) [15] instead.

Herbarium-Field Triplet Loss Network. Once the Herbarium and Field networks are trained, the Herbarium-Field triplet loss network is set up. The network is trained with PlantCLEF 2020 dataset [9] consisting of both herbarium and field images. The network trained in the Non-Frozen Layers setup is set with a learning rate of 0.00001 in the migrated layers and 0.0001 in the newly added layers, whereas the Frozen Front Layers setup is set with a learning rate of zero in the migrated layers.

4 Training Setup

4.1 Data Preparation

As mentioned in the task description, only a subset of species for field images was provided to allow learning a mapping between the herbarium and field domain. We separated the species which possess both herbarium and field images to be used for mapping. Out of 997 classes, 435 classes were identified having both herbarium and field images. These classes were then used for training. Although the total number of classes was reduced from 997 to 435 species, the network was still trained to map the embedding space of 997 classes.

During the training of the Herbarium-Field triplet loss network, the images used for each batch were picked to be balanced for each class. For instance, in a batch of size 16, each class may not comprise more than 4 images, meanwhile, the minimum number of images in each class is 2. This allows a balanced selection of anchors for the triplet loss.

4.2 Data Augmentation

To increase the network generalization and training sample size, data augmentation was applied on the training images. Random cropping, horizontal flipping and colour distortion (brightness, saturation, hue, and contrast) of images were performed on the training dataset. As a result, features and various transforms that are invariant to their original locations can be learned by the network, consequently reducing the likelihood of overfitting [18].

Table 1. Training dataset distribution for different networks.

Network	Number of images		Number of classes	
	Herbarium	Field	Herbarium	Field
Herbarium	305,531	–	997	–
Field	–	1,187,484	–	10,000
Herbarium-Field Triplet Loss	197,552	6,257	435	435

Table 2. Network training parameters.

Parameter	Herbarium and field network	Herbarium-Field triplet loss network
Batch size	256	16
Input image size	$299 \times 299 \times 3$	$299 \times 299 \times 3$
Optimizer	Adam optimizer [16]	Adam optimizer [16]
Initial learning rate	0.0001	0.0001
Weight decay	0.00004	0.00004
Loss function	Softmax cross entropy	Triplet loss

4.3 Training Dataset and Hyperparameters

The training dataset distributions and network setup parameters are summarized in Table 1 and Table 2 respectively.

4.4 Triplet Pairs Selection

For the network to yield better performance, it is wise to choose a hard sample for the network to learn instead of easy pairs [14]. For example, species within the same genus tend to look alike, which makes it difficult to differentiate between them, resulting in a difficult pair. Such a setting would drive the network to learn intra-species variation better. This strategy is employed as part of the optimization in Network 6 in Sect. 5.3.

5 Experiments

The experiments were conducted using Tensorflow 1.13 [1] alongside slim packages. The codes are available at https://github.com/NeuonAI/plantclef2020_challenge.

5.1 Dataset

Due to the limited field training samples, prior to training, a sample of images from each of the "herbarium_photo_associations" and "photo" folders was randomly segregated for validation purposes. 1,219 field images were separated from

Table 3. Dataset of experimented Herbarium-Field triplet loss network.

Network	Herbarium		Field	
Dataset	Train	Test	Train	Test
Number of images	153,867	43,685	5,038	1,219
Number of classes present	435	434	435	345

the test set leaving behind 5,038 field images for training instead of 6,257 as stated in Table 1. The number of images and classes present in the experimented training and testing dataset are summarized in Table 3. Nevertheless, the class number for the Herbarium-Field triplet loss network remains 997 and 10,000 in the Herbarium and Field network stream, respectively.

5.2 Inference Procedure

Herbarium Dictionary
For inference, the embeddings from 997 herbarium classes were first extracted using the trained Herbarium-Field triplet loss network to form the reference embeddings served as a herbarium dictionary. Random samples from each class were picked and fed into the network to obtain the embeddings. The extracted embeddings were then averaged to get a single embedding representation for each class. The embedding for each class was subsequently saved as a dictionary.

Note that the extraction was done with two different types of image cropping, namely, *Center Crop* and *Center and Corner Crop*. The *Center Crop* approach crops the center region of the herbarium sample. Meanwhile, the *Corner Crop* approach crops the top-left, top-right, bottom-left, and bottom-right regions of the herbarium sample. Each region was cropped and resized then passed into the network for the extraction of herbarium embeddings. The process of herbarium dictionary generation is illustrated in Fig. 3.

Feature Similarity
After obtaining the single embedding representation of each class, the saved dictionary is then used to compare the embedding distance between the 997 herbarium representation and the test image. During validation, *Center and Corner Crop* were also applied together with a horizontal flip in obtaining the test images' embeddings. This resulted in 10 different variations for each image which was then averaged to obtain their similarity probability. Cosine similarity was used as the distance metric in measuring the embedding similarity. Then, the cosine distance was obtained by subtracting the cosine similarity from 1. Finally, inverse distance weighting was performed on the cosine distance to obtain the probabilities of each class. The comparison of feature similarity is illustrated in Fig. 4.

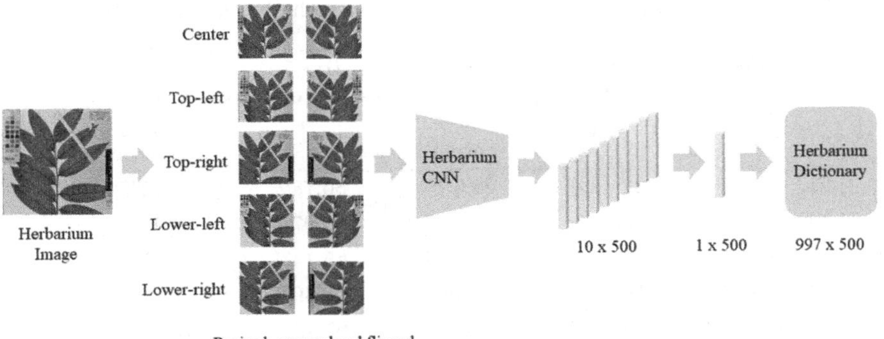

Fig. 3. Process of generating herbarium dictionary.

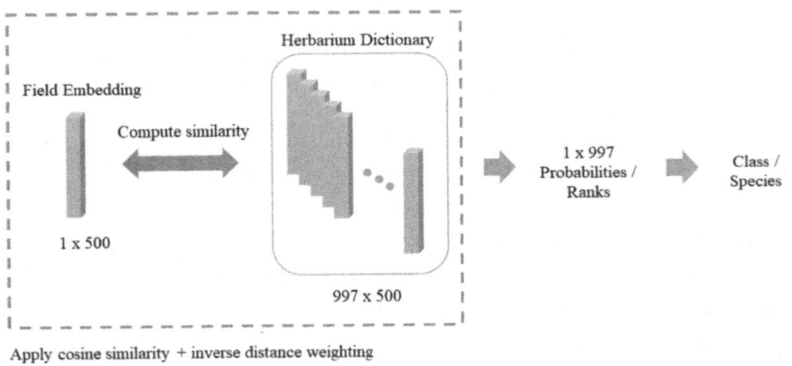

Fig. 4. Process of comparing feature similarity.

5.3 Network and Results

The experimented results are tabulated in Table 4 and Table 5 for *Center Crop* and *Center Crop and Corner Crop* herbarium extraction methods respectively. The networks were tested on the same validation set of 1,219 images in which the Top-1 and Top-5 predictions were evaluated. *Center Crop* and *Corner Crop* were also applied on the field test set before validation. **Five different Herbarium-Field triplet loss networks were experimented, i.e.:**

Network 1: Frozen Front Layers (FL). A network trained with frozen front layers.

Network 2: Non-Frozen Layers (NFL). A network trained with non-frozen layers, or to put simply, trained with all layers.

Table 4. Validation accuracy with *Center Crop* herbarium extraction.

Networks	Top 1 center crop	Top 1 center crop + corner crop	Top 5 center crop	Top 5 center crop + corner crop
FL	27.48%	28.63%	50.78%	52.42%
NFL	32.65%	32.73%	59.97%	58.98%
NFL-ENS	36.42%	37.33%	65.14%	67.51%
NFL-AUG	18.05%	18.46%	42.49%	42.49%
NFL-AUG-ENS	36.42%	7.33%	65.14%	67.51%
TRI-OPT	**58.33%**	**59.72%**	**76.29%**	**77.28%**

Table 5. Validation accuracy with *Center and Corner Crop* herbarium extraction.

Networks	Top 1 center crop	Top 1 center crop + corner crop	Top 5 center crop	Top 5 center crop + corner crop
FL	27.40%	29.20%	50.78%	52.17%
NFL	33.06%	34.29%	59.80%	58.98%
NFL-ENS	36.10%	37.57%	63.82%	6.45%
NFL-AUG	18.29%	18.79%	41.84%	42.74%
NFL-AUG-ENS	36.10%	37.57%	63.82%	66.45%
TRI-OPT	**59.36%**	**61.12%**	**76.37%**	**77.28%**

Network 3: Non-Frozen Layers Ensemble Model (NFL-ENS). A ensemble of 3 different models trained on all layers.

Network 4: Non-Frozen Layers Increased Augmentation (NFL-AUG). A network trained with all layers whereby the training images were pre-processed with more transformations and augmentation.

Network 5: Non-Frozen Layers Increased Augmentation Model Ensemble (NFL-AUG-ENS). An ensemble of Network 3 and Network 4.

Network 6: Triplet Network Optimized Model (TRI-OPT). An optimized network upon the post-PlantCLEF 2020 challenge. The changes were elongated training iteration, input sampling, and reconstruction of herbarium dictionary. This network was not included in any submission run in the 2020 challenge but will be included in the 2021 challenge.

5.4 Discussion

From the experiments, it can be seen that the NFL ensemble models performed the best among the networks. The ensemble of these networks increased the robustness of the system and returned better predictions. On the other hand, the FL network performed the worst among the networks. It can be suggested that the training of all layers does help the prediction model instead of freezing the front layers or extractor layers of the network. It can be seen that the ensemble models with increased augmentation performed equally as the ensemble model without increased augmentation. It can be suggested that the increased augmentation may not have produced enough new significant information for the network to learn. Since a portion of field images was separated from the training set to serve as a test set, some of the classes may miss some field information.

6 Submission

6.1 Inference Procedure

The procedure adopted to produce the submitted results are as follow:

(i) Construct herbarium dictionary by extracting samples of herbarium embeddings for all 997 plant species using the trained Herbarium-Field triplet loss network.
  (a) Apply *Center and Corner Crops* on the images before extraction.
  (b) Average the cropped herbarium embeddings for each species and save them.
(ii) Group the test images belonging to the same observation ID.
(iii) For each image under the same observation ID, apply *Center and Corner Crops* which result in 5 images each.
(iv) Subsequently flip the images horizontally resulting in 10 images each.
(v) Average the 10 images and pass them to the Herbarium-Field triplet loss network.
(vi) Obtain the image embeddings.
(vii) Compute cosine similarity between each of the extracted embeddings with the saved 997 herbarium embeddings.
(viii) Obtain cosine distance by subtracting the cosine similarity from the value of 1.
(ix) Apply inverse distance weighting on the cosine distance.
(x) Obtain the probabilities of the embedding distance.
(xi) Average the probabilities over the total number of images for each observation ID.
(xii) Repeat steps (iii) to (xii) for the remaining observation IDs.
(xiii) Collect the predictions, probabilities and ranks for each observation ID.

6.2 Submitted Runs

The team submitted a total of seven runs based on the networks mentioned in Sect. 5.3.

Run 1. This model was based on (FL). Unlike the rest of the runs, this network was trained with frozen front layers and does not apply image flipping during validation. Moreover, the embedding distances were normalized, inversed then applied with softmax to obtain the probabilities. In addition, the probabilities were based on the averaged embedding instead of all embeddings for each observation ID.

Run 2. This model was based on (NFL). Similar to Run 1, however, it was trained with all layers of the network, the embeddings of each observation IDs were averaged and then applied with Cosine Similarity and Inverse Distance Weighting to obtain the probabilities.

Run 3. This model was based on (NFL). Similar to Run 2, however, by using Cosine Similarity and Inverse Weighting, the probabilities of each embedding were first computed then averaged for each observation IDs.

Run 4. This model was based on (NFL). Similar to Run 3, however, the probabilities take into account the total embeddings of each observation IDs multiplied by their croppings which consist of 10 variations.

Run 5. This model was based on (NFL-ENS). Unlike Run 1 to 4, the network was trained together with the full dataset as stated in Table 1. It is also an ensemble of the predictions from 3 models of the same network.

Run 6. This model was based on (NFL-AUG). Similar to Run 5, which was trained with the full dataset, however, it is not an ensemble of models but trained with increased image processing transformations and augmentations.

Run 7 This model was based on (NFL-AUG-ENS). This run is the ensemble of the predictions from Run 5 and Run 6.

6.3 Submission Results

Our best-submitted runs scored an MRR of 0.121 and 0.108 for the first (whole test set) and second (a subset of test set) metrics, respectively. Our results are tabulated in Table 6. The results of all the participating teams are summarized in Fig. 5 and Fig. 6.

6.4 Discussion

Similar to the experiment results, the ensemble models performed the best among the networks. The ensemble model with increased augmentation, on the other hand, performed best in the whole test set. In addition, the MRR score of the

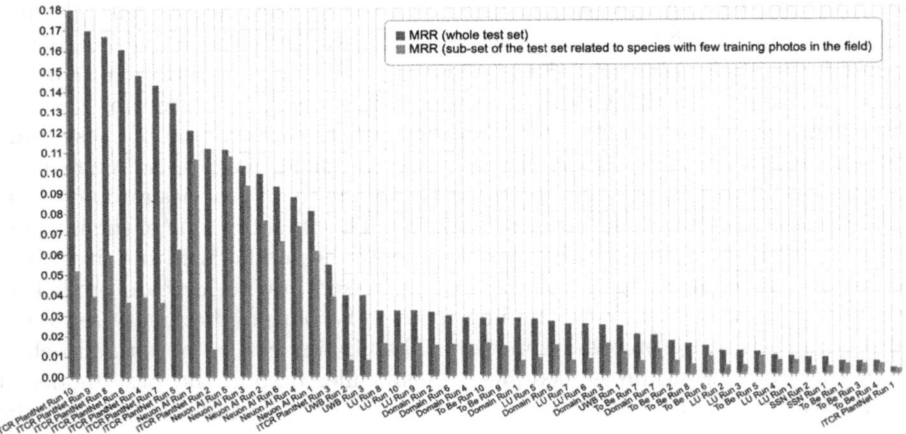

Fig. 5. Official results of PlantCLEF 2020.

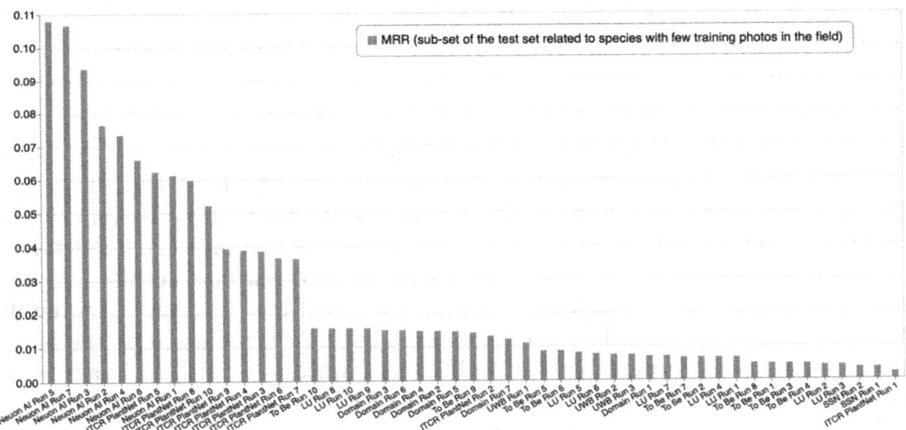

Fig. 6. Official results of PlantCLEF 2020 (second metric evaluation).

Table 6. MRR score of the submitted runs.

Run	MRR whole	MRR subset
7	**0.121**	0.107
5	0.111	**0.108**
3	0.103	0.094
2	0.099	0.076
6	0.093	0.066
4	0.088	0.073
1	0.081	0.061

networks for the first and second metrics are relatively close despite the few training photos in the subset species. It can be suggested that the number of training samples for each class does not directly influence the performance of the model. However, for triplet pairs to form a valid sample, each iteration requires three samples with at least a valid herbarium-field pairs. Some of these pairs are not present for some of the classes where the field image is missing in the training set. In our experiment, we can only train with 435 species instead of the full 997 classes provided due to this limitation. This might be one of the impacts on our current performance. For improvement, the methods in obtaining the herbarium embedding representation can be looked into to increase prediction accuracy. Such methods involve finding the best herbarium dictionary representation. Various image processing methods like flipping can be performed before extracting the herbarium embeddings. Meanwhile, finding the best model of the Herbarium-Field triplet loss network and using it for the extraction of the herbarium embeddings would be significant as well. Moreover, the use of taxonomy classes in training may improve the results. Since the species sharing the same genus and family may share common features, the species lacking field photos may be indirectly helped by species of the same genus or family. Therefore, the utilization of taxonomy during training could help improve the classification.

7 Conclusion

In this paper, we have presented our approach in PlantCLEF 2020. This challenge focused on the cross-domain plant identification between herbarium sheets and in-field photos. We adopted a two-streamed Herbarium-Field triplet loss network which performed relatively equal regardless if few field training images were given. Based on the similarity between our MRR metrics 1 and 2 scored, it is proven that the proposed network feature is not directly affected by the plant class, yet, it learns to perceive the similarity between a given field image with herbarium images.

It is shown that even with a minimal amount of field images for each species, cross-domain plant identification can be performed. However, the absolute performance remains low for practical usage. Nevertheless, utilizing the Herbarium-Field triplet loss network demonstrates to be more effective in classifying species with fewer or no herbarium-field pairs. It offers a step in alleviating the tedious task of plant identification with few field photo samples, or rare species, which requires high-level expertise. For future work, the extraction of herbarium embeddings to form a more powerful dictionary can be investigated to find the best representation of herbarium embeddings for the herbarium-field similarity comparison. Furthermore, the use of taxonomy in training can be implemented to improve the results of classification.

Acknowledgment. The resources of this project is supported by NEUON AI SDN. BHD., Malaysia.

References

1. Abadi, M., et al.: TensorFlow: large-scale machine learning on heterogeneous systems (2015). https://www.tensorflow.org/
2. Argüeso, D., et al.: Few-shot learning approach for plant disease classification using images taken in the field. Comput. Electron. Agric. **175**, 105542 (2020)
3. Chandra, M., Patil, P.S., Roy, S., Redkar, S.S.: Classification of various plant diseases using deep siamese network (2020)
4. Chulif, S., Chang, Y.L.: Herbarium-field triplets network for cross-domain plant identification-NEUON submission to LifeCLEF 2020 plant. CLEF working notes (2020)
5. Chulif, S., Heng, K.J., Chan, T.W., Al Monnaf, M.A., Chang, Y.L.: Plant identication on amazonian and guiana shield flora: NEUON submission to LifeCLEF 2019 plant. In: CLEF (Working Notes) (2019)
6. Funk, V.A.: 100 uses for an herbarium: well at least 72. American Society of Plant Taxonomists Newsletter (2003)
7. Goëau, H., Bonnet, P., Joly, A.: Plant identification in an open-world (LifeCLEF 2016). In: CLEF: Conference and Labs of the Evaluation Forum, no. 1609, pp. 428–439 (2016)
8. Goëau, H., Bonnet, P., Joly, A.: Overview of LifeCLEF plant identification task 2019: diving into data deficient tropical countries. In: CLEF 2019-Conference and Labs of the Evaluation Forum, vol. 2380, pp. 1–13. CEUR (2019)
9. Goëau, H., Bonnet, P., Joly, A.: Overview of the LifeCLEF 2020 plant identification task. In: CLEF working notes 2020, CLEF: Conference and Labs of the Evaluation Forum, September 2020, Thessaloniki, Greece (2020)
10. Goëau, H., et al.: The ImageCLEF 2011 plant images classi cation task. In: ImageCLEF 2011 (2011)
11. Goëau, H., et al.: The ImageCLEF plant identification task 2013. In: Proceedings of the 2nd ACM International Workshop on Multimedia Analysis for Ecological Data, pp. 23–28 (2013)
12. Goëau, H., et al.: LifeCLEF plant identification task 2014. In: CLEF: Conference and Labs of the Evaluation Forum, no. 1180, pp. 598–615 (2014)
13. Göeau, H., Joly, A., Pierre, B.: LifeCLEF plant identification task 2015. CLEF Working Notes 2015 (2015)
14. Hermans, A., Beyer, L., Leibe, B.: In defense of the triplet loss for person re-identification. arXiv preprint arXiv:1703.07737 (2017)
15. Joly, A., et al.: LifeCLEF 2017 lab overview: multimedia species identification challenges. In: Jones, G.J.F., et al. (eds.) CLEF 2017. LNCS, vol. 10456, pp. 255–274. Springer, Cham (2017). https://doi.org/10.1007/978-3-319-65813-1_24
16. Kingma, D.P., Ba, J.: Adam: a method for stochastic optimization. arXiv preprint arXiv:1412.6980 (2014)
17. Krizhevsky, A., Sutskever, I., Hinton, G.E.: ImageNet classification with deep convolutional neural networks. In: Advances in Neural Information Processing Systems, pp. 1097–1105 (2012)
18. Mikołajczyk, A., Grochowski, M.: Data augmentation for improving deep learning in image classification problem. In: 2018 international Interdisciplinary PhD Workshop (IIPhDW), pp. 117–122. IEEE (2018)
19. Picek, L., Sulc, M., Matas, J.: Recognition of the Amazonian flora by inception networks with test-time class prior estimation. In: CLEF (Working Notes) (2019)

20. Russakovsky, O., et al.: ImageNet large scale visual recognition challenge. Int. J. Comput. Vis. **115**(3), 211–252 (2015)
21. Schroff, F., Kalenichenko, D., Philbin, J.: FaceNet: a unified embedding for face recognition and clustering. In: Proceedings of the IEEE Conference on Computer Vision and Pattern Recognition, pp. 815–823 (2015)
22. Szegedy, C., Ioffe, S., Vanhoucke, V., Alemi, A.A.: Inception-v4, inception-ResNet and the impact of residual connections on learning. In: Thirty-First AAAI Conference on Artificial Intelligence (2017)
23. Wäldchen, J., Rzanny, M., Seeland, M., Mäder, P.: Automated plant species identification—trends and future directions. PLoS Comput. Biol. **14**(4), e1005993 (2018)

BERT-Based Transformers for Early Detection of Mental Health Illnesses

Rodrigo Martínez-Castaño[1,2(✉)], Amal Htait[2], Leif Azzopardi[2], and Yashar Moshfeghi[2]

[1] Centro Singular de Investigación en Tecnoloxías Intelixentes (CiTIUS), Universidade de Santiago de Compostela, Santiago, Spain
rodrigo.martinez@usc.es

[2] Department of Computer and Information Sciences, University of Strathclyde, Glasgow, UK
{amal.htait,leif.azzopardi,yashar.moshfeghi}@strath.ac.uk

Abstract. This paper briefly describes our research groups' efforts in tackling Task 1 (Early Detection of Signs of Self-Harm), and Task 2 (Measuring the Severity of the Signs of Depression) from the CLEF eRisk Track. Core to how we approached these problems was the use of BERT-based classifiers which were trained specifically for each task. Our results on both tasks indicate that this approach delivers high performance across a series of measures, particularly for Task 1, where our submissions obtained the best performance for precision, F1, latency-weighted F1 and ERDE at 5 and 50. This work suggests that BERT-based classifiers, when trained appropriately, can accurately infer which social media users are at risk of self-harming, with precision up to 91.3% for Task 1. Given these promising results, it will be interesting to further refine the training regime, classifier and early detection scoring mechanism, as well as apply the same approach to other related tasks (e.g., anorexia, depression, suicide).

Keywords: Self-harm · Depression · Classification · Social media · Early detection · BERT · XLM-RoBERTa

1 Introduction

The eRisk CLEF track aims to explore the development of methods for early risk detection on the Internet, their evaluation, and the application of such methods for improving the health and well being of individuals [12–15]. Early detection technologies can be employed in different areas, particularly those related to health and safety. For instance, in [13] the authors examined whether it was possible to identify grooming activities of paedophiles given posts to online forums.

Complementary content: https://github.com/brunneis/ilab-erisk-2020/.

K. S. Candan et al. (Eds.): CLEF 2021, LNCS 12880, pp. 189–200, 2021.
https://doi.org/10.1007/978-3-030-85251-1_15

While in [14,15], they explored whether it was possible to detect users that were depressed or anorexic from their posts, and crucially how quickly this could be detected. This year the focus is on detecting the early signs of self-harm from people's posts to social media (Task 1), and whether it is possible to infer how depressed people are given such posts (Task 2) [16]. Below is an elaborated description of each task.

Task 1: Early Detection of Signs of Self-harm. This first task consists of triggering alerts for users that present early signs of committing self-harm. A tagged set of users and their posts to Reddit[1] groups was provided for training purposes. The different methods were benchmarked using a system that simulates a real-time scenario introduced in [15]. The posts from the users of the test dataset are served in rounds, one post at a time (simulating their live posting to the Reddit groups). The task then is to provide a decision about each user given their posts, and to do so as early as possible (i.e., with the fewest posts). For the evaluation, the correctness of the prediction (i.e., whether the user will cause self-harm or not) is not the only factor taken into account, but also the delay needed to emit the alerts. Clearly, the sooner a person who is likely to self-harm is identified, the sooner the intervention can be provided.

Task 2: Measuring the Severity of the Signs of Depression. This task consists of automatically estimating the level of several symptoms associated with depression. For that, a questionnaire with 21 questions related to different feelings and well-being (e.g., sadness, pessimism, fatigue) is provided. Each question has between four and seven possible answers which are related to different levels of severity (or relevance) of the symptom or behaviour. A sample of users with their answers to the questionnaire and their writings at Reddit was given. To benchmark the different approaches, a new set of users and their writings is provided, for which every team has to predict their answers.

The goal of this paper is to explore the potential of a BERT-based classifier coupled with a novel scoring mechanism for the early detection of self-harm and depression. This paper is structured as follows. In Sect. 2 we analyse the related work. In Sect. 3 we describe our general approach for both tasks by using BERT-based models for sentence classification. In Sect. 4 and Sect. 5 we explain how the classifiers were trained and applied for Task 1 and Task 2 respectively. Section 6 covers the analysis of our results, where our approach performs the best across a number of metrics for both tasks. Finally, in Sect. 7 we summarise the contributions of these working notes.

2 Related Work

Analyzing mental health-related discourse and language usage in social media is getting an increasing attention from researchers [4,24], and the specific subject of self-harm had been highlighted on in various efforts investigating approaches for detecting the self-harm risk of mental health forum online posts. The early

[1] https://reddit.com/.

related work in this subject mainly used variations of linear classifiers with feature engineering. For example, in the work of [5], the authors used lexicons as a feature in their supervised classifier that identifies posts showing signs of self-harm, with various other features including psycho-linguistic and topic modeling features. To abandon the feature engineering process, researchers exploited deep learning approaches, such as CNN (Convolutional Neural Network), that learns documents representations by considering only their textual content [19,26].

In 2019, the workshop eRisk [15] introduced a new task concerning the early detection of self-harm signs with the participation of 8 teams. The best performing team was UNSL [3] with their text classifier SS3 [2], where their system was extremely fast at making classification decisions but slightly modest in the effectiveness of these decisions. As a continuation of eRisk 2019, eRisk 2020 [16] hosted 12 participants including our team iLab [17]. Our BERT-based classifiers were able to achieve the best performance in terms of Precision, F1, ERDE measures and latency-weighted F1.

3 Approach

A breakthrough in the use of machine learning for Natural Language Processing (NLP) appeared with the generative pre-training of language models on a diverse corpus of unlabelled text, such as ELMo [21], BERT [8], OpenAI GPT [22], XLM [10], and RoBERTa [11]. Such a technique demonstrated large gains on a variety of NLP tasks (e.g., sequence or token classification, question answering, semantic similarity assessment, document classification). In particular, BERT (Bidirectional Encoder Representations from Transformers) [7,8], the model by Google AI, proved to be one of the most powerful tools for text classification [9, 18,20]. BERT is based on the Transformer architecture [25] and it was trained for both masked word prediction and next sentence prediction at the same time. As input, BERT takes two concatenated segments of text which are delimited with special tokens and whose length respects a defined maximum. The model was pre-trained on a huge dataset of unlabelled text. It is typically used within a text classifier for sentence tokenisation and text representation.

As for RoBERTa [11] (a replication study of BERT pre-training by Facebook AI), it shares a similar architecture with BERT but with a different pre-training approach. RoBERTa was trained over ten times more data, the next sentence prediction objective was removed, and the masked word prediction task was improved with the introduction of a dynamic masking pattern applied to the training data.

In another attempt to improve the language model, Facebook AI presented XLM-RoBERTa [6] with the pre-training of *multilingual* language models. This new improvement led to significant performance gains in text classification. For our participation at the eRisk challenges of 2020, variety of pre-trained language models were tested: BERT, DistillBERT, RoBERTa, and XLM-RoBERTa, among others. However, the best performance was achieved when using

XLM-RoBERTa on our training data. In our work, we used Ernie[2], a Python library for sentence classification built on top of Hugging Face Transformers[3], the main library that implements state-of-the-art general-purpose Transformer-based architectures.

Most of the pre-trained language models, including XLM-RoBERTa, have a maximum input length of 512 tokens. In our work, we experimented with input sentences of sizes between 32 and 128 tokens due to GPU memory restrictions. The best results were achieved with an input size of 128 tokens. Note that Reddit posts are usually shorter than 128 tokens. Therefore, using an input size larger than 128 would not substantially increase performance, but it would significantly increase the required computational resources. In the few cases where the Reddit posts were longer, we split them based on punctuation marks in an attempt to respect the context of the writings posted by the users. When training the classifiers, the weights of the pre-trained base models (e.g., XLM-RoBERTa) are updated, in addition to the classification head.

For our participation at the eRisk challenges of 2020, both Task 1 and Task 2, we used the previously explained approach for sentence classification. However, in each task, the employed training schedule and training data were varied and tailored to fit the task scenarios, as explained in the following sections.

4 Task 1

We fine-tuned a number of different language models based on the original BERT architecture with a classification head to predict whether a sentence was written by a subject that self-harms or not. Those models are the base to predict if a user is likely to self-harm and thus, triggering an alert, given a stream of texts. All of our final models were based on XLM-RoBERTa, which demonstrated better performance for this task.

4.1 Data

To train our models, we avoided using the training dataset provided by the eRisk organisers for two reasons. First, during the beginning of our experimentation, we found that the results obtained with our BERT-based approach were not promising enough to improve on the existing approaches used in 2019. Second, the training dataset matches the test data of the eRisk 2019's task. Taking it out from the training stage led us to be able to compare our results with those obtained by the last year's participants in our search for models with greater performance.

The data collected and used for training our models were obtained from the Pushshift Reddit Dataset [1] through its public API, which exposes a repository with constantly updated and almost complete dataset of all the public Reddit data. We downloaded all the available submissions and comments written

[2] https://github.com/labteral/ernie/.

[3] https://github.com/huggingface/transformers/.

to the most popular subreddit about self-harm (r/selfharm). From those posts, we extracted 42,839 authors. In addition, we collected all of the posts in any other subreddit for those authors (SELFHARM-USERS-TEXTS dataset). Then, we obtained an equivalent amount of random users from which we also extracted all their posts (RANDOM-USERS-TEXTS dataset). We filtered the obtained datasets in several ways. First, we checked that there were no user collision between the two collections. After identifying some of the main self-harm related subreddits (r/selfharm, r/Cutters, r/MadeOfStyrofoam, r/SelfHarmScars, r/StopSelfHarm, r/CPTSD and r/SuicideWatch), we removed the users from RANDOM-USERS-TEXTS having at least one post in any of them. All the users with more than 5,000 submissions were removed since those with an extremely high number of posts seem more likely to be bots. Besides, the vast majority of the users had posted fewer times so we presumed to have more chances to profile the average user below that threshold. We also pruned the less active users under 50 submissions. The number of sentences was expanded by splitting the users' texts that were too long for the parameters we utilised in our models. Otherwise, the sentences would be truncated during training, potentially losing valuable information. We split the large posts into groups of contiguous sentences of approximately the maximum length in tokens utilised in our models and following the punctuation marks hierarchy (e.g., prioritising the splits on full stops over commas). As commented before, a maximum length of 128 tokens was set so the models could be fine-tuned in commercial GPUs.

As a result, we created several datasets mainly derived from SELFHARM-USERS-TEXTS and RANDOM-USERS-TEXTS for training our model candidates. These datasets are presented in Table 1, and explained below.

REAL-SELFHARMERS-TEXTS: This dataset was manually created with the aim of obtaining a bigger but similar dataset to the one provided by the eRisk organisers. We manually tagged 354 users as real self-harmers from the users of the SELFHARM-USERS-TEXTS dataset. Then, we filtered by the last 1,000 submissions and comments for every user. We also pruned the writing sequences just before their first writing at r/selfharm. After that, we filtered out users with less than 10 writings remaining, ending up with a total of 120 real self-harmers. For the negative class, we took a sample of random users from the dataset RANDOM-USERS-TEXTS in the same proportion as in the provided training data: ~7.3 random users per self-harmer.

We also generated datasets automatically from SELFHARM-USERS-TEXTS and RANDOM-USERS-TEXTS after removing common users with REAL-SELFHARMERS-TEXTS:

USERS-TEXTS-200K. This dataset was generated by random sampling $200K$ writings from both SELFHARM-USERS-TEXTS (as self-harmers) and RANDOM-USERS-TEXTS (as non self-harmers), with $100K$ from each dataset. Note that we experimented by replicating last years' task with different sizes of sampling such as $2K$, $20K$, $100K$, $300K$, $400K$ and $500K$ writings, but the best results were achieved with a sampling size of $200K$ writings.

USERS-TEXTS-2M: This dataset is a variant of USERS-TEXTS-200K; a balanced dataset with ten times more sentences, totalling $2M$ writings. Note that, during our experimentation replicating last years' task, using a training set larger than $200K$ did not improve the results except for the $ERDE_5$ metric with the $2M$ writings.
USERS-SUBMISSIONS-200K: This dataset was generated in a similar procedure as USERS-TEXTS-200K, with $200K$ randomly sampled writings, but with the difference of avoiding comments. Therefore, sampling users' submissions exclusively.

Table 1. Some statistics of the datasets used to train the classifiers.

Dataset	Class	Users	Subreddits	Sentences	Years
REAL-SELFHARMERS-TEXTS	Selfharm	120	1,346	8,943	2013–2020
	Random	875	5,585	87,260	2009–2020
USERS-TEXTS-200K	Selfharm	9,487	9,797	107,277	2006–2020
	Random	14,280	9,793	107,152	2006–2020
USERS-TEXTS-2M	Selfharm	10,454	26,931	1,075,476	2006–2020
	Random	17,548	26,409	1,076,707	2005–2020
USERS-SUBMISSIONS-200K	Selfharm	10,319	13,681	131,233	2006–2020
	Random	15,937	14,913	128,064	2005–2020

4.2 Method

For our participation in Task 1 of eRisk we trained three models for binary sentence classification, all of them based on the XLM-RoBERTa-base language model (since it behaved better than other variants we tried such as BERT, Distill-BERT, XLNet, etc.): XLMRB-SELFHARM-200K trained with the dataset USERS-TEXTS-200K, XLMRB-SELFHARM-2M trained with the dataset USERS-TEXTS-2M, and XLMRB-SELFHARM-SUB-200K trained with the dataset USERS-SUBMISSIONS-200K. We established a maximum length of tokens as 128 per sentence, a training rate of $2e^{-5}$ and a validation size of the 20%.

In order to predict if a user has or has not risk of self-harm, we averaged the predicted probability of the known writings for every user. We omitted the prediction of sentences with less than 10 tokens as we concluded that the performance on smaller sentences is poor. Since the provided training set was the test set of the last year's task, we used it to compare the performance of our models with the participants of the previous year. We defined several parameters to determine if the system should trigger an alert given a list of known user's texts: the minimum average probability threshold (θ), the minimum number of texts necessary to trigger an alert, and the maximum number of texts that the system will take into account to make its decisions on the subjects. Given a growing list of texts from a user, the system will trigger an alert if the average probability of the known texts for that user is equal or greater than θ, the number of known texts is greater or equal to the established minimum number of texts, and lower or equal to the maximum.

The parameters were adjusted in five variants by finding their optimal values for F1 and the eRisk related metrics: latency-weighted F1, $ERDE_5$ and $ERDE_{50}$ with the REAL-SELFHARMERS-TEXTS dataset. We chose the model with the best performance for each target metric. The selected parameters for each variant can be observed in Table 2.

After choosing the parameters with the REAL-SELFHARMERS-TEXTS dataset, we tested the classifiers with the last year's test data for the same task as showed in Table 3, where we compare the obtained results with the best performer of 2019 for that task: UNSL. That team obtained the best results for precision, F1, $ERDE_5$, $ERDE_{50}$ and latency-weighted F1. With the classifiers that we used in our submission, we improved their results for F1, $ERDE_5$, $ERDE_{50}$ and latency-weighted F1.

Table 2. Combinations of models and parameters for the five submitted runs.

Run	Model	Target Metric	θ	Min. posts	Max. posts
0	XLMRB-SELFHARM-200K	*latency-weighted F1*	0.75	10	50
1	XLMRB-SELFHARM-2M	*latency-weighted F1*	0.76	10	50
2	XLMRB-SELFHARM-2M	*ERDE_5*	0.69	2	5
3	XLMRB-SELFHARM-SUB-200K	*ERDE_50*	0.64	45	45
4	XLMRB-SELFHARM-200K	*F1*	0.68	100	100

Table 3. Results obtained by our five final variants with the 2019 dataset compared to the results obtained by UNSL.

Team	Run	P	R	F1	ERDE 5	ERDE 50	Latency TP	Speed	Latency-weighted F1
UNSL 2019	0	**0.71**	0.41	0.52	0.090	0.073	2	1	0.52
UNSL 2019	4	0.31	**0.88**	0.46	0.082	0.049	3	.99	0.45
iLab	0	0.68	0.66	**0.67**	0.125	0.046	10	0.97	**0.64**
iLab	1	0.69	0.59	0.63	0.124	0.054	10	0.97	0.61
iLab	2	0.33	0.71	0.45	**0.062**	0.057	2	1	0.44
iLab	3	0.34	0.83	0.48	0.144	**0.045**	45	0.83	0.40
iLab	4	0,68	0.66	**0.67**	0.125	0.125	100	0.63	0.42

5 Task 2

5.1 Data

For our participation in Task 2 of eRisk, we used the training dataset provided by the task's organisers. Both training and test datasets consist of Reddit posts written by users who have answered the questionnaire. The training dataset includes a total of 10,941 posts by 20 users, and the test dataset includes 35,562 posts by 70 users.

An analogous approach as the one employed for Task 1, with random posts from users connected solely by a common subreddit, was not possible this time. Therefore, and due to the small dataset for training (only 20 different users), we used the full provided training dataset in order to train the classifiers. For each question of the questionnaire, we modified the training dataset by assigning the same class to all the texts posted by a given user (i.e., each class matches one of the available answers). Thus, we obtained a different training set for each question of the questionnaire, and, therefore, one multi-class classifier.

5.2 Method

For this task, we applied a similar method as the one employed in Task 1, but we treated the problem as a multi-class labelling problem. We created three variants: run 1 with XLM-RoBERTa-base and runs 2 and 3 with RoBERTa-base. For the runs 1 and 2, we expanded the training by splitting texts larger than 128 tokens in the same way as in Task 1. For Run 3, sentences larger than 128 tokens were truncated during the training phase.

For each variant, we fine-tuned the base language model with a head for multi-class classification for every question. We balanced the class weights of every question model for all the variants. The RoBERTa-based classifiers were trained for 4 epochs, whereas we executed 5 epochs for the XLM-RoBERTa-based ones. Those numbers of epochs were found to be optimal in all the models we created during our experimentation for Task 1. We established the maximum sentence length to 128 tokens and the learning rate to $2e^{-5}$ to train all the models. We assigned a 20% of the training data for validation.

For a given user and variant, we predict the questionnaire answer in the following way: given a question and the associated classifier, we obtain the *softmax* prediction vector for every text written by that user and we sum them. The class with the highest accumulated value is the answer to the questionnaire we predict. As in Task 1, during prediction, if the input texts are larger than 128 tokens, we split them and average the predictions of the chunks.

6 Results

Table 4 shows the performance of our runs for Task 1, while Table 5 shows the performance of our runs for Task 2. In each table, the best scores among all the participants are highlighted in bold. Other runs from other teams have also been included to show the best performing runs for each task on each metric.

For Task 1, the evaluation metrics used were [15]:

The standard classification measures **precision (P)**, **recall (R)** and **F1**, are computed with respect to the positive class, which is the only triggering alerts.

ERDE (Early Risk Detection Error) [12], is an error measure that introduces a penalty for late correct alerts (true positives) and depends on the number of user writings seen before the alert. Two sets of user writing numbers are taken into consideration in this challenge: 5 and 50. Contrary to the other metrics, the lower the value of ERDE, the better the performance of the system.
Latency$_{TP}$ measures the delay in detecting true positives, defined as the median number of writings used to detect positive cases.
Speed is the system's overall speed factor, where it will be equal to 1 for a system whose true positives are detected right at the first writing, and almost 0 for a slow system, which detects true positives after hundreds of writings.
Latency-weighted F1 [23] score is equal to $F1 \cdot speed$, and a perfect system gets latency-weighted F1 equals to 1.

Table 4. The performance for each run we submitted on Task 1: Early detection of signs of self-harm. Note that for each bolded metric our run gave the highest performance.

Run	P	R	F1	ERDE 5	ERDE 50	Latency TP	Speed	Latency-Weighted F1
0	0.833	0.577	0.682	0.252	0.111	10	0.965	**0.658**
1	**0.913**	0.404	0.560	0.248	0.149	10	0.965	0.540
2	0.544	0.654	0.594	**0.134**	0.118	2	0.996	0.592
3	0.564	0.885	0.689	0.287	**0.071**	45	0.830	0.572
4	0.828	0.692	**0.754**	0.255	0.255	100	0.632	0.476

Table 5. The performance for each run we submitted on Task 2: Measuring the severity of the signs of depression, along with the runs from other teams that scored higher.

Team	Run	AHR	ACR	ADODL	DCHR
BioInfo@UAVR	0	**38.30%**	69.21%	76.01%	30.00%
prhlt-upv	0	34.01%	67.07%	80.05%	**35.71%**
prhlt-upv	1	34.56%	67.44%	80.63%	**35.71%**
RELAI	0	36.39%	68.32%	**83.15%**	34.29%
iLab	0	36.73%	68.68%	81.07%	27.14%
iLab	1	37.07%	**69.41%**	81.70%	27.14%
iLab	2	35.99%	69.14%	82.93%	34.29%

For Task 2, the following metrics were used [15]:

AHR (Average Hit Rate) is the average of Hit Rate (HR) across all users, and HR is the ratio of cases where the automatic questionnaire has exactly the same answer as the actual questionnaire.
ACR (Average Closeness Rate) is the average of Closeness Rate (CR) across all users, and CR is equal to *(mad - ad)/mad*, where *mad* is the maximum absolute difference, which is equal to the number of possible answers minus one, and *ad* is the absolute difference between the real and the automated answer.
ADODL (Average DODL) is the averaged of Difference between Overall Depression Levels (DODL) across all users. DODL computes the overall depression level (sum of all the answers) for the real and automated questionnaire and, next, the absolute difference (ad_overall) between the real and the automated score is computed. DODL is normalised into [0,1] as follows: *DODL = (63 - ad_overall)/63.*
DCHR (Depression Category Hit Rate) computes the fraction of cases where the automated questionnaire led to a depression category (out of 4 categories: nonexistence, mild, moderate and severe) that is equivalent to the depression category obtained from the real questionnaire.

For Task 1, our team's performance for each of the key metrics was the best compared to the other teams this year. Given our training schedule which tried to maximise the performance for each metric per run, we can see that no specific run was the best across all the metrics, but rather there is a trade-off between metrics. For example, Run 1 obtains a precision score of 0.913, but has the lowest recall, while Run 4 obtains the highest F1, but not the best precision or recall. Of most interest is the performance on the eRisk-specific metrics, where our runs obtained notably the best results. With Run 0 we obtained a latency-weighted F1 of 0.66, where the second-best result was obtained by the team UNSL with their run 1 at 0.61. For $ERDE_5$, Run 2 scored 0.134, whereas the second-best team was again UNSL with their run 1 at 0.172 (where lower is better). For $ERDE_{50}$, our Run 3 obtained a score of 0.071, whereas all the other runs ranged between 0.11 to 0.25.

For Task 2, our team's performance was the best for ACR, and competitive for the other metrics. For AHR, ADODL and DCHR our performances were within 1–2% of the best performances submitted. Interestingly, while the ADODL scores were around 81–83%, this did not translate into a better classification of depression category as surmised by DCHR, which was 34% at best. This disparity may be due to how we employed the BERT based classifier (i.e., we made separate models to predict the results of each question). However, it may be more appropriate to jointly predict the results of all questions and the final depression category. This is because the questions will have a high correlation between answers, and information for inferring the answer for one question, may be useful in inferring others when taken together.

7 Summary

In this paper, we have described how we employed a BERT-based classifier for the tasks of the CLEF eRisk Track: Task 1, early risk detection of self-harm; and Task 2, inferring answers to a depression survey. Our results on both tasks indicated that this approach works very well and obtains very good performance (the best on Task 1 and very competitive performance on Task 2). These results are perhaps not too surprising, given the impact that BERT-based models have been making in improving many other tasks. However, a key difference in this work is how we trained the model. In future work, we will explore and compare different training schedules and classifiers extensions for these tasks, but also for other related tasks (e.g., classifying whether someone is like to suffer from anorexia, depression).

Acknowledgements. The first author would like to thank the following funding bodies for their support: FEDER/Ministerio de Ciencia, Innovación y Universidades, Agencia Estatal de Investigación/Project (RTI2018-093336-B-C21), Consellería de Educación, Universidade e Formación Profesional and the European Regional Development Fund (ERDF) (accreditation 2019–2022 ED431G-2019/04, ED431C 2018/29, ED431C 2018/19).

The second and third authors would like to thank the UKRI's EPSRC Project *Cumulative Revelations in Personal Data* (Grant Number: EP/R033897/1) for their support. We would also like to thank David Losada for arranging this collaboration.

References

1. Baumgartner, J., Zannettou, S., Keegan, B., Squire, M., Blackburn, J.: The pushshift reddit dataset. In: Proceedings of the International AAAI Conference on Web and Social Media, vol. 14, pp. 830–839 (2020)
2. Burdisso, S.G., Errecalde, M., Montes-y Gómez, M.: A text classification framework for simple and effective early depression detection over social media streams. Expert Syst. Appl. **133**, 182–197 (2019)
3. Burdisso, S.G., Errecalde, M., Montes-y Gómez, M.: UNSL at eRisk 2019: a unified approach for anorexia, self-harm and depression detection in social media. In: CLEF (Working Notes) (2019)
4. Chancellor, S., De Choudhury, M.: Methods in predictive techniques for mental health status on social media: a critical review. NPJ Digit. Med. **3**(1), 1–11 (2020)
5. Cohan, A., Young, S., Goharian, N.: Triaging mental health forum posts. In: Proceedings of the Third Workshop on Computational Linguistics and Clinical Psychology, pp. 143–147 (2016)
6. Conneau, A., et al.: Unsupervised cross-lingual representation learning at scale. In: Proceedings of the 58th Annual Meeting of the Association for Computational Linguistics, pp. 8440–8451 (2020)
7. Devlin, J., Chang, M.W.: Open sourcing BERT: state-of-the-art pre-training for natural language processing (2018). http://aiweb.techfak.uni-bielefeld.de/content/bworld-robot-control-software/. Accessed 22 Apr 2021
8. Devlin, J., Chang, M.W., Lee, K., Toutanova, K.: BERT: pre-training of deep bidirectional transformers for language understanding. arXiv preprint arXiv:1810.04805 (2018)

9. Gao, Z., Feng, A., Song, X., Wu, X.: Target-dependent sentiment classification with BERT. IEEE Access **7**, 154290–154299 (2019)
10. Lample, G., Conneau, A.: Cross-lingual language model pretraining. arXiv preprint arXiv:1901.07291 (2019)
11. Liu, Y., et al.: RoBERTa: a robustly optimized BERT pretraining approach. arXiv preprint arXiv:1907.11692 (2019)
12. Losada, D.E., Crestani, F.: A test collection for research on depression and language use. In: Fuhr, N., et al. (eds.) CLEF 2016. LNCS, vol. 9822, pp. 28–39. Springer, Cham (2016). https://doi.org/10.1007/978-3-319-44564-9_3
13. Losada, D.E., Crestani, F., Parapar, J.: CLEF 2017 eRisk overview: early risk prediction on the internet: experimental foundations. In: CEUR Workshop Proceedings, vol. 1866 (2017)
14. Losada, D.E., Crestani, F., Parapar, J.: Overview of eRisk 2018: early risk prediction on the internet (extended lab overview). In: CEUR Workshop Proceedings, vol. 2125 (2018)
15. Losada, D.E., Crestani, F., Parapar, J.: Overview of eRisk 2019 early risk prediction on the internet. In: Crestani, F., et al. (eds.) CLEF 2019. LNCS, vol. 11696, pp. 340–357. Springer, Cham (2019). https://doi.org/10.1007/978-3-030-28577-7_27
16. Losada, D.E., Crestani, F., Parapar, J.: Overview of eRisk 2020: early risk prediction on the internet. In: Arampatzis, A., et al. (eds.) CLEF 2020. LNCS, vol. 12260, pp. 272–287. Springer, Cham (2020). https://doi.org/10.1007/978-3-030-58219-7_20
17. Martínez-Castaño, R., Htait, A., Azzopardi, L., Moshfeghi, Y.: Early risk detection of self-harm and depression severity using BERT-based transformers: iLab at CLEF eRisk 2020. Early Risk Prediction on the Internet (2020)
18. Nikolov, A., Radivchev, V.: Nikolov-Radivchev at SemEval-2019 task 6: offensive tweet classification with BERT and ensembles. In: Proceedings of the 13th International Workshop on Semantic Evaluation, pp. 691–695 (2019)
19. Obeid, J.S., et al.: Identifying and predicting intentional self-harm in electronic health record clinical notes: deep learning approach. JMIR Med. Inform. **8**(7), e17784 (2020)
20. Parikh, P., et al.: Multi-label categorization of accounts of sexism using a neural framework. In: EMNLP/IJCNLP (1) (2019)
21. Peters, M., et al.: Deep contextualized word representations. In: Proceedings of the 2018 Conference of the North American Chapter of the Association for Computational Linguistics: Human Language Technologies, vol. 1 (Long Papers), pp. 2227–2237 (2018)
22. Radford, A., Narasimhan, K., Salimans, T., Sutskever, I.: Improving language understanding by generative pre-training (2018). https://s3-us-west-2.amazonaws.com/openai-assets/research-covers/language-unsupervised/language_understanding_paper.pdf. Accessed 22 Apr 2021
23. Sadeque, F., Xu, D., Bethard, S.: Measuring the latency of depression detection in social media. In: Proceedings of the Eleventh ACM International Conference on Web Search and Data Mining, pp. 495–503 (2018)
24. Skaik, R., Inkpen, D.: Using social media for mental health surveillance: a review. ACM Comput. Surv. (CSUR) **53**(6), 1–31 (2020)
25. Vaswani, A., et al.: Attention is all you need. In: Advances in Neural Information Processing Systems, pp. 5998–6008 (2017)
26. Yates, A., Cohan, A., Goharian, N.: Depression and self-harm risk assessment in online forums. CoRR **abs/1709.01848** (2017)

Dowsing for Math Answers

Yin Ki Ng[1], Dallas J. Fraser[2], Besat Kassaie[1], and Frank Wm. Tompa[1(✉)]

[1] David R. Cheriton School of Computer Science, University of Waterloo, Waterloo, ON N2L 3G1, Canada
fwtompa@uwaterloo.ca

[2] Knowledgehook Inc., 151 Charles St W, Kitchener, ON N2G 1H6, Canada

Abstract. Mathematical Information Retrieval (MathIR) focuses on using mathematical formulas and terminology to search and retrieve documents that include mathematical content. To index mathematical documents, we convert each formula into a token list that is compatible with natural language text. Then, given a natural language query that includes formulas, we select key terms and formulas from the query, again convert the query formulas into token lists, and finally search and rank results using standard search engine techniques. In this paper, we describe our approach in detail for a Community Question Answering task and evaluate the weight to be given to formula tokens versus text tokens. We also evaluate a regression-based approach to re-ranking based on metadata associated with the documents returned from the search.

Keywords: Community Question Answering (CQA) · Mathematical Information Retrieval (MathIR) · Symbol Layout Tree (SLT) · Lucene · Mathematics Stack Exchange (MSE) · ARQMath lab

1 Introduction

Because content expressed in formal mathematics and formulas is often crucial in the STEM literature, the Mathematics Information Retrieval (MathIR) research community has been growing and developing ever-improved math-aware search systems [6,9,16,17,23]. These efforts have been encouraged by a series of MathIR evaluation workshops through NTCIR [2,3,19]. These workshops have provided corpora derived from arXiv and Wikipedia for traditional ad-hoc retrieval tasks and formula search tasks, and the data and tasks have since served as benchmarks for the research community.

The ARQMath Lab (ARQMath) [22] provided the first Community Question Answering (CQA) task with questions involving math formulas, using data from Math Stack Exchange (MSE),[1] a math question answering site. Like the NTCIR

[1] https://math.stackexchange.com.

K. S. Candan et al. (Eds.): CLEF 2021, LNCS 12880, pp. 201–212, 2021.
https://doi.org/10.1007/978-3-030-85251-1_16

workshops that preceded it, the ARQMath Lab poses an evaluation exercise that aims to advance math-aware search and the semantic analysis of mathematical notation and texts. The main task of ARQMath is answer retrieval, in which participating systems need to find and rank answers to a set of mathematical questions among previously posted answers on MSE. A secondary task is to retrieve formulas that match those selected from MSE questions.

A related math question answering task was held recently as part of SemEval-2019 [7], following earlier CQA challenges [11–13]. The math question answering task at SemEval-2019 includes a math question set derived from College Board Scholastic Aptitude Test practice exams, including high school algebra and geometry questions. This task differs from the ARQMath CQA task, in that it does not require a search system to rank answers from a community forum, but rather the task is to identify which of five multiple-choice answers is correct or to compute a numerical answer to a question. On the other hand, the earlier CQA challenges at SemEval involved question-comment threads from the Qatar Living Forum, which is a data collection that is similar to the MSE collection. This CQA challenge series, however, differs from the ARQMath CQA task in that the questions are not necessarily mathematical, and the task objective is answer-ranking instead of answer retrieval from a corpus. Besides SemEval tasks, related tasks under the question-answering context were also held previously at TREC, CLEF, and NTCIR [1,15], but the data involved was not drawn from mathematics and the data was not structured as a community forum.

Tangent-L[2] is a traditional math-aware search system recently developed at Waterloo using the data provided for all three NTCIR math search workshops [5]. In this paper, we show that Tangent-L performs well for the ARQMath Lab question-answering task, and we present initial answers to the following research problems:

RQ1: What is an effective way to convert each mathematical question (expressed in mathematical natural language) into a formal query consisting of keywords and formulas?
RQ2: Should keywords or formulas be assigned heavier weights in a query?
RQ3: What is the effect of a re-ranking algorithm that makes use of metadata?

We present an overview of Tangent-L in Sect. 2. In Sect. 3, we describe our approach to CQA and provide details on how we retrieve and rank answer matches for a mathematical question from an indexed MSE corpus with the use of Tangent-L. Our experimental results are discussed in Sect. 4, and in Sect. 5, we present our conclusions.

2 Overview of Tangent-L

Tangent-L is a traditional search system, built on Lucene by adding methods adapted from an earlier, custom-built Tangent-3 [21] to answer queries with

[2] https://cs.uwaterloo.ca/brushsearch.

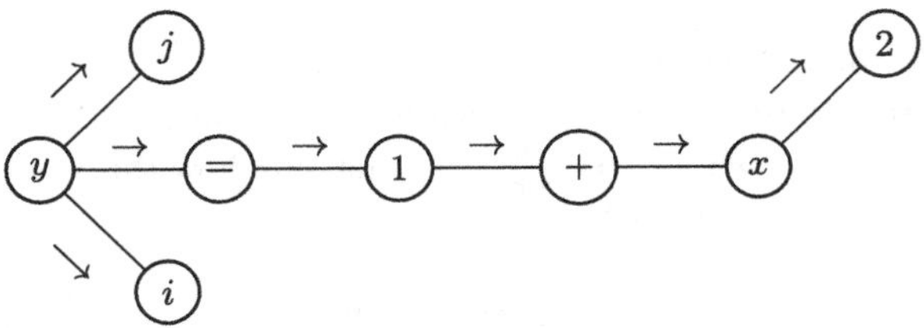

Fig. 1. Symbol layout tree for $y_i^j = 1 + x^2$.

Feature Type	*Definition and Extracted Features*		
Symbol pairs	For each edge, start and end symbols and edge label		
	$(y, j, \nearrow)$	$(y, =, \rightarrow)$	$(y, i, \searrow)$
	$(=, 1, \rightarrow)$	$(1, +, \rightarrow)$	$(+, x, \rightarrow)$
	$(x, 2, \nearrow)$		
Terminal symbols	List of symbols with no outedges		
	$(j, \triangle)$	$(i, \triangle)$	$(2, \triangle)$
Compound symbols	List of outedge labels for nodes with more than one outedge		
	$(y, \nearrow\searrow\rightarrow)$		
Augmented locations	For each feature of the first three types, that feature together with the path to the feature's (first) symbol		
	$(y, j, \nearrow, \emptyset)$	$(y, =, \rightarrow, \emptyset)$	$(y, i, \searrow, \emptyset)$
	$(=, 1, \rightarrow, \rightarrow)$	$(1, +, \rightarrow, \rightarrow\rightarrow)$	$(+, x, \rightarrow, \rightarrow\rightarrow\rightarrow)$
	$(x, 2, \nearrow, \rightarrow\rightarrow\rightarrow\rightarrow)$	$(j, \triangle, \nearrow)$	$(i, \triangle, \searrow)$
	$(2, \triangle, \rightarrow\rightarrow\rightarrow\rightarrow\nearrow)$	$(y, \nearrow\searrow\rightarrow, \emptyset)$	

Fig. 2. Extracted features (22 "math tuples") to represent the formula in Fig. 1.

keywords and formulas. Given a formula in Presentation MathML [10] format,[3] Tangent-L converts it into a *symbol layout tree* (SLT) [20,21], where nodes represent the math symbols and edges represent spatial relationships between these symbols (Fig. 1). Thereafter, this tree-like representation is traversed to extract a list of tokens, or "math tuples", of four types to capture local characteristics of a math formula as depicted in Fig. 2. In preparation for search, the math tuples replace the formula itself in the document and are then treated as if each were a term in the text to be matched.

After formula conversion and standard text pre-processing, including stemming and stop word removal, Tangent-L applies BM25$^+$ ranking [8] to the query terms and the document terms. Specifically, given a corpus of documents D containing $|D|$ documents and a query q consisting of a set of query terms, the score for a document $d \in D$ is given by

[3] A formula in LaTeX representation can be converted into MathML by using LaTeXML (https://dlmf.nist.gov/LaTeXML/).

Topic-ID: A.75
Title: Prove that for each integer m, $\lim_{u\to\infty} \frac{u^m}{e^u} = 0$
Body: I'm unsure how to show that for each integer m, $\lim_{u\to\infty} \frac{u^m}{e^u} = 0$. Looking at the solutions it starts with $e^u > \frac{u^{m+1}}{(m+1)!}$ but not sure how this is a logical step.
Tags: real-analysis, calculus, limits

Fig. 3. A question from MSE, framed as a *topic*, with topic-ID, title, body, and tags.

$$\mathrm{BM25}^{+}(q,d) = \sum_{w\in q} \left(\frac{(k+1)\mathit{tf}_{w,d}}{k\left(1.0 - b + b\frac{|d|}{\overline{d}}\right) + \mathit{tf}_{w,d}} + \delta \right) \log\left(\frac{|D|+1}{|D_w|}\right) \tag{1}$$

where k, b, and δ are constants (following common practice, chosen to be 1.2, 0.75, and 1, respectively); $\mathit{tf}_{w,d}$ is the number of occurrences of term w in document d; $|d|$ is the total number of terms in document d; $\overline{d} = \sum_{d\in D} \frac{|d|}{|D|}$ is the average document length; and $|D_w|$ is the number of documents in D containing term w. To allow for math tuples to be given a weight that differs from natural language terms, we assign weights to query terms as follows:

$$\mathrm{BM25}_{\mathrm{w}}^{+}(q_t \cup q_m, d) = \mathrm{BM25}^{+}(q_t, d) + \alpha \cdot \mathrm{BM25}^{+}(q_m, d) \tag{2}$$

where q_t is the set of keywords in a query, q_m is the set of math tuples in that query, and α is a parameter to adjust the relative weight applied to math tuples.

In the NTCIR-12 arXiv Main task benchmark, where queries are composed of formulas and keywords, Tangent-L gives a comparable performance to other MathIR systems [5]. We are interested in determining how Tangent-L could be adapted to address the ARQLab CQA task.

3 Methodology

After indexing the corpus available from the task organizers,[4] we adopt a three-phase architecture to return answer matches for a mathematical question:

1. *Conversion*: Transform the input (a mathematical question posed on MSE) into a well-formulated query consisting of a *bag* of formulas and keywords.
2. *Searching*: Use Tangent-L to execute the formal query to find the best matches against the indexed corpus.
3. *Re-ranking*: Re-order the best matches by considering additional metadata (such as votes and tags) associated with question-answer pairs.

3.1 Conversion: Creating Search Queries from MSE Questions

For the CQA task, participants are given 98 real-world mathematical questions selected from MSE posts in 2019. As illustrated in Fig. 3, a MSE question is

[4] https://www.cs.rit.edu/~dprl/ARQMath/.

represented by a *topic* that includes a *topic-ID*, *title*, *body*, and list of *tags*. The title and body are free text fields describing a question in mathematical natural language (as opposed to formal logic, for example), and the tags indicate the question's academic areas.

We adopt the following automated mechanism to extract a list of query formulas and keywords that can be used as input for Tangent-L:

Formulas: All formulas within the title are selected as query formulas. Formulas within the body text are selected as long as they are not single variables (e.g., n or i) nor isolated numbers (e.g., 1 or 25). For the topic in Fig. 3, m and $\lim_{u\to\infty} \frac{u^m}{e^u} = 0$ are extracted from the title and $\lim_{u\to\infty} \frac{u^m}{e^u} = 0$ and $e^u > \frac{u^{m+1}}{(m+1)!}$ are selected from the body.

Keywords: Each of the topic's tags is selected to be a query keyword, and if a tag is hyphenated, each component is added as another keyword. Thus, for the topic in Fig. 3, we extract five keywords: "real-analysis", "calculus", "limits", "real", "analysis". For the topic's title and body text, we first tokenize the text and then also select a token as a keyword if it contains a hyphen (such as "Euler-Totient" or "Cesáro-Stolz") or if its *stem* appears on a pre-constructed list of *mathematical stems* created in a pre-processing step by automatically extracting terms from two sources: (1) all available tags from the MSE collection and (2) titles from English Wikipedia articles comprising the corpus for the NTCIR-12 MathIR Wikipedia task [19]. Thus, for the topic in Fig. 3, we extract ten additional keywords: "Prove", "integer", "show", "integer", "Looking", "solutions", "sure", "this", "logical", "step".

Using this approach for each of the 98 topics in the CQA task, on average 8 (ranging from 1 to 35) formulas and on average 38 (ranging from 5 to 155) keywords are extracted for our queries.[5]

3.2 Searching: Retrieving Answers from the Indexed Corpus

Indexing. The ARQMath dataset contains approximately 1.1 million mathematical questions and 1.4 million answers, covering MSE threads from the year 2010 to 2018 [22]. Like the questions used as topics, each question in the dataset comprises a title, body, and list of tags. In addition, it is associated with a set of answers (each of which is assigned the number of votes it receives along with information about the contributor) and a set of comments, and it is possibly linked to related questions or duplicate questions posted earlier on MSE.

The indexed corpus is constructed as follows: each indexing unit is a question-answer pair that includes an MSE answer along with its associated question.[6] For each of these pairs, we extract the following content from the dataset:

from the answer: the body text and the number of votes;

[5] All extracted formulas and keywords can be found in our Working Notes [14].

[6] As our teachers admonished: "Always include the question as part of your answer!".

from the associated question: the title, body, tags of the question plus comments associated with each question. Additionally, we also include the *titles* of all related and duplicate posts for this question.[7]

All formulas within the text are represented by their Presentation MathML form, and an HTML file for this content is then assembled as an indexing unit. The resulting HTML version of the corpus, including a total of 1,445,488 documents, is then indexed by Tangent-L in preparation for search.

Searching. Searching the corpus is a straightforward application of Tangent-L for the converted topics. Each list of extracted formulas (in Presentation MathML) and keywords constitutes a formal query for the search engine, which computes the $BM25^+$ scores using Eq. 2, with the parameter α depending on the experimental setup for the run.

3.3 Re-ranking: Incorporating Answers' Metadata

Having the highest score based on similarity matching of keywords and formulas does not guarantee that an answer best addresses a math question. We wish to make use of the answers' metadata provided in the MSE collection to build a model that reflects how valuable a potential answer might be with respect to any question. We hypothesize that a linear function of the following four variables might serve well:

similarity: The similarity score returned from Tangent-L is clearly an important indicator.
tags: The number of matching tags reflects how well the question and potential answer share academic area(s).
votes: The *vote score* (number of up-votes minus the number of down-votes) received by the answer when posted with its associated question, reflects the community's belief in the answer's value.
reputation: The reputation of the contributor who wrote an answer (computed from the user reputation score and the number of up-votes and down-votes for that user) implies the trustworthiness of that answer.

The remaining problem is to determine what coefficient values to use when linearly combining these inputs. For this we need a training set that includes relevance assessments, which are not available as part of the dataset.

Mock Relevance Assessments. As a substitute for assessed relevance, we build a training set of queries from postings in the MSE collection, with the hypothesis that relevant answers include those that were actually provided for a posted question as well as those provided for *related* and *duplicate* questions.

We use tags, related posts, and duplicate posts of a question, and the vote score for each answer to calculate mock relevance assessments for answers to the training queries, based on the following two observations:

[7] For completeness, all one-way links between posts are converted to two-way links.

1. Considering the target answer's associated question, the more "on-topic" that associated question is to a query question, the more relevant the target answer is likely to be for that query. A posted question is related to a query question if they have matching tags, but are more related if one is marked as a related post of the other, and still more related if it is marked as a duplicate post of the other (or is, in fact, the same question).
2. If two potential answers are associated with the same question, the one with a higher vote score should be preferred.

With these assumptions, a mock assessment value can be computed as follows:

Integral assessment value:

1. An answer gets an assessment value of **2** if its associated question *is* the query question or a duplicate post to the query question.
2. An answer gets an assessment value of **1** if its associated question is a related post to the query question;
3. Otherwise, the answer gets an integral assessment value of **0**

Fractional assessment value:

1. If the associated question is not the same or a duplicate or related post to the query question, or if the associated question contains no matching tags with the query question, or if the associated question has no votes, then the answer gets a fractional assessment of **0**.
2. Otherwise for an answer a, let q be its associated question and A_q be the set of all answers to question q. Then the answer a gets a normalized fractional assessment value F that is computed as follows:

$$F(a,q) = \frac{V_a + \sum\limits_{\substack{s \in A_q \\ V_s < 0}} |V_s|}{\sum\limits_{s \in A_q} |V_s|} \text{ if } V_a > 0 \text{ and } \frac{V_a}{\sum\limits_{s \in A_q} |V_s|} \text{ otherwise} \tag{3}$$

where V_x is the vote score for an answer x.

The final mock relevance assessment is the sum of the integral and fractional assessment values and, when all answers have non-negative vote scores, ranges from 0 to 3 (matching the assessment range expected in the CQA task).

Linear Regression Formula. The final training set is built with queries converted from 1300 randomly-selected questions from the MSE collection. We use Tangent-L with its default $\alpha = 1.0$ (in Eq. 2) to retrieve the top 10,000 answers for each valid query question, resulting in a total of 12,970,000 answers. For each retrieved answer with respect to the query, we then generate the mock relevance assessment and associate the assessment with the values for similarity, tags, votes, and reputation as discussed above. Finally, a linear regression model is trained with these 12,970,000 tuples.

We validate the trained linear regression model by first applying the model to predict a relevance score for the top 1000 retrieved answers of a separate set of another 100 randomly selected query questions, and then re-ranking the answers according to the predicted mock relevance score. Finally, we adopt the normalized Discounted Cumulative Gain (nDCG), which measures the gain of a document based on its position in the result list and its graded relevance. We compare the nDCG value of the results for those 100 topics according to the mock relevance assessment before and after re-ranking. This simple model gives a slight improvement in nDCG after re-ranking (from 0.3192 to 0.3318).

4 Experiments

4.1 Description of Runs

Each participant in the ARQMath Lab was invited to submit up to five runs, each returning up to 1000 answers for each topic question, ranked by their deemed relevance to that question [22]. Our submitted primary run (labelled alpha05) is chosen to be a combination of our hypotheses for the best configuration for all research objectives: auto-extracted keywords and formulas as described in Sect. 3.1, Tangent-L's α parameter (Eq. 2) set to 0.5 so that each math tuple is weighted half as much as a keyword, and re-ranking as described in Sect. 3.3. The other submitted runs each vary these choices to test our hypotheses:

RQ1 *Topic Conversion*
To compare the effectiveness of our extraction algorithm with human understanding of the questions, alternate runs take as input lists of up to five keywords and up to two formulas per topic, all manually chosen by the lab organizers and made available to all participants. Runs with manual selection of keywords and formulas are labelled as such (e.g., alpha05-trans).

RQ2 *Formula Weight*
Previous experiments showed some improvement when reducing the weight of math formulas with respect to the weight for keywords [5]. The value of α is reflected in the label of the run (e.g., alpha02 uses $\alpha = 0.2$ and alpha10 uses $\alpha = 1.0$).

RQ3 *Re-ranking*
Runs with no re-ranking are labelled as such (e.g., alpha05-noR).

4.2 Effectiveness Results and Observations

The primary effectiveness measure for the task is the Normalized Discounted Cumulative Gain (nDCG) with unjudged documents removed (thus nDCG′). Following the organizers' practice [22], we also measure Mean Average Precision with unjudged documents removed (MAP′) and Precision at top-10 matches with unjudged documents removed (P′@10). Additionally, we calculate the bpref measure, which other researchers have found useful, and the count for *Unjudged Answers* within the top-k retrieved answers for each topic.[8]

[8] Having many unjudged answers implies that the evaluation might not be truly informative.

Table 1. CQA (main task) results, averaged over 77 topics. Parentheses indicate a result from an approach using privately held data not available to participants.

		Evaluation Measures				Unjudged Answers		
		nDCG'	*MAP'*†	*P'@10*†	*bpref*†	*top-10*	*top-20*	*top-50*
Baselines								
Linked MSE posts		(0.279)	(0.194)	(0.386)	(0.214)	15	33	45
Approach0		0.247	0.099	0.183	0.115	587	1215	3202
TF-IDF + Tangent-S		0.248	0.047	0.073	0.044	0	1	6
TF-IDF		0.204	0.049	0.074	0.043	1	2	4
Tangent-S		0.158	0.033	0.051	0.033	1	7	20
Tangent-L								
alpha10	*	0.267	0.063	0.079	0.042	0	2	236
alpha10-noR		0.327	0.134	0.158	0.123	4	79	1865
alpha10-trans-noR		0.357	0.149	0.208	0.137	211	557	2253
alpha05	¶	0.278	0.063	0.073	0.041	0	1	3
alpha05-trans	*	0.298	0.074	0.079	0.050	0	1	3
alpha05-noR	*	0.345	0.139	0.162	0.126	2	3	1796
alpha05-trans-noR		0.365	0.152	0.200	0.140	207	545	2227
alpha02	*	0.301	0.069	0.075	0.044	0	1	530
alpha02-noR		0.368	0.146	0.179	0.134	35	157	1784
alpha02-trans-noR		0.372	0.153	0.209	0.138	193	535	2205
alpha01-noR		**0.388**	0.153	0.204	0.142	105	362	1930
alpha01-trans-noR		0.387	**0.158**	0.212	0.142	198	560	2203
alpha001-noR		0.247	0.091	0.156	0.100	616	1271	3296
alpha001-trans-noR		0.348	0.157	**0.236**	**0.155**	371	884	2734

¶ submitted primary run † using H+M binarization
∗ submitted alternate run

The lab organizers obtained relevance assessments from human judges for approximately 500 answers for each of 77 of the 98 topics, and these assessments form the basis for comparing participating systems' performance. With respect to the primary measure, our system placed in the top three positions out of all 23 submissions [22]. This confirms our underlying hypothesis: Tangent-L outperforms other contemporary approaches to math-aware document retrieval, including some based on fusing several rankings and some attempting to build on pre-trained transformers. Our retrieval performance, including additional runs not submitted as part of the formal Lab evaluation, is summarized in Table 1, along with the performance of baseline systems provided by the lab organizers. Boldface is used to highlight the overall best-performing run for each measure.[9]

Our primary run alpha05, with presumed best configuration, actually performs worse than many of our alternate runs; the best performing run with

[9] One of the five baselines, *Linked MSE posts*, uses privately-held data, not available to Lab participants. The other four are traditional text or math-aware search systems adapted for the task.

respect to nDCG′ is alpha01-noR, which uses automated term extraction, $\alpha = 0.1$, and no re-ranking. Summarizing our insights to the research questions:

RQ1: Using automated term extraction is competitive with, but often outperformed by, runs using manually extracted formulas and keywords.
RQ2: Lowering the weight placed on math terms improves performance.
RQ3: Our proposed re-ranking is detrimental to effectiveness.

These observations generally hold with respect to all other evaluation measures.

An analysis based on topic categorization [14] also shows that our system performs particularly well for computational and proof-like topics that rely heavily on formulas. We attribute this strength to our core component, Tangent-L,[10] and conclude that in spite of our observation that performance improves for lower values of α, setting $\alpha = 0$ (i.e., assigning no weight to math terms in a query) would be a poor design decision.

Finally, we note that part of the success results from the search engine indexing question-answer pairs instead of answers only. In fact, when indexed documents include only the answer text, nDCG' scores deteriorate significantly. We hypothesize that question-answer pairs provide a context for evaluating the suitability of each answer in serving as an answer to newly posed topic questions.

4.3 Computational Resources and Efficiency

The size of our question-answer corpus is 24.3 GB with an index size of 5.0 GB. Using an Ubuntu 16.04.6 LTS server, with two Intel Xeon E5-2699 V4 Processors (22 cores 44 threads, 2.20 GHz for each), 1024 GB RAM, and 8TB disk space (on an USB3 external hard disk), it takes less than an hour to index all documents with parallel processing.

When query formulation and searching are executed on a Linux Mint 19.1 machine, with an Intel Core i5-8250U Processor (4 cores 8 threads, up to 3.40 GHz), 24 GB RAM, and 512 GB disk space,[11] retrieval time for the top 1000 matches is on average 13 s for each converted topic (with a maximum of just under a minute).

When re-ranking uses this same Mint machine, model training using the scikit-learn library[12] takes less than 30 s, and re-ranking for all 98 topics requires approximately 3 s per run.

5 Conclusions and Future Work

We conclude that a traditional math-aware search system remains a viable option for addressing a CQA task specialized in the mathematical domain. In particular, Tangent-L is a math-aware search engine well-suited to retrieve answers to

[10] We acknowledge that we have not tested this hypothesis by substituting another math-aware search engine in place of Tangent-L within our experimental apparatus. However, such engines were used for four baselines and by other Lab participants.

[11] A NVIDIA GeForce MX150 graphics card with 2 GB on-card RAM is available on the machine, but it is not used for the experiments.

[12] https://scikit-learn.org.

many computational and proof-like math questions that rely on the presence of formulas.

Nevertheless, several of our initial experimental design decisions turn out to be somewhat disappointing and leave room for improvement.

- Constraining the maximum number of keywords and formulas and the sizes of formulas extracted from a topic description might be worthwhile [18].
- Research related to Automatic Term Extraction (ATE) in technical domains, or in mathematical domains, might provide valuable insights into our problem [4].
- The many re-ranking approaches described in the SemEval CQA Challenge series [11–13] are worthy of further investigation, as they have proven to be successful in modelling CQA-type features that might also be present in the MSE collection.

For future research, the relevance assessments released at the conclusion of the Lab evaluation will certainly constitute important training data for evaluating alternative approaches to mathematical question-answering. The availability of more training data will likely make transformer-based methods much more competitive, especially as researchers improve their ability to design information-rich embeddings of mathematical formulas.

Acknowledgements. This research has been funded by the Waterloo-Huawei Joint Innovation Lab and NSERC, the Natural Science and Engineering Research Council of Canada. George Labahn, Mirette Marzouk, and Kevin Wang provided useful guidance during our weekly research meetings. Gordon Cormack provided his research machine for indexing the corpus. The ARQMath Lab organizers (including, notably, Behrooz Mansouri) developed the idea for the Lab, submitted the proposal to CLEF, and prepared the dataset, the topics, the manual translation of the topic questions into formulas and keywords, and the relevance assessments. The NTCIR Math-IR dataset was made available through an agreement with the National Institute of Informatics. Andrew Kane and anonymous reviewers made valuable suggestions for improving our presentation.

References

1. Abacha, A.B., Agichtein, E., Pinter, Y., Demner-Fushman, D.: Overview of the medical question answering task at TREC 2017 LiveQA. In: TREC 2017. NIST Special Publication, vol. 500-324 (2017)
2. Aizawa, A., Kohlhase, M., Ounis, I.: NTCIR-10 math pilot task overview. In: NTCIR-10, pp. 654–661 (2013)
3. Aizawa, A., Kohlhase, M., Ounis, I., Schubotz, M.: NTCIR-11 math-2 task overview. In: NTCIR-11, pp. 88–98 (2014)
4. Astrakhantsev, N.A., Fedorenko, D.G., Turdakov, D.Y.: Methods for automatic term recognition in domain-specific text collections: a survey. Program. Comput. Softw. **41**(6), 336–349 (2015)
5. Fraser, D.J., Kane, A., Tompa, F.W.: Choosing math features for BM25 ranking with Tangent-L. In: DocEng 2018, pp. 17:1–17:10 (2018)

6. Guidi, F., Sacerdoti Coen, C.: A survey on retrieval of mathematical knowledge. Math. Comput. Sci. **10**(4), 409–427 (2016)
7. Hopkins, M., Le Bras, R., Petrescu-Prahova, C., Stanovsky, G., Hajishirzi, H., Koncel-Kedziorski, R.: SemEval-2019 task 10: math question answering. In: SemEval-2019, pp. 893–899, June 2019
8. Lv, Y., Zhai, C.: Lower-bounding term frequency normalization. In: CIKM 2011, pp. 7–16 (2011)
9. Mansouri, B., Zanibbi, R., Oard, D.W.: Characterizing searches for mathematical concepts. In: JCDL 2019, pp. 57–66. IEEE (2019)
10. Miner, R.R., Carlisle, D., Ion, P.D.F.: Mathematical markup language (MathML) version 3.0, 2nd edn. W3C recommendation, W3C, April 2014
11. Nakov, P., et al.: SemEval-2017 task 3: community question answering. In: SemEval-2017. pp. 27–48, December 2018
12. Nakov, P., Màrquez, L., Magdy, W., Moschitti, A., Glass, J., Randeree, B.: SemEval-2015 task 3: answer selection in community question answering. In: SemEval-2015, pp. 269–281 (2015)
13. Nakov, P., et al.: SemEval-2016 task 3: community question answering. In: SemEval-2016, pp. 525–545 (2016)
14. Ng, Y.K., et al.: Dowsing for math answers with Tangent-L. In: CLEF 2020. CEUR Workshop Proceedings, vol. 2696 (2020)
15. Olvera-Lobo, M.-D., Gutiérrez-Artacho, J.: Question answering track evaluation in TREC, CLEF and NTCIR. In: Rocha, A., Correia, A.M., Costanzo, S., Reis, L.P. (eds.) New Contributions in Information Systems and Technologies. AISC, vol. 353, pp. 13–22. Springer, Cham (2015). https://doi.org/10.1007/978-3-319-16486-1_2
16. Pineau, D.C.: Math-aware search engines: physics applications and overview. CoRR abs/1609.03457 (2016)
17. Sojka, P., Novotný, V., Ayetiran, E.F., Lupták, D., Stefánik, M.: Quo Vadis, math information retrieval. In: RASLAN 2019, pp. 117–128. Tribun EU (2019)
18. Stoica, E., Evans, D.: Dynamic term selection in learning a query from examples. In: RIAO 2000, pp. 1703–1719. CID (2000)
19. Zanibbi, R., Aizawa, A., Kohlhase, M., Ounis, I., Topić, G., Davila, K.: NTCIR-12 MathIR task overview. In: NTCIR-12, pp. 299–308 (2016)
20. Zanibbi, R., Blostein, D.: Recognition and retrieval of mathematical expressions. Int. J. Doc. Anal. Recognit. **15**(4), 331–357 (2012)
21. Zanibbi, R., Davila, K., Kane, A., Tompa, F.W.: Multi-stage math formula search: using appearance-based similarity metrics at scale. In: SIGIR 2016, pp. 145–154 (2016)
22. Zanibbi, R., Oard, D.W., Agarwal, A., Mansouri, B.: Overview of ARQMath 2020 (updated working notes version): CLEF lab on answer retrieval for questions on math. In: CLEF 2020. CEUR Workshop Proceedings, vol. 2696 (2020)
23. Zanibbi, R., Orakwue, A.: Math search for the masses: multimodal search interfaces and appearance-based retrieval. In: Kerber, M., Carette, J., Kaliszyk, C., Rabe, F., Sorge, V. (eds.) CICM 2015. LNCS (LNAI), vol. 9150, pp. 18–36. Springer, Cham (2015). https://doi.org/10.1007/978-3-319-20615-8_2

Overviews 2021 Labs

Overview of ARQMath-2 (2021): Second CLEF Lab on Answer Retrieval for Questions on Math

Behrooz Mansouri[1(✉)], Richard Zanibbi[1], Douglas W. Oard[2], and Anurag Agarwal[1]

[1] Rochester Institute of Technology, Rochester, USA
{bm3302,rxzvcs,axasma}@rit.edu
[2] University of Maryland, College Park, USA
oard@umd.edu

Abstract. This paper provides an overview of the second year of the Answer Retrieval for Questions on Math (ARQMath-2) lab, run as part of CLEF 2021. The goal of ARQMath is to advance techniques for mathematical information retrieval, in particular retrieving answers to mathematical questions (Task 1), and formula retrieval (Task 2). Eleven groups participated in ARQMath-2, submitting 36 runs for Task 1 and 17 runs for Task 2. The results suggest that some combination of experience with the task design and the training data available from ARQMath-1 was beneficial, with greater improvements in ARQMath-2 relative to baselines for both Task 1 and Task 2 than for ARQMath-1 relative to those same baselines. Tasks, topics, evaluation protocols, and results for each task are presented in this lab overview.

Keywords: Community Question Answering (CQA) · Mathematical Information Retrieval (MIR) · Math-aware search · Math formula search

1 Introduction

This second Answer Retrieval for Questions on Math (ARQMath-2) lab[1] at the Conference and Labs of the Evaluation Forum (CLEF) continues a multi-year effort to build new test collections for Mathematics Information Retrieval (Math IR) from content found on Math Stack Exchange,[2] a Community Question Answering (CQA) forum. Using the question posts from Math Stack Exchange, participating systems are given a question or a formula from a question, and asked to return a ranked list of either potential answers to the question or potentially useful formulae (in the case of a formula query). Relevance is determined by the expected utility of each returned item. These tasks allow participating

[1] https://www.cs.rit.edu/~dprl/ARQMath.
[2] https://math.stackexchange.com.

K. S. Candan et al. (Eds.): CLEF 2021, LNCS 12880, pp. 215–238, 2021.
https://doi.org/10.1007/978-3-030-85251-1_17

Table 1. Examples of relevant and not-relevant results for tasks 1 and 2 [9]. For Task 2, formulae are associated with posts, indicated with ellipses at right (see Fig. 1 for more details). Query formulae are from question posts (here, the question at left), and retrieved formulae are from either an answer or a question post.

TASK 1: QUESTION ANSWERING	TASK 2: FORMULA RETRIEVAL
QUESTION I have spent the better part of this day trying to show from first principles that this sequence tends to 1. Could anyone give me an idea of how I can approach this problem? $$\lim_{n\to+\infty} n^{\frac{1}{n}}$$	QUERY FORMULA $\ldots \quad \lim_{n\to+\infty} n^{\frac{1}{n}} \quad \ldots$
RELEVANT You can use AM $\geq$ GM. $$\frac{1+1+\cdots+1+\sqrt{n}+\sqrt{n}}{n} \geq n^{1/n} \geq 1$$ $$1-\frac{2}{n}+\frac{2}{\sqrt{n}} \geq n^{1/n} \geq 1$$	RELEVANT $\ldots \quad \lim_{n\to\infty} \sqrt[n]{n} \quad \ldots$
NOT RELEVANT If you just want to show it converges, then the partial sums are increasing but the whole series is bounded above by $$1+\int_1^\infty \frac{1}{x^2}dx = 2$$	NOT RELEVANT $\ldots \quad \sum_{k=1} \frac{1}{k^2} = \frac{\pi^2}{6} \quad \ldots$

teams to explore leveraging math notation together with text to improve the quality of retrieval results. Table 1 illustrates these two tasks, and Fig. 1 shows the topic format for each task.

For the CQA task, 146,989 questions from 2020 that contained some text and at least one formula were considered as search topics, from which 100 were selected for use in ARQMath-2. For the question answering task, the title and body of the question were provided to participating teams, although other associated data (e.g., comments, answers, and links to related questions) were excluded. For the formula search task, an individual formula from the question post is specified as the query, and systems return a ranked list of other potentially useful instances of formulae found in the collection. Each of the 60 formula queries is a single formula extracted from a question used in the CQA task. For both tasks, participating teams had the option to construct queries using only the text or math portions of each question, or to use both math and text. Following convention, we refer to both questions and formula queries as *topics*.

The ARQMath labs have three objectives:

1. Create test collections for training and evaluating Math IR systems.
2. Establish state-of-the-art results on those test collections to which future researchers can compare their results.
3. Foster the growth of the Math IR research community.

Task 1: Question Answering

```
<Topics>
  ...
  <Topic number="A.9">
    <Title>Simplifying this series</Title>
    <Question>
      I need to write the series
      <span class=''math-container'' id=''q_52''>
        $$\sum_{n=0}^N nx^n$$
      </span>
      in a form that does not involve the summation
      notation, for example
      <span class=''math-container'' id=''q_53''>
        $\sum_{i=0}^n i^2 = \frac{(n^2+n)(2n+1)}{6}$
      </span>
      Does anyone have any idea how to do this?
      I have attempted multiple ways including using
      generating functions however no luck.
    </Question>
    <Tags>sequences-and-series</Tags>
  </Topic>
  ...
</Topics>
```

Task 2: Formula Retrieval

```
<Topics>
  ...
  <Topic number="B.9">
    <Formula_Id>q_52</Formula_Id>
    <Latex>\sum_{n=0}^N nx^n</Latex>
    <Title>Simplifying this series</Title>
    <Question>
      ...
    </Question>
    <Tags>sequences-and-series</Tags>
  </Topic>
  ...
</Topics>
```

Fig. 1. XML Topic File Formats for Tasks 1 and 2. Formula queries in Task 2 are taken from questions for Task 1. Here, ARQMath-1 formula topic B.9 is a copy of ARQMath-1 question topic A.9 with two additional tags for the query formula identifier and LaTeX before the question post.

ARQMath-2 saw progress on each of these goals, roughly doubling the size of the available test collections, nearly doubling the number of participating teams, and demonstrating that substantial improvements over the results reported in ARQMath-1 are possible.

2 Related Work

Math IR shares many commonalities with information retrieval more generally. For example, both exploratory search and refinding are common tasks, and query autocompletion and diversity ranking can be a useful capabilities. Math IR is a special case of cross-modal retrieval, since both text and math can be used to express the same idea, and those two modalities can be productively used together in the query, the document, or both.

The nature of mathematics, however, introduces some unique challenges. Here we need to distinguish between mathematics as a field and mathematical notation as a language. The notion of relevance in Math IR is grounded in mathematics as a field, whereas many of the implementation details are grounded in mathematical notation as a language. To see the difference, consider the notion of equality: many people would consider that $3 + 2$, $2 + 3$, and 5 express the same idea, being equally happy to find formulae that contain any of those. However, many might regard $cos^2(x) + sin^2(x)$ and 1 as different, despite their equality, because the first is specific to some uses of mathematics, and thus not an appropriate formulation for others.

Indeed, thinking of mathematics as a field is itself too reductionist – mathematics is used in many disciplines (e.g., computer science, physics, chemistry, quantum mechanics, economics, and nearly every branch of engineering). In some cases, relevance may be defined within one of those disciplines, with economists looking for other work in economics, for example. In other cases, relevance might be defined in a way that spans disciplines, such as when an engineer might be looking for the work of mathematicians that can help them to solve some specific problem, even when they don't know the notation the mathematicians would have used in formulating or solving that problem.

No single evaluation design could possibly model the full complexity of information needs for Math IR, so every evaluation has been specialized in some way. Mathematicians naturally find Math IR potentially interesting, and one motivation for early work on Math IR has been to support mathematics education. Students can use search engines to find references for assignments, to solve problems, increase knowledge, or clarify concepts. In general math-aware search can be used to find similarities between a piece of mathematics being developed, on the one hand, and proved theorems and well-developed theories in the same or different parts of mathematics, on the other hand.

Complementing this somewhat underdeveloped focus on task design among Math IR researchers is a quite well developed lower-level focus on what has been called Mathematical Knowledge Management (MKM), a research community concerned with the representations of, and operations on, mathematical notation. Among other accomplishments, their activities informed the development of MathML[3] for math on the Web, and novel techniques for math representation and applications such as theorem proving. This community meets annually at the Conference on Intelligent Computer Mathematics (CICM) [8].

Math IR naturally draws on both of these traditions. Math formula search has been studied since the mid-1990's for use in solving integrals, and publicly available math+text search engines have been around since the DLMF[4] system in the early 2000's [6,17]. Prior to ARQMath, the most widely used evaluation resources for math-aware information retrieval were initially developed over a five-year period at the National Institute of Informatics (NII) Testbeds and Community for Information access Research (at NTCIR-10 [1], NTCIR-11 [2] and NTCIR-12 [16]). NTCIR-12 used two collections, one a set of arXiv papers from physics that is split into paragraph-sized documents, and the other a set of articles from English Wikipedia. The NTCIR Mathematical Information

[3] https://www.w3.org/Math.
[4] https://dlmf.nist.gov.

Retrieval (MathIR) tasks developed evaluation methods and allowed participating teams to establish baselines for both "text + math" queries (i.e., keywords and formulae) and isolated formula queries.

At NTCIR-11 and NTCIR-12, formula retrieval was considered in a variety of settings, including the use of wildcards and constraints on symbols or subexpressions (e.g., requiring matched argument symbols to be variables or constants). Our Task 2, Formula Retrieval, has similarities in design to the NTCIR-12 Wikipedia Formula Browsing task, but differs in how queries are defined and how evaluation is performed. In particular, relevance is defined contextually in ARQMath, and ARQMath evaluation is based on *visually distinct* formulae, rather than all (possibly identical) formula instances, as had been done in NTCIR-12. The NTCIR-12 formula retrieval test collection also had a smaller number of queries, with 20 fully specified formula queries (plus 20 variants of those same queries with subexpressions replaced by wildcard characters). NTCIR-11 also had a formula retrieval task, with 100 queries, but in that case systems searched only for exact matches [15].

Another related effort was the SemEval 2019 [7] question answering task. Question sets from MathSAT (Scholastic Achievement Test) practice exams in three categories were used: Closed Algebra, Open Algebra and Geometry. A majority of the questions were multiple choice, with some having numeric answers. This is a valuable parallel development; the questions considered in the CQA task of ARQMath are more informal and open-ended, and selected from actual Math Stack Exchange user posts (a larger and less constrained set).

3 The ARQMath Stack Exchange Collection

For ARQMath-2, we reused the test collection from the first ARQMath. The test collection was constructed using the March 1st, 2020 Math Stack Exchange snapshot from the Internet Archive.[5] Questions and answers from 2010–2018 are included in the collection. The ARQMath test collection contains roughly 1 million questions and 28 million formulae. Formulae in the collection are annotated using <`span`> tags with the class attribute `math-container`, and a unique integer identifier given in the `id` attribute. Formulae are also provided separately in three index files for different formula representations (LaTeX, Presentation MathML, and Content MathML), which we describe in more detail below.

HTML views of question threads, similar to those on the Math Stack Exchange web site (a question, along with answers and other related information) are also included in the ARQMath test collection. The threads are constructed automatically from Math Stack Exchange snapshot XML files. The threads are intended for those performing manual runs, or who wish to examine search results (on queries other than evaluation queries) for formative evaluation purposes. These threads are also used by assessors during evaluation. The HTML thread files were intended only for viewing threads; participants were asked to use provided XML and formula index files to train their models.

[5] https://archive.org/download/stackexchange.

Questions posted after 2018 are used to create test topics: questions from 2019 were used for the first ARQMath, and questions from 2020 are used for ARQMath-2. Additional details may be found in the ARQMath-1 task overview paper [18].

Formula Index Files and Visually Distinct Formulae. In addition to LaTeX, it is common for math-aware information retrieval systems to represent formulae as one or both of two types of rooted trees. Appearance is represented by the spatial arrangement of symbols on writing lines (in Symbol Layout Trees (SLTs)), and mathematical syntax (sometimes referred to as (shallow) semantics) is represented using a hierarchy of operators and arguments (in Operator Trees (OPTs)) [5,11,19]. The standard representations for these are Presentation MathML (SLT) and Content MathML (OPT).

To reduce effort for participants, and to maximize comparability across submitted runs, we used LaTeXML[6] 0.8.5 to generate Presentation MathML and Content MathML from LaTeX for each formula in the ARQMath collection. Some LaTeX formulae were malformed, and LaTeXML has some processing limitations, resulting in conversion failures for 0.14% of both SLTs and OPTs.[7] Participants could elect to do their own formula extraction and conversions, although the formulae that could be submitted in system runs for Task 2 were limited to those with identifiers in the provided LaTeX formula index file.

During evaluation we learned that LaTeX formulae that could not be processed by LaTeXML had their visual identifiers assigned incorrectly, and this may have affected adjacent formulae in the formula index files. This had a small effect on evaluation metrics (our best estimate is that no more than 1.3 visually distinct formulae in the pool for each topic were affected).

ARQMath formulae are provided in LaTeX, SLT, and OPT representations, as Tab Separated Value (TSV) index files. Each line of a TSV file represents a single instance of a formula, containing the formula id, the id of the post in which the formula instance appeared, the id of the thread in which the post is located, a post type (title, question, answer or comment), and the formula representation in either LaTeX, SLT (Presentation MathML), or OPT (Content MathML).

For ARQMath-2, in the formula TSV index files we added a new field for *visually distinct* formula identifiers used in evaluation for Task 2 (Formula Retrieval).[8] The idea is to identify formulae sharing the same appearance. So for example, two occurrences of x^2 in a TSV formula index have different formula *instance* identifiers, but the same *visually distinct* formula identifier. All ARQMath-2 formula index files provide visually distinct identifiers for each formula in the collection.

There are three sets of formula index files: one set is for the collection (i.e., for posts from 2018 and before), while the second and third sets are for search

[6] https://dlmf.nist.gov/LaTeXML.

[7] We thank Deyan Ginev and Vit Novotny for helping reduce LaTeXML failures: for ARQMath-1 conversion failures affected 8% of SLTs, and 10% of OPTs.

[8] We thank Frank Tompa for sharing this suggestion at CLEF 2020.

topics from 2020 (ARQMath-2), and 2019 (ARQMath-1). Only the collection index files have visually distinct formula identifiers.

Distribution. The Math Stack Exchange test collection was distributed to participants as XML files on Google Drive.[9] To facilitate local processing, the organizers provided python code on GitHub[10] for reading and iterating over the XML data, and generating the HTML question threads.

4 Task 1: Answer Retrieval

The main task in ARQMath is the answer retrieval task. Participating systems are given a Math Stack Exchange question post from 2019, and return a ranked list of up to 1,000 answer posts from 2010–2018. System results ('runs') are evaluated using rank quality measures that characterize the extent to which annotated answers with higher relevance come before answers with lower relevance (e.g., nDCG′). This makes Task 1 a ranking task rather than a set retrieval task.

In the following we describe the Task 1 search topics, runs from participant and baseline systems, the assessment and evaluation procedures used, and a summary of the results.

4.1 Topics

In Task 1, participants were given 100 Math Stack Exchange questions posted in 2020 as topics. We used a sampling strategy similar to ARQMath-1, where we chose from questions containing text and at least one formula. To help ensure that most topics had relevant answers available in the collection, we calculated the number of duplicate and related posts for each question, and then chose the majority of topics (89 out of 100) from those with at least one duplicate or related post.[11] To increase the difficulty and diversity of topics, we selected the remaining topics from those without annotated duplicates or related posts.[12]

Because we were interested in a diverse range of search tasks, we also calculated the number of formulae for each question. Finally, we noted the asker's reputation and the tags assigned for each question. We manually drew a sample of 100 questions stratified along those dimensions. In the end, pools for 71 of these questions were evaluated and found to have a sufficient number of relevant responses, and thus were included in the ARQMath-2 test collection.

The topics were selected from various domains to capture a broad spectrum of mathematical areas. The difficulty level of the topics spanned from easy problems that a beginning undergraduate student might be interested in to difficult problems that would be of interest to more advanced users. The bulk of the

[9] https://drive.google.com/drive/folders/1ZPKIWDnhMGRaPNVLi1reQxZWTfH2R4u3.

[10] https://github.com/ARQMath/ARQMathCode.

[11] Participating systems did not have access to this information.

[12] In ARQMath-1, all topics had links to at least one duplicate or related post that were available to the organizers.

topics were aimed at the level of undergraduate math majors (in their 3rd or 4th year) or engineering majors fulfilling their math requirements.

As organizers, we labeled each question with one of three broad categories, *computation*, *concept* or *proof*. Out of the 71 assessed questions, 25 were categorized as *computation*, 19 as *concept*, and 27 as *proof*. We also categorized questions based on their perceived difficulty level, with 32 categorized as easy, 20 as medium, and 19 as hard. Our last categorization was based on whether a question is dependent on text, formula or both. 10 questions were (in our opinion) dependent on text, 21 on formula and 40 on both.

The topics were published as an XML file with the format shown in Fig. 1, where the topic number is an attribute of the Topic tag, and the Title, Question and asker-provided Tags are from the Math Stack Exchange question post. To facilitate system development, we provided python code that participants could use to load the topics. As in the collection, the formulae in the topic file are placed in '`math-container`' tags, with each formula instance represented by a unique identifier and its LaTeX representation. And, as with the collection, we provided three TSV files, one each for the LaTeX, OPT and SLT representations of the formulae, in the same format as the collection's TSV files.

4.2 Participant Runs

Participating teams submitted runs using Google Drive. A total of 36 runs were received from a total of 9 teams. Of these, 28 runs were declared to be automatic, meaning that queries were automatically processed from the topic file, that no changes to the system had been made after seeing the queries, and that ranked lists for each query were produced with no human intervention. 8 runs were declared to be manual, meaning that there was some type of human involvement in generating the ranked list for each query. Manual runs can contribute diversity to the pool of documents that are judged for relevance, since their error characteristics can differ from those of automatic runs. The teams and submissions are shown in Table 2. Please see the participant papers in the working notes for descriptions of the systems that generated these runs.

4.3 Baseline Runs: TF-IDF, Tangent-S, Linked Posts

The organizers ran four baseline systems for Task 1. These baselines were also run for ARQMath 2020, and we re-ran them on the same systems as last year, obtaining very similar run-times [18]. Here is a description of our baseline runs.

1. **TF-IDF.** A term frequency, inverse document frequency) model using the Terrier system [13], with formulae represented using their LaTeX strings. Default parameters from Terrier were used.
2. **Tangent-S.** Formula search engine using SLT and OPT formula representations [5]. One formula was selected from each Task 1 question title if possible; if there was no formula in the title, then one formula was instead chosen from the question's body. If there were multiple formulae in the selected field, a formula with the largest number of symbols (nodes) in its SLT representation

Table 2. Submitted runs for Task 1 (36 runs) and Task 2 (17 runs). Additional baselines for Task 1 (4 runs) and Task 2 (1 run) were also generated by the organizers.

	Automatic		Manual	
	Primary	Alternate	Primary	Alternate
Task 1: Answers				
Baselines	2	2		
Approach0			1	4
BetterThanG		2	1	2
DPRL	1	2		
GoogolFuel	1	4		
MathDowsers	1	1		
MIRMU	1	4		
MSM	1	4		
PSU	1			
TU_DBS	1	4		
Task 2: Formulas				
Baseline	1			
Approach0			1	4
DPRL	1	3		
MathDowsers	1	1		
NLP-NITS	1			
TU_DBS	1	3		
XY_PHOC_DPRL	1			

was chosen; if more than one formula had the largest number of symbols, we chose randomly between them.

3. **TF-IDF + Tangent-S.** Averaging similarity scores from the TF-IDF and Tangent-S baselines. The relevance scores from both systems were normalized in [0,1] using min-max normalization, and then combined using an unweighted average.
4. **Linked Math Stack Exchange Posts.** This is a simple oracle "system" that is able to see duplicate post links from 2020 in the Math Stack Exchange collection (which were not available to participants). It returns *all* answer posts from 2018 or earlier that were in threads that Math Stack Exchange moderators had marked as duplicating the topic question post. Answer posts are sorted in descending order by their vote scores.

4.4 Assessment

Pooling. Participants were asked to rank up to 1,000 answer posts for each topic, which were then sampled for assessment using Top-k pooling. The top 45

Table 3. Relevance assessment criteria for tasks 1 and 2.

Score	Rating	Definition
Task 1: Answer retrieval		
3	High	Sufficient to answer the complete question on its own
2	Medium	Provides some path towards the solution. This path might come from clarifying the question, or identifying steps towards a solution
1	Low	Provides information that could be useful for finding or interpreting an answer, or interpreting the question
0	Not relevant	Provides no information pertinent to the question or its answers. A post that restates the question without providing any new information is considered non-relevant
Task 2: Formula retrieval		
3	High	Just as good as finding an exact match to the query formula would be
2	Medium	Useful but not as good as the original formula would be
1	Low	There is some chance of finding something useful
0	Not relevant	Not expected to be useful

results were combined from all primary runs. To this, we added the top 15 results from each alternate run. The baseline systems, TF-IDF + Tangent-S and Linked Math Stack Exchange Posts, were considered as primary runs and the other two (TF-IDF and Tangent-S) were considered as alternative. Duplicates were then deleted, and the resulting pool was sorted randomly for display to assessors. The pooling depth was designed to identify as many relevant answer posts as possible given our assessment resources. On average, the pools contained 448.12 answers per topic.

Relevance Definition. We used the same relevance definitions created for ARQMath-1. To avoid assessors needing to guess about the level of mathematical knowledge available to the Math Stack Exchange users who originally posted the questions, we asked assessors to base their judgments on the degree of usefulness for an expert (modeled in this case as a math professor), who might then try to use that answer to help the person who had asked the original question. We defined four levels of relevance, as shown in Table 3.

Assessors were allowed to consult external sources to familiarize themselves with the topic of a question, but relevance judgments were made using only information available within the ARQMath test collection. For example, if an answer contained a Math Stack Exchange link such as https://math.stackexchange.com/questions/163309/pythagorean-theorem, they could follow that link to better understand the intent of the person writing the answer, but an external link to the Wikipedia page https://en.wikipedia.org/wiki/Pythagorean_theorem would not be followed.

Training. Unlike ARQMath-1, for ARQMath-2 participants could use the 77 annotated topics for ARQMath-1 Task 1 as a training set [10,18]. For sanity checking results and comparison, results were collected from participants for both the ARQMath-1 and ARQMath-2 topics, and results for both training (ARQMath-1) and testing (ARQMath-2) are provided at the end this document.

Assessment System. For ARQMath-2, assessments were again performed using Turkle[13], a locally installed system with functionality similar to Amazon Mechanical Turk. As Fig. 4 at the end of this document illustrates, there were two panels in the Turkle user interface. The question was shown on the left panel, with the Title on top in a grey bar; below that was the question body. There was also a Thread link, through which assessors could access the Math Stack Exchange post in context, with the question and all answers given for this question (in 2020). In the right panel, the answer to be judged was shown at the top, along with another thread link that allows assessors to view the original thread in which the answer post appeared, which could be helpful for clarifying the context of the answer post, for example by viewing the original question to which it had been posted as a response. Finally, below the answer in the right panel was where assessors selected relevance ratings.

In addition to four levels of relevance, two additional choices were available: 'System failure' indicated system issues such as unintelligible rendering of formulae, or the thread link not working (when it was essential for interpretation). If after viewing the threads, the assessors were still not able to decide the relevance degree, they were asked to choose 'Do not know'. The organizers asked the assessors to leave a comment in the event of a system failure or a 'Do not know' selection. As it happened, the ARQMath-2 assessors did not use these options for Task 1; for each answer, they decided a relevance degree.

Assessor Training. Seven paid undergraduate and graduate mathematics and computer science students from RIT and St. John Fisher College were paid to perform relevance judgments. One assessor had worked with us previously on ARQMath-1. Due to the COVID pandemic, all training sessions were performed remotely over Zoom. For ARQMath-1, relevance criteria had been developed interactively with assessors, leading to four rounds of training; we found the resulting relevance criteria worked well, and so we reused them for ARQMath-2. This allowed us to reduce assessor training time: the four assessors who worked exclusively on Task 1 participated in three meetings, and just two rounds of training assessments. The remaining three assessors initially worked on Task 2, and were later moved to Task 1 after Task 2 assessment was completed. Those three assessors had an initial training meeting when they returned to Task 1 to introduce the task, and then they performed a single round of training assessments, with subsequent discussion at a second meeting. One of those three assessors had previously worked on both Task 1 and Task 2 assessments for ARQMath-1.

At the first assessor meeting, the lab and administrative details were discussed. After this, the assessors were divided into two groups, for Task 1 and Task 2. After this we began training sessions. In the first Task 1 training session, the task was explained, making reference to specific topics and previously assessed answers from ARQMath-1. For each training/practice assessment round, the same 7 topics were assigned to every assessor and the assessors worked independently, thus permitting inter-assessor agreement measures to be computed. After

[13] https://github.com/hltcoe/turkle.

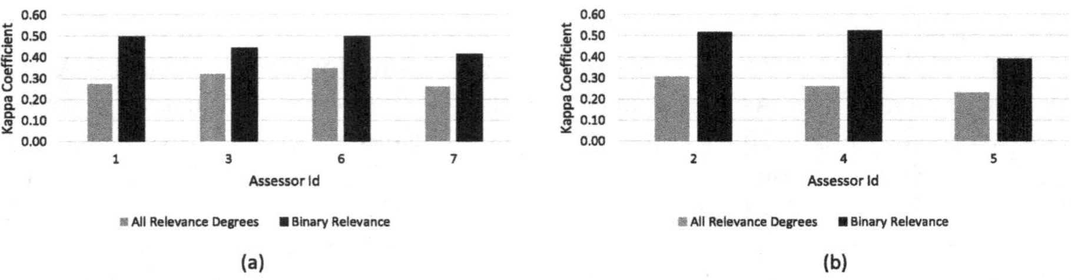

Fig. 2. Inter-annotator agreement (Average Cohen' kappa) over 7 assessors during the last Task 1 training (7 topics from ARQMath-1); four-way classification (gray) and two-way (H+M binarized) classification (black). Chart (a) shows the agreement between the assessors who did only Task 1 and had an additional training session. Chart (b) shows the agreement between the assessors who started with Task 2, and then moved to Task 1.

completing training assessments, a meeting was held to discuss disagreements in relevance scores between with the organizers, along with clarifications of the relevance criteria. The assessors discussed the reasoning for their choices, with the fourth author of this paper (an expert Math Stack Exchange user) sharing their own assessment and reasoning. The primary goal of training was to help assessors make self-consistent annotations, as question interpretations will vary across individuals.

Some of the question topics would not be typically covered in regular undergraduate courses, so that was a challenge that required the assessors to get a basic understanding of those topics before they could do the assessment. The assessors found the questions threads made available in the Turkle interface helpful in this regard (see Fig. 4).

Figure 2 shows agreement between assessors in our two groups over the course of the training process. As shown, collapsing relevance to be binary by considering high and medium as relevant and low and not-relevant as a not-relevant (henceforth "H+M binarization") yielded better agreement among the assessors.[14]

Assessment. A total of 81 topics were assessed for Task 1. 10 judgment pools (for topics A.208, A.215, A.216, A.221, A.230, A.236, A.266, A.277, A.278 and A.280) had zero or one posts with relevance levels of high or medium; these topics were removed from the collection because topics with no relevant posts cannot be used to distinguish between ranked retrieval systems, and because topics with only a single relevant post result in coarsely quantized values for the

[14] H+M binarization corresponds to the definition of relevance usually used in the Text Retrieval Conference (TREC). The TREC definition is "If you were writing a report on the subject of the topic and would use the information contained in the document in the report, then the document is relevant. Only binary judgments ('relevant' or 'not relevant') are made, and a document is judged relevant if any piece of it is relevant (regardless of how small the piece is in relation to the rest of the document)." (source: https://trec.nist.gov/data/reljudge_eng.html).

evaluation measures that we report. For the remaining 71 topics, an average of 447.7 answers were assessed, with an average assessment time of 83.3 s per answer post. The average number of answers labeled with any degree of relevance (high, medium, or low; henceforth "H+M+L binarization") was 49.0 per question, with the highest number of relevant answers being 134 (for topic A.237) and the lowest being 4 (for topic A.227).

Post Assessment. After assessments were completed for Task 1, each assessor was assigned one topic that had originally been completed by another assessor.[15] We were particularly interested in confirming cases in which non relevant documents were found, so for each assessor we selected the topic with the fewest relevant topics. Among the 6 dual-assessed topics, 4 had no high or medium relevant answers according to at least one of the two assessors[16]; meaningful values of kappa for binary relevance can not be calculated in such cases. Averaged over the remaining two questions, kappa was 0.21 on the four-way assessment task, and using H+M binarization it was 0.32.

4.5 Evaluation Measures

For a complex task where rich training data is not yet available, it is possible that a large number of relevant answers may be missed during assessment. Measures which treat unjudged documents as not relevant can be used when directly comparing systems contributing to the judgment pools, but non-contributing systems can be disadvantaged by treating unjudged documents as not relevant, which may prove to be relevant in later analysis. We therefore chose the nDCG$'$ measure (read as "nDCG-prime") introduced by Sakai and Kando [14] as the primary measure for the task.

nDCG is a widely used measure for graded relevance judgments, used to produce a single figure of merit over a set of ranked lists. For ARQMath, each retrieved document earns a gain value (relevance score) $g \in \{0, 1, 2, 3\}$, discounted by a slowly decaying function of the rank position of each result. Discounted gain values are accumulated and then normalized to [0,1] by dividing by the maximum possible Discounted Cumulative Gain (i.e., from all relevant documents sorted in decreasing order of gain value). This results in normalized Discounted Cumulative Gain (nDCG).

The only difference when computing nDCG$'$ is that unjudged documents are removed from the ranked list before performing the computation. It has been shown that nDCG$'$ has somewhat better discriminative power and somewhat better system ranking stability (with judgement ablation) than the bpref measure [4] used recently for formula search (e.g., [11]). Moreover, nDCG$'$ yields a single-valued measure with graded relevance, whereas bpref, Precision@k, and Mean Average Precision (MAP) all require binarized relevance judgments. In addition to nDCG$'$, we also compute Mean Average Precision (MAP) with unjudged

[15] One assessor (with id 7) was not able to continue assessment.

[16] Two of the 4 dual-assessed topics had no high or medium relevant answers found by either assessor.

posts removed (thus MAP′), and Precision at 10 with unjudged posts removed (P′@10).[17] For MAP′ and P′@10 we used H+M binarization.

The ARQMath Task 1 evaluation script removes unjudged posts as a pre-processing step where required, and then computes evaluation measures using `trec_eval`.[18]

4.6 Results

Table 4 in the appendix shows the results for baselines along with teams and their systems ranked by nDCG′. nDCG′ values can be interpreted as the average (over topics) of the fraction of the score for the best possible that was actually achieved. As can be seen, the best nDCG′ value that was achieved was 0.434, by the MathDowsers team. MAP′ with H+M binarization generally ranks systems in the same order as nDCG′ does with graded relevance judgments. However, the results for P′@10 with H+M binarization differ, the TU_DBS team doing best among the participating teams by that measure (exceeded only by the *Linked MSE posts* baseline, which uses human-built links that were not available to participating teams). There are some noticeable differences in system orderings for several participating teams when using ARQMath-2 topics compared with what was seen when those same teams used the same systems (in 2021) on ARQMath-1 topics.

Now comparing results from 2021 with results from 2020, we see that the best improvement over the strongest fully automated baseline in both years (*TF-IDF + Tangent-S*) was substantially larger in 2021 than in 2020. Specifically, in 2020 the MathDowsers team outperformed that baseline by 39% as measured by nDCG′; in 2021 they outperformed that same baseline by 116% as measured by nDCG′.

5 Task 2: Formula Retrieval

In the formula retrieval task, participants were presented with one formula from a 2020 question used in Task 1, and asked to return a ranked list of up to 1,000 formula instances from questions or answers from the evaluation epoch (2018 or earlier). Formulae were returned by their identifiers in `math-container` tags and the companion TSV LaTeX formula index file, along with their associated post identifiers.

As with Task 1, ranked lists were evaluated using rank quality measures, making this a ranking task rather than a set retrieval task. Three key details differentiate Task 2 from Task 1:

[17] Pooling to at least depth 10 ensures that there are no unjudged posts above rank 10 for any baseline, primary, or alternative run. Note that P′@10 cannot achieve a value of 1 because some topics have fewer than 10 relevant posts.

[18] https://github.com/usnistgov/trec_eval.

1. Unlike Task 1, in Task 2 the goal is not answering questions, but to instead show the searcher formulae that might be useful as they seek to satisfy their information need. Task 2 is thus still grounded in the question, but the relevance of a retrieved formula is defined by a formula's expected utility, not just the post in which any one formula instance was found.
2. In Task 1 only answer posts were returned, but for Task 2 the formulae may appear in answer posts or in question posts.
3. For Task 2 we distinguish visually distinct formulae from instances of those formulae, and evaluate by the ranking of visually distinct formulae returned. We call formulae appearing in posts *formula instances*, and of course the same formula may appear in more than one post. By *a visually distinct formula* we mean a set of formula instances that are visually identical when viewed in isolation. For example, x^2 is a formula, $x \cdot x$ is a different visually distinct formula, and each time x^2 appears is a distinct instance of the visually distinct formula x^2. Although systems in Task 2 rank formula instances in order to support the relevance judgment process, the evaluation measure for Task 2 is based on the ranking of visually distinct formulae.

The remainder of this section describes for Task 2 the search topics, the submissions and baselines, the process used for creating relevance judgments, the evaluation measures, and the results.

5.1 Topics

In Task 2, participating teams were given 100 mathematical formulae, each found in a different Math Stack Exchange question from Task 1 (posted in 2020). They were asked to find relevant formulae instances from either question or answer posts in the test collection (from 2018 and earlier). The topics for Task 2 were provided in an XML file similar to those of Task 1, in the format shown in Fig. 1. Task 2 topics differ from their corresponding Task 1 topics in three ways:

1. **Topic number.** For Task 2, topic ids are in the form "B.x" where x is the topic number. There is a correspondence between topic id in tasks 1 and 2. For instance, topic id "B.209" indicates the formula is selected from topic "A.209" in Task 1, and both topics include the same question post (see Fig. 1).
2. **Formula_Id.** This added field specifies the unique identifier for the query formula instance. There may be other formulae in the Title or Body of the question post, but the query is only the formula instance specified by this Formula_Id.
3. **LaTeX.** This added field is the LaTeX representation of the query formula instance as found in the question post.

Because query formulae are drawn from Task 1 question posts, the same LaTeX, SLT and OPT TSV files that were provided for the Task 1 topics can be consulted when SLT or OPT representations for a query formula are needed.

Formulae for Task 2 were manually selected using a heuristic approach to stratified sampling over three criteria: complexity, elements, and text dependence. Formulae complexity was labeled low, medium or high by the fourth author. For example, $\frac{df}{dx} = f(x+1)$ is low complexity, $\sum_{k=0}^{n} \binom{n}{k} k$ is medium complexity, and

$$x - \frac{x^3}{3 \times 3!} + \frac{x^5}{5 \times 5!} - \frac{x^7}{7 \times 7!} + \cdots = \sum_{n=0}^{\infty} (-1)^n \frac{x^{(2n+1)}}{(2n+1) \times (2n+1)!}$$

is high complexity.

Text dependence reflected the first author's opinion of the degree to which text in the Title and Question fields were likely to yield related search results. For instance, for one Task 2 topic, the query formula is $\frac{df}{dx} = f(x+1)$ whereas the complete question is: "How to solve differential equations of the following form: $\frac{df}{dx} = f(x+1)$." When searching for this formula, perhaps the surrounding text could safely be ignored. At most one formula was selected from each Task 1 question topic to produce Task 2 topics. For cases in which suitable formulae were present in both the title and the body of the Task 1 question, we selected the Task 2 formula query from the title.

5.2 Participant Runs

A total of 17 runs were received for Task 2 from a total of six teams, as shown in Table 2. Each run contained at most 1,000 formula instances for each topic, ranked in decreasing order of system-estimated relevance to that query. For each formula instance in a ranked list, participating teams provided the `formula_id` and the associated `post_id` for that formula. Please see the participant papers in the working notes for descriptions of the systems that generated these runs.

5.3 Baseline Run: Tangent-S

We again used Tangent-S [5] as our baseline. Unlike Task 1, a single formula is specified for each Task 2 query, so no formula selection step was needed. This Tangent-S baseline makes no use of the question text. Timing was similar to the use of Tangent-S in ARQMath-1.

5.4 Assessment

Pooling. The retrieved items for Task 2 are formula instances, but pooling was done based on the visually distinct formulae, and not individual formula instances. Visually distinct formulae were identified by clustering all formula instances in the collection.[19] Pooling was performed by then proceeding down each results list until at least one instance of some number of visually distinct formulae had been seen. For primary runs and for the baseline run, the pool depth was the rank of the first instance of the 20th visually distinct formula; for alternate runs the pool depth was the rank of the first instance of the 10th visually distinct formulae.[20]

[19] This differs from the approach used for ARQMath-1, when only submitted formula instances were clustered. For ARQMath-2 the full formula collection was clustered to facilitate post hoc use of the resulting test collection.

[20] In ARQMath-2, Task 1 pools were not used to seed task 2 pools.

Clustering of visually distinct formulae instances was performed using the SLT representation when possible,[21] and the LaTeX representation otherwise. We first converted the Presentation MathML representation to a string representation using Tangent-S, which performed a depth-first traversal of the SLT, with each SLT node and edge generating a single character of the SLT string. Formula instances with identical SLT strings were considered to be the same formula; note that this ignores differences in font. For formula instances with no Tangent-S SLT string available, we removed the white space from their LaTeX strings and grouped formula instances with identical strings. This process is simple and appears to be reasonably robust, but it is possible that some visually identical formula instances were not captured due to LaTeXML conversion failures, or where different LaTeX strings produce the same formula (e.g., if subscripts and superscripts appear in a different order in LaTeX).

Assessment was done on formula instances: for each visually distinct formula we selected at most five instances to assess. We did this differently than last year; in order to prefer highly-ranked instances and instances returned in multiple runs, we selected the 5 instances using a simple voting protocol, where each instance votes by the sum of its reciprocal ranks within each run, breaking ties randomly. Out of 8,129 visually distinct formulae that were assessed, 117 (1.4%) had instances in more than 5 pooled posts.[22]

Relevance Definition. The relevance judgment task was defined for assessors as follows: for a formula query, if a search engine retrieved one or more instances of this retrieved formula, would that have been expected to be useful for the task that the searcher was attempting to accomplish?

Assessors were presented with formula instances in context (i.e., in the question or answer in which they had been found). They were then asked to decide their relevance by considering whether retrieving either that instance or some other instance of that formula could have helped the searcher to address their information need. To make this judgment, they were shown the query formula within the question post where it appeared. Each formula instance in the judgment pool was assigned one of four relevance levels as defined in Table 3.

For example, if the formula query was $\sum \frac{1}{n^{2+\cos n}}$, and the formula instance to be judged is $\sum_{n-1}^{\infty} \frac{1}{n^2}$, the assessors could look at the formula's associated post, compare the formula's variable types and operations with the query, identify the area of mathematics it concerns, and then decide whether finding the second formula rather than the first would be expected to yield good results. Further, they could consider the content of the question post containing the query (and, optionally, the thread containing that question post) in order to understand the searcher's information need. Thus the question post fills a role akin to Borlund's

[21] For ARQMath-1, 92% of formula instances had an SLT representation; for ARQMath-2 we reparsed the collection and improved this to 99.9%.

[22] As mentioned in Sect. 3, a relatively small number of formulae per topic had incorrectly generated visual ids. In 6 cases assessors indicated that a pooled formula for a single visual id was 'not matching' the other formulae in hits grouped for a visual id, rather than assign a relevance score for the formula.

simulated work task [3], although in this case the title, body and tags from the question post are included in the topic and thus can optionally be used by the retrieval system.

The assessor could also consult the post containing a retrieved formula instance (which may be another question post, or an answer post) along with the associated thread, to see if in that case the formula instance would indeed have been a useful basis for a search. Note, however, that the assessment task is not to determine whether the specific post containing the retrieved formula instance is useful, but rather to use that context as a basis for estimating the degree to which useful content would likely be found if this or other instances of the retrieved formula were returned by a search engine.

We then defined the relevance score for a formula to be the maximum relevance score for any judged instance of that formula. This relevance definition essentially asks "if instances of this formula were returned, would we reasonably expect some of those instances to be useful?"

Assessment System. We again used Turkle to build the assessment system for Task 2. As shown in Fig. 4 (at the end of this document), there are two main panels. In the left panel, the question is shown as in Task 1, but now with the formula query highlighted in yellow. In the right panel, up to five retrieval posts (question posts or answer posts) containing instances of the same retrieved formula are displayed, with the retrieved formula instance highlighted in each case. For example, the formula $\sum_{n=1}^{\infty} a_n$ shown in Fig. 4 was retrieved both in an answer post (shown first) and in a question post (shown second). As in Task 1, buttons are provided for the assessor to record their judgment; unlike Task 1, judgments for each instance of the same retrieved formula (up to 5) are recorded separately, and later used to produce a *single* maximum score for each visually distinct formula.

Assessor Training. Three assessors were assigned to perform relevance judgements for Task 2, one of whom had also assessed Task 2 for ARQMath-1 in 2020. Three rounds of training were performed.

In the first training round, the assessors were familiarized with the task. To illustrate how formula search might be used, we interactively demonstrated formula suggestion in MathDeck [12] and the formula search capability of Approach0 [19]. Then the task was defined using examples, showing a formula query with some retrieved results, talking through the relevance definitions and how to apply those definitions in specific cases. Two topics from ARQMath-1 (B.1, B.18) were selected as examples. During the training session, the assessors saw different example results for topics and discussed their relevance based on criteria defined for them with the organizers. These examples were manually selected from ARQMath-1 relevance judgments having different relevance degrees, and included examples from dual-assessed topics that 2020 assessors had disagreements on. The assessors also received feedback from the fourth author of this paper, an expert Math Stack Exchange user.

All three assessors were then assigned 7 other Task 2 topics from ARQMath-1 (B.29, B.32, B.33, B.41, B.59, B.62, B.70) to independently assess. The formulae

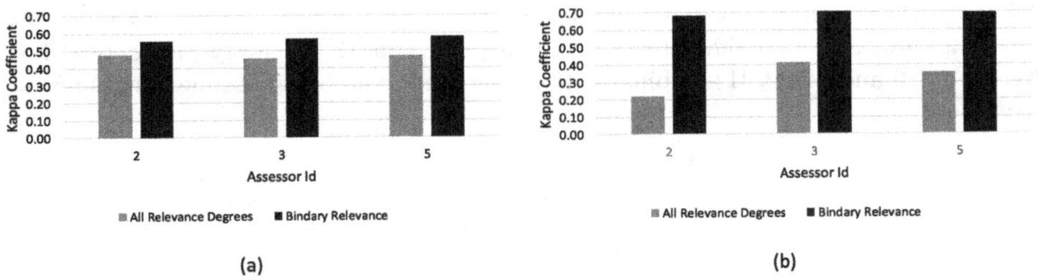

Fig. 3. Inter-assessor agreement (Cohen's kappa) over 3 assessors. Chart (a) shows the agreement on the last training round (7 topics from ARQMath-1). Chart (b) shows the agreement after official Task 2 assessment. Each assessor evaluated two topics, one by each the other two assessors. Shown are four-way classification (gray) and two-way (H+M binarized) classification (black).

to assess were chosen manually using the same process as the first training round. After assessment, the assessors and organizers met by Zoom to discuss and resolve disagreements. The assessors used this opportunity to refine their understanding of the relevance criteria, and the application of those criteria to specific cases. Assessor agreement was found to be fairly good (kappa = 0.281 over four relevance levels and kappa = 0.417 with H+M binary relevance). The assessors were then each assigned another 7 ARQMath-1 topics (B.8, B.69, B.83, B.89, B.92, B.95, B.98) and a third round of assessment practice followed by discussion was performed. The average kappa on the these topics was 0.467 over four relevance levels, and 0.565 for H+M binary relevance, agreement levels consistent with those observed at the end of Task 2 assessor training in 2020 [18]. Figure 3(a) shows the Cohen's kappa coefficient values for each assessor in the last training round.

Assessment. A total of 60 topics were assessed for Task 2. Two queries (B.243 and B.266) had fewer than two relevant answers after H+M binarization and were removed. Of the remaining 58 queries, an average of 140.0 visually distinct formulae were assessed per topic, with an average assessment time of 39.5 s per formulae. The average number of formula instances labeled as relevant after H+M binarization was 30.9 per topic, with the highest being 107 for topic B.296 and the lowest being 3 for topics B.211 and B.255.

Post Assessment. After assessment for Task 2 was completed, each of the three assessors were assigned two topics, one of which had been assessed by each of the other two assessors. Figure 3 shows the Cohen's kappa coefficient values for each assessor. A kappa of 0.329 was achieved on the four-way assessment task, and with H+M binarization the average kappa value was 0.694.

5.5 Evaluation Measures

As for Task 1, the primary evaluation measure for Task 2 is nDCG′, and MAP′ and P′@10 were also computed. Participants submitted ranked lists of formula

Table 4. ARQMath-2 Task 1 (CQA) results. **P** indicates a primary run, **M** indicates a manual run, and (✓) indicates a baseline pooled at the primary run depth. For Precision@10 and MAP, H+M binarization was used. The best baseline results are in parentheses.

Run	Data	Run type		ARQMath-1			ARQMath-2		
				77 Topics			71 Topics		
		P	M	nDCG′	MAP′	P′@10	nDCG′	MAP′	P′@10
Baselines									
Linked MSE posts	n/a	(✓)		(0.279)	(0.194)	(**0.386**)	0.203	0.120	(**0.282**)
TF-IDF + Tangent-S	Both	(✓)		0.248	0.047	0.073	0.201	0.045	0.086
TF-IDF	Both			0.204	0.049	0.074	0.185	0.046	0.063
Tangent-S	Math			0.158	0.033	0.051	0.111	0.027	0.052
MathDowsers									
primary	Both	✓		**0.433**	0.191	0.249	**0.434**	**0.169**	0.211
proximityReRank	Both			0.373	0.117	0.131	0.335	0.081	0.049
DPRL									
QASim	Both			0.417	0.234	0.369	0.388	0.147	0.193
RRF	Both	✓		0.422	**0.247**	**0.386**	0.347	0.101	0.132
Math Stack Exchange	Both			0.409	0.232	0.322	0.323	0.083	0.078
TU_DBS									
TU_DBS_P	Both	✓		0.380	0.198	0.316	0.377	0.158	**0.227**
TU_DBS_A2	Both			0.356	0.173	0.291	0.367	0.147	0.217
TU_DBS_A3	Both			0.359	0.173	0.299	0.357	0.141	0.194
TU_DBS_A1	Both			0.362	0.178	0.304	0.353	0.132	0.180
TU_DBS_A4	Both			0.045	0.016	0.071	0.028	0.004	0.009
Approach0									
B60	Both		✓	0.364	0.173	0.256	0.351	0.137	0.189
B60RM3	Both		✓	0.360	0.168	0.252	0.349	0.137	0.192
B55	Both	✓	✓	0.364	0.173	0.251	0.344	0.135	0.180
A55	Both		✓	0.364	0.171	0.256	0.343	0.134	0.194
P50	Both		✓	0.361	0.171	0.255	0.327	0.122	0.155
MIRMU									
WIBC	Both			0.381	0.135	0.161	0.332	0.087	0.106
RBC	Both	✓		0.392	0.153	0.220	0.322	0.088	0.132
IBC	Both			0.338	0.114	0.153	0.286	0.073	0.117
CompuBERT	Both			0.304	0.114	0.207	0.262	0.083	0.135
SCM	Both			0.324	0.119	0.156	0.250	0.059	0.072
MSM									
MG	Both	✓		0.310	0.114	0.170	0.278	0.077	0.127
PZ	Both			0.336	0.126	0.181	0.275	0.085	0.124
MP	Both			0.203	0.059	0.094	0.154	0.036	0.047
MH	Both			0.184	0.057	0.108	0.131	0.028	0.037
LM	Both			0.178	0.058	0.107	0.128	0.029	0.048
PSU									
PSU	Both	✓		0.317	0.116	0.165	0.242	0.065	0.110
GoogolFuel									
2020S41R71	Both	✓		0.292	0.086	0.153	0.203	0.050	0.092
2020S41R81	Both			0.290	0.085	0.153	0.203	0.050	0.089
2020S41R91	Both			0.289	0.084	0.157	0.203	0.050	0.089
2020S51R71	Both			0.288	0.082	0.140	0.202	0.049	0.089
2020S41	Both			0.281	0.076	0.135	0.201	0.048	0.080
BetterThanG									
Combiner1vs1	Both	✓	✓	0.233	0.046	0.073	0.157	0.031	0.051
Combiner2vs1	Both		✓	0.229	0.044	0.069	0.153	0.030	0.054
CombinerNorm	Both		✓	0.215	0.045	0.073	0.141	0.026	0.042
LuceneBM25	Text			0.179	0.052	0.079	0.119	0.025	0.032
Tangent-S	Math			0.158	0.033	0.051	0.110	0.026	0.061

Table 5. ARQMath-2 Task 2 (Formula Retrieval) results, computed over visually distinct formulae. **P** indicates a primary run, and **(✓)** shows the baseline pooled at the primary run depth. For MAP and P@10, relevance was thresholded H+M binarization. All runs were automatic. Baseline results are in parentheses.

Run	Data	Run type		ARQMath-1			ARQMath-2		
				45 Topics			58 Topics		
		P	M	nDCG′	MAP′	P′@10	nDCG′	MAP′	P′@10
Baseline									
Tangent-S	Math	(✓)		(0.692)	(0.446)	(0.453)	(0.492)	(0.272)	(0.419)
Approach0									
P300	Math		✓	0.507	0.342	0.441	**0.555**	**0.361**	**0.488**
B	Math		✓	0.493	0.340	0.425	0.519	0.336	0.461
B30	Math		✓	0.527	0.358	0.446	0.516	0.295	0.393
C30	Math		✓	0.527	0.358	0.446	0.516	0.295	0.393
P30	Math	✓	✓	0.527	0.358	0.446	0.505	0.284	0.371
MathDowsers									
formulaBase	Both	✓		0.562	0.370	0.447	0.552	0.333	0.450
docBase	Both			0.404	0.251	0.386	0.433	0.257	0.359
XY-PHOC-DPRL									
XY-PHOC	Math	✓		0.611	0.423	0.478	0.548	0.323	0.433
DPRL									
ltr29	Math			0.736	0.522	0.520	0.454	0.221	0.317
ltrall	Math	✓		**0.738**	**0.525**	**0.542**	0.445	0.216	0.333
TangentCFT2-TED	Math			0.648	0.480	0.502	0.410	0.253	0.464
TangentCFT-2	Math			0.607	0.437	0.480	0.338	0.188	0.297
TU_DBS									
TU_DBS_A3	Math			0.426	0.298	0.386	–	–	–
TU_DBS_A1	Math			0.396	0.271	0.391	–	–	–
TU_DBS_A2	Math			0.157	0.085	0.122	0.154	0.071	0.217
TU_DBS_P	Both	✓		0.152	0.080	0.122	0.153	0.069	0.216
NLP_NITS									
FormulaEmbedding_P	Math	✓		0.233	0.140	0.271	0.161	0.059	0.197
FormulaEmbedding_A	Math			–	–	–	0.114	0.039	0.152
Baseline	Math			–	–	–	0.091	0.032	0.151

instances, but we computed these measures over visually distinct formulae. The ARQMath-2 Task 2 evaluation script replaces each formula instance with its associated visually distinct formula, and then deduplicates from the top of the list downward, producing a ranked list of visually distinct formulae, from which our prime evaluation measures are then computed using `trec_eval`.

5.6 Results

Table 5 in the appendix shows the results, with the baseline run shown first, and then teams and their systems ranked by nDCG′. For ARQMath 2 topics, we see that the best results by nDCG′ were achieved by the Approach0 team, with the

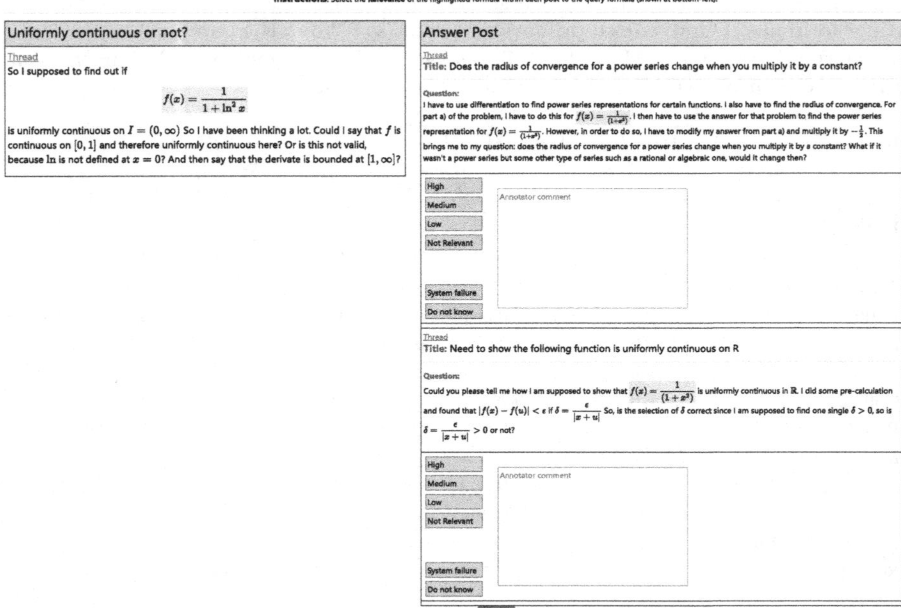

Fig. 4. Turkle Assessment Interface. Shown are hits for Formula Retrieval (Task 2). In the left panel, the formula query is highlighted. In the right panel, one answer post and one question post containing the same retrieved formula are shown. For Task 1, a similar interface was used, but without formula highlighting, and just one returned answer post viewed at a time.

MathDowsers team doing almost as well by that measure, and the XY-PHOC-DPRL team a close third. The order between the best runs from each of those three teams is the same when evaluated on ARQMath-2 topics using MAP′ and P′@10.

Comparing ARQMath-2 results from 2021 with the last year's (2020) ARQMath-1 results, we see that (as with Task 1) for Task 2 the performance relative to the baseline is substantially improved in 2021 over 2020. Specifically, in 2020 the team with the best nDCG′ (DPRL) was 15% below the Tangent-S baseline by that measure; in 2021 the team with the best nDCG′ (Approach0) outperformed the Tangent-S baseline by 13%, as measured by nDCG′.

6 Conclusion

This second year of ARQMath resulted in an improved test collection, more participation, and better results. We anticipate continuing ARQMath for a third year, with participants in ARQMath benefiting from a mature evaluation infrastructure, a larger (and perhaps now also somewhat better) set of relevance judgements on which to train, and a larger and more diverse community of researchers with whom to share ideas.

Acknowledgements. We thank our student assessors from RIT and St. John Fisher College: Josh Anglum, Dominick Banasick, Aubrey Marcsisin, Nathalie Petruzelli, Siegfried Porterfield, Chase Shuster, and Freddy Stock. This material is based upon work supported by the National Science Foundation (USA) under Grant No. IIS-1717997 and the Alfred P. Sloan Foundation under Grant No. G-2017-9827.

References

1. Aizawa, A., Kohlhase, M., Ounis, I.: NTCIR-10 math pilot task overview. In: NTCIR (2013)
2. Aizawa, A., Kohlhase, M., Ounis, I., Schubotz, M.: NTCIR-11 Math-2 task overview. NTCIR **11**, 88–98 (2014)
3. Borlund, P.: The IIR evaluation model: a framework for evaluation of interactive information retrieval systems. Inf. Res. **8**(3) (2003)
4. Buckley, C., Voorhees, E.M.: Retrieval evaluation with incomplete information. In: Proceedings of the 27th Annual International ACM SIGIR Conference on Research and Development in Information Retrieval, pp. 25–32 (2004)
5. Davila, K., Zanibbi, R.: Layout and semantics: combining representations for mathematical formula search. In: Proceedings of the 40th International ACM SIGIR Conference on Research and Development in Information Retrieval, pp. 1165–1168 (2017)
6. Guidi, F., Sacerdoti Coen, C.: A survey on retrieval of mathematical knowledge. In: Kerber, M., Carette, J., Kaliszyk, C., Rabe, F., Sorge, V. (eds.) CICM 2015. LNCS (LNAI), vol. 9150, pp. 296–315. Springer, Cham (2015). https://doi.org/10.1007/978-3-319-20615-8_20
7. Hopkins, M., Le Bras, R., Petrescu-Prahova, C., Stanovsky, G., Hajishirzi, H., Koncel-Kedziorski, R.: SemEval-2019 task 10: math question answering. In: Proceedings of the 13th International Workshop on Semantic Evaluation (2019)
8. Kaliszyk, C., Brady, E., Kohlhase, A., Sacerdoti Coen, C. (eds.): CICM 2019. LNCS (LNAI), vol. 11617. Springer, Cham (2019). https://doi.org/10.1007/978-3-030-23250-4
9. Mansouri, B., Agarwal, A., Oard, D., Zanibbi, R.: Finding old answers to new math questions: the ARQMath Lab at CLEF 2020. In: Jose, J.M., et al. (eds.) ECIR 2020. LNCS, vol. 12036, pp. 564–571. Springer, Cham (2020). https://doi.org/10.1007/978-3-030-45442-5_73
10. Mansouri, B., Oard, D.W., Zanibbi, R.: DPRL systems in the CLEF 2020 ARQMath lab. In: Cappellato, L., Eickhoff, C., Ferro, N., Névéol, A. (eds.) Working Notes of CLEF 2020 - Conference and Labs of the Evaluation Forum, Thessaloniki, Greece, 22–25 September 2020. CEUR Workshop Proceedings, vol. 2696. CEUR-WS.org (2020). http://ceur-ws.org/Vol-2696/paper_223.pdf
11. Mansouri, B., Rohatgi, S., Oard, D.W., Wu, J., Giles, C.L., Zanibbi, R.: Tangent-CFT: an embedding model for mathematical formulas. In: Proceedings of the 2019 ACM SIGIR International Conference on Theory of Information Retrieval (ICTIR), pp. 11–18 (2019)

12. Nishizawa, G., Liu, J., Diaz, Y., Dmello, A., Zhong, W., Zanibbi, R.: MathSeer: a math-aware search interface with intuitive formula editing, reuse, and lookup. In: Jose, J.M., et al. (eds.) ECIR 2020. LNCS, vol. 12036, pp. 470–475. Springer, Cham (2020). https://doi.org/10.1007/978-3-030-45442-5_60
13. Ounis, I., Amati, G., Plachouras, V., He, B., Macdonald, C., Johnson, D.: Terrier information retrieval platform. In: Losada, D.E., Fernández-Luna, J.M. (eds.) ECIR 2005. LNCS, vol. 3408, pp. 517–519. Springer, Heidelberg (2005). https://doi.org/10.1007/978-3-540-31865-1_37
14. Sakai, T., Kando, N.: On information retrieval metrics designed for evaluation with incomplete relevance assessments. Inf. Retrieval **11**(5), 447–470 (2008)
15. Schubotz, M., Youssef, A., Markl, V., Cohl, H.S.: Challenges of mathematical information retrieval in the NTCIR-11 math Wikipedia task. In: SIGIR, pp. 951–954. ACM (2015)
16. Zanibbi, R., Aizawa, A., Kohlhase, M., Ounis, I., Topic, G., Davila, K.: NTCIR-12 MathIR task overview. In: NTCIR (2016)
17. Zanibbi, R., Blostein, D.: Recognition and retrieval of mathematical expressions. Int. J. Doc. Anal. Recogn. (IJDAR) **15**(4), 331–357 (2012)
18. Zanibbi, R., Oard, D.W., Agarwal, A., Mansouri, B.: Overview of ARQMath 2020: CLEF lab on answer retrieval for questions on math. In: Arampatzis, A., et al. (eds.) CLEF 2020. LNCS, vol. 12260, pp. 169–193. Springer, Cham (2020). https://doi.org/10.1007/978-3-030-58219-7_15
19. Zhong, W., Zanibbi, R.: Structural similarity search for formulas using leaf-root paths in operator subtrees. In: Azzopardi, L., Stein, B., Fuhr, N., Mayr, P., Hauff, C., Hiemstra, D. (eds.) ECIR 2019. LNCS, vol. 11437, pp. 116–129. Springer, Cham (2019). https://doi.org/10.1007/978-3-030-15712-8_8

Overview of BioASQ 2021: The Ninth BioASQ Challenge on Large-Scale Biomedical Semantic Indexing and Question Answering

Anastasios Nentidis[1,2](✉), Georgios Katsimpras[1], Eirini Vandorou[1], Anastasia Krithara[1], Luis Gasco[3], Martin Krallinger[3], and Georgios Paliouras[1]

[1] National Center for Scientific Research "Demokritos", Athens, Greece
{tasosnent,gkatsibras,evandorou,akrithara,paliourg}@iit.demokritos.gr
[2] Aristotle University of Thessaloniki, Thessaloniki, Greece
[3] Barcelona Supercomputing Center, Barcelona, Spain
{lgasco,martin.krallinger}@bsc.es

Abstract. Advancing the state-of-the-art in large-scale biomedical semantic indexing and question answering is the main focus of the BioASQ challenge. BioASQ organizes respective tasks where different teams develop systems that are evaluated on the same benchmark datasets that represent the real information needs of experts in the biomedical domain. This paper presents an overview of the ninth edition of the BioASQ challenge in the context of the Conference and Labs of the Evaluation Forum (CLEF) 2021. In this year, a new question answering task, named Synergy, is introduced to support researchers studying the COVID-19 disease and measure the ability of the participating teams to discern information while the problem is still developing. In total, 42 teams with more than 170 systems were registered to participate in the four tasks of the challenge. The evaluation results, similarly to previous years, show a performance gain against the baselines which indicates the continuous improvement of the state-of-the-art in this field.

Keywords: Biomedical knowledge · Semantic indexing · Question answering

1 Introduction

In this paper, we present the shared tasks and the datasets of the ninth BioASQ challenge in 2021, as well as we as an overview of the participating systems and their performance. The remainder of this paper is organized as follows. Section 2 provides an overview of the shared tasks, that took place from December 2020 to May 2021, and the corresponding datasets developed for the challenge. Section 3 presents a brief overview of the systems developed by the participating teams for the different tasks. Detailed descriptions for some of the systems are available in the proceedings of the lab. Then, in Sect. 4, we focus on evaluating the

K. S. Candan et al. (Eds.): CLEF 2021, LNCS 12880, pp. 239–263, 2021.
https://doi.org/10.1007/978-3-030-85251-1_18

performance of the systems for each task and sub-task, using state-of-the-art evaluation measures or manual assessment. Finally, Sect. 5 draws some conclusions regarding this version of the BioASQ challenge.

2 Overview of the Tasks

In this year, the ninth version of the BioASQ challenge offered four tasks: (1) a large-scale biomedical semantic indexing task (task 9a), (2) a biomedical question answering task (task 9b), both considering documents in English, (3) a medical semantic indexing in Spanish (task MESINESP9 using literature, patents and clinical trial abstracts), and (4) a new task on biomedical question answering on the developing problem of COVID-19 (task Synergy). In this section, we describe the two established tasks 9a and 9b with focus on differences from previous versions of the challenge [25]. Detailed information about these tasks can be found in [39]. Additionally, we discuss the second version of the MESINESP task and also present the new Synergy task on biomedical question answering for developing problems, which was introduced this year, providing statistics about the dataset developed for each task.

2.1 Large-Scale Semantic Indexing - Task 9a

Table 1. Statistics on test datasets for Task 9a.

Batch	Articles	Annotated articles	Labels per article
1	7967	7808	12.61
	10053	9987	12.40
	4870	4854	12.16
	5758	5735	12.34
	5770	5666	12.49
Total	34418	34050	12.42
2	6376	6374	12.39
	9101	6403	11.76
	7013	6590	12.15
	6070	5914	12.62
	6151	5904	12.63
Total	34711	31185	12.30
3	5890	5730	12.81
	10818	9910	13.03
	4022	3493	12.21
	5373	4005	12.62
	5325	2351	12.97
Total	31428	25489	12.71

The aim of Task 9a is to classify articles from the PubMed/MedLine[1] digital library into concepts of the MeSH hierarchy. Specifically, the test sets for the evaluation of the competing systems consist of new PubMed articles that are not yet annotated by the indexers in the National Library of Medicine (NLM). Table 1 illustrates a more detailed view of each test. As in the previous years, the task is realized in three independent runs of 5 weekly test sets each. Two scenarios are provided: i) on-line and ii) large-scale. The test sets are a collection of new articles without any restriction on the journal published. For the evaluation of the competing systems standard flat information retrieval measures are used, as well as hierarchical ones, comparing the predictions of the participants with the annotations from the NLM indexers, once available. Similarly to the previous years, for each test set, participants are required to submit their answers in 21 h. Furthermore, a training dataset was available for Task 9a which contains 15,559,157 articles with 12.68 labels per article, on average, and covers 29,369 distinct MeSH labels in total.

2.2 Biomedical Semantic QA - Task 9b

Task 9b focuses on enabling the competing teams to develop systems for all the stages of question answering in the biomedical domain by introducing a large-scale question answering challenge. Again this year, four types of questions are considered: "yes/no", "factoid", "list" and "summary" questions [9]. A total of 3,743 questions, which are annotated with golden relevant elements and answers from previous versions of the task, consist of the available training dataset for this task. The dataset is used by the participating teams to develop their systems. Table 2 provides detailed information about both training and testing sets.

Table 2. Statistics on the training and test datasets of Task 9b. The numbers for the documents and snippets refer to averages per question.

Batch	Size	Yes/No	List	Factoid	Summary	Documents	Snippets
Train	3,743	1033	719	1092	899	9.43	12.32
Test 1	100	27	21	29	23	3.40	4.66
Test 2	100	22	20	34	24	3.43	4.88
Test 3	100	26	19	37	18	3.21	4.29
Test 4	100	25	19	28	28	3.10	4.01
Test 5	100	19	18	36	27	3.59	4.69
Total	4,243	1152	816	1256	1019	8.71	11.40

Task 9b is divided into two phases: (phase A) the retrieval of the required information and (phase B) answering the question. Moreover, it is split into five independent bi-weekly batches and the two phases for each batch run during two consecutive days. In each phase, the participants receive the corresponding test set and have 24 h to submit the answers of their systems. More precisely, in

[1] https://pubmed.ncbi.nlm.nih.gov/.

phase A, a test set of 100 questions written in English is released and the participants are expected to identify and submit relevant elements from designated resources, including PubMed/MedLine articles, snippets extracted from these articles, concepts and RDF triples. In phase B, the manually selected relevant articles and snippets for these 100 questions are also released and the participating systems are asked to respond with *exact answers*, that is entity names or short phrases, and *ideal answers*, that is natural language summaries of the requested information.

2.3 Medical Semantic Indexing in Spanish - MESINESP

Over the last year, scientific production has increased significantly and has made more evident than ever the need to improve the information retrieval methods under a multilingual IR or search scenario for medical content beyond data only in English [38]. The scenario faced during the year 2020 demonstrates the need to improve access to information in demanding scenarios such as a disease outbreaks or public health threats at multinational/cross-border scale. In a health emergency scenario, access to scientific information is essential to accelerate research and healthcare progress and to enable resolving the health crisis more effectively. During the COVID-19 health crisis, the need to improve multilingual search systems became evermore significant, since a considerable fraction of medical publications (especially clinical case reports on COVID patients) were written in the native language of medical professionals.

MESINESP was created in response to the lack of resources for indexing content in languages other than English, and to improve the lack of semantic interoperability in the search process when attempting to retrieve medically relevant information across different data sources.

The MESINESP 2021 track [14], promoted by the Spanish Plan for the Advancement of Language Technology (Plan TL)[2] and organized by the Barcelona Supercomputing Center (BSC) in collaboration with BioASQ, aims to improve the state of the art of semantic indexing for content written in Spanish, ranking among the highest number of native speakers in the world[3]. In an effort to improve interoperability in semantic search queries, this edition was divided into three subtracks to index scientific literature, clinical trials and medical patents.

MESINESP-L (subtrack 1) required the automatic indexing with DeCS[4] terms of a set of abstracts from scientific articles (titles and abstracts) from two widely used literature databases with content in Spanish: IBECS[5] and LILACS[6].

[2] https://plantl.mineco.gob.es.

[3] https://www.ethnologue.com/guides/ethnologue200.

[4] DeCS (*Descriptores Descriptores en Ciencias de la Salud*, Health Science Descriptors) is a structured controlled vocabulary created by BIREME to index scientific publications on BvSalud (*Biblioteca Virtual en Salud*, Virtual Health Library).

[5] IBECS includes bibliographic references from scientific articles in health sciences published in Spanish medical journals. http://ibecs.isciii.es.

[6] LILACS is a resource comprising scientific and technical literature from Latin America and the Caribbean countries. It includes 26 countries, 882 journals and 878,285 records, 464,451 of which are full texts https://lilacs.bvsalud.org.

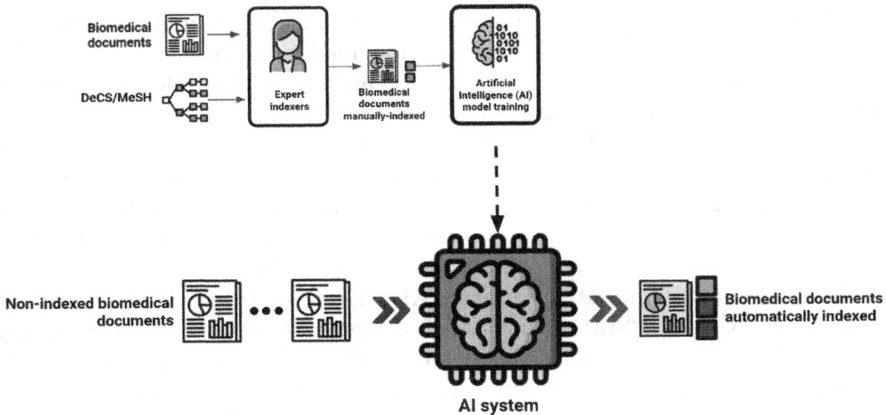

Fig. 1. Simplified MESINESP2 workflow showing the importance of annotation for the generation of automatic semantic indexing systems.

We built the corpora for the task from the data available in BvSalud, the largest database of scientific documents in Spanish, which integrates records from LILACS, MEDLINE, IBECS and other databases. First, we downloaded the whole collection of 1.14 million articles present in the platform. Then, only journal articles with titles and abstracts written in Spanish that had been previously manually indexed by LILACS and IBECS experts with DeCS codes were selected, obtaining a final training dataset of 237,574 articles. A development set of records manually indexed by expert annotators was also provided. This development corpus included 1,065 articles manually annotated (indexed) by the three human indexers who obtained the best IAA in the last MESINESP edition. To generate the test set, 500 publications were selected to be indexed by the three experts. We also incorporated a background set of 9,676 Spanish-language clinical practice guidelines to evaluate the performance of the models on this type of biomedical documents (Fig. 1).

Clinical Trials subtrack (MESINESP-T) asked participating teams to generate models able to automatically predict DeCS codes for clinical trials from the REEC database[7].

Last year's task generated a silver standard (automatically assigned codes by participating teams) with a set of REEC clinical trials. The predictions of the best performing team was used as a substitute or surrogate data collection for training systems, pooling a total of 3,560 clinical trials. For the development set, 147 records manually annotated by expert indexers in MESINESP 2020 were provided. For the test set, we calculated the semantic similarity between MESINESP-L training corpus and a pre-selection of 416 clinical trials published after 2020. Then, the top 250 most similar clinical trials, which included many

[7] Registro Español de Estudios Clínicos, a database containing summaries of clinical trials https://reec.aemps.es/reec/public/web.html.

COVID-19 related trials, were annotated by our indexers. Similar to what was done for the scientific literature track, we included a background set of 5,669 documents from medicine data sheets to be automatically indexed by teams (generating thus a silver standard collection).

Finally, for the patents subtrack (MESINESP-P), the aim was to explore and evaluate indexing strategies of medical patents written in Spanish providing only a very small manually annotated patent collection (in addition to the literature corpus). We presented the track as a cross-corpus training challenge, in which participants should transfer/adapt previous models to the patent language without a large manually annotated data set. All patents written in Spanish having the assigned IPC codes “A61P” and “A61K31” were retrieved using Google Big Query[8], only these codes were considered as they cover medicinal chemistry related topics [18]. After data harvesting, 65,513 patents were obtained, out of which the 228 most semantically similar to the MESINESP-L training set were chosen. After an annotation process, 119 were used as the development set and 109 as the test set. Some summary statistics of the used datasets can be seen in the Table 3 and 4.

Table 3. Summary statistics of the MESINESP corpora.

Corpus	Docs	DeCS	Unique DeCS	Tokens	Avg.DeCS/doc	Avg.token/doc
MESINESP-L training	237574	∼1.98M	22434	∼43.1M	8.37(3.5)	181.45(72.3)
MESINESP-L development	1065	11283	3750	211420	10.59(4.1)	198.52(64.2)
MESINESP-L test	491	5398	2124	93645	10.99(3.9)	190.72(63.6)
MESINESP-T training	3560	52257	3940	∼4.13M	14.68(1.19)	1161.0(553.5)
MESINESP-T development	147	2038	771	146791	13.86(5.53)	998.58(637.5)
MESINESP-T test	248	3271	905	267031	13.19(4.49)	1076.74(553.68)
MESINESP-P development	109	1092	520	38564	10.02(3.11)	353.79(321.5)
MESINESP-P test	119	1176	629	9065	9.88(2.76)	76.17(27.36)

Table 4. Summary statistics on the number of entities of each type extracted for each corpus.

Corpus	Diseases	Medications	Procedures	Symptoms
MESINESP - L	711751	87150	362927	127810
MESINESP - T	129362	86303	52566	10140
MESINESP - P	171	180	25	12

Some additional resources were published in order to serve as complementary annotations for participating teams. Since the BSC text mining unit had already implemented several competitive medical named entity recognition tools adapted to content in Spanish [19–21], four different NER systems were applied to each of

[8] https://cloud.google.com/blog/topics/public-datasets/google-patents-public-datasets-connecting-public-paid-and-private-patent-data.

the corpora to annotate automatically mentions of medical entities that may help improve model performance, namely diseases, procedures, medications/drugs and symptoms. Many DeCS terms do actually correspond to these semantic classes, in particular diseases. Overall, the semantic annotation results for the MESINESP included around 840,000 disease mentions, 170,000 medicine/drug mentions, 415,000 medical procedures mentions and 137,000 symptoms mentions.

2.4 Synergy Task

The established question answering BioASQ task (Task B) is structured in a sequence of phases. First comes the annotation phase; then with a partial overlap runs the challenge; and only when this is finished does the assessment phase start. This leads to restricted interaction between the participating systems and the experts, which is acceptable due to the nature of the questions, that have a clear, undisputed answer. However, a more interactive model is necessary for open questions on developing research topics, such as the case of COVID-19, where new issues appear every day and most of them remain open for some time. In this context, a model based on the synergy between the biomedical experts and the automated question answering systems is needed.

In this direction, we introduced the BioASQ Synergy task envisioning a continuous dialog between the experts and the systems. In this model, the experts pose open questions and the systems provide relevant material and answers for these questions. Then, the experts assess the submitted material (documents and snippets) and answers, and provide feedback to the systems, so that they can improve their responses. This process proceeds with new feedback and new predictions from the systems in an iterative way.

This year, Task Synergy took place in two versions, focusing on unanswered questions for the developing problem of the COVID-19 disease. Each version was structured into four rounds, of systems responses and expert feedback for the same questions. However, some new questions or new modified versions of some questions could be added to the test sets. The details of the datasets used in task Synergy are available in Table 5.

Table 5. Statistics on the datasets of Task Synergy. "Answer" stands for questions marked as having enough relevant material from previous rounds to be answered".

Version	Round	Size	Yes/No	List	Factoid	Summary	Answer	Feedback
1	1	108	33	22	17	36	0	0
1	2	113	34	25	18	36	53	101
1	3	113	34	25	18	36	80	97
1	4	113	34	25	18	36	86	103
2	1	95	31	22	18	24	6	95
2	2	90	27	22	18	23	10	90
2	3	66	17	14	18	17	25	66
2	4	63	15	14	17	17	33	63

Contrary to the task B, this task was not structured into phases, but both relevant material and answers were received together. However, for new questions only relevant material (documents and snippets) is required until the expert considers that enough material has been gathered during the previous round and mark the questions as "ready to answer". When a question receives a satisfactory answer that is not expected to change, the expert can mark the question as "closed", indicating that no more material and answers are needed for it.

In each round of this task, we consider material from the current version of the COVID-19 Open Research Dataset (CORD-19) [41] to reflect the rapid developments in the field. As in task B, four types of questions are supported, namely yes/no, factoid, list, and summary, and two types of answers, exact and ideal. The evaluation of the systems will be based on the measures used in Task 9b. Nevertheless, for the information retrieval part we focus on new material. Therefore, material already assessed in previous rounds, available in the expert feedback, should not be re-submitted. Overall, through this process, we aim to facilitate the incremental understanding of COVID-19 and contribute to the discovery of new solutions.

3 Overview of Participation

3.1 Task 9a

This year, 6 teams participated with a total of 21 different systems. Below, we provide a brief overview of those systems for which a description was available, stressing their key characteristics. The participating systems along with their corresponding approaches are listed in Table 6. Detailed descriptions for some of the systems are available at the proceedings of the workshop.

Table 6. Systems and approaches for Task 9a. Systems for which no description was available at the time of writing are omitted.

System	Approach
bert_dna, pi_dna	SentencePiece, BioBERT, multiple binary classifiers
NLM	SentencePiece, CNN, embeddings, ensembles, PubMedBERT
dmiip_fdu	d2v, tf-idf, SVM, KNN, LTR, DeepMeSH, AttentionXML, BERT, PLT
Iria	Luchene Index, multilabel k-NN, stem bigrams, ensembles, UIMA ConceptMapper

The team of Roche and Bogazici University participated in task 9a with four different systems ("*bert_dna*" and "*pi_dna*" variations). In particular, their systems are based on the BERT framework with SentencePiece tokenization, and multiple binary classifiers. The rest of the teams build upon existing systems that had already competed in previous versions of the task. The National Library of Medicine (NLM) team competed with five different systems [31]. To improve their previously developed CNN model [32], they utilized a pretrained transformer model, PubMedBERT, which was fine-tuned to rank candidates obtained from the CNN. The Fudan University ("*dmiip_fdu*") team also relied on their previous "*AttentionXML*" [1], "*DeepMeSH*" [30], and "*BERTMeSH*" models [46]. Differently from their previous version, they extended AttentionXML with BioBERT. Finally, the team of Universidade de Vigo and Universidade da Coruña competed with two systems ("*Iria*") that followed the same approach used by the systems in previous versions of the task [34].

As in previous versions of the challenge, two systems developed by NLM to facilitate the annotation of articles by indexers in MedLine/PubMed, where available as baselines for the semantic indexing task. MTI [24] as enhanced in [47] and an extension based on features suggested by the winners of the first version of the task [40].

3.2 Task 9b

This version of Task 9b was undertaken by 90 different systems in total, developed by 24 teams. In phase A, 9 teams participated, submitting results from 34 systems. In phase B, the numbers of participants and systems were 20 and 70 respectively. There were only three teams that engaged in both phases. An overview of the technologies employed by the teams is provided in Table 7 for the systems for which a description was available. Detailed descriptions for some of the systems are available at the proceedings of the workshop.

Table 7. Systems and approaches for Task9b. Systems for which no information was available at the time of writing are omitted.

Systems	Phase	Approach
bio-answerfinder	A, B	Bio-AnswerFinder, ElasticSearch, Bio-ELECTRA, ELECTRA, BioBERT, SQuAD, wRWMD
RYGH	A	BM25, BioBERT, PubMedBERT, T5
bioinfo	A	BM25, ElasticSearch, distant learning, DeepRank, universal weighting passage mechanism (UPWM), BERT
KU-DMIS	B	BioBERT, NLI, MultiNLI, SQuAD, BART, beam search, BERN, language_check, sequence_tagging
MQ	B	BERT, ROUGE
Ir_sys	B	BM25, T5, BERT, SpanBERT, XLNet, PubmedBERT, BART
CRJ	B	Proximal Policy Optimization (PPO), word2vec, BERT, Reinforcement Learning
LASIGE_ULISBOA	B	BioBERT, transfer learning
UvA	B	encoder-decoder model, seq2seq, BART
MDS_UNCC	B	BioBERT
ALBERT	B	DistilBERT, ALBERT, SQuAD
UDEL-LAB	B	BioM-ALBERT, BioM-ELECTRA, SQuAD
MQU	B	BERT, summarization
NCU-IISR/AS-GIS	B	BioBERT, PubMedBERT, logistic-regression

The "*UCSD*" team [27] participated in both phases of the task with two systems ("*bio-answerfinder*"). Specifically, for phase A they relied on previously developed Bio-AnswerFinder system [28], but instead of LSTM based keyword selection classifier, they used a Bio-ELECTRA++ model based keyword selection classifier together with the Bio-ELECTRA Mid based re-ranker [26]. This model was also used as an initial step for their systems in phase B, in order to re-rank candidate sentences. For factoid and list questions they fine-tuned a Bio-ELECTRA model using both SQuad and BioASQ training data. The answer candidates are then scored considering classification probability, the top ranking of corresponding snippets and number of occurrences. Finally a normalization and filtering step is performed and, for list questions, an enrichment step based on coordinated phrase detection. For yes/no questions, they used a Bio-ELECTRA model based ternary yes/no/neutral classifier. The final decision is made by score voting. For summary questions, they follow two approaches. First, they employ hierarchical clustering, based on weighted relaxed word mover's distance (wRWMD) similarity [28] to group the top sentences, and select the sentence ranked highest by Bio-AnswerFinder to be concatenated to form the summary. Secondly, an abstractive summarization system based on the unified text-to-text transformer model t5 [33] is used.

In phase A, the team from the University of Aveiro participated with four distinct "*bioinfo*" systems [5]. Relying on their previous model [3], they improved the computation flow and experimented with the transformer architecture. In the end, they developed two variants that used the passage mechanism from [3] and the BERT model. The "*RYGH*" team participated in phase A with five systems. They adopted a pipeline that utilized the BM25 along with several pre-trained models including BioBERT, PubMedBERT, PubMedBERT-FullText and T5.

In phase B, this year the "*KU-DMIS*" team [2] participated in both exact and ideal answers. Their systems are based on the transformers models and follow either a model-centric or a data-centric approach. The former, which is based on the sequence tagging approach [45], is used for list questions while the latter, which relies on the characteristics of the training datasets and therefore data cleaning and sampling are important aspects of its architecture, is used for factoid questions. For yes/no questions, they utilized the BioBERT-large model, as a replacement of the previously used BioBERT-BASE model. For ideal questions, they followed the last year's strategy, where their BART model utilizes the predicted exact answer as a input for generating an ideal answer.

There were four teams from the Macquarie University that participated in task 9b. The first team ("*MQ*") [23] competed with five systems which are based on the use of BERT variants in a classification setting. The classification task takes as input the question, a sentence, and the sentence position, and the target labels are based on the ROUGE score of the sentence with respect to the ideal answer. The second team ("*CRJ*") competed with three systems that followed the Proximal Policy Optimization (PPO) approach to Reinforcement Learning [22], and also utilized word2vec and BERT word embeddings. The third team (ALBERT) [16] competed with four systems that were based on the transformer-based language models, DistilBERT and ALBERT. The pretrained models were fine-tuned first on the SQuAD dataset and then on the BioASQ dataset. Finally, the fourth team ("*MQU*") participated with five systems. Their systems utilized sentence transformers fine-tuned for passage retrieval, as well as abstractive summarizers trained on news media data.

The Fudan University team participated with four systems ("*Ir_sys*"). All systems utilized variants of the BERT framework. For yes/no questions they used BioBERT, while for factoid/list questions they combined SpanBERT, PubmedBERT and XLNet. For summary questions, they utilized both extractive and abstractive methods. For the latter, they performed conditional generation of answers by employing the BART model. The "*LASIGE_ULISBOA*" team [10], from the University of Lisboa, competed with four systems which are based on BioBERT. The models are fine-tuned on larger non-medical datasets prior to training on the task's datasets. The final decisions for the list questions are computed by applying a voting scheme, while a softmax is utilized for the remaining questions.

The University of Delaware team [6] participated with four systems ("*UDEL-LAB*") which are based on BioM-Transformets models [7]. In particular, they used both BioM-ALBERT and BioM-ELECTRA, and also applied transfer learning by fine tuning the models on MNLI and SQuAD datasets. The "*NCU-IISR*" team [48], as in the previous version of the challenge, participated in both parts of phase B, constructing various BERT-based models. In particular, they utilized BioBERT and PubMedBERT models to score candidate sentences. Then, as a second step a logistic regressor, trained on predicting the similarity between a question and each snippet sentence, re-ranks the sentences.

The "*Universiteit van Amsterdam*" team submitted three systems ("*UvA*") that focused on ideal answers. They reformulated the task as a seq2seq language generation task in an encoder-decoder setting. All systems utilized variants of pre-trained language generation models. Specifically, they used BART and MT5 [43].

In this challenge too, the open source OAQA system proposed by [44] served as baseline for phase B exact answers. The system which achieved among the highest performances in previous versions of the challenge remains a strong baseline for the exact answer generation task. The system is developed based on the UIMA framework. ClearNLP is employed for question and snippet parsing. MetaMap, TmTool [42], C-Value and LingPipe [8] are used for concept identification and UMLS Terminology Services (UTS) for concept retrieval. The final steps include identification of concept, document and snippet relevance based on classifier components and scoring and finally ranking techniques.

3.3 Task MESINESP

MESINESP track received greater interest from the public in this second edition. Out of 35 teams registered for CLEF Labs 2021, 7 teams from China, Chile, India, Spain, Portugal and Switzerland finally took part in the task. These teams provided a total of 25 systems for MESINESP-L, 20 for MESINESP-T and 20 for

MESINESP-P. Like last year, the approaches were pretty similar to those of the English track, relying mainly on deep language models for text representation using BERT-based systems and extreme multilabel classification strategies.

Table 8 describes the general methods used by the participants. Most of the teams used sophisticated systems such as AttentionXML, graph-based entity linking, or label encoding systems. But unlike the first edition, this year some teams have also tested models with more traditional technologies such as TF-IDF to evaluate their performance in the indexing of documents in Spanish.

This year's baseline was an improved textual search system that searches the text for both DeCS descriptors and synonyms to assign codes to documents. This approach got an MiF of 0.2876 for scientific literature, 0.1288 for clinical trials and 0.2992 for patents.

Table 8. Systems and approaches for Task MESINESP 2021. Systems for which no description was available at the time of writing are omitted.

System	Ref	Approach
Iria		k-NN, Luchene Index, lemmas, syntactic dependencies, NP, chunks, name entities, Sentence embeddings
Fudan University	-	AttentionXML, Multilingual BERT, label-level attention
Roche	[15]	SentencePiece, NER, BETO, multiple binary classifiers, synonym matching
Vicomtech	[13]	BERT based classifier, label encoding
LASIGE	[36]	Graph-based entity linking, Personalized PageRank, semantic similarity-based filter, X-Transformer, Multilingual BERT
Universidad de Chile	-	TF-IDF, word embeddings, cosine similarity

3.4 Task Synergy

In the first two versions of the new task Synergy, introduced this year, 15 teams participated submitting the results from 39 distinct systems. An overview of systems and approaches employed in this task is provided in Table 9 for the systems for which a description was available. More detailed descriptions for some of the systems are available at the proceedings of the workshop.

The *Fudan University* team, uses BM25 to fetch the top documents and then they use BioBERT, SciBERT, ELECTRA and T5 models to score the relevance of each document and query. Finally, the reciprocal rank fusion (RRF) is used to get the final document ranking results by integrating the previous results. Similarly, for snippet retrieval task, we use the same method with the focus in sentence. They also participate in all four types of questions. For the Yes/No type, they use the BERT encoder, a linear transformation layer and the sigmoid function to calculate the yes or no probability. For Factoid/List questions, they

Table 9. Systems and their approaches for Task Synergy. Systems for which no description was available at the time of writing are omitted.

System	Approach
RYGH	BM25, BioBERT, SciBERT, ELECTRA, Text-to-Text Transfer Transformer (T5), Reciprocal Rank Fusion (RRF), Named Entity Recognition, BERT, SQuAD, SpanBERT
bio-answerfinder	Bio-ELECTRA++, BERT, weighted relaxed word mover's distance (wRWMD), pyserini with MonoT5, SQuAD, GloVe
AUEB	BM25, Word2Vec, Graph-Node Embeddings, SciBERT, DL (JPDRMM)
MQ	Word2Vec, BERT, LSTM, Reinforcement Learning (PPO)
bioinfo	BM25, ElasticSearch, distant learning, DeepRank, universal weighting passage mechanism (UPWM), BERT
NLM	BM25 model, T5, BART
pa-synergy	Lucene full-text search, BERT

again employ BERT as the backbone and fine-tune the model with SQuAD. For Summary questions, they perform conditional generation of answers by adopting BART as the backbone of the model. As this is a collaborative task, they use experts' feedback data in two aspects: one is to expand query by Named Entity Recognition, and the other is to finetune the model by using feedback data.

The *"MQ"* team [23] focused on the question answering component of the task, section ideal answers using one of their systems that participated in BioASQ 8b [22] Phase B For document retrieval, they used the top documents returned by the API provided by BioASQ. For snippet retrieval, they re-ranked the document sentences based on tfidf-cosine similarity with the question or the sentence score predicted by their QA system. In run 4, they experimented with a variant of document retrieval based on an independent retrieval system, tuned with the BioASQ data. What is more, they incorporated feedback from previous rounds to remove false negatives in documents and snippets and omit all documents and snippets that had been previously judged.

The *"bio-answerfinder"* team [27] used the Bio-AnswerFinder end-to-end QA system they had previously developed [28]. For exact answers and ideal answers they used re-ranked candidate sentences as input to the Synergy challenge subsystems. For factoid and list questions they used an answer span classifier fine-tuned ELECTRA_Base [11] using combined SQuAD v1.1 and BioASQ 8b training data. For list questions, answer candidates were enriched by coordinated phrase detection and processing. For Yes/No questions, they used a binary classifier fine-tuned on ELECTRA Base using training data created/annotated from BioASQ 8b training set (ideal answers). For summary questions, they used the top 10 selected sentences to generate an answer summary. Hierarchical clustering using weighted relaxed word mover's distance (wRWMD) similarity was used to group sentences, with similarity threshold to maximize ROGUE-2 score. They used the feedback provided to augment the training data used for the BERT [3] based reranker classifier used by Bio-AnswerFinder, after weighted relaxed word mover's distance (wRWMD) similarity based ranking and focus-word-based filtering. At each round, the BERT-Base based reranker was retrained with the cumulative Synergy expert feedback.

The *"University of Aveiro"* team [4] built on their BioASQ Task 8b implementation [3] modifying it to fit the Synergy Task by adding methodology for the given feedback of each round. Their approach was to create a strong baseline using simple relevance feedback technique, using a tf-idf score they expanded the query and finally processed it using the BM25 algorithm. This approach was adopted for questions having some feedback from previous rounds, for the new questions they used the BM25 algorithm along with reranking, similarly to the BioASQ Task 8b. The *"NLM"* team [37] first used the BM25 model to retrieve relevant articles and reranked them with the Text-to-Text Transfer Transformer (T5) relevance-based reranking model. For snippets, after splitting the relevant articles into sentences and chunks they used a re-ranking model based on T5 relevance. For ideal answers they used extractive and abstractive approaches. For the former they concatenated the top-n snippets, while for the later they finetuned their model using Bidirectional and Auto-Regressive Transformers (BART) on multiple biomedical datasets.

The *"AUEB"* team also built on their implementation from BioASQ Task 8b [29] exploiting the feedback to filter out the material that was already assessed. They participated in all stages of the Synergy Task. They use mostly JPDRMM-based methods with ElasticSearch for document retrieval and SEMantic Indexing for SEntence Retrieval (SEMISER) for snippet retrieval. The *"JetBrains"* team were based on their BioASQ Task 8b approach as well. In short, they used Lucene full-text search combined with BERT based reranker for document retrieval and BERT-based models for exact answers, without using the feedback provided by the experts. The *"MQU"* team used sentence vector similarities on the entire CORD-19 dataset, not considering the expert feedback either.

4 Results

4.1 Task 9a

In Task 9a, each of the three batches were independently evaluated as presented in Table 10. As in previous versions of the task, standard evaluation measures [9] were used for measuring the classification performance of the systems, both flat and hierarchical. In particular, the official measures used to identify the winners for each batch were the micro F-measure (MiF) and the Lowest Common Ancestor F-measure (LCA-F) [17]. As suggested by Demšar [12], the appropriate way to compare multiple classification systems over multiple datasets is based on their average rank across all the datasets.

In this task, the system with the best performance in a test set gets rank 1.0 for this test set, the second best rank 2.0 and so on. In case two or more systems

Table 10. Average system ranks across the batches of the task 9a. A hyphenation symbol (-) is used whenever the system participated in fewer than 4 test sets in the batch. Systems participating in fewer than 4 test sets in all three batches are omitted.

System	Batch 1		Batch 2		Batch 3	
	MiF	LCA-F	MiF	LCA-F	MiF	LCA-F
dmiip_fdu	**1.25**	**1.25**	**1.375**	**1.875**	**2**	**2.25**
deepmesh_dmiip_fdu	2.25	2	3.375	2.75	3.25	2.75
attention_dmiip_fdu	2.75	3	1.5	**1.875**	2.25	**2.25**
deepmesh_dmiip_fdu_	3.5	3.5	3	2.375	2.75	2.875
NLM System 3	4	4	4.75	4.75	3	2.875
NLM System 1	5.25	5.25	6.5	6.5	7.5	7.5
MTI First Line Index	6.75	6.5	7.75	7.75	8.5	8.5
Default MTI	7.75	7.5	8.5	8.5	10	9.5
NLM CNN	8.75	8.75	9.75	9.75	11.25	12.5
pi_dna_2	-	-	11.375	12	14.25	14.25
pi_dna	-	-	12.25	12.5	9.25	10.25
bert_dna	-	-	12.75	12.75	12.375	11.5
iria-1	-	-	14.875	15.125	16.125	16.25
iria-mix	-	-	15.125	14.875	17.25	17.125
DeepSys1	-	-	15.5	15.25	-	-
NLM System 2	-	-	-	-	5.5	5
NLM System 4	-	-	-	-	6.5	6.5
pi_dna_3	-	-	-	-	12.75	13
DeepSys2	-	-	-	-	15.25	15.25

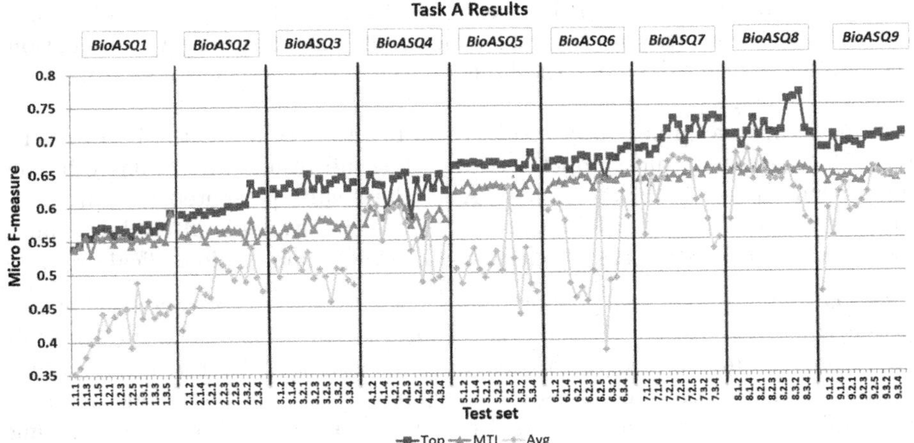

Fig. 2. The micro f-measure (MiF) achieved by systems across different years of the BioASQ challenge. For each test set the MiF score is presented for the best performing system (Top) and the MTI, as well as the average micro f-measure of all the participating systems (Avg).

tie, they all receive the average rank. Based on the rules of the challenge, the average rank of each system for a batch is the average of the four best ranks of the system in the five test sets of the batch. The average rank of each system, based on both the flat MiF and the hierarchical LCA-F scores, for the three batches of the task are presented in Table 10.

The results of Task 9a reveal that several participating systems manage to outperform the strong baselines in all test batches and considering either the flat or the hierarchical measures. Namely, the "*dmiip_fdu*" systems from the Fudan University team achieve the best performance and the "NLM" systems the second best in all three batches of the task. More detailed results can be found in the online results page[9]. Figure 2 presents the improvement of the MiF scores achieved by both the MTI baseline and the top performing participant systems through the nine years of the BioASQ challenge.

4.2 Task 9b

Phase A: The evaluation of phase A in Task 9b is based on the Mean Average Precision (MAP) measure for each of the three types of annotations, namely documents, concepts and RDF triples. For snippets, where several distinct snippets may overlap with the same golden snippet, interpreting the MAP, which is based on the number of relevant elements, is more complicated. Therefore, this year, the F-measure is used for the official ranking of the systems in snippet retrieval, which is calculated based on character overlaps[10].

As in BioASQ8, a modified version of Average Precision (AP) is adopted. In brief, since BioASQ3, the participant systems are allowed to return up to 10 relevant items (e.g. documents), and the calculation of AP was modified to reflect this change. However, some questions with fewer than 10 golden relevant items have been observed in the last years, resulting to relatively small AP values even for submissions with all the golden elements. Therefore, the AP calculation was modified to consider both the limit of 10 elements and the actual number of golden elements [25].

Some indicative preliminary results from batch 4 are presented in Tables 11 and 12 for document and snippet retrieval. The full results are available in the online results page of Task 9b, phase A[11]. The results presented here are preliminary, as the final results for the task 9b will be available after the manual assessment of the system responses by the BioASQ team of biomedical experts.

Phase B: In phase B of task 9b, both exact and ideal answers are expected by the participating systems. For the sub-task of ideal answer generation, the BioASQ experts assign manual scores to each answer submitted by the participating systems during the assessment of system responses [9]. Then these scores are used for the official ranking of the systems. Regarding exact answers, the participating systems are ranked based on their average ranking in the three question types

[9] http://participants-area.bioasq.org/results/9a/.
[10] http://participants-area.bioasq.org/Tasks/b/eval_meas_2021/.
[11] http://participants-area.bioasq.org/results/9b/phaseA/.

Table 11. Preliminary results for document retrieval in batch 4 of phase A of Task 9b. Only the top-10 systems are presented, based on MAP.

System	Mean precision	Mean recall	Mean F-measure	MAP	GMAP
bioinfo-2	0.1280	0.5213	0.1873	**0.4236**	0.0125
pa-5	**0.2421**	0.5132	**0.2902**	0.4192	0.0128
RYGH-4	0.1170	0.5118	0.1733	0.4179	0.0123
RYGH-3	0.1150	0.5120	0.1726	0.4174	**0.0132**
RYGH	0.1140	0.5083	0.1701	0.4166	0.0120
RYGH-5	0.1160	0.5118	0.1733	0.4109	0.0122
bioinfo-3	0.1270	**0.5280**	0.1865	0.4042	0.0131
bioinfo-4	0.1270	**0.5280**	0.1865	0.4042	0.0131
RYGH-1	0.1160	0.5110	0.1725	0.4027	0.0111
pa-1	0.1410	0.4773	0.1930	0.3893	0.0092

Table 12. Preliminary results for snippet retrieval in batch 4 of phase A of Task 9b. Only the top-10 systems are presented, based on F-measure.

System	Mean precision	Mean recall	Mean F-measure	MAP	GMAP
pa-5	**0.1932**	0.3147	**0.2061**	**0.9696**	0.0026
RYGH-4	0.1416	**0.3337**	0.1764	0.4561	**0.0068**
RYGH-1	0.1369	0.3334	0.1737	0.4697	0.0062
pa-1	0.1567	0.2777	0.1733	0.8515	0.0018
RYGH-5	0.1397	0.3257	0.1733	0.4492	0.0064
pa-2	0.1563	0.2745	0.1722	0.8372	0.0015
RYGH	0.1382	0.3271	0.1722	0.4595	0.0059
RYGH-3	0.1382	0.3234	0.1721	0.4490	0.0064
pa-3	0.1567	0.2686	0.1718	0.8437	0.0012
pa-4	0.1567	0.2686	0.1718	0.8437	0.0012

Table 13. Results for batch 4 for exact answers in phase B of Task 9b. Only the top-10 systems based on Yes/No F1 and the BioASQ Baseline are presented.

System	Yes/No		Factoid			List		
	F1	Acc	Str. Acc	Len. Acc	MRR	Prec	Rec	F1
KU-DMIS-1	**0.9480**	**0.9600**	0.5000	0.6071	0.5310	0.6454	**0.8202**	**0.7061**
lr_sys1	**0.9480**	**0.9600**	**0.6429**	**0.7857**	**0.6929**	0.5929	0.7675	0.6312
KU-DMIS-5	0.9008	0.9200	0.5000	0.7143	0.5726	0.6245	0.7377	0.6470
KU-DMIS-2	0.8904	0.9200	0.5000	0.6786	0.5589	0.5568	0.7465	0.6001
KU-DMIS-3	0.8904	0.9200	0.5000	0.6429	0.5429	0.5991	0.7860	0.6430
KU-DMIS-4	0.8904	0.9200	0.4286	0.6786	0.5101	0.5521	0.7149	0.5802
NCU-IISR...1	0.8441	0.8800	0.3571	0.6071	0.4232	0.5263	0.3991	0.4261
NCU-IISR...2	0.8441	0.8800	0.3571	0.6071	0.4232	0.5263	0.3991	0.4261
NCU-IISR...3	0.8441	0.8800	0.3571	0.6071	0.4232	0.5263	0.3991	0.4261
lr_sys2	0.8252	0.8800	0.6071	0.7500	0.6464	0.6027	0.6614	0.5780
BioASQ_Baseline	0.3506	0.3600	0.1429	0.3571	0.2077	0.1767	0.3202	0.1857

where exact answers are required. Summary questions are not considered as no exact answers are submitted for them. For yes/no questions, the systems are ranked based on the F1-measure, macro-averaged over the class of no and yes. For factoid questions, the ranking is based on mean reciprocal rank (MRR) and for list questions on mean F1-measure. Indicative preliminary results for exact answers from the fourth batch of Task 9b are presented in Table 13. The full results of phase B of Task 9b are available online[12]. These results are preliminary, as the final results for Task 9b will be available after the manual assessment of the system responses by the BioASQ team of biomedical experts.

The top performance of the participating systems in exact answer generation for each type of question during the nine years of BioASQ is presented in Figure 3. These results reveal that the participating systems keep improving in all types of questions. In batch 4, for instance, presented in Table 13, in yes/no questions most systems manage to outperform by far the strong baseline, which is based on a version of the OAQA system that achieved top performance in previous years. Improvements are also observed in the preliminary results For list and factoid questions, some improvements are also observed in the preliminary results compared to the previous years, but there is still more room for improvement.

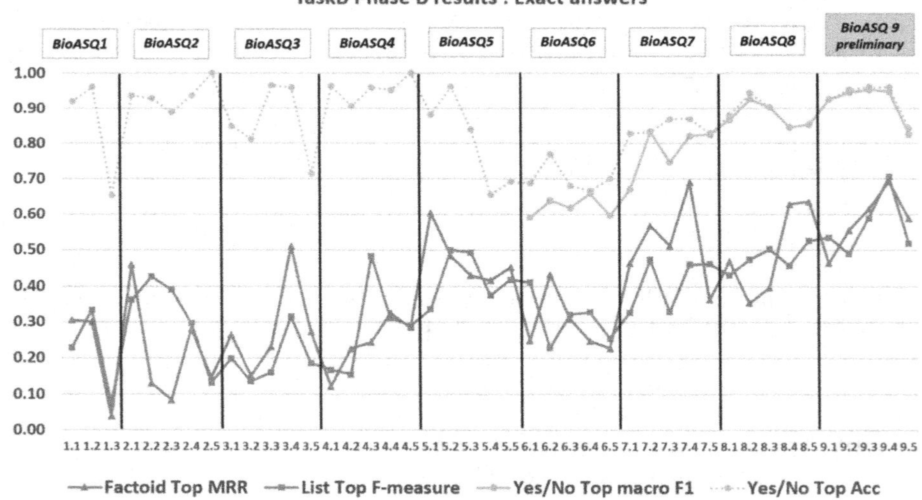

Fig. 3. The official evaluation scores of the best performing systems in Task B, Phase B, exact answer generation, across the nine years of the BioASQ challenge. Since BioASQ6 the official measure for Yes/No questions is the macro-averaged F1 score (macro F1), but accuracy (Acc) is also presented as the former official measure.

[12] http://participants-area.bioasq.org/results/9b/phaseB/.

4.3 Task MESINESP

The performance of participating teams this year is higher than last year. There has been an increase in f-score of 0.06 for scientific literature, and the state of the art of clinical trials and patents semantic indexing with DeCS has been established in 0.3640 and 0.4514.

As shown in Table 14, once again, the top performer this year was the Bert-DeCS system developed by Fudan University. Their system was based on an AttentionXML architecture with an Multilingual BERT encoding layer that was trained with MEDLINE articles and then fine-tuned with MESINESP corpora. This architecture obtained the best MiF score performance in scientific literature, clinical trials and patents. However, the best code prediction accuracy was achieved by Roche's "*pi_dna*" system. Comparing the performance of the models with the baseline, it is noteworthy that only 7 of the models implemented for patents have been able to outperform the look-up system, highlighting the good performance of *iria-2*.

Table 14. Results of models

		MESINESP-L	MESINESP-T	MESINESP-P
Team	System	MiF	MiF	MiF
Fudan University	BERTDeCS-CooMatInfer	0.4505	0.1095	0.4489
	BERTDeCS version 2	0.4798	*0.3640*	*0.4514*
	BERTDeCS version 3	0.4808	0.3630	0.4480
	BERTDeCS version 4	*0.4837*	0.3563	0.4514
	bertmesh-1	0.4808	0.3600	0.4489
Roche	bert_dna	0.3989	0.2710	0.2479
	pi_dna	*0.4225*	*0.2781*	*0.3628*
	pi_dna_2	0.3978	0.2680	-
	pi_dna_3	0.4027	-	-
	bert_dna_2	0.3962	0.2383	0.2479
Universidade de Lisboa	LASIGE_BioTM_1	*0.2007*	-	-
	LASIGE_BioTM_2	0.1886	-	-
	clinical_trials_1.0	-	0.0679	-
	clinical_trials_0.25	-	*0.0686*	-
	patents_1.0	-	-	*0.0314*
Vicomtech	Classifier	*0.3825*	0.2485	0.1968
	CSSClassifier025	0.3823	*0.2819*	0.2834
	CSSClassifier035	0.3801	0.2810	0.2651
	LabelGlosses01	0.3704	0.2807	0.2908
	LabelGlosses02	0.3746	-	*0.2921*
Uni Vigo, Uni. Coruña	iria-1	0.3406	*0.2454*	0.1871
	iria-2	0.3389	-	*0.3203*
	iria-3	0.2537	0.1562	0.0793
	iria-4	0.3656	0.2003	0.2169
	iria-mix	*0.3725*	0.2003	0.2542
Universidad de Chile	tf-idf-model	*0.1335*	-	-
YMCA University	AnujTagging	*0.0631*	-	-
	Anuj_ml	-	*0.0019*	-
	Anuj_NLP	0.0035	-	-
	Anuj_Ensemble	-	-	*0.0389*
Baseline		0.2876	0.1288	0.2992

The results of the task show a drop in performance compared to the English task despite teams using similar technologies. This drop in performance could be associated with a lower number of training documents and inconsistencies in the manual indexing of these documents because they come from two different bibliographic sources [35]. Alternatively, this could also be explained by the delay in updating deprecated DeCS codes from the historical database. DeCS add and remove new terms twice a year, and the lack of temporal alignment in the update process could lead to inconsistencies between training and test data and decrease overall performance.

Regarding MESINESP-T track, there is no similar task in English to compare the results. The performance of the models is systematically lower than those generated for scientific literature. Because participants reported that they reused the models trained with scientific literature, incorporating the development set to make their predictions, a low quality Gold Standard cannot be associated with the drop in performance. However, given that the length of clinical trial documents is much longer than article abstracts, and that most systems use BERT models with an input size limit of 512 tokens, it is possible that a significant part of the documents will not be processed by the models and relevant information will be lost for indexing.

The patents subtrack presented a major challenge for the participants as they did not have a large training and development dataset. Since the statistics between the MESINESP-T and MESINESP-P corpora were similar, the participants solved the lack of data using the same models generated for scientific literature. The resulting models were promising, and the performance of some of the systems, such as Fudan, Roche and Iria, remained at the same level as scientific literature track.

On the other hand, although the performance of the models is lower than that of the English task, we used the participants' results to see whether the manual annotation process could be improved. To this end, a module for indexing assistance was developed in the ASIT tool, and a set of pre-annotated documents with the predictions of the best-performing team was provided to our expert indexers. After tracking annotation times, we observed that this type of system could improve annotation times by **up to 60%**[14].

4.4 Synergy Task

In task Synergy the participating systems were expected to retrieve documents and snippets, as in phase A of task B, and, at the same time, provide answers for some of these questions, as in phase B of task B. In contrast to task B, it is possible that no answer exists for some questions. Therefore only some of the questions provided in each test set, that were indicated to have enough relevant material gathered from previous rounds, require the submission of exact and ideal answers. Also in contrast to task B, during the first round no golden documents and snippets were given, while on the rest of the rounds a separate file with feedback from the experts, based on the previously submitted responses, was provided.

The feedback concept was introduced in this task to further assist the collaboration between the systems and the BioASQ team of biomedical experts. The feedback includes the already judged documentation and answers along with their evaluated relevancy to the question. The documents and snippets included in the feedback are not considered valid for submission in the following rounds, and even if accidentally submitted, they will not be taken into account for the evaluation of that round. The evaluation measures for the retrieval of documents and snippets are the MAP and F-measure respectively, as in phase A of task B.

Regarding the ideal answers, the systems are ranked according to manual scores assigned to them by the BioASQ experts during the assessment of systems responses as in phase B of task B [9]. For the exact answers, which are required for all questions except the summary ones, the measure considered for ranking the participating systems depends on the question type. For the yes/no questions, the systems were ranked according to the macro-averaged F1-measure on prediction of no and yes answer. For factoid questions, the ranking was based on mean reciprocal rank (MRR) and for list questions on mean F1-measure.

Some indicative results for the first round of Synergy Task, version 1, are presented for document retrieval in Table 15. The full results of Synergy Task are available online[13]. As regards the extraction of exact answers, despite the moderate scores in list and factoid questions the experts found useful the submissions of the participants, as most of them (more than 70%) stated they would be interested in using a tool following the BioASQ Synergy process to identify interesting material and answers for their research.

Table 15. Results for document retrieval in round 1 of the first version of Synergy task. Only the top-10 systems are presented.

System	Mean precision	Mean recall	Mean F-Measure	MAP	GMAP
RYGH-5	**0.4963**	**0.3795**	**0.3457**	**0.3375**	**0.0829**
RYGH-3	0.4948	0.354	0.3454	0.3363	0.0418
RYGH-1	0.4892	0.3523	0.3358	0.3248	0.0471
RYGH-4	0.4799	0.3603	0.328	0.3236	0.0598
NLM-1	0.4773	0.3251	0.3383	0.2946	0.0459
NLM-2	0.4773	0.3251	0.3383	0.2946	0.0459
NLM-3	0.4438	0.331	0.3078	0.2735	0.0635
NLM-4	0.4438	0.331	0.3078	0.2735	0.0635
RYGH	0.4225	0.3308	0.3016	0.3008	0.0281
bio-answerfinder	0.4105	0.216	0.2372	0.1935	0.014

13 http://participants-area.bioasq.org/results/synergy/.

5 Conclusions

An overview of the ninth BioASQ challenge is provided in this paper. This year, the challenge consisted of four tasks: The two tasks on biomedical semantic indexing and question answering in English, already established through the previous eight years of the challenge, the second version of the MESINESP task on semantic indexing of medical content in Spanish, and the new task Synergy on question answering for COVID-19.

In the second version of the MESINESP task we introduced two new challenging sub-tracks, beyond the one on medical literature. Namely, on patents and clinical trials in Spanish. Due to the lack of big datasets in these new tracks, the participants were pushed to experiment with transferring knowledge and models from the literature track, highlighting the importance of adequate resources for the development of systems to effectively help biomedical experts dealing with non-English resources.

The introduction of the Synergy Task, in an effort to enable a dialogue between the participating systems with biomedical experts revealed that state-of-the-art systems, despite they still have room for improvement, can be a useful tool for biomedical experts that need specialized information in the context of the developing problem of the COVID-19 pandemic.

The overall shift of participant systems towards deep neural approaches observed during the last years, is even more apparent this year. State-of-the-art methodologies have been successfully adapted to biomedical question answering and novel ideas have been explored leading to improved results, particularly for exact answer generation this year. Most of the teams developed systems based on neural embeddings, such as BERT, SciBERT, and BioBERT models, for all tasks of the challenge. In the QA tasks in particular, different teams attempted transferring knowledge from general domain QA datasets, notably SQuAD, or from other NLP tasks such as NER and NLI.

Overall, the top preforming systems were able to advance over the state of the art, outperforming the strong baselines on the challenging tasks offered in BioASQ, as in previous versions of the challenge. Therefore, BioASQ keeps pushing the research frontier in biomedical semantic indexing and question answering, extending beyond the English language, through MESINESP, and beyond the already established models for the shared tasks, by introducing Synergy. The future plans for the challenge include the extension of the benchmark data for question answering though a community-driven process, as well as extending the Synergy task into other developing problems beyond COVID-19.

Acknowledgments. Google was a proud sponsor of the BioASQ Challenge in 2020. The ninth edition of BioASQ is also sponsored by Atypon Systems inc. BioASQ is grateful to NLM for providing the baselines for task 9a and to the CMU team for providing the baselines for task 9b. The MESINESP task is sponsored by the Spanish Plan for the Advancement of Language Technologies (Plan TL). BioASQ would also like to thank LILACS, SCIELO, Biblioteca Virtual en Salud, Instituto de Salud Carlos III, and BIREME for providing data and help in organizing the BioASQ MESINESP task.

References

1. attentionxml: Label tree-based attention-aware deep model for high-performance extreme multi-label text classification
2. ku-dmis at bioasq 9: Data-centric and model-centric approaches for biomedical question answering
3. Almeida, T., Matos, S.: BIT.UA at BioASQ 8: lightweight neural document ranking with zero-shot snippet retrieval. In: CLEF (Working Notes) (2020)
4. Almeida, T., Matos, S.: BioASQ synergy: a strong and simple baseline rooted in relevance feedback. In: CLEF (Working Notes) (2021)
5. Almeida, T., Matos, S.: Universal passage weighting mechanism (UPWM) in BioASQ 9b. In: CLEF (Working Notes) (2021)
6. Alrowili, S., Shanker, K.: Large biomedical question answering models with ALBERT and ELECTRA. In: CLEF (Working Notes) (2021)
7. Alrowili, S., Shanker, V.: BioM-transformers: building large biomedical language models with BERT, ALBERT and ELECTRA. In: Proceedings of the 20th Workshop on Biomedical Language Processing, pp. 221–227. Association for Computational Linguistics, June 2021. https://www.aclweb.org/anthology/2021.bionlp-1.24
8. Baldwin, B., Carpenter, B.: LingPipe. World Wide Web (2003). http://alias-i.com/lingpipe
9. Balikas, G., et al.: Evaluation framework specifications. Project deliverable D4.1, UPMC, May 2013
10. Campos, M., Couto, F.: Post-processing BioBERT and using voting methods for biomedical question answering. In: CLEF (Working Notes) (2021)
11. Clark, K., Luong, M.T., Le, Q.V., Manning, C.D.: ELECTRA: pre-training text encoders as discriminators rather than generators. arXiv preprint arXiv:2003.10555 (2020)
12. Demsar, J.: Statistical comparisons of classifiers over multiple data sets. J. Mach. Learn. Res. **7**, 1–30 (2006)
13. García-Pablos, A., Perez, N., Cuadros, M.: Vicomtech at MESINESP2: BERT-based multi-label classification models for biomedical text indexing (2021)
14. Gasco, L., et al.: Overview of BioASQ 2021-MESINESP track. Evaluation of advance hierarchical classification techniques for scientific literature, patents and clinical trials (2021)
15. Huang, Y., Buse, G., Abdullatif, K., Ozgur, A., Ozkirimli, E.: Pidna at BioASQ MESINESP: hybrid semantic indexing for biomedical articles in Spanish (2021)
16. Khanna, U., Molla, D.: Transformer-based language models for factoid question answering at bioasq9b. In: CLEF (Working Notes) (2021)
17. Kosmopoulos, A., Partalas, I., Gaussier, E., Paliouras, G., Androutsopoulos, I.: Evaluation measures for hierarchical classification: a unified view and novel approaches. Data Min. Knowl. Disc. **29**(3), 820–865 (2015)
18. Krallinger, M., et al.: Overview of the CHEMDNER patents task. In: Proceedings of the Fifth BioCreative Challenge Evaluation Workshop, pp. 63–75 (2015)
19. Miranda-Escalada, A., Farré, E., Krallinger, M.: Named entity recognition, concept normalization and clinical coding: Overview of the cantemist track for cancer text mining in Spanish, corpus, guidelines, methods and results. In: Proceedings of the Iberian Languages Evaluation Forum (IberLEF 2020). CEUR Workshop Proceedings (2020)

20. Miranda-Escalada, A.: The ProfNER shared task on automatic recognition of occupation mentions in social media: systems, evaluation, guidelines, embeddings and corpora. In: Proceedings of the Sixth Social Media Mining for Health (# SMM4H) Workshop and Shared Task, pp. 13–20 (2021)
21. Miranda-Escalada, A., Gonzalez-Agirre, A., Armengol-Estapé, J., Krallinger, M.: Overview of automatic clinical coding: annotations, guidelines, and solutions for non-English clinical cases at CodiEsp track of CLEF eHealth 2020. In: Working Notes of Conference and Labs of the Evaluation (CLEF) Forum. CEUR Workshop Proceedings (2020)
22. Molla, D., Jones, C., Nguyen, V.: Query focused multi-document summarisation of biomedical texts. arXiv preprint arXiv:2008.11986 (2020)
23. Molla, D., Khanna, U., Galat, D., Nguyen, V., Rybinski, M.: Query-focused extractive summarisation for finding ideal answers to biomedical and COVID-19 questions. In: CLEF (Working Notes) (2021)
24. Mork, J.G., Demner-Fushman, D., Schmidt, S.C., Aronson, A.R.: Recent enhancements to the NLM medical text indexer. In: Proceedings of Question Answering Lab at CLEF (2014)
25. Nentidis, A., et al.: Overview of BioASQ 2020: the eighth BioASQ challenge on large-scale biomedical semantic indexing and question answering. In: Arampatzis, A., et al. (eds.) CLEF 2020. LNCS, vol. 12260, pp. 194–214. Springer, Cham (2020). https://doi.org/10.1007/978-3-030-58219-7_16
26. Ozyurt, I.B.: On the effectiveness of small, discriminatively pre-trained language representation models for biomedical text mining. In: Proceedings of the First Workshop on Scholarly Document Processing, pp. 104–112 (2020)
27. Ozyurt, I.B.: End-to-end biomedical question answering via bio-answerfinder and discriminative language representation models. In: CLEF (Working Notes) (2021)
28. Ozyurt, I.B., Bandrowski, A., Grethe, J.S.: Bio-AnswerFinder: a system to find answers to questions from biomedical texts. Database **2020** (2020)
29. Pappas, D., Stavropoulos, P., Androutsopoulos, I.: AUEB-NLP at BioASQ 8: biomedical document and snippet retrieval (2020)
30. Peng, S., You, R., Wang, H., Zhai, C., Mamitsuka, H., Zhu, S.: DeepMesh: deep semantic representation for improving large-scale mesh indexing. Bioinformatics **32**(12), i70–i79 (2016)
31. Rae, A., Mork, J., Demner-Fushman, D.: A neural text ranking approach for automatic mesh indexing. In: CLEF (Working Notes) (2021)
32. Rae, A.R., Pritchard, D.O., Mork, J.G., Demner-Fushman, D.: Automatic mesh indexing: revisiting the subheading attachment problem. In: AMIA Annual Symposium Proceedings, vol. 2020, p. 1031. American Medical Informatics Association (2020)
33. Raffel, C.: Exploring the limits of transfer learning with a unified text-to-text transformer. arXiv preprint arXiv:1910.10683 (2019)
34. Ribadas, F.J., De Campos, L.M., Darriba, V.M., Romero, A.E.: CoLe and UTAI at BioASQ 2015: experiments with similarity based descriptor assignment. CEUR Workshop Proc. **1391** (2015)
35. Rodriguez-Penagos, C.: Overview of MESINESP8, a Spanish medical semantic indexing task within BioASQ 2020 (2020)
36. Ruas, P., Andrade, V.D.T., Couto, F.M.: LASIGE-BioTM at MESINESP2: entity linking with semantic similarity and extreme multi-label classification on Spanish biomedical documents (2021)

37. Sarrouti, M., Gupta, D., Abacha, A.B., Demner-Fushman, D.: NLM at BioASQ 2021: deep learning-based methods for biomedical question answering about COVID-19. In: CLEF (Working Notes) (2021)
38. Torres-Salinas, D., Robinson-Garcia, N., van Schalkwyk, F., Nane, G.F., Castillo-Valdivieso, P.: The growth of COVID-19 scientific literature: a forecast analysis of different daily time series in specific settings. arXiv preprint arXiv:2101.12455 (2021)
39. Tsatsaronis, G., et al.: An overview of the BioASQ large-scale biomedical semantic indexing and question answering competition. BMC Bioinform. **16**, 138 (2015). https://doi.org/10.1186/s12859-015-0564-6
40. Tsoumakas, G., Laliotis, M., Markontanatos, N., Vlahavas, I.: Large-scale semantic indexing of biomedical publications. In: 1st BioASQ Workshop: A Challenge on Large-Scale Biomedical Semantic Indexing and Question Answering (2013)
41. Wang, L.L., et al.: CORD-19: the COVID-19 open research dataset. ArXiv (2020)
42. Wei, C.H., Leaman, R., Lu, Z.: Beyond accuracy: creating interoperable and scalable text-mining web services. Bioinform. (Oxford, Engl.) **32**(12), 1907–10 (2016). https://doi.org/10.1093/bioinformatics/btv760
43. Xue, L., et al.: mT5: a massively multilingual pre-trained text-to-text transformer. arXiv preprint arXiv:2010.11934 (2020)
44. Yang, Z., Zhou, Y., Eric, N.: Learning to answer biomedical questions: OAQA at BioASQ 4b. ACL **2016**, 23 (2016)
45. Yoon, W., Jackson, R., Kang, J., Lagerberg, A.: Sequence tagging for biomedical extractive question answering. arXiv preprint arXiv:2104.07535 (2021)
46. You, R., Liu, Y., Mamitsuka, H., Zhu, S.: BERTMeSH: deep contextual representation learning for large-scale high-performance MeSH indexing with full text. Bioinformatics **37**(5), 684–692 (2021)
47. Zavorin, I., Mork, J.G., Demner-Fushman, D.: Using learning-to-rank to enhance NLM medical text indexer results. ACL **2016**, 8 (2016)
48. Zhang, Y., Han, J.C., Tsai, R.T.H.: NCU-IISR/AS-GIS: results of various pre-trained biomedical language models and logistic regression model in BioASQ task 9b phase b. In: CLEF (Working Notes) (2021)

Overview of the CLEF–2021 CheckThat! Lab on Detecting Check-Worthy Claims, Previously Fact-Checked Claims, and Fake News

Preslav Nakov[1], Giovanni Da San Martino[2], Tamer Elsayed[3], Alberto Barrón-Cedeño[4], Rubén Míguez[5], Shaden Shaar[1], Firoj Alam[1(✉)], Fatima Haouari[3], Maram Hasanain[3], Watheq Mansour[3], Bayan Hamdan[11], Zien Sheikh Ali[3], Nikolay Babulkov[6], Alex Nikolov[6], Gautam Kishore Shahi[7], Julia Maria Struß[8], Thomas Mandl[9], Mucahid Kutlu[10], and Yavuz Selim Kartal[10]

[1] Qatar Computing Research Institute, HBKU, Doha, Qatar
{pnakov,sshaar,fialam}@hbku.edu.qa
[2] University of Padova, Padova, Italy
dasan@math.unipd.it
[3] Qatar University, Doha, Qatar
{telsayed,200159617,maram.hasanain,wm1900793,zs1407404}@qu.edu.qa
[4] DIT, Università di Bologna, Bologna, Italy
a.barron@unibo.it
[5] Newtral Media Audiovisual, Madrid, Spain
ruben.miguez@newtral.es
[6] Sofia University, Sofia, Bulgaria
nbabulkov@gmail.com, alexnickolow@gmail.com
[7] University of Duisburg-Essen, Duisburg, Germany
gautam.shahi@uni-due.de
[8] University of Applied Sciences Potsdam, Potsdam, Germany
struss@fh-potsdam.de
[9] University of Hildesheim, Hildesheim, Germany
mandl@uni-hildesheim.de
[10] TOBB University of Economics and Technology, Ankara, Turkey
{m.kutlu,ykartal}@etu.edu.tr
[11] Amman, Jordan

Abstract. We describe the fourth edition of the CheckThat! Lab, part of the 2021 Conference and Labs of the Evaluation Forum (CLEF). The lab evaluates technology supporting tasks related to factuality, and covers Arabic, Bulgarian, English, Spanish, and Turkish. Task 1 asks to predict which posts in a Twitter stream are worth fact-checking, focusing on COVID-19 and politics (in all five languages). Task 2 asks to determine whether a claim in a tweet can be verified using a set of previously fact-checked claims (in Arabic and English). Task 3 asks to predict the veracity of a news article and its topical domain (in English). The

B. Hamdan—Independent Researcher.

K. S. Candan et al. (Eds.): CLEF 2021, LNCS 12880, pp. 264–291, 2021.
https://doi.org/10.1007/978-3-030-85251-1_19

evaluation is based on mean average precision or precision at rank k for the ranking tasks, and macro-F_1 for the classification tasks. This was the most popular CLEF-2021 lab in terms of team registrations: 132 teams. Nearly one-third of them participated: 15, 5, and 25 teams submitted official runs for tasks 1, 2, and 3, respectively.

Keywords: Fact-checking · Disinformation · Misinformation · Check-worthiness estimation · Verified claim retrieval · Fake news detection · COVID-19

1 Introduction

The mission of the `CheckThat!` lab is to foster the development of technology to enable the (semi-)automatic verification of claims. Systems for claim identification and verification can be very useful as supportive technology for investigative journalism, as they could provide help and guidance, thus saving time [34,45,47,54,98]. A system could automatically identify check-worthy claims, make sure they have not been fact-checked already by a reputable fact-checking organization, and then present them to a journalist for further analysis in a ranked list. Additionally, the system could identify documents that are potentially *useful* for humans to perform manual fact-checking of a claim, and it could also estimate a *veracity score* supported by evidence to increase the journalist's understanding and trust in the system's decision.

`CheckThat!` at CLEF 2021 is the fourth edition of the lab. The 2018 edition [65] focused on the identification and verification of claims in political debates. The 2019 edition [31,32] featured political debates and isolated claims, in conjunction with a closed set of Web documents to retrieve evidence from.

In 2020 [15], the focus was on social media—in particular on *Twitter*—as information posted on this platform is not checked by an authoritative entity before posting and such posts tend to disseminate very quickly. Moreover, social media posts lack context due to their short length and conversational nature; thus, identifying a claim's context is sometimes key for effective fact-checking [23].

In the 2021 edition of the `CheckThat!` lab, we feature three tasks: 1. check-worthiness estimation, 2. detecting previously fact-checked claims, and 3. predicting the veracity of news articles and their domain. In these tasks, we focus on (*i*) *tweets*, (*ii*) *political debates and speeches*, and (*iii*) *news articles*. Moreover, besides Arabic and English, we extend our language coverage to Bulgarian, Spanish, and Turkish. We further add a new task (task 3) on multi-class fake news detection for news articles and topical domain identification, which can help direct the article to the right fact-checking expert [68].

2 Previously on `CheckThat!`

Three editions of the `CheckThat!` lab have been held so far, and some of the tasks in the 2021 edition are reformulated from previous editions. Below, we discuss some relevant tasks from previous years.

2.1 CheckThat! 2020

Task 1$_{2020}$. *Given a topic and a stream of potentially related tweets, rank the tweets by check-worthiness for the topic* [43,82]. The most successful runs adopted state-of-the-art transformer models. The top-ranked teams for the English version of this task used BERT [24] and RoBERTa [70,99]. For the Arabic version, the top systems used AraBERT [52,99] and the multilingual BERT [42].

Task 2$_{2020}$. *Given a check-worthy claim and a dataset of verified claims, rank the verified claims, so that those that verify the input claim (or a sub-claim in it) are ranked on top of the list* [82]. The most effective approaches fine-tuned large-scale pre-trained transformers such as BERT and RoBERTa. In particular, the top-ranked run fine-tuned RoBERTa [18].

Task 4$_{2020}$. *Given a check-worthy claim on a specific topic and a set of potentially-relevant Web pages, predict the veracity of the claim* [43]. Two runs were submitted for the task [95], using a scoring function that computes the degree of concordance and negation between a claim and all input text snippets for that claim.

Task 5$_{2020}$. *Given a political debate or a speech, segmented into sentences, together with information about who the speaker of each sentence is, prioritize the sentences for fact-checking* [82]. For this task, only one out of eight runs outperformed a strong bi-LSTM baseline [59].

2.2 CheckThat! 2019

Task 1$_{2019}$. *Given a political debate, an interview, or a speech, segmented into sentences, rank the sentences by the priority with which they should be fact-checked* [10]. The most successful approaches used neural networks for the classification of the individual instances. For example, Hansen et al. [40] learned domain-specific word embeddings and syntactic dependencies and used an LSTM with a classification layer onn top of it.

Task 2$_{2019}$. *Given a claim and a set of potentially relevant Web pages, identify which of the pages (and passages thereof) are useful for assisting a human to fact-check that claim. There was also a second subtask, asking to determine the factuality of the claim* [44]. The most effective approach for this task used textual entailment and external data [35].

2.3 CheckThat! 2018

Task 1$_{2018}$ [9] was identical to Task 1_{2019}. The best approaches used *pseudo-speeches* as a concatenation of all interventions by a debater [105], and represented the entries with embeddings, part-of-speech tags, and syntactic dependencies [39].

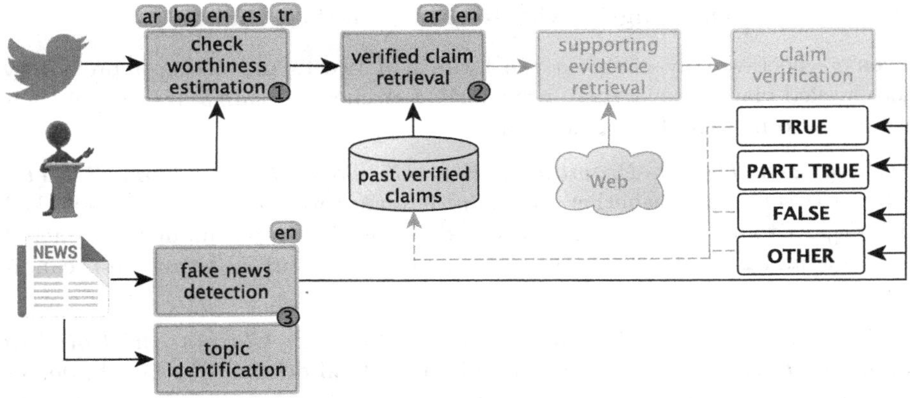

Fig. 1. The full verification pipeline. The 2021 lab covers three tasks from that pipeline: (*i*) check-worthiness estimation, (*ii*) verified claim retrieval, and (*iii*) fake news detection. The gray tasks were addressed in previous editions of the lab [16,32].

Task 2_{2018}. *Given a check-worthy claim in the form of a (transcribed) sentence, determine whether the claim is likely to be true, half-true, or false* [17]. The best approach retrieved relevant information from the Web, and fed the claim with the most similar Web-retrieved text to a convolutional neural network [39].

3 Description of the Tasks

The lab is organized around three tasks, each of which in turn has several subtasks. Figure 1 shows the full `CheckThat!` verification pipeline, and the three tasks we target this year are highlighted.

3.1 Task 1: Check-Worthiness Estimation

The aim of Task 1 is to determine whether a piece of text is worth fact-checking. In order to do that, we either resort to the judgments of professional fact-checkers or we ask human annotators to answer several auxiliary questions [3,4], such as "does it contain a verifiable factual claim?", "is it harmful?" and "is it of general interest?", before deciding on the final check-worthiness label.

Subtask 1A: Check-Worthiness of Tweets. Given a tweet, produce a ranked list of tweets, ordered by their check-worthiness. This is a ranking task, focusing either on COVID-19 or politics. It was offered in Arabic, Bulgarian, English, Spanish, and Turkish. The participants were free to work on any language(s) of their choice, and they could also use multilingual approaches that make use of all datasets for training.

Subtask 1B: Check-Worthiness of Debates or Speeches. Given a political debate/speech, return a ranked list of its sentences, ordered by their check-worthiness. This is a ranking task, and it was offered in English.

3.2 Task 2: Detecting Previously Fact-Checked Claims

Given a check-worthy claim in the form of a tweet, and a set of previously fact-checked claims, rank these previously fact-checked claims in order of their usefulness to fact-check that new claim.

Subtask 2A: Detect Previously Fact-Checked Claims from Tweets. Given a tweet, detect whether the claim it makes was previously fact-checked with respect to a collection of fact-checked claims. This is a ranking task, offered in Arabic and English, where the systems need to return a list of top-n candidates.

Subtask 2B: Detect Previously Fact-Checked Claims in Political Debates or Speeches. Given a claim in a political debate or a speech, detect whether the claim has been previously fact-checked with respect to a collection of previously fact-checked claims. This is a ranking task, and it was offered in English.

3.3 Task 3: Fake News Detection

Task 3 was offered for the first time, as a pilot task. In includes two subtasks.

Subtask 3A: Multi-class Fake News Detection of News Articles. Given the text of a news article, determine whether the claims made in the article are *true*, *partially true*, *false*, or *other*. This is a classification task, offered in English.

Subtask 3B: Given the Text of a News Article, Determine the Topical Domain of the Article. This is a classification task to determine the topical domain of a news article [87]. It involves six categories (health, crime, climate, election, and education), and was offered in English.

4 Datasets

Here, we briefly describe the datasets for each of the three tasks. For more details, refer to the task description paper for each individual task [80,81,89].

4.1 Task 1: Check-Worthiness Estimation

Subtask 1A: Check-Worthiness for Tweets. We produced datasets in five languages with tweets covering COVID-19, politics, and other topics. We refer to these datasets as the CT–CWT–21 corpus, which stands for `CheckThat!` check-worthiness for tweets 2021. Table 1 shows statistics about the corpus.

For **Arabic**, the training set is sampled from the corpus used in the 2020 edition of the `CheckThat!` lab [43]; we only kept tweets with full agreement between the annotators. The tweets mainly cover politics and COVID-19. The newly collected testing set covers two political events: Gulf reconciliation and US Capitol riots. They were labelled by two expert annotators, and the disagreements were resolved by discussion between the annotators.

Table 1. Task 1A (Check-worthiness in tweets): Statistics about the CT–CWT–21 corpus for all five languages. The bottom part of the table shows the main topics.

Partition	Arabic	Bulgarian	English	Spanish	Turkish	Total
Training	3,444	3,000	822	2,495	1,899	11,660
Development	661	350	140	1,247	388	2,786
Testing	600	357	350	1,248	1,013	3,568
Total	4,705	3,707	1,312	4,990	3,300	18,014
Main topics						
COVID-19	■	■	■		■	
Politics	■			■	■	

For **Bulgarian**, we created a new dataset focusing on COVID-19. The tweets were annotated by three annotators, and disagreements were resolved by majority voting, and then by a consolidator.

For **English**, the dataset also focused on COVID-19. For training, we released the data used in the `CheckThat!` lab of 2020 [82]. For testing, we annotated new instances, where we had three annotators per example, and we resolved the disagreements by majority voting, and then by a consolidator.

For **Spanish**, we had a new dataset. The tweets were manually annotated by journalists from Newtral—a Spanish fact-checking organization—and came from the Twitter accounts of 300 Spanish politicians.

For **Turkish**, the training set came from the TrClaim-19 dataset [53], whereas the testing set was labelled for this task by three annotators. We applied majority voting for aggregation. The training set covers important events in Turkey in 2019 (e.g., the earthquake in Istanbul, and the military operation in Syria), whereas the test set focuses on COVID-19.

The datasets for Arabic, Bulgarian, and English have annotations for some auxiliary questions. For example, annotators were asked question such as "Is the claim of interest to the public?" and "Would the claim cause harm?"

Subtask 1B: Check-Worthiness for Debates/Speeches. For training, we collected 57 debates/speeches from 2012–2018, and we selected sentences from the transcript that were checked by human fact-checkers. After a political debate/speech, PolitiFact journalists publish an article fact-checking some of the claims made in it. We collected all such sentences and considered them check-worthy, and the rest non check-worthy. However, as PolitiFact journalists only fact-check a few claims made in the claims, there is an abundance of false negative examples in the dataset. To address this issue at test time, we manually looked over the debates from the test set and we attempted to check whether each sentence contains a verified claim using BM25 suggestions. Table 2 shows some statistics about the data. Note the higher proportion of positive examples in the test set compared to the training and the development sets.

Further details about the CT–CWT–21 corpus for Task 1 can be found in [81].

Table 2. Task 1B (Check-worthiness in Debates/Speeches): Statistics about the CT–CWT–21 corpus for subtask 1B.

Dataset	# of debates	# of sentences	
		Check-worthy	Non-check-worthy
Training	40	429	41,604
Development	9	69	3,517
Test	8	298	5,002
Total	57	796	50,123

4.2 Task 2: Detecting Previously Fact-Checked Claims

Subtask 2A: Detecting Previously Fact-Checked Claims from Tweets. For **English**, we have 1,401 annotated tweets, each matching a single claim in a set of 13,835 verified claims from Snopes.

For **Arabic**, we have 858 tweets, matching 1,039 verified claims (some tweets match more than one verified claim) in a collection of 30,329 previously fact-checked claims. The latter include 5,921 Arabic claims from AraFacts [5] and 24,408 English claims from ClaimsKG [93], translated to Arabic using the Google translate API (http://cloud.google.com/translate).

Subtask 2B: Detecting Previously Fact-Checked Claims in Political Debates/Speeches. We have 669 claims from political debates [79], matched against 804 verified claims (some input claims match more than one verified claim) in a collection of 19,250 verified claims in PolitiFact.

Table 3 shows statistics about the CT–VCR–21 corpus for Task 2, including both subtasks and languages. CT–VCR–21 stands for `CheckThat!` verified claim retrieval 2021. *Input–VerClaim* pairs represent input claims with their corresponding verified claims by a fact-checking source. The input for subtask 2A (2B) is a tweet (sentence from a political debate or a speech). More details about the corpus construction can be found in [80].

4.3 Task 3: Fake News Detection

The process of corpus creation for Task 3 extends the AMUSED framework [83]. Starting with articles written by fact-checking organizations, we scraped the links to the original articles they verified, together with the factuality judgments. This process was done in two steps. First, in an automatic filtering step, all links with posts from social media channels or to multimedia documents were filtered out. In a second step, the remaining links were subjected to a manual checking process. During this step, we additionally made sure that the scraped link actually pointed to the checked document and that the document still existed (thus, eliminating error pages, articles with other content, etc.). After successful verification for each article, we scraped its title and full text.

Table 3. Task 2: Statistics about the CT–VCR–21 corpus, including the number of *Input–VerClaim* pairs and the number of *VerClaim* claims to match the input claim against.

	2A–Arabic	2A–English	2B–English
Input claims	**858**	**1,401**	**669**
Training	512	999	472
Development	85	200	119
Test	261	202	78
Input–*VerClaim* pairs	**1,039**	**1,401**	**804**
Training	602	999	562
Development	102	200	139
Test	335	202	103
Verified claims (to match against)	**30,329**	**13,835**	**19,250**

Subtask 3A: Multi-class Fake News Categorization of News Articles. This subtask was offered in English only. We collected a total of 900 news articles for training and 354 news articles for testing from 11 fact-checking websites such as PolitiFact. The label for the original fact-checking site was given as a rating. However, due to the heterogeneous labeling schemes of different fact-checking organizations (e.g., *false*: incorrect, inaccurate, misinformation; *partially false*: mostly false, half false), we merged labels with shared meaning according to [84,85], resulting in the following four classes: *false*, *partially false*, *true* and *other*. We provided an ID, the title of the article, the text of the article, and our rating as data to the participants. No further metadata about the article was made available in the dataset. The ID is a unique identifier created for the dataset, the title is the title given in the target article, the text is the full-text content of the article, and our rating is the normalized rating provided in one of the above four label categories.

Subtask 3B: Topical Domain Identification of News Articles. This subtask is also offered in English only. We annotated a subset of the articles from subtask 3A with their topic: 318 articles for training, and 137 articles for testing in six different classes as shown in Table 4 based on [86]. We refer to the corpus as CT-FAN-21, which stands for `CheckThat!` 2021 Fake News. We provided the ID, the title, the text, and our rating as the metadata for the dataset. Here, ID is the unique ID, title is the title of the fake news article, the text is the full-text content of the article, and domain is the domain, expressed in terms of one of the above six categories.

The datasets for subtasks 3A and 3B are available in Zenodo [88]. We did not provide any other information (e.g., a link to the article, a publication date, eventual tags, authors, location of publication, etc.).

Table 4. Task 3: Statistics about the number of documents and class distribution for the CT-FAN-21 corpus for fake news detection (left) and for topic identification (right).

Class	Training	Test
False	465	111
True	142	65
Partially false	217	138
Other	76	40
Total	900	354

Topic	Training	Test
Health	127	54
Climate	49	21
Economy	43	19
Crime	39	17
Elections	32	14
Education	28	12
Total	318	137

5 Evaluation

For the ranking tasks, as in the two previous editions of the `CheckThat!` lab, we used *Mean Average Precision* (MAP) as the official evaluation measure. We further calculated and reported reciprocal rank, and $P@k$ for $k \in \{1, 3, 5, 10, 20, 30\}$, as unofficial measures. For the classification tasks, we used accuracy and macro-F_1 score.

6 Results for Task 1: Check-Worthiness Estimation

Below, we report the evaluation results for task 1 and its two subtasks for all five languages.

6.1 Task 1A. Check-Worthiness of Tweets

Fifteen teams took part in this task, with English and Arabic being the most popular languages. Four out of the fifteen teams submitted runs for all five languages —most of them having trained independent models for each language (yet, team UPV trained a single multilingual model). For all five languages, we had a monolingual baseline based on n-gram representations. Table 5 shows the performance of the official submissions on the test set, in addition to the n-gram baseline. The official run was the last valid blind submission by each team. The table shows the runs ranked on the basis of the official MAP measure and includes all five languages.

Arabic. Eight teams participated for Arabic, submitting a total of 17 runs (yet, recall that only the last submission counts). All participating teams fine-tuned existing pre-trained models, such as AraBERT, and multilingual BERT models. We can see that the top two systems additionally worked on improved training datasets. Team **Accenture** used a label augmentation approach to increase the

Table 5. Task 1A: results for the official submissions in all five languages.

	Team	MAP	MRR	RP	P@1	P@3	P@5	P@10	P@20	P@30
Arabic										
1	Accenture [100]	0.658	1.000	0.599	1.000	1.000	1.000	1.000	0.950	0.840
2	bigIR	0.615	0.500	0.579	0.000	0.667	0.600	0.600	0.800	0.740
3	SCUoL [6]	0.612	1.000	0.599	1.000	1.000	1.000	1.000	0.950	0.780
4	iCompass	0.597	0.333	0.624	0.000	0.333	0.400	0.400	0.500	0.640
4	QMUL-SDS [1]	0.597	0.500	0.603	0.000	0.667	0.600	0.700	0.650	0.720
6	TOBB ETU [101]	0.575	0.333	0.574	0.000	0.333	0.400	0.400	0.500	0.680
7	DamascusTeam	0.571	0.500	0.558	0.000	0.667	0.600	0.800	0.700	0.640
8	UPV [14]	0.548	1.000	0.550	1.000	0.667	0.600	0.500	0.400	0.580
9	ngram-baseline	0.428	0.500	0.409	0.000	0.667	0.600	0.500	0.450	0.440
Bulgarian										
1	bigIR	0.737	1.000	0.632	1.000	1.000	1.000	1.000	1.000	0.800
2	UPV [14]	0.673	1.000	0.605	1.000	1.000	1.000	1.000	0.800	0.700
3	ngram-baseline	0.588	1.000	0.474	1.000	1.000	1.000	0.900	0.750	0.640
4	Accenture [100]	0.497	1.000	0.474	1.000	1.000	0.800	0.700	0.600	0.440
5	TOBB ETU [101]	0.149	0.143	0.039	0.000	0.000	0.000	0.200	0.100	0.060
English										
1	NLP& IR@UNED [49]	0.224	1.000	0.211	1.000	0.667	0.400	0.300	0.200	0.160
2	Fight for 4230 [103]	0.195	0.333	0.263	0.000	0.333	0.400	0.400	0.250	0.160
3	UPV [14]	0.149	1.000	0.105	1.000	0.333	0.200	0.200	0.100	0.120
4	bigIR	0.136	0.500	0.105	0.000	0.333	0.200	0.100	0.100	0.120
5	GPLSI [77]	0.132	0.167	0.158	0.000	0.000	0.000	0.200	0.150	0.140
6	csum112	0.126	0.250	0.158	0.000	0.000	0.200	0.200	0.150	0.160
7	abaruah	0.121	0.200	0.158	0.000	0.000	0.200	0.200	0.200	0.140
8	NLytics [75]	0.111	0.071	0.053	0.000	0.000	0.000	0.000	0.050	0.120
9	Accenture [100]	0.101	0.143	0.158	0.000	0.000	0.000	0.200	0.200	0.100
10	TOBB ETU [101]	0.081	0.077	0.053	0.000	0.000	0.000	0.000	0.050	0.080
11	ngram-baseline	0.052	0.020	0.000	0.000	0.000	0.000	0.000	0.000	0.020
Spanish										
1	TOBB ETU [101]	0.537	1.000	0.525	1.000	1.000	0.800	0.900	0.700	0.680
2	GPLSI [77]	0.529	0.500	0.533	0.000	0.667	0.600	0.800	0.750	0.620
3	bigIR	0.496	1.000	0.483	1.000	1.000	0.800	0.800	0.600	0.620
4	NLP& IR@UNED [49]	0.492	1.000	0.475	1.000	1.000	1.000	0.800	0.800	0.620
5	Accenture [100]	0.491	1.000	0.508	1.000	0.667	0.800	0.900	0.700	0.620
6	ngram-baseline	0.450	1.000	0.450	1.000	0.667	0.800	0.700	0.700	0.660
7	UPV	0.446	0.333	0.475	0.000	0.333	0.600	0.800	0.650	0.580
Turkish										
1	TOBB ETU [101]	0.581	1.000	0.585	1.000	1.000	0.800	0.700	0.750	0.660
2	SU-NLP [22]	0.574	1.000	0.585	1.000	1.000	1.000	0.800	0.650	0.680
3	bigIR	0.525	1.000	0.503	1.000	1.000	1.000	0.800	0.700	0.720
4	UPV [14]	0.517	1.000	0.508	1.000	1.000	1.000	1.000	0.850	0.700
5	Accenture [100]	0.402	0.250	0.415	0.000	0.000	0.400	0.400	0.650	0.660
6	ngram-baseline	0.354	1.000	0.311	1.000	0.667	0.600	0.700	0.600	0.460

number of positive examples, while team **bigIR** augmented the training set with the Turkish training set (which they automatically translated to Arabic).

Bulgarian. Four teams took part for Bulgarian, submitting a total of 11 runs. The top-ranked team was **bigIR**. They did not submit a task description paper, and thus we cannot give much detail about their system. Team **UPV** is the second best system, and they used multilingual sentence transformer representation (SBERT) with knowledge distillation. They also introduced an auxiliary language identification task, aside from the downstream check-worthiness task.

English. Ten teams took part in task 1A for English, with a total of 21 runs. The top-ranked team was **NLP&IR@UNED**, and they fine-tuned several pre-trained transformers models. They reported BERTweet was best on the development set. The model was trained using RoBERTa on 850 million English tweets and 23 million COVID-19 related English tweets. The second best system (Team **Fight for 4230**) also used BERTweet with a dropout layer. It also included pre-processing and data augmentation.

Spanish. Six teams took part for Spanish, with a total of 13 runs. The top team **TOBB ETU** explored different data augmentation strategies, including machine translation and weak supervision. However, they submitted a fine-tuned BETO model without any data augmentation. The first runner up **GPLSI** opted for using the BETO Spanish transformer together with a number of hand-crafted features, such as the presence of numbers or words in the LIWC lexicon.

Turkish. Five teams participated for Turkish, submitting a total of 9 runs. All participants used BERT-based models. The top ranked team **TOBB ETU** fine-tuned BERTurk after removing user mentions and URLs. The runner up team **SU-NLP** applied a pre-processing step that includes removing hashtags, emojis, and replacing URLs and mentions with special tokens. Subsequently, they used an ensemble of BERTurk models fine-tuned with different seed values. The third-ranked team **bigIR** machine-translated the Turkish text to Arabic and then fine-tuned AraBERT on the translated text.

All languages. Table 6 summarizes the MAP performance of all the teams that submitted predictions for all languages in Task 1A. We can see that team **BigIR** performed best overall.

Table 6. MAP performance for the official submissions to **Task 1A** in all five languages. μ shows a standard mean of the five MAP scores; μ_w shows a weighed mean, where each MAP is multiplied by the size of the testing set.

	Team	ar	bg	en	es	tr	μ	μ_w
1	bigIR	0.615	**0.737**	0.136	0.496	0.525	**0.502**	**0.513**
2	UPV [14]	0.548	0.673	**0.149**	0.446	0.517	0.467	0.477
3	TOBB ETU [101]	0.575	0.149	0.081	**0.537**	**0.581**	0.385	0.472
4	Accenture [100]	**0.658**	0.497	0.101	0.491	0.402	0.430	0.456
5	ngram-baseline	0.428	0.588	0.052	0.450	0.354	0.374	0.394

Table 7. Task 1B (English): Official evaluation results, in terms of MAP, MRR, R-Precision, and Precision@k. The teams are ranked by the official evaluation measure: MAP.

Rank	Team	MAP	MRR	RP	P@1	P@3	P@5	P@10	P@20	P@30
1	Fight for 4230 [103]	0.402	0.917	0.403	0.875	0.833	0.750	0.600	0.475	0.350
2	ngram-baseline	0.235	0.792	0.263	0.625	0.583	0.500	0.400	0.331	0.217
3	NLytics [75]	0.135	0.345	0.130	0.250	0.125	0.100	0.137	0.156	0.135

6.2 Task 1B. Check-Worthiness of Debates/Speeches

Two teams took part in this subtask, submitting a total of 3 runs. Table 7 shows the performance of the official submissions on the test set, in addition to the ngram baseline. Similarly to Task 1A, the official run was the last valid blind submission by each team. The table shows the runs ranked on the basis of the official MAP measure.

The top-ranked team, **Fight for 4230**, fine-tuned BERTweet after normalizing the claims, augmenting the data using WordNet-based substitutions and removal of punctuation. They were able to beat the ngram baseline by 18 MAP points absolute.

7 Results for Task 2: Verified Claim Retrieval

7.1 Subtask 2A: Detecting Previously Fact-Checked Claims in Tweets

Table 8 shows the official results for Task 2A in both Arabic and English. A total of four teams participated in this task, and they all managed to improve over the Elastic Search (ES) baseline.

Arabic. One team, bigIR, submitted a run for this subtask. They used AraBERT to rerank a list of candidates retrieved by a BM25 model. Their approach consists of three main steps. First, constructing a balanced training dataset, where the positive examples correspond to the query relevances (qrels) provided by the organizers, while the negative examples were selected from the top retrieved candidates by BM25 such that they were not already labeled as positive. Second, they fine-tuned AraBERT to predict the relevance score for a given tweet–VerClaim pair. They added two neural network layers on top of AraBERT to perform the classification task. Finally, at inference time, they first used BM25 to retrieve the top-20 candidate verified claims. Then, they fed each tweet–VerClaim pair to the fine-tuned model to get a relevance score and to rerank the candidate claims accordingly. As Table 8 shows, team **bigIR** outperformed the Elastic Search baseline by a good margin achieving a MAP@5 of 0.908 versus 0.794 for the baseline.

Table 8. Task 2A: Official evaluation results, in terms of MRR, MAP@k, and Precision@k. The teams are ranked by the official evaluation measure: MAP@5. Here, *ES-baseline* refers to the Elastic Search baseline.

	Team	MRR	MAP					Precision				
			@1	@3	@5	@10	@20	@1	@3	@5	@10	@20
Arabic												
1	bigIR	0.924	0.787	0.905	**0.908**	0.910	0.912	0.908	0.391	0.237	0.120	0.061
2	ES-baseline	0.835	0.682	0.782	**0.794**	0.799	0.802	0.793	0.344	0.217	0.113	0.058
English												
1	Aschern [25]	0.884	0.861	0.880	**0.883**	0.884	0.884	0.861	0.300	0.182	0.092	0.046
2	NLytics [75]	0.807	0.738	0.792	**0.799**	0.804	0.806	0.738	0.289	0.179	0.093	0.048
3	DIPS [60]	0.795	0.728	0.778	**0.787**	0.791	0.794	0.728	0.282	0.177	0.092	0.048
4	ES-baseline	0.761	0.703	0.741	**0.749**	0.757	0.759	0.703	0.262	0.164	0.088	0.046

English. Three teams participated for English, submitting a total of ten runs. All of them managed to improve over the Elastic Search (ES) baseline by a large margin. Team **Aschern** had the top-ranked system, which used TF.IDF, fine-tuned pre-trained sentence-BERT, and the reranking LambdaMART model. The system is 13.4 (MAP@5) points absolute above the baseline. The second best system is the **NLytics**, which used RoBERTa to train their model and this system was 5 (MAP@5) point above the baseline.

7.2 Subtask 2B: Detecting Previously Fact-Checked Claims in Political Debates and Speeches

Table 9 shows the official results for Task 2B, which was offered in English only. We can see that only three teams participated in this subtask, submitting a total of five runs, and no team managed to beat the Elastic Search (ES) baseline, which was based on BM25.

Among the three participating teams, Team **DIPS** was the top-ranked one. They used sentence BERT (S-BERT) embeddings for all claims, and computed the cosine similarity for each pair of an input claim and a verified claim from the dataset of previously fact-checked claims. They made a prediction was made by passing a sorted list of cosine similarities to a neural network. Team **BeaSku** was the second-best team, which used a triplet loss training method to perform fine-tuning of the S-BERT model. Then, they used the scores predicted by the fine-tuned model along with BM25 scores as features to train a reranker based on rankSVM. In addition, they discussed the impact of applying online mining of triplets. They also performed some experiments aiming at augmenting the training dataset with additional examples.

Table 9. Task 2B (English): official evaluation results, in terms of MAP, MAP@k, and Precision@k. The teams are ranked by the official evaluation measure: MAP@5.

	Team	MRR	MAP					Precision				
			@1	@3	@5	@10	@20	@1	@3	@5	@10	@20
1	ES-baseline	0.350	0.304	0.339	**0.346**	0.351	0.353	0.304	0.143	0.091	0.052	0.027
2	DIPS [60]	0.336	0.278	0.313	**0.328**	0.338	0.342	0.266	0.143	0.099	0.059	0.032
3	Beasku [91]	0.320	0.266	0.308	**0.327**	0.332	0.332	0.253	0.139	0.101	0.056	0.028
4	NLytics [75]	0.216	0.171	0.210	**0.215**	0.219	0.222	0.165	0.101	0.068	0.038	0.022

8 Overview of Task 3: Fake News Detection

In this section, we present an overview of all task submissions for tasks 3A and 3B. Overall, there were 88 submissions by 27 teams for Task 3A and 49 submissions by 20 teams for task 3B. For task 3, unlike the other tasks, each participant could submit up to 5 runs. After evaluation, we found that two teams from task 3A and seven teams from task 3B submitted the wrong files, and thus we have not considered them for evaluation; we report the ranking for 25 teams for task 3A and 13 teams for task 3B. In Tables 10 and 11, we report the best submission of each team for task 3A and 3B, respectively. In the following sections, we report the results for each of the subtasks.

8.1 Task 3A. Multi-class Fake News Detection of News Articles

Most teams used deep learning models and in particular the transformer architecture for this pilot task. There have been no attempts to model knowledge with semantic technology, e.g., argument processing [30].

The best submission (team **NoFake**) was ahead of the rest by a rather large margin and achieved a macro-F1 score of 0.838. They applied BERT and made extensive use of external resources and in particular downloaded collections of misinformation datasets from fact-checking sites. The second best submission (team **Saud**) achieved a macro-F1 score of 0.503 and used lexical features, traditional weighting methods as features, and standard machine learning algorithms. This shows, that traditional approaches can still outperform deep learning models for this task. Many teams used BERT and its newer variants. Such systems are ranked after the second position. The most popular model was RoBERTa, which was used by seven teams. Team **MUCIC** used a majority voting ensemble with three BERT variants [12]. The participating teams that used BERT had to find solutions for handling the length of the input: BERT and its variants have limitations on the length of their input, but the length of texts in the CT-FAN-21 dataset, which consists of newspaper articles, is much longer. In most cases, heuristics were used for the selection of part of the text. Overall, most submissions achieved a macro-F1 score below 0.5.

Table 10. Task 3A: Performance of the best run per team based on F_1 score for individual classes, and accuracy and macro-F_1 for the overall measure.

Team		True	False	Partially false	Other	Accuracy	Macro-F1
1	NoFake*[56]	0.824	0.862	0.879	0.785	0.853	0.838
2	Saud*	0.321	0.615	0.502	0.618	0.537	0.514
3	DLRG* [50]	0.250	0.588	0.519	0.656	0.528	0.503
4	NLP& IR@UNED [49]	0.247	0.629	0.536	0.459	0.528	0.468
5	NITK_NLP [57]	0.196	0.617	0.523	0.459	0.517	0.449
6	UAICS [26]	0.442	0.470	0.482	0.391	0.458	0.446
7	CIVIC-UPM [48]	0.268	0.577	0.472	0.340	0.463	0.414
8	Uni. Regensburg [41]	0.231	0.489	0.497	0.400	0.438	0.404
9	Pathfinder* [96]	0.277	0.517	0.451	0.360	0.452	0.401
10	CIC* [8]	0.205	0.542	0.490	0.319	0.410	0.389
11	Black Ops [92]	0.231	0.518	0.327	0.453	0.427	0.382
12	NLytics*	0.130	0.575	0.522	0.318	0.475	0.386
13	Nkovachevich [55]	0.237	0.643	0.552	0.000	0.489	0.358
14	talhaanwar*	0.283	0.407	0.435	0.301	0.367	0.357
15	abaruah	0.165	0.531	0.552	0.125	0.455	0.343
16	Team GPLSI[77]	0.293	0.602	0.226	0.092	0.356	0.303
17	Sigmoid [76]	0.222	0.345	0.323	0.154	0.291	0.261
18	architap	0.154	0.291	0.394	0.187	0.294	0.257
19	MUCIC [12]	0.143	0.446	0.275	0.070	0.331	0.233
20	Probity	0.163	0.401	0.335	0.033	0.302	0.233
21	M82B [7]	0.130	0.425	0.241	0.094	0.305	0.223
22	Spider	0.046	0.482	0.145	0.069	0.316	0.186
23	Qword [97]	0.108	0.458	0.000	0.033	0.277	0.150
24	ep*	0.060	0.479	0.000	0.000	0.319	0.135
25	azaharudue*	0.060	0.479	0.000	0.000	0.319	0.135
Majority class baseline		0.000	0.477	0.000	0.000	0.314	0.119

* Runs submitted after the deadline, but before the release of the results.

The second most popular neural network model was the recurrent neural network, which was used by six teams. Many participants experimented also with traditional text processing methods as they were commonly used for knowledge representation in information retrieval. For example, team **Kovachevich** used a Naïve Bayes classifier with TF.IDF features for the 500 most frequent stems in the dataset [55]. Some lower-ranked teams used additional techniques and resources. These include LIWC [49], data augmentation by inserting artificially created similar documents [8], semantic analysis with the Stanford Empath Tool [26], and the reputation of the sites of a search engine result after searching with the title of the article [49].

Table 11. Task 3B: Performance of the best run per team based on F1-measure for individual classes, and accuracy and macro-F_1 for overall measure.

Team		Climate	Crime	Economy	Education	Elections	Health	Acc	Macro F1
1	NITK_NLP [57]	0.950	0.872	0.824	0.800	0.897	0.946	0.905	0.881
2	NoFake* [56]	0.800	0.875	0.900	0.957	0.692	0.907	0.869	0.855
3	Nkovachevich [55]	0.927	0.872	0.743	0.737	0.857	0.911	0.869	0.841
4	DLRG	0.952	0.743	0.688	0.800	0.828	0.897	0.847	0.818
5	CIC* [8]	0.952	0.750	0.688	0.588	0.889	0.871	0.832	0.790
6	architap	0.900	0.711	0.774	0.609	0.815	0.907	0.825	0.786
7	NLytics	0.826	0.714	0.710	0.500	0.769	0.867	0.788	0.731
8	CIVIC-UPM* [48]	0.864	0.700	0.645	0.421	0.609	0.821	0.745	0.677
9	ep*	0.727	0.476	0.222	0.343	0.545	0.561	0.511	0.479
10	Pathfinder* [96]	0.900	0.348	0.250	0.000	0.526	0.667	0.599	0.448
11	M82B [7]	0.294	0.000	0.000	0.000	0.000	0.576	0.409	0.145
12	MUCIC [12]	0.294	0.000	0.000	0.000	0.000	0.576	0.409	0.145
13	azaharudue*	0.129	0.000	0.000	0.125	0.000	0.516	0.321	0.128
Majority class baseline		0.000	0.000	0.000	0.000	0.000	0.565	0.394	0.094

* Runs submitted after the deadline, but before the release of the results.

8.2 Task 3B. Topical Domain Identification of News Articles

The performance of the systems for task 3B was overall higher than for task 3A. The first three submissions were close together and all used transformer-based architectures. The best submissionm, by team **NITK_NLP**, used an ensemble of three transformers [57]. The second best submission (by team **NoFake**) and the third best submission (by team **Nkovachevich**) used BERT.

9 Related Work

There has been work on checking the factuality/credibility of a claim, of a news article, or of an information source [11,13,51,58,64,69,73,104]. Claims can come from different sources, but special attention has been paid to those from social media [37,62,66,78,79,90,102]. Check-worthiness estimation is still a fairly-new problem especially in the context of social media [34,45–47]. A lot of research was performed on fake news detection for news articles, which is mostly approached as a binary classification problem [71].

`CheckThat!` is related to several other initiatives at SemEval on determining rumour veracity and support for rumours [28,36], on stance detection [63], on fact-checking in community question answering forums [61], on propaganda detection [27,29], and on semantic textual similarity [2,67]. It is also related to the FEVER task [94] on fact extraction and verification, as well as to the Fake News Challenge [38], and the FakeNews task at MediaEval [72].

10 Conclusion and Future Work

We have presented the 2021 edition of the `CheckThat!` Lab, which was the most popular CLEF-2021 lab in terms of team registrations (132 teams registered), and about one-third of them actually participated: 15, 5, and 25 teams submitted official runs for tasks 1, 2, and 3, respectively. The lab featured tasks that span important steps of the verification pipeline: from spotting check-worthy claims to checking whether they have been fact-checked elsewhere before. We further featured a fake news detection task, and we also checked the class and the topical domain of news articles. Together, these tasks support the technology pipeline to assist human fact-checkers. Moreover, in-line with the general mission of CLEF, we promoted multi-linguality by offering our tasks in five different languages.

In future work, we plan to extend the datasets with more examples, more information sources, and also to cover more languages.

Acknowledgments. The work of Tamer Elsayed and Maram Hasanain is made possible by NPRP grant #NPRP-11S-1204-170060 from the Qatar National Research Fund (a member of Qatar Foundation). The work of Fatima Haouari is supported by GSRA grant #GSRA6-1-0611-19074 from the Qatar National Research Fund. The statements made herein are solely the responsibility of the authors.

This research is also part of the Tanbih mega-project, developed at the Qatar Computing Research Institute, HBKU, which aims to limit the impact of "fake news", propaganda, and media bias, thus promoting digital literacy and critical thinking.

Appendix

A Systems for Task 1

The positions in the task ranking appear after each team name. See Tables 5, 6 and 7 for further details.

Team Accenture [100] (1A:ar:1 1A:bg:4 1A:en:9 1A:es:5 1A:tr:5) used BERT and RoBERTa with data augmentation. They further generated additional synthetic training data using lexical substitution. To find the most probable substitutions, they used BERT-based contextual embedding to create synthetic examples for the positive class. They further added a mean-pooling layer and a dropout layer on top of the model before the final classification layer.

Team Fight for 4230 [103] (1A:en:2 1B:en:1) focused its efforts mostly on two fronts: the creation of a pre-processing module able to properly normalize the tweets and the augmentation of the data by means of machine translation and WordNet-based substitutions. The pre-processing included link removal and punctuation cleaning, as well as quantities and contractions expansion. All hashtags related to COVID-19 were normalized into one and the hashtags were expanded. Their best approach was based on BERTweet with a dropout layer and the above-mentioned pre-processing.

Team GPLSI [77] (1A:en:5 1A:es:2) applied the RoBERTa and the BETO transformers together with different manually engineered features, such as the occurrence of dates and numbers or words from LIWC. A thorough exploration of parameters was made using weighting and bias techniques. They also tried to split the four-way classification into two binary classifications and one three-way classification. They further tried oversampling and undersampling.

Team iCompass (`ar:4`) used several prepossessing steps, including (*i*) English word removal, (*ii*) removing URLs and mentions, and (*iii*) data normalization, removing tashkeel and the letter madda from texts, as well as duplicates, and replacing some characters to prevent mixing. They proposed a simple ensemble of two BERT-based models, which include AraBERT and Arabic-ALBERT.

Team NLP&IR@UNED [49] (`1A:en:1 1A:es:4`) used several transformer models, such as BERT, ALBERT, RoBERTa, DistilBERT, and Funnel-Transformer, for the experiments to compare the performance. For English, they obtained better results using BERT trained with tweets. For Spanish, they used Electra.

Team NLytics [74] (`1A:en:8 1B:en:3`) used RoBERTa with a regression function in the final layer, approaching the problem as a ranking task.

Team QMUL-SDS [1] (`1A:ar:4`) used the AraBERT preprocessing function to (*i*) replace URLs, email addressees, and user mentions with standard words, (*ii*) removed line breaks, HTML markup, repeated characters, and unwanted characters, such as emotion icons, and (*iii*) handled white spaces between words and digits (non-Arabic, or English), and/or a combination of both, and before and after two brackets, and also (*iv*) removed unnecessary punctuation. They addressed the task as a ranking problem, and fine-tuned an Arabic transformer (AraBERTv0.2-base) on a combination of the data from this year and the data from the CheckThat! lab 2020 (the CT20-AR dataset).

Team SCUoL [6] (`1A:ar:3`) used typical pre-processing steps, including cleaning the text, segmentation, and tokenization. Their experiments consists of fine-tuning different AraBERT models, and their final results were obtained using AraBERTv2-base.

Team SU-NLP [22] (`1A:tr:2`) also used several pre-possessing steps, including (*i*) removing emojis, hashtags, and (*ii*) replacing all mentions with a special token (@USER), and all URLs with the respective website's domain. If the URL is for a tweet, they replaced the URL with TWITTER and the respective user account name. They reported that this URL expansion method improved the performance. Subsequently, they used an ensemble of BERTurk models fine-tuned using different seed values.

Team TOBB ETU [101] (`1A:ar:6 1A:bg:5 1A:en:10 1A:es:1 1A:tr:1`) investigated different approaches to fine-tune transformer models including data augmentation using machine translation, weak supervision, and cross-lingual training. For their submission, they removed URLs and user mentions from the tweets, and fine-tuned a separate BERT-based models for each language. In particular, they fine-tuned BERTurk[1], AraBERT, BETO[2], and the BERT-base model for Turk-

[1] http://huggingface.co/dbmdz/bert-base-turkish-cased.
[2] http://huggingface.co/dccuchile/bert-base-spanish-wwm-cased.

ish, Arabic, Spanish, and English, respectively. For Bulgarian, they fine-tune a RoBERTa model pre-trained with Bulgarian documents.[3]

Team UPV [14] (1A:ar:8 1A:bg:2 1A:en:3 1A:es:6 1A:tr:4) used a multilingual sentence transformer representation (S-BERT) with knowledge distillation, originally intended for question answering. They further introduced an auxiliary language identification task, aside the downstream check-worthiness task.

B Systems for Task 2

Team Aschern [25] (2A:en:1) used TF.IDF, fine-tuned pre-trained S-BERT, and the reranking LambdaMART model.

Team BeaSku [91] (2B:en:3) used triplet loss training to fine-tune S-BERT. Then, they used the scores predicted by the fine-tuned model along with BM25 scores as features to train a rankSVM re-ranker. They further discussed the impact of applying online mining of triplets. They also experimented with data augmentation.

Team DIPS [60] (2A:en:3 2B:en:2) calculated S-BERT embeddings for all claims, then computed a cosine similarity for each pair of an input claim and a verified claim. The prediction is made by passing a sorted list of cosine similarities to a neural network.

Team NLytics (2A:en:2 2B:en:4) approached the problem as a regression task, and used RoBERTa with a regression function in the final layer.

C Systems for Task 3

Team Black Ops [92] (3A:11) performed data pre-processing by removing stopwords and punctuation marks. Then, they experimented with decision trees, random forest, and gradient boosting classifiers for Task 3A, and found the latter to perform best.

Team CIC [8] (3A:10 3B:5) experimented with logistic regression, multi-layer perceptron, support vector machines, and random forest. Their experiments consisted of using stratified 5-fold cross-validation on the training data. Their best results were obtained using logistic regression for task 3A, and a multi-layer perceptron for task 3B.

Team CIC 3A:11 experimented with a decision tree, a random forest, and a gradient boosting algorithms. They found the latter to perform best.

Team CIVIC-UPM [48] (3A:7 3B:8) participated in the two subtasks of task 3. They performed pre-processing, using a number of tools: (*i*) `ftfy` to repair

[3] http://huggingface.co/iarfmoose/roberta-base-bulgarian.

Unicode and emoji errors, *(ii)* `ekphrasis` to perform lower-casing, normalizing percentages, time, dates, emails, phones, and numbers, *(iii)* `contractions` for abbreviation expansion, and *(iv)* `NLTK` for word tokenization, stop-words removal, punctuation removal and word lemmatization. Then, they combined `doc2vec` with transformer representations (Electra base, T5 small and T5 base, Longformer base, RoBERTa base and DistilRoBERTa base). They further used additional data from Kaggle's Ag News task, Kaggle's KDD2020, and Clickbait news detection competitions. Finally, they experimented with a number of classifiers such as Naïve Bayes, Random Forest, Logistic Regression with L1 and L2 regularization, Elastic Net, and SVMs. The best system for subtask 3A used DistilRoBERTa-base on the text body with oversampling and a sliding window for dealing with long texts. Their best system for task 3B used RoBERTa-base on the title+body text with oversampling but no sliding window.

Team DLRG (3A:3 3B:4) experimented with a number of traditional approaches like Random Forest, Naïve Bayes and Logistic Regression as well as an online passive-aggressive classifier and different ensembles thereof. The best result was achieved by an ensemble of Naïve Bayes, Logistic Regression, and the Passive Aggressive classifier for task 3A. For task 3B, the Online Passive-Aggressive classifier outperformed all other approaches, including the considered ensembles.

Team GPLSI [77] (3A:16) applied the RoBERTa transformer together with different manually-engineered features, such as the occurrence of dates and numbers or words from LIWC. Both the title and the body were concatenated as a single sequence of words. Rather than going for a single multi-class setting, they used two binary models considering the most frequent classes: false vs. other, and true vs. other, followed by one three-class model.

Team MUCIC [12] (3A:19 3B:12) used a majority voting ensemble with three BERT variants. They applied BERT, Distilbert, and RoBERTa, and fine-tuned the pre-trained models.

Team NITK_NLP [57] (3A:5 3B:1) proposed an approach, that included pre-processing and tokenization of the news article, and then experimented with multiple transformer models. The final prediction was made by an ensemble.

Team NKovachevich [55] (3A:13 3B:3) created lexical features. They extracted the 500 most frequent word stems in the dataset, and calculated the TF.IDF values, which they used in a multinomial Naïve Bayes classifier. A much better performance was achieved with an LSTM model that used GloVe embeddings. A little lower F1 value was achieved using BERT. They further found RoBERTa to perform worse than BERT.

Team NLP&IR@UNED [49] (3A:4) experimented with four transformer architectures and input sizes of 150 and 200 words. In the preliminary tests, the best performance was achieved by ALBERT with 200 words. They also experimented with combining TF.IDF values from the text, all the features provided by the

LIWC tool, and the TF.IDF values from the first 20 domain names returned by a query to a search engine. Unlike what was obtained in the dev dataset, in the official competition, the best results were obtained with the approach based on TF.IDF, LIWC, and domain names.

Team NLytics (3A:12 3B:7) fined-tuned RoBERTa on the dataset for each of the sub-tasks. Since the data is unbalanced, they used under-sampling. They also truncated the documents to 512 words to fit into the RoBERTa input size.

Team NoFake [56] (3A:1 3B:2) applied BERT without fine-tuning, but used an extensive amount of additional data for training, downloaded from various fact-checking websites.

Team Pathfinder [96] (3A:9 3A:10) participated in both tasks and used multinomial Naïve Bayes and random forest. The former performed better for both tasks. For task 3A, the they merged the classed *false* and *partially false* into one class, which boosted the model performance by 41% (a non-official score mentioned in the paper).

Team Probity (3A:20) addressed the multiclass fake news detection subtask, they used a simple LSTM architecture where they adopted word2vec embeddings to represent the news articles.

Team Qword [97] (3A:23) applied pre-processing techniques, which included stop-word removal, punctuation removal and lemmatization using a Porter stemmer. The TF.IDF values were calculated for the words. For these features, four classification algorithms were applied. The best result was given by Extreme Gradient Boosting.

Team SAUD (3A:2) used an SVM with TF.IDF. They tried Logistic Regression, Multinomial Naïve Bayes, and Random Forest, and found SVM to work best.

Team Sigmoid [76] (3A:17) experimented with different traditional machine learning approaches, with multinomial Naïve Bayes performing best, and one deep learning approach, namely an LSTM with the Adam optimizer. The latter outperformed the more traditional approaches.

Team Spider (3A:22) applies an LSTM, after a pre-processing consisting of stop-word removal and stemming.

Team UAICS [26] (3A:6) experimented with various models including BERT, LSTM, Bi-LSTM, and feature-based models. Their submitted model is a Gradient Boosting with a weighted combination of three feature groups: bi-grams, POS tags, and lexical categories of words.

Team University of Regensburg [41] (3A:8) used different fine-tuned variants of BERT with a linear layer on top and applied different approaches to address the maximum sequence length of BERT. Besides hierarchical transformer representations, they also experimented with different summarization techniques like extractive and abstractive summarization. They performed oversampling to address the class imbalance, as well as extractive (using DistilBERT) and abstractive summarization (using distil-BART-CNN-12-6), before performing classification using fine-tuned BERT with a hierarchical transformer representation.

References

1. Abumansour, A., Zubiaga, A.: QMUL-SDS at CheckThat! 2021: enriching pre-trained language models for the estimation of check-worthiness of Arabic tweets. In: Faggioli et al. [33]
2. Agirre, E., et al.: SemEval-2016 task 1: semantic textual similarity, monolingual and cross-lingual evaluation. In: Proceedings of the 10th International Workshop on Semantic Evaluation, SemEval 2016, pp. 497–511 (2016)
3. Alam, F., et al.: Fighting the COVID-19 infodemic in social media: a holistic perspective and a call to arms. In: Proceedings of the International AAAI Conference on Web and Social Media. ICWSM 2021, vol. 15, pp. 913–922 (2021)
4. Alam, F., et al.: Fighting the COVID-19 infodemic: modeling the perspective of journalists, fact-checkers, social media platforms, policy makers, and the society. ArXiv preprint 2005.00033 (2020)
5. Ali, Z.S., Mansour, W., Elsayed, T., Al-Ali, A.: AraFacts: the first large Arabic dataset of naturally occurring claims. In: Proceedings of the Sixth Arabic Natural Language Processing Workshop, ANLP 2021, pp. 231–236 (2021)
6. Althabiti, S., Alsalka, M., Atwell, E.: An AraBERT model for check-worthiness of Arabic tweets. In: Faggioli et al. [33]
7. Ashik, S.S., Apu, A.R., Marjana, N.J., Hasan, M.A., Islam, M.S.: M82B at CheckThat! 2021: multiclass fake news detection using BiLSTM based RNN model. In: Faggioli et al. [33]
8. Ashraf, N., Butt, S., Sidorov, G., Gelbukh, A.: Fake news detection using machine learning and data augmentation - CLEF2021. In: Faggioli et al. [33]
9. Atanasova, P., et al.: Overview of the CLEF-2018 CheckThat! Lab on automatic identification and verification of political claims. Task 1: check-worthiness. In: Cappellato et al. [21]
10. Atanasova, P., Nakov, P., Karadzhov, G., Mohtarami, M., Da San Martino, G.: Overview of the CLEF-2019 CheckThat! Lab on automatic identification and verification of claims. Task 1: check-worthiness. In: Cappellato et al. [20]
11. Ba, M.L., Berti-Equille, L., Shah, K., Hammady, H.M.: VERA: a platform for veracity estimation over web data. In: Proceedings of the 25th International Conference on World Wide Web, WWW 2016, pp. 159–162 (2016)
12. Balouchzahi, F., Shashirekha, H., Sidorov, G.: MUCIC at CheckThat! 2021: FaDo-fake news detection and domain identification using transformers ensembling. In: Faggioli et al. [33]
13. Baly, R., et al.: What was written vs. who read it: news media profiling using text analysis and social media context. In: Proceedings of the 58th Annual Meeting of the Association for Computational Linguistics, ACL 2020, pp. 3364–3374 (2020)
14. Baris Schlicht, I., Magnossão de Paula, A., Rosso, P.: UPV at CheckThat! 2021: mitigating cultural differences for identifying multilingual check-worthy claims. In: Faggioli et al. [33]
15. Barrón-Cedeño, A., et al.: Overview of CheckThat! 2020: automatic identification and verification of claims in social media. In: Arampatzis, A., et al. (eds.) CLEF 2020. LNCS, vol. 12260, pp. 215–236. Springer, Cham (2020). https://doi.org/10.1007/978-3-030-58219-7_17

16. Barrón-Cedeño, A., et al.: Overview of CheckThat! 2020: Automatic Identification and Verification of Claims in Social Media. In: Arampatzis, A., et al. (eds.) Experimental IR Meets Multilinguality, Multimodality, and Interaction – 11th International Conference of the CLEF Association, CLEF 2020, Thessaloniki, Greece, 22–25 September 2020, Proceedings. LNCS, vol. 12260, pp. 215–236. Springer, Cham (2020). https://doi.org/10.1007/978-3-030-58219-7_17
17. Barrón-Cedeño, A., et al.: Overview of the CLEF-2018 CheckThat! Lab on automatic identification and verification of political claims. Task 2: factuality. In: Cappellato et al. [21]
18. Bouziane, M., Perrin, H., Cluzeau, A., Mardas, J., Sadeq, A.: Buster.AI at CheckThat! 2020: insights and recommendations to improve fact-checking. In: Cappellato et al. [19]
19. Cappellato, L., Eickhoff, C., Ferro, N., Névéol, A. (eds.): CLEF 2020 Working Notes. CEUR Workshop Proceedings. CEUR-WS.org (2020)
20. Cappellato, L., Ferro, N., Losada, D., Müller, H. (eds.): Working Notes of CLEF 2019 Conference and Labs of the Evaluation Forum. CEUR Workshop Proceedings. CEUR-WS.org (2019)
21. Cappellato, L., Ferro, N., Nie, J.Y., Soulier, L. (eds.): Working Notes of CLEF 2018-Conference and Labs of the Evaluation Forum. CEUR Workshop Proceedings. CEUR-WS.org (2018)
22. Carik, B., Yeniterzi, R.: SU-NLP at CheckThat! 2021: check-worthiness of Turkish tweets. In: Faggioli et al. [33]
23. Cazalens, S., Lamarre, P., Leblay, J., Manolescu, I., Tannier, X.: A content management perspective on fact-checking. In: Proceedings of the International Conference on World Wide Web, WWW 2018, pp. 565–574 (2018)
24. Cheema, G.S., Hakimov, S., Ewerth, R.: Check_square at CheckThat! 2020: claim detection in social media via fusion of transformer and syntactic features. In: Cappellato et al. [19]
25. Chernyavskiy, A., Ilvovsky, D., Nakov, P.: Aschern at CLEF CheckThat! 2021: lambda-calculus of fact-checked claims. In: Faggioli et al. [33]
26. Cusmuliuc, C.G., Amarandei, M.A., Pelin, I., Cociorva, V.I., Iftene, A.: UAICS at CheckThat! 2021: fake news detection. In: Faggioli et al. [33]
27. Da San Martino, G., Barrón-Cedeno, A., Wachsmuth, H., Petrov, R., Nakov, P.: SemEval-2020 task 11: detection of propaganda techniques in news articles. In: Proceedings of the 14th Workshop on Semantic Evaluation, SemEval 2020, pp. 1377–1414 (2020)
28. Derczynski, L., Bontcheva, K., Liakata, M., Procter, R., Wong Sak Hoi, G., Zubiaga, A.: SemEval-2017 task 8: RumourEval: determining rumour veracity and support for rumours. In: Proceedings of the 11th International Workshop on Semantic Evaluation, SemEval 2017, pp. 69–76 (2017)
29. Dimitrov, D., et al.: SemEval-2021 task 6: detection of persuasion techniques in texts and images. In: Proceedings of the International Workshop on Semantic Evaluation, SemEval 2021 (2021)
30. Dumani, L., Neumann, P.J., Schenkel, R.: A framework for argument retrieval - ranking argument clusters by frequency and specificity. In: Jose, J.M., et al. (eds.) ECIR 2020. LNCS, vol. 12035, pp. 431–445. Springer, Cham (2020). https://doi.org/10.1007/978-3-030-45439-5_29
31. Elsayed, T., et al.: CheckThat! at CLEF 2019: automatic identification and verification of claims. In: Advances in Information Retrieval, pp. 309–315 (2019)

32. Elsayed, T., et al.: Overview of the CLEF-2019 CheckThat! lab: automatic identification and verification of claims. In: Crestani, F., et al. (eds.) CLEF 2019. LNCS, vol. 11696, pp. 301–321. Springer, Cham (2019). https://doi.org/10.1007/978-3-030-28577-7_25
33. Faggioli, G., Ferro, N., Joly, A., Maistro, M., Piroi, F. (eds.): CLEF 2021 Working Notes. Working Notes of CLEF 2021-Conference and Labs of the Evaluation Forum. CEUR-WS.org (2021)
34. Gencheva, P., Nakov, P., Màrquez, L., Barrón-Cedeño, A., Koychev, I.: A context-aware approach for detecting worth-checking claims in political debates. In: Proceedings of the International Conference Recent Advances in Natural Language Processing, RANLP 2017, pp. 267–276 (2017)
35. Ghanem, B., Glavaš, G., Giachanou, A., Ponzetto, S., Rosso, P., Rangel, F.: UPV-UMA at CheckThat! lab: verifying Arabic claims using cross lingual approach. In: Cappellato et al. [20]
36. Gorrell, G., et al: SemEval-2019 task 7: RumourEval, determining rumour veracity and support for rumours. In: Proceedings of the 13th International Workshop on Semantic Evaluation, SemEval 2019, pp. 845–854 (2019)
37. Gupta, A., Kumaraguru, P., Castillo, C., Meier, P.: TweetCred: real-time credibility assessment of content on Twitter. In: Aiello, L.M., McFarland, D. (eds.) SocInfo 2014. LNCS, vol. 8851, pp. 228–243. Springer, Cham (2014). https://doi.org/10.1007/978-3-319-13734-6_16
38. Hanselowski, A., et al.: A retrospective analysis of the fake news challenge stance-detection task. In: Proceedings of the 27th International Conference on Computational Linguistics, COLING 2018, pp. 1859–1874 (2018)
39. Hansen, C., Hansen, C., Simonsen, J., Lioma, C.: The Copenhagen team participation in the check-worthiness task of the competition of automatic identification and verification of claims in political debates of the CLEF-2018 fact checking lab. In: Cappellato et al. [21]
40. Hansen, C., Hansen, C., Simonsen, J., Lioma, C.: Neural weakly supervised fact check-worthiness detection with contrastive sampling-based ranking loss. In: Cappellato et al. [20]
41. Hartl, P., Kruschwitz, U.: University of Regensburg at CheckThat! 2021: exploring text summarization for fake newsdetection. In: Faggioli et al. [33]
42. Hasanain, M., Elsayed, T.: bigIR at CheckThat! 2020: multilingual BERT for ranking Arabic tweets by check-worthiness. In: Cappellato et al. [19]
43. Hasanain, M., et al.: Overview of CheckThat! 2020 Arabic: automatic identification and verification of claims in social media. In: Cappellato et al. [19]
44. Hasanain, M., Suwaileh, R., Elsayed, T., Barrón-Cedeño, A., Nakov, P.: Overview of the CLEF-2019 CheckThat! Lab on automatic identification and verification of claims. Task 2: evidence and factuality. In: Cappellato et al. [20]
45. Hassan, N., Li, C., Tremayne, M.: Detecting check-worthy factual claims in presidential debates. In: Proceedings of the 24th ACM International on Conference on Information and Knowledge Management, CIKM 2015, pp. 1835–1838 (2015)
46. Hassan, N., Tremayne, M., Arslan, F., Li, C.: Comparing automated factual claim detection against judgments of journalism organizations. In: Computation Journalism Symposium, pp. 1–5 (2016)
47. Hassan, N., et al.: ClaimBuster: the first-ever end-to-end fact-checking system. Proc. VLDB Endow. **10**(12), 1945–1948 (2017)
48. Álvaro Huertas-Garcıia, Huertas-Tato, J., Martín, A., Camacho, D.: CIVIC-UPM at CheckThat! 2021: integration of transformers in misinformation detection and topic classification. In: Faggioli et al. [33]

49. Juan R. Martinez-Rico, J.M.R., Araujo, L.: NLP&IR@UNED at CheckThat! 2021: check-worthiness estimation and fake news detection using transformer models. In: Faggioli et al. [33]
50. Kannan, R., R, R.: DLRG@CLEF2021: an ensemble approach for fake detection on news articles. In: Faggioli et al. [33]
51. Karadzhov, G., Nakov, P., Màrquez, L., Barrón-Cedeño, A., Koychev, I.: Fully automated fact checking using external sources. In: Proceedings of the International Conference Recent Advances in Natural Language Processing, RANLP 2017, pp. 344–353 (2017)
52. Kartal, Y.S., Kutlu, M.: TOBB ETU at CheckThat! 2020: prioritizing English and Arabic claims based on check-worthiness. In: Cappellato et al. [19]
53. Kartal, Y.S., Kutlu, M.: TrClaim-19: the first collection for Turkish check-worthy claim detection with annotator rationales. In: Proceedings of the 24th Conference on Computational Natural Language Learning, pp. 386–395 (2020)
54. Kazemi, A., Garimella, K., Shahi, G.K., Gaffney, D., Hale, S.A.: Tiplines to combat misinformation on encrypted platforms: a case study of the 2019 Indian election on WhatsApp. arXiv:2106.04726 (2021)
55. Kovachevich, N.: BERT fine-tuning approach to CLEF CheckThat! Fake news detection. In: Faggioli et al. [33]
56. Kumari, S.: NoFake at CheckThat! 2021: fake news detection using BERT. arXiv:2108.05419 (2021)
57. 3 L, H.R., M, A.: NITK_NLP at CLEF CheckThat! 2021: ensemble transformer model for fake news classification. In: Faggioli et al. [33]
58. Ma, J., Gao, W., Mitra, P., Kwon, S., Jansen, B.J., Wong, K.F., Cha, M.: Detecting rumors from microblogs with recurrent neural networks. In: Proceedings of the International Joint Conference on Artificial Intelligence, IJCAI 2016, pp. 3818–3824 (2016)
59. Martinez-Rico, J., Araujo, L., Martinez-Romo, J.: NLP&IR@UNED at CheckThat! 2020: a preliminary approach for check-worthiness and claim retrieval tasks using neural networks and graphs. In: Cappellato et al. [19]
60. Mihaylova, S., Borisova, I., Chemishanov, D., Hadzhitsanev, P., Hardalov, M., Nakov, P.: DIPS at CheckThat! 2021: verified claim retrieval. In: Faggioli et al. [33]
61. Mihaylova, T., Karadzhov, G., Atanasova, P., Baly, R., Mohtarami, M., Nakov, P.: SemEval-2019 task 8: fact checking in community question answering forums. In: Proceedings of the 13th International Workshop on Semantic Evaluation, SemEval 2019, pp. 860–869 (2019)
62. Mitra, T., Gilbert, E.: CREDBANK: a large-scale social media corpus with associated credibility annotations. In: Proceedings of the Ninth International AAAI Conference on Web and Social Media, ICWSM 2015, pp. 258–267 (2015)
63. Mohammad, S., Kiritchenko, S., Sobhani, P., Zhu, X., Cherry, C.: SemEval-2016 task 6: detecting stance in tweets. In: Proceedings of the 10th International Workshop on Semantic Evaluation, SemEval 2016, pp. 31–41 (2016)
64. Mukherjee, S., Weikum, G.: Leveraging joint interactions for credibility analysis in news communities. In: Proceedings of the 24th ACM International Conference on Information and Knowledge Management, CIKM 2015, pp. 353–362 (2015)
65. Nakov, P., et al.: Overview of the CLEF-2018 lab on automatic identification and verification of claims in political debates. In: Working Notes of CLEF 2018 – Conference and Labs of the Evaluation Forum. CLEF 2018 (2018)

66. Nakov, P., et al.: Automated fact-checking for assisting human fact-checkers. In: Proceedings of the 30th International Joint Conference on Artificial Intelligence, IJCAI 2021 (2021)
67. Nakov, P., et al.: SemEval-2016 Task 3: community question answering. In: Proceedings of the 10th International Workshop on Semantic Evaluation, SemEval 2015, pp. 525–545 (2016)
68. Nakov, P., et al.: The CLEF-2021 CheckThat! Lab on detecting check-worthy claims, previously fact-checked claims, and fake news. In: Hiemstra, D., Moens, M.-F., Mothe, J., Perego, R., Potthast, M., Sebastiani, F. (eds.) ECIR 2021, Part II. LNCS, vol. 12657, pp. 639–649. Springer, Cham (2021). https://doi.org/10.1007/978-3-030-72240-1_75
69. Nguyen, V.H., Sugiyama, K., Nakov, P., Kan, M.Y.: FANG: Leveraging social context for fake news detection using graph representation. In: Proceedings of the 29th ACM International Conference on Information & Knowledge Management, CIKM 2020, pp. 1165–1174 (2020)
70. Nikolov, A., Da San Martino, G., Koychev, I., Nakov, P.: Team_Alex at CheckThat! 2020: identifying check-worthy tweets with transformer models. In: Cappellato et al. [19]
71. Oshikawa, R., Qian, J., Wang, W.Y.: A survey on natural language processing for fake news detection. In: Proceedings of the 12th Language Resources and Evaluation Conference, LREC 2020, pp. 6086–6093 (2020)
72. Pogorelov, K., et al.: FakeNews: Corona virus and 5G conspiracy task at MediaEval 2020. In: Proceedings of the MediaEval workshop, MediaEval 2020 (2020)
73. Popat, K., Mukherjee, S., Strötgen, J., Weikum, G.: Credibility assessment of textual claims on the web. In: Proceedings of the 25th ACM International Conference on Information and Knowledge Management, CIKM 2016, pp. 2173–2178 (2016)
74. Pritzkau, A.: NLytics at CheckThat! 2021: check-worthiness estimation as a regression problem on transformers. In: Faggioli et al. [33]
75. Pritzkau, A.: NLytics at CheckThat! 2021: multi-class fake news detection of news articles and domain identification with RoBERTa - a baseline model. In: Faggioli et al. [33]
76. Sardar, A.A.M., Salma, S.A., Islam, M.S., Hasan, M.A., Bhuiyan, T.: Team Sigmoid at CheckThat! 2021: multiclass fake news detection with machine learning. In: Faggioli et al. [33]
77. Sepúlveda-Torres, R., Saquete, E.: GPLSI team at CLEF CheckThat! 2021: fine-tuning BETO and RoBERTa. In: Faggioli et al. [33]
78. Shaar, S., Alam, F., Martino, G.D.S., Nakov, P.: The role of context in detecting previously fact-checked claims. arXiv preprint arXiv:2104.07423 (2021)
79. Shaar, S., Babulkov, N., Da San Martino, G., Nakov, P.: That is a known lie: detecting previously fact-checked claims. In: Proceedings of the 58th Annual Meeting of the Association for Computational Linguistics, ACL 2020, pp. 3607–361 (2020)
80. Shaar, S., et al.: Overview of the CLEF-2021 CheckThat! Lab task 2 on detect previously fact-checked claims in tweets and political debates. In: Faggioli et al. [33]
81. Shaar, S., et al.: Overview of the CLEF-2021 CheckThat! Lab task 1 on check-worthiness estimation in tweets and political debates. In: Faggioli et al. [33]
82. Shaar, S., et al.: Overview of CheckThat! 2020 English: automatic identification and verification of claims in social media. In: Cappellato et al. [19]

83. Shahi, G.K.: AMUSED: an annotation framework of multi-modal social media data. arXiv:2010.00502 (2020)
84. Shahi, G.K., Dirkson, A., Majchrzak, T.A.: An exploratory study of COVID-19 misinformation on Twitter. Online Soc. Netw. Media **22**, 100104 (2021). https://doi.org/10.1016/j.osnem.2020.100104. https://www.sciencedirect.com/science/article/pii/S2468696420300458
85. Shahi, G.K., Majchrzak, T.A.: Exploring the spread of COVID-19 misinformation on Twitter (2021)
86. Shahi, G.K.: A multilingual domain identification using fact-checked articles: a case study on COVID-19 misinformation. arXiv preprint (2021)
87. Shahi, G.K., Nandini, D.: FakeCovid – a multilingual cross-domain fact check news dataset for COVID-19. In: Workshop Proceedings of the 14th International AAAI Conference on Web and Social Media (2020)
88. Shahi, G.K., Struß, J.M., Mandl, T.: CT-FAN-21 corpus: a dataset for fake news detection, April 2021. https://doi.org/10.5281/zenodo.4714517
89. Shahi, G.K., Struß, J.M., Mandl, T.: Overview of the CLEF-2021 CheckThat! Lab: task 3 on fake news detection. In: Faggioli et al. [33]
90. Shu, K., Sliva, A., Wang, S., Tang, J., Liu, H.: Fake news detection on social media: a data mining perspective. SIGKDD Explor. Newsl. **19**(1), 22–36 (2017)
91. Skuczyńska, B., Shaar, S., Spenader, J., Nakov, P.: BeaSku at CheckThat! 2021: fine-tuning sentence BERT with triplet loss and limited data. In: Faggioli et al. [33]
92. Sohan, S., Rajon, H.S., Khusbu, A., Islam, M.S., Hasan, M.A.: Black Ops at CheckThat! 2021: user profiles analyze of intelligent detection on fake tweets notebook in shared task. In: Faggioli et al. [33]
93. Tchechmedjiev, A., et al.: ClaimsKG: a knowledge graph of fact-checked claims. In: Ghidini, C., et al. (eds.) ISWC 2019. LNCS, vol. 11779, pp. 309–324. Springer, Cham (2019). https://doi.org/10.1007/978-3-030-30796-7_20
94. Thorne, J., Vlachos, A., Christodoulopoulos, C., Mittal, A.: FEVER: a large-scale dataset for fact extraction and VERification. In: Proceedings of the Conference of the North American Chapter of the Association for Computational Linguistics: Human Language Technologies, NAACL-HLT 2018, pp. 809–819 (2018)
95. Touahri, I., Mazroui, A.: EvolutionTeam at CheckThat! 2020: integration of linguistic and sentimental features in a fake news detection approach. In: Cappellato et al. [19]
96. Tsoplefack, W.K.: Classifier for fake news detection and topical domain of news articles. In: Faggioli et al. [19]
97. Utsha, R.S., Keya, M., Hasan, M.A., Islam, M.S.: Qword at CheckThat! 2021: an extreme gradient boosting approach for multiclass fake news detection. In: Faggioli et al. [33]
98. Vasileva, S., Atanasova, P., Màrquez, L., Barrón-Cedeño, A., Nakov, P.: It takes nine to smell a rat: neural multi-task learning for check-worthiness prediction. In: Proceedings of the International Conference on Recent Advances in Natural Language Processing, RANLP 2019, pp. 1229–1239 (2019)
99. Williams, E., Rodrigues, P., Novak, V.: Accenture at CheckThat! 2020: if you say so: post-hoc fact-checking of claims using transformer-based models. In: Cappellato et al. [19]
100. Williams, E., Rodrigues, P., Tran, S.: Accenture at CheckThat! 2021: interesting claim identification and ranking with contextually sensitive lexical training data augmentation. In: Faggioli et al. [33]

101. Zengin, M.S., Kartal, Y.S., Kutlu, M.: TOBB ETU at CheckThat! 2021: data engineering for detecting check-worthy claims. In: Faggioli et al. [33]
102. Zhao, Z., Resnick, P., Mei, Q.: Enquiring minds: early detection of rumors in social media from enquiry posts. In: Proceedings of the 24th International Conference on World Wide Web, WWW 2015, pp. 1395–1405 (2015)
103. Zhou, X., Wu, B., Fung, P.: Fight for 4230 at CLEF CheckThat! 2021: domain-specific preprocessing and pretrained model for ranking claims by check-worthiness. In: Faggioli et al. [33]
104. Zubiaga, A., Liakata, M., Procter, R., Hoi, G.W.S., Tolmie, P.: Analysing how people orient to and spread rumours in social media by looking at conversational threads. PLoS One **11**(3), e0150989 (2016)
105. Zuo, C., Karakas, A., Banerjee, R.: A hybrid recognition system for check-worthy claims using heuristics and supervised learning. In: Cappellato et al. [21]

Overview of ChEMU 2021: Reaction Reference Resolution and Anaphora Resolution in Chemical Patents

Yuan Li[1], Biaoyan Fang[1], Jiayuan He[1,4], Hiyori Yoshikawa[1,5], Saber A. Akhondi[2], Christian Druckenbrodt[3], Camilo Thorne[3], Zubair Afzal[2], Zenan Zhai[1], Timothy Baldwin[1], and Karin Verspoor[1,4(✉)]

[1] The University of Melbourne, Melbourne, Australia
[2] Elsevier BV, Amsterdam, The Netherlands
[3] Elsevier Information Systems GmbH, Frankfurt, Germany
[4] RMIT University, Melbourne, Australia
karin.verspoor@rmit.edu.au
[5] Fujitsu Limited, Minato Ward, Japan

Abstract. In this paper, we provide an overview of the Cheminformatics Elsevier Melbourne University (ChEMU) evaluation lab 2021, part of the Conference and Labs of the Evaluation Forum 2021 (CLEF 2021). The ChEMU evaluation lab focuses on information extraction over chemical reactions from patent texts. As the second instance of our ChEMU lab series, we build upon the ChEMU corpus developed for ChEMU 2020, extending it for two distinct tasks related to reference resolution in chemical patents. Task 1—Chemical Reaction Reference Resolution—focuses on paragraph-level references and aims to identify the chemical reactions or general conditions specified in one reaction description referred to by another. Task 2—Anaphora Resolution—focuses on expression-level references and aims to identify the reference relationships between expressions in chemical reaction descriptions. Herein, we describe the resources created for these tasks and the evaluation methodology adopted. We also provide a brief summary of the results obtained in this lab, finding that one submission achieves substantially better results than our baseline models.

Keywords: Reaction reference resolution · Anaphora resolution · Chemical patents · Text mining · Information extraction

1 Introduction

The discovery of new chemical compounds is perceived as a key driver of the chemical industry and many other industrial sectors, and information relevant for this discovery is found in chemical synthesis descriptions in natural language texts. In particular, patents serve as a critical source of information about new chemical compounds. Compared with journal publications, patents provide more

K. S. Candan et al. (Eds.): CLEF 2021, LNCS 12880, pp. 292–307, 2021.
https://doi.org/10.1007/978-3-030-85251-1_20

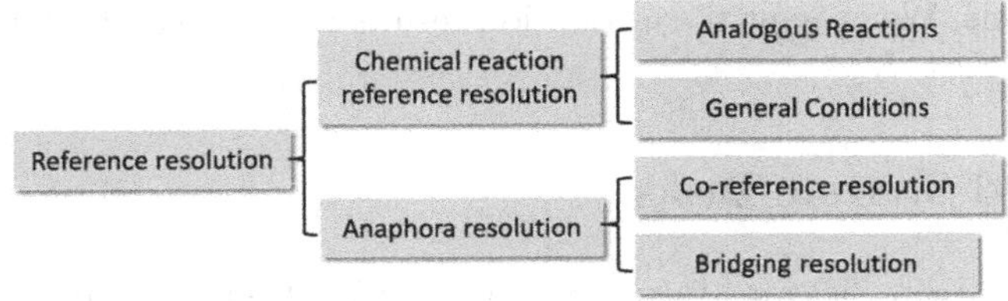

Fig. 1. Illustration of the task hierarchy.

timely and comprehensive information about new chemical compounds [1,4,24], since they are usually the first venues where new chemical compounds are disclosed. Despite the significant commercial and research value of the information in patents, manual extraction of such information is costly, considering the large volume of patents available [12,18]. Thus, developing automatic natural language processing (NLP) systems for chemical patents, which convert text corpora into structured knowledge about chemical compounds, has become a focus of recent research [10,13].

The ChEMU campaign focuses on information extraction tasks over chemical reactions in patents[1]. ChEMU 2020 [10,11,20] provided two information extraction tasks, named entity recognition (NER) and event extraction, and attracted 37 teams around the world to participate. In the ChEMU 2021 lab, we provide two new information extraction tasks: chemical reaction reference resolution and anaphora resolution, focusing on reference resolution in chemical patents. Compared with previous shared tasks dealing with anaphora resolution, e.g., the CRAFT-CR task [3], our proposed tasks extend the scope of reference resolution by considering reference relationships on both paragraph-level and expression-level (see Fig. 1). Specifically, our first task aims at the identification of reference relationships between reaction descriptions. Our second task aims at the identification of reference relationships between chemical expressions, including both coreference and bridging. Moreover, we focus on chemical patents while the CRAFT-CR task focused on journal articles.

Unfortunately, we didn't receive any submissions to Task 1, chemical reaction reference resolution. The complexity of this task in particular combined with relatively short time periods for people to develop their systems may have made it difficult for people to participate. We plan to re-run it in 2022, to give the opportunity for more people to participate since the data and task definitions will have been around for a longer period of time. As a result, the remainder of this paper will focus on the second task, anaphora resolution.

The rest of the paper is structured as follows. We first discuss related work and shared tasks in Sect. 2 and introduce the corpus we created for use in the lab in Sect. 3. Then we give an overview of the task in Sect. 4 and detail the valuation framework of ChEMU in Sect. 5 including the evaluation methods and

[1] Our main website is http://chemu.eng.unimelb.edu.au.

baseline models. We present the evaluation results in Sect. 6 and finally conclude this paper in Sect. 7.

2 Related Shared Tasks

Several shared tasks have addressed reference resolution in scientific literature. BioNLP2011 hosted a subtask on protein coreference [21]. CRAFT 2019 hosted a subtask on coreference resolution (CRAFT-CR) in biomedical articles [3]. However, these shared tasks differ from ours in several respects.

First, previous shared tasks considered different domains of scientific literature. For example, the dataset used in BioNLP2011 is derived from the GENIA corpus [22], which primarily focuses on the biological domain, viz. gene/proteins and their regulations. The dataset used in CRAFT-CR shared task is based on biomedical journal articles in PubMed [2,6]. Our ChEMU shared task, in contrast, focuses on the domain of chemical patents. This difference entails the critical importance for this shared task: information extraction methodologies for general scientific literature or the biomedical domain will not be effective for chemical patents [17]. It is widely acknowledged that patents are written quite differently as compared with general scientific literature, resulting in substantially different linguistic properties. For example, patent authors may trade some clarity in wording for more protection of their intellectual property.

Secondly, our reference resolution tasks include both paragraph-level and entity-level reference phenomena. Our first task aims at identification of reference relationships between reaction descriptions, i.e. paragraph-level. This task is challenging because a reaction description may refer to an extremely remote reaction and thus requires processing of very long documents. Our second task aims at anaphora resolution, similarly to previous entity-level coreference tasks. However, a key difference is that we extend the scope of this task by including both coreference and bridging phenomena. That is, we not only aim at finding expressions referring to the same entity, but also expressions that are semantically related or associated.

3 The ChEMU Chemical Reaction Corpus

In this section, we explain how the dataset is created for the anaphora resolution task. The complete annotation guidelines are made available at [8].

3.1 Corpus Selection

We build on the ChEMU corpus [25] developed for the ChEMU 2020 shared task [11]. The ChEMU corpus contains patents from the European Patent Office and the United States Patent and Trademark Office, available in English in a digital format. It is based on the Reaxys® database,[2] containing reaction entries for patent documents manually created by experts in chemistry. It consists of 'snippets' extracted from chemical patents, where each snippet corresponds to a reaction description. It is common that several snippets are extracted from the same chemical patent.

3.2 Mention Type

We aim to capture anaphora in chemical patents, with a focus on identifying chemical compounds during the reaction process. Consistent with other anaphora corpora [6,9,23], only mentions that are involved in referring relationships (as defined in Sect. 3.3) and related to chemical compounds are annotated. The mention types that are considered for anaphora annotation are listed below. It should be noted that verbs (e.g. *mix*, *purify*, *distil*) and descriptions that refer to events (e.g. *the same process, step 5*) are not annotated in this corpus.

Chemical Names. Chemical names are a critical component of chemical patents. We capture as atomic mentions the formal name of chemical compounds, e.g. *N-[4-(benzoxazol-2-yl)-methoxyphenyl]-S-methyl-N'-phenyl-isothiourea* or *2-Chloro-4-hydroxy-phenylboronic acid.* Chemical names often include nested chemical components, but for the purposes of our corpus, we consider chemical names to be atomic and do not separately annotate internal mentions. Hence *4-(benzoxazol-2-yl)-methoxyphenyl* and *acid* in the examples above will not be annotated as mentions, as they are part of larger chemical names.

Identifiers. In chemical patents, identifiers or labels may also be used to represent chemical compounds, in the form of uniquely-identifying sequences of numbers and letters such as *5i.* These can be abbreviations of longer expressions incorporating that identifier that occur earlier in the text, such as *chemical compound 5i*, or may refer back to an exact chemical name with that identifier. Thus, the identifier is annotated as an atomic mention as well.

Phrases and Noun Types. Apart from chemical names and identifiers, chemical compounds are commonly presented as noun phrases (NPs). An NP consists of a noun or pronoun, and premodifiers; NPs are the most common type of compound expressions in chemical patents. Here we detail NPs that are related to compounds:

1. Pronouns: In chemical patents, pronouns (e.g. *they* or *it*) usually refer to a previously mentioned chemical compounds.

[2] Reaxys® Copyright ©2021 Elsevier Life Sciences IP Limited except certain content provided by third parties. Reaxys is a trademark of Elsevier Life Sciences IP Limited, used under license. https://www.reaxys.com.

2. Definite and indefinite NPs: Commonly used to refer to chemical compounds, e.g. *the solvent, the title compound, the mixture*, and *a white solid, a crude product.*

Furthermore, there are a few types of NPs that need specific handling in chemical patents:

1. Quantified NPs: Chemical compounds are usually described with a quantity. NPs with quantities are considered as atomic mentions if the quantities are provided, e.g. *398.4 mg of the compound 1.*
2. NPs with prepositions: Chemical NPs connected with prepositions (e.g. *in, with, of*) can be considered as a single mention. For example, the phrase *2,4-dichloro-6-(6-triuoromethylpyridin-2-yl)-1,3,5-triazine (5.0 g, 16.9 mmol) in tetrahydrofuran (100 mL)* is a single mention, as it describes a solvent that contains *2,4-dichloro-6-(6-triuoromethylpyridin-2-yl)-1,3,5-triazine (5.0 g, 16.9 mmol)* and *tetrahydrofuran (100 mL).*

NPs describing chemical equipment containing a compound may also be relevant to anaphora resolution. This generally occurs when the equipment that contains the compound undergoes a process that also affects the compound. Thus, equipment expressions such as the flask and the autoclave can also be mentions if they are used to implicitly refer to a contained compound.

Unlike many annotation schemes, our annotation allows discontinuous mentions. For example, the underlined spans of the fragment *114 mg of 4-((4aS,7aS)-6-benzyloctahydro-1-pyrrolo[3,4-b]pyridine-1-yl)-7H-pyrrolo[2,3-d]pyrimidine was obtained with a yield of about 99.1%* are treated as a single discontinuous mention. This introduces further complexity into the task and helps to capture more comprehensive anaphora phenomena.

Relationship to ChEMU 2020 Entities. Since this dataset is built on the ChEMU 2020 corpus [25], annotation of related chemical compounds is available by leveraging existing entity annotations introduced for the ChEMU 2020 named entity recognition (NER) task. However, there are some differences in the definitions of entities for the two tasks.

In the original ChEMU 2020 corpus, entity annotations identify chemical compounds (i.e. REACTION_PRODUCT, STARTING_MATERIAL, REAGENT_CATALYST, SOLVENT, and OTHER COMPOUND), reaction conditions (i.e. TIME, TEMPERATURE), quantity information (i.e. YIELD_PERCENT, YIELD_OTHER), and example labels (i.e. EXAMPLE_LABEL). There is overlap with our definition of mention for the labels relating to chemical compounds. However, in our annotation, chemical names are annotated along with additional quantity information, as we consider this information to be an integral part of the chemical compound description. Furthermore, the original entity annotations do not include generic expressions that corefer with chemical compounds such as *the mixture, the organic layer*, or *the filtrate*, and neither do they include equipment descriptions.

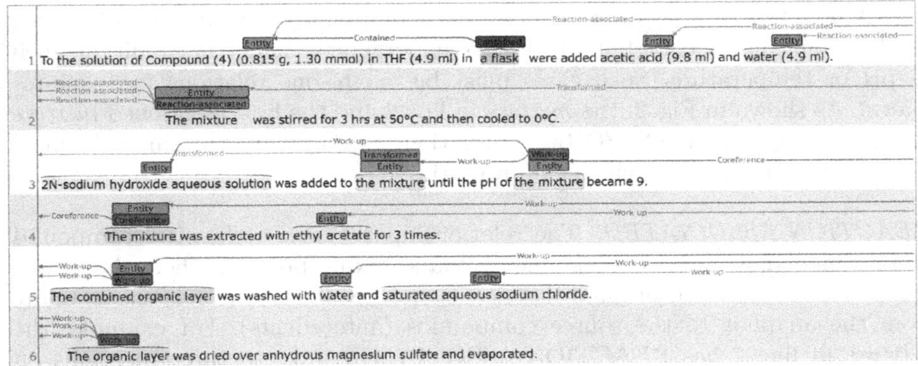

1 To the solution of Compound (4) (0.815 g, 1.30 mmol) in THF (4.9 ml) in a flask were added acetic acid (9.8 ml) and water (4.9 ml).
2 The mixture was stirred for 3 hrs at 50°C and then cooled to 0°C.
3 2N-sodium hydroxide aqueous solution was added to the mixture until the pH of the mixture became 9.
4 The mixture was extracted with ethyl acetate for 3 times.
5 The combined organic layer was washed with water and saturated aqueous sodium chloride.
6 The organic layer was dried over anhydrous magnesium sulfate and evaporated.

Fig. 2. Annotated snippet of anaphora resolution in the chemical patents. The figure is taken from [7]. Different color of links represent different anaphora relation types.

3.3 Relation Types

Anaphora resolution subsumes both coreference and bridging. In the context of chemical patents, we define four sub-types of bridging, incorporating generic and chemical knowledge.

A referring mention which cannot be interpreted on its own, or an indirect mention, is called an *anaphor*, and the mention which it refers back to is called the *antecedent*. In relation annotation, we preserve the direction of the anaphoric relation, from the anaphor to the antecedent. Following similar assumptions in recent work, we restrict annotations to cases where the antecedent appears earlier in the text than the anaphor.

Coreference. Coreference is defined as expressions/mentions that refer to the same entity [5,19]. In chemistry, identifying whether two mentions refer to the same entity needs to consider various chemical properties (e.g. temperature or pH). As such, for two mentions to be coreferent, they must share the same chemical properties. We consider two different cases of coreference:

1. Single Antecedents: the anaphor refers to a single antecedent.
2. Multiple Antecedents: the anaphor refers to multiple antecedents, e.g. *start materials* refers to all the chemical compounds or materials that are used at the beginning.

It is possible for there to be ambiguity as to which mention of a given antecedent an anaphor refers to (where the mention is identical); in these cases the closest mention is selected.

Bridging. As stated above, when we consider the anaphora relations, we take the chemical properties of the mention into consideration. Coreference is insufficient to cover all instances of anaphora in chemical patents, and bridging occurs frequently. We define four bridging types:

TRANSFORMED. Links between chemical compounds that are initially based on the same components, but which have undergone a change in condition, such as pH or temperature. Such cases must be one-to-one relations (not one-to-many). As shown in Fig. 2, the *mixture* in line 2 and the first-mentioned *mixture* in line 3 have the TRANSFORMED relation, as they have the same chemical components but different chemical properties.

REACTION-ASSOCIATED. The relationship between a chemical compound and its immediate source compounds is via a mixing process, where the source compounds retain their original chemical structure. This relation is one-to-many from the anaphor to the source compounds (antecedents). For example, the *mixture* in line 2 has REACTION-ASSOCIATED links to three mentions on line 1 that are combined to form it: (1) *the solution of Compound (4) (0.815 g, 1.30 mmol) in THF (4.9 ml)*; (2) *acetic acid (9.8 ml)*; and (3) *water (4.9 ml))*.

WORK-UP. Chemical compounds are used to isolate or purify an associated output product, in a one-to-many relation, from the anaphor to the compounds (antecedents) that are used for the work-up process. As demonstrated in Fig. 2, *The combined organic layer* in line 5 comes from the extraction of *The mixture and ethyl acetate* in line 4, and they are hence annotated as WORK-UP.

CONTAINED. A chemical compound is contained inside equipment. It is a one-to-many relation from the anaphor (equipment) to the compounds (antecedents) that it contains. An example of this is *a flask* and *the solution of Compound (4) (0.815 g, 1.30 mmol) in THF (4.9 ml)* on line 1, where the compound is contained in the flask.

3.4 Annotation Process

For the corpus annotation, we use the BRAT text annotation tool.[3] In total 1500 snippets have been annotated by two chemical experts, a PhD candidate and a final year bachelor student in Chemistry. A draft of the annotation guideline was created and refined with chemical experts, then four rounds of annotation training were completed prior to beginning official annotation. In each round, the two annotators individually annotated the same 10 snippets (different across each round of annotation), and their annotations were compared and combined by an adjudicator; annotation guidelines were then refined based on discussion. After several rounds of training, we achieved a high inner-annotator agreement of Krippendorff's $\alpha = 0.92$ [14] at the mention annotation level,[4] and $\alpha = 0.84$ for relations. Finally, the development and test sets were double annotated by the two expert annotators, with any disagreements merged by the adjudicator.

[3] https://brat.nlplab.org/.

[4] With the lowest agreement being $\alpha = 0.89$ for coreference mentions.

Table 1. Corpus annotation statistics.

	Training	Development	Test
Snippets	6392	1535	2585
Sentences	763	164	274
Tokens/Sentences	15.8	15.2	15.8
Mentions	19626	4515	7810
Discontinuous mentions	876	235	399
Coreference	3568	870	1491
Bridging	10377	2419	4135
Transformed	493	107	166
Reaction-associated	3308	764	1245
Work-up	6230	1479	2576
Contained	346	69	148

3.5 Data Partitions

We randomly partitioned the whole dataset into three splits for training, development, and test purposes, with a ratio of 0.6/0.15/0.25. The training and development sets were released to participants for model development. Note that participants are allowed to use the combination of training and development sets and to use their own partitions to build models. The test set is withheld for use in the formal evaluation. The statistics of the three splits including their number of snippets, total number of sentences, and average number of tokens per sentence, are summarized in Table 1.

To ensure the snippets included in the training, development, and test splits have similar distributions, we compare the distribution of relation types (five types of relations in total). Based on the numbers in Table 1, we confirm that the label distribution in the three splits are similar, with very little variation ($\leq$2%) across the three splits observed for each relation type.

4 Task Definition

This task requires the resolution of general anaphoric dependencies between expressions in chemical patents. Five types of anaphoric relationships are defined:

1. *Coreference*: two expressions/mentions that refer to the same entity.
2. *Transformed*: two chemical compound entities that are initially based on the same chemical components and have undergone possible changes through various conditions (e.g., pH and temperature).
3. *Reaction-associated*: the relationship between a chemical compound and its immediate sources via a mixing process. The immediate sources do need to be reagents, but they need to end up in the corresponding product. The source compounds retain their original chemical structure.

[Acetic acid (9.8 ml)] and **[water (4.9 ml)]** were added to **[the solution]** in **[a flask]**. **[The mixture]$_1$** was stirred for 3 hrs at 50°C and then cooled to 0°C . 2N-sodium hydroxide aqueous solution was added to **[the mixture]$_2$** until the pH of **[the mixture]$_3$** became 9. **[The mixture]$_4$** was extracted with **[ethyl acetate]** for 3 times. **[The combined organic layer]** was washed with water and saturated aqueous sodium chloride.

ID	Relation type	Anaphor	Antecedent
AR1	Coreference	**[The mixture]$_4$**	**[the mixture]$_3$**
AR2	Transformed	**[the mixture]$_2$**	**[The mixture]$_1$**
AR3	Reaction_associated	**[The mixture]$_1$**	**[water (4.9 ml)]**
AR4	Work-up	**[The combined organic layer]**	**[ethyl acetate]**
AR5	Contained	**[a flask]**	**[the solution]**

Fig. 3. Text snippet containing a chemical reaction, with its anaphoric relationships. The expressions that are involved are highlighted in **bold**. In the cases where several expressions have identical text form, subscripts are added according to their order of appearance.

4. *Work-up*: the relationship between chemical compounds that were used for isolation or purification purposes, and their corresponding output products.
5. *Contained*: the association holding between chemical compounds and the related equipment in which they are placed. The direction of the relation is from the related equipment to the previous chemical compound.

Taking the text snippet in Fig. 3 as an example, several anaphoric relationships can be extracted from it. **[The mixture]$_4$** and **[the mixture]$_3$** refer to the same "mixture" and thus, form a coreference relationship. The two expressions **[The mixture]$_1$** and **[the mixture]$_2$** are initially based on the same chemical components but the property of **[the mixture]$_2$** changes after the "stir" and "cool" action. Thus, the two expressions should be linked as "Transformed". The expression **[The mixture]$_1$** comes from mixing the chemical compounds prior to it, e.g., **[water (4.9 ml)]**. Thus, the two expressions are linked as "Reaction-associated". The expression **[The combined organic layer]** comes from the extraction of **[ethyl acetate]**. Thus, they are linked as "Work-up". Finally, the expression **[the solution]** is contained by the entity **[a flask]**, and the two are linked as "Contained".

5 Evaluation Framework

5.1 Evaluation Methods

We use BRATEval[5] to evaluate all the runs that we receive. Three metrics are used to evaluate the performance of all the submissions: Precision, Recall, and F_1 score. We use two difference matching criteria, exact matching and relaxed matching (approximate matching), as in some practical applications it also makes sense to understand if the model can identify the *approximate* region of mentions.

[5] https://bitbucket.org/nicta_biomed/brateval/src/master/.

Formally, let $E = (ET, A, B)$ denote an entity where ET is the type of E, A and B are the beginning position (inclusive) and end position (exclusive) of the text span of E. Then two entities E_1 and E_2 are exactly matched ($E_1 = E_2$), if $ET_1 = ET_2$, $A_1 = A_2$, and $B_1 = B_2$. While two entities E_1 and E_2 are approximately matched ($E_1 \approx E_2$) if $ET_1 = ET_2$, $A_2 < B_1$, and $A_1 < B_2$, i.e. the two spans $[A_1, B_1)$ and $[A_2, B_2)$ overlaps.

Furthermore, let $R = (RT, E^{ana}, E^{ant})$ be a relation where RT is the type of R, E^{ana} the anaphor of R, E^{ant} the antecedent of R. Then R_1 and R_2 are exactly matched ($R_1 = R_2$) if $RT_1 = RT_2$, $E_1^{ana} = E_2^{ana}$, and $E_1^{ant} = E_2^{ant}$. While R_1 and R_2 are approximately matched ($R_1 \approx R_2$) if $RT_1 = RT_2$, $E_1^{ana} \approx E_2^{ana}$, and $E_1^{ant} \approx E_2^{ant}$.

In summary, we require strict type match in both exact and relaxed matching, but are lenient in span matching.

Exact Matching. With the above definitions, the metrics for exact matching can be easily calculated. The true positives (TP) are exact matching pairs found in gold relations and predicted relations. Then false positives (FP) are the predicted relations that don't have a match, i.e. $FP = \#pred - TP$, where $\#pred$ is the number of predicted relations. Similarly, false negatives FN are the gold relations that are not matched by any predicted relations, i.e. $FN = \#gold - TP$ where $\#gold$ is the number of gold relations. Finally Precision $P = TP/(TP + FP)$, Recall $R = TP/(TP + FN)$, and $F_1 = 2/(1/P + 1/R)$.

Relaxed Matching. Unlike exact matching, relaxed matching is not well-defined and metrics in this setting have more than one way to calculate, therefore we need to clearly define all the metrics.

Let consider an example shown in Fig. 4a where nodes $\{P_i\}_{i=1}^5$ are predicted relations, $\{G_i\}_{i=1}^5$ are gold relations, and every edge between a P node and a G node means they are approximately matched. At first glance, one may think that $FN = FP = 0$ because every gold relation has at least a match and so does every predicted relation. However, it is impossible to find 5 true positive pairs from this graph without using one node more than once. Therefore, if $FN = FP = 0$, then $FN + TP \neq \#gold = 5$ and $FP + TP \neq \#pred = 5$, which is inconsistent with the formulas in exact setting.

So, instead of defining FN as the number of gold relations that don't have a match, we just define $FN = \#gold - TP$. Similarly FP is defined as $\#pred - TP$. Then the problem remained is how to calculate TP. Actually, finding true positive pairs can be considered as bipartite matching. Figure 4b shows a matching with $TP = 3$ but is not optimal. Figure 4c shows one possible maximum bipartite matching with $TP = 4$. Another optimal matching is replacing edge $P_0 - G_0$ with $P_0 - G_1$.

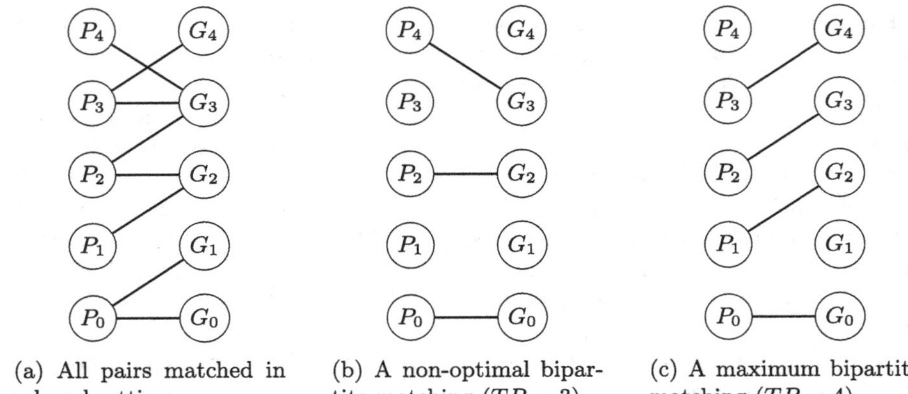

(a) All pairs matched in relaxed setting

(b) A non-optimal bipartite matching ($TP = 3$)

(c) A maximum bipartite matching ($TP = 4$)

Fig. 4. An example matching graph and two bipartite matching for it.

In summary, we define TP as the maximum bipartite matching for the graph constructed by all approximately matched pairs, then $FN = \#gold - TP$ and $FP = \#pred - TP$, finally Precision $P = TP/(TP + FP)$, Recall $R = TP/(TP + FN)$, and $F_1 = 2/(1/P + 1/R)$. This has been implemented in the latest BRATEval.

5.2 Coreference Linkings

We consider two types of coreference linking, i.e. (1) surface coreference linking and (2) atomic coreference linking, due to the existence of *transitive coreference relationships*. By transitive coreference relationships we mean multi-hop coreference such as a link from an expression T1 to T3 via an intermediate expression T2, viz., "T1→T2→T3". Surface coreference linking will restrict attention to one-hop relationships, viz., to: "T1→T2" and "T2→T3". Whereas atomic coreference linking will tackle coreference between an anaphoric expression and its first antecedent, i.e. intermediate antecedents will be collapsed. Thus, these two links will be used for the above example, "T1→T3" and "T2→T3". Note that we only consider transitive linking in coreference relationships.

Note that {T1→T2, T2→T3} infers {T1→T3, T2→T3}, but the reverse is not true. This leads to a problem about how to score a prediction {T1→T3, T2→T3}, when the gold relation is {T1→T2, T2→T3}. Both T1→T3 and T2→T3 are true, but some information is missing here.

Our solution is to first expand both the prediction set and gold set where all valid relations that can be inferred will be generated and added to the set, and then to evaluate the two sets normally. In the above example, the gold set will be expanded to {T1→T2, T2→T3, T1→T3}, and then the result is

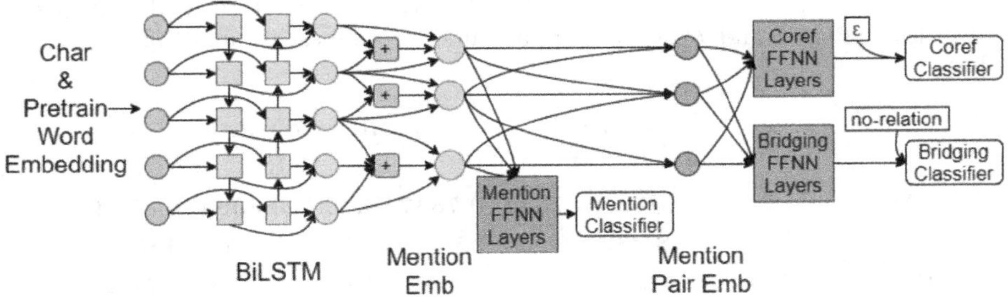

Fig. 5. The architecture of our baseline model. The figure is taken from [7].

$TP = 2$, $FN = 1$. Likewise, when evaluate {T1→T4, T2→T4, T3→T4} against {T1→T2, T2→T3, T3→T4}, the gold set will be expanded into 6 relations, while the prediction set won't be expanded as no new relation can be inferred. So the evaluation result will be $TP = 3$, $FN = 3$. One may worry that if there is a chain of length n then its expanded set will be in $O(n^2)$, when n is large, this local evaluation result will have too much influence on the overall result. But we find in practice that coreference chains are relatively short, with 3 or 4 being the most typical lengths, so it is unlikely to be a big issue.

5.3 Baselines

Our baseline model adopts an end-to-end architecture for coreference resolution [15,16], as depicted in Fig. 5. Following the methods presented in [7], we use GloVe embeddings and a character-level CNN as input to a BiLSTM to obtain contextualized word representations. Then all possible spans are enumerated and fed to a mention classifier which detects if the input is a mention. Based on the same mention representations, pairs of mentions are fed to a coreference classifier and a bridging classifier, where the coreference classifier does binary classification and the bridging one classifies pairs into 4 bridging relation types and a special class for no relation. Training is done jointly with all losses added together.

We released the code for training our baseline models to help the participants to get started on the shared task.[6] Two variants of the baseline model are evaluated on the test set, one using the ELMO embeddings as input to the BiLSTM component, while the other used pretrained ChELMO, based on the embeddings of [26] pre-trained on chemical patents, with the hope of benefiting more from domain-specific pretraining.

[6] Code available at https://github.com/biaoyanf/ChEMU-Ref.

Table 2. Overall performance for all runs on the test set. Here P, R, and F are short for Precision, Recall, and F_1 score. For each metric, the best result is highlighted in **bold**.

	Exact-match			Relaxed-match		
	P	R	F	P	R	F
CMU	0.8177	**0.7542**	**0.7847**	**0.909**	**0.8384**	**0.8723**
Baseline-ChELMO	**0.8566**	0.6882	0.7633	0.9024	0.725	0.8041
Baseline-ELMO	0.8435	0.6676	0.7453	0.8875	0.7025	0.7842
HUKB	0.7132	0.6696	0.6907	0.7702	0.7231	0.7459

6 Results and Discussions

A total of 19 teams registered on our submission website for the shared task. Among them, we finally received 2 submissions on the test set. One team is from Carnegie Mellon University, US (CMU) and the other one is from Hokkaido University, Japan (HUKB). Both of them adopted a two-step approach where mentions are first detected and then relations between them are determined. They also both relied on BERT-like models to extract contextualized representations for mention detection. While the CMU team used a BERT-like model in the relation extraction, the HUKB team chose a rule-based method. In this section, we report their results along with the performance of our two baseline systems.

We report the overall performance of all runs in Table 2. The rankings of different systems are fully consistent across all metrics. The CMU team achieves an F_1 score of 0.7847 in exact matching, outperforming our two baselines which get 0.7633 and 0.7453, followed by the HUKB team who obtains 0.6907. The lead of the CMU team is even larger in relaxed matching, with an F_1 score of 0.8723, about 7 points higher than our baselines. This shows the potential of the CMU model and indicates that the performance in exact matching may be further boosted if the boundary errors of their model could be corrected in a post-processing step.

Our baselines have higher precision in the exact setting and precision in relaxed setting is also very close to the best, which indicates that our models are more conservative and could possibly be enhanced by making more aggressive predictions to improve recall. The use of domain-pretrained embeddings (ChELMO vs. ELMO) does, as expected, benefit performance.

Table 3 provides more details about the performance of all models for each relation type. The CMU team outperforms others on TRANSFORMED relation by a large margin. While our baselines performs the best on CONTAINED relation type. For the other three relation types, the CMU model wins F_1 score and recall, while our models achieve the highest precision, which is similar to our observation on the overall results. Given that the models perform very differently, it would be very interesting to do more analysis when the details of all

Table 3. Performance per relation type for all runs on the test set. Here P, R, and F are short for Precision, Recall, and F_1 score. For each metric, the best result is highlighted in **bold**.

		Exact-match			Relaxed-match		
		P	R	F	P	R	F
COREFERENCE	CMU	0.7568	**0.5822**	**0.6581**	0.8945	**0.6881**	**0.7779**
	Baseline-ChELMO	0.8476	0.4661	0.6015	**0.9244**	0.5084	0.656
	Baseline-ELMO	**0.8497**	0.4474	0.5861	0.9185	0.4836	0.6336
	HUKB	0.6956	0.5319	0.6028	0.7868	0.6016	0.6819
CONTAINED	CMU	0.7727	0.6892	0.7286	0.8561	**0.7635**	0.8071
	Baseline-ChELMO	**0.9211**	**0.7095**	**0.8015**	0.9386	0.723	**0.8168**
	Baseline-ELMO	0.9175	0.6014	0.7265	**0.9794**	0.6419	0.7755
	HUKB	0.7214	0.6824	0.7014	0.7929	0.75	0.7708
REACTION_ASSOCIATED	CMU	0.8037	**0.7631**	0.7829	**0.9019**	**0.8562**	**0.8785**
	Baseline-ChELMO	**0.8381**	0.7357	**0.7836**	0.8673	0.7614	0.8109
	Baseline-ELMO	0.8145	0.7229	0.766	0.8498	0.7542	0.7991
	HUKB	0.668	0.6803	0.6741	0.7224	0.7357	0.729
TRANSFORMED	CMU	**0.9423**	**0.8855**	**0.913**	**0.9423**	**0.8855**	**0.913**
	Baseline-ChELMO	0.7935	0.8795	0.8343	0.7935	0.8795	0.8343
	Baseline-ELMO	0.7877	0.8494	0.8174	0.7877	0.8494	0.8174
	HUKB	0.6611	0.7169	0.6879	0.6611	0.7169	0.6879
WORK_UP	CMU	0.846	**0.8447**	**0.8454**	**0.9195**	**0.9181**	**0.9188**
	Baseline-ChELMO	**0.8705**	0.7803	0.8229	0.9181	0.823	0.868
	Baseline-ELMO	0.8566	0.7605	0.8057	0.899	0.7981	0.8456
	HUKB	0.7467	0.7403	0.7435	0.7929	0.7861	0.7895

the models are disclosed, and hopefully every team can borrow ideas from others and further improve the performance.

7 Conclusions

This paper presents a general overview of the activities and outcomes of the ChEMU 2021 evaluation lab. As the second instance of our ChEMU lab series, ChEMU 2021 targets two new tasks focusing on reference resolution in chemical patents. Our first task aims at identification of reference relationships between chemical reaction descriptions, and our second task aims at identification of reference relationships between expressions in chemical reactions. The evaluation result includes different approaches to tackling the shared task, with one submission clearly outperforming our baseline methods. We look forward to fruitful discussion and deeper understanding of the methodological details of these submissions at the workshop.

Acknowledgements. Funding for the ChEMU project is provided by an Australian Research Council Linkage Project, project number LP160101469, and Elsevier. We acknowledge the support of our ChEMU-Ref annotators, Dr. Sacha Novakovic and Colleen Hui Shiuan Yeow at the University of Melbourne, and the annotation teams supporting the reaction reference task annotation.

References

1. Akhondi, S.A., et al.: Automatic identification of relevant chemical compounds from patents. Database **2019** (2019)
2. Bada, M., et al.: Concept annotation in the CRAFT corpus. BMC Bioinf. **13**, 161 (2012). https://doi.org/10.1186/1471-2105-13-161. https://www.ncbi.nlm.nih.gov/pubmed/22776079
3. Baumgartner Jr., W.A., et al.: CRAFT shared tasks 2019 overview—integrated structure, semantics, and coreference. In: Proceedings of The 5th Workshop on BioNLP Open Shared Tasks, pp. 174–184 (2019)
4. Bregonje, M.: Patents: a unique source for scientific technical information in chemistry related industry? World Patent Inf. **27**(4), 309–315 (2005)
5. Clark, K., Manning, C.D.: Entity-centric coreference resolution with model stacking. In: Proceedings of the 53rd Annual Meeting of the Association for Computational Linguistics and the 7th International Joint Conference on Natural Language Processing of the Asian Federation of Natural Language Processing, ACL 2015, 26–31 July 2015, Beijing, China, Volume 1: Long Papers, pp. 1405–1415. The Association for Computer Linguistics (2015). https://doi.org/10.3115/v1/p15-1136
6. Cohen, K.B., et al.: Coreference annotation and resolution in the colorado richly annotated full text (CRAFT) corpus of biomedical journal articles. BMC Bioinform. **18**(1), 372:1–372:14 (2017). https://doi.org/10.1186/s12859-017-1775-9
7. Fang, B., Druckenbrodt, C., Akhondi, S.A., He, J., Baldwin, T., Verspoor, K.: ChEMU-Ref: a corpus for modeling anaphora resolution in the chemical domain. In: Proceedings of the 16th Conference of the European Chapter of the Association for Computational Linguistics. Association for Computational Linguistics, April 2021
8. Fang, B., et al.: ChEMU-ref dataset for modeling anaphora resolution in the chemical domain (2021). https://doi.org/10.17632/r28xxr6p92
9. Ghaddar, A., Langlais, P.: WikiCoref: an English coreference-annotated corpus of Wikipedia articles. In: Calzolari, N., et al. (eds.) Proceedings of the Tenth International Conference on Language Resources and Evaluation LREC 2016, Portorož, Slovenia, 23-28 May 2016. European Language Resources Association (ELRA) (2016). http://www.lrec-conf.org/proceedings/lrec2016/summaries/192.html
10. He, J., et al.: ChEMU 2020: natural language processing methods are effective for information extraction from chemical patents. Front. Res. Metrics Anal. **6**, 654438 (2021). https://doi.org/10.3389/frma.2021.654438
11. He, J., et al.: Overview of ChEMU 2020: named entity recognition and event extraction of chemical reactions from patents. In: Arampatzis, A., et al. (eds.) CLEF 2020. LNCS, vol. 12260, pp. 237–254. Springer, Cham (2020). https://doi.org/10.1007/978-3-030-58219-7_18
12. Hu, M., Cinciruk, D., Walsh, J.M.: Improving automated patent claim parsing: dataset, system, and experiments. arXiv preprint arXiv:1605.01744 (2016)
13. Krallinger, M., Leitner, F., Rabal, O., Vazquez, M., Oyarzabal, J., Valencia, A.: CHEMDNER: the drugs and chemical names extraction challenge. J. Cheminf. **7**(S1), S1 (2015)
14. Krippendorff, K.: Measuring the reliability of qualitative text analysis data. Qual. Quant. **38**, 787–800 (2004)
15. Lee, K., He, L., Lewis, M., Zettlemoyer, L.: End-to-end neural coreference resolution. In: Palmer, M., Hwa, R., Riedel, S. (eds.) Proceedings of the 2017 Conference

on Empirical Methods in Natural Language Processing, EMNLP 2017, Copenhagen, Denmark, 9–11 September 2017, pp. 188–197. Association for Computational Linguistics (2017). https://doi.org/10.18653/v1/d17-1018
16. Lee, K., He, L., Zettlemoyer, L.: Higher-order coreference resolution with coarse-to-fine inference. In: Walker, M.A., Ji, H., Stent, A. (eds.) Proceedings of the 2018 Conference of the North American Chapter of the Association for Computational Linguistics: Human Language Technologies, NAACL-HLT, New Orleans, Louisiana, USA, 1–6 June 2018, Volume 2 (Short Papers), pp. 687–692. Association for Computational Linguistics (2018). https://doi.org/10.18653/v1/n18-2108
17. Lupu, M., Mayer, K., Kando, N., Trippe, A.J.: Current Challenges in Patent Information Retrieval, vol. 37. Springer, Heidelberg (2017). https://doi.org/10.1007/978-3-662-53817-3
18. Muresan, S., et al.: Making every SAR point count: the development of Chemistry Connect for the large-scale integration of structure and bioactivity data. Drug Discovery Today **16**(23–24), 1019–1030 (2011)
19. Ng, V.: Machine learning for entity coreference resolution: a retrospective look at two decades of research. In: Singh, S.P., Markovitch, S. (eds.) Proceedings of the Thirty-First AAAI Conference on Artificial Intelligence, 4–9 February 2017, San Francisco, California, USA, pp. 4877–4884. AAAI Press (2017). http://aaai.org/ocs/index.php/AAAI/AAAI17/paper/view/14995
20. Nguyen, D.Q., et al.: ChEMU: named entity recognition and event extraction of chemical reactions from patents. In: Jose, J.M., et al. (eds.) ECIR 2020. LNCS, vol. 12036, pp. 572–579. Springer, Cham (2020). https://doi.org/10.1007/978-3-030-45442-5_74
21. Nguyen, N., Kim, J.D., Tsujii, J.: Overview of BioNLP 2011 protein coreference shared task. In: Proceedings of BioNLP Shared Task 2011 Workshop, pp. 74–82 (2011)
22. Ohta, T., Tateisi, Y., Kim, J.D., Mima, H., Tsujii, J.: The GENIA corpus: an annotated research abstract corpus in molecular biology domain. In: Proceedings of the Second International Conference on Human Language Technology Research, pp. 82–86 (2002)
23. Pradhan, S., Moschitti, A., Xue, N., Uryupina, O., Zhang, Y.: CoNLL-2012 shared task: modeling multilingual unrestricted coreference in ontonotes. In: Pradhan, S., Moschitti, A., Xue, N. (eds.) Joint Conference on Empirical Methods in Natural Language Processing and Computational Natural Language Learning - Proceedings of the Shared Task: Modeling Multilingual Unrestricted Coreference in OntoNotes, EMNLP-CoNLL 2012, 13 July 2012, Jeju Island, Korea, pp. 1–40. ACL (2012). https://www.aclweb.org/anthology/W12-4501/
24. Senger, S., Bartek, L., Papadatos, G., Gaulton, A.: Managing expectations: assessment of chemistry databases generated by automated extraction of chemical structures from patents. J. Cheminf. **7**(1), 1–12 (2015)
25. Verspoor, K., et al.: ChEMU dataset for information extraction from chemical patents (2020) https://doi.org/10.17632/wy6745bjfj
26. Zhai, Z., et al.: Improving chemical named entity recognition in patents with contextualized word embeddings. In: Proceedings of the 18th BioNLP Workshop and Shared Task, pp. 328–338. Association for Computational Linguistics, Florence, Italy, August 2019. https://doi.org/10.18653/v1/W19-5035

Overview of the CLEF eHealth Evaluation Lab 2021

Hanna Suominen[1,2,3](✉), Lorraine Goeuriot[4], Liadh Kelly[5], Laura Alonso Alemany[6], Elias Bassani[7,8], Nicola Brew-Sam[1], Viviana Cotik[9,10], Darío Filippo[11], Gabriela González-Sáez[4], Franco Luque[6,12], Philippe Mulhem[4], Gabriella Pasi[7], Roland Roller[13], Sandaru Seneviratne[1], Rishabh Upadhyay[7], Jorge Vivaldi[14], Marco Viviani[7], and Chenchen Xu[1,2]

[1] The Australian National University, Canberra, ACT, Australia
{hanna.suominen,nicola.brew-sam,sandaru.seneviratne, chenchen.xu}@anu.edu.au

[2] Data61/Commonwealth Scientific and Industrial Research Organisation, Canberra, ACT, Australia

[3] University of Turku, Turku, Finland

[4] Université Grenoble Alpes, CNRS, Grenoble INP, LIG, 38000 Grenoble, France
lorraine.goeuriot@imag.fr

[5] Maynooth University, Maynooth, Ireland
liadh.kelly@mu.ie

[6] Universidad Nacional de Córdoba, Córdoba, Argentina
{lauraalonsoalemany,francolq}@unc.edu.ar

[7] University of Milano-Bicocca, DISCo, Milan, Italy
{gabriella.pasi,rishabh.upadhyay,marco.viviani}@unimib.it

[8] Consorzio per il Trasferimento Tecnologico - C2T, Milan, Italy
elias.bassani@consorzioc2t.it

[9] Departamento de Computación, FCEyN, Universidad de Buenos Aires, Buenos Aires, Argentina
vcotik@dc.uba.ar

[10] Instituto de Investigación en Ciencias de la Computación (ICC), CONICET-UBA, Buenos Aires, Argentina

[11] Hospital de Pediatría 'Prof. Dr. Juan P. Garrahan', Buenos Aires, Argentina

[12] CONICET, Buenos Aires, Argentina

[13] German Research Center for Artificial Intelligence (DFKI), Bremen, Germany
roland.roller@dfki.de

[14] Institut de Lingüística Aplicada, Universitat Pompeu Fabra, Barcelona, Spain
jorge.vivaldi@upf.edu

Abstract. In this paper, we provide an overview of the ninth annual edition of the CLEF eHealth evaluation lab. CLEF eHealth 2021 continues our evaluation resource building efforts around the easing and support of patients, their next-of-kins, health care professionals, and health

With equal contribution, HS, LG & LK co-chaired the lab. Task 1 was led by VC and LAA, and organized by LAA, VC, DF, FL, RR, and JV; Task 2 was led by LG, GP, and HS, and organized by EB, NB-S, LG, GG-S, LK, PM, GP, HS, SS, RU, MV, and CX.

K. S. Candan et al. (Eds.): CLEF 2021, LNCS 12880, pp. 308–323, 2021.
https://doi.org/10.1007/978-3-030-85251-1_21

scientists in understanding, accessing, and authoring electronic health information in a multilingual setting. The 2021 lab offered two tasks: Task 1 on multilingual Information Extraction (IE), this year extending to a corpus of Spanish radiology reports; and Task 2 on Consumer Health Search (CHS) that builds on the previous year's Information Retrieval (IR) tasks. In total, 11 teams took part in these tasks (7 in Task 1 on IE and 4 in Task 2 on IR). Herein, we describe the resources created for these tasks and the evaluation methodology adopted, and we provide a brief summary of the participants of this year's challenges as well as the results obtained. As in previous years, the organizers have made data, tools, and more specific overview papers associated with the lab tasks available for future research and development.

Keywords: Entity linking · Evaluation · Health records · Information extraction · Information retrieval · Medical informatics · Self-diagnosis · Test-set generation · Text classification · Text segmentation

1 Introduction

In recent years, electronic health (eHealth) content has become available in a variety of forms, ranging from patient records and medical dossiers, scientific publications, and health-related websites to medical-related topics shared across social networks. Laypeople, clinicians, and policy-makers need to easily retrieve and make sense of such medical content to support their clinical judgement and decision-making. The increasing difficulties experienced by these stakeholders in retrieving and digesting valid and relevant information in their preferred language to make health-centred decisions has motivated CLEF eHealth to organise yearly shared challenges since 2013.

More specifically, CLEF eHealth[1] was established as a lab workshop in 2012 as part of the Conference and Labs of the Evaluation Forum (CLEF, formerly known as Cross-Language Evaluation Forum). Since 2013 it has offered evaluation labs in the fields of layperson and professional health information extraction (IE), management, and retrieval (IR) with the aims of bringing together researchers working on related information access topics and providing them with datasets to work with and validate the outcomes. These labs and their subsequent workshops target:

1. developing processing methods and resources (e.g., dictionaries, abbreviation mappings, and data with model solutions for method development and evaluation) in a multilingual setting:
   (a) to enrich difficult-to-understand eHealth texts,
   (b) to provide personalized reliable access to medical information, and
   (c) to provide valuable documentation;

[1] https://clefehealth.imag.fr/.

2. developing an evaluation setting and releasing evaluation results for these methods and resources;
3. contributing to the participants and organizers' professional networks and interaction with all interdisciplinary actors of the ecosystem for producing, processing, and consuming eHealth information.

The vision for the Lab is two-fold: (1) to develop tasks that potentially impact patient understanding of medical information and (2) to provide the community with an increasingly sophisticated dataset of clinical narratives, enriched with links to standard knowledge bases, evidence-based care guidelines, systematic reviews, and other further information, to advance the state-of-the-art in multilingual IE and IR in health care.

The ninth annual CLEF eHealth evaluation lab, CLEF eHealth 2021, aiming to build upon the resource development and evaluation approaches proposed in the previous years of the lab [10,11,15,18–20,39,40], offered the following two tasks:

- *Task 1.* Multilingual IE [3] and
- *Task 2.* Consumer Health Search (CHS) [16].

The *Multilingual IE* task builds upon the six previous editions of the task (2015–2020) which already addressed the analysis of biomedical text in English, French, Hungarian, Italian, Spanish, and German [25,27–31]. This year, the task focuses on Named Entity Recognition in Spanish ultrasound reports. Ten different classes of concepts in the radiology domain are distinguished, including Anatomical Entities, and Findings, that describe a pathological or abnormal event, negations, and indicators of probability or future outcomes. As well as complex entities, the task includes the challenge of semantic split of the dataset. That is, training, development, and test sets cover different semantic fields. This allows for a more realistic held-out evaluation.

The *Consumer Health Search* task is a continuation of the previous CLEF eHealth IR tasks that ran in 2013–2018, and 2020 [7–9,14,17,33,34,42]. It embraces the Text REtrieval Conference (TREC) -style evaluation process, with a shared collection of documents and queries, the contribution of runs from participants and the subsequent formation of relevance assessments and evaluation of the participants submissions. The 2021 task generates a new representative web corpus and collection of layperson medical queries. The task is structured into a number of optional subtasks as follows: (1) ad-hoc search, (2) weakly-supervised IR, and (3) document credibility assessment.

The remainder of this paper is structured as follows: in Sect. 2, we detail the tasks, evaluation, and datasets created; in Sect. 3, we describe the submission and results for each task; and in Sect. 4, we provide conclusions.

2 Materials and Methods

In this section, we describe the materials and methods used in the two tasks of the CLEF eHealth evaluation lab 2021. After specifying our text documents to process in Sect. 2.1, we address the human annotations, queries, and relevance assessments in Sect. 2.2. Finally, in Sect. 2.3, we introduce our evaluation methods.

2.1 Text Documents

Task 1. The dataset for this task consists of a corpus of Spanish radiology reports, more concretely pediatric ultrasounds from an Argentinian public hospital. These reports are generally written within a hospital information system by direct typing in a computer and are informed in only one section, where the most relevant findings are described. They are written using standard templates that guide physicians on the structure of the report when the findings are normal, but most of the time they are written in free text to be able to describe the findings discovered in abnormal studies. This fact results in great variations in both size and content of the reports, ranging from 8 to 193 words. Also, there are misspellings and inconsistencies in the usage of abbreviations, punctuation, and line breaks, as can be seen in Fig. 1.

```
2a.
HIGADO de forma, tamano y ecoestructura normal.
VIA BILIAR intra y extrahepatica: no dilatada.
VESICULA BILIAR: de paredes finas sin imagenes endoluminales.
BAZO: tamano y ecoestructura normal.
Diametro longitudinal: 6.89 ( cm ) RETROPERITONEO VASCULAR: sin
alteraciones.
No se detectaron adenomegalias.
Ambos rinones de formsa, tamano y situacion habitual.
Adecuada diferenciacion cortico-medular.
RD Diam Long: 5.8 cm RI Diam long: 6.1 cm Vejiga de caracteristicas
normales.
No se observo liquido libre en cavidad abdomino-pelviana.
```

2y.
LIVER of regular form, size and echostructure.
Intra and extrahepatic BILE DUCT: non-dilated.
GALLBLADDER: thin walls and no endoluminal images.
SPLEEN: regular size and echostructure.
Longitudinal diameter: 6.89 (cm) VASCULAR RETROPERITONEAL: no alterations.
No adenomegalies were found.
Both kidneys of regular form, size and location.
Adequate corticomedullary differentiation.
RK Long diam: 5.8 cm LK Long diam: 6.1 cm Bladder of regular characteristics.
No free liquid was observed within the abdomino-pelvian cavity.

Fig. 1. A sample report, with its translation. It shows abbreviations ("RD" for right kidney, "RI" for left kidney, "Diam" for diameter), typos ("formsa" for "forma"), and inconsistencies (capitalization of "Vejiga" because of start of sentence without a full stop).

Task 2. The document corpus used in the CHS task consists of web pages acquired from the CommonCrawl dump of 2021-04[2]. An initial list of websites was acquired from the 2018 CHS task which was built by submitting a set of medical queries to the Microsoft Bing Application Programming Interfaces (through the Azure Cognitive Services) repeatedly over a period of a few weeks, and acquiring the uniform resource Locators (URL) of the retrieved results. The domains of the acquired URLs were then included in the list, except some domains that were excluded for decency reasons. The list was augmented by including a number of known reliable and unreliable health websites, and social media contents of ranging reliability levels, from lists previously compiled by health institutions and agencies [17]. From this initial list of domains, a sample of domains was identified for final acquisition. This list was further extended by including websites, which were highly relevant for the task queries to create the final domain list with 600 domains. This introduced 13 new domains compared to the 2018 collection, and all domains were newly crawled from the latest CommonCrawl 2021-04.

The corpus was complemented with social media documents from *Reddit* and *Twitter*. A list of 150 health topics related to various health conditions was selected. Search queries were manually generated from those topics and were submitted to Reddit to retrieve posts and comments. The same process was applied on Twitter to get related tweets from the platform. A social media document was defined as a text obtained by a single interaction, therefore for Reddit one document is composed by a post, one comment of the post and associated meta-information. For Twitter, a document is a single tweet with its associated meta-information.

2.2 Human Annotations, Queries, and Relevance Assessments

Task 1. The radiology text data is annotated with seven different classes of entities: *Finding, Anatomical Entity, Location, Measure, Degree, Type of Measure* and *Abbreviation.* Additionally, hedges are also identified, distinguishing *Negation, Uncertainty and Conditional Temporal.* An example annotation can be found in Fig. 2, and the frequency of each type of entity can be seen in Fig. 3.

The phenomena under study have some challenging properties. For example, entities can be embedded within other entities. Moreover, entities can be discontinuous, and they can even span over sentence boundaries. The entity type *Finding* is particularly challenging, as it presents great variability in its textual forms. It ranges from a single word to more than ten words in some cases, comprising all kinds of phrases. However, this is also the most informative type of entity for the potential users of these annotations. Another challenging phenomena is the regular polysemy observed between *Anatomical entities* and *Locations.* In the manual annotation process, we have found that human annotators have less agreement on those categories than on the rest, and automatic classifiers also experience difficulties to consistently classify those as well.

[2] https://commoncrawl.org/2021/02/january-2021-crawl-archive-now-available/.

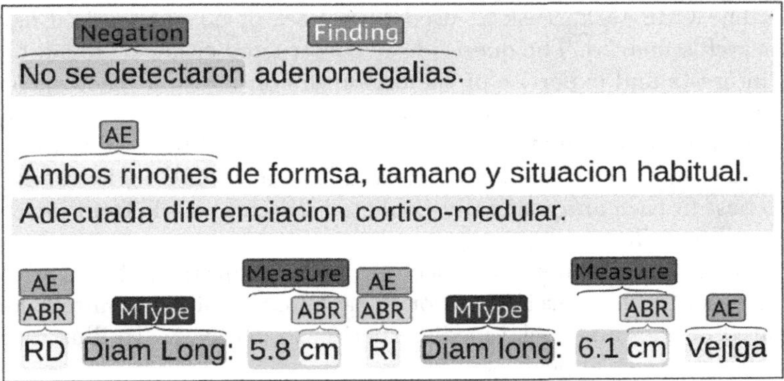

Fig. 2. A snippet of the report in Fig. 1, with manual annotations. Abbreviations: AE—Anatomical Entity, ABR—Abbreviation, MType—Type of Measure.

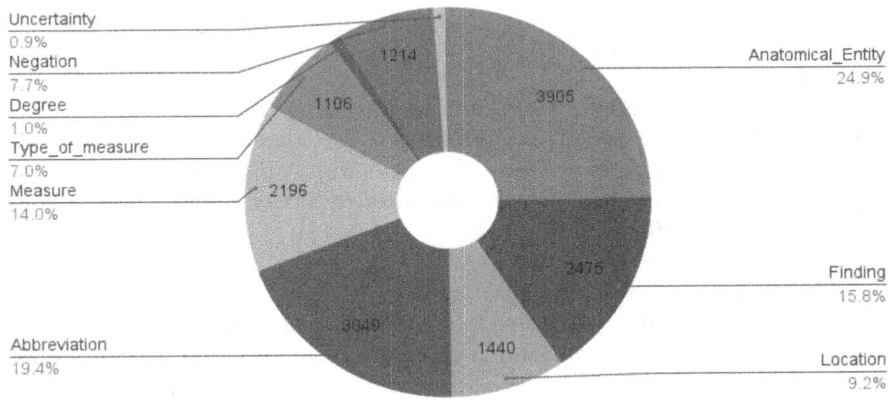

Fig. 3. Number and frequency of occurrences of the different kinds of entities in the annotated dataset for Task 1.

The given corpus consists of a total of 513 ultrasound reports, with 35,000 words and over 15,000 annotated named entities. In order to assess the portability of the approaches, half of the reports were provided as training, and the other half for testing, making sure that the testing partition contained portions of text that belonged to previously unseen phenomena. Reports were manually annotated by clinical experts [4] and then revised by linguists. Annotation guidelines and training were provided for both rounds of annotation. More information about the dataset can be found in [4]. Nevertheless, for the challenge the annotation criteria has been reviewed and some annotations have been modified.

The task, called SpRadIE (for Spanish Radiology Information Extraction), was inspired by previous research on this subject [2,5].

Task 2. The CHS task, Task 2, used a new set of 55 queries in English for realistic search scenarios. The queries were constructed either by hand, based on research interests and expertise of the organizers on multiple sclerosis and diabetes, or by using searches issued by the public to social media search services. Namely, the queries were manually authored and tailored by experts from established search scenarios and manually selected from a list of Google trends related queries to best fit each automatically extracted search scenario from social media (e.g., Twitter and Reddit).

Each query was manually labelled by the organizers with a narrative in English to describe the search intent or to capture the submission text for manually created queries and social medial queries, respectively. To illustrate, some queries and narratives appear as follows:

- Scenario 22:
  - Query: *my risk for developing type 2 diabetes*
  - Narrative: *You read that the risk for developing type 2 diabetes is increasing due to environmental and lifestyle factors, and you want to know more about your own risk.*
- Scenario 68:
  - Query: *List of multiple sclerosis symptoms*
  - Narrative: *I am a 40 year old patient with MS, and I have very vage symptoms, including fatigue, brain fog, foot drop, difficulties passing urine, problems turning right. Are these related to MS or might I have another disease in addition?*
- Scenario 105:
  - Query: *wisdom tooth cuts gum pain*
  - Narrative: *Hi all My wisdom tooth is currently cutting it's way through my bottom right gum the pain is intense throbbing aching jaw and weirdly a sore throat especially when swallowing. I just wonder if this is normal as I've had two wisdom tooth come through before with no pain at all. Thank you!*

People with lived experience of the related medical conditions were consulted to motivate, validate, and refine the narratives. Furthermore, the queries were enriched by the organizers to have a theme (manually created ones) or name (social media) to ease classifying them, but these were neither released to the participants nor used for evaluation.

The subtasks 1, 2, and 3 used these 55 queries with 5 released for training and 50 reserved for testing; the test topics contained a balanced sample of the manually constructed and automatically extracted search scenarios.

Relevance assessments are currently in progress and will be detailed in the CHS task overview [16]. Similar to the 2016 and 2017 pools, we created the pool using the rank-biased precision (RBP)-based Method A (Summing contributions) [26] in which documents are weighted according to their overall contribution to the effectiveness evaluation as provided by the RBP formula (with $p = 0.8$, following a study published in 2007 on RBP [35]). This strategy, named RBPA has been proven more efficient than traditional fixed-depth or stratified pooling to evaluate systems under fixed assessment budget constraints [22], as it is the case for this task. All participants' runs were considered on the document's pool, along with six baselines provided by the organizers. In order to guarantee the judgements of the documents of the participants' runs, half of the pool is composed by their documents and half from documents of the baselines' runs.

Along with relevance assessments, readability and credibility judgments were also collected for the assessment pool; these were used to evaluate systems across different dimensions of relevance (see [12] for further information about the three dimensions).

The relevance, readability, and credibility assessments were performed by 26 volunteers in May–June 2021. Of these assessors, 16 were from Australia, 1 from Finland, 3 from France, 2 from Ireland, and 4 from Italy. The numbers of female and male assessors were 19 and 7, respectively. All assessors were recruited, trained, and supervised by the organizers by using bespoke written materials from April to June 2021. The recruitment took place on social media and via email, using both organizers' existing contacts and snowballing.

Assessments were implemented online by the organizers' expanding and customising the Relevation! tool for relevance assessments [21] to capture our task dimensions, scales, and other preferences (Figs. 4, 5, and 6). Each assessor was initially assigned 2 queries to be assessed, and in the end, every assessor completed 1 to 4 queries. Each query was associated with 250 documents to be assessed with respect to their relevance, readability, and credibility.

Ethical approval (2021/013) was obtained from the Human Research Ethics Committee of the Australian National University. Each study participant provided informed consent.

2.3 Evaluation Methods

Task 1. Participants could submit up to 4 runs. Lenient and exact match precision, recall, and F1 score were calculated. Submissions were evaluated with micro-averaged lenient match F1. The lenient match is calculated using the Jaccard Index, as described in [13] and based on [1].

Task 2. For Subtasks 1, 2, and 3, participants could submit up to 4 runs in TREC format. Evaluation measures for Subtask 1, adhoc search task are Normalized Discounted Cumulative Gain (NDCG) at 10 (NDCG@10), BPref, and RBP, as well as other metrics adapted to other relevance dimensions such

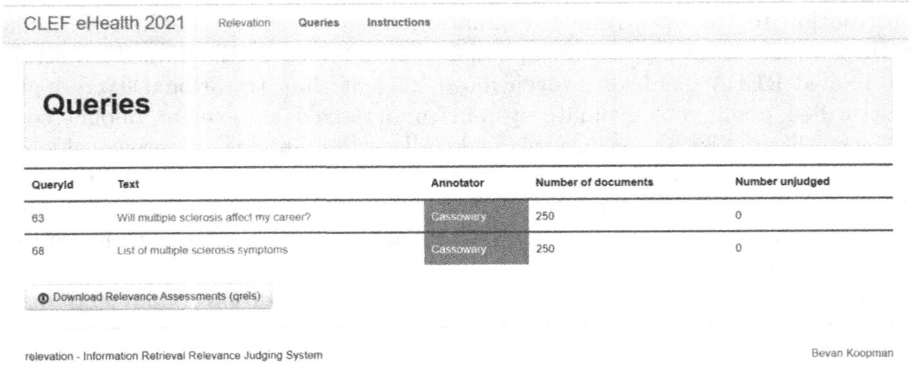

Fig. 4. CLEF eHealth consumer health search task 2021: assessor's landing page

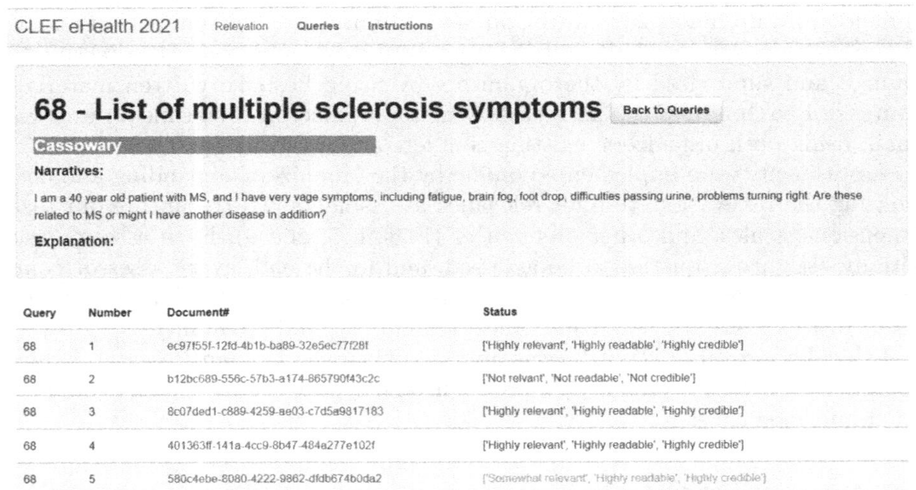

Fig. 5. CLEF eHealth consumer health search task 2021: assessor's documents for a given query

as uRBP and cRBP (with alpha value capturing the user expertise), an adapted metric to measure credibility relevance dimension based on uRBP. Subtask 3 used F1, Area under the receiver operating characteristic Curve (AUC), and Accuracy to measure a given system's ability to predict document credibility.

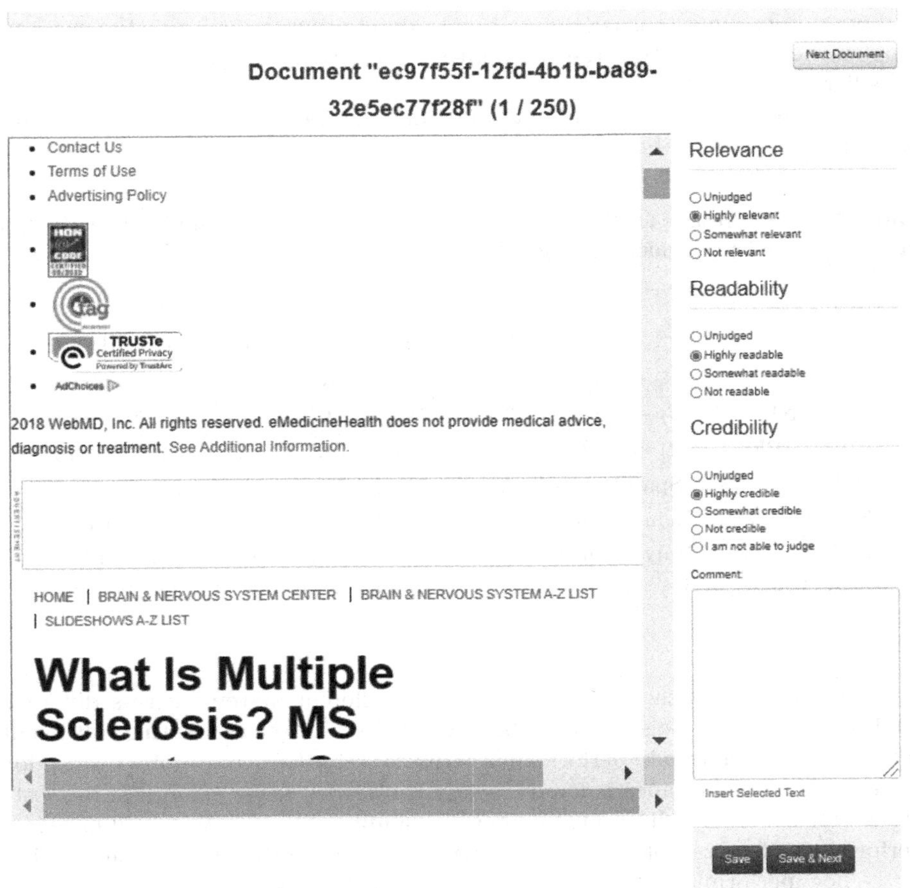

Fig. 6. CLEF eHealth consumer health search task 2021: assessor's document view

3 Results

The number of teams who registered their interest in CLEF eHealth 2021 Tasks 1 and 2 was 58 and 43 (and a total of 67 unique teams). In total, 7 and 4 teams submitted to the two shared tasks, respectively.

Task 1. Overall seven different teams participated in our shared task. Most prominent were participants from Spain, but also from Italy, UK and Colombia. Most participating teams were experimenting with different variations of neural networks, particularly transformer-based approaches [23,36,37,41], but also bi-LSTMs [6]. Besides the challenge also includes submissions of a CRF [24], and a pattern based approach [32]. Overall, overlapping and discontinuous entities of the given dataset were the biggest challenge of the dataset, which made pre-

and post-processing steps necessary. Moreover, in order to deal with the overlapping entities appropriately, the two highest scored teams make usage of multiple classifiers.

Table 1 shows the best result of each team's run. Best lenient precision, recall, and F1 are written in bold.

Table 1. Overall results for the best performing system for each team on the SpRadIE task, sorted by lenient micro-averaged F1.

Team	Lenient			Exact		
	PREC	REC	F1	PREC	REC	F1
EdIE (UnEd, UK) – run2	87.24	**83.85**	**85.51**	81.88	78.70	80.26
LSI (UNED, Spain) – run1	**90.28**	78.33	83.88	86.17	74.76	80.07
CTB (UPM, Spain) – run3	78.62	78.32	78.47	73.27	72.99	73.13
HULAT (UC3M, Spain) – run1	78.38	73.08	75.64	67.28	62.73	64.92
SINAI (UJaen, Spain) – run2	86.07	64.43	73.70	79.37	59.42	67.96
SWAP (UniBA, Italy) – run1	70.18	51.14	59.17	56.75	41.35	47.84
IMS (UniPD, Italy) – run1	9.29	57.62	16.00	5.45	33.77	9.38

The variation of the performance of the different systems across different kinds of entities can be seen in the boxplots in Fig. 7. We can see that, although there is much variation in performance across systems (hence the long boxes), for some entities performance is lower, mostly those with fewer examples. Interestingly, types of entity with a big number of examples, like Location, still have low performance, for example, if compared with Anatomical Entities. It is interesting to see how performance for Abbreviations is very varied across approaches.

Task 2 had 4 teams submitting runs: In Subtask 2.1 on Ad Hoc IR, a 4-member team from the School of Computer Science, Zhongyuan University of Technology (ZUT) in Zhengzhou, China and a team with two members from the Information Management Systems (IMS) Research Group of the Italian University of Padova (UniPd) submitted runs. In Subtasks 2.2 on Weakly Supervised IR and 2.3 on Document Credibility Prediction, the leader of this IMS UniPd team, who has been a regular participant in previous CLEF eHealth IR tasks, submitted runs. Participants submissions were due by May 8th 2021 and the relevance assessments are being collected at the time of writing of this paper. See the Task 2 overview paper for further details and the results of the evaluation [16].

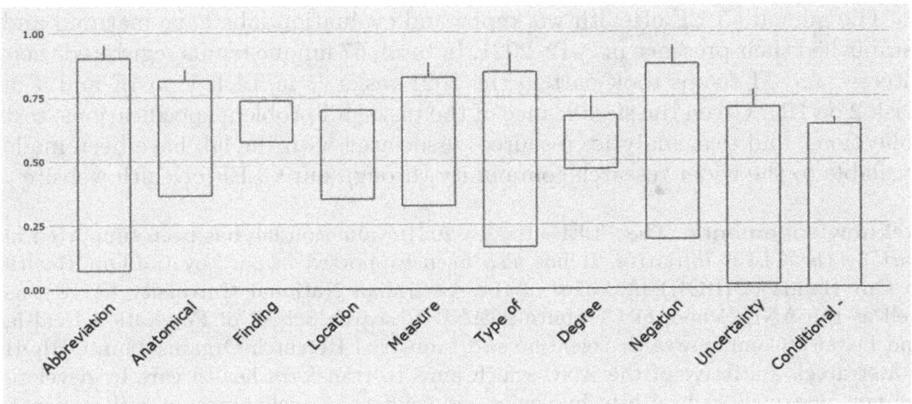

Fig. 7. Variation in the performance of different systems across different kinds of entities.

4 Conclusions

This paper provided an overview of the CLEF eHealth 2021 evaluation lab. The CLEF eHealth workshop series was established in 2012 as a scientific workshop with an aim of establishing an evaluation lab [38]. Since 2013, this annual workshop has been supplemented with two or more preceding shared tasks each year. In other words, they are the CLEF eHealth 2013–2020 evaluation labs [10,11,15,18–20,39,40]. These labs have offered a recurring contribution to the creation and dissemination of text analytics resources, methods, test collections, and evaluation benchmarks in order to ease and support patients, their next-of-kins, clinical staff, and health scientists in understanding, accessing, and authoring eHealth information in a multilingual setting.

In 2021, the CLEF eHealth lab offered two shared task. The first task was on multilingual IE and the second task was on CHS. These tasks built on the IE and IR tasks offered by the CLEF eHealth lab series since its inception in 2013. Test collections generated by these shared tasks offered a specific task definition, implemented in a dataset distributed together with an implementation of relevant evaluation metrics to allow for direct comparability of the results reported by the systems evaluated on the collections. These established CLEF IE and IR tasks used a traditional shared task model for evaluation in which a community-wide evaluation is executed in a controlled setting: independent training and test datasets were used and all participants gained access to the test data at the same time, following which no further updates to systems were allowed. Shortly after releasing the test data (without labels or other solutions), the participating teams submitted their outputs from the frozen systems to the task organizers, who evaluated these results and reported the resulting benchmarks to the community.

The annual CLEF eHealth workhops and evaluation labs have matured and established their presence in 2012–2021. In total, 67 unique teams registered their interest and 11 teams took part in the 2021 tasks (7 in Task 1 on IE and 4 in Task 2 on IR). Given the significance of the tasks, all problem specifications, test collections, and text analytics resources associated with the lab have been made available to the wider research community through our CLEF eHealth website[3].

Acknowledgements. The CLEF eHealth 2021 evaluation lab has been supported in part by the CLEF Initiative. It has also been supported in part by the Our Health in Our Hands (OHIOH) initiative of the Australian National University (ANU), as well as the ANU School of Computing, ANU Research School of Population Health, and Data61/Commonwealth Scientific and Industrial Research Organisation. OHIOH is a strategic initiative of the ANU which aims to transform health care by developing new personalised health technologies and solutions in collaboration with patients, clinicians, and health care providers. Moreover, the lab has been supported in part by the bi-lateral Kodicare (Knowledge Delta based improvement and continuous evaluation of retrieval engines) project funded by the French ANR (ANR-19-CE23-0029) and Austrian FWF. We are also thankful to the people involved in the annotation, query creation, and relevance assessment exercises. Last but not least, we gratefully acknowledge the participating teams' hard work. We thank them for their submissions and interest in the lab.

References

1. Bossy, R., Golik, W., Ratkovic, Z., Bessières, P., Nédellec, C.: BioNLP shared task 2013—an overview of the Bacteria Biotope task. In: Proceedings of the BioNLP Shared Task 2013 Workshop, pp. 161–169. Association for Computational Linguistics, Sofia, August 2013. https://www.aclweb.org/anthology/W13-2024
2. Cotik, V.: Information extraction from Spanish radiology reports. Ph.D. thesis (2018)
3. Cotik, V., et al.: Overview of CLEF eHealth Task 1 - SpRadIE: a challenge on information extraction from Spanish Radiology Reports. In: CLEF 2021 Evaluation Labs and Workshop: Online Working Notes. CEUR-WS, September 2021
4. Cotik, V., Filippo, D., Roller, R., Uszkoreit, H., Xu, F.: Annotation of entities and relations in spanish radiology reports. In: Proceedings of the International Conference Recent Advances in Natural Language Processing, RANLP 2017, pp. 177–184 (2017)
5. Cotik, V., Rodríguez, H., Vivaldi, J.: Spanish named entity recognition in the biomedical domain. In: Lossio-Ventura, J.A., Muñante, D., Alatrista-Salas, H. (eds.) SIMBig 2018. CCIS, vol. 898, pp. 233–248. Springer, Cham (2019). https://doi.org/10.1007/978-3-030-11680-4_23
6. Fabregat, H., Duque, A., Araujo, L., Martinez-Romo, J.: LSI_UNED at CLEF eHealth2021: exploring the effects of transfer learning in negation detection and entity recognition in clinical texts. In: CLEF eHealth 2021. CLEF 2021 Evaluation Labs and Workshop: Online Working Notes. CEUR-WS (2021)
7. Goeuriot, L., et al.: ShARe/CLEF eHealth Evaluation Lab 2013, task 3: information retrieval to address patients' questions when reading clinical reports. CLEF 2013 Online Working Notes 8138 (2013)

[3] http://clef-ehealth.org/.

8. Goeuriot, L., et al.: An Analysis of evaluation campaigns in ad-hoc medical information retrieval: CLEF eHealth 2013 and 2014. Inf. Retrieval J. **21**, 507–540 (2018)
9. Goeuriot, L., et al.: ShARe/CLEF eHealth Evaluation Lab 2014, task 3: user-centred health information retrieval. In: CLEF 2014 Evaluation Labs and Workshop: Online Working Notes. Sheffield, UK (2014)
10. Goeuriot, L., et al.: Overview of the CLEF eHealth evaluation lab 2015. In: Mothe, J., et al. (eds.) Experimental IR Meets Multilinguality, Multimodality, and Interaction. CLEF 2015. LNCS, vol. 9283, pp. 429–443. Springer, Cham (2015). https://doi.org/10.1007/978-3-319-24027-5_44
11. Goeuriot, L., et al.: CLEF 2017 eHealth evaluation lab overview. In: Jones, G.J.F., et al. (eds.) CLEF 2017. LNCS, vol. 10456, pp. 291–303. Springer, Cham (2017). https://doi.org/10.1007/978-3-319-65813-1_26
12. Goeuriot, L., Liu, Z., Pasi, G., Saez, G.G., Viviani, M., Xu, C.: Overview of the CLEF eHealth 2020 task 2: consumer health search with ad hoc and spoken queries. In: Working Notes of Conference and Labs of the Evaluation (CLEF) Forum. CEUR Workshop Proceedings (2020)
13. Goeuriot, L., et al.: CLEF eHealth evaluation lab 2021. In: Hiemstra, D., Moens, M.-F., Mothe, J., Perego, R., Potthast, M., Sebastiani, F. (eds.) ECIR 2021. LNCS, vol. 12657, pp. 593–600. Springer, Cham (2021). https://doi.org/10.1007/978-3-030-72240-1_69
14. Goeuriot, L., et al.: Overview of the CLEF eHealth 2020 task 2: consumer health search with ad hoc and spoken queries. In: Working Notes of Conference and Labs of the Evaluation (CLEF) Forum. CEUR Workshop Proceedings (2020)
15. Goeuriot, L., et al.: Overview of the CLEF eHealth evaluation lab 2020. In: Arampatzis, A., et al. (eds.) CLEF 2020. LNCS, vol. 12260, pp. 255–271. Springer, Cham (2020). https://doi.org/10.1007/978-3-030-58219-7_19
16. Goeuriot, L., et al.: Consumer health search at CLEF eHealth 2021. In: CLEF 2021 Evaluation Labs and Workshop: Online Working Notes. CEUR-WS, September 2021
17. Jimmy, J., Zuccon, G., Palotti, J.: Overview of the CLEF 2018 consumer health search task. In: Working Notes of Conference and Labs of the Evaluation (CLEF) Forum. CEUR Workshop Proceedings (2018)
18. Kelly, L., Goeuriot, L., Suominen, H., Névéol, A., Palotti, J., Zuccon, G.: Overview of the CLEF eHealth evaluation lab 2016. In: Fuhr, N., et al. (eds.) CLEF 2016. LNCS, vol. 9822, pp. 255–266. Springer, Cham (2016). https://doi.org/10.1007/978-3-319-44564-9_24
19. Kelly, L., et al.: Overview of the ShARe/CLEF eHealth evaluation lab 2014. In: Kanoulas, E., et al. (eds.) CLEF 2014. LNCS, vol. 8685, pp. 172–191. Springer, Cham (2014). https://doi.org/10.1007/978-3-319-11382-1_17
20. Kelly, L., et al.: Overview of the CLEF eHealth evaluation lab 2019. In: Crestani, F., et al. (eds.) CLEF 2019. LNCS, vol. 11696, pp. 322–339. Springer, Cham (2019). https://doi.org/10.1007/978-3-030-28577-7_26
21. Koopman, B., Zuccon, G.: Relevation!: an open source system for information retrieval relevance assessment. In: Proceedings of the 37th international ACM SIGIR conference on Research & development in information retrieval, pp. 1243–1244. ACM (2014)
22. Lipani, A., Palotti, J., Lupu, M., Piroi, F., Zuccon, G., Hanbury, A.: Fixed-cost pooling strategies based on IR evaluation measures. In: Jose, J.M., et al. (eds.) ECIR 2017. LNCS, vol. 10193, pp. 357–368. Springer, Cham (2017). https://doi.org/10.1007/978-3-319-56608-5_28

23. López-Úbeda, P., Díaz-Galiano, M.C., Ureña-López, L.A., Martín-Valdivia, M.T.: Pre-trained language models to extract information from radiological reports. In: CLEF eHealth 2021. CLEF 2021 Evaluation Labs and Workshop: Online Working Notes, CEUR-WS (2021)
24. Ángel Martín-Caro García-Largo, M., Bedmar, I.S.: Extracting information from radiology reports by natural language processing and deep learning. In: CLEF eHealth 2021. CLEF 2021 Evaluation Labs and Workshop: Online Working Notes, CEUR-WS (2021)
25. Miranda-Escalada, A., Gonzalez-Agirre, A., Armengol-Estapé, J., Krallinger, M.: Overview of automatic clinical coding: annotations, guidelines, and solutions for non-English clinical cases at CodiEsp track of CLEF eHealth 2020. In: Working Notes of Conference and Labs of the Evaluation (CLEF) Forum. CEUR Workshop Proceedings (2020)
26. Moffat, A., Zobel, J.: Rank-biased precision for measurement of retrieval effectiveness. ACM Trans. Inf. Syst. **27**(1), 2:1-2:27 (2008). https://doi.org/10.1145/1416950.1416952
27. Névéol, A., et al.: Clinical information extraction at the CLEF eHealth evaluation lab 2016. In: Balog, K., Cappellato, L., Ferro, N., Macdonald, C. (eds.) CLEF 2016 Working Notes. CEUR Workshop Proceedings (CEUR-WS.org) (2016). ISSN 1613-0073. http://ceur-ws.org/Vol-1609/
28. Névéol, A., et al.: CLEF eHealth 2017 multilingual information extraction task overview: ICD10 coding of death certificates in English and French. In: CLEF 2017 Online Working Notes. CEUR-WS (2017)
29. Névéol, A., et al.: CLEF eHealth evaluation lab 2015 task 1b: clinical named entity recognition. In: CLEF 2015 Online Working Notes. CEUR-WS (2015)
30. Névéol, A., et al.: CLEF eHealth 2018 multilingual information extraction task overview: ICD10 coding of death certificates in French, Hungarian and Italian. In: CLEF 2018 Online Working Notes. CEUR-WS (2018)
31. Neves, M., et al.: Overview of task 1 in CLEF eHealth 2019: indexing German non-technical summaries of animal experiments. In: CLEF 2019 Online Working Notes. CEUR-WS (2019)
32. Nunzio, G.M.D.: IMS-UNIPD @ CLEF eHealth task 1: a memory based reproducible baseline. In: CLEF eHealth 2021. CLEF 2021 Evaluation Labs and Workshop: Online Working Notes. CEUR-WS (2021)
33. Palotti, J., et al.: CLEF eHealth evaluation lab 2015, task 2: retrieving information about medical symptoms. In: CLEF 2015 Online Working Notes. CEUR-WS (2015)
34. Palotti, J., et al.: CLEF 2017 task overview: the IR task at the ehealth evaluation lab. In: Working Notes of Conference and Labs of the Evaluation (CLEF) Forum. CEUR Workshop Proceedings (2017)
35. Park, L.A., Zhang, Y.: On the distribution of user persistence for rank-biased precision. In: Proceedings of the 12th Australasian Document Computing Symposium, pp. 17–24 (2007)
36. Polignano, M., de Gemmis, M., Semeraro, G.: Comparing transformer-based NER approaches for analysing textual medical diagnoses. In: CLEF eHealth 2021. CLEF 2021 Evaluation Labs and Workshop: Online Working Notes. CEUR-WS (2021)
37. Solarte-Pabón, O., Montenegro, O., Blazquez-Herranz, A., Saputro, H., Rodriguez-González, A., Menasalvas, E.: Information extraction from Spanish radiology reports using multilingual BERT. In: CLEF eHealth 2021. CLEF 2021 Evaluation Labs and Workshop: Online Working Notes. CEUR-WS (2021)

38. Suominen, H.: CLEFeHealth2012—the CLEF 2012 workshop on cross-language evaluation of methods, applications, and resources for ehealth document analysis. In: Forner, P., Karlgren, J., Womser-Hacker, C., Ferro, N. (eds.) CLEF 2012 Working Notes, vol. 1178. CEUR Workshop Proceedings (CEUR-WS.org) (2012)
39. Suominen, H., et al.: Overview of the CLEF eHealth evaluation lab 2018. In: Bellot, P., et al. (eds.) CLEF 2018. LNCS, vol. 11018, pp. 286–301. Springer, Heidelberg (2018). https://doi.org/10.1007/978-3-319-98932-7_26
40. Suominen, H., et al.: Overview of the ShARe/CLEF eHealth evaluation lab 2013. In: Forner, P., Müller, H., Paredes, R., Rosso, P., Stein, B. (eds.) CLEF 2013. LNCS, vol. 8138, pp. 212–231. Springer, Heidelberg (2013). https://doi.org/10.1007/978-3-642-40802-1_24
41. Suárez-Paniagua, V., Dong, H., Casey, A.: A multi-BERT hybrid system for named entity recognition in spanish radiology reports. In: CLEF eHealth 2021. CLEF 2021 Evaluation Labs and Workshop: Online Working Notes. CEUR-WS (2021)
42. Zuccon, G., et al.: The IR task at the CLEF eHealth evaluation lab 2016: user-centred health information retrieval. In: CLEF 2016 Evaluation Labs and Workshop: Online Working Notes. CEUR-WS, September 2016

Overview of eRisk 2021: Early Risk Prediction on the Internet

Javier Parapar[1(✉)], Patricia Martín-Rodilla[1], David E. Losada[2], and Fabio Crestani[3]

[1] Information Retrieval Lab, Centro de Investigación en Tecnoloxías da Información e as Comunicacións (CITIC), Universidade da Coruña, A Coruña, Spain
{javierparapar,patricia.martin.rodilla}@udc.es

[2] Centro Singular de Investigación en Tecnoloxías Intelixentes (CiTIUS), Universidade de Santiago de Compostela, Santiago de Compostela, Spain
david.losada@usc.es

[3] Faculty of Informatics, Universitá della Svizzera Italiana (USI), Lugano, Switzerland
fabio.crestani@usi.ch

Abstract. This paper gives an outline of eRisk 2021, the CLEF conference's fifth edition of this lab. The main goal of eRisk is to explore issues of evaluation methodology, effectiveness metrics and other processes related to early risk detection. Early alerting models may be used in a variety of situations, including those involving health and safety. This edition of eRisk had three tasks. The first task focused on early detecting signs of pathological gambling. The second challenge was to spot early signs of self-harm. The third required participants to fill out a depression questionnaire (automatically, based on user writings on social media).

Keywords: Early risk · Pathological gambling · Self-harm · Depression

1 Introduction

The primary goal of eRisk is to investigate topics such as evaluation methodologies, metrics, and other factors relevant to developing research collections and identifying problems for early risk identification. Early detection technologies have the potential to be useful in a variety of fields, especially those related to safety and health. Early alerts may be issued, for example, when a person begins to exhibit symptoms of a psychotic illness, when a sexual abuser begins interacting with an infant, or when a suspected criminal begins publishing antisocial threats on the Internet.

While the evaluation methodology (strategies for developing new research sets, innovative evaluation metrics, etc.) can be extended across various domains, eRisk has so far concentrated on psychological issues (essentially, depression,

K. S. Candan et al. (Eds.): CLEF 2021, LNCS 12880, pp. 324–344, 2021.
https://doi.org/10.1007/978-3-030-85251-1_22

self-harm and eating disorders). We conducted an exploratory task on the early diagnosis of depression in 2017 [4,5]. This pilot task was focused on the evaluation methods and test dataset described in [3]. In 2018, we continued the task on early identification of symptoms of depression while also launching a new task on early detection of signs of anorexia [6,7].

In 2019, we ran the continuation of the challenge on early identification of symptoms of anorexia, a challenge on early detection of signs of self-harm, and a third task aimed at estimating a user's responses to a depression questionnaire focused on her social media interactions [8–10]. Finally, in 2020, we continued with the early detection of self-harm and the task on severity estimation of depression symptoms [11–13].

Over the years, we've been able to compare a variety of solutions that use diverse technologies and models (e.g. Natural Language Processing, Machine Learning, or Information Retrieval). We discovered that the interplay between psychological disorders and language use is challenging and that the effectiveness of most contributing systems is low. For example, most participants had performance levels (e.g., in terms of F1) that were less than 70%. This suggests that this kind of early prediction tasks requires additional investigation, and the solutions offered so far have a lot of space for improvement.

In 2021, the lab had three campaign-style tasks [16]. The first task explores a new domain: pathological gambling. We designed this new task in the same fashion as previous early detection challenges. The second task is a continuation of the early detection of the self-harm task. Finally, we provided the third edition of the depression severity estimation task, where participants were required to analyse the user's posts and then estimate the user's answers to a standard depression questionnaire. These tasks are described in greater detail in the next sections of this overview article. We had 76 teams registered for the lab. We finally received results from 18 of them: 26 runs for Task 1, 55 runs for Task 2 and 36 for Task 3.

2 Task 1: Early Detection of Pathological Gambling

This was a new task in 2021. The challenge was to conduct a study on early risk detection of pathological gambling. Pathological gambling (ICD-10-CM code F63.0) is also called ludomania and usually referred to as *gambling addiction* (it is an urge to gamble independently of its negative consequences). According to the World Health Organization [1], in 2017, adult gambling addiction had prevalence rates ranged from 0.1% to 6.0%. The task entailed sequentially processing evidence and detecting early signs of pathological gambling, also known as compulsive gambling or disordered gambling, as soon as possible. The task is primarily concerned with evaluating Text Mining solutions and focuses on texts written in Social Media. Participating systems had to read and process the posts in the order in which they were created on Social Media. As a result, systems that effectively perform this task could be used to sequentially monitor user interactions in blogs, social networks, and other types of online media.

Table 1. Task 1 (pathological gambling). Main statistics of test collection

	Test	
	Pathological Gamblers	*Control*
Num. subjects	164	2,184
Num. submissions (posts & comments)	54,674	1,073,883
Avg num. of submissions per subject	333.37	491.70
Avg num. of days from first to last submission	≈560	≈662
Avg num. words per submission	30.64	20.08

The test collection for this task had the same format as the collection described in [3]. The source of data is also the same used for previous eRisks. It is a collection of writings (posts or comments) from a set of Social Media users. There are two categories of users, pathological gamblers and non-pathological gamblers, and, for each user, the collection contains a sequence of writings (in chronological order). We set up a server that iteratively gave user writings to the participating teams. More information about the server can be found at the lab website[1].

This was an "*only test*" task. No training data was provided to the participants. The test stage consisted of participants connecting to our server and iteratively receiving user writings and sending responses. At any point in the user chronology, each participant could stop and issue an alert. After reading each user post, the teams had to choose between: i) alerting about the user (the system predicts the user will develop the risk) or ii) not alerting about the user. Alerts were regarded as final (i.e. further decisions about this individual were ignored), while *no alerts* were considered as non-final (i.e. the participants could later submit an alert about this user if they detected the appearance of signs of risk). This choice had to be made for each user in the test split. The accuracy of the decisions and the number of user writings required to make the decisions were used to evaluate the systems (see below). To support the testing stage, we deployed a REST service. The server iteratively distributed user writings to each participant while waiting for their responses (no new user data was distributed to a specific participant until the service received a decision from that team). The service was open for submissions from February 1st, 2021, until April 23rd 2021.

In order to build the ground truth assessments, we followed existing approaches that optimize the use of assessors time [14,15]. These methods allow to build test collections using simulated pooling strategies. Table 1 reports the main statistics of the test collection used for T1. Evaluation measures are discussed in the next sections.

[1] https://early.irlab.org/server.html.

2.1 Decision-Based Evaluation

This form of evaluation revolves around the (binary) decisions taken for each user by the participating systems. Besides standard classification measures (Precision, Recall and F1[2]), we computed $ERDE$, the early risk detection error used in previous editions of the lab. A full description of $ERDE$ can be found in [3]. Essentially, $ERDE$ is an error measure that introduces a penalty for late correct alerts (true positives). The penalty grows with the delay in emitting the alert, and the delay is measured here as the number of user posts that had to be processed before making the alert.

Since 2019, we complemented the evaluation report with additional decision-based metrics that try to capture additional aspects of the problem. These metrics try to overcome some limitations of $ERDE$, namely:

- the penalty associated to true positives goes quickly to 1. This is due to the functional form of the cost function (sigmoid).
- a perfect system, which detects the true positive case right after the first round of messages (first chunk), does not get error equal to 0.
- with a method based on releasing data in a chunk-based way (as it was done in 2017 and 2018) the contribution of each user to the performance evaluation has a large variance (different for users with few writings per chunk vs users with many writings per chunk).
- $ERDE$ is not interpretable.

Some research teams have analysed these issues and proposed alternative ways for evaluation. Trotzek and colleagues [18] proposed $ERDE_o^{\%}$. This is a variant of ERDE that does not depend on the number of user writings seen before the alert but, instead, it depends on the *percentage* of user writings seen before the alert. In this way, user's contributions to the evaluation are normalized (currently, all users weight the same). However, there is an important limitation of $ERDE_o^{\%}$. In real life applications, the overall number of user writings is not known in advance. Social Media users post contents online and screening tools have to make predictions with the evidence seen. In practice, you do not know when (and if) a user's thread of messages is exhausted. Thus, the performance metric should not depend on knowledge about the total number of user writings.

Another proposal of an alternative evaluation metric for early risk prediction was done by Sadeque and colleagues [17]. They proposed $F_{latency}$, which fits better with our purposes. This measure is described next.

Imagine a user $u \in U$ and an early risk detection system that iteratively analyzes u's writings (e.g. in chronological order, as they appear in Social Media) and, after analyzing k_u user writings ($k_u \geq 1$), takes a binary decision $d_u \in \{0, 1\}$, which represents the decision of the system about the user being a risk case. By $g_u \in \{0, 1\}$, we refer to the user's golden truth label. A key component of an early risk evaluation should be the delay on detecting true positives (we do

[2] computed with respect to the positive class.

not want systems to detect these cases too late). Therefore, a first and intuitive measure of delay can be defined as follows[3]:

$$\text{latency}_{TP} = \text{median}\{k_u : u \in U, d_u = g_u = 1\} \tag{1}$$

This measure of latency is calculated over the true positives detected by the system and assesses the system's delay based on the median number of writings that the system had to process to detect such positive cases. This measure can be included in the experimental report together with standard measures such as Precision (P), Recall (R) and the F-measure (F):

$$P = \frac{|u \in U : d_u = g_u = 1|}{|u \in U : d_u = 1|} \tag{2}$$

$$R = \frac{|u \in U : d_u = g_u = 1|}{|u \in U : g_u = 1|} \tag{3}$$

$$F = \frac{2 \cdot P \cdot R}{P + R} \tag{4}$$

Furthermore, Sadeque et al. proposed a measure, $F_{latency}$, which combines the effectiveness of the decision (estimated with the F measure) and the delay[4] in the decision. This is calculated by multiplying F by a penalty factor based on the median delay. More specifically, each individual (true positive) decision, taken after reading k_u writings, is assigned the following penalty:

$$penalty(k_u) = -1 + \frac{2}{1 + \exp^{-p \cdot (k_u - 1)}} \tag{5}$$

where p is a parameter that determines how quickly the penalty should increase. In [17], p was set such that the penalty equals 0.5 at the median number of posts of a user[5]. Observe that a decision right after the first writing has no penalty (i.e. $penalty(1) = 0$). Figure 1 plots how the latency penalty increases with the number of observed writings.

The system's overall speed factor is computed as:

$$speed = (1 - \text{median}\{penalty(k_u) : u \in U, d_u = g_u = 1\}) \tag{6}$$

[3] Observe that Sadeque et al. (see [17], pg 497) computed the latency for all users such that $g_u = 1$. We argue that latency should be computed only for the true positives. The false negatives ($g_u = 1$, $d_u = 0$) are not detected by the system and, therefore, they would not generate an alert.

[4] Again, we adopt Sadeque et al.'s proposal but we estimate latency only over the true positives.

[5] In the evaluation we set p to 0.0078, a setting obtained from the eRisk 2017 collection.

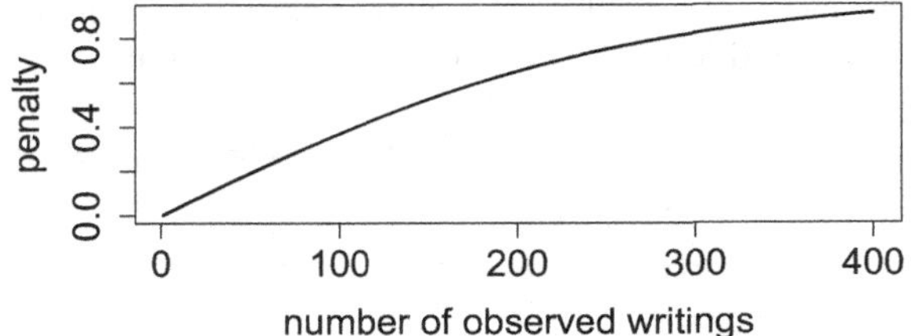

Fig. 1. Latency penalty increases with the number of observed writings (k_u)

where speed equals 1 for a system whose true positives are detected right at the first writing. A slow system, which detects true positives after hundreds of writings, will be assigned a speed score near 0.

Finally, the *latency-weighted* F score is simply:

$$F_{latency} = F \cdot speed \tag{7}$$

Since 2019 user's data were processed by the participants in a post by post basis (i.e. we avoided a chunk-based release of data). Under these conditions, the evaluation approach has the following properties:

- smooth grow of penalties;
- a perfect system gets $F_{latency} = 1$;
- for each user u the system can opt to stop at any point k_u and, therefore, now we do not have the effect of an imbalanced importance of users;
- $F_{latency}$ is more interpretable than $ERDE$.

2.2 Ranking-Based Evaluation

This section discusses an alternative form of evaluation, which was used as a complement of the evaluation described above. After each release of data (new user writing) the participants had to send back the following information (for each user in the collection): i) a decision for the user (alert/no alert), which was used to compute the decision-based metrics discussed above, and ii) a score that represents the user's level of risk (estimated from the evidence seen so far). We used these scores to build a ranking of users in decreasing estimation of risk. For each participating system, we have one ranking at each point (i.e., ranking after 1 writing, ranking after 2 writings, etc.). This simulates a continuous re-ranking approach based on the evidence seen so far. In a real life application, this ranking would be presented to an expert user who could take decisions (e.g. by inspecting the rankings).

Each ranking can be scored with standard IR metrics, such as P@10 or NDCG. We therefore report the ranking-based performance of the systems after seeing k writings (with varying k).

Table 2. Participating teams in Task 1: number of runs, number of user writings processed by the team, and lapse of time taken for the whole process.

Team	#Runs processed	#User writings	Lapse of time (from 1st to last response)
RELAI	5	1231	9 days 05:42:11
UPV-Symanto	5	801	18:42:54
UNSL	5	2000	5 days 01:23:26
BLUE	5	1828	1 days 23:43:28
CeDRI	2	271	1 days 05:44:10
EFE	4	2000	3 days 03:02:22

2.3 Task 1: Results

Table 2 shows the participating teams, the number of runs submitted and the approximate lapse of time from the first response to the last response. This time lapse is indicative of the degree of automation of each team's algorithms. A few of the submitted runs processed the entire thread of messages (2000), but many variants opted for stopping earlier. Three teams processed the thread of messages in a reasonably fast way (around a day for processing the entire history of user messages). The rest of the teams took several days to run the whole process. Some teams took even more than a week. This suggests that they incorporated some form of offline processing.

Table 3 reports the decision-based performance achieved by the participating teams. In terms of Precision, $F1$, $ERDE_{50}$ and latency-weighted $F1$, the best performing run was submitted by the UNSL team. This run (#2) also has a quite high level of Recall (.939). Many teams achieved perfect Recall at the expense of very low Precision figures. In terms of $ERDE_5$, the best performing run is RELAI #0. This run, however, shows poor performance in terms of classification accuracy. The majority of teams made quick decisions. Overall, these findings indicate that some systems achieved a relatively high level of effectiveness with only a few dozen user submissions. Social and public health systems may use the best predictive algorithms to assist expert humans in detecting signs of pathological gambling as early as possible.

Table 4 presents the ranking-based results. Because some teams only processed a few dozens of user writings, we could only compute their user rankings for the initial number of processed writings.

Some runs (e.g., UNSL runs #0 #1 #2, RELAI #2) have the same levels of ranking-based shallow effectiveness over multiple points (after one writing, after 100 writings, and so forth). However, for the 100 cut-off, only UNSL #2 obtains the highest NDCG after one writing. This run is consistently the best performing one in terms of ranking for every cut-off, metric and number of writings. The UPV-Symanto team seems to have some bug on their model as it consistently yielded zero performance.

Table 3. Decision-based evaluation for Task 1

Team	Run	P	R	$F1$	$ERDE_5$	$ERDE_{50}$	$latency_{TP}$	*speed*	*latency-weighted* $F1$
UNSL	0	0.326	0.957	0.487	0.079	0.023	11	0.961	0.468
UNSL	1	0.137	0.982	0.241	0.060	0.035	4	0.988	0.238
UNSL	2	**0.586**	0.939	**0.721**	0.073	**0.020**	11	0.961	**0.693**
UNSL	3	0.084	0.963	0.155	0.066	0.060	1	**1**	0.155
UNSL	4	0.086	0.933	0.157	0.067	0.060	1	**1**	0.157
RELAI	0	0.138	0.988	0.243	**0.048**	0.036	1	**1**	0.243
RELAI	1	0.108	**1**	0.194	0.057	0.045	1	**1**	0.194
RELAI	2	0.071	**1**	0.132	0.067	0.064	1	**1**	0.132
RELAI	3	0.071	**1**	0.132	0.066	0.064	1	**1**	0.132
RELAI	4	0.070	**1**	0.131	0.066	0.065	1	**1**	0.131
BLUE	0	0.107	0.994	0.193	0.067	0.046	2	0.996	0.192
BLUE	1	0.157	0.988	0.271	0.054	0.036	2	0.996	0.270
BLUE	2	0.121	0.994	0.215	0.065	0.045	2	0.996	0.215
BLUE	3	0.095	**1**	0.174	0.071	0.051	2	0.996	0.173
BLUE	4	0.110	0.994	0.198	0.068	0.048	2	0.996	0.197
UPV-Symanto	0	0.042	0.415	0.077	0.088	0.087	1	**1**	0.077
UPV-Symanto	1	0.040	0.457	0.074	0.097	0.091	1	**1**	0.074
UPV-Symanto	2	0.030	0.238	0.053	0.093	0.091	1	**1**	0.053
UPV-Symanto	3	0.035	0.409	0.064	0.098	0.097	1	**1**	0.064
UPV-Symanto	4	0.028	0.256	0.051	0.098	0.095	1	**1**	0.051
CeDRI	0	0.076	**1**	0.142	0.079	0.060	2	0.996	0.141
CeDRI	1	0.070	**1**	0.131	0.066	0.065	1	**1**	0.131
EFE	0	0.251	0.640	0.361	0.079	0.037	16	0.942	0.340
EFE	1	0.296	0.537	0.382	0.076	0.043	31	0.884	0.337
EFE	2	0.233	0.750	0.356	0.082	0.033	11	0.961	0.342
EFE	3	0.292	0.549	0.381	0.076	0.044	31	0.884	0.337

Table 4. Ranking-based evaluation for Task 1

Team	Run	1 writing			100 writings			500 writings			1000 writings		
		$P@10$	$NDCG@10$	$NDCG@100$	$P@10$	$NDCG@10$	$NDCG@100$	$P@10$	$NDCG@10$	$NDCG@100$	$P@10$	$NDCG@10$	$NDCG@100$
UNSL	0	**1**	**1**	0.81	**1**	**1**	**1**	**1**	**1**	**1**	**1**	**1**	**1**
UNSL	1	**1**	**1**	0.79	0.8	0.73	0.87	0.8	0.69	0.86	0.8	0.62	0.84
UNSL	2	**1**	**1**	**0.85**	**1**	**1**	**1**	**1**	**1**	**1**	**1**	**1**	**1**
UNSL	3	0.9	0.92	0.74	**1**	**1**	0.76	**1**	**1**	0.72	**1**	**1**	0.72
UNSL	4	**1**	**1**	0.69	0	0	0.25	0	0	0.11	0	0	0.13
RELAI	0	0.9	0.92	0.73	**1**	**1**	0.93	**1**	**1**	0.92	**1**	**1**	0.91
RELAI	1	**1**	**1**	0.72	**1**	**1**	0.91	**1**	**1**	0.91	**1**	**1**	0.91
RELAI	2	0.8	0.81	0.49	0.5	0.43	0.32	0.5	0.55	0.42	0.5	0.55	0.41
RELAI	3	0.8	0.88	0.61	0.6	0.68	0.49	0.7	0.77	0.55	0.8	0.85	0.55
RELAI	4	0.6	0.63	0.45	0	0	0.04	0	0	0.03	0	0	0.07
BLUE	0	0.9	0.88	0.61	0.8	0.73	0.57	0.9	0.93	0.64	0.7	0.78	0.60
BLUE	1	**1**	**1**	0.61	0.8	0.82	0.53	**1**	**1**	0.56	**1**	**1**	0.56
BLUE	2	0.6	0.70	0.73	0.8	0.87	0.76	0.8	0.88	0.75	0.9	0.90	0.76
BLUE	3	0.6	0.65	0.60	0.8	0.87	0.61	0.7	0.71	0.60	0.7	0.67	0.60
BLUE	4	0.9	0.81	0.73	**1**	**1**	0.77	**1**	**1**	0.76	**1**	**1**	0.78
UPV-Symanto	0	0	0	0	0	0	0	0	0	0			
UPV-Symanto	1	0	0	0	0	0	0	0	0	0			
UPV-Symanto	2	0	0	0	0	0	0	0	0	0			
UPV-Symanto	3	0	0	0	0	0	0	0	0	0			
UPV-Symanto	4	0	0	0	0	0	0	0	0	0			
CeDRI	0	0.9	0.93	0.64	0.7	0.63	0.40						
CeDRI	1	0	0	0.02	0	0	0.03						
EFE	0	0.2	0.29	0.28	0.6	0.64	0.52	0.6	0.62	0.53	0.6	0.62	0.52
EFE	1	0.2	0.29	0.28	0.6	0.64	0.52	0.6	0.62	0.53	0.6	0.62	0.52
EFE	2	0.5	0.45	0.40	0.6	0.56	0.50	0.6	0.57	0.54	0.6	0.57	0.52
EFE	3	0.5	0.45	0.40	0.6	0.56	0.50	0.6	0.57	0.54	0.6	0.57	0.52

In summary, UNSL #2 is overall the best performing run in ranking and decision-based evaluation.

3 Task 2: Early Detection of Self-Harm

This is a continuation of 2019 task 2 and 2020 task 1. This task proposes the early risk detection of self-harm in the very same way as described for pathological gambling in Sect. 2. The test collection for this task also had the same format as the collection described in [3]. The source of data is also the same used for previous eRisks. Here are two categories of users, self-harm and non-self-harm, and, for each user, the collection contains a sequence of writings (in chronological order). We set up a server that iteratively gave user writings to the participating teams. More information about the server can be found at the lab website[6].

Table 5. Task 2 (self-harm). Main statistics of test collection

	Train		Test	
	Self-Harm	Control	Self-Harm	Control
Num. subjects	145	618	152	1296
Num. submissions (posts & comments)	18,618	254,642	51,104	688,823
Avg num. of submissions per subject	128.4	412.0	336.2	531.5
Avg num. of days from first to last submission	$\approx$ 312	$\approx$461	$\approx$346	$\approx$510
Avg num. words per submission	22.4	15.2	26.03	20.74

This was a train and a test task. The test phase followed the same procedure as Task 1 (see Sect. 2). For the training stage, the teams had access to training data where we released the whole history of writings for training users. We indicated what users had explicitly mentioned that they had done self-harm. The participants could therefore tune their systems with the training data. In 2021, the training data for Task 2 was composed of all 2019's Task 2 users and 2020's Task 1 test users.

Again, we followed existing methods to build the assessments using simulated pooling strategies, which optimize the use of assessors time [14,15]. Table 5 reports the main statistics of the train and test collections used for T2. The same decision and ranking based measures as discussed in Sects. 2.1 and 2.2 were used for this task.

6 https://early.irlab.org/server.html.

Table 6. Participating teams in Task 2: number of runs, number of user writings processed by the team, and lapse of time taken for the whole process.

Team	#Runs processed	#User writings	Lapse of time (from 1st to last response)
NLP-UNED	5	472	07:08:37
AvocadoToast	3	379	10 days 13:20:37
Birmingham	5	11	2 days 08:01:32
NuFAST	3	6	17:07:57
NaCTeM	5	1999	5 days 20:22:04
EFE	4	1999	1 days 15:17:18
BioInfo@UAVR	2	91	1 days 02:21:30
NUS-IDS	5	46	3 days 08:11:46
RELAI	5	1561	11 days 00:49:27
CeDRI	3	369	1 days 09:51:27
BLUE	5	156	1 days 04:57:23
UPV-Symanto	5	538	11:56:33
UNSL	5	1999	3 days 17:36:10

3.1 Task 2: Results

Table 6 shows the participating teams, the number of runs submitted and the approximate lapse of time from the first response to the last response. The lapse of time is indicative of the degree of automation of each team's algorithms. A few of the submitted runs processed the entire thread of messages (about 2000), but many variants opted for stopping earlier or were not able to process the users' history in time. Only one team was able to process the entire set of writings in a reasonable amount of time (around a day or so for processing the entire history of user messages). The remaining teams took several days to complete the process. Some teams required more than a week. Again, this suggests that they used some form of offline processing.

Table 7 reports the decision-based performance achieved by the participating teams. In terms of Precision, Birmingham run #2 obtains the highest values but at the expenses of low Recall. Similarly, CEDRI systems #1 and #2 obtain perfect Recall but with low Precision values. When considering the Precision-Recall trade-off, UNSL #4 is the best performance being the only run over 0.6 (highest $F1$). Regarding latency-penalized metrics, UPV-Symanto #1 obtains the best $ERDE_5$ and UNSL #0 the best $ERDE_5$ error value. It is again UNSL #4, the one achieving the best latency-weighted $F1$. This run seems to be quite balanced overall. When comparing the best values with the ones from last year, the best values for Precision and F1 are lower than those reported in 2020. This year the amount of released training data more than doubled, but the availability of a larger training set was apparently no beneficial for the 2021 participants.

Table 7. Decision-based evaluation for Task 2

Team	Run	P	R	$F1$	$ERDE_5$	$ERDE_{50}$	$latency_{TP}$	$speed$	$latency$-$weighted$ $F1$
NLP-UNED	0	0.442	0.75	0.556	0.080	0.042	6	0.981	0.545
NLP-UNED	1	0.442	0.796	0.568	0.091	0.041	11	0.961	0.546
NLP-UNED	2	0.422	0.73	0.535	0.088	0.047	7	0.977	0.522
NLP-UNED	3	0.419	0.77	0.543	0.093	0.047	10	0.965	0.524
NLP-UNED	4	0.453	0.816	0.582	0.088	0.040	9	0.969	0.564
AvocadoToast	0	0.214	0.757	0.334	0.111	0.069	11	0.961	0.321
AvocadoToast	1	0.245	0.401	0.304	0.078	0.076	**1**	**1**	0.304
AvocadoToast	2	0.215	0.757	0.335	0.111	0.069	11	0.961	0.322
Birmingham	0	0.584	0.526	0.554	0.068	0.054	2	0.996	0.551
Birmingham	1	0.644	0.309	0.418	0.097	0.074	8	0.973	0.406
Birmingham	2	**0.757**	0.349	0.477	0.085	0.070	4	0.988	0.472
Birmingham	3	0.629	0.434	0.514	0.084	0.062	5	0.984	0.506
Birmingham	4	0	0	0	0.105	0.105			
NuFAST	0	0.124	0.283	0.172	0.101	0.097	**1**	**1**	0.172
NuFAST	1	0.124	0.283	0.172	0.101	0.097	**1**	**1**	0.172
NuFAST	2	0.124	0.283	0.172	0.101	0.097	**1**	**1**	0.172
NaCTeM	0	0.108	0.882	0.193	0.185	0.184	1999	0.0	0.0
NaCTeM	1	0.108	0.882	0.193	0.185	0.184	1999	0.0	0.0
NaCTeM	2	0.108	0.882	0.193	0.185	0.184	1999	0.0	0.0
NaCTeM	3	0.108	0.882	0.193	0.184	0.184	1999	0.0	0.0
NaCTeM	4	0.108	0.882	0.193	0.184	0.184	1999	0.0	0.0
EFE	0	0.381	0.717	0.498	0.118	0.050	17	0.938	0.467
EFE	1	0.434	0.605	0.505	0.114	0.063	32	0.880	0.445
EFE	2	0.366	0.796	0.501	0.120	0.043	12	0.957	0.48
EFE	3	0.422	0.605	0.497	0.114	0.063	32	0.88	0.437
BioInfo@UAVR	0	0.233	0.862	0.367	0.136	0.050	22	0.918	0.337
BioInfo@UAVR	1	0.274	0.789	0.407	0.128	0.047	22	0.918	0.374
NUS-IDS	0	0.133	0.987	0.234	0.108	0.073	3	0.992	0.232
NUS-IDS	1	0.131	0.98	0.232	0.116	0.073	4	0.988	0.229
NUS-IDS	2	0.134	0.993	0.236	0.117	0.072	4	0.988	0.233
NUS-IDS	3	0.128	0.987	0.227	0.106	0.075	3	0.992	0.225
NUS-IDS	4	0.135	0.987	0.237	0.104	0.071	3	0.992	0.235
RELAI	0	0.138	0.967	0.242	0.140	0.073	5	0.984	0.238
RELAI	1	0.114	0.993	0.205	0.146	0.086	5	0.984	0.202
RELAI	2	0.488	0.276	0.353	0.087	0.082	2	0.996	0.352
RELAI	3	0.207	0.875	0.335	0.079	0.056	2	0.996	0.334
RELAI	4	0.119	0.868	0.209	0.120	0.089	2	0.996	0.208
CeDRI	0	0.110	0.993	0.199	0.109	0.090	2	0.996	0.198
CeDRI	1	0.116	**1**	0.207	0.113	0.085	2	0.996	0.206
CeDRI	2	0.105	**1**	0.190	0.096	0.094	**1**	**1**	0.190
BLUE	0	0.283	0.934	0.435	0.084	0.041	5	0.984	0.428
BLUE	1	0.142	0.875	0.245	0.117	0.081	4	0.988	0.242
BLUE	2	0.454	0.849	0.592	0.079	0.037	7	0.977	0.578
BLUE	3	0.394	0.868	0.542	0.075	0.035	5	0.984	0.534
BLUE	4	0.249	0.928	0.393	0.085	0.044	4	0.988	0.388
UPV-Symanto	0	0.307	0.678	0.422	0.097	0.051	5	0.984	0.416
UPV-Symanto	1	0.276	0.638	0.385	**0.059**	0.056	**1**	**1**	0.385
UPV-Symanto	2	0.313	0.645	0.422	0.072	0.053	2	0.996	0.420
UPV-Symanto	3	0.301	0.770	0.433	0.089	0.044	5	0.984	0.426
UPV-Symanto	4	0.198	0.711	0.310	0.082	0.063	3	0.992	0.307
UNSL	0	0.336	0.914	0.491	0.125	**0.034**	11	0.961	0.472
UNSL	1	0.110	0.987	0.198	0.093	0.092	**1**	**1**	0.198
UNSL	2	0.129	0.934	0.226	0.098	0.085	**1**	**1**	0.226
UNSL	3	0.464	0.803	0.588	0.064	0.038	3	0.992	0.583
UNSL	4	0.532	0.763	**0.627**	0.064	0.038	3	0.992	**0.622**

Table 8. Ranking-based evaluation for Task 2

Team	Run	1 writing			100 writings			500 writings			1000 writings		
		$P@10$	$NDCG@10$	$NDCG@100$	$P@10$	$NDCG@10$	$NDCG@100$	$P@10$	$NDCG@10$	$NDCG@100$	$P@10$	$NDCG@10$	$NDCG@100$
NLP-UNED	0	0.8	0.82	0.47	0.8	0.74	0.47	0	0	0	0	0	0
NLP-UNED	1	0.7	0.68	0.39	0.8	0.86	0.55	0	0	0	0	0	0
NLP-UNED	2	0.9	0.81	0.39	0.6	0.44	0.44	0	0	0	0	0	0
NLP-UNED	3	0.6	0.6	0.37	0.6	0.58	0.47	0	0	0	0	0	0
NLP-UNED	4	0.5	0.47	0.32	**0.9**	**0.94**	0.55	0	0	0	0	0	0
AvocadoToast	0	0	0	0.11	0.7	0.5	0.52	0	0	0	0	0	0
AvocadoToast	1	0	0	0.1	0.3	0.28	0.26	0	0	0	0	0	0
AvocadoToast	2	0.1	0.06	0.12	0.7	0.5	0.52	0	0	0	0	0	0
Birmingham	0	0.3	0.41	0.12	0	0	0	0	0	0	0	0	0
Birmingham	1	0	0	0.03	0	0	0	0	0	0	0	0	0
Birmingham	2	0.1	0.19	0.07	0	0	0	0	0	0	0	0	0
Birmingham	3	0.1	0.07	0.08	0	0	0	0	0	0	0	0	0
Birmingham	4	0	0	0.11	0	0	0	0	0	0	0	0	0
NuFAST	0	0	0	0.08	0	0	0	0	0	0	0	0	0
NuFAST	1	0	0	0.08	0	0	0	0	0	0	0	0	0
NuFAST	2	0	0	0.08	0	0	0	0	0	0	0	0	0
NaCTeM	0	0.1	0.06	0.07	0	0	0.08	0.1	0.06	0.15	0	0	0.06
NaCTeM	1	0.1	0.06	0.14	0.1	0.07	0.09	0	0	0.1	0.1	0.06	0.07
NaCTeM	2	0.2	0.19	0.15	0.2	0.19	0.11	0.1	0.06	0.13	0.1	0.06	0.09
NaCTeM	3	0.1	0.06	0.07	0.1	0.06	0.08	0	0	0.11	0.1	0.19	0.18
NaCTeM	4	0	0	0.07	0.1	0.06	0.06	0.1	0.06	0.1	0.1	0.06	0.08
EFE	0	0.5	0.35	0.37	0.8	0.74	0.63	0.8	0.74	0.6	0.8	0.81	0.62
EFE	1	0.5	0.35	0.37	0.8	0.74	0.63	0.8	0.74	0.6	0.8	0.81	0.62
EFE	2	0.7	0.68	0.49	0.5	0.44	0.56	0.6	0.55	0.59	0.6	0.55	0.59
EFE	3	0.7	0.68	0.49	0.5	0.44	0.56	0.6	0.55	0.59	0.6	0.55	0.59
BioInfo@UAVR	0	0.1	0.06	0.13	0	0	0	0	0	0	0	0	0
BioInfo@UAVR	1	0.1	0.06	0.07	0	0	0	0	0	0	0	0	0
NUS-IDS	0	0.8	0.86	0.55	0	0	0	0	0	0	0	0	0
NUS-IDS	1	0.8	0.75	0.49	0	0	0	0	0	0	0	0	0
NUS-IDS	2	0.9	0.81	0.49	0	0	0	0	0	0	0	0	0
NUS-IDS	3	0.6	0.73	0.46	0	0	0	0	0	0	0	0	0
NUS-IDS	4	0.8	0.85	0.52	0	0	0	0	0	0	0	0	0
RELAI	0	0.1	0.06	0.11	0.4	0.37	0.46	0.4	0.32	0.38	0.5	0.47	0.41
RELAI	1	0	0	0.12	0.2	0.12	0.36	0	0	0.27	0.1	0.06	0.28
RELAI	2	0.8	0.71	0.4	0.4	0.28	0.40	**1**	**1**	0.6	**1**	**1**	0.57
RELAI	3	0.7	0.76	0.43	0	0	0.31	0.9	0.88	0.59	0.8	0.75	0.56
RELAI	4	0.4	0.44	0.34	0	0	0.21	0.4	0.34	0.27	0.5	0.5	0.31
CeDRI	0	0.3	0.35	0.35	0.5	0.54	0.31	0	0	0	0	0	0
CeDRI	1	0.3	0.38	0.19	0.4	0.54	0.2	0	0	0	0	0	0
CeDRI	2	0.1	0.1	0.07	0.2	0.25	0.12	0	0	0	0	0	0
BLUE	0	0.7	0.75	0.54	0.8	0.82	0.59	0	0	0	0	0	0
BLUE	1	0.2	0.13	0.26	0.4	0.41	0.29	0	0	0	0	0	0
BLUE	2	0.6	0.49	0.50	**0.9**	**0.94**	0.55	0	0	0	0	0	0
BLUE	3	0.6	0.43	0.49	0.8	0.87	0.54	0	0	0	0	0	0
BLUE	4	0.7	0.61	0.52	0.8	0.88	0.55	0	0	0	0	0	0
UPV-Symanto	0	0.8	0.83	0.53	**0.9**	**0.94**	0.67	0.9	0.94	0.67	0	0	0
UPV-Symanto	1	0.8	0.88	0.5	0.8	0.69	0.64	0.8	0.69	0.64	0	0	0
UPV-Symanto	2	0.8	0.82	0.55	0.8	0.83	0.59	0.8	0.83	0.59	0	0	0
UPV-Symanto	3	0.6	0.70	0.51	**0.9**	**0.94**	0.69	0.9	0.94	0.69	0	0	0
UPV-Symanto	4	0.9	0.93	0.53	**0.9**	0.81	0.65	0.9	0.81	0.65	0	0	0
UNSL	0	**1**	**1**	**0.70**	0.7	0.74	**0.82**	0.8	0.81	0.8	0.8	0.81	**0.80**
UNSL	1	0.8	0.82	0.61	0.8	0.73	0.59	0.9	0.94	0.58	**1**	**1**	0.61
UNSL	2	0.3	0.27	0.28	0	0	0	0	0	0	0	0	0
UNSL	3	**1**	**1**	0.63	**0.9**	0.81	0.76	0.9	0.81	**0.71**	0.8	0.73	0.69
UNSL	4	**1**	**1**	0.63	**0.9**	0.81	0.76	0.9	0.81	**0.71**	0.8	0.73	0.69

Therefore, these results seem to suggest the need of models that better exploit existing information.

Table 8 presents the ranking-based results. Some runs perform equally for some of the ranking-based effectiveness over different cut-off values (e.g., UNSL runs #0 #3 #4 after one writing or NLP-UNED#4, BLUE #2 or UPV-Symanto #0 and #3 after 100 writings). After 500 and 1000 writings, RELAI #1 obtains the best values for shallow cut-offs. UNSL #4 obtains the highest NDCG and Precision at the 10 cut-off after one writing and very good values under the other situations. This seems to point out that this effective run keeps the same good overall behaviour as in the case of the decision-based evaluation.

4 Task 3: Measuring the Severity of the Signs of Depression

This task is a continuation of Task 3 from 2019 and Task 2 from 2020. The task consists of estimating the degree of depression based on a thread of user submissions. Participants were given the full history of postings for each user (in a single release of data), and they were required to fill out a standard depression questionnaire based on the evidence found in the history of postings. Participants in 2021 had the option of using 2019 and 2020 data as training data (filled questionnaires and social media submissions from the users, i.e. a training set composed of 90 users).

The questionnaire is derived from the Beck's Depression Inventory (BDI) [2], which assesses the presence of feelings like sadness, pessimism, loss of energy, etc., for the detection of depression. The questionnaire contains the 21 questions reported in Table 9.

The task aims at exploring the viability of automatically estimating the severity of the multiple symptoms associated with depression. Given the user's history of writings, the algorithms had to estimate the user's response to each individual question. We collected questionnaires filled by Social Media users together with their history of writings (we extracted each history of writings right after the user provided us with the filled questionnaire). The questionnaires filled by the users (ground truth) were used to assess the quality of the responses provided by the participating systems.

The participants were given a dataset with 80 test users and they were asked to produce a file with the following structure:

```
username1 answer1 answer2 .... answer21
username2 ....
....
```

Each line has a user identifier and 21 values. These values correspond to the responses to the questions of the depression questionnaire (the possible values are 0, 1a, 1b, 2a, 2b, 3a, 3b -for questions 16 and 18- and 0, 1, 2, 3 -for the rest of the questions-).

4.1 Task 3: Evaluation Metrics

For consistency purposes, we employed the same evaluation metrics utilised in 2019 and 2020. These metrics assess the quality of a questionnaire filled by a system in comparison with the real questionnaire filled by the actual Social Media user:

- **Average Hit Rate** (AHR): Hit Rate (HR) averaged over all users. HR is a stringent measure that computes the ratio of cases where the automatic questionnaire has the same answer as the actual answers to the questionnaire.

For example, an automatic questionnaire with five matches gets HR equal to 5/21 (because there are 21 questions in the form).

- **Average Closeness Rate** (ACR): Closeness Rate (CR) averaged over all users. CR takes into account that the answers of the depression questionnaire represent an ordinal scale. For example, consider the #17 question:

```
17. Irritability
0. I am no more irritable than usual.
1. I am more irritable than usual.
2. I am much more irritable than usual.
3. I am irritable all the time.
```

Imagine that the real user answered "0". A system S1 whose answer is "3" should be penalised more than a system S2 whose answer is "1". For each

Table 9. Beck's Depression Inventory

```
Instructions:

This questionnaire consists of 21 groups of statements. Please read each group of statements
carefully, and then pick out the one statement in eachgroup that best describes the way you
feel. If several statements in thegroup seem to apply equally well, choose the highest number
for that group.

1. Sadness
 0. I do not feel sad.
 1. I feel sad much of the time.
 2. I am sad all the time.
 3. I am so sad or unhappy that I can't stand it.

2.Pessimism
 0. I am not discouraged about my future.
 1. I feel more discouraged about my future than I used to be.
 2. I do not expect things to work out for me.
 3. I feel my future is hopeless and will only get worse.

3.Past Failure
 0. I do not feel like a failure.
 1. I have failed more than I should have.
 2. As I look back, I see a lot of failures.
 3. I feel I am a total failure as a person.

4. Loss of Pleasure
 0. I get as much pleasure as I ever did from the things I enjoy.
 1. I don't enjoy things as much as I used to.
 2. I get very little pleasure from the things I used to enjoy.
 3. I can't get any pleasure from the things I used to enjoy.

5. Guilty Feelings
 0. I don't feel particularly guilty.
 1. I feel guilty over many things I have done or should have done.
 2. I feel quite guilty most of the time.
 3. I feel guilty all of the time.

6. Punishment Feelings
 0. I don't feel I am being punished.
 1. I feel I may be punished.
 2. I expect to be punished.
 3. I feel I am being punished.
```

(continued)

Table 9. *(continued)*

```
7. Self-Dislike
 0. I feel the same about myself as ever.
 1. I have lost confidence in myself.
 2. I am disappointed in myself.
 3. I dislike myself.

8. Self-Criticalness
 0. I don't criticize or blame myself more than usual.
 1. I am more critical of myself than I used to be.
 2. I criticize myself for all of my faults.
 3. I blame myself for everything bad that happens.

9. Suicidal Thoughts or Wishes
 0. I don't have any thoughts of killing myself.
 1. I have thoughts of killing myself, but I would not carry them out.
 2. I would like to kill myself.
 3. I would kill myself if I had the chance.

10.Crying
 0. I don't cry anymore than I used to.
 1. I cry more than I used to.
 2. I cry over every little thing.
 3. I feel like crying, but I can't.

11.Agitation
 0. I am no more restless or wound up than usual.
 1. I feel more restless or wound up than usual.
 2. I am so restless or agitated that it's hard to stay still.
 3. I am so restless or agitated that I have to keep moving or doing something.

12.Loss of Interest
 0. I have not lost interest in other people or activities.
 1. I am less interested in other people or things than before.
 2. I have lost most of my interest in other people or things.
 3. It's hard to get interested in anything.

13. Indecisiveness
 0. I make decisions about as well as ever.
 1. I find it more difficult to make decisions than usual.
 2. I have much greater difficulty in making decisions than I used to.
 3. I have trouble making any decisions.

14. Worthlessness
 0. I do not feel I am worthless.
 1. I don't consider myself as worthwhile and useful as I used to.
 2. I feel more worthless as compared to other people.
 3. I feel utterly worthless.

15. Loss of Energy
 0. I have as much energy as ever.
 1. I have less energy than I used to have.
 2. I don't have enough energy to do very much.
 3. I don't have enough energy to do anything.

16. Changes in Sleeping Pattern
 0. I have not experienced any change in my sleeping pattern.
 1a. I sleep somewhat more than usual.
 1b. I sleep somewhat less than usual.
 2a. I sleep a lot more than usual.
 2b. I sleep a Iot less than usual.
 3a. I sleep most of the day.
 3b. I wake up 1-2 hours early and can't get back to sleep.
```

(continued)

Table 9. (*continued*)

```
17. Irritability
 0. I am no more irritable than usual.
 1. I am more irritable than usual.
 2. I am much more irritable than usual.
 3. I am irritable all the time.

18. Changes in Appetite
 0. I have not experienced any change in my appetite.
 1a. My appetite is somewhat less than usual.
 1b. My appetite is somewhat greater than usual.
 2a. My appetite is much less than before.
 2b. My appetite is much greater than usual.
 3a. I have no appetite at all.
 3b. I crave food all the time.

19. Concentration Difficulty
 0. I can concentrate as well as ever.
 1. I can't concentrate as well as usual.
 2. It's hard to keep my mind on anything for very long.
 3. I find I can't concentrate on anything.

20.Tiredness or Fatigue
 0. I am no more tired or fatigued than usual.
 1. I get more tired or fatigued more easily than usual.
 2. I am too tired or fatigued to do a lot of the things I used to do.
 3. I am too tired or fatigued to do most of the things I used to do.

21.Loss of Interest in Sex
 0. I have not noticed any recent change in my interest in sex.
 1. I am less interested in sex than I used to be.
 2. I am much less interested in sex now.
 3. I have lost interest in sex completely.
```

question, CR computes the absolute difference (ad) between the real and the automated answer (e.g. ad=3 and ad=1 for S1 and S2, respectively) and, next, this absolute difference is transformed into an effectiveness score as follows: $CR = (mad - ad)/mad$, where mad is the maximum absolute difference, which is equal to the number of possible answers minus one[7]

- **Average DODL (ADODL)**: Difference between overall depression levels (DODL) averaged over all users. The previous measures assess the systems' ability to answer each question in the form. DODL, instead, does not look at question-level hits or differences but computes the overall depression level (sum of all the answers) for the real and automated questionnaire and, next, the absolute difference ($ad\_overall$) between the real and the automated score is computed.
  Depression levels are integers between 0 and 63 and, thus, DODL is normalised into [0,1] as follows: $DODL = (63 - ad\_overall)/63$.
- **Depression Category Hit Rate (DCHR)**. In the psychological domain, it is customary to associate depression levels with the followingcategories:

[7] In the two questions (#16 and #18) that have seven possible answers $\{0, 1a, 1b, 2a, 2b, 3a, 3b\}$ the pairs $(1a, 1b)$, $(2a, 2b)$, $(3a, 3b)$ are considered equivalent because they reflect the same depression level. As a consequence, the difference between $3b$ and 0 is equal to 3 (and the difference between $1a$ and $1b$ is equal to 0).

```
minimal depression (depression levels 0-9)
mild depression (depression levels 10-18)
moderate depression (depression levels 19-29)
severe depression (depression levels 30-63)
```

The last effectiveness measure consists of computing the fraction of cases where the automated questionnaire led to a depression category that is equivalent to the depression category obtained from the real questionnaire.

4.2 Task 3: Results

Table 10 presents the results achieved by the participants in this task.

Starting with the AHR scores, the results in the task show that the best teams get rates below 40% of correct answers. These results do not improve but are aligned with the results obtained in the tasks of previous years (eRisk's Task 3 in 2019 and Task 2 in 2020), whose best AHR ratios were around 40%. This suggests that analyzing user posts can help extract some signals or symptoms related to depression. In the case of ACR, the best performing run (UPV-Symanto 4_symanto_upv_lingfeat_cor) shows a 73.17%, exceeding the 70% ACR barrier established in previous years, which represents a sustained improvement in the results of this metric for this task. However, this value is only slightly better than the näive all 1s algorithm (72.90%). This metric penalizes high distances between the correct answer and the answer given by the system and, thus, it somehow favours conservative answers. By always choosing 1, the all 1s algorithm sets an upper limit of the distance equal to 2 (it gets 2 when the correct answer is 3). In terms of AHR, some participating runs outperform the näive baseline algorithms (all 1s = 23.03%, all 0s = 32.02%). This implies that the distance-based ACR metric penalizes system failures in estimating response to an item more effectively.

These results put forth an existing barrier in the generalization process: from the specific estimation of individual answers (to each question in the questionnaire) to the overall estimation of the subject's depression level. In terms of ADODL, the best run (CYUT run 2) shows rates around 83.59%, representing a tiny percentage improvement compared to previous years (the best ADODL result obtained in Task 2 2020 was 83.15%).

Several teams offer values greater than 80% in the ADODL metric, strengthening the values obtained in previous years. However, the difficulty in the generalization process is clearly appreciated when we analyze the DCHR metric. In this case, the best performing run (CYUT run 2) gets the depression category right for only 41.25% of the individuals. This result is slightly lower than the maximum obtained in previous years (around 45% of individuals in Task 2 2020). This value is better than the baseline variants but, still, there is much room for improvement, and the trend in the data remains consistent throughout successive editions.

These results confirm the task's viability for automatically extracting some depression-related evidence from social media activity. Still, there is a need to

Table 10. Task 3 Results. Participating teams and runs with corresponding scores in AHR, ACR, ADODL and DCHR metrics. Stared runs did not submit decisions for every subject.

Run	AHR	ACR	ADODL	DCHR
BLUE run0	27.86%	64.66%	74.15%	17.50%
BLUE run1	30.00%	64.58%	70.65%	11.25%
BLUE run2	30.36%	65.42%	75.42%	21.25%
BLUE run3	29.52%	64.70%	73.63%	13.75%
BLUE run4	29.76%	65.04%	74.84%	15.00%
CYUT run1	32.02%	66.33%	75.34%	20.00%
CYUT run2	32.62%	69.46%	**83.59%**	**41.25%**
CYUT run3	28.39%	63.51%	80.10%	38.75%
DUTH_ATHENA MaxFT	31.43%	64.86%	74.46%	15.00%
DUTH_ATHENA MeanFT	32.02%	65.63%	73.81%	12.50%
DUTH_ATHENA MeanPosts	25.06%	63.97%	80.28%	30.00%
DUTH_ATHENA MeanPostsAB	33.04%	67.86%	80.32%	27.50%
DUTH_ATHENA MeanPostsSVM	**35.36**%	67.18%	73.97%	15.00%
NaCTeM run1	31.43%	64.54%	74.98%	18.75%
NaCTeM run2	31.55%	65.00%	75.04%	21.25%
NaCTeM run3	32.86%	66.67%	76.23%	22.50%
RELAI dmknn_dan	34.64%	67.58%	78.69%	23.75%
RELAI dmknn_danb	30.18%	65.26%	78.91%	25.00%
RELAI etm *	38.78%	72.56%	80.27%	35.71%
RELAI k_nn_dan	34.82%	66.07%	72.38%	11.25%
RELAI lda	28.33%	63.19%	68.00%	10.00%
Tanvi_Darci run 0	35.12%	67.76%	75.81%	22.50%
Unior_NLP uniorA	31.67%	63.95%	69.42%	08.75%
Unior_NLP uniorB	31.61%	64.66%	74.74%	15.00%
Unior_NLP uniorC	28.63%	63.31%	76.45%	20.00%
Unior_NLP uniorD	28.10%	64.25%	71.27%	15.00%
uOttawa1_sim_BERT_base+	28.39%	65.73%	78.91%	25.00%
uOttawa2_Top2Vec_USE+	28.04%	63.00%	77.32%	27.50%
uOttawa3_sim_BERT_large+	25.83%	59.68%	71.23%	27.50%
uOttawa4_Ensemble_BERT_QA	27.68%	62.08%	76.92%	20.00%
uOttawa5_sim_ROBERTA+	26.31%	62.60%	76.45%	30.00%
UPV-Symanto 0_symanto_upv_svm_linear_drb	34.58%	67.32%	75.62%	26.25%
UPV-Symanto 1_symanto_upv_svm_linear_mt30	32.20%	66.05%	77.28%	26.25%
UPV-Symanto 2_symanto_upv_svm_linear	33.15%	66.05%	75.42%	23.75%
UPV-Symanto 3_symanto_upv_rfc_df40_mt30	33.09%	66.39%	76.87%	23.75%
UPV-Symanto 4_symanto_upv_lingfeat_cors	34.17%	**73.17%**	82.42%	32.50%
All 0s Baseline	23.03%	54.92%	54.92%	7.50%
All 1s Baseline	32.02%	72.90%	81.63%	33.75%

improve the generalization process in order to advance towards a more comprehensive, more effective depression screening tool. Some of our future plans include to further analyze the participants' estimations (e.g., to determine which particular BDI questions are easier or harder to answer automatically) and to study whether or not specific questions of the questionnaire are more influential to the global depression score (ADODL and DCHR).

5 Conclusions

This paper provided an overview of eRisk 2021. The fifth edition of this lab focused on two types of tasks. On the one hand, two tasks were on early detection of pathological gambling and self-harm (Task 1 and 2, respectively), where participants had sequential access to the user's social media posts and had to send alerts about at-risk individuals. On the other hand, one task was released to measuring the severity of the signs of depression (Task 3), where the participants were given the full user history, and their systems had to automatically estimate the user's responses to a standard depression questionnaire

The proposed tasks received 117 runs from 18 teams in total. Although the effectiveness of the proposed solutions is still limited, the experimental results show that evidence extracted from social media is valuable, and automatic or semi-automatic screening tools could be developed to detect at-risk individuals. These results encourage us to further investigate the development of benchmarks for text-based screening of risk indicators.

Acknowledgements. This work was supported by projects RTI2018-093336-B-C21, RTI2018-093336-B-C22 (Ministerio de Ciencia e Innvovación & ERDF). The first and second authors thank the financial support supplied by the Consellería de Educación, Universidade e Formación Profesional (accreditation 2019–2022 ED431G/01, ED431B 2019/03) and the European Regional Development Fund, which acknowledges the CITIC Research Center in ICT of the University of A Coruña as a Research Center of the Galician University System. The third author also thanks the financial support supplied by the Consellería de Educación, Universidade e Formación Profesional (accreditation 2019–2022 ED431G-2019/04, ED431C 2018/29) and the European Regional Development Fund, which acknowledges the CiTIUS-Research Center in Intelligent Technologies of the University of Santiago de Compostela as a Research Center of the Galician University System.

References

1. Abbott, M.: The epidemiology and impact of gambling disorder and other gambling-related harm. In: WHO Forum on Alcohol, Drugs and Addictive Behaviours, Geneva, Switzerland (2017)
2. Beck, A.T., Ward, C.H., Mendelson, M., Mock, J., Erbaugh, J.: An inventory for measuring depression. JAMA Psychiatry **4**(6), 561–571 (1961)

3. Losada, D.E., Crestani, F.: A test collection for research on depression and language use. In: Fuhr, N., et al. (eds.) CLEF 2016. LNCS, vol. 9822, pp. 28–39. Springer, Cham (2016). https://doi.org/10.1007/978-3-319-44564-9_3
4. Losada, D.E., Crestani, F., Parapar, J.: eRISK 2017: CLEF lab on early risk prediction on the internet: experimental foundations. In: Jones, G.J.F., et al. (eds.) CLEF 2017. LNCS, vol. 10456, pp. 346–360. Springer, Cham (2017). https://doi.org/10.1007/978-3-319-65813-1_30
5. Losada, D.E., Crestani, F., Parapar, J.: eRisk 2017: CLEF lab on early risk prediction on the internet: experimental foundations. In: CEUR Proceedings of the Conference and Labs of the Evaluation Forum, CLEF 2017, Dublin, Ireland (2017)
6. Losada, D.E., Crestani, F., Parapar, J.: Overview of eRisk 2018: early risk prediction on the internet (extended lab overview). In: CEUR Proceedings of the Conference and Labs of the Evaluation Forum, CLEF 2018, Avignon, France (2018)
7. Losada, D.E., Crestani, F., Parapar, J.: Overview of eRisk: early risk prediction on the internet. In: Bellot, P., et al. (eds.) CLEF 2018. LNCS, vol. 11018, pp. 343–361. Springer, Cham (2018). https://doi.org/10.1007/978-3-319-98932-7_30
8. Losada, D.E., Crestani, F., Parapar, J.: Early detection of risks on the internet: an exploratory campaign. In: Azzopardi, L., Stein, B., Fuhr, N., Mayr, P., Hauff, C., Hiemstra, D. (eds.) ECIR 2019. LNCS, vol. 11438, pp. 259–266. Springer, Cham (2019). https://doi.org/10.1007/978-3-030-15719-7_35
9. Losada, D.E., Crestani, F., Parapar, J.: Overview of eRisk 2019 early risk prediction on the internet. In: Crestani, F., et al. (eds.) CLEF 2019. LNCS, vol. 11696, pp. 340–357. Springer, Cham (2019). https://doi.org/10.1007/978-3-030-28577-7_27
10. Losada, D.E., Crestani, F., Parapar, J.: Overview of eRisk at CLEF 2019: early risk prediction on the internet (extended overview). In: CEUR Proceedings of the Conference and Labs of the Evaluation Forum, CLEF 2019, Lugano, Switzerland (2019)
11. Losada, D.E., Crestani, F., Parapar, J.: erisk 2020: self-harm and depression challenges. In: Advances in Information Retrieval - 42nd European Conference on IR Research, ECIR 2020, Lisbon, Portugal, 14–17 April 2020, Proceedings, Part II, pp. 557–563 (2020)
12. Losada, D.E., Crestani, F., Parapar, J.: Overview of eRisk 2020: early risk prediction on the internet. In: Arampatzis, A., et al. (eds.) CLEF 2020. LNCS, vol. 12260, pp. 272–287. Springer, Cham (2020). https://doi.org/10.1007/978-3-030-58219-7_20
13. Losada, D.E., Crestani, F., Parapar, J.: Overview of erisk at CLEF 2020: early risk prediction on the internet (extended overview). In: Working Notes of CLEF 2020 - Conference and Labs of the Evaluation Forum, Thessaloniki, Greece, 22–25 September 2020 (2020)
14. Otero, D., Parapar, J., Barreiro, Á.: Beaver: efficiently building test collections for novel tasks. In: Proceedings of the First Joint Conference of the Information Retrieval Communities in Europe (CIRCLE 2020), Samatan, Gers, France, 6–9 July 2020 (2020)
15. Otero, D., Parapar, J., Barreiro, Á.: The wisdom of the rankers: a cost-effective method for building pooled test collections without participant systems. In: SAC '21: The 36th ACM/SIGAPP Symposium on Applied Computing, Virtual Event, Republic of Korea, 22–26 March 2021, pp. 672–680 (2021)

16. Parapar, J., Martín-Rodilla, P., Losada, D.E., Crestani, F.: erisk 2021: pathological gambling, self-harm and depression challenges. In: Advances in Information Retrieval - 43rd European Conference on IR Research, ECIR 2021, Virtual Event, 28 March–1 April 2021, Proceedings, Part II, pp. 650–656 (2021)
17. Sadeque, F., Xu, D., Bethard, S.: Measuring the latency of depression detection in social media. In: WSDM, pp. 495–503. ACM (2018)
18. Trotzek, M., Koitka, S., Friedrich, C.: Utilizing neural networks and linguistic metadata for early detection of depression indications in text sequences. IEEE Trans. Knowl. Data Eng. **32**, 588–601 (2018)

Overview of the ImageCLEF 2021: Multimedia Retrieval in Medical, Nature, Internet and Social Media Applications

Bogdan Ionescu[1(✉)], Henning Müller[2], Renaud Péteri[3], Asma Ben Abacha[4], Mourad Sarrouti[4], Dina Demner-Fushman[4], Sadid A. Hasan[5], Serge Kozlovski[6], Vitali Liauchuk[6], Yashin Dicente Cid[7], Vassili Kovalev[6], Obioma Pelka[8], Alba García Seco de Herrera[9], Janadhip Jacutprakart[9], Christoph M. Friedrich[8], Raul Berari[10], Andrei Tauteanu[10], Dimitri Fichou[10], Paul Brie[10], Mihai Dogariu[1], Liviu Daniel Ştefan[1], Mihai Gabriel Constantin[1], Jon Chamberlain[9], Antonio Campello[11], Adrian Clark[9], Thomas A. Oliver[12], Hassan Moustahfid[12], Adrian Popescu[13], and Jérôme Deshayes-Chossart[13]

[1] University Politehnica of Bucharest, Bucharest, Romania
bogdan.ionescu@upb.ro
[2] University of Applied Sciences Western Switzerland (HES-SO), Delémont, Switzerland
[3] University of La Rochelle, La Rochelle, France
[4] National Library of Medicine, Bethesda, USA
[5] CVS Health, Wellesley, MA, USA
[6] United Institute of Informatics Problems, Minsk, Belarus
[7] University of Warwick, Coventry, UK
[8] University of Applied Sciences and Arts Dortmund, Dortmund, Germany
[9] University of Essex, Colchester, UK
[10] teleportHQ, Cluj-Napoca, Romania
[11] Wellcome Trust, London, UK
[12] Pacific Islands Fisheries Science Center, Silver Spring, USA
[13] Université Paris-Saclay, CEA, List, Palaiseau, France

Abstract. This paper presents an overview of the ImageCLEF 2021 lab that was organized as part of the Conference and Labs of the Evaluation Forum – CLEF Labs 2021. ImageCLEF is an ongoing evaluation initiative (first run in 2003) that promotes the evaluation of technologies for annotation, indexing and retrieval of visual data with the aim of providing information access to large collections of images in various usage scenarios and domains. In 2021, the 19th edition of ImageCLEF runs four main tasks: (i) a *medical* task that groups three previous tasks, i.e., caption analysis, tuberculosis prediction, and medical visual question answering and question generation, (ii) a *nature* coral task about segmenting and labeling collections of coral reef images, (iii) an *Internet* task addressing the problems of identifying hand-drawn and digital user interface components, and (iv) a new *social media* aware task on estimating potential real-life effects of online image sharing. Despite the current pandemic situation, the benchmark campaign received a strong participation with over 38 groups submitting more than 250 runs.

K. S. Candan et al. (Eds.): CLEF 2021, LNCS 12880, pp. 345–370, 2021.
https://doi.org/10.1007/978-3-030-85251-1_23

Keywords: Visual question answering and generation · Medical image classification · Coral image segmentation and classification · Recognition of website user interface components · Prediction of effects of online image sharing · ImageCLEF lab

1 Introduction

ImageCLEF[1] is the image retrieval and classification lab of the CLEF (Conference and Labs of the Evaluation Forum) conference. ImageCLEF has started in 2003 with only four participants [12]. It increased its impact with the addition of medical tasks in 2004 [11], attracting over 20 participants already in the second year. An overview of ten years of the medical tasks can be found in [25]. It continued the ascending trend, reaching over 200 participants in 2019 and over 110 in 2020 despite the outbreak of the covid-19 pandemic. The tasks have changed much over the years but the general objective has always been the same, i.e., *to combine text and visual data to retrieve and classify visual information.* Tasks have evolved from more general object classification and retrieval to many specific application domains, e.g., nature, security, medical, Internet. A detailed analysis of several tasks and the creation of the data sets can be found in [31]. ImageCLEF has shown to have an important impact over the years, already detailed in 2010 [44,45].

Since 2018, ImageCLEF uses the crowdAI platform, now migrated to AIcrowd[2] from 2020, to distribute the data and receive the submitted results. The system allows having an online leader board and gives the possibility to keep data sets accessible beyond competition, including a continuous submission of runs and addition to the leader board. Over the years, ImageCLEF and also CLEF have shown a strong scholarly impact that was analyzed in [44,45]. For instance, the term "ImageCLEF" returns on Google Scholar[3] over 5,800 article results (search on June 11th, 2021). This underlines the importance of evaluation campaigns for disseminating best scientific practices. We introduce here the four tasks that were run in the 2021 edition[4], namely: ImageCLEFmedical, ImageCLEFcoral ImageCLEFdrawnUI, and the new ImageCLEFaware.

2 Overview of Tasks and Participation

ImageCLEF 2021 consists of four main tasks with the objective of covering a *diverse range* of multimedia retrieval applications, namely: *medicine*, *nature*, *Internet*, and *social media* applications. It followed the 2019 tradition [24] of diversifying the use cases [4,5,9,26,33,37]. The 2021 tasks are presented as follows (Fig. 1):

[1] http://www.imageclef.org/.
[2] https://www.aicrowd.com/.
[3] https://scholar.google.com/.
[4] https://www.imageclef.org/2021/.

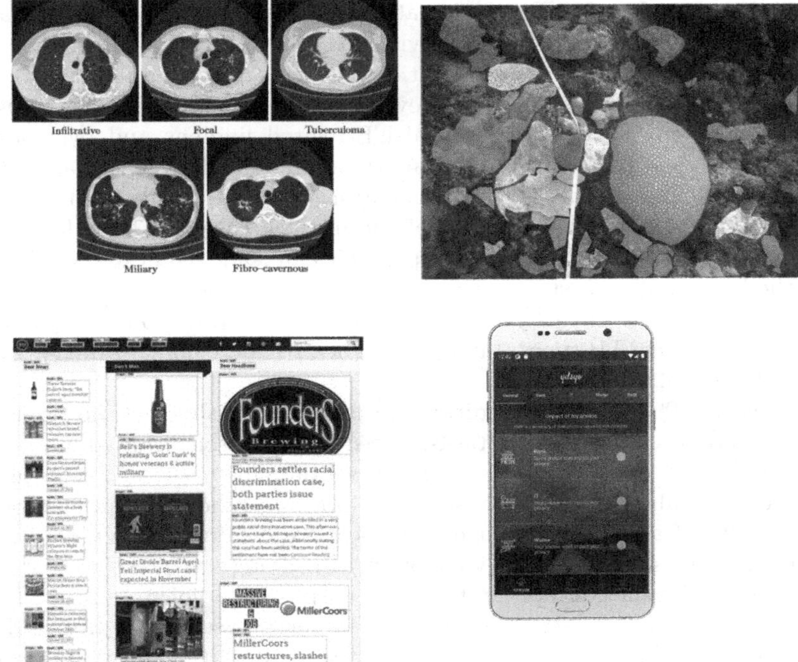

Fig. 1. Sample images from (left to right, top to bottom): ImageCLEFmedical tuberculosis prediction, ImageCLEFcoral with segmenting and labeling collections of coral reef images, ImageCLEFdrawnUI with recognition of website UIs, and ImageCLEFaware with estimating potential real-life effects of online image sharing.

- **ImageCLEFmedical**. Medical tasks have been part of ImageCLEF every year since 2004. In 2018, all but one task were medical, but little interaction happened between the medical tasks. For this reason, starting with 2019, the medical tasks were focused towards one specific problem but combined as a single task with several subtasks. This allows exploring synergies between the domains:
  - *Visual Question Answering*: This is the fourth edition of the VQA-Med task. With the increasing interest in artificial intelligence (AI) to support clinical decision making and improve patient engagement, opportunities to generate and leverage algorithms for automated medical image interpretation are currently being explored. In view of this and inspired by the success of the previous VQA-Med editions [2,3,21], we propose this year two tasks on visual question answering (VQA) and visual Question Generation (VQG) [4]. For the VQA task, given a radiology image accompanied with a relevant question, participating systems are tasked with answering the question based on the visual image content, while for the VQG task,

given a radiology image, participating systems are tasked with generating relevant questions based on the visual content of the medical image;
  - *Tuberculosis*: This is the fifth edition of the task. The main objective is to provide an automatic CT-based evaluation of tuberculosis (TB) patients. This is done by detecting visual TB-related findings and by assessing the TB type based on the automatic analysis of lung CT scans. Being able to generate this automatic analysis from the image data allows to have a preliminary assessment of the medical case and limit laboratory analyses to determine the TB type. This can lead to quicker decisions on the best treatment strategy, reduced use of antibiotics, and lower impact on the patient. In this year edition, participants need to directly classify one of the five TB types: Infiltrative, Focal, Tuberculoma, Miliary, Fibro-cavernous [26].
  - *Caption*: This is the fifth edition of the task in this format, however, it is based on previous medical tasks. Based on the lessons learned in previous years [15,22,23,34,35], this year [33] we brought back the "caption prediction" subtask which focuses on composing coherent captions for the entirety of a radiology image. This year we continue with the "concept detection" subtask which focuses on identifying the presence and location of relevant concepts in the same corpus of radiology images. In the 2021 edition, the dataset is the same as the dataset of the ImageCLEF-VQAMed 2021 task. This encourages teams to participate in both tasks, as detected concepts can be used as building blocks for the VQA tasks. But also generated questions and answers can be used to evaluate the concept detection models.
- **ImageCLEFdrawnUI**. Traditionally, user interfaces (UI) are drawn by designers before being translated into code by developers. As this process is error prone and time consuming, the use of deep learning to automatize it and help UI professionals is gaining traction. In this second edition of the task [5], participants need to develop a machine learning system able to detect the position and type of UI elements in images. The task is separated into two subtasks. The wireframe subtask takes, as in the last edition, hand drawn wireframes as input. Issues from last year, such as class imbalance have been addressed by adding new images. The new screenshot subtask takes digital images as input and is a more difficult challenge due to the ambiguous way the images can be analyzed.
- **ImageCLEFcoral**. This is the third edition of the task. As in previous years [7,8], the task addresses the problem of automatically segmenting and labeling a collection of images that can be used in combination to create 3D models for the monitoring of coral reefs. The task is separated into two subtasks which aim to label the images with types of benthic substrate. The first subtask uses bounding boxes to annotate the images while the second subtask segment the images pixel-wise using polygons. This year [9], the training and test data form the complete set of images required to form a 3D reconstruction of the environment.

Table 1. Key figures regarding participation in ImageCLEF 2021.

Task	Completed registrations	Groups that subm. results	Submitted runs	Submitted working notes
VQ answering	33	13	75	8
Tuberculosis	29	11	64	9
Caption	23	10	75	8
Coral	3	3	8	3
DrawnUI	8	3	28	2
Aware	7	2	6	0
Overall	103	42	256	30

- **ImageCLEFaware**. This was the first edition of the task [26]. The disclosure of personal data is done in a particular context and users are often unaware that their data can be reused in other contexts. It is thus important to give feedback to users about the effects of personal data sharing. The objective was to automatically provide a rating of a visual user profile in different real-life situations. A new dataset was created specifically for this task and will be shared publicly in the following months. Data were sampled from YFCC100 and were further anonymized in order to comply with GPDR.

To participate in the evaluation campaign, the research groups had to register by following the instructions on the ImageCLEF 2021 web page[5]. To ease the overall management of the campaign, in 2021 the challenge was organized through the AIcrowd platform[6]. To actually get access to the data sets, the participants were required to submit a signed End User Agreement (EUA). Table 1 summarizes the participation in ImageCLEF 2021, including the number of completed registrations, indicated both per task and for the overall lab. The table also shows the number of groups that submitted runs and the ones that submitted a working notes paper describing the techniques used. Teams were allowed to register for participating in several different tasks.

After a decrease in participation in 2016, the participation increased in 2017 and 2018, and increased again in 2019. In 2018, 31 teams completed the tasks and 28 working notes papers were received. In 2019, 63 teams completed the tasks and 50 working notes papers were retrieved. In 2020, 40 teams completed the tasks and submitted working notes papers. In 2021, 42 teams completed the tasks and we received 30 working notes papers. Although there is a slight increase in the number of teams succeeding to conclude the tasks, we can clearly see a drop in participation compared to 2019. We expect that this is mostly due to the current pandemic situation which caught us for the second time during the organizing of the lab. Nevertheless, we still received a hefty number

[5] https://www.imageclef.org/2021/.

[6] https://www.aicrowd.com/.

of systems, i.e., 256 runs, which allow for an effective comparison of the results of the proposed solutions.

In the following sections, we present the tasks. Only a short overview is reported, including general objectives, description of the tasks and data sets, and a short summary of the results. A detailed review of the received submissions for each task is provided with the task overview working notes: ImageCLEFmedical VQA [4], Tuberculosis [26], and Caption [33], ImageCLEFcoral [9], ImageCLEFdrawnUI [5], and ImageCLEFaware [37].

3 The Visual Question Answering Task

Visual Question Answering is an exciting problem that combines natural language processing (NLP) and computer vision (CV) techniques. With the increasing interest in artificial intelligence (AI) technologies to support clinical decision making and improve patient engagement, opportunities to generate and leverage algorithms for automated medical image interpretation are being explored at a faster pace. To offer more training data and evaluation benchmarks, we organized the first visual question answering (VQA) task in the medical domain in 2018 [21], and continued the task in 2019 [3] and 2020 [2]. Following the strong engagement from the research community in the previous editions of VQA in the medical domain (VQA-Med) and the ongoing interests from both computer vision and medical informatics communities, we continued the task this year (VQA-Med 2021) [4] with an enhanced focus on (i) answering medical questions about abnormalities and (ii) generating relevant natural language questions about radiology images based on their visual content[7].

3.1 Task Setup

Two subtasks were proposed:

- Visual question answering (VQA) task: given a radiology image accompanied by a relevant question, participating systems in VQA-Med 2021 were tasked with answering the question based on the visual image content.
- Visual question generation (VQG) task: given a radiology image, participating systems were tasked with generating relevant natural language questions about the abnormality present in the image.

3.2 Data Set

For the visual question answering task, we automatically constructed the training, validation, and test sets by: (i) applying several filters to select relevant images and associated annotations, and, (ii) creating patterns to generate the

[7] https://www.imageclef.org/2021/medical/vqa.

questions and their answers. We selected relevant medical images from the MedPix[8] database with filters based on their captions, localities, and diagnosis methods. We selected only the cases where the diagnosis was made based on the image. Finally, we considered the most frequent abnormality question categories to create the data set, which included a training set of 4,500 radiology images with 4,500 question-answer (QA) pairs (the same dataset used in 2020), a new validation set of 500 radiology images with 500 QA pairs, and a new test set of 500 radiology images with 500 questions about Abnormality. To further ensure the quality of the data, the reference answers of the test set were manually validated by a medical doctor.

For the visual question generation task, we automatically constructed the validation and test sets by using a collection of radiology images and their associated captions. We automatically generated questions from the images and their captions using two different approaches. To generate questions from the images, we used a variational autoencoder-based model called VQGR [40] trained on the VQA-RAD dataset (A CNN was used to encode the images and an LSTM to decode the questions). The second approach used a T5-based model fine-tuned on the SQuAD and MS MARCO datasets to generate questions from the image captions. Then, a medical doctor curated the list of created questions. The final curated corpus for the VQG task was comprised of 85 radiology images with 200 questions for validation, and 100 radiology images with 302 reference questions for the test set. For more details, please refer to the VQA-Med 2021 overview paper [4].

3.3 Participating Groups and Submitted Runs

Out of 48 online registrations, 33 participants submitted signed end user agreement forms. Finally, 13 teams submitted a total of 75 successful runs; 68 runs for the VQA task and 7 runs for the VQG task, indicating a notable interest in the VQA-Med challenge. Table 2 gives an overview of all participating teams and the number of submitted runs (please note that were allowed only 10 runs per team).

3.4 Results

Similar to the evaluation setup of the VQA-Med 2020 challenge [2], the evaluation of the participant systems for the VQA task in VQA-Med 2021 is also conducted based on two primary metrics: accuracy and BLEU. We used an adapted version of accuracy from the general domain VQA[9] task that strictly considers exact matching of a participant provided answer and the ground truth answer. To compensate for the strictness of the accuracy metric, BLEU [32] is used to capture the word overlap-based similarity between a system-generated answer and the ground truth answer. The overall methodology and resources for the

[8] https://medpix.nlm.nih.gov/.

[9] https://visualqa.org/evaluation.html.

Table 2. Participating groups in the VQA-Med 2021 tasks.

Team	Institution	# Valid runs
Zhao_Ling_Ling	Yunnan University (China)	10
Zhao_Shi_	School of Information Science and Engineering, Yunnan University (China)	2
dua_dua	School of Computer Science and Engineering, Sun Yat-sen University (China)	10
Li_Yong_	South China Normal University (China)	10
TeamS	D4L data4life gGmbH& Hasso Plattner Institute (Germany)	10
sheerin	Siva Subramaniya Nadar College of Engineering (India)	5
IALab_PUC	IALab group of the Pontifical Catholic University (Chile)	5
Chabbiimen	Research Groups in Intelligent Machines& Higher Institute of Informatics and Communication Technologies (Tunisia)	5

Table 3. Maximum Accuracy and Maximum BLEU Scores for the VQA Task (out of each team's submitted runs).

Team	Accuracy	BLEU
dua_dua	0.382	0.416
Zhao_Ling_Ling	0.362	0.402
TeamS	0.348	0.391
zhao_shi_	0.316	0.352
IALab_PUC	0.236	0.276
Li_Yong_	0.222	0.255
sheerin	0.196	0.227
Baseline 1	0.288	0.326
Baseline 2	0.134	0.156

Table 4. Maximum Average BLEU Scores for the VQG Task (out of each team's submitted runs).

Team	Average BLEU
Chabbiimen	0.383
Baseline	0.274

BLEU metric are essentially similar to last year's VQA task. The BLEU metric is also used to evaluate the submissions for the VQG task, where we essentially compute the word overlap-based average similarity score between the system-generated questions and the ground truth question for each given test image[10]. The overall results of the participating systems are presented in Table 3 and Table 4 in a descending order of the accuracy and average BLEU scores respectively (the higher the better).

3.5 Lessons Learned

Similar to last three years, participants continued to use state-of-the-art deep learning techniques to build their VQA-Med systems for both VQA and VQG tasks [2,3,21]. In particular, most systems leveraged encoder-decoder architectures with, e.g., deep convolutional neural networks (CNNs) like VGGNet or ResNet. A variety of pooling strategies were explored, e.g., global average pooling to encode image features and transformer-based architectures like BERT or recurrent neural networks (RNN) to extract question features (for the VQA task). Various types of attention mechanisms are also used coupled with different pooling strategies such as multimodal factorized bilinear (MFB) pooling or multi-modal factorized high-order pooling (MFH) in order to combine multimodal features followed by bilinear transformations to finally predict the possible answers in the VQA task and generate possible question words in the VQG task.

Analyses of the results in Table 3 suggest that in general, participating systems performed well for the VQA task. For the VQG task, results in Table 4 suggest that the task was comparatively challenging than the VQA task, but participating systems achieved better BLEU scores compared to last year's VQG results [2].

4 The Tuberculosis Task

Tuberculosis (TB) is a bacterial infection caused by a germ called Mycobacterium tuberculosis. About 130 years after its discovery, the disease remains a persistent threat and one of the top 10 causes of death worldwide according to the WHO [47]. The bacteria usually attack the lungs and generally TB can be cured with antibiotics. However, the different types of TB require different treatments, and therefore detection of the specific case characteristics is an important real-world task.

In the previous editions of this task, the setup evolved from year to year. In the first two editions [15,17] participants had to detect Multi-drug resistant patients (MDR subtask) and to classify the TB type (TBT subtask) both based only on the CT image. After 2 editions it was concluded to drop the MDR subtask because it seemed impossible to solve based only on the image, and the TBT subtask was also suspended because of a very little improvement in

[10] https://github.com/abachaa/VQA-Med-2021/tree/main/EvaluationCode.

the results between the 1st and the 2nd editions. At the same time, most of the participants obtained good results in the severity scoring (SVR) subtask introduced in 2018. In the 3d edition Tuberculosis task [16] was restructured to allow usage of the uniform dataset, and included two subtasks - continued Severity Score (SVR) prediction subtask and a new subtask based on providing an automatic report (CT Report) on the TB case. In the 4th edition [27], the SVR subtask was dropped and the automated CT report generation task was modified to be lung-based rather than CT-based.

Because of the fairly high results achieved by the participants in the CTR task last year, we decided to discontinue the CTR task at the moment and switch to the task which was not yet solved with high quality. So in this year's edition, it was decided to bring back to life the Tuberculosis Type classification task from the 1st and 2nd ImageCLEFmed Tuberculosis editions. The task dataset was updated, extended in size, and some additional information was added for part of the CT scans.

We hoped that utilizing the newest deep learning approaches together with available at the moment pre-trained models and additional data sets will allow the participants to achieve better results for the TB Type classification compared to the early editions of the task.

4.1 Task Setup

In this task, participants had to automatically categorize each TB case into one of the following five types: (1) Infiltrative, (2) Focal, (3) Tuberculoma, (4) Miliary, (5) Fibro-cavernous. So the task is a multi-label classification problem.

4.2 Data Set

In this edition, the data set containing chest CT scans of 1,338 TB patients was used: 917 images for the training (development) data set and 421 for the test set. Some of the scans were accompanied by additional meta-information, depending on data available for different cases. Each CT image corresponded to only one TB type and to one unique patient. For all patients, we provided 3D CT images with a slice size of 512×512 pixels and a variable number of slices (the median number was 128).

Same as in the previous year, for all patients we provided two versions of automatically extracted masks of the lungs obtained using the methods described in [14,29].

4.3 Participating Groups and Submitted Runs

In 2021, 11 groups from 9 countries submitted at least one run. Similar to the previous editions, each group could submit up to 10 runs. 64 scored runs were submitted in total. All groups used CNNs in some way, and two groups used a combination of CNN and RNN. Several groups tried a few different methods during their experiments, all reported approaches are listed below.

The majority of participants (seven groups) used 2D CNN to analyze either selected projections of CT images or all slices. Two of these groups further used per-slice features output of 2D CNN to train RNN in order to extract inter-slice information. Four groups tried to utilize 3D CNNs for whole CT analysis. Different neural network architectures and model training tweaks were used by participants, the majority of participants also used transfer learning techniques. All participants used some approaches for artificial data set enlargement and a few pre-processing steps, such as resizing, normalization, slice filtering etc.

Table 5. Results obtained by the participants of the task. Only the best run of each participant is reported here.

Group name	Run ID	Kappa	Accuracy	Run rank
SenticLab.UAIC	135715	0.221	0.466	1
hasibzunair	135720	0.200	0.423	4
SDVA-UCSD	135721	0.190	0.371	8
Emad_Aghajanzadeh	135689	0.181	0.404	11
MIDL-NCAI-CUI	134939	0.140	0.333	23
uaic2021	135708	0.129	0.333	28
IALab_PUC	134688	0.120	0.401	30
KDE-lab	133407	0.117	0.382	31
JBTTM	134791	0.038	0.221	42
Zhao_Shi_	133103	0.015	0.380	47
YNUZHOU	133288	−0.008	0.385	55

4.4 Results

The task was evaluated as a multi-label classification problem and scored using unweighted Cohen's Kappa and accuracy metrics. The ranking of this task is done first by Kappa and then by accuracy. Table 5 shows the final results for each group's best run and includes the run rank. More detailed results, including other performance measures, are presented in the overview article [26].

4.5 Lessons Learned and Next Steps

The results obtained in the task should be compared to the same TBT sub-task presented in the 2018 edition. Before comparison, we should note, that although the task setup is the same in both editions, the data set was significantly changed, which means participants needed to deal with different images and labels distribution, so the scores can't be compared directly.

Top scores in the 2018 and 2021 editions are pretty close. The best result of 2021 achieved by SenticLab.UAIC group is slightly worse than the best result of 2018 - 0.221 vs 0.231 (−0.01 drop). On the other hand, four groups overcome 2nd best result from 2018. We should also mention that the group SDVA-UCSD participated in both editions and was able to improve Kappa score from 0.15 to 0.19. The best performer, SenticLab.UAIC group used per-slice analysis, which combined selection of relevant slices and their analysis by EfficientNet-B4 network. The 2nd-ranked hasibzunair group developed a hybrid CNN-RNN model and used pre-training on human action videos. The 3rd ranked SDVA-UCSD group used 3D ResNet34 with convolutional block attention.

Results analysis shows, that while the best result was not improved this year compared to the similar 2018 subtask, overall the top-5 scores of 2021 look better than in the 2018 edition, and the group which participated in both editions was able to improve its result. Analyzing participants working notes we observed the variability of participants approaches (top-3 groups used very different methods) and usage of modern machine learning techniques and methods. As a result, we can conclude that the task is successful and its outcome is informative and useful.

Possible updates for future editions of TBT task should consider: (i) extending the additional meta-information for CT scans; (ii) including some kind of lesion location information to the data set.

5 The Caption Task

The caption task was first proposed as part of the ImageCLEFmedical [23] in 2016. In 2017 and 2018 [15,22] the ImageCLEFcaption task comprised two subtasks: concept detection and caption prediction. In 2019 [34] and 2020 [35], the task concentrated on extracting Unified Medical Language System® (UMLS) Concept Unique Identifiers (CUIs) [6] from radiology images.

In 2021 [33], both subtasks, concept detection and caption prediction, were running again due to participants demands. To make the task more realistic, the focus in ImageCLEF 2021 lies in using real radiology images annotated by medical doctors in contrast to earlier years where images have been extracted from medical publications. Since this task can be considered as a first step of the Visual Question Answering Task 3, this year both tasks used the same dataset.

5.1 Task Setup

The ImageCLEFmed Caption 2021 [33] follows the format of the ImageCLEFmed caption previous tasks. In 2021, the overall task comprises two subtasks: "Concept Detection" and "Caption prediction". The concept detection subtask focuses on predicting Unified Medical Language System® (UMLS) Concept Unique Identifiers (CUIs) [6] based on the visual image representation in a given image. The caption prediction subtask focuses composing coherent captions for the entirety of the images.

The detected concepts are evaluated using the balanced precision and recall trade-off in terms of F1-scores, as in previous years. The predicted captions are evaluated using the BLEU score independent from the first subtask and designed to be robust to variability in style and wording.

5.2 Data Set

In 2021, the dataset is the same as the ImageCLEFVQA task [4] (see details in Sect. 4.2). The VQA-Med collection of radiology images and their annotations were used as a basis for the extraction of the concepts and captions. Semi-automatic text preprocessing was then applied to improve the quality of the annotations.

Following this approach, we provided new training, validation, and test sets for both tasks:

- The Caption and Concept training sets contain 2,756 radiology images and associated captions and concepts.
- The validation sets contain 500 radiology images and associated captions and concepts.
- The test sets contain 500 radiology images and associated reference captions and concepts.

We have also validated all the captions manually and checked the coherence of the generated concepts in the training, validation, and test sets.

As an additional source for training machine learning systems, the ROCO dataset [36], that has been used in the preceding years could be used by the participants.

Table 6. Performance of the participating teams in the ImageCLEF 2021 Concept Detection Task. The best run per team is selected. Teams with previous participation in 2020 are marked with an asterix.

Team	Institution	F1 Score
AUEB NLP Group*	Information Processing Laboratory, Department of Informatics, Athens University of Economics and Business, Athens, Greece	0.505
NLIP-Essex*-ITESM	School of Computer Science and Electronic Engineering, University of Essex, Colchester, UK and Instituto Tecnologico y de Estudios Superiores de Monterrey, Monterrey, Mexico	0.469
ImageSem	Institute of Medical Information and Library, Chinese Academy of Medical Sciences and Peking Union Medical College, Beijing, China	0.419
IALab PUC	Department of Computer Science, Pontificia Universidad Católica de Chile, Región Metropolitana, Chile	0.360
RomiBed	The Center for machine vision and signal analysis, University of Oulu, Oulu, Finland	0.143

Table 7. Performance of the participating teams in the ImageCLEF 2021 Caption Prediction Task. The best run per team is selected.

Team	Institution	BLEU Score
IALab PUC	Department of Computer Science, Pontificia Universidad Católica de Chile, Región Metropolitana, Chile	0.5098
AUEB NLP Group	Information Processing Laboratory, Department of Informatics, Athens University of Economics and Business, Athens, Greece	0.4610
AEHRC-CSIRO	Australian e-Health Research Centre, Commonwealth Scientific and Industrial Research Organisation, Herston, Australia	0.4319
kdelab	Department of Computer Science and Engineering, Toyohashi University of Technology, Aichi, Japan	0.3616
jeanbenoit_delbrouck	Laboratory of Quantitative Imaging and Artificial Intelligent, Department of Biomedical Data Science, Stanford University, Stanford, United States	0.2850
ImageSem	Institute of Medical Information and Library, Chinese Academy of Medical Sciences and Peking Union Medical College, Beijing, China	0.2565
RomiBed	Center for machine vision and signal analysis, University of Oulu, Finland	0.2427
ayushnanda14	Department of Computer Science and Engineering, Siva Subramaniya Nadar College of Engineering, Kalavakkam, India	0.1029

5.3 Participating Groups and Submitted Runs

In the fifth edition of the ImageCLEFcaption task, 23 teams registered and signed the End-User-Agreement license, needed to download the development data. 75 graded runs were submitted for evaluation by 10 teams (8 submitted working notes) attracting more attention than last year. Each of the group was allowed 10 graded runs per subtask. In the concept detection task 5 teams participated and 2 teams also took part in the 2020 challenge. The caption prediction task raised interest of 8 teams, that submitted their results, 2 teams decided not to submit working notes.

In the concept detection subtask, the groups typically used deep learning models trained as multi-label classificators or more Information Retrieval oriented solutions. For the IR solutions, image embeddings from deep learning models are typically used. In this year, more modern deep learning architectures like EfficientNets [41] and Visual Transformers (ViT) [18] have been proposed for the solutions. In the caption prediction task, several teams used variations of the

Show, Attend and Tell model. New has been the occurrence of Transformer based architectures and general language models like GPT-2 [38]. Transfer Learning has frequently been used and some teams in both subtasks tried to pretrain with more medically oriented datasets like ROCO or CheXpert.

To get a better overview of the submitted runs, the best results for each team are presented in Tables 6 and 7.

5.4 Results

This years models for concept detection show again increased F1-scores in comparison to earlier years. This could partly be explained by a smaller number of potential concepts in the images. More modern architectures have been used and show improvements. Transformer based architectures and solutions arrived at both tasks. For concept detection in this year machine learning based methods and information retrieval oriented solutions have been used more equally by all groups. In former years the majority of proposed solutions used multi-label approaches. Some participants noticed, that less complex solutions showed the best results. An in-depth analysis is presented in [33].

5.5 Lessons Learned and Next Steps

The participants appreciated, that more realistic medical images have been used in contrast to the publication based images from last years. On the other hand the size of the training and testing datasets is small in comparison to other datasets. This leads to simpler solutions as less concepts are present and the captions show less variation. One expectable next step would be to increase the number of concepts and variation of image descriptions further by increasing the dataset size. The use of the ROCO dataset as a pretraining solutions showed no improvement for the groups that used it. It can be assumed, that the descriptions/captions of the VQA-task images have a different focus in comparison to the ROCO images.

6 The DrawnUI Task

Creating high quality User Interfaces (UI) is a complex process involving several actors such as designers and developers. As more companies push to increase their online presence, the automatization of this process is gaining interest. Pix2Code [1] and UI2Code [10] were proposed in 2018 to tackle this challenge, those solutions took as input a screenshot and output a domain specific language representing the UI.

The first edition of the ImageCLEFdrawnUI task [20] took place in 2020 with a data set of 3,000 wireframe. Participants were tasked to create a computer vision system to localize and identify different UI elements in the drawings. Two of the three participating teams obtained results exceeding the baseline using various object detection algorithm combined with data preprocessing, cleaning and augmentation.

6.1 Task Setup

The 2021 ImageCLEFdrawnUI task (see the detailed overview paper [5]) is the second edition of the task and consist of two challenges. Given hand drawn (wireframes) and digital (screenshots) images of user interfaces, participants must develop a machine learning models to predict the bounding boxes coordinates and type of each UI elements in the images. For each task, the data sets are separated in 75% for training and 25% for validation. The $MAP0.5IoU$ and $R0.5IoU$ [19] were used to evaluate the submissions.

6.2 Data Set

For the wireframe task, the data set contained 4,291 hand-drawn wireframe images. Each images was drawn based on actual screenshots of mobile and web UIs. Images from the RICO data set [13] were used for the mobile UI while a custom parser was used to obtain the web pages UIs. For the drawing itself, three persons were involved and had to use a predefined dictionary of 21 shapes and were instructed to focus on an unambiguous drawing instead of fidelity to the original screenshot to facilitate the following annotation step and thereafter the computer vision task. The VOTT software[11] was used for annotation by two different annotators and verified by a single person afterward. In the previous edition, there was a large class imbalance in the dataset, to overcome this, new images containing a larger proportion of the rare class were introduce and the class distribution was more carefully monitored during the creation of both train and validation set.

Table 8. Participation in the DrawUI 2021 task, wireframe subtask: the best score from all runs for each team.

Team	#Runs	MAP@0.5	R@0.5
vyskocj	10	0.900	0.934
pwc	10	0.836	0.865
AIMultimediaLab	1	0.216	0.319

Table 9. Participation in the DrawUI 2021 task, screenshot subtask: the best score from all runs.

Team	#Runs	MAP@0.5	R@0.5
vyskocj	7	0.628	0.83

For the screenshot task, the data set consisted of 9,276 screenshots. A custom parser was used to obtain the images, In addition to the screenshot, the parser

[11] https://github.com/microsoft/VoTT.

also screened the Document Oriented Model to extract the position and type of each HTML element of the webpages. Those UI elements were then attributed when applicable to one of the 6 elements of the retained dictionary (TEXT, IMAGE, HEADING, BUTTON, INPUT, LINK).

6.3 Participating Groups and Submitted Runs

8 teams registered for both tasks. For the wireframe task, 3 teams from 3 countries submitted 21 runs. For the screenshot task, 1 team submitted 7 run. Teams were limited to submit 10 runs (Tables 8 and 9).

6.4 Results

The $MAP0.5IoU$ and $R0.5IoU$ scores have been compiled using the Python API of COCO[12]. For both subtasks, the participants used recent object detection model architectures such as YOLOv5 and Faster R-CNN supplemented by a Feature Pyramid Network. Data augmentation methods were also employed, ranging from color and contrast normalization, to random cutting out of objects and relative resizing of the images. In the screenshot subtask, low-quality data points were filtered out based on color similarity checking. Overall, these experiments brought the mAP score to 0.900 for the wireframe subtask and 0.628 for the screenshot one, representing a promising improvement compared to the 2020 edition.

6.5 Lessons Learned and Next Steps

Based on the high scores obtained when tackling it, the wireframe challenge is nearing full completion. For the screenshot subtask, it was also demonstrated that a smaller sized model converged faster to an adequate level, indicating that large resource allocation is not a necessity for satisfactory results. Although the participation rate was very low, our baseline scores were still surpassed and the contestants proposed uniquely adapted modifications of the data set and the models for solving the subtasks.

For the next editions of the task, the further development and extension the two data sets remains a priority. We will stress making them more challenging from a technical perspective, as well as showcasing them to the UI-based communities, attracting more participants interested in the ML-facilitated development of user interfaces.

7 The Coral Task

There is a crucial need to implement effective monitoring techniques to protect coral reefs immediately and in the long term [46]. This monitoring process can

[12] https://github.com/cocodataset/cocoapi.

be made by collecting 3D visual data using autonomous underwater vehicles which will provide useful information for both annotation and further study of the coral. The ImageCLEFcoral task organisers have developed a novel multi-camera system that allows large amounts of imagery to be captured by a SCUBA diver or autonomous underwater vehicle in a single dive.

In its 3rd edition, the ImageCLEFcoral data form the complete set of images required to form a 3D reconstruction of the environment. This allows the participants to explore novel probabilistic computer vision techniques based around image overlap and transposition of data points.

7.1 Task Setup

Following the format of previous editions of the ImageCLEFcoral task [7,8], in 2021 participants were again asked to devise and implement algorithms for automatically annotating regions in a collection of images containing several types of benthic substrate, such as hard coral or sponge. As in previous editions, the overall task comprises two sub-tasks: "Coral reef image annotation and localisation" and "Coral reef image pixel-wise parsing" subtasks. The "Coral reef image annotation and localisation" subtask uses bounding boxes for the annotation, with sides parallel to the edges of the image, around identified features. The "Coral reef image pixel-wise parsing" subtasks uses a series of boundary image coordinates which form a single polygon around each identified feature; this has been dubbed *pixel-wise parsing* (these polygons should not have self-intersections). Participants were invited to make submissions for either or both tasks.

Algorithmic performance is evaluated on the unseen test data using the popular intersection over union metric from the PASCAL VOC[13] exercise. This computes the area of intersection of the output of an algorithm and the corresponding ground truth, normalising that by the area of their union to ensure its maximum value is bounded.

7.2 Data Set

As in previous editions, the data for this ImageCLEFcoral task originates from a growing, large-scale collection of images taken from coral reefs around the world as part of a coral reef monitoring project with the Marine Technology Research Unit at the University of Essex. The images contain annotations of the following 13 types of substrates: Hard Coral – Branching, Hard Coral – Submassive, Hard Coral – Boulder, Hard Coral – Encrusting, Hard Coral – Table, Hard Coral – Foliose, Hard Coral – Mushroom, Soft Coral, Soft Coral – Gorgonian, Sponge, Sponge – Barrel, Fire Coral – Millepora and Algae - Macro or Leaves.

In 2021, the training and test data form the complete set of images required to form a 3D reconstruction of the environment. The training dataset contains images from 6 subsets from 4 locations. 1 subset is complete (containing all the

[13] http://host.robots.ox.ac.uk/pascal/VOC/.

images to build the 3D model) and 5 subsets contain a partial collection. The test data contains the images required to complete 4 of the partial image sets from each of the 4 locations (the final partial subset is not used for testing, only training).

In addition, participants are encouraged to use the publicly available NOAA NCEI data[14] and/or CoralNet[15] to train their approaches.

7.3 Participating Groups and Submitted Runs

In this third edition of the ImageCLEFcoral task, 8 teams registered, of which 3 teams submitted 8 runs. Teams were limited to submit 10 runs per subtask. To get a better overview of the submitted runs, the best results for each team are presented in Tables 10 and 11. An in-depth analysis is presented in [9].

Table 10. Coral reef image annotation and localisation performance in terms of $MAP0.5IoU$. The best run per team is selected.

Run id	Team	MAP 0.5 IoU
139118	UAlbany	0.457
138115	University of West Bohemia	0.121

Table 11. Pixel-wise coral reef parsing performance in terms of $MAP0.5IoU$. The best run per team is selected.

Run id	Team	MAP 0.5 IoU
139084	University of West Bohemia	0.075
138389	MTRU	0.021

7.4 Results

The results from both tasks showed lower performance than has been achieved in previous years. More detailed analysis of the results is presented in [9], where pixel accuracy per class is investigated. This gives us a better indication as to which classes are difficult to train for and identify. Previous years' tasks used only training data from a single location, so the reason for obtaining good performance when testing with a dataset from the same area is clear. By contrast, this year both the training and test datasets were from multiple locations. In addition, some participants included large-scale training datasets from a fifth location.

[14] https://www.ncei.noaa.gov/.
[15] https://coralnet.ucsd.edu/.

7.5 Lessons Learned and Next Steps

The varied morphology and distribution of substrates across different datasets and locations suggest that trying to develop a single generic algorithm to detect coral reef substrate type will be challenging. This proved to be the case for the datasets used in this task, even with the incorporation of considerably larger datasets from other sources as training corpora. The next steps for this work are to leverage the image overlap of the data to develop probabilistic labelled models in 3D and develop cross-compatibility in large datasets for use in this task.

8 The Aware Task

Social networks engage the users to share their personal data in order to interact with other users. The context of the sharing is chosen by the users but they do not have control on further data use. These data are automatically aggregated into profiles which are exploited by social networks to propose personalized advertising/services to users. Depending on their visibility, data can be also consulted by other entities to make decisions which have a high impact on the user's life. It is thus important to give users feedback about the potential real-life effects of their personal data sharing.

We designed a task focused on the automatic rating of visual user profile in four impactful situations. Each profile includes 100 photos and its appeal is manually evaluated via crowdsourcing. Participants are asked to provide automatic visual profile ratings obtained by using a training set which includes visual- and situation-related information. These ratings are then ranked and compared to manual ones in order to assess the feasibility of providing automatic feedback related to the effects of personal photos sharing. Two teams submitted results for this first edition of the task.

8.1 Task Setup

This is the first edition of the task and consists of one challenge. Participants are provided with automatic object detections for the images and with object ratings per situation. Then, the objective is to propose a ranking of user profiles which is as close as possible to the crowdsourced one. Data were split into 360/40/100 profiles for training/validation and test. The Pearson correlation coefficient between manual and automatic profile rankings was used to evaluate the quality of proposed runs. The final scores were calculated by averaging correlations obtained for individual situations.

8.2 Data Set

A data set of 500 user profiles with 100 photos per profile was created and annotated with an "appeal" score for four real-life situations via crowdsourcing.

The modeled situations are demands for: a bank credit, an accommodation, a job as an IT engineer, a job as a waiter. Participants to the experiment were asked to provide a global rating of each profile in each situation modeled using a 7-points Likert scale ranging from "strongly unappealing" to "strongly appealing". The averaged "appeal" score was used to create a ground truth composed of ranked users in each modeled situation. User profiles are created by repurposing a subset of the YFCC100M dataset [43].

Situations are modeled by crowdsourcing visual objects ratings. Similar to profile crowdsourcing, object ratings are collected for each situation using a 7-points Likert scale with ratings between -3 (strongly negative influence) to +3 (strongly positive influence). The averaged rating is computed and provided to participants. A Faster R-CNN object detector was trained in order to detect objects in images. The detection dataset combines objects from OpenImages [28], ImageNet [39] and COCO [30]. Only objects with at least one non-zero situation rating were kept. All objects detected in the 100 images of a profile were provided to participants, along with the detection probability and the associated bounding box. Given a situation, the combination of the ratings of objects and of their automatic detection enables the automatic computation of a profile score.

Given the personal nature of the included profiles, the dataset was anonymized in order to comply with GDPR. Participants did not have access to the images, and the user IDs and the object names were hashed.

8.3 Participating Groups and Submitted Runs

We received in total 6 valid submissions from 2 teams. SIP_Team was from the University of Paris, France. v18nguye is an independent researcher. None of the two participants provided details about their participation.

Table 12. Results of the Aware 2021 task.

Team	# Runs	Pearson
SIP_Team	3	0.597
v18nguye	3	0.388

8.4 Lessons Learned and Next Steps

While no details were provided about the implemented methods, the scores reported in Table 12 give a good correlation between automatic and manual profile rankings. This means that automatic methods for computing visual profile ratings are effective.

These initial results encourage us to pursue the task next year. We plan to: (1) enrich the dataset with new objects which have a strong influence in at least one of the modeled situations, (2) use more recent object detectors, such as EfficientDet [42], which should boost results via an improved photo analysis and (3) increase the number of user profiles in order to have a more representative training set.

9 Conclusion

This paper presents a general overview of the activities and outcomes of the ImageCLEF 2021 evaluation campaign. Four tasks were organised, covering challenges in the medical domain (visual question answering and visual question generation, tuberculosis prediction, and caption analysis), nature (segmenting and labeling collections of coral images), Internet (identifying website user interface components), and social networks (analysis of the real-life effects of personal data sharing). Despite the outbreak of the COVID-19 pandemic and lock-down during the benchmark, 103 teams registered, 42 teams completed the tasks and submitted over 256 runs.

As anticipated already, most of the proposed solutions evolved around state-of-the-art deep neural network architectures. In the VQA task most systems leveraged encoder-decoder architectures with, e.g., deep convolutional neural networks (CNNs) like VGGNet or ResNet. Systems were able to solve the VQA task with good performance. The VQG task proved to be more challenging, however, results improved compared to the last year's edition. In the tuberculosis task, the best result was not improved this year compared to the similar 2018 task. However, overall, the top-5 scores of 2021 look better than in the 2018 edition, and the group which participated in both editions was able to improve its result. The methods employed a variety of different approaches. In the caption task, the more realistic medical images were closer to a real-world use case scenario. On the other hand, the size of the training and testing datasets is smaller. This led to simpler solutions as less concepts are present and the captions show less variation.

In the drawnUI task, the wireframe challenge achieved close to perfect solutions. For the screenshot task, it was also demonstrated that a smaller sized model converged faster to an adequate level, indicating that large resource allocation is not a necessity for satisfactory results. In the coral task, the varied morphology and distribution of substrates across different datasets and locations suggest that trying to develop a single generic algorithm to detect coral reef substrate type will be challenging. This was also visible from the results which are still low for an on-the-field application. The aware task is a new concept and was in its first edition this year. Despite the incipient participation, achieved results prove the feasibility of the concept.

ImageCLEF 2021 brought again together an interesting mix of tasks and approaches and we are looking forward to the fruitful discussions at the CLEF 2021 workshop.

Acknowledgements. Data collection for the Tuberculosis task was supported by the National Institute of Allergy and Infectious Diseases, National Institutes of Health, US Department of Health and Human Services, CRDF project DAA9-19-65987-1.

The aware task was fully supported and the drawnUI was partially supported under project AI4Media, A European Excellence Centre for Media, Society and Democracy, H2020 ICT-48-2020, grant #951911.

References

1. Beltramelli, T.: pix2code: generating code from a graphical user interface screenshot. In: Proceedings of the ACM SIGCHI Symposium on Engineering Interactive Computing Systems, pp. 1–9 (2018)
2. Ben Abacha, A., Datla, V.V., Hasan, S.A., Demner-Fushman, D., Müller, H.: Overview of the VQA-med task at ImageCLEF 2020: visual question answering and generation in the medical domain. In: CLEF 2020 Working Notes. CEUR Workshop Proceedings, CEUR-WS.org, Thessaloniki, Greece, 22–25 September 2020 (2020)
3. Ben Abacha, A., Hasan, S.A., Datla, V.V., Liu, J., Demner-Fushman, D., Müller, H.: VQA-Med: overview of the medical visual question answering task at ImageCLEF 2019. In: CLEF2019 Working Notes. CEUR Workshop Proceedings, CEUR-WS.org, Lugano, Switzerland, 09–12 September 2019 (2019). http://ceur-ws.org
4. Ben Abacha, A., Sarrouti, M., Demner-Fushman, D., Hasan, S.A., Müller, H.: Overview of the VQA-med task at ImageCLEF 2021: visual question answering and generation in the medical domain. In: CLEF 2021 Working Notes. CEUR Workshop Proceedings, CEUR-WS.org, Bucharest, Romania, 21–24 September 2021 (2021)
5. Berari, R., et al.: Overview of ImageCLEFdrawnUI 2021: the detection and recognition of hand drawn and digital website UIs task. In: CLEF2021 Working Notes. CEUR Workshop Proceedings, CEUR-WS.org, Bucharest, Romania, 21–24 September 2021 (2021). http://ceur-ws.org
6. Bodenreider, O.: The Unified Medical Language System (UMLS): integrating biomedical terminology. Nucleic Acids Res. **32**(Database-Issue), 267–270 (2004). https://doi.org/10.1093/nar/gkh061
7. Chamberlain, J., Campello, A., Wright, J.P., Clift, L.G., Clark, A., García Seco de Herrera, A.: Overview of ImageCLEFcoral 2019 task. In: CLEF2019 Working Notes. CEUR Workshop Proceedings. CEUR-WS.org (2019)
8. Chamberlain, J., Campello, A., Wright, J.P., Clift, L.G., Clark, A., García Seco de Herrera, A.: Overview of the ImageCLEFcoral 2020 task: automated coral reef image annotation. In: CLEF2020 Working Notes. CEUR Workshop Proceedings. CEUR-WS.org (2020)
9. Chamberlain, J., García Seco de Herrera, A., Campello, A., Clark, A., Oliver, T.A., Moustahfid, H.: Overview of the ImageCLEFcoral 2021 task: coral reef image annotation of a 3D environment (2021)
10. Chen, C., Su, T., Meng, G., Xing, Z., Liu, Y.: From UI design image to GUI skeleton: a neural machine translator to bootstrap mobile GUI implementation. In: International Conference on Software Engineering, vol. 6 (2018)
11. Clough, P., Müller, H., Sanderson, M.: The CLEF 2004 cross-language image retrieval track. In: Peters, C., Clough, P., Gonzalo, J., Jones, G.J.F., Kluck, M., Magnini, B. (eds.) CLEF 2004. LNCS, vol. 3491, pp. 597–613. Springer, Heidelberg (2005). https://doi.org/10.1007/11519645_59
12. Clough, P., Sanderson, M.: The CLEF 2003 cross language image retrieval task. In: Proceedings of the Cross Language Evaluation Forum (CLEF 2003) (2004)
13. Deka, B., et al.: Rico: a mobile app dataset for building data-driven design applications. In: Proceedings of the 30th Annual ACM Symposium on User Interface Software and Technology, UIST 2017, pp. 845–854 (2017). https://doi.org/10.1145/3126594.3126651
14. Dicente Cid, Y., Jimenez-del-Toro, O., Depeursinge, A., Müller, H.: Efficient and fully automatic segmentation of the lungs in CT volumes. In: Goksel, O., Jimenez-del-Toro, O., Foncubierta-Rodriguez, A., Müller, H. (eds.) Proceedings of the VIS-

CERAL Challenge at ISBI. CEUR Workshop Proceedings, vol. 1390, pp. 31–35, April 2015

15. Dicente Cid, Y., Kalinovsky, A., Liauchuk, V., Kovalev, V., Müller, H.: Overview of ImageCLEFtuberculosis 2017 - predicting tuberculosis type and drug resistances. In: CLEF2017 Working Notes. CEUR Workshop Proceedings, CEUR-WS.org, Dublin, Ireland, 11–14 September 2017 (2017). http://ceur-ws.org
16. Dicente Cid, Y., Liauchuk, V., Klimuk, D., Tarasau, A., Kovalev, V., Müller, H.: Overview of ImageCLEFtuberculosis 2019 - automatic CT-based report generation and tuberculosis severity assessment. In: CLEF2019 Working Notes. CEUR Workshop Proceedings, CEUR-WS.org, Lugano, Switzerland, 9–12 September 2019 (2019). http://ceur-ws.org
17. Dicente Cid, Y., Liauchuk, V., Kovalev, V., Müller, H.: Overview of ImageCLEFtuberculosis 2018 - detecting multi-drug resistance, classifying tuberculosis type, and assessing severity score. In: CLEF2018 Working Notes. CEUR Workshop Proceedings, CEUR-WS.org, Avignon, France, 10–14 September 2018 (2018). http://ceur-ws.org
18. Dosovitskiy, A., et al.: An image is worth 16 × 16 words: transformers for image recognition at scale. In: Proceedings of the 9th International Conference on Learning Representations (ICLR 2021): 03–07 May 2021, Online Event (2021). https://openreview.net/forum?id=YicbFdNTTy
19. Everingham, M., Gool, L.V., Williams, C.K.I., Winn, J., Zisserman, A.: The PASCAL Visual Object Classes (VOC) challenge. Int. J. Comput. Vis. **88**, 303–338 (2010). https://doi.org/10.1007/s11263-009-0275-4
20. Fichou, D., et al.: Overview of ImageCLEFdrawnUI 2020: the detection and recognition of hand drawn website UIs task. In: CLEF2020 Working Notes. CEUR Workshop Proceedings, CEUR-WS.org, Thessaloniki, Greece, 22–25 September 2020 (2020). http://ceur-ws.org
21. Hasan, S.A., Ling, Y., Farri, O., Liu, J., Lungren, M., Müller, H.: Overview of the ImageCLEF 2018 medical domain visual question answering task. In: CLEF2018 Working Notes. CEUR Workshop Proceedings, CEUR-WS.org, Avignon, France, 10–14 September 2018 (2018). http://ceur-ws.org
22. García Seco de Herrera, A., Eickhoff, C., Andrearczyk, V., Müller, H.: Overview of the ImageCLEF 2018 caption prediction tasks. In: CLEF2018 Working Notes. CEUR Workshop Proceedings, CEUR-WS.org, Avignon, France, 10–14 September 2018 (2018). http://ceur-ws.org
23. García Seco de Herrera, A., Schaer, R., Bromuri, S., Müller, H.: Overview of the ImageCLEF 2016 medical task. In: Working Notes of CLEF 2016 (Cross Language Evaluation Forum), September 2016
24. Ionescu, B., et al.: ImageCLEF 2019: multimedia retrieval in lifelogging, medical, nature, and security applications. In: Azzopardi, L., Stein, B., Fuhr, N., Mayr, P., Hauff, C., Hiemstra, D. (eds.) ECIR 2019. LNCS, vol. 11438, pp. 301–308. Springer, Cham (2019). https://doi.org/10.1007/978-3-030-15719-7_40
25. Kalpathy-Cramer, J., et al.: Evaluating performance of biomedical image retrieval systems: Overview of the medical image retrieval task at ImageCLEF 2004–2014. Comput. Med. Imaging Graph. **39**, 55–61 (2015)
26. Kozlovski, S., Liauchuk, V., Dicente Cid, Y., Kovalev, V., Müller, H.: Overview of ImageCLEFtuberculosis 2021 - CT-based tuberculosis type classification. In: CLEF2021 Working Notes. CEUR Workshop Proceedings, CEUR-WS.org, Bucharest, Romania, 21–24 September 2021 (2021). http://ceur-ws.org

27. Kozlovski, S., Liauchuk, V., Dicente Cid, Y., Tarasau, A., Kovalev, V., Müller, H.: Overview of ImageCLEFtuberculosis 2020 - automatic CT-based report generation. In: CLEF2020 Working Notes. CEUR Workshop Proceedings, CEUR-WS.org, Thessaloniki, Greece, 22–25 September 2020 (2020). http://ceur-ws.org
28. Kuznetsova, A., et al.: The open images dataset V4: unified image classification, object detection, and visual relationship detection at scale. CoRR abs/1811.00982 (2018). arxiv.org/abs/1811.00982
29. Liauchuk, V., Kovalev, V.: ImageCLEF 2017: supervoxels and co-occurrence for tuberculosis CT image classification. In: CLEF2017 Working Notes. CEUR Workshop Proceedings, CEUR-WS.org, Dublin, Ireland, 11–14 September 2017 (2017). http://ceur-ws.org
30. Lin, T.-Y., et al.: Microsoft COCO: common objects in context. In: Fleet, D., Pajdla, T., Schiele, B., Tuytelaars, T. (eds.) ECCV 2014. LNCS, vol. 8693, pp. 740–755. Springer, Cham (2014). https://doi.org/10.1007/978-3-319-10602-1_48
31. Müller, H., Clough, P., Deselaers, T., Caputo, B. (eds.): ImageCLEF - Experimental Evaluation in Visual Information Retrieval, The Springer International Series On Information Retrieval, vol. 32. Springer, Heidelberg (2010)
32. Papineni, K., Roukos, S., Ward, T., Zhu, W.J.: BLEU: a method for automatic evaluation of machine translation. In: Proceedings of the 40th Annual Meeting on Association for Computational Linguistics, pp. 311–318. Association for Computational Linguistics (2002)
33. Pelka, O., Ben Abacha, A., García Seco de Herrera, A., Jacutprakart, J., Friedrich, C.M., Müller, H.: Overview of the ImageCLEFmed 2021 concept & caption prediction task. In: CLEF2021 Working Notes. CEUR Workshop Proceedings, CEUR-WS.org, Bucharest, Romania, 21–24 September 2021 (2021)
34. Pelka, O., Friedrich, C.M., García Seco de Herrera, A., Müller, H.: Overview of the ImageCLEFmed 2019 concept prediction task. In: CLEF2019 Working Notes. CEUR Workshop Proceedings, CEUR-WS.org, Lugano, Switzerland, 09–12 September 2019 (2019). http://ceur-ws.org
35. Pelka, O., Friedrich, C.M., García Seco de Herrera, A., Müller, H.: Overview of the ImageCLEFmed 2020 concept prediction task: medical image understanding. In: CLEF2020 Working Notes. CEUR Workshop Proceedings, CEUR-WS.org, Thessaloniki, Greece, 22–25 September 2020 (2020)
36. Pelka, O., Koitka, S., Rückert, J., Nensa, F., Friedrich, C.M.: Radiology Objects in COntext (ROCO): a multimodal image dataset. In: Stoyanov, D., et al. (eds.) LABELS/CVII/STENT -2018. LNCS, vol. 11043, pp. 180–189. Springer, Cham (2018). https://doi.org/10.1007/978-3-030-01364-6_20
37. Popescu, A., Deshayes-Chossart, J., Ionescu, B.: Overview of ImageCLEFaware 2021: estimating potential real-life effects of online image sharing task. In: CLEF2021 Working Notes. CEUR Workshop Proceedings, CEUR-WS.org, Bucharest, Romania, 21–24 September 2021 (2021). http://ceur-ws.org
38. Radford, A., Wu, J., Child, R., Luan, D., Amodei, D., Sutskever, I.: Language models are unsupervised multitask learners. Technical report, Open-AI (2019)
39. Russakovsky, O., et al.: ImageNet large scale visual recognition challenge. Int. J. Comput. Vis. **115**(3), 211–252 (2015)
40. Sarrouti, M., Ben Abacha, A., Demner-Fushman, D.: Visual question generation from radiology images. In: Proceedings of the First Workshop on Advances in Language and Vision Research, pp. 12–18. Association for Computational Linguistics, Online, July 2020. https://www.aclweb.org/anthology/2020.alvr-1.3

41. Tan, M., Le, Q.: EfficientNet: rethinking model scaling for convolutional neural networks. In: Chaudhuri, K., Salakhutdinov, R. (eds.) Proceedings of the 36th International Conference on Machine Learning (ICML 2019), Long Beach, California, USA, 10–15 June 2019, vol. 97, pp. 6105–6114, June 2019. http://proceedings.mlr.press/v97/tan19a.html
42. Tan, M., Pang, R., Le, Q.V.: EfficientDet: scalable and efficient object detection. In: Proceedings of the IEEE/CVF Conference on Computer Vision and Pattern Recognition, pp. 10781–10790 (2020)
43. Thomee, B., et al.: YFCC100M: the new data in multimedia research. Commun. ACM **59**(2), 64–73 (2016)
44. Tsikrika, T., de Herrera, A.G.S., Müller, H.: Assessing the scholarly impact of ImageCLEF. In: Forner, P., Gonzalo, J., Kekäläinen, J., Lalmas, M., de Rijke, M. (eds.) CLEF 2011. LNCS, vol. 6941, pp. 95–106. Springer, Heidelberg (2011). https://doi.org/10.1007/978-3-642-23708-9_12
45. Tsikrika, T., Larsen, B., Müller, H., Endrullis, S., Rahm, E.: The scholarly impact of CLEF (2000–2009). In: Forner, P., Müller, H., Paredes, R., Rosso, P., Stein, B. (eds.) CLEF 2013. LNCS, vol. 8138, pp. 1–12. Springer, Heidelberg (2013). https://doi.org/10.1007/978-3-642-40802-1_1
46. Wilkins, K.W., Rosa-Marín, A., Cziesielski, M., Hughes, H., Love, C., Nowakowski, C.: Short and long-term visions for protecting coral reefs. Limnol. Oceanogr. Bull. **30** (2021)
47. World Health Organization, et al.: Global tuberculosis report 2019 (2019)

Overview of LifeCLEF 2021: An Evaluation of Machine-Learning Based Species Identification and Species Distribution Prediction

Alexis Joly[1(✉)], Hervé Goëau[2], Stefan Kahl[6], Lukáš Picek[10], Titouan Lorieul[1], Elijah Cole[9], Benjamin Deneu[1], Maximillien Servajean[7], Andrew Durso[11], Isabelle Bolon[8], Hervé Glotin[3], Robert Planqué[4], Rafael Ruiz de Castañeda[8], Willem-Pier Vellinga[4], Holger Klinck[6], Tom Denton[12], Ivan Eggel[5], Pierre Bonnet[2], and Henning Müller[5]

[1] Inria, LIRMM, Univ Montpellier, CNRS, Montpellier, France
alexis.joly@inria.fr
[2] CIRAD, UMR AMAP, Montpellier, Occitanie, France
[3] Univ. Toulon, Aix Marseille Univ., CNRS, LIS, DYNI Team, Marseille, France
[4] Xeno-canto Foundation, Amsterdam, The Netherlands
[5] HES-SO, Sierre, Switzerland
[6] KLYCCB, Cornell Lab of Ornithology, Cornell University, Ithaca, USA
[7] LIRMM, AMI, Univ. Paul Valéry Montpellier, Univ. Montpellier, CNRS, Montpellier, France
[8] ISG, Department of Community Health and Medicine, UNIGE, Geneva, Switzerland
[9] Department of Computing and Mathematical Sciences, Caltech, Pasadena, USA
[10] Department of Cybernetics, FAV, University of West Bohemia, Pilsen, Czechia
[11] Department of Biological Sciences, Florida Gulf Coast University, Fort Myers, USA
[12] Google LLC, San Francisco, USA

Abstract. Building accurate knowledge of the identity, the geographic distribution and the evolution of species is essential for the sustainable development of humanity, as well as for biodiversity conservation. However, the difficulty of identifying plants and animals is hindering the aggregation of new data and knowledge. Identifying and naming living plants or animals is almost impossible for the general public and is often difficult even for professionals and naturalists. Bridging this gap is a key step towards enabling effective biodiversity monitoring systems. The LifeCLEF campaign, presented in this paper, has been promoting and evaluating advances in this domain since 2011. The 2021 edition proposes four data-oriented challenges related to the identification and prediction of biodiversity: (i) PlantCLEF: cross-domain plant identification based on herbarium sheets, (ii) BirdCLEF: bird species recognition in audio soundscapes, (iii) GeoLifeCLEF: remote sensing based prediction of species, and (iv) SnakeCLEF: Automatic Snake Species Identification with Country-Level Focus.

K. S. Candan et al. (Eds.): CLEF 2021, LNCS 12880, pp. 371–393, 2021.
https://doi.org/10.1007/978-3-030-85251-1_24

1 LifeCLEF Lab Overview

Accurately identifying organisms observed in the wild is an essential step in ecological studies. Unfortunately, observing and identifying living organisms requires high levels of expertise. For instance, plants alone account for more than 400,000 different species and the distinctions between them can be quite subtle. Since the Rio Conference of 1992, this *taxonomic gap* has been recognized as one of the major obstacles to the global implementation of the Convention on Biological Diversity[1]. In 2004, Gaston and O'Neill [10] discussed the potential of automated approaches for species identification. They suggested that, if the scientific community were able to (i) produce large training datasets, (ii) precisely evaluate error rates, (iii) scale up automated approaches, and (iv) detect novel species, then it would be possible to develop a generic automated species identification system that would open up new vistas for research in biology and related fields.

Since the publication of [10], automated species identification has been studied in many contexts [3,12,22,35,41,50,51,59]. This area continues to expand rapidly, particularly due to advances in deep learning [2,11,36,42,52,54–56]. In order to measure progress in a sustainable and repeatable way, the LifeCLEF[2] research platform was created in 2014 as a continuation and extension of the plant identification task that had been run within the ImageCLEF lab[3] since 2011 [14–16]. Since 2014, LifeCLEF expanded the challenge by considering animals in addition to plants, and including audio and video content in addition to images [23–29]. Four challenges were evaluated in the context of LifeCLEF 2021 edition:

1. **PlantCLEF 2021**: Identifying plant pictures from herbarium sheets.
2. **BirdCLEF 2021**: Bird species recognition in audio soundscapes.
3. **GeoLifeCLEF 2021**: Species presence prediction at given locations based on occurrence, environmental and remote sensing data.
4. **SnakeCLEF 2021**: Automated snake species identification with Country-Level Focus.

The system used to run the challenges (registration, submission, leaderboard, etc.) was the AICrowd platform[4] for the PlantCLEF and ths SnakeCLEF challenge and the Kaggle platform[5] for GeoLifeCLEF and BirdCLEF challenges. In total, 834 teams/persons participated to LifeCLEF 2021 edition by submitting runs to at least one of the four challenges. In the following sections, we provide a synthesis of the methodology and main results of each of the four challenges. More details can be found in the overview reports of each challenge and the individual reports of the participants (references provided below).

[1] https://www.cbd.int/.
[2] http://www.lifeclef.org/.
[3] http://www.imageclef.org/.
[4] https://www.aicrowd.com.
[5] https://www.kaggle.com.

2 PlantCLEF Challenge: Identifying Plant Pictures from Herbarium Sheets

A detailed description of the task and a more complete discussion of the results can be found in the dedicated working note [13].

2.1 Objective

Automated identification of plants has recently improved considerably thanks to the progress of deep learning and the availability of training data with more and more photos in the field. In the context of LifeCLEF 2018, we measured a top-1 classification accuracy over 10K species up to 90% and we showed that automated systems are not so far from human expertise [23]. However, this profusion of field images only concerns a few tens of thousands of species, mostly located in North America and Western Europe, with fewer images from the richest regions in terms of biodiversity such as tropical countries. On the other hand, for several centuries, botanists have collected, catalogued and systematically stored plant specimens in herbaria, particularly in tropical regions. Recent huge efforts by the biodiversity informatics community such as iDigBio[6] or e-ReColNat[7] made it possible to put millions of digitized collections online. Thus, the 2020 and 2021 editions of the PlantCLEF challenge were designed to evaluate to what extent automated plant species identification on tropical data deficient regions can be improved by the use of herbarium sheets. Herbarium collections potentially represent a large reservoir of data for training species prediction models. However, their visual appearance is very different from field photographs because the specimens are first dried and then crushed on a herbarium board before being digitized (see examples Fig. 1). This difference in appearance represents a very severe domain shift which makes the task of learning from one domain to the other very difficult. The main novelty of the 2021 edition over 2020 is that we provide new training data related to species *traits*, i.e. attributes of the species such as their growth form, woodiness or habitat. Traits are a very valuable information that can potentially help improve the prediction of the models. Indeed, it can be assumed that species which share the same traits also share to some extent common visual appearances. This information can then potentially be used to guide the learning of a model through auxiliary loss functions for instance.

2.2 Dataset and Evaluation Protocol

The challenge is based on a dataset of 997 species mainly focused on the South America's Guiana Shield (Fig. 2), an area known to have one of the greatest diversity of plants in the world. It as evaluated as a cross-domain classification task where the training set consist of 321,270 herbarium sheets and 6,316 photos in the field to enable learning a mapping between the two domains. A valuable

[6] http://portal.idigbio.org/portal/search.

[7] https://explore.recolnat.org/search/botanique/type=index.

Fig. 1. Field photos and herbarium sheets of the same specimen (*Tapirira guianensis* Aubl.). Despite the very different visual appearances between the two types of images, similar structures and shapes of flowers, fruits and leaves can be observed.

asset of this training set is that a set of 354 plant observations are provided with both herbarium sheets and field photos to potentially allow a more precise mapping between the two domains. In addition to the images, the training data includes the values of 5 traits for each 997 species. These trait data items were collected through the Encyclopedia of Life API[8] and were selected as the most exhaustive ones, i.e.: "plant growth form", "habitat", "plant lifeform", "trophic guild" and "woodiness". Each of them was double-checked and completed by experts of the Guyanese flora, in order to ensure that each of the 1000 species have a validated value for each trait.

The test set relies on the data of two highly trusted experts and is composed of 3,186 photos in the fields related to 638 plant observations.

Participants were allowed to use complementary training data (e.g. for pre-training purposes) but on the condition that (i) the experiment is entirely reproducible, i.e. that the used external resource is clearly referenced and accessible to any other research group in the world, (ii) the use of external training data or not is mentioned for each run, and (iii) the additional resource does not contain any of the test observations. External training data was allowed but participants had to provide at least one submission that used only the data provided this year.

The main evaluation measure for the challenge is the Mean Reciprocal Rank (MRR), which is defined as

$$\frac{1}{Q}\sum_{q=1}^{Q}\frac{1}{\text{rank}_q}$$

where Q is the number of plant observations and rank_q is the predicted rank of the true label for the qth observation.

A second MRR score is computed on a subset of test set composed of the most difficult species, i.e. the ones that are the least frequently photographed in the field. They were selected based on the most comprehensive estimates of the available amount of field pictures from different data sources (IdigBio, GBIF, Encyclopedia of Life, Bing and Google Image search engines, previous datasets

[8] https://eol.org/docs/what-is-eol/data-services.

related to PlantCLEF and ExpertCLEF challenges). These difficult species are much more challenging in the sense that the discriminant features must necessary be learned from the herbarium data.

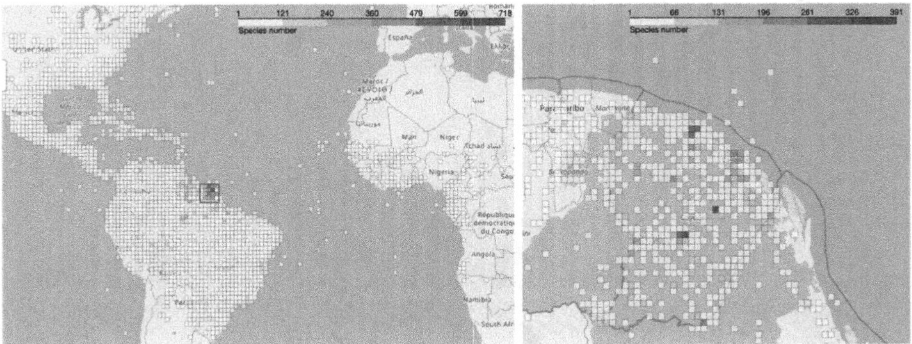

Fig. 2. Density grid maps of the number of species of geolocated plants in PlantCLEF2021. Many species have also been collected to a lesser extent in other regions outside French Guiana, such as the Americas and Africa.

2.3 Participants and Results

About 40 teams registered for the PlantCLEF challenge 2021 (PC21) and 4 of them finally submitted runs, *i.e.* files containing the predictions of the system(s) they ran. Details of the methods and systems used in the runs are synthesized in the overview working note paper of the task [13] and further developed in the individual working notes of participants (NeuonAI [5], Lehigh University [58]). Complementary runs based on the best performing approach during PlantCLEF2020 (a Few Shot Adversarial Domain Adaptation approach - FSADA - [53]) were also submitted by the organisers. In particular, we focused on assessing the impact of the trait information introduced this year. We report in Fig. 3 the performance achieved by the 33 collected runs.

The main outcomes we can derive from that results are the following:

The Most Difficult PlantCLEF Challenge Ever. Traditional classification models based on CNNs perform very poorly on the task. Domain Adaptation methods (DA) based on CNNs perform much better but the task remains difficult even with these dedicated techniques. The best submitted run barely approaches a MRR of 0.2.

Genericity and Stability. Regarding the difference between the two MRR metrics (whole test set vs. difficult species), the NeuonAI team demonstrated that it is possible to achieve equivalent and quite good performance for all species, even those that have few or no field photos at all in the training dataset. Rather than focusing on learning a common feature invariant domain as for the other

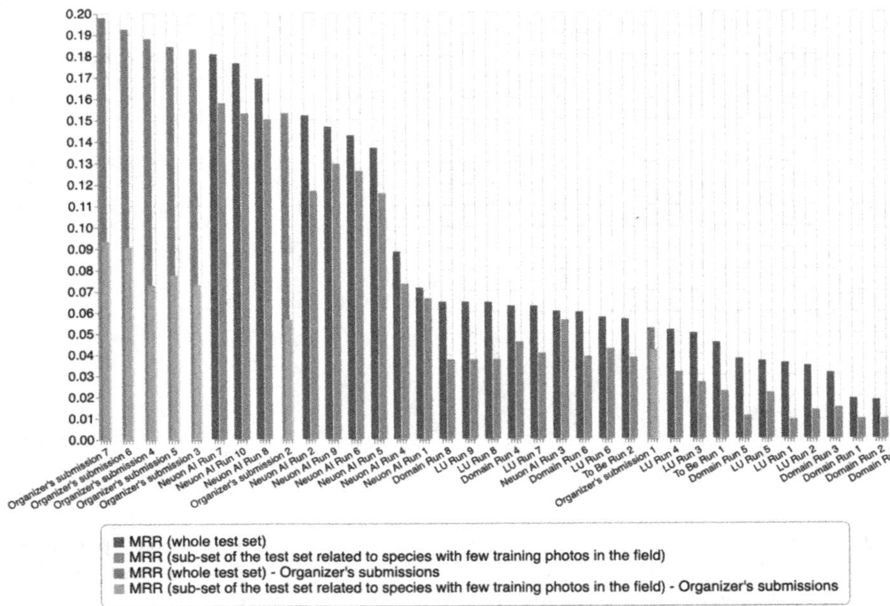

Fig. 3. PlantCLEF 2021 results

team's submissions, the NeuonAI's approach focuses on a deep metric learning on features embeddings. Looking solely at the the second MRR score, this approach seems to be more effective in transferring knowledge to the least frequently photographed species (which is the most challenging objective). The FSADA approach, on the other side, offers a better trade off considering all species together.

The Most Informative Species Trait is the "Plant Growth Form". Organizer's submissions 4, 5 and 6 demonstrate that adding an auxiliary task related based on species traits to the FSADA approach improve performance. As hypothesised, it seems to help gathering and discriminating wide groups of plant species sharing similar visual aspects (such as tendrils for climber plants, typical large leaves for tropical trees against smaller leaves for shrubs or long thin leaves and frequent flowers for herbs).

3 BirdCLEF Challenge: Bird Call Identification in Soundscape Recordings

A detailed description of the task and a more complete discussion of the results can be found in the dedicated overview paper [31].

3.1 Objective

The *LifeCLEF Bird Recognition Challenge* (BirdCLEF) launched in 2014 and has since become the largest bird sound recognition challenge in terms of dataset size and species diversity with multiple tens of thousands of recordings covering up to 1,500 species [17,30,32]. Birds are ideal indicators to identify early warning signs of habitat changes that are likely to affect many other species. They have been shown to respond to various environmental changes over many spatial scales. Large collections of (avian) audio data are an excellent resource to conduct research that can help to deal with environmental challenges of our time. The community platform Xeno-canto[9] launched in 2005 and hosts bird sounds from all continents and daily receives new recordings from some of the remotest places on Earth. The Xeno-canto archive currently consists of more than 635,000 focal recordings covering over 10,000 species of birds, making it one of the most comprehensive collections of bird sound recordings worldwide, and certainly the most comprehensive collection shared under Creative Commons licenses. Xeno-canto data was used for BirdCLEF in all past editions to provide researchers with large and diverse datasets for training and testing.

In recent years, research in the domain of bioacoustics shifted towards deep neural networks for sound event recognition [33,49]. In past editions, we have seen many attempts to utilize convolutional neural network (CNN) classifiers to identify bird calls based on visual representations of these sounds (i.e., spectrograms) [18,34,40]. Despite their success for bird sound recognition in focal recordings, the classification performance of CNN on continuous, omnidirectional soundscapes remained low. Passive acoustic monitoring can be a valuable sampling tool for habitat assessments and the observation of environmental niches which often are endangered. However, manual processing of large collections of soundscape data is not desirable and automated attempts can help to advance this process [57]. Yet, the lack of suitable validation and test data prevented the development of reliable techniques to solve this task. Bridging the acoustic gap between high-quality training recordings and soundscapes with high ambient noise levels is one of the most challenging tasks in the domain of audio event recognition.

The main goal of the 2021 edition of BirdCLEF was to open the field of bird song identification to a broader audience by providing both a challenging research task and a low barrier to entry. The competition was hosted on Kaggle[10] to attract machine learning experts from around the world to participate and submit. While the overall task was consistent with previous editions, the organization focused on providing entry-level resources to enable participants to achieve baseline results without the need for extensive dataset analysis and workflow implementation.

[9] https://www.xeno-canto.org/.

[10] https://www.kaggle.com/c/birdclef-2021.

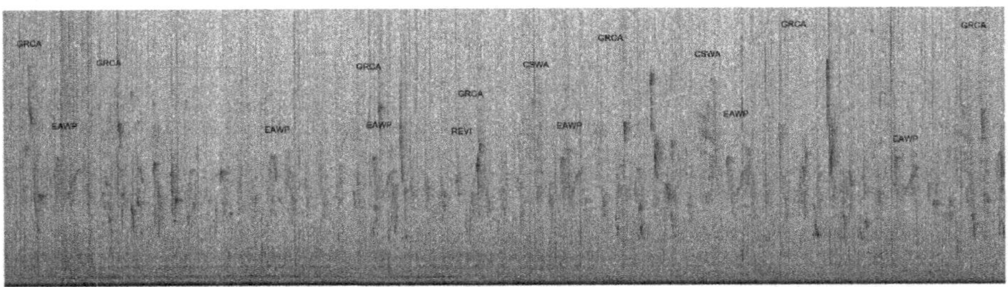

Fig. 4. Dawn chorus soundscapes often have an extremely high call density. The 2021 BirdCLEF dataset contained 100 fully annotated soundscapes recorded in South and North America.

3.2 Dataset and Evaluation Protocol

Deploying a bird sound recognition system to a new recording and observation site requires classifiers that generalize well across different acoustic domains. Focal recordings of bird species from around the world form an excellent base to develop such a detection system. However, the lack of annotated soundscape data for a new deployment site poses a significant challenge. As in previous editions, training data was provided by the Xeno-canto community and consisted of more than 60,000 recordings covering 397 species from two continents (South and North America). Participants were allowed to use metadata to develop their systems. Most notably, we provided detailed location information on recording sites of focal and soundscape recordings, allowing participants to account for migration and spatial distribution of bird species. A validation dataset with 200 min of soundscape data was also provided.

The hidden test data contained 80 soundscape recordings of 10-minute duration covering four distinct recording locations. Validation data only contained soundscapes for two of the four locations. All audio data were collected with passive acoustic recorders from deployments in Colombia (COL), Costa Rica (COR), the Sierra Nevada (SNE) of California, USA and the Sapsucker Woods area (SSW) in Ithaca, New York, USA. Expert ornithologists provided annotations for a variety of quiet and extremely dense acoustic scenes (see Fig. 4).

The goal of the task was to localize and identify all audible birds within the provided soundscape test set. Each soundscape was divided into segments of 5 s, and a list of audible species had to be returned for each segment. The used evaluation metric was the row-wise micro-averaged F1-score. In previous editions, ranking metrics were used to assess the overall classification performance. However, when applying bird call identification systems to real-world data, confidence thresholds have to be set in order to provide meaningful results. The F1-score as balanced metric between recall and precision appears to better reflect this circumstance. Precision and recall were determined based on the total number of true positives (TP), false positives (FP) and false negatives (FN) for each segment (i.e., row of the submission). More formally:

$$Micro\text{-}Precision = \frac{TP_{sum}}{TP_{sum} + FP_{sum}}, \qquad Micro\text{-}Recall = \frac{TP_{sum}}{TP_{sum} + FN_{sum}}$$

The micro F1-score as harmonic mean of the micro-precision and micro-recall for each segment is defined as:

$$Micro\text{-}F1 = 2 \times \frac{Micro\text{-}Precision \times Micro\text{-}Recall}{Micro\text{-}Precision + Micro\text{-}Recall}$$

The average across all (segment-wise) F1-scores was used as the final metric. Segments that did not contain a bird vocalizations had to be marked with the "nocall" label, which acted as an additional class label for non-events. The micro-averaged F1-score reduces the impact of rare events, which only contribute slightly to the overall metric if misidentified. The classification performance on common classes (i.e., species with high vocal presence) is well reflected in the metric.

3.3 Participants and Results

1,004 participants from 70 countries on 816 teams entered the BirdCLEF 2021 competition and submitted a total of 9,307 runs. Details of the best methods and systems used are synthesized in the overview working notes paper of the task [31] and further developed in the individual working notes of participants. In Fig. 5 we report the performance achieved by the top 50 collected runs. The private leaderboard score is the primary metric and was revealed to participants after the submission deadline to avoid probing the hidden test data. Public leaderboard scores were visible to participants over the course of the entire challenge.

The baseline F1-score in this year's edition was 0.4799 (public 0.5467) with all segments marked as non-events, and 686 teams managed to score above this threshold. The best submission achieved a F1-score of 0.6932 (public 0.7736) and the top 10 best performing systems were within only 2% difference in score. The vast majority of approaches was based on convolutional neural network ensembles and mostly differed in pre- and post-processing and neural network backbone. Interestingly, the choice of CNN backbone does not seem to have significant impact on the overall score. Off-the-shelve architectures like MobileNet, EfficientNet, or DenseNet all seem to perform well on this task. Participants mostly used mel scale spectrograms as model inputs and the most commonly used augmentation method was mix-up (i.e., overlapping samples to emulate simultaneously vocalizing birds). Post-processing in the form of bagging and thresholding scores, location based filtering, or even decision trees as separate stage to combine scores and metadata appeared to be the most important measure to achieve high scores.

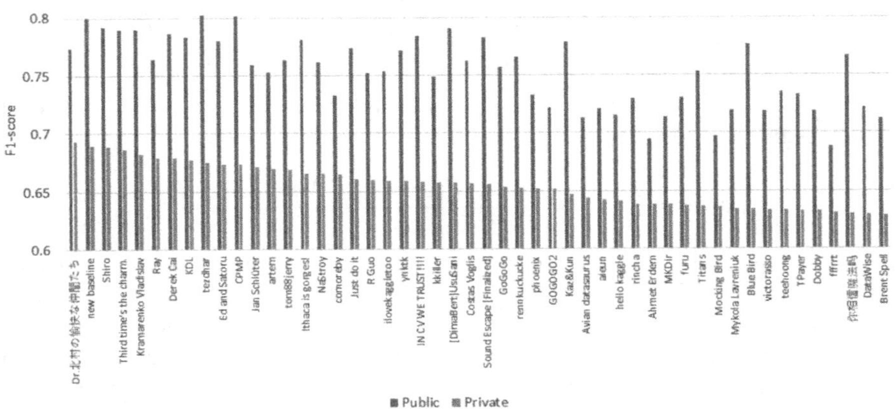

Fig. 5. Scores achieved by the best systems evaluated within the bird identification task of LifeCLEF 2021.

4 GeoLifeCLEF Challenge: Species Prediction Based on Occurrence Data, Environmental Data and Remote Sensing Data

A detailed description of the task and a more complete discussion of the results can be found in the dedicated working note [37].

4.1 Objective

Automatic prediction of the list of species most likely to be present at a given location is useful for many scenarios related to biodiversity management and conservation. First, it can improve species identification tools (whether automatic, semi-automatic or based on traditional field guides) by reducing the list of candidate species observable at a given site.

Moreover, it can facilitate decision making related to land use and land management with regard to biodiversity conservation obligations (e.g. to determine new buildable areas or new natural areas to be protected).

Last but not least, it can be used in the context of educational and citizen science initiatives, e.g. to determine regions of interest with a high species richness or vulnerable habitats to be monitored carefully.

4.2 Data Set and Evaluation Protocol

Data Collection. The data for this year's challenge is the same as last year reorganized in a more easy-to-use and compact format. A detailed description of the GeoLifeCLEF 2020 dataset is provided in [6]. In a nutshell, it consists of over 1.9 million observations covering 31, 435 plant and animal species distributed

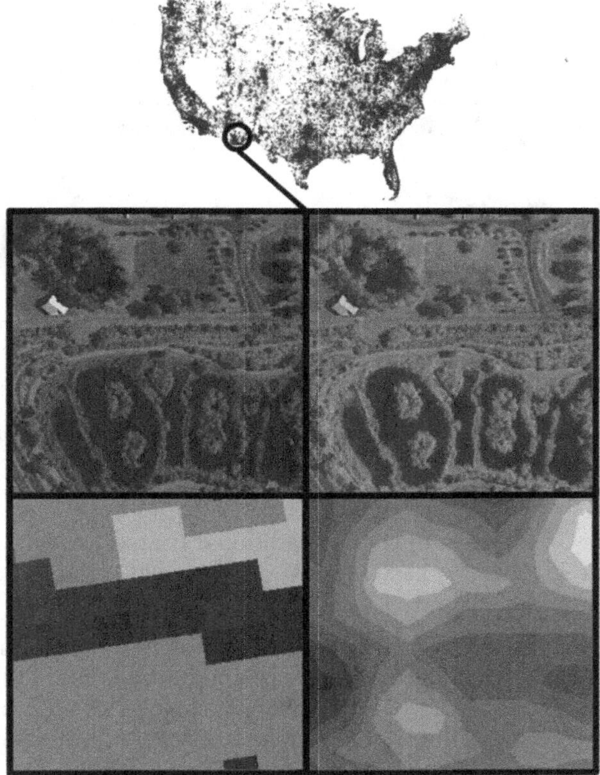

Fig. 6. In the GeoLifeCLEF dataset, each species observation is paired with high-resolution covariates (clockwise from top left: RGB imagery, IR imagery, altitude, land cover).

across US and France (as shown in Fig. 7). Each species observation is paired with high-resolution covariates (RGB-IR imagery, land cover and altitude) as illustrated in Fig. 6. These high-resolution covariates are resampled to a spatial resolution of 1 m per pixel and provided as 256 × 256 images covering a 256 m × 256 m square centered on each observation. RGB-IR imagery come from the 2009–2011 cycle of the National Agriculture Imagery Program (NAIP) for the U.S.[11], and from the BD-ORTHO® 2.0 and ORTHO-HR® 1.0 databases from the IGN for France[12]. Land cover data originates from the National Land Cover Database (NLCD) [21] for the U.S. and from CESBIO[13] for France. All elevation data comes from the NASA Shuttle Radar Topography Mission (SRTM)[14].

[11] https://www.fsa.usda.gov.
[12] https://geoservices.ign.fr.
[13] http://osr-cesbio.ups-tlse.fr/~oso/posts/2017-03-30-carte-s2-2016/.
[14] https://lpdaac.usgs.gov/products/srtmgl1v003/.

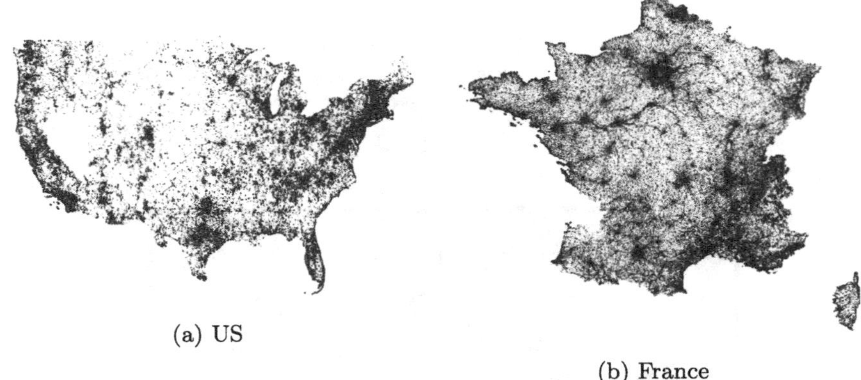

(a) US

(b) France

Fig. 7. Occurrences distribution over the US and France in GeoLifeCLEF 2021. Blue dots represent training data, red dots represent test data. (Color figure online)

In addition, the dataset also includes traditional coarser resolution covariates: bio-climatic rasters ($1\,\text{km}^2$/pixel, from WorldClim [20]) and pedologic rasters ($250\,\text{m}^2$/pixel, from SoilGrids [19]).

Train-Test Split. The full set of occurrences was split in a training and testing set using a spatial block holdout procedure as illustrated in Fig. 7. This limits the effect of *spatial auto-correlation* in the data [46]. Using this splitting procedure, a model cannot achieve a high performance by simply interpolating between training samples. The split was based on a global grid of $5\,\text{km} \times 5\,\text{km}$ quadrats. 2.5% of these quadrats were randomly sampled and the observations falling in those formed the test set. 10% of those observations were used for the public leaderboard on Kaggle while the remaining 90% allowed to compute the private leaderboard providing the final results of the challenge. Similarly, another 2.5% of the quadrats were randomly sampled to provide an official validation set. The remaining quadrats and their associated observations were assigned to the training set.

Evaluation Metric. For each occurrence in the test set, the goal of the task was to return a candidate set of species likely to be present at that location. To measure the precision of the predicted sets, top-30 error rate was chosen as the main evaluation criterion. Each observation i is associated with a single ground-truth label y_i corresponding to the observed species. For each observation, the submissions provided 30 candidate labels $\hat{y}_{i,1}, \hat{y}_{i,2}, \ldots, \hat{y}_{i,30}$. The top-30 error rate is then computed using

$$\text{Top-30 error rate} = \frac{1}{N}\sum_{i=1}^{N} e_i \quad \text{where} \quad e_i = \begin{cases} 1 & \text{if } \forall k \in \{1,\ldots,30\},\ \hat{y}_{i,k} \neq y_i \\ 0 & \text{otherwise} \end{cases}$$

Note that this evaluation metric does not try to correct the sampling bias inherent to present-only observation data (linked to the density of population, etc.).

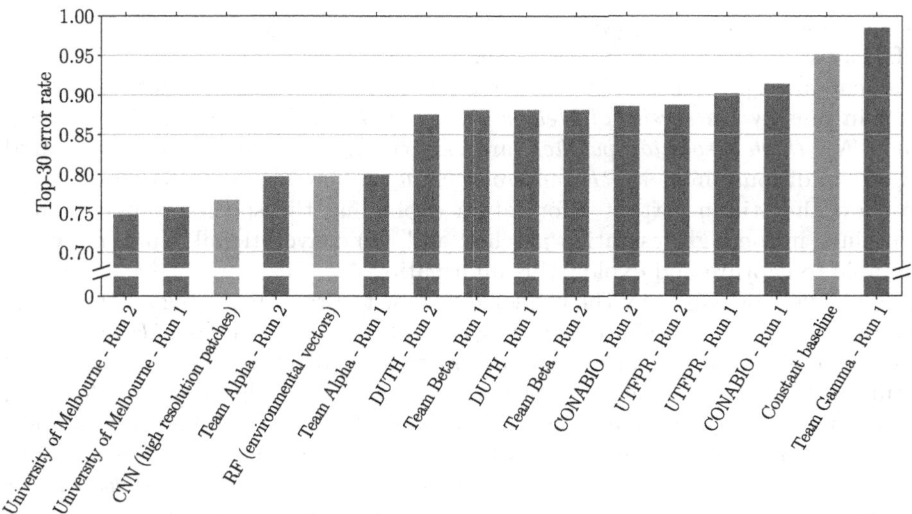

Fig. 8. Results of the GeoLifeCLEF 2021 task. The top-30 error rates of the submissions of each participant are shown in blue. The provided baselines are shown in orange. (Color figure online)

The absolute value of the resulting figures should thus be taken with care. Nevertheless, this metric does allow to compare the different approaches and to determine which type of input data and of models are useful for the species presence detection task.

4.3 Participants and Results

Seven teams participated to the GeoLifeCLEF 2021 challenge (hosted on Kaggle[15]) and submitted a total of 26 submissions: *University of Melbourne*, *DUTH* (Democritus University of Thrace), *CONABIO* (Comisión Nacional para el Conocimiento y Uso de la Biodiversidad), *UTFPR* (Federal University of Technology – Paraná) as well as three participants for which we could not identify the affiliation and which we denote here, respectively, as *Team Alpha*, *Team Beta* and *Team Gamma*. Details of the methods used in the submitted runs are synthesized in the overview working note paper for this task [37]. Runs of the winning team are further developed in the individual working note [48].

In Fig. 8, we report the performance achieved by the collected runs. The main outcome of the challenge is that a method based on a convolutional neural network (CNN) trained solely on RGB imagery (*University of Melbourne - Run 1*) easily beats a classical model used for species distribution modelling [9] consisting of a random forest using punctual environmental variables (*RF (environmental vectors)*). This might come as a surprise as it did not make use

[15] https://www.kaggle.com/c/geolifeclef-2021/.

of any bioclimatic or soil type variable which are often considered as the most informative in the ecological literature.

Generally speaking, CNN-based models trained on high resolution patches used in runs by *University of Melbourne* and *Team Alpha* as well as in the baseline *CNN (high resolution patches)* are very competitive and efficient compared to the traditional model (*RF (environmental vectors)*). This observation tends to show that (i) important information explaining the species composition is contained in the high-resolution patches, and, (ii) convolutional neural networks are able to capture and exploit this information.

One question raised by the challenge is how to properly aggregate the different variables provided as input. Adding altitude data to the model (*University of Melbourne - Run 2*) provides an improvement in prediction accuracy backing the intuition that this variable is informative of the species distribution. However, aggregating all the variables does not mechanically lead to higher performance: *CNN (high resolution patches)* makes use of the additional land cover data but its performance is not as good as the two runs from *University of Melbourne.* It seems that it is important not to aggregate the features representation of those variables too early in the architectures of the networks: concatenation of higher-level features (*University of Melbourne - Run 2*) is more efficient than early aggregation (*CNN (high resolution patches)*). Furthermore, it is unclear for now whether the information contained in the high-resolution patches is complementary or redundant to the one captured from the bioclimatic and soil variables and whether they should be used together or not. Finally, there remains considerable room for improvement on this challenge as the winning solution does not make use of all the different patches provided and its top-30 error rate is still high, near 75% error rate.

5 SnakeCLEF Challenge: Automated Snake Species Identification with Country-Level Focus

A detailed description of the task and a more complete discussion of the results can be found in the dedicated overview paper [44].

5.1 Objective

To build an automatic and robust image-based system for snake species identification is an important goal for biodiversity, conservation, and global health. With over half a million victims of death and disability from venomous snakebite annually, such a system could significantly improve eco-epidemiological data and treatment outcomes (e.g. based on the specific use of antivenoms) [1,4]. This applies especially in remote geographic areas, where snake species identification assistance has a bigger potential to save lives.

Fig. 9. *Naja nigricincta* from northern Namibia (left) and South Africa (right), demonstrating geographical variation within a species. ©*Di Franklin* - iNaturalist , *and* ©*bryanmaritz* - iNaturalist

Fig. 10. Variation in *Vipera berus* (European Adder) color and pattern. Examples from Germany, Switzerland and Poland. ©*Thorsten Stegmann* - iNaturalist, ©*jandetka* - iNaturalist, ©*jandetka* - iNaturalist, *and* ©*chorthippus* - iNaturalist.

Snake species identification difficulty lies in the high intra-class and low inter-class variance in appearance, which may depend on geographic location, color morph, sex, or age (Fig. 10 and Fig. 9). At the same time, many species are visually similar to other species (e.g. mimicry). Our knowledge of which snake species occur in which countries is incomplete, and it is common that most or all images of a given snake species might originate from a small handful of countries or even a single country. Furthermore, many snake species resemble species found on other continents, with which they are entirely allopatric. Knowing the geographic origin of an unidentified snake can narrow down the possible correct identifications considerably. In no location on Earth do more than 125 of the approximate 3,900 snake species co-occur [47]. Thus, regularization to all countries is a critical component of an automated snake identification system.

5.2 Dataset and Evaluation Protocol

Dataset Overview: For this year's challenge, we have prepared a dataset consisting of 386,006 images belonging to 772 snake species from 188 countries and all continents. The dataset has a heavy long-tailed class distribution, where the most frequent species (*Thamnophis sirtalis*) is represented by 22,163 images and the least frequent by just 10 (*Achalinus formosanus*).

Such a distribution with small inter-class variance and high intra-class variance creates a challenging task. We provide a simple train/val (90%/10%) split to validate preliminary results while ensuring the same species distributions. The test set data consist of 23,673 images submitted to the iNaturalist platform within the first four months of 2021. Unlike in previous years, where the final testing set remained undisclosed, we provided the test data without labels to the participants.

Metadata: Besides images, we provided 3 level hierarchical taxonomic labels (family, genus, species) and location context (continent, country). The geographical information was included for approximately 85% of the development images and all test images. Additionally, we provide a mapping matrix (MM) describing species-country presence to allow better worldwide regularization.

$$\mathrm{MM}_{cs} = \begin{cases} 1 & \text{ifspecies } S \in \text{country } C \\ 0 & \text{otherwise} \end{cases} \tag{1}$$

The vast majority (77%) of all images came from the United States and Canada, with 9% from Latin American and the Caribbean, 5.7% from Europe, 4.5% from Asia, 1.8% from Africa, and 1.5% from Australia/Oceania. Bias at smaller spatial scales undoubtedly exists as well [38], largely due to where participants in citizen science projects are concentrated. Nevertheless, snake species from nearly every country were represented, with 46/215 (21%) of countries having all of their snake species represented, mostly in Europe. Nearly half of all countries (106/215; 49%) had more than 50% of their snake species represented (Fig. 11). Priority areas for improvement of the training dataset in future rounds are countries with high diversity and low citizen science participation, especially Indonesia, Papua New Guinea, Madagascar, and several central African and Caribbean countries (Fig. 12).

Evaluation: The main goal of this challenge was to build a system that is capable of recognizing 772 snake species based on the given unseen image and relevant geographical location, with a focus on worldwide performance. To assure that,

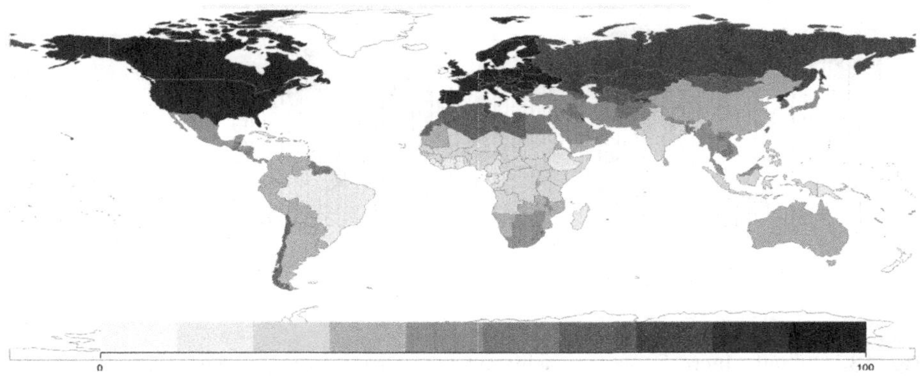

Fig. 11. Percentage of snake species per country included in SnakeCLEF2021. The countries with biggest coverage are in Europe, Oceania, and North America.

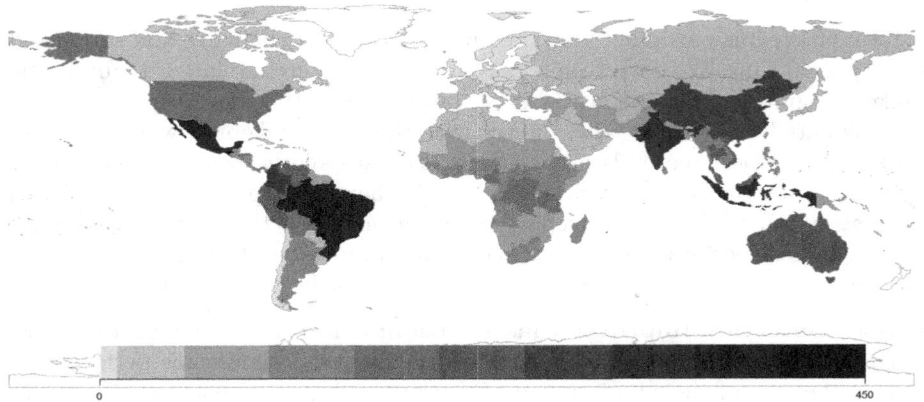

Fig. 12. Worldwide snake species distribution, showing the number of species that are found in each country. Large countries in the tropics (Brazil, Mexico, Colombia, India, Indonesia) have more than 300 species.

we defined the macro F1 country performance Macro F_{1_c} as the main metric. We calculate it as the mean of country F1 scores:

$$\text{Macro } F_{1_c} = \frac{1}{N}\sum_{c=0}^{N} F_{1_c}, \quad F_{1_c} = \frac{1}{\sum_{s=1}^{k} MM_{cs}} \times \sum_{s=0}^{N} F_{1_s} MM_{cs} \tag{2}$$

where c is country index, s is species index, and country performance (F_{1_c}). To get the $F1_S$ we use following formula for each species:

$$F_{1_s} = 2 \times \frac{P_s \times R_s}{P_s + R_s} \tag{3}$$

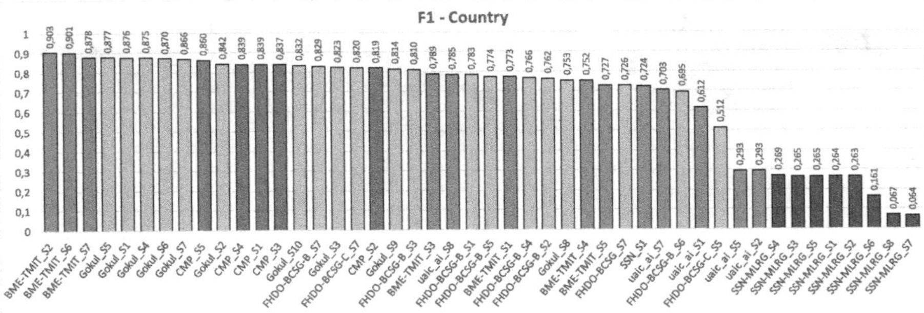

Fig. 13. Official Macro F_{1_c} scores achieved by all runs to the SnakeCLEF 2021 competition.

5.3 Participants and Results

A total of 7 teams participated in the SnakeCLEF 2021 challenge and submitted a total of 46 runs. We have seen a vast increase in interest related to automatic snake recognition from the last year [8]. Interestingly, three participating teams are originated from India – the country with the most snakebites worldwide [39]. Details of the best methods and systems used are synthesized in the overview working notes paper of the task [44] and further developed in the individual working notes. In Fig. 13, we report the performance achieved by all collected runs. The best performing model achieved an impressive Macro F_{1_c} of 0.903.

The main outcomes we can derive from that results are the following:

Object Detection Improves Classification: Utilization of the detection network for a better region of interest selection showed a significant performance gain in the case of the winning team. However, such an approach requires additional labelling procedure and the build of two neural network models. Furthermore, a two-stage solution might be too heavy for deployment on edge devices; thus, its usage is probably impossible.

CNN Outperforms ViT in Snake Recognition: Similarly to last year challenge [43], all participants featured deep convolutional neural networks. Besides CNNs, Vision Transformers (ViT) [7] were utilized by two teams. Interestingly, the performance of the ViT was slightly worst, which is contradictory to their performance in fungi recognition [45], thus showing that ViT might not be the best option for all fine-grained tasks.

6 Conclusions and Perspectives

The main outcome of this collaborative evaluation is a new snapshot of the performance of state-of-the-art computer vision, bio-acoustic and machine learning techniques towards building real-world biodiversity monitoring systems. This study shows that recent deep learning techniques still allow some consistent progress for most of the evaluated tasks. One of the main new outcomes of this edition of LifeCLEF is the appearance of Visual Transformers among the best models of the SnakeCLEF task, which is the most straightforward task of LifeCLEF to experiment this new type of models. Even if their performance is still slightly inferior to that of convolutional neural networks, there is no doubt that they are now an alternative to be considered in the future. On the contrary, the 50 best methods of the BirdCLEF sound recognition task are solely based on convolutional neural networks ensembles. Interestingly, the choice of the CNN backbone does not seem to be the most determining factor of the better performance. The devil is in the detail, typically in the pre-processing and post-processing methodologies. The geolifeclef task also confirms the power of convolutional neural networks for this type of task, revealing their ability to recognise species habitats even when they are only trained on remote sensing images only (i.e. without any additional environmental data as input). Regarding the cross-domain plant identification task, the main outcome was that the performance of state-of-the-art domain adaptation methods such as FSDA can be improved by bringing additional information to the adversarial discriminator such as species traits or species taxonomy.

Acknowledgements. This project has received funding from the European Union's Horizon 2020 research and innovation programme under grant agreement No° 863463 (Cos4Cloud project), and the support of #DigitAG.

References

1. Bolon, I., et al.: Identifying the snake: First scoping review on practices of communities and healthcare providers confronted with snakebite across the world. PLoS one **15**(3), e0229989 (2020)
2. Bonnet, P., et al.: Plant identification: experts vs. machines in the era of deep learning. In: Joly, A., Vrochidis, S., Karatzas, K., Karppinen, A., Bonnet, P. (eds.) Multimedia Tools and Applications for Environmental & Biodiversity Informatics. MSA, pp. 131–149. Springer, Cham (2018). https://doi.org/10.1007/978-3-319-76445-0_8
3. Cai, J., Ee, D., Pham, B., Roe, P., Zhang, J.: Sensor network for the monitoring of ecosystem: bird species recognition. In: Intelligent Sensors, Sensor Networks and Information, 2007. ISSNIP 2007. 3rd International Conference on (2007). https://doi.org/10.1109/ISSNIP.2007.4496859
4. de Castañeda, R.R., et al.: Snakebite and snake identification: empowering neglected communities and health-care providers with AI. Lancet Digital Health **1**(5), e202–e203 (2019)
5. Chulif, S., Chang, Y.L.: Improved herbarium-field triplet network for cross-domain plant identification: neuon submission to lifeclef 2021 plant. In: Working Notes of CLEF 2021 - Conference and Labs of the Evaluation Forum (2021)
6. Cole, E., et al.: The GeoLifeCLEF 2020 dataset. arXiv preprint arXiv:2004.04192 (2020)
7. Dosovitskiy, A., et al.: An image is worth 16x16 words: Transformers for image recognition at scale. arXiv preprint arXiv:2010.11929 (2020)

8. Durso, A.M., Moorthy, G.K., Mohanty, S.P., Bolon, I., Salathé, M., Ruiz De Castañeda, R.: Supervised learning computer vision benchmark for snake species identification from photographs: implications for herpetology and global health. Front. Artif. Intell. **4**, 17 (2021)
9. Evans, J.S., Murphy, M.A., Holden, Z.A., Cushman, S.A.: Modeling species distribution and change using random forest. In: Drew, C., Wiersma, Y., Huettmann, F. (eds.) Predictive Species and Habitat Modeling in Landscape Ecology. Springer, New York (2011). https://doi.org/10.1007/978-1-4419-7390-0_8
10. Gaston, K.J., O'Neill, M.A.: Automated species identification: why not? Philos. Trans. R. Soc. Lond. B Biol. Sci. **359**(1444), 655–667 (2004)
11. Ghazi, M.M., Yanikoglu, B., Aptoula, E.: Plant identification using deep neural networks via optimization of transfer learning parameters. Neurocomputing **235**, 228–235 (2017)
12. Glotin, H., Clark, C., LeCun, Y., Dugan, P., Halkias, X., Sueur, J.: Proceedings of the 1st workshop on Machine Learning for Bioacoustics - ICML4B. ICML, Atlanta USA (2013). http://sabiod.org/ICML4B2013_book.pdf
13. Goëau, H., Bonnet, P., Joly, A.: Overview of PlantCLEF 2021: cross-domain plant identification. In: Working Notes of CLEF 2021 - Conference and Labs of the Evaluation Forum (2021)
14. Goëau, H., et al.: The imageclef 2013 plant identification task. In: CLEF task overview 2013, CLEF: Conference and Labs of the Evaluation Forum, September 2013, Valencia, Spain. Valencia (2013)
15. Goëau, H., et al.: The imageclef 2011 plant images classification task. In: CLEF task overview 2011, CLEF: Conference and Labs of the Evaluation Forum, September 2011, Amsterdam, Netherlands (2011)
16. Goëau, H., et al.: Imageclef 2012 plant images identification task. In: CLEF task overview 2012, CLEF: Conference and Labs of the Evaluation Forum, September 2012, Rome, Italy. Rome (2012)
17. Goëau, H., Glotin, H., Planqué, R., Vellinga, W.P., Stefan, K., Joly, A.: Overview of birdclef 2018: monophone vs. soundscape bird identification. In: CLEF task overview 2018, CLEF: Conference and Labs of the Evaluation Forum, September 2018, Avignon, France (2018)
18. Grill, T., Schlüter, J.: Two convolutional neural networks for bird detection in audio signals. In: 2017 25th European Signal Processing Conference (EUSIPCO), pp. 1764–1768 (Aug 2017). https://doi.org/10.23919/EUSIPCO.2017.8081512
19. Hengl, T., et al.: Soilgrids250m: global gridded soil information based on machine learning. PLoS one **12**(2), e0169748 (2017)
20. Hijmans, R.J., Cameron, S.E., Parra, J.L., Jones, P.G., Jarvis, A.: Very high resolution interpolated climate surfaces for global land areas. Int. J. Climatol. J. R. Meteorol. Soc. **25**(15), 1965–1978 (2005)
21. Homer, C., et al.: Completion of the 2011 national land cover database for the conterminous united states - representing a decade of land cover change information. Photogramm. Eng. Remote. Sens. **81**(5), 345–354 (2015)
22. Joly, A., et al.: Interactive plant identification based on social image data. Ecol. Inform. **23**, 22–34 (2014)
23. Joly, A., et al.: Overview of LifeCLEF 2018: a large-scale evaluation of species identification and recommendation algorithms in the era of AI. In: Bellot, P., et al. (eds.) CLEF 2018. LNCS, vol. 11018, pp. 247–266. Springer, Cham (2018). https://doi.org/10.1007/978-3-319-98932-7_24

24. Joly, A., et al.: Overview of LifeCLEF 2019: identification of Amazonian plants, South & North American Birds, and niche prediction. In: Crestani, F., et al. (eds.) CLEF 2019. LNCS, vol. 11696, pp. 387–401. Springer, Cham (2019). https://doi.org/10.1007/978-3-030-28577-7_29
25. Joly, A., et al.: LifeCLEF 2016: multimedia life species identification challenges. In: Fuhr, N., et al. (eds.) CLEF 2016. LNCS, vol. 9822, pp. 286–310. Springer, Cham (2016). https://doi.org/10.1007/978-3-319-44564-9_26 https://hal.archives-ouvertes.fr/hal-01373781
26. Joly, A., et al.: LifeCLEF 2017 lab overview: multimedia species identification challenges. In: Jones, G.J., et al. (eds.) CLEF 2017. LNCS, vol. 10456, pp. 255–274. Springer, Cham (2017). https://doi.org/10.1007/978-3-319-65813-1_24 https://hal.archives-ouvertes.fr/hal-01629191
27. Joly, A., et al.: LifeCLEF 2014: multimedia life species identification challenges. In: Kanoulas, E., et al. (eds.) CLEF 2014. LNCS, vol. 8685, pp. 229–249. Springer, Cham (2014). https://doi.org/10.1007/978-3-319-11382-1_20 https://hal.inria.fr/hal-01075770
28. Joly, A., et al.: LifeCLEF 2015: multimedia life species identification challenges. In: Mothe, J., et al. (eds.) CLEF 2015. LNCS, vol. 9283, pp. 462–483. Springer, Cham (2015). https://doi.org/10.1007/978-3-319-24027-5_46
29. Joly, A., et al.: Overview of LifeCLEF 2020: a system-oriented evaluation of automated species identification and species distribution prediction. In: Arampatzis, A., et al. (eds.) CLEF 2020. LNCS, vol. 12260, pp. 342–363. Springer, Cham (2020). https://doi.org/10.1007/978-3-030-58219-7_23
30. Kahl, S., et al.:Overview of birdclef 2020: bird sound recognition in complex acoustic environments. In: CLEF task overview 2020, CLEF: Conference and Labs of the Evaluation Forum, September 2020, Thessaloniki, Greece (2020)
31. Kahl, S., et al.: Overview of BirdCLEF 2021: bird call identification in soundscape recordings. In: Working Notes of CLEF 2021 - Conference and Labs of the Evaluation Forum (2021)
32. Kahl, S., Stöter, F.R., Glotin, H., Planqué, R., Vellinga, W.P., Joly, A.: Overview of birdclef 2019: large-scale bird recognition in soundscapes. In: CLEF task overview 2019, CLEF: Conference and Labs of the Evaluation Forum, September 2019, Lugano, Switzerland (2019)
33. Kahl, S., Wood, C.M., Eibl, M., Klinck, H.: Birdnet: a deep learning solution for avian diversity monitoring. Ecol. Inform. **61**, 101236 (2021)
34. Lasseck, M.: Audio-based bird species identification with deep convolutional neural networks. In: CLEF working notes 2018, CLEF: Conference and Labs of the Evaluation Forum, September 2018, Avignon, France (2018)
35. Lee, D.J., Schoenberger, R.B., Shiozawa, D., Xu, X., Zhan, P.: Contour matching for a fish recognition and migration-monitoring system. In: Optics East, pp. 37–48. International Society for Optics and Photonics (2004)
36. Lee, S.H., Chan, C.S., Remagnino, P.: Multi-organ plant classification based on convolutional and recurrent neural networks. IEEE Trans. Image Process. **27**(9), 4287–4301 (2018)
37. Lorieul, T., Cole, E., Deneu, B., Servajean, M., Joly, A.: Overview of GeoLifeCLEF 2021: predicting species distribution from 2 million remote sensing images. In: Working Notes of CLEF 2021 - Conference and Labs of the Evaluation Forum (2021)
38. Millar, E.E., Hazell, E.C., Melles, S.: The 'cottage effect'in citizen science? spatial bias in aquatic monitoring programs. Int. J. Geogr. Inf. Sci. **33**(8), 1612–1632 (2019)

39. Mohapatra, B., et al.: Snakebite mortality in india: a nationally representative mortality survey. PLoS Negl Trop Dis **5**(4), e1018 (2011)
40. Mühling, M., Franz, J., Korfhage, N., Freisleben, B.: Bird species recognition via neural architecture search. In: CLEF working notes 2020, CLEF: Conference and Labs of the Evaluation Forum, September 2020, Thessaloniki, Greece (2020)
41. NIPS International Conference: Proceedings of the Neural Information Processing Scaled for Bioacoustics, from Neurons to Big Data (2013). http://sabiod.org/nips4b
42. Norouzzadeh, M.S., Morris, D., Beery, S., Joshi, N., Jojic, N., Clune, J.: A deep active learning system for species identification and counting in camera trap images. Methods Ecol. Evolut. **12**(1), 150–161 (2021)
43. Picek, L., Ruiz De Castañeda, R., Durso, A.M., Sharada, P.M.: Overview of the snakeclef 2020: automatic snake species identification challenge. In: CLEF task overview 2020, CLEF: Conference and Labs of the Evaluation Forum, September 2020, Thessaloniki, Greece (2020)
44. Picek, L., Durso, A.M., Ruiz De Castañeda, R., Bolon, I.: Overview of SnakeCLEF 2021: automatic snake species identification with country-level focus. In: Working Notes of CLEF 2021 - Conference and Labs of the Evaluation Forum (2021)
45. Picek, L., et al.: Danish fungi 2020 - not just another image recognition dataset (2021)
46. Roberts, D.R., et al.: Cross-validation strategies for data with temporal, spatial, hierarchical, or phylogenetic structure. Ecography **40**(8), 913–929 (2017)
47. Roll, U., et al.: The global distribution of tetrapods reveals a need for targeted reptile conservation. Nat. Ecol. Evol. **1**(11), 1677–1682 (2017)
48. Seneviratne, S.: Contrastive representation learning for natural world imagery: habitat prediction for 30,000 species. In: CLEF working notes 2021, CLEF: Conference and Labs of the Evaluation Forum, September 2021, Bucharest, Romania (2021)
49. Shiu, Y., et al.: Deep neural networks for automated detection of marine mammal species. Sci. Rep. **10**(1), 1–12 (2020)
50. Towsey, M., Planitz, B., Nantes, A., Wimmer, J., Roe, P.: A toolbox for animal call recognition. Bioacoustics **21**(2), 107–125 (2012)
51. Trifa, V.M., Kirschel, A.N., Taylor, C.E., Vallejo, E.E.: Automated species recognition of antbirds in a mexican rainforest using hidden markov models. J. Acoust. Soc. Am. **123**, 2424 (2008)
52. Van Horn, G., et al.: The inaturalist species classification and detection dataset. CVPR (2018)
53. Villacis, J., Goëau, H., Bonnet, P., Mata-Montero, E., Joly, A.: Domain adaptation in the context of herbarium collections: a submission to plantclef 2020. In: CLEF working notes 2020, CLEF: Conference and Labs of the Evaluation Forum, September 2020, Thessaloniki, Greece (2020)
54. Villon, S., Mouillot, D., Chaumont, M., Subsol, G., Claverie, T., Villéger, S.: A new method to control error rates in automated species identification with deep learning algorithms. Sci. Rep. **10**(1), 1–13 (2020)
55. Wäldchen, J., Mäder, P.: Machine learning for image based species identification. Methods Ecol. Evol. **9**(11), 2216–2225 (2018)
56. Wäldchen, J., Rzanny, M., Seeland, M., Mäder, P.: Automated plant species identification-trends and future directions. PLoS Comput. Biol. **14**(4), e1005993 (2018)

57. Wood, C.M., Kahl, S., Chaon, P., Peery, M.Z., Klinck, H.: Survey coverage, recording duration and community composition affect observed species richness in passive acoustic surveys. Methods Ecol. Evol. **12**(5), 885–896 (2021)
58. Youshan Zhang, B.D.D.: Weighted pseudo labeling refinement for plant identifiation. In: Working Notes of CLEF 2021 - Conference and Labs of the Evaluation Forum (2021)
59. Yu, X., Wang, J., Kays, R., Jansen, P.A., Wang, T., Huang, T.: Automated identification of animal species in camera trap images. EURASIP J. Image Video Process. **2013**(1), 1–10 (2013)

Overview of LiLAS 2021 – Living Labs for Academic Search

Philipp Schaer[1(✉)], Timo Breuer[1], Leyla Jael Castro[2], Benjamin Wolff[2], Johann Schaible[3], and Narges Tavakolpoursaleh[3]

[1] TH Köln – University of Applied Sciences, Cologne, Germany
{philipp.schaer,timo.breuer}@th-koeln.de
[2] ZB MED – Information Centre for Life Sciences, Cologne, Germany
{ljgarcia,wolff}@zbmed.de
[3] GESIS – Leibniz Institute for the Social Sciences, Cologne, Germany
{johann.schaible,narges.tavakolpoursaleh}@gesis.org

Abstract. The Living Labs for Academic Search (LiLAS) lab aims to strengthen the concept of user-centric living labs for academic search. The methodological gap between real-world and lab-based evaluation should be bridged by allowing lab participants to evaluate their retrieval approaches in two real-world academic search systems from life sciences and social sciences. This overview paper outlines the two academic search systems LIVIVO and GESIS Search, and their corresponding tasks within LiLAS, which are ad-hoc retrieval and dataset recommendation. The lab is based on a new evaluation infrastructure named STELLA that allows participants to submit results corresponding to their experimental systems in the form of pre-computed runs and Docker containers that can be integrated into production systems and generate experimental results in real-time. Both submission types are interleaved with the results provided by the productive systems allowing for a seamless presentation and evaluation. The evaluation of results and a meta-analysis of the different tasks and submission types complement this overview.

1 Introduction

The Living Labs for Academic Search (LiLAS) lab aims to strengthen the concept of user-centric living labs for the domain of academic search. By allowing lab *participants* to evaluate their retrieval approaches in two real-world academic search portals (called *sites*) from life sciences and social sciences, the methodological gap between real-world and lab-based evaluations is effectively reduced.

This gap is based on the different opportunities available to researchers in academia and industry. While industry-based research in the field of information retrieval (IR) has the opportunity to conduct experiments in-vivo – thanks to the availability of large systems, with a wide range and correspondingly large user base – these opportunities usually remain closed to academic research. In-vivo here describes the possibility to perform IR experiments integrated into real-world systems and to conduct experiments where the actual interaction with

K. S. Candan et al. (Eds.): CLEF 2021, LNCS 12880, pp. 394–418, 2021.
https://doi.org/10.1007/978-3-030-85251-1_25

Fig. 1. Overview of the live evaluation pipeline.

these systems takes place. It should be emphasized here that these are not classic user experiments in which the focus is on the individual interactions of users (e.g., to investigate questions of UI design), but rather aggregated usage data is collected in large quantities in order to generate reliable quantitative research results. The potential of living labs and real-world evaluation techniques has been shown in previous CLEF labs such as NewsREEL [10] and LL4IR [14], or TREC OpenSearch [2]. In a similar vein, LiLAS is designed around the living lab evaluation concept and introduces different use cases in the broader field of academic search. Academic search solutions, which have to deal with the phenomena around the exponential growing rate [15] of scientific information and knowledge, tend to fall behind the real-world requirements and demands. The vast amount of scientific information does not only include traditional journal publication, but also a constantly growing amount of pre-prints, research datasets, code, survey data, and many other research objects. This heterogeneity and mass of documents and datasets introduces new challenges to the disciplines of information retrieval, recommender systems, digital libraries, and related fields. Academic search is a conceptional umbrella to subsume all these different disciplines and is well-known through (mostly domain-specific) search systems and portals such as PubMed, arXiv.org, or dblp. While those three are examples of open-science-friendly systems as they allow re-use of metadata, usage data and/or access to fulltext data, other systems such as Google Scholar or ResearchGate. The later offer no access at all to their internal algorithms and data and are therefore representatives of a closed-science (and commercial) mindset.

Progress in the field of academic search and its corresponding domains is usually evaluated by means of shared tasks that are based on the principles of Cranfield/TREC-style studies [13]. Most recently the TREC-COVID evaluation campaign run by NIST attracted a high number of participants and showed the high impact of scientific retrieval tasks in the community. Within TREC-COVID a wide range of systems and retrieval approaches participated and generally showed the massive retrieval performance that recent BERT and other transformer-based machine learning approaches are capable of. However, classic vector-space retrieval was also highly successful and showed the limitations of the test collection-based evaluation approach of TREC-COVID and the general need for innovation in the field of academic search and IR. Meta-evaluation studies of system performances in TREC and CLEF showed a need for innovation in IR evaluation [1]. The field of academic search is no exception to this. The central concern of academic search is finding both relevant and high-quality documents.

The question of what constitutes relevance in academic search is multilayered [4] and an ongoing research area.

In 2020 we held a first iteration of LiLAS as a so-called workshop lab. This year we provide participants exclusive access to real-world systems, their document base (in our case a very heterogeneous set of research articles and research data including, for instance, surveys), and the actual interactions including the query string and the corresponding click data (see overview on the setup in Fig. 1). To foster different experimental settings we compile a set of head queries and candidate documents to allow pre-computed submissions. Using the STELLA-infrastructure, we allow participants to easily integrate their approaches into the real-world systems using Docker containers and provide the possibility to compare different approaches at the same time.

This lab overview is structured as follows: In Sects. 2 and 3 we introduce the two main use cases of LiLAS which are bond to the sites granting us access to their retrieval systems: LIVIVO and GESIS Search. In these two sections the systems, the provided datasets, and task are described. In Sect. 4 we outline the evaluation setup and STELLA, our living lab evaluation framework, and the two submission types, namely pre-computed runs and Docker container submissions. Section 4 also includes the description of the evaluation metrics used with in the lab and a short overview on the organizational structure of the lab. In Sect. 5 we introduce the participating groups and approaches. We outline the results of the evaluation rounds in Sect. 6 and conclude in Sect. 7.

2 Ad-Hoc Search in LIVIO

2.1 LIVIVO Literature Search Portal

LIVIVO[1] [11] is a literature search portal developed and supported by ZB MED – Information Centre for Life Sciences. ZB MED is a non-profit organization providing specialized literature in Life Sciences at a national (German) and international level and hosting one of the largest stock of life science literature in Europe. Since 2015, ZB MED supports users including librarians, students, general practitioners and researchers with LIVIVO, a comprehensive and interdisciplinary search portal for Life Sciences.

LIVIVO integrates various literature resources from medicine, health, environment, agriculture and nutrition, covering a variety of scholarly publication types (e.g., conferences, preprints, peer-review journals). LIVIVO corpus includes about 80 million documents from more than 50 data sources in multiple languages (e.g., English, German, French). To better support its users, LIVIVO offers an end-user interface in English and German, an automatically and semantically enhanced search capability, and a subject-based categorization covering the different areas it supports (e.g., environment, agriculture, nutrition, medicine). Precision of search queries is improved by using descriptors with semantic support; in particular, LIVIVO uses three multilingual vocabularies to

[1] https://www.livivo.de.

```
# Sample head query
{ "qid": 1001, "qstr": "integrierte AND versorgung", "freq": 12 }

# Sample documents
{ "DBRECORDID": "AGRISFR2016215853",
  "TITLE": ["Dissection ..."],
  "AUTHOR": ["Teyssèdre, Simon"],
  "SOURCE": ["Dissection ..."],
  "LANGUAGE": ["fra"],
  "DATABASE": ["AGRIS"] }

# Sample candidate list
{ "qid": 1001,
  "qstr": "integrierte AND versorgung",
  "candidates": ["C951899619", "C676171", "848078", "C765841" ... ] }
```

Fig. 2. Examples for head queries, documents, and candidate lists for the LIVIVO system.

this end (Medical Subject Headings MeSH, UMTHES, and AGROVOC. In addition to its search capabilities, LIVIVO also integrates functionality supporting inter-library loans at a national level in Germany. Since 2020, LIVIVO also offers a specialized collection on COVID-19[2]

2.2 LIVIVO Dataset

For the LiLAS challenge, we prepared training and test datasets comprising head queries together with 100-document candidate list. In Fig. 2 we include an excerpt of the different elements included in the data. Data was formatted in JSON and presented as JSONL files to facilitate processing. Participating head queries were restricted to keywords-based search and keywords-based search plus AND, OR and NOT operators.

Head queries were assigned an identifier, namely *qid*, a query string, *qstr* and as an additional information the query frequency, *freq*. For each head query, a candidate list was also provided. Candidate lists include the query identifier as well as corresponding string, together with a list of 100 document identifiers (i.e. the native identifier used in the LIVIVO database).

In addition to head queries and candidate lists, we also provided a set of documents in LIVIVO corresponding to three of the major bibliographic scholarly databases so participants could create their own indexes. The document set contains metadata for approx. 35 million documents and is provided as a JSONL file. To reduce complexity and keep the data manageable, we decided to provide only the 6 most important data fields (DBRECORDID, TITLE, AUTHOR, SOURCE, LANGUAGE, DATABASE). Additional metadata and fulltext is mostly available from the original database curators.

[2] https://www.livivo.de//covid19.

The aformentioned databases correspond to Medline, the National Library of Medicine's (NLM) bibliographic database for life sciences and biomedical information including about 20 million of abstracts; the NLM catalog, providing access to bibliographic data for over 1.4 million journals, books and similar data; and the Agricultural Science and Technology Information (AGRIS) database, a Food and Agriculture Organization of the United Nations initiative compiling information on agricultural research with 8.9 million structured bibliographical records on agricultural science and technology.

2.3 Task

Finding the most relevant publications in relation to a head query remains a challenge in scholarly Information Retrieval systems. While most repositories or registries deal mostly with publications in English, LIVIVO, the production system used at LiLAS, supports multilingualism, adding an extra layer of complexity and presenting a challenge to participants.

The goal of this ad-hoc search task is supporting researchers to find the most relevant literature regarding a head query. Participants were asked to define and implement their ranking approach using as basis a multi-lingual candidate documents list. A good ranking should present users with the most relevant documents on top of the result set. An interesting aspect of this task is the multilingualism as multiple languages can be used to pose a query (e.g. English, German, French); however, regardless of the language used on the query, the retrieval can include documents in other languages as part of the result set.

3 Research Data Recommendations in GESIS-Search

3.1 GESIS Search Portal

GESIS Search[3] is a search portal for social science research data and open access publications developed and supported by GESIS - Leibniz Institute for the Social Sciences. GESIS is a member of the Leibniz Association with the purpose to promote social science research. It provides essential and internationally relevant research-based services for the social sciences, and as the largest European infrastructure institute for the social sciences, GESIS offers advice, expertise and services to scientists at all stages of their research projects.

GESIS Search aims at helping its users find appropriate scholarly information on the broad topic of social sciences [6]. To this end, it provides different types of information from the social sciences in multiple languages, comprising literature (114.7k publications), research data (84k), questions and variables (13.6k), as well as instruments and tools (440). A well-configured relevance ranking together with a well-defined structure and faceting mechanism allow to address the users' information needs, however, the most interesting aspect is the inclusion of scientific literature with research data. Typically, those types of information are

[3] https://search.gesis.org/.

```
# Sample publication document
{ "id": "csa201419416",
  "title": "The Changing Value...",
  "abstract": "This article reviews...",
  "topic":[
    "Children",
    "Child Mortality",
    "Values"] }

# Sample research dataset document
{ "id": "DA3433",
  "title": "Kindheit, Jugend und Erwachsenwerden...",
  "title_en": "Childhood, Adolencence, and Becoming an Adult...",
  "abstract": "Die Hauptthemen der Studie...",
  "abstract_en": "The primary topics of the study...",
  "topic": ["Familie und Ehe", "Kinder"],
  "topic_en": ["Family life and marriage", "Children"] }

# Sample candidate list
{ "s_id": "gesis-ssoar-62031",
  "candidate_docs": {
    "ZA6752": 0.1856689453125,
    "ZA6751": 0.183837890625,
    "ZA6749": 0.181396484375,
    "ZA6782": 0.1795654296875} }
```

Fig. 3. Examples for publication documents, research dataset documents, and candidate lists for the GESIS Search system.

accessible through different portals only, posing the problem of a lack of links between these two types of information. GESIS Search provides such an integrated access to research data as well as to publications. The information items are connected to each other based on links that are either manually created or automatically extracted by services that find data references in full texts. Such linking allows researchers to explore the connections between information items interactively.

3.2 GESIS Search Dataset

For LiLAS, we focus on all publications and research data comprised by GESIS Search. The publications are mostly in English and German, and are annotated with further textual metadata including title, abstract, topic, persons, and others. Metadata on research data comprises (among others) a title, topics, datatype, abstract, collection method, primary investigators, and contributors in English and/or German.

The data provided to participants comprises the mentioned metadata on social science literature and research data on social science topics comprised in the GESIS Search. In Fig. 3 we include an excerpt of the different elements included in the data. For the dataset recommendation task with pre-computed results (see details in Sect. 3.3), in addition, the participants were given the set of research data candidates that are recommended for each publication. This candidate set is computed based on context similarity between publications and research data. It is created by applying the TF-IDF score to vectorize the combination of title, abstract, and topics for each document type and computing the cosine similarities between cross-data types. It contains a list of research data for each publication with the highest similarities to the publication among other research data in the corpus.

3.3 Task

Research data is of high importance in scientific research, especially when making progress in experimental investigations. However, finding useful research data can be difficult and cumbersome, even if using dataset search engines, such as Google Dataset Search[4]. Another approach is scanning scientific publication for utilized or mentioned research data; however, this allows to find explicitly stated research data and not other research data relevant to the subject. To alleviate the situation, we aim at evolving the recommendation of appropriate research data beyond explicitly mentioned or cited research data. To this end, we propose to recommend research data based on publications of the user's interest between a scientific publication and possible research data candidates.

The main task is: given a seed-document, participants are asked to calculate the best fitting research data recommendations with regards to the seed-document. This resembles the use case of providing highly useful recommendations of research data relevant to the publication that the user is currently viewing. For example, the user is interested in the impact of religion on political elections. She finds a publication regarding that topic, which has a set of research data candidates covering the same topic.

The participants were allowed to submit pre-computed and live runs (see Sect. 4.2 for more details). For submitting the pre-computed run, the participants also received a first candidate list comprising 1k publication each having a list of recommended research data. The task here was to re-rank this candidate list. On the contrary, for submitting the live runs, such a candidate list was not needed, as the recommended candidates needed to be calculated first. To do so, participants are provided metadata on publications as well as on the research data comprised in GESIS Search (see Sect. 3.1 for more details on the provided data).

[4] https://datasetsearch.research.google.com/.

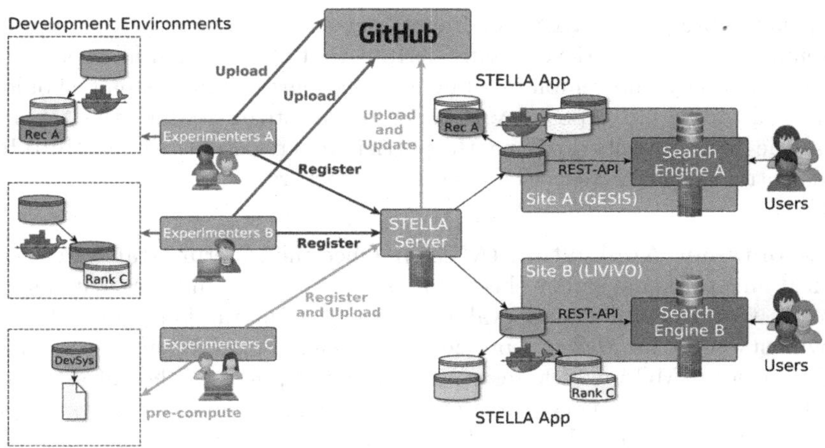

Fig. 4. Overview of the STELLA infrastructure

4 Evaluation Setup

4.1 STELLA Infrastructure

The technical infrastructure and platform was provided by our evaluation service called STELLA [3] (as illustrated in Fig. 4). It complements existing shared task platforms by allowing experimental ranking and recommendation systems to be fully integrated into an evaluation environment, with no interference in the interaction between the users and the system as the whole process is transparent for users. Besides transparency and reproduciblity, one of the STELLA main principles is the integration of experimental systems as micro-services. More specifically, lab participants package their single systems as Docker containers that are bundled in a multi-container application (MCA). Providers of academic research infrastructures deploy the MCA in their back-end and use the REST-API either to get ranking and recommendations or to post the corresponding user feedback that is mainly used for our evaluations. Intermediate evaluation results are available through a public dashboard service that is hosted on a central server, also part of the STELLA infrastructure. After authentication, participants can register experimental systems at this central instance and access feedback data that can be used to optimize their systems. In the following, each component of the infrastructure is briefly described to give the reader a better idea on how STELLA serves as a proxy for user-oriented experiments with ranking and recommendation systems.

Micro-services. As pointed out before, we request our lab participants to package their systems with Docker. For the sake of compatibility, we provide templates for these micro-services to implement minimal REST-based web services. Participants can adapt their systems to these templates as they see it fits as long as the pre-defined REST endpoints deliver technically correct responses. The templates can be retrieved from GitHub[5] that is fundamental to our infrastructure. Not only the templates, but also the participant systems should be hosted in a public Git repository in order to be integrated into the MCA. As soon as the developments are done, the participants register their Git(Hub) URL at the central dashboard service of the infrastructure.

Multi-container Application (MCA). Once the experimental systems pass technical unit tests and sanity checks for selected queries and target items, they are ready to be deployed and evaluated via user interactions. To reduce the deployments costs for the site providers, the single experimental systems are bundled into an MCA which serves as the entry point to the infrastructure. The MCA handles the query distribution among the experimental systems and also sends user feedback data to the central server at regular intervals. After the REST-API corresponding to the MCA is connected to the search interface, the user traffic can be redirected to the MCA which will actually deliver the experimental results. We then interleave results of single experimental systems with those from the baseline system by using a Team-Draft-Interleaving (TDI) approach. This results in two benefits: 1) we prevent users from subpar retrieval results that also might affect the site's reputation, and 2), as shown before, interleaved results can be used to infer statistically significant results with less user data as compared to conventional A/B tests. The site providers rely on their own logging tools. STELLA expects a minimal set of information required when sending feedback; however, sites are free to add any additional JSON-formatted feedback information and interactions to the data payload, for instance logged clicks on site-specific SERP elements. The underlying source code of the MCA is hosted in a public GitHub repository[6].

Central Server. The central server instance of the infrastructure fulfills four functionalities: 1) participants, sites and administrators visit the server to register user accounts and systems; 2) a dashboard service provides visual analytics and first insights about the performance of experimental systems; 3) likewise, feedback data in the form of user interactions is stored in a database that can be downloaded for system optimizations and further evaluations; and 4) the server implements an automated update job of the MCA in order to integrate newly submitted systems if suitable.

Each MCA that is instantiated with legitimate credentials posts the logged user feedback to the central infrastructure server. Even though the infrastructure would allow continuous integration of newly submitted systems, we stuck to the official dates of round 1 and 2 when updating the MCAs at the sites. Due to moderate traffic, we run the central server on a lightweight single core virtual

[5] https://github.com/stella-project/stella-micro-template.
[6] https://github.com/stella-project/stella-app.

machine with 2 GB RAM and 50 GB storage capacity[7]. More technical details about the implementations can be found in the public GitHub repository[8].

4.2 Submission Types

Participants can choose between two different submission types for both tasks (i.e. ad-hoc search and dataset recommendation). Similar to previous living labs, **Type A** are pre-computed runs that contain rankings and recommendations of the most frequent queries and the most frequently viewed document, respectively for reach task. Alternatively, it is possible to integrate the entire experimental system as a micro-service as part of a **Type B** submission. Both submission types have their own distinct merits as described below.

Type A - Pre-computed Runs. Even though the primary goal of the STELLA framework is the integration of entire systems as micro-services, we offer the possibility to participate in the experiments by submitting system outputs, i.e. in the form of pre-computed rankings and recommendations. We do so for two reasons. First, the Type A submissions resemble those of previous living labs and serve as the baseline in order to evaluate the feasibility of our new infrastructure design. Second, we hope to lower technical barriers for some participants that want to submit the system outputs only. To make it easier for participants, we follow the familiar TREC run file syntax.

Depending on the chosen task, for each of the selected top-k queries or target items (identified by `<qid>`) a ranking or recommendation has to be computed in advance and then uploaded to the dashboard service. The upload process is tightly integrated into the GitHub ecosystem. Once the run file is uploaded, a new repository is automatically created from the previously described micro-template to which the uploaded run is committed. This is made possible thanks to GitHub API and access tokens. The run file itself is loaded as a pandas `DataFrame` into the running micro-service when the *indexing* endpoint is called. Upon request, the queries and target items are translated into the corresponding `<qid>` to filter the `DataFrame`. Due to manageable sizes of top-k queries and target items, the entire (compressed) run file can be uploaded to the repository and can be kept in memory after it is indexed as a `DataFrame`. As a technical safety check, we also integrate a dedicated verification tool[9] in combination with GitHub Actions to verify that the uploaded files follow the correct syntax.

Type B - Docker Containers. Running fully-fledged ranking and recommendation systems as micro-services overcomes the restrictions of responses that are limited to top-k queries and target items. Therefore, we offer the possibility to integrate the entire systems as a Docker container into the STELLA infrastructure as part of Type B submissions. As pointed out earlier, participants fork the

[7] https://lilas.stella-project.org/.
[8] https://github.com/stella-project/stella-server.
[9] https://github.com/stella-project/syntax_checker_CLI.

template of the micro-services and adapt it to their experimental system. While Docker and the implementation of pre-defined REST endpoints are hard requirements, participants have total freedom w.r.t. the implementation and tools they use within their container, i.e., they do not even have to build up on the Python web application that is provided in the template. Solely, the *index* endpoint and, depending on the chosen task, either the *ranking* or *recommendation* endpoint have to deliver technically correct results. For this purpose, we include unit tests in the template repository that can be run in order to verify that the Docker containers can be properly integrated. If these unit tests pass, the participants register the URL of the corresponding Git repository at the dashboard service. Later on, the system URL is added to the build file of the MCA when an update process is invoked. If the MCA is updated at the sites, newly submitted experimental systems are build from the Dockerfiles in the specified repositories.

4.3 Baseline Systems

LIVIVO baseline system for ranking is built on Apache Solr and Apache Lucene. The index contains about 80 million documents from more than 50 data sources in multiple languages and about 120 searchable fields ranging from basic data such as Title, Abstract, Authors to more specific such as MeSH-Terms, availability or OCR-Data. For ranking, LIVIVO uses the Lucene default ranker which is a variant of TF-IDF; on top of it, a custom boosting is added. Newer documents as well as search queries occurring in title or author fields are boosted. An exact match of search phrases in title-field results in a very high boosting. Moreover LIVIVO uses a Lucene-based plugin which executes NLP-tasks like stemming, lemmatization, multilingual search; it also makes use of semantic technologies, mainly based on the Medical Subject Headings (MeSH) vocabulary.

The baseline system for recommendation of research data based on publications in Gesis Search utilizes Pyserini, a Python interface to the IR toolkit built on Lucene designed to support reproducible IR research. The baseline system for recommendation applies the SimpleSearcher of Pyserini that provides the entry point for sparse retrieval BM25 ranking using bag-of-words representations. The Lucene-based index contains abstracts and titles of all research data. The publication identifier (target item of the recommendation) is translated into the publication title, which, in turn, is used to query the index with a BM25 algorithm. Accordingly, the research data recommendations are based on the title and abstracts of the research data and queries made from the publication titles.

4.4 Evaluation Metrics

Our logging infrastructure allows us to track search sessions and the corresponding interactions made by users. Each session comprises a specific site user, multiple queries (or target items) as wells as the corresponding results and feedback data in the form of user interactions, primarily logged as clicks with timestamps.

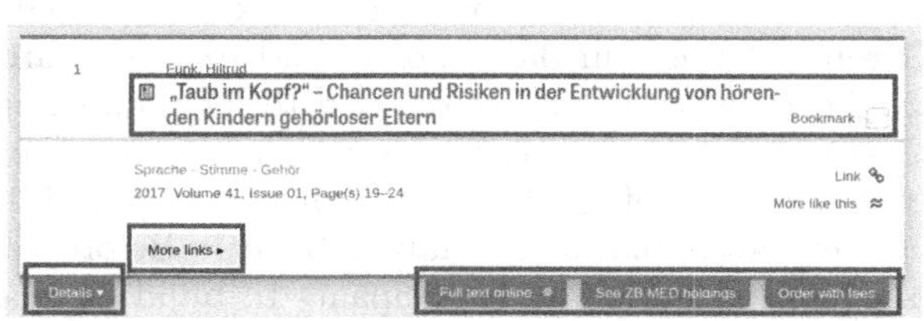

SERP Element	w_s
Bookmark	10
Order	10
Fulltext	8
In Stock	8
More Links	2
Title	1
Details	1

Fig. 5. Table : Example illustrating the SERP elements for that clicks were logged at LIVIVO and the corresponding weights w_s according to Eq. 1.

Similar to previous living lab initiatives, we design our user-oriented experiments with interleaved result lists. Given a list with interleaved results and the corresponding clicks of users, we determine *Wins*, *Losses*, *Ties*, and the derived *Outcomes* for relative comparisons of the experimental and baseline systems [14]. Following previous living lab experiments, we implement the interleaving method by the *Team-Draft-Interleaving* algorithm [12]. More specifically, we refactored exactly the same implementation[10] for the highest degree of comparability.

Furthermore we follow Gingstad et al.'s proposal of a weighted score based on click events [5] and define the *Reward* as

$$Reward = \sum_{s \epsilon S} w_s c_s \tag{1}$$

where S denotes the set of all elements on a search engine result page (SERP) for which clicks are considered, w_s denotes the corresponding weight of the SERP element s that was clicked, and c_s denotes the total number of clicks on the SERP element s. The *Normalized Reward* is defined as

$$nReward = \frac{Reward_{\text{exp}}}{Reward_{\text{exp}} + Reward_{\text{base}}} \tag{2}$$

that is the sum of all weighted clicks on experimental results ($Reward_{\text{exp}}$) normalized by the total *Reward* given by $Reward_{\text{exp}} + Reward_{\text{base}}$. Note that, only those clicks from the experimental systems where rankings were interleaved with results of the two compared systems are considered. Figure 5 shows the SERP elements that were logged at LIVIVO and the corresponding weights for our evaluations. We do not implement the *Mean Normalized Reward* proposed by Gingstad et al. due to a different evaluation setup. Our lab is organized in rounds during which the systems as well as the underlying document collections are not modified and we already determine the *Normalized Reward* over all aggregated clicks of a specific round.

[10] https://bitbucket.org/living-labs/ll-api/src/master/ll/core/interleave.py.

4.5 Lab Rounds and Overall Lab Schedule

The lab was originally split in two separated rounds of 4 weeks each. Due to technical issues for LIVIVO round 1 was four days shorter and round 2 started one week later as planned. To compensate this, we decided to let round 2 last until 24 May 2021, so in total round 2 lasted nearly six instead of four weeks. Each participating groups received a set of feedback data after each round; the feedback was also made publicly available on the lab website[11]. Before each round a training phase was offered to allow the participants to build or adapt their systems to the new datasets or click feedback data.

5 Participation

5.1 Team Lemuren

Team lemuren participated in both rounds with pre-computed results and dockerized systems for the ad-hoc search task at LIVIVO [17]. For both rounds, they submitted two different approaches.

The pre-computed ranking results of `lemuren elk` are based on built-in functions of Elasticsearch. This system uses a combination between the divergence from randomness model and the Jelinek-Mercer smoothing method for re-ranking candidate documents. The preprocessing pipeline implements stop-word removal, stemming and considers synonyms for medical and COVID19-related terms. The system was tuned only to the results in English.

`save fami` is another pre-computed system. It also uses Elasticsearch combined with natural language processing (NLP) modules implemented with the Python package spaCy. Similar to the second submission for the pre-computed round, this dockerized system is build on top of Elasticsearch and spaCy. The indexing pipeline follows a multilingual approach supporting English and German languages. For both languages the system implements full solutions available in spaCy, either by the models `en_core_sci_lg` (English biomedical texts) or `de_core_news_lg` (general German texts). The system uses the Google Translator API[12] for language detection and automatic translating of incoming queries (from German to English and vice versa). For indexing and document-retrieval Elasticsearch was used with a custom boosting for MeSH and Chemical-tokens. `lemuren elastic only (LEO)` is the second dockerized system by this team which, different from LEPREP, relies only on Elasticsearchs built-in tools for indexing documents and processing queries. For indexing documents a custom ingestion pipeline is used to detect the documents language (English or German) and creating the corresponding language fields. Handling of basic acronyms was modeled by using the built-in word-delimiter function. Similar to LEPREP-System, LEO uses Google Translator API for automatic query translation. The system is complemented by a fuzzy match and fuzzy query-expansion to obtain better results for mistyped queries. Like `lemuren elk` in round one, LEO also uses DFR and LMJelinekMercer to calculate a score and a similarity distance.

[11] https://th-koeln.sciebo.de/s/OBm0NLEwz1RYl9N.
[12] https://pypi.org/project/google-trans-new/.

5.2 Team Tekma

Team tekma contributed experiments to both rounds. In the first round, they submitted the pre-computed results of the system `tekma_s` for the ad-hoc search task at LIVIVO [8]. In the second round, they submitted pre-computed recommendations (covering the entire volume of publications) for the corresponding task at GESIS. Both systems are described below.

`tekma_s` used Apache Solr to index the document and used pseudo-relevance feedback to extend the queries for the ad-hoc search task. The system only considers documents in English. The system got few impressions and clicks in comparison to the baseline system. `tekma_n` participated in the second round producing pre-computed recommendations. They used Apache Solr BM25 ranking function and applied query expansion and data enrichment by adding the metadata translations and re-ranking the retrieved result using user feedback and KNN. To generate the primary recommendations for a publication, they used publication fields as a query to search the indexed dataset.

5.3 Team GESIS Research

In addition to the baseline system, team GESIS Research contributed a fully dockerized system in both rounds [16]. `gesis_rec_pyterrier` implements a naive content-based recommendation without any advanced knowledge about user preferences and usage metrics. It uses the metadata available in both entity types, i.e., title, abstract, and topics. They employed the classical tfidf-based weighting model from the PyTerrier framework to obtain first-hand experience with the online evaluation. The indexing and query have been made of the combination of words in title, abstract, and research data topics and publications. They decided to submit the same experimental system for both rounds to gain more user feedback for their unique system. Even though only tfidf-based recommendations are implemented at the current state, it offers a good starting point for further experimentation with PyTerrier and the declarative manner of defining retrieval pipelines.

6 Results

Our experimental evaluations are twofold. First, we evaluate overall statistics of both rounds and sites. Second, we evaluate the performance of all participating systems based on the click data logged during the active periods. As mentioned before, the first round ran during four weeks from March 1st, 2021 to March 28th, 2021 and the second round for five weeks from April 17th, 2021 until May 24th, 2021 at LIVIVO and for six weeks from April 12th, 2021 until May 24th, 2021 at GESIS. To foster transparency and reproducibility of the evaluations, we release the corresponding evaluation scripts in an open-source GitHub repository[13].

[13] https://github.com/stella-project/stella-evaluations.

Table 1. Number of Sessions, impressions, clicks and click through rate (CTR).

Evaluation round	Site	Sessions	Impressions	Clicks	CTR
Round 1	LIVIVO	2852	4658	2452	0.5264
Round 1	GESIS	4568	8390	152	0.0181
Round 2	LIVIVO	12962	25830	11562	0.4476
Round 2	GESIS	6576	12068	250	0.0207

6.1 Overall Evaluations of both Rounds and Sites

Table 1 provides an overview of the traffic logged in both rounds. In sum, substantially more sessions, impressions, and clicks were logged in the second round not only due a longer period but also because more systems contributed as Type B submissions. In the first round, systems deployed at LIVIVO were mostly contributed as Type A submissions, meaning their responses were restricted to pre-selected head queries. LIVIVO started the second round with full systems which delivered results for arbitrary queries and thus more session data was logged. GESIS started both rounds with the majority of systems contributed as type B submissions. In comparison to LIVIVO, more sessions and impressions were logged in the first round, but less recommendations were clicked. Similarly, there are less clicks in the second round in comparison to LIVIVO, which is also reflected by the Click-Through Rate (CTR) that is determined by the ratio between Clicks and Impressions. As mentioned before, GESIS introduced the recommendations of research datasets as a new service, and, presumably, users were not aware of this new feature.

During the first two weeks of the first round, the amount of logged data at LIVIVO is comparatively low due to systems with pre-computed results for pre-selected head queries. After that, the first type B systems was deployed and increasingly more user traffic could be redirected to our infrastructure. Figure 6 illustrates these effects. The cumulative sums of logged sessions, impressions, and clicks rapidly increased after the first Type B system got online in mid-March.

The logged impressions follow a power-law distribution for both rankings and recommendations as shown in Fig. 7. Most of the impressions can be attributed to a few top-k queries (rankings) or documents (recommendations). The COVID-19 pandemic has a clear influence on the query distributions: the most frequent and the fifth most frequent query are "covid19" and "covid", respectively. Three of the ten most frequent queries are German queries ("demenz", "pflege", "schlaganfall"); others are either domain-specific or can be interpreted as English queries. In Table 2 we report statistics about the queries logged during both rounds at LIVIVO. In both rounds, interaction data was logged for 11,822 unique queries with an average length of 2.9840 terms and each session had 1.9340 queries on average. Nine out of the ten most frequent target items of the recommendations at GESIS are publications with German titles.

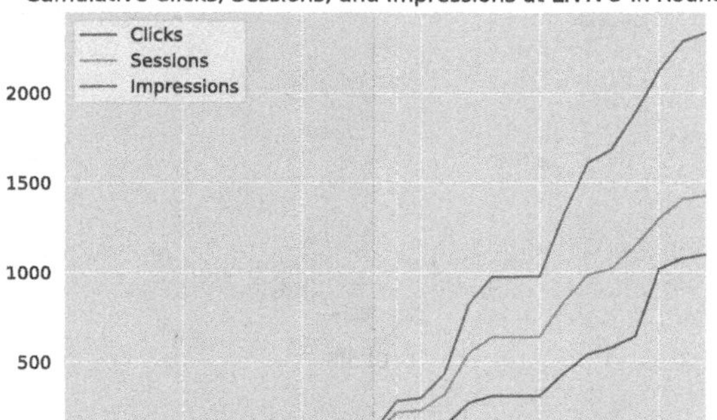

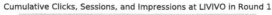

Fig. 6. Cumulative sum of logged session data at LIVIVO before (blue) and after (green) the first fully dockerized system went online in the first round.

Table 2. Statistics of the queries at LIVIVO

Number of Unique Queries	11822
Average Query Length [Terms]	2.9840
Average Number of Queries per Session	1.9340
Average Number of Clicks per Query	0.4547

Another important aspect to be considered as part of the system evaluations is the position bias inherent in the logged data. Click decisions are biased towards the top ranks of the result lists as shown in Fig. 8. For both use cases, the rankings and recommendations were displayed to users as vertical lists. Note that, GESIS restricted the recommendations to the first six recommended datasets and no pagination over the following recommended items was possible. LIVIVO shows ten results per page to its users, and as it can be seen from the logged data, users rarely click results beyond the fifth page.

In addition to "simple" clicks on ranked items, we logged specific SERP elements that were clicked at LIVIVO. Table 4 already provided an overview on which elements were logged and Fig. 9 shows the CTR of these elements also follows a power-law distribution. The number of clicks is the highest for the *Details* button and it is followed by the *Title* and *Fulltext* click options. In comparison, the other four logged elements receive substantially less clicks.

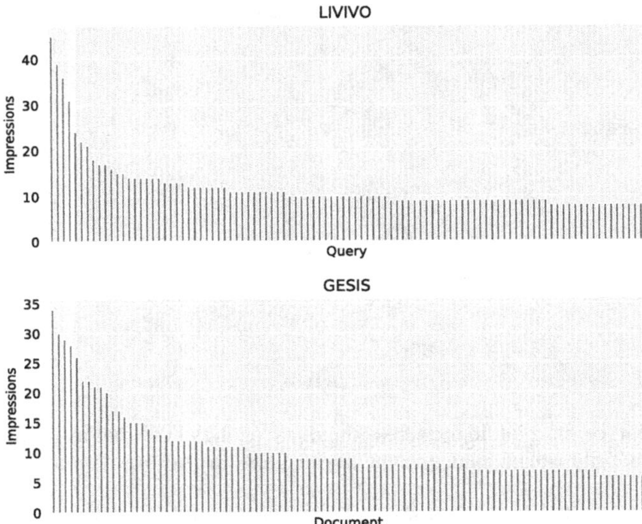

Fig. 7. Impressions vs. Query/Document

6.2 System Evaluations

An overview of all systems participating in our experiments is provided in Table 3. In the first round, three type A systems (`lemuren_elk`, `tekmas`, `save_fami`) were submitted and deployed at LIVIVO. They were also deployed in the second round, but did not receive any updates between the two rounds. Since there were no type B submissions in the first round for LIVIVO, we deployed the type B system `livivo_rank_pyserini` after two weeks in mid-March. It provided results for the entire volume of publications and rankings were based on the BM25 method. It was implemented with Pyserini [9] and the corresponding default settings[14]. In contrast to the other systems, it was online for the last two weeks of the first round only. In the second round, it was online in the first days until the other type B systems were ready to be deployed since we wanted to distribute the user traffic among the participants' systems only. In the second round, two type B systems `lemuren_elastic_only` and `lemuren_elastic_preprocessing` were contributed. Both systems build up on Elasticsearch, whereas they differ by the pre-processing as outlined before. At GESIS, `gesis_rec_pyterrier`, submitted as type B system, was online in both rounds. In the first round, the only type A submission was `gesis_rec_precom` that was substituted in the second round by `tekma_n`. Both baseline systems at LIVIVO (`livivo_base`) and GESIS (`gesis_rec_pyserini`) were integrated as type B systems, remained unmodified, and could deliver results for every request.

[14] https://github.com/stella-project/livivo_rank_pyserini.

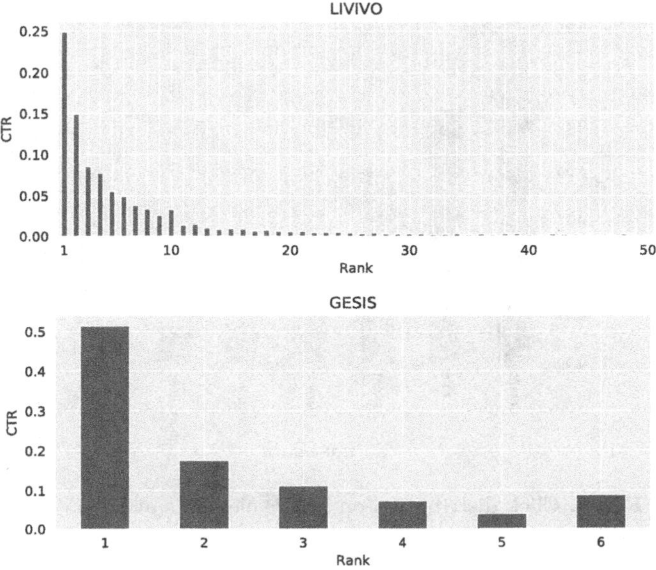

Fig. 8. Click-through Rate (CTR) vs. Rank

Table 4 compares the experimental systems' outcomes and the corresponding logged interactions and session data during the first round. Regarding the *Outcome* measure, none of the experimental systems was able to outperform the baseline systems. Note that the reported *Outcomes* of the baseline systems result from comparisons against all experimental systems. The systems with pre-computed rankings (type A submissions) received a total number of 32 clicks over a period of four weeks at LIVIVO. Since interaction data was sparse in the first round, we only received enough data for `livivo_rank_pyserini` to conduct significance tests. The reported p-value results from a Wilcoxon signed-rank test and shows a significant difference between the experimental and baseline system.

Table 5 shows the results of the second round. `tekma_n` was contributed as type A submission, but results were pre-computed for the entire volume of publications at GESIS. It replaced `gesis_rec_precom` and achieved a higher CTR compared to the other recommender systems. Likewise, it achieves an *Outcome* of 0.62, which might be an indicator that it outperforms the baseline recommendations given by `gesis_rec_pyserini`. Unfortunately, we are not able to conduct any meaningful significance tests due to the sparsity of click data. At LIVIVO, the systems with pre-computed rankings (type A submissions) received a comparable amount of clicks similar to the first round. In sum, all three systems received a total number of 35 clicks over a period of five weeks. Even though, click data is sparse and interpretations have to be made carefully, the relative ranking order of these three systems is preserved in the second round (e.g. in terms of the *Outcome*, total number of clicks, or CTR).

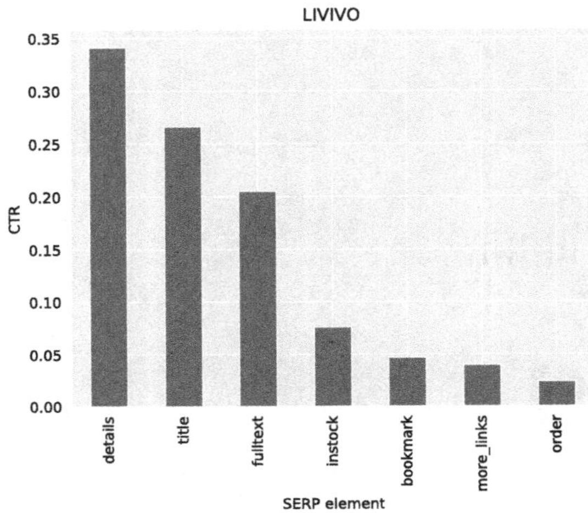

Fig. 9. Click distribution on SERP elements at LIVIVO

In the second round, no experimental system could outperform the baseline system at LIVIVO. Both experimental type B systems `lemuren_elastic_only` and `lemuren_elastic_preprocessing` achieve significantly lower *Outcome* scores as the baseline. However, the second system has substantially lower *Outcome* and CTR scores. Both systems share a fair amount of the same methodological approach and only differ by the processing of the input text. In this case, the system performance does not seem to benefit from this specific pre-processing step, when interpreting clicks as positive relevance signals. The third type B system at LIVIVO `livivo_rank_pyserini` did not participate the entire second round, since we took it offline as soon as the other type B systems were available. Despite having participated in comparatively less experiments than in the first round (1260 sessions vs. 243 sessions), the system achieves in both rounds comparable results in terms of *Outcome* and CTR scores. This circumstance raises the question for how long systems have to be online to deliver reliable performance estimates.

Previous studies showed that a system is more likely to win if its documents are ranked at higher positions [7]. As part of our experimental evaluations, we can confirm this circumstance. We also determined the Spearman correlation between an interleaving outcome (1: win, −1: loss, 0: tie) and the highest ranked position of a document contributed by an experimental system. At both sites, we see a weak but significant correlation (LIVIVO: $\rho = -0.0883$, $p = 1.3535e-09$; GESIS: $\rho = -0.3480$, $p = 4.7422e-07$).

One shortcoming of the previous measures derived from interleaving experiments is the simplified interpretation of click interactions. As outlined in Sect. 4, by weighting clicks differently, it is possible to account for the meaning of the corresponding SERP elements. Table 6 shows the total number of clicks on SERP elements for each systems and the *Normalized Reward* (nReward) resulting from

Table 3. System overview

System name	Task	Type	Experimental	Round 1	Round 2
lemuren_elk	1	A	●	●	●
tekmas	1	A	●	●	●
save_fami	1	A	●	●	●
livivo_rank_pyserini	1	B	●	◑	◑
lemuren_elastic_only	1	B	●	○	●
lemuren_elastic_preprocessing	1	B	●	○	●
livivo_base	1	B	○	●	●
tekma_n	2	A	●	○	●
gesis_rec_precom	2	A	●	●	○
gesis_rec_pyterrier	2	B	●	●	●
gesis_rec_pyserini	2	B	○	●	●

Table 4. Outcomes of Round 1. Dagger symbols (†) indicate baseline systems. Significant differences are denoted by an asterisk symbol (∗).

System	Win	Loss	Tie	Outcome	Sessions	Impressions	Clicks	CTR
gesis_rec_pyserini†	36	36	1	0.50	2284	4195	37	0.0088
gesis_rec_pyterrier	26	28	1	0.48	1968	3675	28	0.0076
gesis_rec_precom	10	8	0	0.56	316	520	11	0.0212
livivo_base†	332	234	67	0.59	1426	2329	677	0.2907
livivo_rank_pyserini	215	302	64	0.42*	1260	2135	517	0.2422
lemuren_elk	4	8	1	0.33	45	55	10	0.1818
tekmas	6	10	1	0.38	64	77	8	0.1039
save_fami	9	12	1	0.43	57	62	14	0.2258

the weighting scheme given in Fig. 5. We compare the total number of clicks of those (interleaving) experiments in which the experimental and baseline systems delivered results. As it can be seen, comparing systems by clicks on different SERP elements, provides a more diverse analysis. For instance, some of the systems achieve higher numbers of clicks (and CTRs) for some SERP elements in direct comparison to the baseline systems. `livivo_rank_pyserini`, `lemuren_elastic_only` got more clicks on the *Bookmark* element than the baseline system, while all systems achieve lower numbers of total clicks.

None of the systems could outperform the baseline system in terms of the nReward measure, but in comparison to the *Outcome* scores, there is a more balanced ratio between the nReward scores that also accounts for the meaning of specific clicks. Likewise, it accounts for clicks even if the experimental system did not "win" in the interleaving experiment. In Table 6 we compare the total number of clicks over multiple sessions. While the Win, Loss, Tie, and Outcome only

Table 5. Outcomes of Round 2. Dagger symbols (†) indicate baseline systems. Significant differences are denoted by an asterisk symbol ($*$).

System	Win	Loss	Tie	Outcome	Sessions	Impressions	Clicks	CTR
gesis_rec_pyserini†	51	68	2	0.43	3288	6034	53	0.0088
gesis_rec_pyterrier	26	25	1	0.51	1529	2937	27	0.0092
tekma_n	42	26	1	0.62	1759	3097	45	0.0145
livivo_base†	2447	1063	372	0.70	6481	12915	3791	0.2935
livivo_rank _pyserini	48	71	15	0.40	243	434	112	0.2581
lemuren_elastic _only	707	1042	218	0.40*	3131	6274	1273	0.2029
lemuren_elastic _preprocessing	291	1308	135	0.18*	2948	6026	570	0.0946
lemuren_elk	6	13	0	0.32	61	69	10	0.1449
tekma_s	4	7	1	0.36	36	42	5	0.1190
save_fami	7	6	3	0.54	62	70	20	0.2857

Table 6. Experimental systems of round 2 and the corresponding number of clicks on SERP elements, total number of clicks, and the *Reward* score.

	Bookmark	Details	Fulltext	In Stock	More Links	Order	Title	Total Clicks	nReward
livivo_rank _pyserini	182	341	176	55	62	28	263	1107	0.4367
livivo_base	180	443	228	154	57	29	329	1420	0.5633
lemuren_elastic _only	63	832	481	107	105	54	638	2280	0.4045
livivo_base	56	1066	646	295	129	85	858	3135	0.5955
lemuren _elastic _preprocessing	23	355	257	23	28	21	285	992	0.2143
livivo_base	69	1190	762	301	119	82	934	3457	0.7857
lemuren_elk	1	13	16	0	2	0	10	42	0.4242
livivo_base	1	24	7	14	1	0	20	67	0.5758
tekmas	2	11	2	2	1	0	6	24	0.3430
livivo_base	0	13	6	7	0	1	9	36	0.6570
save_fami	11	21	9	3	1	1	16	62	0.5496
livivo_base	8	13	7	5	2	1	6	42	0.4504
All experimental systems	282	1573	941	190	199	104	1218	4507	0.3485
livivo_base	314	2749	1656	776	308	198	2156	8157	0.6515

measure if there have been more clicks in a single experiment, the nReward also considers those clicks that were made in experiments in which the experimental system did not necessarily win.

7 Conclusions

The Living Labs for Academic Search (LiLAS) lab re-introduced the living lab paradigm with a focus on tasks in the domain of academic search. The lab offered the possibility to participate in two different tasks, which were either dedicated to ad-hoc search in the Life Sciences or research data recommendations in the Social Sciences. Participants were provided with datasets and access to the underlying search portals for experimentation. For both tasks, participants could contribute their experimental systems either by pre-computed outputs for selected queries (or target items) or as fully-fledged dockerized systems. In total, we evaluated nine experimental systems out of which seven were contributed by three participating groups. In sum, two groups contributed experiments that cover pre-computed rankings and fully dockerized systems at LIVIVO and pre-computed recommendations at GESIS. The GESIS research team contributed another completely dockerized recommendation system. Our experimental setup is based on interleaving experiments that combine experimental results with those from the corresponding baseline systems at LIVIVO and GESIS. In accordance with the living lab paradigm, our evaluations are based on user interactions, i.e. in the form of click feedback.

A key component of the underlying infrastructure is the integration of experimental ranking and recommendation systems as micro-services that are implemented with the help of Docker. The LiLAS lab was the first test-bed to use this evaluation service and it exemplified some of the benefits resulting from the new infrastructure design. First of all, completely dockerized systems can overcome the restrictions of results limited to filtered lists of top-k queries or target items. Significantly more data and click interactions can be logged if the experimental systems can deliver results on-the-fly for arbitrary requests of rankings and recommendations. As a consequence, this allows much more data aggregation in a shorter period of time and provides a solid basis for statistical significance tests.

Furthermore, the deployment effort for site providers and organizers is considerably reduced. Once the systems are properly described with the corresponding Dockerfile, they can be rebuild on purpose, exactly as the participants and developers intended them to be. Likewise, the entire infrastructure service can be migrated with minimal costs due to Docker. However, we hypothesize that one reason for the low participation might be the technical overhead for those who were not already familiar with Docker. On the other hand, the development efforts pay off. If the systems are properly adapted to the required interface and the source code is available in a public repository, the (IR) research community can rely on these artifacts that make the experiments transparent and reproducible.

Thus, we address the reproducibility of these living lab experiments mostly from a technological point of view, in the sense that we can repeat the experiments in the future with reduced efforts, since the participating systems are openly available and should be reconstructible with the help of the corresponding Dockerfiles. Future work should investigate how feasible it is to rely on the Dockerfiles for the long-term preservation. Since experimental systems are rebuilt each time with the help of the Dockerfile, updates of the underlying dependencies might be a threat to the reproducibility. An intuitive solution would be the integration of pre-built Docker images that may allow a longer reproducibility. Apart from the underlying technological aspects, the reproducibility of the actual experimental results has to be investigated. Our experimental setup would allow to answer questions with regard to the reproducibility of the experimental results over time and also across different domains (e.g. Life vs. Social Sciences).

Most of the evaluation measures are made for interleaving experiments that also depend on the results of the baseline system and not solely on those of an experimental system. We have not investigated yet, if the experimental results follow a transitive relation: if the experimental system A outperforms the baseline system B, denoted as $A \succ B$, and the baseline system B outperforms another experimental system C ($B \succ C$), can we conclude that system A would also outperform system C ($A \succ C$)? As the evaluations showed, click results are heavily biased towards the first ranks and likewise they are context-dependent, i.e. they depend on the entire result list and single click decisions have to be interpreted in relation to neighboring and previously seen results and further evaluations in these directions would require counterfactual reasoning. Nonetheless, in the second round it was illustrated how our infrastructure service can be used for incremental developments and component-wise analysis of experimental systems. The two experimental systems `lemuren_elastic_only` and `lemuren_elastic_preprocessing` follow a similar approach and only differ by the pre-processing component that has been shown not to be of any benefit.

In addition to established outcome measures of interleaving experiments (Win, Loss, Tie, Outcome), we also account for the meaning of clicks on different SERP elements. In this context, we implement the Reward measure that is the weighted sum of clicks on different elements corresponding to a specific result. Even though most of the experimental systems could not outperform the baseline systems in terms of the overall scores, we see some clear differences between the system performance, which allow us to assess a system's merits more thoroughly, when the evaluations are based on different SERP elements.

Overall, we consider our lab as a successful advancement to previous living lab experiments. We were able to exemplify the benefits of fully dockerized systems delivering results for arbitrary results on-the-fly. Furthermore, we could confirm several previous findings, for instance the power laws underlying the click distributions. Additionally, we were able to conduct more diverse comparison by differentiating between clicks on different SERP elements and accounting for their meaning. Unfortunately, we could not attract many participants, leaving some aspects not tested, e.g. how many systems/experiments can be run simultaneously considering the limitations of the infrastructure design, hardware requirements, server load and user traffic. Likewise, no experimental ranking system could outperform the baseline system. In the future, it might be helpful to provide participants with open and more transparent baseline systems they can build upon. Some of the pre-computed experimental ranking and recommendations seem to deliver promising results; however, the evaluations need to be interpreted with care due to the sparsity of the available click data. As a way out, we favor continuous evaluations freed from the time limits of rounds, in order to re-frame the introduced living lab service as an ongoing evaluation challenge. The corresponding source code can be retrieved from a public GitHub project[15] and we plan to release the aggregated session data as a curated research dataset.

Acknowledgments. This paper is supported by DFG (project no. 407518790).

References

1. Armstrong, T.G., Moffat, A., Webber, W., Zobel, J.: Improvements that don't add up: ad-hoc retrieval results since 1998. In: Proceeding of the 18th ACM conference on information and knowledge management, pp. 601–610. CIKM 2009, ACM, Hong Kong, China (2009). https://doi.org/10.1145/1645953.1646031
2. Balog, K., Schuth, A., Dekker, P., Schaer, P., Tavakolpoursaleh, N., Chuang, P.Y.: Overview of the trec 2016 open search track. In: Proceedings of the Twenty-Fifth Text REtrieval Conference (TREC 2016). NIST (2016)
3. Breuer, T., Schaer, P.: A living lab architecture for reproducible shared task experimentation. In: Information between Data and Knowledge, Schriften zur Informationswissenschaft, vol. 74, pp. 348–362. Werner Hülsbusch, Glückstadt (2021). https://doi.org/10.5283/epub.44953
4. Carevic, Z., Schaer, P.: On the connection between citation-based and topical relevance ranking: results of a pretest using iSearch. In: Proceedings of the First Workshop on Bibliometric-enhanced Information Retrieval co-located with 36th European Conference on Information Retrieval (ECIR 2014), Amsterdam, The Netherlands, 13 April 2014. CEUR Workshop Proceedings, vol. 1143, pp. 37–44. CEUR-WS.org (2014)
5. Gingstad, K., Jekteberg, Ø., Balog, K.: Arxivdigest: a living lab for personalized scientific literature recommendation. In: d'Aquin, M., Dietze, S., Hauff, C., Curry, E., Cudré-Mauroux, P. (eds.) CIKM 2020: The 29th ACM International Conference on Information and Knowledge Management, Virtual Event, Ireland, 19–23 October 2020, pp. 3393–3396. ACM (2020). https://doi.org/10.1145/3340531.3417417
6. Hienert, D., Kern, D., Boland, K., Zapilko, B., Mutschke, P.: A digital library for research data and related information in the social sciences. In: 19th ACM/IEEE Joint Conference on Digital Libraries, JCDL 2019, Champaign, IL, USA, 2–6 June 2019, pp. 148–157 (2019). https://doi.org/10.1109/JCDL.2019.00030
7. Jagerman, R., Balog, K., de Rijke, M.: Opensearch: lessons learned from an online evaluation campaign. J. Data Inf. Qual. **10**, 1–15 (2018)
8. Keller, J., Munz, L.P.M.: Tekma at clef-2021: BM-25 based rankings for scientific publication retrieval and data set recommendation. In: Faggioli, G., Ferro, N., Joly, A., Maistro, M., Piroi, F. (eds.) Working Notes of CLEF 2021 - Conference and Labs of the Evaluation Forum. CEUR Workshop Proceedings (2021)
9. Lin, J., Ma, X., Lin, S., Yang, J., Pradeep, R., Nogueira, R.: Pyserini: an easy-to-use python toolkit to support replicable IR research with sparse and dense representations. CoRR abs/2102.10073 (2021)
10. Lommatzsch, A., Kille, B., Hopfgartner, F., Ramming, L.: Newsreel multimedia at mediaeval 2018: news recommendation with image and text content. In: Working Notes Proceedings of the MediaEval 2018 Workshop. CEUR-WS (2018)

[15] https://github.com/stella-project.

11. Müller, B., Poley, C., Pössel, J., Hagelstein, A., Gübitz, T.: LIVIVO - the vertical search engine for life sciences. Datenbank-Spektrum **17**(1), 29–34 (2017). https://doi.org/10.1007/s13222-016-0245-2
12. Radlinski, F., Kurup, M., Joachims, T.: How does clickthrough data reflect retrieval quality? In: Shanahan, J.G., et al. (eds.) Proceedings of the 17th ACM Conference on Information and Knowledge Management, CIKM 2008, Napa Valley, California, USA, 26–30 October 2008, pp. 43–52. ACM (2008). https://doi.org/10.1145/1458082.1458092
13. Schaible, J., Breuer, T., Tavakolpoursaleh, N., Müller, B., Wolff, B., Schaer, P.: Evaluation infrastructures for academic shared tasks. Datenbank-Spektrum **20**(1), 29–36 (2020). https://doi.org/10.1007/s13222-020-00335-x
14. Schuth, A., Balog, K., Kelly, L.: Overview of the living labs for information retrieval evaluation (LL4IR) CLEF Lab 2015. In: Mothe, J., et al. (eds.) CLEF 2015. LNCS, vol. 9283, pp. 484–496. Springer, Cham (2015). https://doi.org/10.1007/978-3-319-24027-5_47
15. de Solla Price, D.J.: Little Science. Big Science. Columbia University Press, New York (1963)
16. Tavakolpoursaleh, N., Schaible, S.: Pyterrier-based research data recommendations for scientific articles in the social sciences. In: Faggioli, G., Ferro, N., Joly, A., Maistro, M., Piroi, F. (eds.) Working Notes of CLEF 2021 - Conference and Labs of the Evaluation Forum. CEUR Workshop Proceedings (2021)
17. Tran, A.H.M., et al.: Ad-hoc retrieval of scientific documents on the livivo search portal. In: Faggioli, G., Ferro, N., Joly, A., Maistro, M., Piroi, F. (eds.) Working Notes of CLEF 2021 - Conference and Labs of the Evaluation Forum. CEUR Workshop Proceedings (2021)

Overview of PAN 2021: Authorship Verification, Profiling Hate Speech Spreaders on Twitter, and Style Change Detection

Janek Bevendorff[1], Berta Chulvi[2], Gretel Liz De La Peña Sarracén[2], Mike Kestemont[3], Enrique Manjavacas[3], Ilia Markov[3], Maximilian Mayerl[4], Martin Potthast[5], Francisco Rangel[6], Paolo Rosso[2], Efstathios Stamatatos[7], Benno Stein[1], Matti Wiegmann[1(✉)], Magdalena Wolska[1], and Eva Zangerle[4]

[1] Bauhaus-Universität Weimar, Weimar, Germany
{janek.bevendorff,benno.stein,matti.wiegmann, magdalena.wolska}@uni-weimar.de
[2] Universitat Politècnica de València, Valencia, Spain
berta.chulvi@uv.es, prosso@dsic.upv.es
[3] University of Antwerp, Antwerp, Belgium
{mike.kestemont,enrique.manjavacas,Ilia.Markov}@uantwerpen.be
[4] University of Innsbruck, Innsbruck, Austria
{Maximilian.Mayerl,eva.zangerle}@uibk.ac.at
[5] Universität Leipzig, Leipzig, Germany
martin.potthast@uni-leipzig.de
[6] Symanto Research, Nürnberg, Germany
[7] University of the Aegean, Mytilene, Greece
stamatatos@aegean.gr
pan@webis.de https://pan.webis.de

Abstract. The paper gives a brief overview of the three shared tasks organized at the PAN 2021 lab on digital text forensics and stylometry hosted at the CLEF conference. The tasks include authorship verification across domains, author profiling for hate speech spreaders, and style change detection for multi-author documents. In part the tasks are new and in part they continue and advance past shared tasks, with the overall goal of advancing the state of the art, providing for an objective evaluation on newly developed benchmark datasets.

1 Introduction

The PAN workshop series has been organized since 2007 and has included shared tasks on specific computational challenges related to authorship analysis, computational ethics, and determining the originality of a piece of writing. Over the years, the respective organizing committees of the 51 shared tasks have assembled evaluation resources for the aforementioned research disciplines that amount to 48 datasets plus nine datasets contributed by the community.[1] Each new

[1] https://pan.webis.de/data.html.

K. S. Candan et al. (Eds.): CLEF 2021, LNCS 12880, pp. 419–431, 2021.
https://doi.org/10.1007/978-3-030-85251-1_26

dataset introduced new variants of author identification, profiling, and author obfuscation tasks as well as multi-author analysis and determining the morality, quality, or originality of a text. The 2021 edition of PAN continues in the same vein, introducing new resources and previously unconsidered problems to the community. As in earlier editions, PAN is committed to reproducible research in IR and NLP and all shared tasks will ask for software submissions on our TIRA platform [22]. The following sections outline the task definitions and summarize the participants' results.

2 Author Profiling

Author profiling is the problem of distinguishing between classes of authors by studying how language is shared by people. This helps in identifying authors' individual characteristics, such as age, gender, and language variety, among others. During the years 2013–2020 we addressed several of these aspects in the shared tasks organised at PAN.[2] In 2013 the aim was to identify gender and age in social media texts for English and Spanish [31]. In 2014 we addressed age identification from a continuous perspective (without gaps between age classes) in the context of several genres, such as blogs, Twitter, and reviews (in Trip Advisor), both in English and Spanish [28]. In 2015, apart from age and gender identification, we addressed also personality recognition on Twitter in English, Spanish, Dutch and Italian [33]. In 2016, we addressed the problem of cross-genre gender and age identification (training on Twitter data and testing on blogs and social media data) in English, Spanish, and Dutch [34]. In 2017, we addressed gender and language variety identification in Twitter in English, Spanish, Portuguese, and Arabic [32]. In 2018, we investigated gender identification in Twitter from a multimodal perspective, considering also the images linked within tweets; the dataset was composed of English, Spanish, and Arabic tweets [30]. In 2019 the focus was on profiling bots and discriminating bots from humans on the basis of textual data only [27]. We used Twitter data both in English and Spanish. Bots play a key role in spreading inflammatory content and also fake news. Advanced bots that generated human-like language, also with metaphors, were the most difficult to profile. It is interesting to note that when bots were profiled as humans, they were mostly confused with males. In 2020 we focused on profiling fake news spreaders [25]. The easiness of publishing content in social media has led to an increase in the amount of disinformation that is published and shared. The goal was to profile those authors who have shared some fake news in the past. Early identification of possible fake news spreaders on Twitter should be the first step towards preventing fake news from further dissemination.

Author Profiling at PAN'21: Hate Speech Spreaders on Twitter. Having previously profiled bots and fake news spreaders, at PAN'21 we have focused on PROFILING HATE SPEECH SPREADERS in social media, more specifically on

[2] To generate the datasets, we have followed a methodology that complies with the EU General Data Protection Regulation [26].

Twitter, addressing the problem both in English and Spanish, as we did in the previous author profiling tasks. The goal has been to identify those Twitter users that can be considered haters, depending on the number of tweets with hateful content that they had spread.

Hate speech (HS) is commonly defined as any communication that disparages a person or a group on the basis of some characteristic, such as race, colour, ethnicity, gender, sexual orientation, nationality, religion, or others [20]. Given the huge amount of user-generated content on the Web and, in particular, on social media, the problem of detecting and, if possible, contrasting the HS diffusion, is becoming fundamental, for instance, in the fight against misogyny and xenophobia [1]. While most of the approaches focus on detecting whether a text is hateful or not, few works focus on the user account level detection. In [17] the authors studied the flow of posts generated by users on Gab, analysing the profiles and network of hateful and non-hateful users, focusing on the diffusion dynamics of hateful users. The observations suggested that hateful content propagates farther, wider and faster. Unlike this work, where the analysis was carried out statically, in [18] dynamic graphs were employed to investigate the temporal effects of hate speech. In [4] the authors presented a comparative study of hate speech users on Twitter. They investigated the distinctive characteristics of hateful users and targeted users in terms of their profile, activities, and online visibility. They found that hateful users can be more popular and that participating in hate speech can result in a greater online visibility. In [35] the focus was also on users for hate speech detection on Twitter. This study used a methodology to obtain a graph given the entire profile of users, and investigated the difference between hateful users and normal ones in terms of activity patterns, word usage and network structure. The authors observed that hateful users are densely connected, thus they focused on exploiting the network of connections. In [23] the authors proposed a model that considers intra-user and inter-user representation learning for hate speech detection. In [6] the focus was on studying the use of emojis in white nationalist conversation on Twitter. A difference between the 'pro' and 'anti' nationalist was observed.

Dataset and Task. As an evaluation setup, we have created a collection that contains Spanish and English tweets posted by users on Twitter. To build the PAN-AP-2021 corpus[3] we have proceeded as follows. Firstly, we have looked for users considered potential haters. To do so, we have followed two approaches: (1) a keyword-based one (e.g. searching for hateful words towards women or immigrants); and (2) a user-based one, by inspecting users known as haters (e.g. users appearing in reports and/or press) and following their networks (followers and followees). Secondly, for the identified users, we have collected their timelines and manually annotated those tweets conveying hate. Thirdly, we have labelled

[3] We should highlight that we are aware of the legal and ethical issues related to collecting, analysing and profiling social media data [26] and that we are committed to legal and ethical compliance in our scientific research and its outcomes. For instance, we have anonymised the user name, masked all the user mentions and also the class has been changed in order to avoid any explicit mention.

as "keen to spread hate speech" those users with more than ten hateful tweets. Finally, we have collected two hundred tweets per Twitter user to build up the final dataset. This dataset consists of three hundred users per language, with two hundred tweets per user. Two hundred users per language have been provided for training purposes, keeping the remaining one hundred for testing purposes. The dataset is completely balanced per class (hater vs. not hater) as well as by the number of tweets per user.

The goal in the task is to classify the user as hater or not hater (binary classification). Given that we have a balanced dataset (even though this is not a realistic scenario,[4] we balance the dataset to prevent machine/deep learning models from being skewed towards the majority class) we use accuracy as the evaluation metric for the binary classification. Then, we average both accuracies for English and Spanish to come up with the final ranking.

Evaluation and Results. We have had a total number of 66 participants. The best performing team has used a 100-dimension word embedding representation to feed a Convolutional Neural Network. We have also run seven baselines covering the different technologies our participants usually use:

- LDSE [29]: This method represents documents based on the probability distribution of the occurrence of their words in the different classes. The key concept of LDSE is a weight representing the probability of a term to belong to one of the two categories: hate speech spreader/non hate speech spreader. The distribution of weights for a given document should be closer to the weights of its corresponding category;
- Character n-grams with n ranging from 2 to 6 and a SVM;
- Word n-grams with n ranging from 1 to 3 and a Neural Network (NN);
- Universal Sentence Encoder (USE) feeding up a BiLSTM;
- XLM-Roberta (XLMR) transformer feeding up a BiLSTM;
- Multilingual BERT (MBERT) transformer to feed up a BiLSTM;
- TFIDF vectors representing each user's text to feed up a BiLSTM.

The baseline results are shown in Table 1. Out of the 66 participants only 7 outperformed LDSE and SVM with char n-grams baselines, further 7 participants also outperformed the NN with word n-grams baseline, and only one was worse than the TFIDF+LSTM baseline. Only 4 teams participated just in English. More details will be available in the overview paper [24].

[4] In a realistic scenario, we would need to know a priori the distribution of haters vs non-haters; depending on the study, the number of hatred messages in Twitter ranges from 1% [21] to 10%–15% [39], although when the target are communities such as the LGBT, up to 78% of respondents had experienced online anti-LGBT and hate speech in the last 5 years (https://www.report-it.org.uk/files/online-crime-2020_0.pdf). Furthermore, one of the aims of this shared task is to foster research on profiling haters in order to address this problem automatically.

Table 1. Baselines performance in terms of accuracy on the PAN-AP-2021 dataset on Hate Speech Spreaders identification.

Baseline	English	Spanish	Average
LDSE	70.0	82.0	76.0
SVM + char n-grams	69.0	83.0	76.0
NN + word n-grams	65.0	83.0	74.0
USE-LSTM	56.0	79.0	67.5
XLMR-LSTM	62.0	73.0	67.5
MBERT-LSTM	59.0	75.0	67.0
TFIDF-LSTM	61.0	51.0	56.0

3 Authorship Verification

Author identification is concerned with the automated identification of the individual(s) who authored an anonymous document on the basis of text-internal properties related to language and writing style [9,16,37]. Computational author identification has been a long-running subtask at PAN with a reasonably steady number of participants over the years. While authorship has been studied via quantitative means for several decades by now, the academic and industrial interest in this task shows no signs of abating. The history of this field is characterized by a number of interesting developments and the seminal application of machine learning to the problem has been a clear landmark near the end of the previous century.[5] Today, machine learning can be considered the dominant paradigm in the field, though certain otherwise ubiquitous methods have been slow to gain a foothold. Deep learning via neural networks, for example, has become the dominant form of machine learning in many fields, yet has remained relatively uncommon in recent editions of the authorship track at PAN and in the field of computational authorship studies in general. In the past, we tentatively ascribed this absence to (1) the lack of large-scale training resources in this field and (2) the increased infrastructural challenges that come with the hardware requirements of large neural networks [14]. This problem is exacerbated by our requirement for participants to submit fully-fledged software systems to the TIRA platform [22] instead of only their finished runs. This has been a clear incentive for us to try scaling up the training resources that we can make available to participants.

Scaling up Resources for Authorship Verification at PAN'21. With the view to benchmarking authorship systems at a much larger scale, our tasks in

[5] Machine learning emerged as a methodology in authorship attribution in the 1990s. The first paper to apply a text classification approach in this domain is [19] to the best of our knowledge.

recent years [12,14] have focused on transformative literature, so-called "fanfiction" [8], a text variety that is nowadays abundantly available on the internet [5] with rich metadata and in many languages. Additionally, fanfiction is an excellent source of material for studies of cross-domain scenarios, since users often publish "fics" ranging over multiple topical domains ("fandoms"), such as Harry Potter, Twilight, or Marvel comics. The datasets we provided for our tasks at PAN'20 and PAN'21 were crawled from the long-established fanfiction community `fanfiction.net`. Access to the data can be requested on Zenodo.[6]

Dataset and Task. The 2021 edition of the authorship verification task built upon last year's edition [10] with the same task layout and training data, yet with a conceptually different test set. The basic task remained authorship verification, the most fundamental and generally more demanding setup in the field, where one is to approximate the target function $\phi : (D_k, d_u) \rightarrow \{T, F\}$, D_k being a set of documensets of known authorship by the same author and d_u being a document of unknown or disputed authorship. If $\phi(D_k, d_u) = T$, then the author of D_k is also the author of d_u and if $\phi(D_k, d_u) = F$, then the author of D_k is not the same as the author of d_u. In our case, D_k contains only a single document, since our datasets consist of document *pairs*. For the 2021 edition, we adopted a cross-domain setting in which D_k and d_u do not share the topic or genre, which was accomplished by sampling the texts from different fandoms.

The training resources were identical to those from last year and came in the form of a "small" and "large" dataset. The large dataset contains 148,000 same-author and 128,000 different-authors pairs across 1,600 fandoms. Each single author has written in at least two, but not more than six fandoms. The small training set is a subset of the large training set with 28,000 same-author and 25,000 different-author pairs from the same 1,600 fandoms. The test set, however (19,999 text pairs in total) is conceptually different. While the overall sampling strategy remained the same, we shifted to an "open-set" verification scenario. Whereas last year's "closed-set" test problems included only texts from fandoms and authors that were already present in the training data, this year's test set included only fresh and previously unseen authors and fandoms. This setup forces participants into a "true" verification problem, while the previous "closed-set" task (in principle) could have also been re-cast as an attribution task (although this was not known to the participants beforehand). The pure verification task is generally considered more difficult than attribution because of the stylistic idiosyncrasies of human authors which often require bespoke ad-hoc models.

Evaluation and Results. For each of the 19,999 problems (or text pairs) in the test set, the systems had to produce a scalar score a_i (in the $[0, 1]$ range) indicating the (scaled) probability that the pair was written by the same author ($a_i > 0.5$) or different authors ($a_i < 0.5$). Systems could choose to leave problems too difficult to answer undecided by submitting a score of precisely $a_i = 0.5$

[6] https://zenodo.org/record/3716403.

Table 2. Final results for the cross-domain, open-set authorship verification task at PAN'21. Submitted systems are ranked by their mean performance across five evaluation metrics. Best result per column is shown in bold. Participants were allowed to make one submission for both the small and the large calibration datasets.

System	Dataset	AUC-ROC	c@1	F_1	$F_{0.5u}$	BRIER	Overall
boenninghoff21	Large	**0.9869**	**0.9502**	**0.9524**	**0.9378**	**0.9452**	**0.9545**
embarcaderoruiz21	Large	0.9697	0.9306	0.9342	0.9147	0.9305	0.9359
weerasinghe21	Large	0.9719	0.9172	0.9159	0.9245	0.9340	0.9327
weerasinghe21	Small	0.9666	0.9103	0.9071	0.9270	0.9290	0.9280
menta21	Large	0.9635	0.9024	0.8990	0.9186	0.9155	0.9198
peng21	Small	0.9172	0.9172	0.9167	0.9200	0.9172	0.9177
embarcaderoruiz21	Small	0.9470	0.8982	0.9040	0.8785	0.9072	0.9070
menta21	Small	0.9385	0.8662	0.8620	0.8787	0.8762	0.8843
rabinovits21	Small	0.8129	0.8129	0.8094	0.8186	0.8129	0.8133
ikae21	Small	0.9041	0.7586	0.8145	0.7233	0.8247	0.8050
unmasking21	Small	0.8298	0.7707	0.7803	0.7466	0.7904	0.7836
tyo21	Large	0.8275	0.7594	0.7911	0.7257	0.8123	0.7832
naive21	Small	0.7956	0.7320	0.7856	0.6998	0.7867	0.7600
compressor21	Small	0.7896	0.7282	0.7609	0.7027	0.8094	0.7581
futrzynski21	Large	0.7982	0.6632	0.8324	0.6682	0.7957	0.7516
liaozhihao21	Small	0.4962	0.4962	0.0067	0.0161	0.4962	0.3023

which is rewarded by some metrics. For this year's evaluation, we used the same four evaluations metrics as last year (AUC-ROC, F_1, c@1 and $F_{0.5u}$), to allow for a diverse assessment of the submitted systems. As a result of discussions at last year's workshop, we also included the complement of the BRIER score [3] as an additional metric.[7] The submitted systems are ranked by their mean performance across all 5 metrics. Two baseline systems were made available to the participants: a compression-based approach [7] and a naive distance-based, first-order bag-of-words model [13]. We use a short-text variant of Koppel and Schler's unmasking [2,15] as a third baseline whose source code is also freely available, but which was not given explicitly to the participants. The overall results can be found in Table 2. As in previous years, we also carried out pair-wise significance tests (based on approximate randomization, with the score as a reference metric) to be able to assess whether the answers between systems were considered significantly different according to conventional statistics. The outcome of this procedure is summarized in Table 3.

As can be seen, most of the submitted systems reach an excellent performance (many scoring > 0.9 for multiple metrics) in spite of the anticipated difficulty of the test set in comparison to last year. Last year's best performing team again tops the list, though interestingly, the runner-up is a first-time participant. Most

[7] Thanks to Fabrizio Sebastiani (Consiglio Nazionale delle Ricerche, Italy) for this suggestion.

systems produced significantly differing set of answers, with the exception of the dense cohort following the system in first place. Like last year, it is striking that systems calibrated on the large dataset invariably and significantly outperform their counterparts trained on the smaller dataset indicating that these systems are capable of harnessing the increased size of the calibration resources well. Most systems outperform the three baselines, which encouragingly demonstrates how the field is making progress. More details on the results will be available in the overview paper [11].

4 Multi-author Writing Style Analysis

The goal of the style change detection task is to identify – based on an intrinsic style analysis – the text positions at which the author switches within a given multi-author document. Detecting these positions is a crucial part of the authorship identification process and multi-author document analysis, but multi-author documents have been largely understudied in general.

This task has been part of PAN since 2016 with varying task definitions, datasets, and evaluation procedures. In 2016, participants were asked to identify and group fragments of a given document that correspond to individual authors [36]. In 2017, we asked participants to detect whether a given document is multi-authored and, if this is indeed the case, to determine the positions at which authorship changes [38]. Since this task was deemed as highly complex, its complexity was reduced in 2018 to asking participants only to predict whether a given document is single- or multi-authored [14]. Following the promising results, participants were asked in the 2019 task installment to first detect whether a document was single- or multi-authored and then, if it was indeed written by multiple authors, to predict the number of authors [42]. In 2020, based on the advances made over the previous years, we decided to go back towards the original definition of the task, i.e., finding the positions in a text where authorship changes. Participants first had to determine whether a document was written by one or by multiple authors and – in the case of a multi-author document – to detect at which paragraphs the author changes [41].

Style Change Detection at PAN'21. For style change detection, a fundamental question is the following: If multiple authors wrote a text together, can we find evidence of this fact, e.g., do we have a means to detect variations in the writing style? Answering this question is one of the most difficult and most interesting challenges in author identification and represents the only means to detecting plagiarism in a document if no other texts are given for comparison. Likewise, it can help to uncover "gifted authorship", to verify a claimed authorship, or to develop new technologies for writing assistance. We tackle this challenge by providing three style change detection tasks in increasing difficulty: (1) Single vs. Multiple Authors: given a text, find out whether the text was written by a single author or by multiple authors, (2) Style Change Basic: given a text written by two authors that contains only a single style change, find the

Table 3. Pairwise significance tests for approximate randomization with 10,000 bootstrap iterations, using F_1 as reference metric. Symbols: '=' (not significantly different with $p > 0.5$), '*', '**', '***' (significantly different with $p < 0.05$, $p < 0.01$, $p < 0.001$). Only the top-performing systems are shown here: a full comparison will be offered in the detailed overview paper.

	embarcaderoruiz21-large	weerasinghe21-large	weerasinghe21-small	menta21-large	peng21-small
boenninghoff21-large	***	***	***	***	***
embarcaderoruiz21-large		*	=	***	**
weerasinghe21-large			***	***	=
weerasinghe21-small				**	***
menta21-large					***

position of this change, i.e., cut the text into two based on stylometric information (note that this task corresponds to authorship verification where the two authors are responsible only for the first and the remaining part of a text, respectively), (3) Style Change "Real-World": given a text written by two or more authors, find all positions of writing style changes, i.e., assign all paragraphs of a text uniquely to exactly one of all the authors you deem responsible for the multi-author document.

Dataset and Evaluation. As in previous years, a novel dataset was created from posts from the popular StackExchange network of Q&A sites. To generate the documents for the task, we used a dump of questions and answers from the StackExchange network as our data source, of which we used a subset of communities[8]. We cleaned the data by removing questions and answers that were edited after they were originally posted and by removing images, URLs, code snippets, block quotes and bullet lists from all questions and answers. Subsequently, we split all questions and answers into paragraphs, dropping all paragraphs with fewer than 100 characters. To reduce the potential impact of topic changes, each document was generated from a single question thread this year. Hence, for each document, we pick a question thread to draw paragraphs from. Then, we decided randomly how many authors the document should have, settling a

[8] The following StackExchange sites were used: Code Review, Computer Graphics, CS Educators, CS Theory, Data Science, DBA, DevOps, GameDev, Network Engineering, Raspberry Pi, Superuser, and Server Fault.

Table 4. Overall results for the style change detection task, ranked by average performance across all three tasks.

Participant	Task1 F_1	Task2 F_1	Task3 F_1
Zhang et al.	0.753	**0.751**	**0.501**
Strøm	**0.795**	0.707	0.424
Singh et al.	0.634	0.657	0.432
Deibel et al.	0.621	0.669	0.263
Nath	0.704	0.647	–
Baseline	0.457	0.470	0.329

number between one and four authors per case. Following that, we randomly chose a corresponding number of authors from the authors who contributed to the question thread we were drawing paragraphs from. We then took all the paragraphs written by those authors and shuffled them to create the final documents. If a document created in this way had fewer than two paragraphs, or was fewer than 1,000 or more than 10,000 characters long, we discarded it. Applying this procedure, we created a total of 16,000 documents. We split the resulting set of documents into a training, a test and a validation set; the training set consisted of 70% of all generated documents whereas the test and validation set each consisted of 15% of all documents. Submissions were evaluated using the F_α measure for each task and for each document, with α set to 1.

Results. The style change detection task received five software submissions. Table 4 presents the individual results achieved by the participants. We list the F_1 measures for all three tasks. The approach by Strøm achieved the highest score for Task 1, whereas Zhang et al. achieved the highest score for Tasks 2 and 3. All of the submitted approaches outperformed the random baseline. Further details on the approaches taken can be found in the overview paper [40].

Acknowledgments. The work of the researchers from Universitat Politècnica de València was partially funded by the Spanish MICINN under the project MISMIS-FAKEnHATE on MISinformation and MIScommunication in social media: FAKE news and HATE speech (PGC2018-096212-B-C31), and by the Generalitat Valenciana under the project DeepPattern (PROMETEO/2019/121). This article is also based upon work from the DigForAsp COST Action 17124 on Digital Forensics: evidence analysis via intelligent systems and practices, supported by European Cooperation in Science and Technology.

References

1. Basile, V., et al.: SemEval-2019 Task 5: multilingual detection of hate speech against immigrants and women in Twitter. In: Proceedings of the 13th International Workshop on Semantic Evaluation (SemEval-2019), Co-located with the

Annual Conference of the North American Chapter of the Association for Computational Linguistics: Human Language Technologies (NAACL-HLT 2019) (2019)
2. Bevendorff, J., Stein, B., Hagen, M., Potthast, M.: Generalizing unmasking for short texts. In: Burstein, J., Doran, C., Solorio, T. (eds.) 14th Conference of the North American Chapter of the Association for Computational Linguistics: Human Language Technologies (NAACL 2019), pp. 654–659. Association for Computational Linguistics, June 2019. https://www.aclweb.org/anthology/N19-1068
3. BRIER, G.W.: Verification of forecasts expressed in terms of probability. Monthly Weather Rev. **78**(1), 1–3 (1950). https://doi.org/10.1175/1520-0493(1950)078⟨0001:VOFEIT⟩2.0.CO;2. https://journals.ametsoc.org/view/journals/mwre/78/1/1520-0493_1950_078_0001_vofeit_2_0_co_2.xml
4. ElSherief, M., Nilizadeh, S., Nguyen, D., Vigna, G., Belding, E.: Peer to peer hate: hate speech instigators and their targets. In: Proceedings of the International AAAI Conference on Web and Social Media, vol. 12 (2018)
5. Fathallah, J.: Fanfiction and the Author. How FanFic Changes Popular Cultural Texts, Amsterdam University Press, Amsterdam (2017)
6. Hagen, L., et al.: Emoji use in Twitter white nationalism communication. In: Conference Companion Publication of the 2019 on Computer Supported Cooperative Work and Social Computing, pp. 201–205 (2019)
7. Halvani, O., Graner, L.: Cross-domain authorship attribution based on compression: notebook for PAN at CLEF 2018. In: Cappellato, L., Ferro, N., Nie, J., Soulier, L. (eds.) Working Notes of CLEF 2018 - Conference and Labs of the Evaluation Forum, Avignon, France, 10–14 September 2018, CEUR Workshop Proceedings, vol. 2125. CEUR-WS.org (2018). http://ceur-ws.org/Vol-2125/paper_90.pdf
8. Hellekson, K., Busse, K.: (eds.): The Fan Fiction Studies Reader. University of Iowa Press (2014)
9. Juola, P.: Authorship attribution. Found. Trends Inf. Retr. **1**(3), 233–334 (2006)
10. Kestemont, M., et al.: Overview of the cross-domain authorship verification task at PAN 2020. In: Cappellato, L., Eickhoff, C., Ferro, N., Névéol, A. (eds.) Working Notes of CLEF 2020 - Conference and Labs of the Evaluation Forum, Thessaloniki, Greece, 22–25 September 2020, CEUR Workshop Proceedings, vol. 2696. CEUR-WS.org (2020). http://ceur-ws.org/Vol-2696/paper_264.pdf
11. Kestemont, M., et al.: Overview of the authorship verification task at PAN 2021. In: Faggioli, G., Ferro, N., Joly, A., Maistro, M., Piroi, F. (eds.) CLEF 2021 Labs and Workshops, Notebook Papers. CEUR-WS.org (2021)
12. Kestemont, M., Stamatatos, E., Manjavacas, E., Daelemans, W., Potthast, M., Stein, B.: Overview of the cross-domain authorship attribution task at PAN 2019. In: CLEF 2019 Labs and Workshops, Notebook Papers (2019)
13. Kestemont, M., Stover, J.A., Koppel, M., Karsdorp, F., Daelemans, W.: Authenticating the writings of Julius Caesar. Expert Syst. Appl. **63**, 86–96 (2016). https://doi.org/10.1016/j.eswa.2016.06.029
14. Kestemont, M., et al.: Overview of the author identification task at PAN 2018: cross-domain authorship attribution and style change detection. In: CLEF 2018 Labs and Workshops, Notebook Papers (2018)
15. Koppel, M., Schler, J.: Authorship verification as a one-class classification problem. In: Brodley, C.E. (ed.) Machine Learning, Proceedings of the Twenty-first International Conference (ICML 2004), Banff, Alberta, Canada, 4–8 July 2004, ACM International Conference Proceeding Series, vol. 69. ACM (2004). https://doi.org/10.1145/1015330.1015448
16. Koppel, M., Schler, J., Argamon, S.: Computational methods in authorship attribution. J. Am. Soc. Inform. Sci. Technol. **60**(1), 9–26 (2009)

17. Mathew, B., Dutt, R., Goyal, P., Mukherjee, A.: Spread of hate speech in online social media. In: Proceedings of the 10th ACM Conference on Web Science, pp. 173–182 (2019)
18. Mathew, B., Illendula, A., Saha, P., Sarkar, S., Goyal, P., Mukherjee, A.: Hate begets hate: a temporal study of hate speech. Proc. ACM on Hum.-Comput. Interact. **4**(CSCW2), 1–24 (2020)
19. Matthews, R.A.J., Merriam, T.V.N.: Neural computation in Stylometry I: an application to the works of shakespeare and fletcher. Lit. Linguist. Comput. **8**(4), 203–209 (1993). https://doi.org/10.1093/llc/8.4.203. ISSN 0268–1145
20. Nockleby, J.T.: Hate speech. In: Levy, L.W., Karst, K.L., et al. (eds.) Encyclopedia of the American Constitution. 2nd edn., pp. pp. 1277–1279. Macmillan, New York (2000)
21. Pereira-Kohatsu, J.C., Quijano-Sánchez, L., Liberatore, F., Camacho-Collados, M.: Detecting and monitoring hate speech in Twitter. Sensors **19**(21), 4654 (2019)
22. Potthast, M., Gollub, T., Wiegmann, M., Stein, B.: TIRA integrated research architecture. In: Ferro, N., Peters, C. (eds.) Information Retrieval Evaluation in a Changing World. TIRS, vol. 41, pp. 123–160. Springer, Cham (2019). https://doi.org/10.1007/978-3-030-22948-1_5
23. Qian, J., ElSherief, M., Belding, E.M., Wang, W.Y.: Leveraging intra-user and inter-user representation learning for automated hate speech detection. arXiv preprint arXiv:1804.03124 (2018)
24. Rangel, F., De-La-Peña-Sarracén, G.L., Chulvi, B., Fersini, E., Rosso, P.: Profiling hate speech spreaders on twitter task at PAN 2021. In: Faggioli, G., Ferro, N., Joly, A., Maistro, M., Piroi, F. (eds.) CLEF 2021 Labs and Workshops, Notebook Papers. CEUR-WS.org (2021)
25. Rangel, F., Giachanou, A., Ghanem, B., Rosso, P.: Overview of the 8th author profiling task at PAN 2019: profiling fake news spreaders on Twitter. In: CLEF 2020 Labs and Workshops, Notebook Papers. CEUR Workshop Proceedings (2020)
26. Rangel, F., Rosso, P.: On the implications of the general data protection regulation on the organisation of evaluation tasks. Lang. Law/Linguagem Direito **5**(2), 95–117 (2019)
27. Rangel, F., Rosso, P.: Overview of the 7th author profiling task at pan 2019: bots and gender profiling. In: CLEF 2019 Labs and Workshops, Notebook Papers (2019)
28. Rangel, F., et al.: Overview of the 2nd author profiling task at PAN 2014. In: CLEF 2014 Labs and Workshops, Notebook Papers (2014)
29. Rangel, F., Franco-Salvador, M., Rosso, P.: A low dimensionality representation for language variety identification. In: Gelbukh, A. (ed.) CICLing 2016. LNCS, vol. 9624, pp. 156–169. Springer, Cham (2018). https://doi.org/10.1007/978-3-319-75487-1_13
30. Rangel, F., Rosso, P., Montes-y-Gómez, M., Potthast, M., Stein, B.: Overview of the 6th author profiling task at PAN 2018: multimodal gender identification in Twitter. In: CLEF 2019 Labs and Workshops, Notebook Papers (2018)
31. Rangel, F., Rosso, P., Moshe Koppel, M., Stamatatos, E., Inches, G.: Overview of the author profiling task at PAN 2013. In: CLEF 2013 Labs and Workshops, Notebook Papers (2013)
32. Rangel, F., Rosso, P., Potthast, M., Stein, B.: Overview of the 5th author profiling task at PAN 2017: gender and language variety identification in Twitter. Working Notes Papers of the CLEF (2017)
33. Rangel, F., Rosso, P., Potthast, M., Stein, B., Daelemans, W.: Overview of the 3rd author profiling task at PAN 2015. In: CLEF 2015 Labs and Workshops, Notebook Papers (2015)

34. Rangel, F., Rosso, P., Verhoeven, B., Daelemans, W., Potthast, M., Stein, B.: Overview of the 4th author profiling task at PAN 2016: cross-genre evaluations. In: CLEF 2016 Labs and Workshops, Notebook Papers (2016). ISSN 1613–0073
35. Ribeiro, M., Calais, P., Santos, Y., Almeida, V., Meira Jr., W.: Characterizing and Detecting Hateful Users on Twitter. In: Proceedings of the International AAAI Conference on Web and Social Media, vol. 12 (2018)
36. Rosso, P., Rangel, F., Potthast, M., Stamatatos, E., Tschuggnall, M., Stein, B.: Overview of PAN'16–new challenges for authorship analysis: cross-genre profiling, clustering, diarization, and obfuscation. In: Experimental IR Meets Multilinguality, Multimodality, and Interaction. 7th International Conference of the CLEF Initiative (CLEF 16) (2016)
37. Stamatatos, E.: A survey of modern authorship attribution methods. JASIST **60**(3), 538–556 (2009). https://doi.org/10.1002/asi.21001
38. Tschuggnall, M., et al.: Overview of the author identification task at PAN 2017: style breach detection and author clustering. In: CLEF 2017 Labs and Workshops, Notebook Papers (2017)
39. Waseem, Z.: Are you a racist or am i seeing things? Annotator influence on hate speech detection on Twitter. In: Proceedings of the First Workshop on NLP and Computational Social Science, pp. 138–142. Association for Computational Linguistics, Austin, November 2016. https://doi.org/10.18653/v1/W16-5618. https://www.aclweb.org/anthology/W16-5618
40. Zangerle, E., Mayerl, M., Potthast, M., Stein, B.: Overview of the style change detection task at PAN 2021. In: Faggioli, G., Ferro, N., Joly, A., Maistro, M., Piroi, F. (eds.) CLEF 2021 Labs and Workshops, Notebook Papers. CEUR-WS.org (2021)
41. Zangerle, E., Mayerl, M., Specht, G., Potthast, M., Stein, B.: Overview of the style change detection task at PAN 2020. In: CLEF 2020 Labs and Workshops, Notebook Papers (2020)
42. Zangerle, E., Tschuggnall, M., Specht, G., Stein, B., Potthast, M.: Overview of the style change detection task at PAN 2019. In: CLEF 2019 Labs and Workshops, Notebook Papers (2019)

Overview of SimpleText 2021 - CLEF Workshop on Text Simplification for Scientific Information Access

Liana Ermakova[1(✉)], Patrice Bellot[2], Pavel Braslavski[3], Jaap Kamps[4], Josiane Mothe[5], Diana Nurbakova[6], Irina Ovchinnikova[7], and Eric SanJuan[8]

[1] Université de Bretagne Occidentale, HCTI - EA 4249, Brest, France
liana.ermakova@univ-brest.fr
[2] Aix Marseille Univ, Université de Toulon, CNRS, LIS, Marseille, France
[3] Ural Federal University, Yekaterinburg, Russia
[4] University of Amsterdam, Amsterdam, The Netherlands
[5] Université de Toulouse, IRIT, Toulouse, France
[6] Institut National des Sciences Appliquées de Lyon, Lyon, France
[7] Sechenov University, Moscow, Russia
[8] Avignon Université, LIA, Avignon, France

Abstract. Information retrieval has moved from traditional document retrieval in which search is an isolated activity, to modern information access where search and the use of the information are fully integrated. But non-experts tend to avoid authoritative primary sources such as scientific literature due to their complex language, internal vernacular, or lacking prior background knowledge. Text simplification approaches can remove some of these barriers, thereby avoiding that users rely on shallow information in sources prioritizing commercial or political incentives rather than the correctness and informational value. The CLEF 2021 SimpleText track addresses the opportunities and challenges of text simplification approaches to improve scientific information access head-on. We aim to provide appropriate data and benchmarks, starting with pilot tasks in 2021, and create a community of NLP and IR researchers working together to resolve one of the greatest challenges of today.

Keywords: Scientific text simplification · (Multi-document) summarization · Contextualization · Background knowledge

> Everything should be made as simple as possible, but no simpler
>
> *Albert Einstein*

1 Introduction

Scientific literacy, including health related questions, is important for people to make right decisions, evaluate the information quality, maintain physiological

K. S. Candan et al. (Eds.): CLEF 2021, LNCS 12880, pp. 432–449, 2021.
https://doi.org/10.1007/978-3-030-85251-1_27

and mental health, avoid spending money on useless items. For example, the stories the individuals find credible can determine their response to the COVID-19 pandemic, including the application of social distancing, using dangerous fake medical treatments, or hoarding. Unfortunately, stories in social media are easier for lay people to understand than the research papers. Scientific texts such as scientific publications can also be difficult to understand for non domain-experts or scientists outside the publication domain. Improving text comprehensibility and its adaptation to different audience remains an unresolved problem. Although there are some attempts to tackle the issue of text comprehensibility, they are mainly based on readability formulas, which have not convincingly demonstrated the ability to reduce the difficulty of text [30].

To put a step forward to automatically reduce difficulty of text understanding, we propose a new workshop called SimpleText which aims to create a community interested in generating simplified summaries of scientific documents. Thus, the goal of this workshop is to connect researchers from different domains, such as Natural Language Processing, Information Retrieval, Linguistics, Scientific Journalism etc. in order to work together on automatic popularization of science.

Improving text comprehensibility and its adaptation to different audience bring societal, technical, and evaluation challenges. There is a large range of important *societal challenges* SimpleText is linked to. Open science is one of them. Making the research really open and accessible for everyone implies providing it in a form that can be readable and understandable; referring to the "comprehensibility" of the research results, making science understandable [20]. Another example of those societal challenges is offering means to develop counter-speech to fake news based on scientific results. SimpleText also tackles *technical challenges* related to data (passage) selection and summarization, comprehensibility and readability of texts.

To face these challenges, SimpleText provides an open forum aiming at answering questions like:

- **Information selection:** Which information should be simplified (e.g., in terms of document and passage selection and summarisation)?
- **Comprehensibility:** What kind of background information should be provided (e.g., which terms should be contextualized by giving a definition and/or application)? What information is the most relevant or helpful?
- **Readability:** How to improve the readability of a given short text (e.g., by reducing vocabulary and syntactic complexity) without information distortion?

We provides data and benchmarks, and addresses evaluation challenges underlying the technical challenges, including:

- How to evaluate information selection?
- How to evaluate background information?
- How to measure text simplification?

2 Related Work

In order to simplify scientific texts, one has to (1) select the information to be included in a simplified summary, (2) decide whether the selected information is sufficient and comprehensible or provide some background knowledge if not, (3) improve the readability of the text [15]. Our workshop is organized around this pipeline.

2.1 Information Selection

People have to manage the constantly growing amount of information, e.g. according to research platform Dimensions[1], from 01/01/20–01/10/20, about 180K articles on COVID-19 were published. To deal with this data volume, a concise overview, i.e. a summary, is needed. Thus, summarization is already a step towards text simplification as it reduces the amount of information to be processed. Besides, people prefer to read a short document instead of a long one. Since motivation to understand a scientific text is of importance for readers, the simplified options depends on the motivation of readers [38]. Thus, the information in a summary designed for a scientist from a specific field should be different from that adapted for general public and we should take into account differences in narrative and information texts comprehension while evaluating the comprehensibility level of simplified texts in different readership. Thus, the main challenge is to choose which information should be included in a simplified text. Despite recent significant progress in the domains of information retrieval (IR) and natural language processing (NLP), the problem of constructing a consistent overview has not been solved yet [17].

Automatic summarization can simplify access to primary source scientific documents - the resulting concise text is expected to highlight the most important parts of the document and thus reduces the reader's efforts. Evaluation initiatives in the 2000s such as the Document Understanding Conference (DUC) and the Summarization track at the Text Analysis Conference[2] (TAC) have focused primarily on the automatic summarization of news in various contexts and scenarios. Scientific articles are typically provided with a short abstract written by the authors. Thus, automatic generation of an abstract for a standalone article does not seem to be a practical task. However, if we consider a large collection of scientific articles and citations between them, we can come to the task of producing an abstract that would contain the important aspects of a paper from the perspective of the community. Such a task has been offered to the participants of the TAC 2014 Biomedical Summarization Track, as well as of the CL-SciSumm shared task series. Another close work is CLEF-IP 2012–2013: Retrieval in the Intellectual Property Domain (novelty search). Given a patent claim, the task was to retrieve the passages relevant to this claim from a document collection; the retrieved passages were compared to the relevant passages indicated by a patent examiner in her/his search report, but this relevancy

[1] https://www.dimensions.ai.

[2] https://tac.nist.gov/2014/BiomedSumm.

relationship between claims and text passages in other documents cannot be considered as text simplification nor summarization.

Sentence selection is a crucial but understudied task in document simplification [59] as existing works mainly focus on word/phrase-level (simplification of difficult words and constructions) [5,23,34,44,49,57] or sentence-level simplifications [9,14,51,56,60,61]. The state-of-the-art in automatic summarization is achieved by deep learning models, in particular by pretrained Bidirectional Encoder Representations from Transformers (BERT) which can be used for both extractive and abstractive models [32] However, the information in a summary designed for an expert might be different from that for a general audience. Therefore, a major step in training artificial intelligence (AI) text simplification models is the creation of high quality data. Zhong et al. studied various discourse factors associated with sentence deletion on the Newsela corpus containing manually simplified sentences from news articles [59] (contrary to SimpleText which focuses on scientific literature). They found that professional editors utilize different strategies to meet the readability standards of elementary and middle schools. It is important to study the limits of existing models, like GPT-2 for English and CamemBERT for French [35], and how it is possible to overcome them.

How to evaluate the information in a simplified summary? Summary informativeness metrics can mainly be divided into two classes: (1) questionnaire-based metrics and (2) overlap-based metrics [17]. In case of questionnaire-based metrics, an assessor should answer a set of questions issued from the source text or evaluate the importance of each sentence/passage [17], e.g. Responsiveness metric was introduced at the Document Understanding Conference (DUC) [42]. A Pyramid score is in the middle between the questionnaire based and overlap-based metrics since it calculates the number of repetitions of information units of variable length inside a sentence labeled by experts in their own words [41]. Overlap-based measures estimate the proportion of shared words between the reference summary and the summary under consideration, e.g. a widely used ROUGE metric (short for Recall-Oriented Understudy for Gisting Evaluation) and its variants [31]. The overlap metrics require a set of reference summaries. Providing a collection of simplified texts makes it possible to apply overlap metrics like ROUGE to text simplification.

2.2 Comprehensibility (Background Knowledge)

Comprehensibility of a text varies for different readerships. Readers of popular science texts have a basic background, are able to process logical connections and recognize novelty [26]. In the popular science text, a reader looks for rationalization and clear links between well known and new [39]. In order to really understand new concepts, readers need to include them into their mental representation of the scientific domain. Models of mental representation of knowledge are mostly based on propositional structures, but we consider embodied (grounded) reading comprehension to be useful for the SimpleText project because embodied cognition can provide a mental bridge between a personal experience and semantic representation of knowledge in the long-term semantic memory [47]. Therefore, a simplified scientific text has to be able to evoke clear associations with embodied cognition.

According to The Free Dictionary[3], background knowledge is "information that is essential to understanding a situation or problem". The lack of basic knowledge can become a barrier to reading comprehension and there is a knowledge threshold allowing reading comprehension [43]. Scientific text simplification presupposes the facilitation of readers' understanding of complex content by establishing links to basic lexicon, avoiding distortion connections among objects within the domain. Traditional methods of text simplification try to eliminate complex concepts and constructions [5,23,34,44,49,57]. However, it is not always possible, especially in the case of scientific literature. In contrast to previous research, SimpleText is not limited to a "Split and Rephrase" task but also aims to provide a sufficient context to a scientific text as the lack of background knowledge could be a major obstacle for text comprehension [43]. Entity linking (Wikification, task of tying named entities from the text to the corresponding knowledge base items, e.g. Wikipedia) could help mitigate the background knowledge problem, by providing definitions, illustrations, examples, and related entities. However, the existing entity linking datasets are focused primarily on such entities as people, places, and organizations [25], while a lay reader of a scientific article needs assistance with new concepts and methods. Wikification is close to the task of terminology and key-phrase extraction from scientific texts [3]. The idea of contextualizing news was further developed in the Background Linking task at TREC 2020 News Track aiming at a list of links to the articles that a person should read next [2]. It is also important to remember that the goal is to keep the text simple and short, as long texts can discourage potential readers. Thus, in contrast to previous projects, SimpleText aims to provide lacking background knowledge but keeping the text as short as possible in order to help a user understand a complex text which cannot be further simplified without severe information distortion. Searching for background knowledge is close to INEX/CLEF Tweet Contextualization track 2011–2014 [4] and CLEF Cultural micro-blog Contextualization 2016, 2017 Workshop [18], but SimpleText differs from them by making a focus on a selection of notions to be explained and the helpfulness of the information provided rather than its relevance.

2.3 Readability (Language Simplification)

Sentence compression can be seen as a middle ground between text simplification and summarization. The task is to remove redundant or less important parts of an input sentence, preserving its grammaticality and original meaning. Recent works have applied the BERT neural network model [19,36,58], in order to simplify sentences. These approaches are mainly reduced to the "Split and Rephrase" task. Moreover, simplification systems are mainly limited by deleting

[3] https://www.thefreedictionary.com/background+knowledge.

words [33]. Besides, although large pre-trained BERT models like GPT2 outperformed other state-of-the-art models on several NLP tasks, researchers point to several serious issues of these models – consistency and coherency (coreference errors) [52]. In any case, to train and evaluate an AI model one should have a corpus of scientific articles and their simplified versions with a benchmarking system. In previous works, some datasets were developed such as WebSplit et WikiSplit, however the text simplification task was reduced to "Split and Rephrase" [1,6,40]. Another dataset was based on Simple Wikipedia but there is no direct correspondence between Wikipedia and Simple Wikipedia articles [11]. The comparable WikiLarge dataset combines aligned sentence pairs in [29], the aligned and revision sentence pairs in [53], and WikiSmall corpus [60]. To have parallel data (not comparable) is important as the efficiency of a text simplification system depends on the quality and quantity of training data [27]. The dataset Newsela contains 1,932 English news articles re-written by professional editors into four simpler versions [55]. In contrast to that, we focus on scientific texts. CL-SciSumm-2020 features LaySummary subtask[4], where a participating system must produce a text summary of a scientific paper (overall scope, goal and potential impact without using technical jargon) on epilepsy, archaeology, and materials engineering intended for a non-technical audience. However, in most cases, the names of the objects are not replaceable in the process of text transformation or simplification due to the risk of information distortion [12,37]. In this case, complex concepts should be explained to a reader.

Grabar and Cardon introduced a corpus of technical and simplified medical texts in French [7,24]. The corpus contains 663 pairs of comparable sentences issued from encyclopedias, drug leaflets and scientific summaries, and aligned by two annotators. In [7], they proposed an automatic method for sentence alignment. In their further work, using different ratios of general and specialized sentences, they trained neural models on (1) the health comparable corpus in French, (2) the WikiLarge corpus translated from English to French, and (3) and a lexicon that associates medical terms with paraphrases [8]. Jiang et al. proposed a neural CRF alignment model and constructed two text simplification datasets: Newsela-Auto and Wiki-Auto [27]. Their transformer-based seq2seq model established a new state-of-the-art for text simplification in both automatic and human evaluation. In contrast to that, our corpus is not comparable (when simplified sentences are not issued from original sentences but are similar to them), but parallel (source sentences are directly simplified, so they carry the same information). Besides, their work tackles language simplification only without considering content selection for popularized texts which can be different from those designed for experts.

Readability formulas have not convincingly demonstrated the ability to reduce the difficulty of the text [10,21,30,48]. Automatic evaluation metrics have been designed to measure the results of text simplification: SARI [55] targets lexical complexity, while SAMSA estimates the structural complexity of a sentence [50]. Formality style transfer is a cognate task, where a system rewrites

[4] https://ornlcda.github.io/SDProc/sharedtasks.html#laysumm.

a text in a different style preserving its meaning [46]. These tasks are frequently evaluated with lexical overlap metrics such as BLEU [45] or ROUGE [31] to compare the system's output against gold standard. SimpleText is also aimed at providing adequate evaluation metrics for text simplification. Since traditional readability indices can be misleading [54], we rely on human evaluation.

3 Data Set

3.1 Collection

For this edition we use the Citation Network Dataset: DBLP+Citation, ACM Citation network[5]. An elastic search index is provided to participants accessible through a GUI API. This Index is adequate to:

- apply basic passage retrieval methods based on vector or language IR models;
- generate Latent Dirichlet Allocation models;
- train Graph Neural Networks for citation recommendation as carried out in StellarGraph[6] for example;
- apply deep bi directional transformers for query expansion;
- and much more ...

While structured abstracts with distinct, labeled sections for rapid comprehension are an emerging trend since they tend to be informative [16,22], several approaches were proposed to classify sentences in non-structured abstracts [13,16,28]. However, non-expert are usually interested in other types of information. We selected passages that are adequate to be inserted as plain citations in the original journalistic article. The comparison of the journalistic articles with the scientific ones as well as the analysis we carried out to choose topics demonstrated that non-expert, the most important information is the application of an object (which problem can be solved? how to use this information/object? what are examples?).

One of the important problems in manual text simplification is a cognitive bias called the curse of knowledge, which occurs when an individual assumes that their interlocutor has the background to understand them. To leverage this issue, we simplify text passages issued from computer science articles abstracts by a pair of experts. One annotator is a computer scientist who understands the text and simplifies passages. Then each pair of passages (simplified and not) is reread by a professional translator from the University of Western Brittany Translation Office[7] who is an English native speaker but not a specialist in computer science. Each passage is discussed and rewritten multiple times until it becomes clear for non computer scientists. The observation of the obtained simplification examples revealed opposite strategies in making text understandable. On the one hand, shortening passages by eliminating details and generalization

[5] https://www.aminer.org/citation.
[6] https://stellargraph.readthedocs.io/.
[7] https://www.univ-brest.fr/btu.

seem an efficient strategy. On the other hand, simplified sentences are longer and more concrete, e.g. the sentence from an article on exposing image tampering "The learning classifiers are applied for classification" was simplified as "The machine learning algorithms are applied to detect image manipulation". For a computer scientist, it is evident that the detection problem is a special case of a binary classification task, but in order to make this sentence understandable for a non computer scientist, the abstract term "classification" should be replaced with a concrete use-case "to detect image manipulation". Thus, on the one hand our methodology of passage simplification ensures data quality. On the other hand, it provides interesting insights to simplification strategies. 57 manually simplified passages were provided to participants for training.

We manually searched for difficult terms and ranked them from 1 to 10 according to their complexity. 1 corresponds to the terms that very difficult and unknown to the general public. Lower ranks shows that the term might be explained if there is a room. Notice, that the final ranking can be obtained by binary comparison of each pair of candidate terms.

We continue to simplify passages and search for difficult terms.

3.2 Queries

For this edition 13 queries are a selection of recent n press titles from *The Guardian* enriched with keywords manually extracted from the content of the article. It has been checked that each keyword allows to extract at least 5 relevant abstracts. The use of these keywords is optional.

Input format for all tasks:

- Topics in the MD format (see Fig. 1);
- Full text articles from The Guardian (link, folder query_related_content with full texts in the MD format);
- ElasticSearch index on the data server:[8];
- DBLP full dump in the JSON.GZ format;
- DBLP abstracts extracted for each topic in the following MD format (doc_id, year, abstract) (see Fig. 2).

[8] https://guacamole.univ-avignon.fr/nextcloud/index.php/apps/files/?dir=/simpleText/.

Query 1: Digital assistants like Siri and Alexa entrench gender biases, says UN

https://www.theguardian.com/technology/2019/may/22/digital-voice-assistants-siri-alexa-gender-biases-unesco-says

Topic 1.1: Digital assistant

https://inex:qatc2011@guacamole.univ-avignon.fr/dblp1/_search?q="Digital assistant"&size=1000

Topic 1.2: Biases

https://inex:qatc2011@guacamole.univ-avignon.fr/dblp1/_search?q=biases&size=1000

Fig. 1. Query example

1564531496	2002	In this short paper we describe the architectural cc
2988211052	2002	In this short paper we describe the architectural cc
3006661050	2003	Modern Personal Digital Assistant (PDA) architecture
1970213811	2006	This demonstration presents a new interaction techni
2797641221	2018	Digital assistants are emerging to become more preva
2158159346	2004	Abstract Mobile devices are significantly changing
2463945949	2016	DIANE is a digital assistant system that aims to fas

Fig. 2. DBLP abstract examples

4 Pilot Tasks

In 2021, SimpleText was run as a CLEF workshop. The goal was to create a community interested in generating a simplified summary of scientific documents and to define tasks and evaluation setup.

We proposed three pilot tasks to help to better understand the challenges as well as discuss these challenges and the way to evaluate solutions. Details on the tasks, guideline and call for contributions can be found at the SimpleText website[9], in this paper we just briefly introduce the planned pilot tasks. Note that the pilot tasks are means to help the discussions and to develop a research community around text simplification. Contributions are not exclusively rely on the pilot tasks.

43 teams were registered for the SimpleText workshop with 23 participants subscribed on our Google group and 24 followers on Twitter. Although data was downloaded from the server by several participants, they did not submit their runs on our pilot tasks due to the lack of time. We continue to enrich

[9] https://simpletext-madics.github.io/2021/clef/en/.

data prepared for the pilot tasks for the SimpleText@CLEF-2021 workshop to prepare an evaluation lab in 2022. As we did not perform evaluation this year, we present only potential evaluation metrics that can be used in the 2022 edition of SimpleText.

4.1 Task 1: Selecting Passages to Include in a Simplified Summary - Content Simplification

Given an article from a major international newspaper general audience, this pilot task aims at retrieving from a large scientific bibliographic database with abstracts, all passages that would be relevant to illustrate this article. Extracted passages should be adequate to be inserted as plain citations in the original paper.

Sentence pooling and automatic metrics can be used to evaluate these results. The relevance of the source document can be evaluated as well as potential unresolved anaphora issues.

Output: A maximum of 1000 passages to be included in a simplified summary in a TSV (Tab-Separated Values) file with the following fields:

- *run_id*: Run ID starting with *team_id_*;
- *manual*: Whether the run is manual 0,1;
- *topic_id*: Topic ID;
- *doc_id*: Source document ID;
- *passage*: Text of the selected passage;
- *rank*: Passage rank.

An output example is given in Table 1.

4.2 Task 2: Searching for Background Knowledge

The goal of this pilot task is to decide which terms (up to 10) require explanation and contextualization to help a reader to understand a complex scientific text - for example, with regard to a query, terms that need to be contextualized (with a definition, example and/or use-case). Terms should be ranked from 1 to 10 according to their complexity. *1* corresponds to the most difficult term, while lower ranks show that the term might be explained if there is a room.

Output: List of terms to be contextualized in a tabulated file TSV with the following fields:

- *run_id*: Run ID starting with *team_id_*;
- *manual*: Whether the run is manual 0,1;
- *topic_id*: Topic ID;
- *passage_text*: Passage text;
- *term*: Term or other phrase to be explained;
- *rank*: Importance of the explanation for a given term.

An output example for task 2 is given in Table 2.

Table 1. Task 1 output example

run_id	Manual	topic_id	doc_id	Passage	Rank
ST_1	1	1	3000234933	People are becoming increasingly comfortable using Digital Assistants (DAs) to interact with services or connected objects	1
ST_1	1	1	3003409254	Big data and machine learning (ML) algorithms can result in discriminatory decisions against certain protected groups defined upon personal data like gender, race, sexual orientation etc.	2
ST_1	1	1	3003409254	Such algorithms designed to discover patterns in big data might not only pick up any encoded societal biases in the training data, but even worse, they might reinforce such biases resulting in more severe discrimination	3

Term pooling and automatic metrics (NDCG, ...) will be used to evaluate these results in the future edition.

4.3 Task 3: Scientific Text Simplification

The goal of this pilot task is to provide a simplified version of text passages. Participants are provided with queries and abstracts of scientific papers. The abstracts can be split into sentences as in the example. The simplified passages will be evaluated manually with eventual use of aggregating metrics in the future edition.

Output: Simplified passages in a TSV tabulated file with the following fields:

- *run_id*: Run ID starting with *team_id_*;
- *manual*: Whether the run is manual 0,1;
- *topic_id*: Topic ID;
- *doc_id*: Source document ID;
- *source_passage*: Source passage text;
- *simplified_passage*: Text of the simplified passage.

An output example for task 3 is given in Table 3.

Table 2. Task 2 output example

run_id	Manual	topic_id	passage_text	Term	Rank
ST_1	1	1	Automated decision making based on big data and machine learning (ML) algorithms can result in discriminatory decisions against certain protected groups defined upon personal data like gender, race, sexual orientation etc. Such algorithms designed to discover patterns in big data might not only pick up any encoded societal biases in the training data, but even worse, they might reinforce such biases resulting in more severe discrimination	Machine learning	1
ST_1	1	1	Automated decision making based on big data and machine learning (ML) algorithms can result in discriminatory decisions against certain protected groups defined upon personal data like gender, race, sexual orientation etc. Such algorithms designed to discover patterns in big data might not only pick up any encoded societal biases in the training data, but even worse, they might reinforce such biases resulting in more severe discrimination	Societal biases	2
ST_1	1	1	Automated decision making based on big data and machine learning (ML) algorithms can result in discriminatory decisions against certain protected groups defined upon personal data like gender, race, sexual orientation etc. Such algorithms designed to discover patterns in big data might not only pick up any encoded societal biases in the training data, but even worse, they might reinforce such biases resulting in more severe discrimination	ML	3

Table 3. Task 3 output example

run_id	Manual	topic_id	doc_id	source_passage	simplified_passage
ST_1	1	1	3003409254	Automated decision making based on big data and machine learning (ML) algorithms can result in discriminatory decisions against certain protected groups defined upon personal data like gender, race, sexual orientation etc. Such algorithms designed to discover patterns in big data might not only pick up any encoded societal biases in the training data, but even worse, they might reinforce such biases resulting in more severe discrimination	Automated decision-making may include sexist and racist biases and even reinforce them because their algorithms are based on the most prominent social representation in the dataset they use

5 Conclusion and Future Work

The paper introduced the CLEF 2021 SimpleText track, consisting of a workshop and pilot tasks on text simplification for scientific information access. Although 43 teams were registered for the SimpleText workshop and the data was downloaded from the server by several participants, they did not submit their runs on our pilot tasks due to the lack of time and therefore we did not perform evaluation this year. We continue to enrich data prepared for the tasks for the next edition of SimpleText.

The created collection of simplified texts makes it possible to apply overlap metrics like ROUGE to text simplification. However, we will work on a new evaluation metric that can take into account unresolved anaphora [4] and information types.

In future, we will perform deeper analysis of queries collected from different sources. We will reconsider source data: research papers/preprints and their abstracts (e.g. from HAL[10], arXiv[11], or ISTEX[12] platforms using unpaywall API[13] to search for open access versions), Wikipedia/SimpleWikipedia articles, science journalism articles (e.g. ScienceX[14] instead of The Guardian, as it can be freely shared for research purposes), forums like ELI5[15]. We will propose an evaluation lab at CLEF (instead of a workshop). The objective of the Task 1 will be to decide automatically which passages of the scientific articles/abstracts should be included in extractive summaries in order to get a simplified summary of the initial texts taking into account that the information in a summary designed for an expert should be different from that aimed at a general audience. For the pilot task 2, participants will be asked to provide context for difficult terms.

We will prepare datasets in French and enrich datasets in English. We will also propose baselines for all three tasks.

References

1. Aharoni, R., Goldberg, Y.: Split and rephrase: better evaluation and a stronger baseline. arXiv:1805.01035 [cs], May 2018. http://arxiv.org/abs/1805.01035
2. Anand Deshmukh, A., Sethi, U.: IR-BERT: leveraging bert for semantic search in background linking for news articles. arXiv e-prints **2007**. arXiv:2007.12603, July 2020. http://adsabs.harvard.edu/abs/2020arXiv200712603A
3. Augenstein, I., Das, M., Riedel, S., Vikraman, L., McCallum, A.: Semeval 2017 task 10: scienceie-extracting keyphrases and relations from scientific publications. arXiv preprint arXiv:1704.02853 (2017)

[10] https://hal.archives-ouvertes.fr/.
[11] https://arxiv.org/.
[12] https://istex.fr/.
[13] https://unpaywall.org/products/api.
[14] https://sciencex.com/.
[15] https://www.reddit.com/r/explainlikeimfive/.

4. Bellot, P., Moriceau, V., Mothe, J., SanJuan, E., Tannier, X.: INEX tweet contextualization task: evaluation, results and lesson learned. Inf. Process. Manage. **52**(5), 801–819 (2016). https://doi.org/10.1016/j.ipm.2016.03.002
5. Biran, O., Brody, S., Elhadad, N.: Putting it simply: a context-aware approach to lexical simplification. In: Proceedings of the 49th Annual Meeting of the Association for Computational Linguistics: Human Language Technologies, pp. 496–501. Association for Computational Linguistics, Portland, June 2011. https://www.aclweb.org/anthology/P11-2087
6. Botha, J.A., Faruqui, M., Alex, J., Baldridge, J., Das, D.: Learning to split and rephrase from Wikipedia edit history. In: Proceedings of the 2018 Conference on Empirical Methods in Natural Language Processing, pp. 732–737. Association for Computational Linguistics, Brussels, October 2018. https://doi.org/10.18653/v1/D18-1080. https://www.aclweb.org/anthology/D18-1080
7. Cardon, R., Grabar, N.: Détection automatique de phrases paralléles dans un corpus biomédical comparable technique/simplifié. In: TALN 2019, Toulouse, France, July 2019. https://hal.archives-ouvertes.fr/hal-02430446
8. Cardon, R., Grabar, N.: French biomedical text simplification: when small and precise helps. In: Proceedings of the 28th International Conference on Computational Linguistics, pp. 710–716. International Committee on Computational Linguistics, Barcelona, December 2020. https://doi.org/10.18653/v1/2020.coling-main.62. https://www.aclweb.org/anthology/2020.coling-main.62
9. Chen, P., Rochford, J., Kennedy, D.N., Djamasbi, S., Fay, P., Scott, W.: Automatic text simplification for people with intellectual disabilities. In: Artificial Intelligence Science and Technology, pp. 725–731. World Scientific, November 2016. https://doi.org/10.1142/9789813206823_0091. https://www.worldscientific.com/doi/abs/10.1142/97898132068230091
10. Collins-Thompson, K., Callan, J.: A language modeling approach to predicting reading difficulty. In: Proceedings of HLT/NAACL, vol. 4 (2004)
11. Coster, W., Kauchak, D.: Simple English Wikipedia: a new text simplification task. In: Proceedings of the 49th Annual Meeting of the Association for Computational Linguistics: Human Language Technologies, pp. 665–669 (2011)
12. Cram, D., Daille, B.: Terminology extraction with term variant detection. In: Proceedings of ACL-2016 System Demonstrations, pp. 13–18. Association for Computational Linguistics, Berlin, August 2016. https://doi.org/10.18653/v1/P16-4003. https://www.aclweb.org/anthology/P16-4003
13. Dernoncourt, F., Lee, J.Y.: PubMed 200k RCT: a dataset for sequential sentence classification in medical abstracts. In: Proceedings of the Eighth International Joint Conference on Natural Language Processing (Volume 2: Short Papers), pp. 308–313. Asian Federation of Natural Language Processing, Taipei, November 2017. https://www.aclweb.org/anthology/I17-2052
14. Dong, Y., Li, Z., Rezagholizadeh, M., Cheung, J.C.K.: EditNTS: an neural programmer-interpreter model for sentence simplification through explicit editing. In: Proceedings of the 57th Annual Meeting of the Association for Computational Linguistics, pp. 3393–3402. Association for Computational Linguistics, Florence, July 2019. https://doi.org/10.18653/v1/P19-1331. https://www.aclweb.org/anthology/P19-1331
15. Ermakova, L., et al..: Text simplification for scientific information access: CLEF 2021 simpletext workshop. In: Proceedings of Advances in Information Retrieval - 43nd European Conference on IR Research, ECIR 2021, Lucca, Italy, 28 March–1 April 2021. Lucca, Italy (2021)

16. Ermakova, L., Bordignon, F., Turenne, N., Noel, M.: Is the abstract a mere teaser? Evaluating generosity of article abstracts in the environmental sciences. Front. Res. Metrics Anal. **3** (2018). https://doi.org/10.3389/frma.2018.00016. https://www.frontiersin.org/articles/10.3389/frma.2018.00016/full
17. Ermakova, L., Cossu, J.V., Mothe, J.: A survey on evaluation of summarization methods. Inf. Process. Manage. **56**(5), 1794–1814 (2019). https://doi.org/10.1016/j.ipm.2019.04.001. http://www.sciencedirect.com/science/article/pii/S0306457318306241
18. Ermakova, L., Goeuriot, L., Mothe, J., Mulhem, P., Nie, J.Y., SanJuan, E.: CLEF 2017 microblog cultural contextualization lab overview. In: Proceedings of Experimental IR Meets Multilinguality, Multimodality, and Interaction - 8th International Conference of the CLEF Association, CLEF 2017, Dublin, Ireland, 11–14 September 2017,pp. 304–314 (2017). https://doi.org/10.1007/978-3-319-65813-1_27
19. Fang, F., Stevens, M.: Sentence simplification with transformer-XL and paraphrase rules, p. 10 (2019)
20. Fecher, B., Friesike, S.: Open science: one term, five schools of thought. In: Bartling, S., Friesike, S. (eds.) Opening Science, pp. 17–47. Springer, Cham (2014). https://doi.org/10.1007/978-3-319-00026-8_2
21. Flesch, R.: A new readability yardstick. J. Appl. Psychol. **32**(3), 221–233 (1948)
22. Fontelo, P., Gavino, A., Sarmiento, R.F.: Comparing data accuracy between structured abstracts and full-text journal articles: implications in their use for informing clinical decisions. Evidence-Based Med. **18**(6), 207–11 (2013). https://doi.org/10.1136/eb-2013-101272. http://www.researchgate.net/publication/240308203_Comparing_data_accuracy_between_structured_abstracts_and_full-text_journal_articles_implications_in_their_use_for_informing_clinical_decisions
23. Glavaš, G., Štajner, S.: Simplifying lexical simplification: do we need simplified corpora? In: Proceedings of the 53rd Annual Meeting of the Association for Computational Linguistics and the 7th International Joint Conference on Natural Language Processing (Volume 2: Short Papers). pp. 63–68. Association for Computational Linguistics, Beijing, July 2015. https://doi.org/10.3115/v1/P15-2011. https://www.aclweb.org/anthology/P15-2011
24. Grabar, N., Cardon, R.: CLEAR-simple corpus for medical French, November 2018. https://halshs.archives-ouvertes.fr/halshs-01968355
25. Hoffart, J., et al.: Robust disambiguation of named entities in text. In: Proceedings of the 2011 Conference on Empirical Methods in Natural Language Processing, pp. 782–792 (2011)
26. Jarreau, P.B., Porter, L.: Science in the social media age: profiles of science blog readers. J. Mass Commun. Q. **95**(1), 142–168 (2018). https://doi.org/10.1177/1077699016685558
27. Jiang, C., Maddela, M., Lan, W., Zhong, Y., Xu, W.: Neural CRF model for sentence alignment in text simplification. arXiv:2005.02324 [cs], June 2020. http://arxiv.org/abs/2005.02324
28. Jin, D., Szolovits, P.: Hierarchical neural networks for sequential sentence classification in medical scientific abstracts. In: Proceedings of the 2018 Conference on Empirical Methods in Natural Language Processing, pp. 3100–3109. Association for Computational Linguistics, Brussels, October 2018. https://doi.org/10.18653/v1/D18-1349. https://www.aclweb.org/anthology/D18-1349

29. Kauchak, D.: Improving text simplification language modeling using unsimplified text data. In: Proceedings of the 51st Annual Meeting of the Association for Computational Linguistics (Volume 1: Long Papers), pp. 1537–1546. Association for Computational Linguistics, Sofia, August 2013. https://www.aclweb.org/anthology/P13-1151
30. Leroy, G., Endicott, J.E., Kauchak, D., Mouradi, O., Just, M.: User evaluation of the effects of a text simplification algorithm using term familiarity on perception, understanding, learning, and information retention. J. Med. Internet Res. **15**(7), e144 (2013)
31. Lin, C.Y.: ROUGE: a package for automatic evaluation of summaries. In: Text Summarization Branches Out: Proceedings of the ACL–04 Workshop, pp. 74–81 (2004)
32. Liu, Y., Lapata, M.: Text summarization with pretrained encoders. arXiv:1908.08345 [cs], September 2019. http://arxiv.org/abs/1908.08345
33. Maddela, M., Alva-Manchego, F., Xu, W.: Controllable text simplification with explicit paraphrasing. arXiv:2010.11004 [cs], April 2021.http://arxiv.org/abs/2010.11004
34. Maddela, M., Xu, W.: A word-complexity lexicon and a neural readability ranking model for lexical simplification. In: Proceedings of the 2018 Conference on Empirical Methods in Natural Language Processing, pp. 3749–3760. Association for Computational Linguistics, Brussels (2018). https://doi.org/10.18653/v1/D18-1410. https://www.aclweb.org/anthology/D18-1410
35. Martin, L., et al.: CamemBERT: a tasty French language model. In: Proceedings of the 58th Annual Meeting of the Association for Computational Linguistics, pp. 7203–7219. Association for Computational Linguistics (2020). https://doi.org/10.18653/v1/2020.acl-main.645. https://www.aclweb.org/anthology/2020.acl-main.645
36. Maruyama, T., Yamamoto, K.: Extremely low resource text simplification with pre-trained transformer language model. In: International Conference on Asian Language Processing p. 6 (2019)
37. McCarthy, P.M., Guess, R.H., McNamara, D.S.: The components of paraphrase evaluations. Behav. Res. Methods **41**(3), 682–690 (2009). https://doi.org/10.3758/BRM.41.3.682. https://doi.org/10.3758/BRM.41.3.682
38. Michalsky, T.: When to scaffold motivational self-regulation strategies for high school students' science text comprehension. Front. Psychol. **12** (2021). https://doi.org/10.3389/fpsyg.2021.658027. https://www.frontiersin.org/articles/10.3389/fpsyg.2021.658027/full
39. Molek-Kozakowska, K.: Communicating environmental science beyond academia: stylistic patterns of newsworthiness in popular science journalism. Discour. Commun. **11**(1), 69–88 (2017). https://doi.org/10.1177/1750481316683294
40. Narayan, S., Gardent, C., Cohen, S.B., Shimorina, A.: Split and rephrase. In: Proceedings of the 2017 Conference on Empirical Methods in Natural Language Processing, pp. 606–616. Association for Computational Linguistics, Copenhagen, September 2017. https://doi.org/10.18653/v1/D17-1064. https://www.aclweb.org/anthology/D17-1064
41. Nenkova, A., Passonneau, R., McKeown, K.: The pyramid method: incorporating human content selection variation in summarization evaluation. ACM Trans. Speech Lang. Process. **4**(2) (2007). https://doi.org/10.1145/1233912.1233913
42. Owczarzak, K., Dang, H.T.: Overview of the TAC 2011 summarization track: guided task and AESOP task. In: Proceedings of the Text Analysis Conference (TAC 2011), Gaithersburg, Maryland, USA, November 2011

43. O'Reilly, T., Wang, Z., Sabatini, J.: How much knowledge is too little? When a lack of knowledge becomes a barrier to comprehension. Psychol. Sci. (2019). https://doi.org/10.1177/0956797619862276. https://journals.sagepub.com/doi/10.1177/0956797619862276
44. Paetzold, G., Specia, L.: Lexical simplification with neural ranking. In: Proceedings of the 15th Conference of the European Chapter of the Association for Computational Linguistics: Volume 2, Short Papers, pp. 34–40. Association for Computational Linguistics, Valencia, April 2017. https://www.aclweb.org/anthology/E17-2006
45. Papineni, K., Roukos, S., Ward, T., Zhu, W.J.: BLEU: a method for automatic evaluation of machine translation. In: Proceedings of the 40th Annual Meeting on Association for Computational Linguistics, pp. 311–318. Association for Computational Linguistics (2002)
46. Rao, S., Tetreault, J.: Dear sir or madam, may i introduce the GYAFC dataset: corpus, benchmarks and metrics for formality style transfer. In: Proceedings of the 2018 Conference of the North American Chapter of the Association for Computational Linguistics: Human Language Technologies, Volume 1 (Long Papers), pp. 129–140 (2018)
47. Sadoski, M.: Reading comprehension is embodied: theoretical and practical considerations. Educ. Psychol. Rev. **30**(2), 331–349 (2018). https://doi.org/10.1007/s10648-017-9412-8
48. Si, L., Callan, J.: A statistical model for scientific readability. In: Proceedings of the Tenth International Conference on Information and Knowledge Management, CIKM 2001, pp. 574–576. ACM, New York (2001). https://doi.org/10.1145/502585.502695
49. Specia, L., Jauhar, S.K., Mihalcea, R.: SemEval-2012 task 1: english lexical simplification. In: *SEM 2012: The First Joint Conference on Lexical and Computational Semantics – Volume 1: Proceedings of the main conference and the shared task, and Volume 2: Proceedings of the Sixth International Workshop on Semantic Evaluation (SemEval 2012), pp. 347–355. Association for Computational Linguistics, Montréal (2012). https://www.aclweb.org/anthology/S12-1046
50. Sulem, E., Abend, O., Rappoport, A.: Semantic structural evaluation for text simplification. In: Proceedings of the 2018 Conference of the North American Chapter of the Association for Computational Linguistics: Human Language Technologies, Volume 1 (Long Papers), pp. 685–696 (2018)
51. Wang, T., Chen, P., Rochford, J., Qiang, J.: Text simplification using neural machine translation. In: Proceedings of the AAAI Conference on Artificial Intelligence, vol. 30, no. 1, March 2016. https://ojs.aaai.org/index.php/AAAI/article/view/9933
52. Wang, W., Li, P., Zheng, H.T.: Consistency and coherency enhanced story generation. arXiv:2010.08822 [cs], October 2020. http://arxiv.org/abs/2010.08822
53. Woodsend, K., Lapata, M.: Learning to simplify sentences with quasi-synchronous grammar and integer programming. In: Proceedings of the 2011 Conference on Empirical Methods in Natural Language Processing, pp. 409–420. Association for Computational Linguistics, Edinburgh, July 2011. https://www.aclweb.org/anthology/D11-1038
54. Wubben, S., van den Bosch, A., Krahmer, E.: Sentence simplification by monolingual machine translation. In: Proceedings of the 50th Annual Meeting of the Association for Computational Linguistics (Volume 1: Long Papers), pp. 1015–1024 (2012)

55. Xu, W., Callison-Burch, C., Napoles, C.: Problems in current text simplification research: new data can help. Trans. Assoc. Comput. Linguist. **3**, 283–297 (2015). https://doi.org/10.1162/tacl_a_00139. https://www.mitpressjournals.org/doi/abs/10.1162/tacla00139
56. Xu, W., Napoles, C., Pavlick, E., Chen, Q., Callison-Burch, C.: Optimizing statistical machine translation for text simplification. Trans. Assoc. Comput. Linguist. **4**, 401–415 (2016)
57. Yatskar, M., Pang, B., Danescu-Niculescu-Mizil, C., Lee, L.: For the sake of simplicity: unsupervised extraction of lexical simplifications from Wikipedia. In: Human Language Technologies: The 2010 Annual Conference of the North American Chapter of the Association for Computational Linguistics, pp. 365–368. Association for Computational Linguistics, Los Angeles, June 2010. https://www.aclweb.org/anthology/N10-1056
58. Zhao, S., Meng, R., He, D., Saptono, A., Parmanto, B.: Integrating transformer and paraphrase rules for sentence simplification. In: Proceedings of the 2018 Conference on Empirical Methods in Natural Language Processing, pp. 3164–3173. Association for Computational Linguistics, Brussels, October 2018. https://doi.org/10.18653/v1/D18-1355. https://www.aclweb.org/anthology/D18-1355
59. Zhong, Y., Jiang, C., Xu, W., Li, J.J.: Discourse level factors for sentence deletion in text simplification. In: Proceedings of the AAAI Conference on Artificial Intelligence, vol. 34, no. 05, pp. 9709–9716, April 2020. https://doi.org/10.1609/aaai.v34i05.6520. https://ojs.aaai.org/index.php/AAAI/article/view/6520
60. Zhu, Z., Bernhard, D., Gurevych, I.: A monolingual tree-based translation model for sentence simplification. In: Proceedings of the 23rd International Conference on Computational Linguistics (Coling 2010), pp. 1353–1361. Coling 2010 Organizing Committee, Beijing, August 2010. https://www.aclweb.org/anthology/C10-1152
61. Štajner, S., Nisioi, S.: A detailed evaluation of neural sequence-to-sequence models for in-domain and cross-domain text simplification. In: Proceedings of the Eleventh International Conference on Language Resources and Evaluation (LREC 2018). European Language Resources Association (ELRA), Miyazaki, Japan, May 2018. https://www.aclweb.org/anthology/L18-1479

Overview of Touché 2021: Argument Retrieval

Alexander Bondarenko[1(✉)], Lukas Gienapp[2], Maik Fröbe[1], Meriem Beloucif[3], Yamen Ajjour[1], Alexander Panchenko[4], Chris Biemann[3], Benno Stein[5], Henning Wachsmuth[6], Martin Potthast[2], and Matthias Hagen[1]

[1] Martin-Luther-Universität Halle-Wittenberg, Halle, Germany
touche@webis.de
[2] Leipzig University, Leipzig, Germany
[3] Universität Hamburg, Hamburg, Germany
[4] Skolkovo Institute of Science and Technology, Moscow, Russia
[5] Bauhaus-Universität Weimar, Weimar, Germany
[6] Paderborn University, Paderborn, Germany
https://touche.webis.de

Abstract. This paper is a condensed report on the second year of the Touché shared task on argument retrieval held at CLEF 2021. With the goal to provide a collaborative platform for researchers, we organized two tasks: (1) supporting individuals in finding arguments on controversial topics of social importance and (2) supporting individuals with arguments in personal everyday comparison situations.

Keywords: Argument retrieval for controversial questions · Argument retrieval for comparative questions · Shared task

1 Introduction

Informed decision making and opinion formation are natural routine tasks. Generally, both of these tasks often involve weighing two or more options. Any choice to be made may be based on personal prior knowledge and experience, but they may also often require searching and processing new knowledge. With the ubiquitous access to various kinds of information on the web—from facts over opinions and anecdotes to arguments—everybody has the chance to acquire knowledge for decision making or opinion formation on almost any topic. However, large amounts of easily accessible information imply challenges such as the need to assess their relevance to the specific topic of interest and to estimate how well an implied stance is justified; no matter whether it is about topics of social importance or "just" about personal decisions. In the simplest form, such a

K. S. Candan et al. (Eds.): CLEF 2021, LNCS 12880, pp. 450–467, 2021.
https://doi.org/10.1007/978-3-030-85251-1_28

justification might be a collection of basic facts and opinions. More complex justifications are often grounded in argumentation, though; for instance, a complex relational aggregation of assertions and evidence pro or con either side, where different assertions or evidential statements support or refute each other.

Furthermore, while web resources such as blogs, community question answering sites, news articles, or social platforms contain an immense variety of opinions and argumentative texts, a notable proportion of these may be of biased, faked, or populist nature. This has motivated argument retrieval research to focus not only on the relevance of arguments, but also on the aspect of their quality. While conventional web search engines support the retrieval of factual information fairly well, they hardly address the deeper analysis and processing of argumentative texts, in terms of mining argument units from these texts, assessing the quality of the arguments, or classifying their stance. To address this, the argument search engine args.me [51] was developed to retrieve arguments relevant to a given controversial topic and to account for the pro or con stance of individual arguments in the result presentation. So far, however, it is limited to a document collection crawled from a few online debate portals, and largely disregards quality aspects. Other argument retrieval systems such as ArgumenText [45] and TARGER [13] take advantage of the large web document collection Common Crawl, but their ability to reliably retrieve arguments to support sides in a decision process is limited. The comparative argumentation machine CAM [44], a system for argument retrieval in comparative search, tries to support decision making in comparison scenarios based on billions of individual sentences from the Common Crawl. Still, it lacks a proper ranking of diverse longer argumentative texts.

To foster research on argument retrieval and to establish more collaboration and exchange of ideas and datasets among researchers, we organized the second Touché lab on argument retrieval at CLEF 2021 [8,9].[1] Touché is a collaborative platform[2] to develop and share retrieval approaches that aim to support decisions at a societal level (e.g., "Should hate speech be penalized more, and why?") and at a personal level (e.g., "Should I major in philosophy or psychology, and why?"), respectively. The second year of Touché featured two tasks:

1. Argument retrieval for *controversial* questions from a focused collection of debates to support opinion formation on topics of social importance.
2. Argument retrieval for *comparative* questions from a generic web crawl to support informed decision making.

Approaches to these two tasks, which do not only consider the relevance of arguments but also facets of argumentative quality, will help search engines to deliver more accurate argumentative results. Additionally, they will also be an important part of open-domain conversational agents that "discuss"

[1] The name of the lab is inspired by the usage of the term 'touché' as an exclamation "used to admit that someone has made a good point against you in an argument or discussion." [https://dictionary.cambridge.org/dictionary/english/touche].

[2] https://touche.webis.de/.

controversial societal topics with humans—as showcased by IBM's Project Debater [4,5,32].[3]

The teams that participated in the second year of Touché were able to use the topics and relevance judgments from the first year to develop their approaches. Many trained and optimized learning-based rankers as part of their retrieval pipelines and employed a large variety of pre-processing methods (e.g., stemming, duplicate removal, query expansion), argument quality features, or comparative features (e.g., credibility, part-of-speech tags). In this paper, we report the results and briefly describe the most effective participants' retrieval approaches submitted at Touché 2021; a more comprehensive overview of each approach will be covered in the forthcoming extended overview [9].

2 Previous Work

Queries in argument retrieval often are phrases that describe a controversial topic, questions that ask to compare two options, or even complete arguments themselves [53]. In the Touché lab, we address the first two types in two different shared tasks. Here, we briefly summarize the related work for both tasks.

2.1 Argument Retrieval

Argument retrieval aims for delivering arguments to support users in making a decision or to help persuading an audience of a specific point of view. An argument is usually modeled as a conclusion with supporting or attacking premises [51]. While a conclusion is a statement that can be accepted or rejected, a premise is a more grounded statement (e.g., a statistical evidence).

The development of an argument search engine is faced with challenges that range from mining arguments from unstructured text to assessing their relevance and quality [51]. Argument retrieval follows several paradigms that start from different sources and perform argument mining and retrieval tasks in different orders [1]. Wachsmuth et al. [51], for instance, extract arguments offline using heuristics that are tailored to online debate portals. Their argument search engine args.me uses BM25F to rank the indexed arguments while giving conclusions more weight than premises. Also Levy et al. [29] use distant supervision to mine arguments offline for a set of topics from Wikipedia before ranking them. Following a different paradigm, Stab et al. [45] retrieve documents from the Common Crawl[4] in an online fashion (no prior offline argument mining) and use a topic-dependent neural network to extract arguments from the retrieved documents at query time. With the two Touché tasks, we address the paradigms of Wachsmuth et al. [51] (Task 1) and Stab et al. [45] (Task 2), respectively.

Argument retrieval should rank arguments according to their topical relevance but also to their quality. What makes a good argument has been studied

[3] https://www.research.ibm.com/artificial-intelligence/project-debater/.

[4] http://commoncrawl.org.

since the time of Aristotle [3]. Recently, Wachsmuth et al. [48] categorized the different aspects of argument quality into a taxonomy that covers three dimensions: logic, rhetoric, and dialectic. Logic concerns the local structure of an argument, i.e., the conclusion and the premises and their relations. Rhetoric covers the effectiveness of the argument in persuading an audience with its conclusion. Dialectic addresses the relations of an argument to other arguments on the topic. For example, an argument that has many attacking premises might be rather vulnerable in a debate. The relevance of an argument to a query's topic is categorized by Wachsmuth et al. [48] under dialectic quality.

Researchers assess argument relevance by measuring an argument's similarity to a query's topic or incorporating its support/attack relations to other arguments. Potthast et al. [40] evaluate four standard retrieval models at ranking arguments with regard to the quality dimensions: relevance, logic, rhetoric, and dialectic. One of the main findings is that DirichletLM is better at ranking arguments than BM25, DPH, and TF-IDF. Gienapp et al. [21] extend this work by proposing a pairwise strategy that reduces the costs of crowdsourcing argument retrieval annotations in a pairwise fashion by 93% (i.e., annotating only a small subset of argument pairs).

Wachsmuth et al. [52] create a graph of arguments by connecting two arguments when one uses the other's conclusion as a premise. Later on, they exploit this structure to rank the arguments in the graph using PageRank scores [37]. This method is shown to outperform several baselines that only consider the content of the argument and its local structure (conclusion and premises). Dumani et al. [15] introduce a probabilistic framework that operates on semantically similar claims and premises. The framework utilizes support/attack relations between clusters of premises and claims and between clusters of claims and a query. It is found to outperform BM25 in ranking arguments. Later, Dumani et al. [16] also proposed an extension of the framework to include the quality of a premise as a probability by using the fraction of premises which are worse with regard to the three quality dimensions cogency, reasonableness, and effectiveness. Using a pairwise quality estimator trained on the Dagstuhl-15512 ArgQuality Corpus [50], their probabilistic framework with the argument quality component outperformed the one without it on the 50 Task 1 topics of Touché 2020.

2.2 Retrieval for Comparisons

Comparative information needs in web search have first been addressed by basic interfaces where two to-be-compared products are entered separately in a left and a right search box [34,46]. Comparative sentences are then identified and mined from product reviews in favor or against one or the other to-be-compared entity using opinion mining approaches [23,24,26]. Recently, the identification of the comparison preference (the "winning" entity) in comparative sentences has been tackled in a more broad domain (not just product reviews) by applying feature-based and neural classifiers [31,39]. Such preference classification forms the basis of the comparative argumentation machine CAM [44] that takes two entities and some comparison aspect(s) as input, retrieves comparative sentences in favor of one or the other entity using BM25, and then classifies their preference for a final merged result table presentation. A proper argument ranking, however, is still missing in CAM. Chekalina et al. [11] later extend the system to accept comparative questions as input and to return a natural language answer to the user. A comparative question is parsed by identifying the comparison objects, aspect(s), and predicate. The system's answer is either generated directly based on Transformers [14] or by retrieval from an index of comparative sentences.

3 Lab Overview and Statistics

The second edition of Touché received 36 registrations (compared to 28 registrations in the first year), with a majority coming from Germany and Italy, but also from the Americas, Europe, Africa, and Asia (16 from Germany, 10 from Italy, 2 from the United States and Mexico, and 1 each from Canada, India, the Netherlands, Nigeria, the Russian Federation, and Tunisia). Aligned with the lab's fencing-related title, the participants were asked to select a real or fictional swordsman character (e.g., Zorro) as their team name upon registration.

We received result submissions from 27 of the 36 registered teams (up from 20 submissions in the first year). As in the previous edition of Touché, we paid attention to foster the reproducibility of the developed approaches by using the TIRA platform [41]. Upon registration, each team received an invitation to TIRA to deploy actual software implementations of their approaches. TIRA is an integrated cloud-based evaluation-as-a-service research architecture on which participants can install their software on a dedicated virtual machine. By default, the virtual machines operate the server version of Ubuntu 20.04 with one CPU (Intel Xeon E5-2620), 4 GB of RAM, and 16 GB HDD, but we adjusted the resources to the participants' requirements when needed (e.g., one team asked for 30 GB of RAM, 3 CPUs, and 30 GB of HDD). The participants had full administrative access to their virtual machines. Still, we pre-installed the latest versions of reasonable standard software (e.g., Docker and Python) to simplify the deployment of the approaches.

Using TIRA, the teams could create result submissions via a click in the web UI that then initiated the following pipeline: the respective virtual machine is shut down, disconnected from the internet, and powered on again in a sandbox mode, mounting the test datasets for the respective tasks, and running a team's deployed approach. The interruption of the internet connection ensures that the participants' software works without external web services that may disappear or become incompatible—possible causes of reproducibility issues—but it also means that downloading additional external code or models during the execution was not possible. We offered our support when this connection interruption caused problems during the deployment, for instance, with spaCy that tries to download models if they are not already available on the machine, or with PyTerrier that, in its default configuration, checks for online updates. To simplify participation of teams that do not want to develop a fully-fledged retrieval pipeline on their end, we enabled two exceptions from the interruption of the internet connection for all participants: the APIs of args.me and ChatNoir were available even in the sandbox mode to allow accessing a baseline system for each of the tasks. The virtual machines that the participants used for their submissions will be archived such that the respective systems can be re-evaluated or applied to new datasets as long as the APIs of ChatNoir and args.me remain available—that are both maintained by us.

In cases where a software submission in TIRA was not possible, the participants could submit just run files. Overall, 5 of the 27 teams submitted traditional run files instead of software in TIRA. Per task, we allowed each team to submit up to 5 runs that should follow the standard TREC-style format.[5] We checked the validity of all submitted run files, asking participants to resubmit their run files (or software) if there were any validity issues—again, also offering our support in case of problems. All 27 teams submitted valid runs, resulting in 90 valid runs (doubling the 42 result submissions that we received in the first year).

4 Task 1: Argument Retrieval for Controversial Questions

The goal of the Touché 2021 lab's first task was to advance technologies that support individuals in forming opinions on socially important controversial topics such as: "Should hate speech be penalized more?". For such topics, the task was to retrieve relevant and high-quality argumentative texts from the args.me corpus [1], a focused crawl of online debate portals. In this scenario, relevant arguments should help users to form an opinion on the topic and to find arguments that are potentially useful in debates or discussions.

The results of last year's Task 1 participants indicated that improving upon "classic" argument-agnostic baseline retrieval models (such as BM25 and DirichletLM) in the ranking of arguments from a focused crawl is difficult, but, at the same time, the results of these baselines still left some room for improvements. Also, the detection of the degree of argumentativeness and the assessment of the quality of an argument were not "solved" in the first year, but identified as potentially interesting contributions of submissions to the task's second iteration.

4.1 Task Definition

Given a controversial topic formulated as a question, approaches to Task 1 needed to retrieve relevant and high-quality arguments from the args.me corpus, which covers a wide range of timely controversial topics. To enable approaches that leverage training and fine-tuning, the topics and relevance judgments from the 2020 edition of Task 1 were provided.

[5] The expected format of submissions was also described at https://touche.webis.de.

Table 1. Example topic for Task 1: Argument Retrieval for Controversial Questions.

Number	89
Title	Should hate speech be penalized more?
Description	Given the increasing amount of online hate speech, a user questions the necessity and legitimacy of taking legislative action to punish or inhibit hate speech.
Narrative	Highly relevant arguments include those that take a stance in favor of or opposed to stronger legislation and penalization of hate speech and that offer valid reasons for either stance. Relevant arguments talk about the prevalence and impact of hate speech, but may not mention legal aspects. Irrelevant arguments are the ones that are concerned with offensive language that is not directed towards a group or individuals on the basis of their membership in the group.

4.2 Data Description

Topics. We formulated 50 new search questions on controversial topics. Each topic consisted of (a) a title in form of a question that a user might submit as a query to a search engine, (b) a description that summarizes the particular information need and search scenario, and (c) a narrative that guides the assessors in recognizing relevant results (an example topic is given in Table 1). We carefully designed the topics by clustering the debate titles in the args.me corpus, formulating questions for a balanced mix of frequent and niche topics—manually ensuring that at least some relevant arguments are contained in the args.me corpus for each topic.

Document Collection. The document collection for Task 1 was the args.me corpus [1], which is freely available for download[6] and also accessible via the args.me API.[7] The corpus contains about 400,000 structured arguments (from debatewise.org, idebate.org, debatepedia.org, and debate.org), each with a conclusion (claim) and one or more supporting or attacking premises (reasons).

4.3 Submitted Approaches

Twenty-one participating teams submitted at least one valid run to Task 1. The submissions partly continued the trend of Touché 2020 [7] by deploying "classical" retrieval models, however with an increased focus on machine learning models (especially for query expansion and for assessing argument quality). Overall, we observed two kinds of contributions: (1) Reproducing and fine-tuning approaches from the previous year by increasing their robustness, and (2) developing new, mostly neural approaches for argument retrieval by fine-tuning pretrained models for the domain-specific search task at hand.

[6] https://webis.de/data.html#args-me-corpus.
[7] https://www.args.me/api-en.html.

Like in the first year, combining "classical" retrieval models with various query expansion methods and domain-specific re-ranking features remained a frequent choice of approaches to Task 1. Not really surprising—given last year's baseline results—DirichletLM was employed most often as the initial retrieval model, followed by BM25. For query expansion, most participating teams continued to leverage WordNet [17]. However, transformer-based approaches received increased attention, such as query hallucination, which was successfully used by Akiki and Potthast [2] in the previous Touché lab. Similarly, utilizing deep semantic phrase embeddings to calculate the semantic similarity between a query and possible result documents gained widespread adoption. Moreover, many approaches tried to use some form of argument quality estimation as one of their features for ranking or re-ranking.

This year's approaches benefited from the judgments released for Touché in 2020. Many teams used them for general parameter optimization but also to evaluate intermediate results of their approaches and to fine-tune or select the best configurations. For instance, comparing different kinds of pre-processing methods based on the available judgments from last year received much attention (e.g., stopword lists, stemming algorithms, or duplicate removal).

4.4 Task Evaluation

The teams' result rankings should be formatted in the "standard" TREC format where document IDs are sorted by descending relevance score for each search topic (i.e., the most relevant argument/document occurs at Rank 1). Prior to creating the assessment pools, we ran a near-duplicate detection for all submitted runs using the CopyCat framework [18], since near-duplicates might impact evaluation results [19,20]. The framework found only 1.1% of the arguments in the top-5 results to be near-duplicates (mostly due to debate portal users reusing their arguments in multiple debate threads). We created duplicate-free versions of each result list by removing the documents for which a higher-ranked document is a near-duplicate; in such cases, the next ranked non-near-duplicate then just moved up the ranked list. The top-5 results of the original and the deduplicated runs then formed the judgment pool—created with TrecTools [38]—resulting in 3,711 unique documents that were manually assessed with respect to their relevance and argumentative quality.

For the assessment, we used the Doccano tool [35] and followed previously suggested annotation guidelines [21,40]. Our eight graduate and undergraduate student volunteers (all with a computer science background) assessed each argument's relevance to the given topic with four labels (0: not relevant, 1: relevant, 2: highly relevant, or -2: spam) and the argument's rhetorical quality [50] with three labels (0: low quality, 1: sufficient quality, and 2: high quality). To calibrate the annotators' interpretations of the guidelines (i.e., the topics including the narratives and instructions on argument quality), we performed an initial κ-test in which each annotator had to label the same 15 documents from three topics (5 documents from each topic). The observed Fleiss' κ values of 0.50 for argument relevance (moderate agreement) and of 0.39 for argument quality (fair

Table 2. Results for Task 1: Argument Retrieval for Controversial Questions. The left part (a) shows the evaluation results of a team's best run according to the results' relevance, while the right part (b) shows the best runs according to the results' quality. An asterisk (*) indicates that the runs with the best relevance and the best quality differ for a team. The baseline DirichletLM ranking is shown in bold.

(a) Best relevance score per team

	nDCG@5	
Team	**Rel.**	**Qual.**
Elrond*	0.720	0.809
Pippin Took*	0.705	0.798
Robin Hood*	0.691	0.756
Asterix*	0.681	0.802
Dread Pirate Roberts*	0.678	0.804
Skeletor*	0.667	0.815
Luke Skywalker	0.662	0.808
Shanks*	0.658	0.790
Heimdall*	0.648	0.833
Athos	0.637	0.802
Goemon Ishikawa	0.635	0.812
Jean Pierre Polnareff	0.633	0.802
Swordsman	**0.626**	**0.796**
Yeagerists	0.625	0.810
Hua Mulan*	0.620	0.789
Macbeth*	0.611	0.783
Blade*	0.601	0.751
Deadpool	0.557	0.679
Batman	0.528	0.695
Little Foot	0.521	0.718
Gandalf	0.486	0.603
Palpatine	0.401	0.562

(b) Best quality score per team

	nDCG@5	
Team	**Qual.**	**Rel.**
Heimdall*	0.841	0.639
Skeletor*	0.827	0.666
Asterix*	0.818	0.663
Elrond*	0.817	0.674
Pippin Took*	0.814	0.683
Goemon Ishikawa	0.812	0.635
Hua Mulan*	0.811	0.620
Dread Pirate Roberts*	0.810	0.647
Yeagerists	0.810	0.625
Robin Hood*	0.809	0.641
Luke Skywalker	0.808	0.662
Macbeth*	0.803	0.608
Athos	0.802	0.637
Jean Pierre Polnareff	0.802	0.633
Swordsman	**0.796**	**0.626**
Shanks*	0.795	0.639
Blade*	0.763	0.588
Little Foot	0.718	0.521
Batman	0.695	0.528
Deadpool	0.679	0.557
Gandalf	0.603	0.486
Palpatine	0.562	0.401

agreement) are similar to previous studies [21,49,50]. However, we still had a final discussion with all the annotators to clarify potential misinterpretations. Afterwards, each annotator independently judged the results for disjoint subsets of the topics (i.e., each topic was judged by one annotator only).

4.5 Task Results

The results of the runs with the best nDCG@5 scores per participating team are reported in Table 2. Below, we briefly summarize the best configurations of the teams ranked in the top-5 of either the relevance or the quality evaluation. A more comprehensive discussion including all teams' approaches will be part of the forthcoming extended lab overview [9].

Team *Elrond* combined DirichletLM retrieval with a pre-processing pipeline consisting of Krovetz stemming [27], stopword removal using a custom list, removing terms with certain part-of-speech tags, and enriching the document representations using WordNet-based synonyms.

Team *Pippin Took* also used DirichletLM as their basic retrieval model (parameter optimization based on the Touché 2020 judgments) combined with WordNet-based query expansion.

Team *Robin Hood* combined RM3 [28] query expansion with phrase embeddings for retrieval. Their system represents the premise and the conclusion of each argument in two separate vector spaces using the Universal Sentence Encoder [10], and then ranks the arguments based on their cosine similarity to the embedded query.

Team *Asterix* combined BM25 as basic retrieval model with WordNet-based query expansion and a quality-aware re-ranking approach (linear regression model trained on the Webis-ArgQuality-20 dataset [21]). In their system, arguments are ranked based on a combination of the predicted quality score and a normalized BM25 score.

Team *Dread Pirate Roberts* trained a LambdaMART model on the Task 1 relevance labels of Touché 2020 to re-rank the top-100 results of an initial DirichletLM ranking. Using greedy feature selection, they identified the four to nine features with the best nDCG scores in a 5-fold cross-validation setup.

Team *Heimdall* represented arguments using k-means cluster centroids in a vector space constructed using phrase embeddings. Their system combines the cosine similarity of a query to a centroid with DirichletLM retrieval scores, and derives an argument quality score from an SVM regression model that uses $tf \cdot idf$ features and was trained on the overall quality ratings from the Webis-ArgQuality-20 dataset.

Team *Skeletor*, finally, combined a fine-tuned BM25 model with the cosine similarity of passages calculated by a phrase embedding model fine-tuned for question answering. They included pseudo-relevance feedback using the 50 arguments that are most similar in the embedding space to the top-3 initially retrieved arguments. The final retrieval score of a candidate result passage is approximated in their system by its similarity to the relevance feedback passages determined with manifold approximation and summed as the argument's score.

5 Task 2: Argument Retrieval for Comparative Questions

The goal of the Touché 2021 lab's second task was to support individuals making informed decisions in "everyday" or personal comparison situations—in its simplest form for questions such as "Is X or Y better for Z?". Decision making in such situations benefits from finding balanced justifications for choosing one or the other option, for instance, in the form of pro/con arguments.

Table 3. Example topic for Task 2: Argument Retrieval for Comparative Questions.

Number	88
Title	Should I major in philosophy or psychology?
Description	A soon-to-be high-school graduate finds themself at a crossroad in their live. Based on their interests, majoring in philosophy or in psychology are the potential options and the graduate is searching for information about the differences and similarities, as well as advantages and disadvantages of majoring in either of them (e.g., with respect to career opportunities or gained skills).
Narrative	Relevant documents will overview one of the two majors in terms of career prospects or developed new skills, or they will provide a list of reasons to major in one or the other. Highly relevant documents will compare the two majors side-by-side and help to decide which should be preferred in what context. Not relevant are study program and university advertisements or general descriptions of the disciplines that do not mention benefits, advantages, or pros/cons.

Similar to Task 1, the results of last year's Task 2 participants indicated that improving upon an argument-agnostic BM25 baseline is quite difficult. Promising proposed approaches tried to re-rank based on features capturing "comparativeness" or "argumentativeness".

5.1 Task Definition

Given a comparative question, an approach to Task 2 needed to retrieve documents from the general web crawl ClueWeb12[8] that help to come to an informed decision on the comparison. Ideally, the retrieved documents should be argumentative with convincing arguments for or against one or the other option. To identify arguments in web documents, the participants were not restricted to any system; they could use own technology or any existing argument taggers such as MARGOT [30]. To lower the entry barriers for participants new to argument mining, we offered support for using the neural argument tagger TARGER [13] hosted on our own servers and accessible via an API.[9]

5.2 Data Description

Topics. For the second task edition, we manually selected 50 new comparative questions from the MS MARCO dataset [36] (questions from Bing's search logs) and the Quora dataset [22] (questions asked on the Quora question answering

[8] https://lemurproject.org/clueweb12/.

[9] https://demo.webis.de/targer-api/apidocs/.

website). We ensured to include questions on diverse topics, for example asking about electronics, culinary, house appliances, life choices, etc. Table 3 shows an example topic for Task 2 that consists of a title (i.e., a comparative question), a description of the possible search context and situation, and a narrative describing what makes a retrieved result relevant (meant as a guideline for human assessors). We manually ensured that relevant documents for each topic were actually contained in the ClueWeb12 (i.e., avoiding questions on comparison options not known at the ClueWeb12 crawling time in 2012).

Document Collection. The retrieval corpus was formed by the ClueWeb12 collection that contains 733 million English web pages (27.3 TB uncompressed) crawled by the Language Technologies Institute at Carnegie Mellon University between February and May 2012. For participants of Task 2 who could not index the ClueWeb12 on their side, we provided access to the indexed corpus through the BM25F-based search engine ChatNoir [6] via its API.[10]

5.3 Submitted Approaches

For Task 2, six teams submitted approaches that all used ChatNoir for an initial document retrieval. Most teams then applied a document "preprocessing" on the ChatNoir results (e.g., removing HTML markups) and re-ranked them with feature-based or neural classifiers trained on last year's judgments. Commonly used techniques further included (1) query processing (e.g., lemmatization and POS-tagging), (2) query expansion (e.g., synonyms from WordNet [17], or generated with the word2vec [33] or sense2vec embeddings [47]), and (3) calculating argumentativeness, credibility, or comparativeness scores used as features in the re-ranking. The teams predicted document relevance labels by using a random forest classifier, XGBoost [12], LightGBM [25], or a fine-tuned BERT [14].

5.4 Task Evaluation

Using the CopyCat framework [18], we found that on average 11.6% of the documents in the top-5 results of a run were near-duplicates—a non-negligible redundancy that might have negatively impacted the reliability and validity of an evaluation, since rankings containing multiple relevant duplicates tend to overestimate the actual retrieval effectiveness [19,20]. Following the strategy used in Task 1, we pooled the top-5 documents from the original and the deduplicated runs, resulting in 2,076 unique documents that needed to be judged.

Our eight volunteer annotators (same as for Task 1) labeled a document for its topical relevance (three labels; 0: not relevant, 1: relevant, and 2: highly relevant) and for whether rhetorically well-written arguments [50] were contained (three labels; 0: low quality or no arguments in the document, 1: sufficient quality, and 2: high quality). Similar to Task 1, our eight volunteer assessors went through an initial κ-test on 15 documents from three topics (five documents

[10] https://www.chatnoir.eu/doc/.

Table 4. Results for Task 2 Argument Retrieval for Comparative Questions. The left part (a) shows the evaluation results of a team's best run according to the results' relevance, while the right part (b) shows the best runs according to the results' quality. An asterisk (*) indicates that the runs with the best relevance and the best quality differ for a team. The baseline ChatNoir ranking is shown in bold.

(a) Best relevance score per team

	nDCG@5	
Team	**Rel.**	**Qual.**
Katana*	0.489	0.675
Thor	0.478	0.680
Rayla*	0.473	0.670
Jack Sparrow	0.467	0.664
Mercutio	0.441	0.651
Puss in Boots	**0.422**	**0.636**
Prince Caspian	0.244	0.548

(b) Best quality score per team

	nDCG@5	
Team	**Qual.**	**Rel.**
Rayla*	0.688	0.466
Katana*	0.684	0.460
Thor	0.680	0.478
Jack Sparrow	0.664	0.467
Mercutio	0.651	0.441
Puss in Boots	**0.636**	**0.422**
Prince Caspian	0.548	0.244

per topic). As in case of Task 1, the observed Fleiss' κ values of 0.46 for relevance (moderate agreement) and of 0.22 for quality (fair agreement) are similar to previous studies [21,49,50]. Again, however, we had a final discussion with all the annotators to clarify some potential misinterpretations. Afterwards, each annotator independently judged the results for disjoint subsets of the topics (i.e., each topic was judged by one annotator only).

5.5 Task Results

The results of the runs with the best nDCG@5 scores per participating team are reported in Table 4. Below, we briefly summarize the best configurations of the teams. A more comprehensive discussion including all teams' approaches will be part of the forthcoming extended lab overview [9].

Team *Katana* re-ranked the top-100 ChatNoir results using an XGBoost [12] approach (overall relevance-wise most effective run) or a LightGBM [25] approach (team Katana's quality-wise best run), respectively. Both approaches were trained on judgments from Touché 2020 employing relevance features (e.g., ChatNoir relevance score) and "comparativness" features (e.g., number of identified comparison objects, aspects, or predicates [11]).

Team *Thor* re-ranked the top-110 ChatNoir results by locally creating an Elasticsearch BM25F index (fields: original and lemmatized document titles, bodies, and argument units (premises and claims) as identified by TARGER; BM25 parameters b and k_1 optimized on the Touché 2020 judgments). This new index was then queried with the topic title expanded by WordNet synonyms [17].

Team *Rayla* re-ranked the top-120 ChatNoir results by linearly combining different scores such as a relevance score, PageRank, SpamRank (all returned by ChatNoir), or an argument support score (ratio of argumentative sentences (premises and claims) in documents found with their own DistilBERT-based [43] classifier). The weights of the individual scores were optimized in a grid search on the Touché 2020 judgments.

Team *Mercutio* re-ranked the top-100 ChatNoir results returned for the topic titles expanded with synonyms (word2vec [33] or nouns in GPT-2 [42] extensions when prompted with the topic title). The re-ranking was based on the relative ratio of premises and claims in the documents (as identified by TARGER).

Team *Prince Caspian* re-ranked the top-40 ChatNoir results using a logistic regression classifier (features: $tf \cdot idf$-weighted 1- to 4-grams; training on the Touché 2020 judgments) that predicts the probability of a result being relevant (final ranking by descending probability).

6 Summary and Outlook

From the 36 teams that registered for the Touché 2021 lab, 27 actively participated by submitting at least one valid run to one of the two shared tasks:(1) argument retrieval for controversial questions, and (2) argument retrieval for comparative questions. Most of the participating teams used the judgments from the first lab's edition to train feature-based or neural approaches that predict argument quality or that re-rank some initial retrieval result. Overall, many more approaches could improve upon the argumentation-agnostic baselines (DirichletLM or BM25) than in the first year, indicating that progress was achieved. For a potential next iteration of the Touché lab, we currently plan to enrich the tasks by including further argument quality dimensions in the evaluation by focusing on the most relevant/argumentative text passages in the retrieval and by detecting the pro/con stance of the returned results.

Acknowledgments. We are very grateful to the CLEF 2021 organizers and the Touché participants, who allowed this lab to happen. We also want to thank Jan Heinrich Reimer for setting up Doccano, Christopher Akiki for providing the baseline DirichletLM implementation, our volunteer annotators who helped to create the relevance and argument quality assessments, and our reviewers for their valuable feedback on the participants' notebooks.

This work was partially supported by the DFG through the project "ACQuA: Answering Comparative Questions with Arguments" (grants BI 1544/7-1 and HA 5851/2-1) as part of the priority program "RATIO: Robust Argumentation Machines" (SPP 1999).

References

1. Ajjour, Y., Wachsmuth, H., Kiesel, J., Potthast, M., Hagen, M., Stein, B.: Data acquisition for argument search: the args.me corpus. In: Proceedings of the 42nd German Conference on Artificial Intelligence (KI 2019). pp. 48–59. Springer, Berlin, Heidelberg, New York (2019). https://doi.org/10.1007/978-3-030-30179-8_4
2. Akiki, C., Potthast, M.: Exploring argument retrieval with transformers. In: Working Notes Papers of the CLEF 2020 Evaluation Labs, vol. 2696 (2020). http://ceur-ws.org/Vol-2696/

3. Kennedy, G.A.: On Rhetoric: A Theory of Civic Discourse. Oxford University Press, Oxford (2006)
4. Bar-Haim, R., Eden, L., Friedman, R., Kantor, Y., Lahav, D., Slonim, N.: From arguments to key points: towards automatic argument summarization. In: Proceedings of the 58th Annual Meeting of the Association for Computational Linguistics (ACL 2020), pp. 4029–4039. Association for Computational Linguistics (2020). https://doi.org/10.18653/v1/2020.acl-main.371
5. Bar-Haim, R., et al.: From surrogacy to adoption; from bitcoin to cryptocurrency: debate topic expansion. In: Proceedings of the 57th Conference of the Association for Computational Linguistics (ACL 2019), pp. 977–990. Association for Computational Linguistics (2019). https://doi.org/10.18653/v1/p19-1094
6. Bevendorff, J., Stein, B., Hagen, M., Potthast, M.: Elastic ChatNoir: search engine for the clueweb and the common crawl. In: Pasi, G., Piwowarski, B., Azzopardi, L., Hanbury, A. (eds.) ECIR 2018. LNCS, vol. 10772, pp. 820–824. Springer, Cham (2018). https://doi.org/10.1007/978-3-319-76941-7_83
7. Bondarenko, A., et al.: Overview of Touché 2020: argument retrieval. In: Working Notes Papers of the CLEF 2020 Evaluation Labs. CEUR Workshop Proceedings, vol. 2696 (2020). http://ceur-ws.org/Vol-2696/
8. Bondarenko, A., et al.: Overview of Touché 2021: argument retrieval. In: Hiemstra, D., Moens, M.-F., Mothe, J., Perego, R., Potthast, M., Sebastiani, F. (eds.) ECIR 2021. LNCS, vol. 12657, pp. 574–582. Springer, Cham (2021). https://doi.org/10.1007/978-3-030-72240-1_67
9. Bondarenko, A., et al.: Overview of Touché 2021: argument retrieval. In: Working Notes of CLEF 2021 - Conference and Labs of the Evaluation Forum, p. (to appear). CEUR Workshop Proceedings, CLEF and CEUR-WS.org (2021)
10. Cer, D., et al.: Universal Sentence Encoder. CoRR **abs/1803.11175** (2018). http://arxiv.org/abs/1803.11175
11. Chekalina, V., Bondarenko, A., Biemann, C., Beloucif, M., Logacheva, V., Panchenko, A.: Which is better for deep learning: python or MATLAB? Answering comparative questions in natural language. In: Proceedings of the 16th Conference of the European Chapter of the Association for Computational Linguistics: System Demonstrations (EACL 2021), pp. 302–311. Association for Computational Linguistics (2021). https://www.aclweb.org/anthology/2021.eacl-demos.36/
12. Chen, T., Guestrin, C.: XGBoost: a scalable tree boosting system. In: Proceedings of the 22nd ACM SIGKDD International Conference on Knowledge Discovery and Data Mining, pp. 785–794. ACM (2016). https://doi.org/10.1145/2939672.2939785
13. Chernodub, A., et al.: TARGER: neural argument mining at your fingertips. In: Proceedings of the 57th Annual Meeting of the Association for Computational Linguistics (ACL 2019), pp. 195–200. Association for Computational Linguistics (2019). https://www.aclweb.org/anthology/P19-3031
14. Devlin, J., Chang, M., Lee, K., Toutanova, K.: BERT: pre-training of deep bidirectional transformers for language understanding. In: Proceedings of the 2019 Conference of the North American Chapter of the Association for Computational Linguistics: Human Language Technologies (NAACL-HLT 2019), pp. 4171–4186. Association for Computational Linguistics (2019). https://doi.org/10.18653/v1/n19-1423
15. Dumani, L., Neumann, P.J., Schenkel, R.: A framework for argument retrieval - ranking argument clusters by frequency and specificity. In: Jose, J.M., et al. (eds.) ECIR 2020. LNCS, vol. 12035, pp. 431–445. Springer, Cham (2020). https://doi.org/10.1007/978-3-030-45439-5_29

16. Dumani, L., Schenkel, R.: Quality aware ranking of arguments. In: Proceedings of the 29th ACM International Conference on Information & Knowledge Management, pp. 335–344. CIKM 2020, Association for Computing Machinery (2020). https://doi.org/10.1007/978-3-030-45439-5_29
17. Fellbaum, C.: WordNet: An Electronic Lexical Database. Bradford Books (1998)
18. Fröbe, M., et al.: CopyCat: near-duplicates within and between the ClueWeb and the common crawl. In: Proceedings of the 44th International ACM Conference on Research and Development in Information Retrieval (SIGIR 2021). ACM (2021). https://doi.org/10.1145/3404835.3463246
19. Fröbe, M., Bevendorff, J., Reimer, J., Potthast, M., Hagen, M.: Sampling bias due to near-duplicates in learning to rank. In: Proceedings of the 43rd International ACM Conference on Research and Development in Information Retrieval (SIGIR 2020), pp. 1997–2000. ACM (2020). https://doi.org/10.1145/3397271.3401212
20. Fröbe, M., Bittner, J.P., Potthast, M., Hagen, M.: The effect of content-equivalent near-duplicates on the evaluation of search engines. In: Jose, J.M., et al. (eds.) ECIR 2020. LNCS, vol. 12036, pp. 12–19. Springer, Cham (2020). https://doi.org/10.1007/978-3-030-45442-5_2
21. Gienapp, L., Stein, B., Hagen, M., Potthast, M.: Efficient pairwise annotation of argument quality. In: Proceedings of the 58th Annual Meeting of the Association for Computational Linguistics (ACL 2020), pp. 5772–5781. Association for Computational Linguistics, Online (2020). https://www.aclweb.org/anthology/2020.acl-main.511/
22. Iyer, S., Dandekar, N., Csernai, K.: First Quora Dataset Release: Question Pairs (2017). https://data.quora.com/First-Quora-Dataset-Release-Question-Pairs
23. Jindal, N., Liu, B.: Identifying comparative sentences in text documents. In: Proceedings of the 29th Annual International Conference on Research and Development in Information Retrieval (SIGIR 2006), pp. 244–251. ACM (2006). https://doi.org/10.1145/1148170.1148215
24. Jindal, N., Liu, B.: Mining comparative sentences and relations. In: Proceedings of the 21st National Conference on Artificial Intelligence and the 18th Innovative Applications of Artificial Intelligence Conference (AAAI 2006), pp. 1331–1336. AAAI Press (2006). http://www.aaai.org/Library/AAAI/2006/aaai06-209.php
25. Ke, G., et al.: LightGBM: a highly efficient gradient boosting decision tree. In: Proceedings of the Annual Conference on Neural Information Processing Systems (NeurIPS 2017), pp. 3146–3154 (2017)
26. Kessler, W., Kuhn, J.: A corpus of comparisons in product reviews. In: Proceedings of the 9th International Conference on Language Resources and Evaluation (LREC 2014), pp. 2242–2248. European Language Resources Association (ELRA) (2014). http://www.lrec-conf.org/proceedings/lrec2014/summaries/1001.html
27. Krovetz, R.: Viewing morphology as an inference process. In: Proceedings of the 16th Annual International Conference on Research and Development in Information Retrieval (SIGIR 1993), pp. 191–202. ACM (1993). https://doi.org/10.1145/160688.160718
28. Lavrenko, V., Croft, W.B.: Relevance-based language models. In: Proceedings of the 24th Annual International Conference on Research and Development in Information Retrieval (SIGIR 2001), pp. 120–127. ACM (2001). https://doi.org/10.1145/383952.383972

29. Levy, R., Bogin, B., Gretz, S., Aharonov, R., Slonim, N.: Towards an argumentative content search engine using weak supervision. In: Proceedings of the 27th International Conference on Computational Linguistics (COLING 2018), pp. 2066–2081. Association for Computational Linguistics (2018). https://www.aclweb.org/anthology/C18-1176/
30. Lippi, M., Torroni, P.: MARGOT: a web server for argumentation mining. Expert Syst. Appl. **65**, 292–303 (2016). https://doi.org/10.1016/j.eswa.2016.08.050
31. Ma, N., Mazumder, S., Wang, H., Liu, B.: Entity-aware dependency-based deep graph attention network for comparative preference classification. In: Proceedings of the 58th Annual Meeting of the Association for Computational Linguistics (ACL 2020), pp. 5782–5788. Association for Computational Linguistics (2020). https://www.aclweb.org/anthology/2020.acl-main.512/
32. Mass, Y., et al.: Word emphasis prediction for expressive text to speech. In: Proceedings of the 19th Annual Conference of the International Speech Communication Association (Interspeech 2018), pp. 2868–2872. ISCA (2018). https://doi.org/10.21437/Interspeech.2018-1159
33. Mikolov, T., Chen, K., Corrado, G., Dean, J.: Efficient estimation of word representations in vector space. In: Proceedings of the 1st International Conference on Learning Representations (ICLR 2013) (2013). http://arxiv.org/abs/1301.3781
34. Nadamoto, A., Tanaka, K.: A comparative web browser (CWB) for browsing and comparing web pages. In: Proceedings of the 12th International World Wide Web Conference (WWW 2003), pp. 727–735. ACM (2003). https://doi.org/10.1145/775152.775254
35. Nakayama, H., Kubo, T., Kamura, J., Taniguchi, Y., Liang, X.: doccano: Text Annotation Tool for Human (2018). https://github.com/doccano/doccano
36. Nguyen, T., et al.: MS MARCO: a human generated machine reading comprehension dataset. In: Proceedings of the Workshop on Cognitive Computation: Integrating neural and symbolic approaches 2016 co-located with the 30th Annual Conference on Neural Information Processing Systems (NIPS 2016). CEUR Workshop Proceedings, vol. 1773. CEUR-WS.org (2016). http://ceur-ws.org/Vol-1773/CoCoNIPS_2016_paper9.pdf
37. Page, L., Brin, S., Motwani, R., Winograd, T.: The PageRank Citation Ranking: Bringing Order to the Web. Technical Report 1999–66, Stanford InfoLab (1999). http://ilpubs.stanford.edu:8090/422/
38. Palotti, J.R.M., Scells, H., Zuccon, G.: TrecTools: an open-source python library for information retrieval practitioners involved in TREC-like campaigns. In: Proceedings of the 42nd International Conference on Research and Development in Information Retrieval (SIGIR 2019), pp. 1325–1328. ACM (2019). https://doi.org/10.1145/3331184.3331399
39. Panchenko, A., Bondarenko, A., Franzek, M., Hagen, M., Biemann, C.: Categorizing comparative sentences. In: Proceedings of the 6th Workshop on Argument Mining (ArgMining@ACL 2019), pp. 136–145. Association for Computational Linguistics (2019). https://doi.org/10.18653/v1/w19-4516
40. Potthast, M., et al.: Argument search: assessing argument relevance. In: Proceedings of the 42nd International Conference on Research and Development in Information Retrieval (SIGIR 2019), pp. 1117–1120. ACM (2019). https://doi.org/10.1145/3331184.3331327
41. Potthast, M., Gollub, T., Wiegmann, M., Stein, B.: TIRA integrated research architecture. In: Information Retrieval Evaluation in a Changing World. TIRS, vol. 41, pp. 123–160. Springer, Cham (2019). https://doi.org/10.1007/978-3-030-22948-1_5

42. Radford, A., Wu, J., Child, R., Luan, D., Amodei, D., Sutskever, I.: Language models are unsupervised multitask learners. OpenAI blog **1**(8), 9 (2019)
43. Sanh, V., Debut, L., Chaumond, J., Wolf, T.: DistilBERT, a Distilled Version of BERT: Smaller, Faster, Cheaper and Lighter. CoRR abs/1910.01108 (2019). http://arxiv.org/abs/1910.01108
44. Schildwächter, M., Bondarenko, A., Zenker, J., Hagen, M., Biemann, C., Panchenko, A.: Answering comparative questions: better than ten-blue-links? In: Proceedings of the Conference on Human Information Interaction and Retrieval (CHIIR 2019), pp. 361–365. ACM (2019). https://doi.org/10.1145/3295750.3298916
45. Stab, C., et al.: ArgumenText: searching for arguments in heterogeneous sources. In: Proceedings of the Conference of the North American Chapter of the Association for Computational Linguistics (NAACL-HLT 2018), pp. 21–25. Association for Computational Linguistics (2018). https://doi.org/10.18653/v1/n18-5005
46. Sun, J., Wang, X., Shen, D., Zeng, H., Chen, Z.: CWS: a comparative web search system. In: Proceedings of the 15th International Conference on World Wide Web (WWW 2006), pp. 467–476. ACM (2006). https://doi.org/10.1145/1135777.1135846
47. Trask, A., Michalak, P., Liu, J.: Sense2vec - A Fast and Accurate Method for Word Sense Disambiguation in Neural Word Embeddings. CoRR **abs/1511.06388** (2015). http://arxiv.org/abs/1511.06388
48. Wachsmuth, H., et al.: Argumentation quality assessment: theory vs. practice. In: Proceedings of the 55th Annual Meeting of the Association for Computational Linguistics (ACL 2017), pp. 250–255. Association for Computational Linguistics (2017). https://doi.org/10.18653/v1/P17-2039
49. Wachsmuth, H., et al.: Argumentation quality assessment: theory vs. practice. In: Proceedings of the 55th Annual Meeting of the Association for Computational Linguistics (ACL 2017), pp. 250–255. Association for Computational Linguistics (2017)
50. Wachsmuth, H., et al.: Computational argumentation quality assessment in natural language. In: Proceedings of the 15th Conference of the European Chapter of the Association for Computational Linguistics (EACL 2017), pp. 176–187 (2017). http://aclweb.org/anthology/E17-1017
51. Wachsmuth, H., et al.: Building an argument search engine for the web. In: Proceedings of the 4th Workshop on Argument Mining (ArgMining@EMNLP 2017), pp. 49–59. Association for Computational Linguistics (2017). https://doi.org/10.18653/v1/w17-5106
52. Wachsmuth, H., Stein, B., Ajjour, Y.: "PageRank" for argument relevance. In: Proceedings of the 15th Conference of the European Chapter of the Association for Computational Linguistics (EACL 2017), pp. 1117–1127. Association for Computational Linguistics (2017). https://doi.org/10.18653/v1/e17-1105
53. Wachsmuth, H., Syed, S., Stein, B.: Retrieval of the best counterargument without prior topic knowledge. In: Proceedings of the 56th Annual Meeting of the Association for Computational Linguistics (ACL 2018), pp. 241–251. Association for Computational Linguistics (2018). https://www.aclweb.org/anthology/P18-1023/

Author Index